BARENTS SEA

NORTH CAPE

Hammerfest

RUSSIA

Arctic Ci

WHITE SEA

FINNMARK

Muonio R.

Narvik

Torne R

LAPPLAND

NORDLANDET

VÄSTERBOTTEN

ÖSTERBOTTEN

SEA

Luleå

Oulu

FINLAND

Lake
Oneg

THE·KEEL

JÄMTLAND

Umeå

Gulf of Bothnia

Vasa (Vaasa)

KARELIA

Lake
Ladoga

OLD FINLAND

Trondheim

TRØNDELAG

NORRLAND

SWEDEN

Tammerfors
(Tampere)

Viborg
(Viipuri)

St. Petersburg
(Leningrad)

Anjala

Borgå (Porvoo)

Fredrikshamn
(Hamina)

NORWAY

Eidsvoll

DALARNA

Gävle

Åbo (Turku)

Helsingfors
(Helsinki)

Narva

ergen

Christiania
(Oslo)

VÄRMLAND

SVEALAND

Uppsala

ÅLAND
ISLANDS

GULF OF
FINLAND

Revel
(Tallinn)

Karlstad

Lake Mälaren

Stockholm

DAGÖ

ESTONIA

RUSSIA

VESTLANDET

Moss

Lake
Vänern

Örebro

ÖSEL

LIVONIA

ØSTLANDET

Norrköping

avanger

SØRLANDET

Arendal

Lake
Vättern

Visby

GOTLAND

Riga

W. Dvina R.

Christiansand

Marstrand

Jönköping

Gothenburg
(Göteborg)

GÖTALAND

ÖLAND

Skagerrak

Kattegat

Kalmar

BALTIC SEA

Tilsit

POLAND

Ålborg

ANHOLT

Karlskrona

Aarhus

SKÅNE

DENMARK

Lund

Copenhagen

Malmö

BORNHOLM

RÜGEN

Danzig

Stettin

TCH

UBLIC

Berlin

Oder R.

HANOVER

PRUSSIA

# THE NORDIC SERIES

## Volume 12

# Scandinavia in the Revolutionary Era, 1760-1815

H. Arnold Barton

University of Minnesota Press     Minneapolis

The University of Minnesota Press gratefully
acknowledges publication assistance from the Swedish
Council for Research in the Humanities and Social
Sciences, Stockholm, and the National Endowment for
the Humanities, a federal agency which supports study
in such fields as history, philosophy, literature, and
languages.

Published by the University of Minnesota Press
2037 University Avenue Southeast, Minneapolis MN 55414
Published simultaneously in Canada
by Fitzhenry & Whiteside Limited, Markham.
Printed in the United States of America.

**Library of Congress Cataloging in Publication Data**
Barton, H. Arnold (Hildor Arnold), 1929–
   Scandinavia in the Revolutionary era, 1760–1815.
   (The Nordic series; v. 12)
   Bibliography: p.
   Includes index.
   1. Scandinavia—History—18th century.   2. Scandinavia
—History—19th century. I. Title. II. Series.
DL78.B37 1986     948'.05     84-26972
ISBN 0-8166-1392-3
ISBN 0-8166-1393-1 (pbk.)

To the memory of my parents,
Sven Hildor Barton
Marguerite Arnhold Barton

# Contents

# Preface

The Seven Years' War ushered in a new era in the history of the West. By its conclusion in 1763, nearly a quarter century of intermittent warfare on land and sea had severely strained the resources of most European states, which thereafter made determined efforts to recoup their losses and prepare economically for fresh trials of strength. Ambitious programs of reform during the following decades bore the impress of the rationalism and empiricism of the Enlightenment, as well as something of its humanitarianism; in much of Europe governments practiced in varying degree what later generations would describe as enlightened despotism. They sought to assert undivided authority over all subjects of the state and to draw upon its full resources.

Such reforms encountered resistance—sometimes amounting to full-scale insurrection—from social groups or regions that traditionally had enjoyed the protection of special rights and immunities. At times the defense of privilege in turn provoked antiaristocratic or antioligarchical reactions by those less favored in the social hierarchy, who came to challenge the very concept of special status based on birth or tradition.

In Great Britain's North American colonies and later in France, such conflicts led to revolutions exercising a profound influence throughout the Western world. The French Revolution resulted in another quarter-century of war and in the emergence of the Napoleonic empire. Under occupation by the conquering French, or to resist their onslaught, much of Europe was reorganized territorially, administratively, and in varying degree socially, with far-reaching consequences for the future.

The rise of the middle classes in numbers, wealth, and assertiveness, which so largely underlay the social and political upheavals of the period, to a great extent reflected economic transformations, in both agriculture and industry, which by 1760 were entering their dynamic phase. Whereas political revolution centered in France, economic revolution centered in Great Britain. The influences of both radiated out into the European world, tending ultimately toward the same basic restructuring of society.

By the early 1760s, the Enlightenment was at its zenith. Everywhere, the *philosophes* made bold to proclaim, the light of Reason was breaking through the clouds of obscurantism. French speech, thought, and manners seemed to carry all before them in the cosmopolitan world of taste, refinement, and ideas. Yet signs of a growing Counter-Enlightenment were already apparent. Religious pietisms and secular mysticisms were on the rise, while the Pre-Romantic mood in literature and the arts exalted the emotions, individuality, and local distinctiveness, in rebellion against classical canons and French cultural hegemony.

How did these developments, between the Seven Years' War and the end of the Napoleonic conflict, affect that large corner of northern Europe known as Scandinavia, or often simply as "the North" (*Norden*)? Little has ever been said about the region in historical writing on Europe as a whole in this crucial period, even though it can add much to our understanding of the era. Historians in the Nordic countries have tended to write for each other, or at least for their compatriots, in their own languages. Among them, strong traditions of meticulous monographic research utilizing original sources, while producing admirable historical literatures, have meanwhile discouraged broad, synthetic, or speculative studies of a type often congenial to French or Anglo-Saxon scholars. They have thus not attempted any regional survey or comparative history of their lands during this era.

With a license reserved—perhaps—for the outsider, I have sought in the present study to provide such an overview, with emphasis upon lines of development common to the European world of the time. While examining ways in which such developments proceeded from local conditions and traditions, it endeavors to trace the impact in Scandinavia of impulses from the larger world beyond. In so doing, it draws parallels and comparisons between the different Nordic lands, as well as between Scandinavia as a region and the West as a whole. Since the involvement of the Nordic states in the wider European arena of diplomacy and war is already the most familiar part of the story, the focus is principally upon internal and inter-Nordic developments.

From all of this emerges that the Nordic countries—in no lesser degree than the rest of the Western world—underwent the great transformations of the era, even though never occupied or reorganized by Revolutionary or Napoleonic France, and though not yet experiencing an industrial revolution on the British model. The main initiatives, moreover, were already well under way in the

North before the convening of the French Estates-General and the storming of
the Bastille in 1789. The changes of these years would be crucial to the evolution
of modern Scandinavia.

The rendering of foreign terms, personal and place names from an earlier
time is invariably problematical. Without entering into lengthy explanations, let
me simply say that I have sought a pragmatic middle way between the usages
of the period and present-day orthography and form.

The Selected Bibliography contains only what I consider the most basic
works, while giving a certain emphasis to those available to non-Nordic scholars
in English, French, and German. All translations are my own, unless otherwise
noted.

Many persons played their parts, directly or indirectly, in this work. Robert
R. Palmer, Jerome Blum, and Franklin D. Scott long ago encouraged me in
directions manifested here. Over the years, Sten Carlsson, Georg Nørregård,
Kåre D. Tønnesson, Göran Rystad, Michael Roberts, Stewart Oakley, Raymond
E. Lindgren, Jørgen Schou-Christensen, Michael F. Metcalf, J. R. Christian-
son, H. Peter Krosby, John Ervin, Jr., and the late Peter A. Munch in particular
gave encouragement, criticism, advice, and ideas important to my widening
insight and understanding.

I received much welcome assistance from various institutions, above all from
the Royal Library in Stockholm and from the Morris Library at Southern Illinois
University at Carbondale, where with his usual wizardry Charles Holliday
managed to provide the most unlikely materials through interlibrary loans. Lisa
Lee and Lorie Allen expertly prepared the manuscript on a word processor
under Vincent A. Lacey's technical coordination. Lillian J. Wonders of the
University of Alberta in Edmonton, Canada, was my expert cartographer.

Permission to make use of material from certain of my earlier publications
has been graciously granted by: Twayne Publishers, Boston, for *Count Hans
Axel von Fersen: Aristocrat in an Age of Revolution* (1975); by *Eighteenth-
Century Studies*, for "Gustav III of Sweden and the Enlightenment," 6 (1972),
1–34; by the *William [ Mary Quarterly*, for "Sweden and the War of American
Independence," 3rd ser., 23 (1966), 408–30; by *Scandinavian Studies*, for "The
Swedish Succession Crises of 1809 and 1810, and the Question of Scandinavian
Union," 42 (1970), 309–33, and "Late Gustavian Autocracy in Sweden: Gustav
IV Adolf and His Opponents, 1792–1809," 46 (1974), 265–84.

I am deeply indebted to the National Endowment for the Humanities for a
fellowship making possible a year's research at the beginning of this project and
for underwriting a part of the publication costs, to the Swedish Council for
Research in the Humanities and Social Sciences for a generous publication

grant, and to Southern Illinois University at Carbondale for sabbatical leave and research support.

As always, my wife, Aina, has played her own quiet role in seeing this daunting undertaking through to its completion. How great that has been, only she and I can ever know.

H. A. B.

# Scandinavia in the Revolutionary Era, 1760–1815

# CHAPTER 1

# The Setting
# Scandinavia around 1760

Scandinavia is presently understood to include five countries—Denmark, Finland, Iceland, Norway, and Sweden. It includes a sizable part of Europe, some 445,500 square miles, a land area more than twice the size of France and nearly five times that of Great Britain.

The region is nonetheless based on no single unifying factor. Geographically Norway and Sweden—divided along the crest of a mountain range, the "Keel"—constitute the Scandinavian Peninsula. Denmark, geographically an extension of the north German plain, as well as Iceland and the Færø Islands in the North Atlantic, belong to the Scandinavian world through ethnic and linguistic ties. Finland is contiguous with Russia, and the majority of its population speak a Ural-Altaic tongue. Yet on grounds of history, culture, and tradition, Finland too belongs to the Scandinavian community.

By the eighteenth century this region had long been organized into two dynastic states, the Danish and the Swedish. Norway, with its old tributary lands—Iceland, the Færø Islands, and Greenland—had been united with Denmark since 1380. The Swedish kingdom included Finland since the Christianization of that country beginning in the twelfth century. In 1397 the whole of the Scandinavian North formed the Kalmar Union under the Danish royal house, but Sweden-Finland broke away in 1520 to reestablish its independence under the new Vasa dynasty.

By the eighteenth century both monarchies possessed territories in northern Germany. The Danish kings held Schleswig, the old Danish South Jutland (Sønderjylland), as an independent duchy, and the adjoining duchy of Holstein as a fief of the Holy Roman Empire; since 1460 "the duchies" were joined in an "indissoluble union" that prevented their outright incorporation, individually or together, into "the kingdom." Their internal consolidation under the sole rule of the Danish royal house meanwhile took centuries to complete; not until the eighteenth century were the last autonomous enclaves liquidated. Since the accession of Christian I in 1448, the Danish crown was held by the house of Oldenburg. With the extinction of the ducal line in 1667, the small ancestral county (*Grafschaft*) of Oldenburg, with the county of Delmenhorst, fiefs of the Holy Roman Empire west of the Weser River, also passed to the Danish royal line. The Swedish monarchy acquired western or ducal Pomerania and the port of Wismar on the Mecklenburg coast, likewise as fiefs of the empire, during the seventeenth century.

Finally, the Danish monarchy was also a colonial power on a modest scale. During the seventeenth century it had established trading posts and colonies in India, on the Guinea coast of West Africa, and in the Virgin Islands in the West Indies. In 1721 the Norwegian pastor Hans Egede recolonized Greenland, where the old Norse population had died out by the fifteenth century.[1]

Scandinavia lies on Europe's northern periphery. It extended in the eighteenth century from around 54 degrees north latitude on the Holstein border to 71 degrees at the North Cape, from about 33 degrees east longitude on Finland's north Karelian frontier to 24 degrees west on the outermost tip of Iceland. Oslo, Stockholm, and Helsinki lie at roughly the same latitude as Cape Farewell on the southern tip of Greenland. Nearly a third of peninsular Scandinavia lies above the Arctic Circle.

Within this vast region there are immense variations of topography and climate, from well-tilled and densely populated landscapes of the middle European type to great areas of western Europe's most undisturbed wilderness. Denmark, with the Scandinavian possessions in North Germany and Sweden's southernmost province of Skåne, represented the richest agricultural region. Most of Sweden and all of Finland lie fairly close to sea level, though the terrain is often broken and rugged. Norway is a mountainous region, with an average altitude nearly twice that of Europe as a whole. Iceland and the Færøes are treeless, sub-Arctic islands.

By European standards, much of the Scandinavian world is a hard environment. Yet it also contains valuable resources. Most important in the preindustrial age was arable land, which varied greatly in extent, distribution, and quality. It is presently estimated to comprise about 75 percent of Denmark's area, 10 percent of Finland, 9 percent of Sweden, and only 3 percent of Norway, although what may be considered cultivatable is naturally open to varying interpretation. Outside Denmark, Skåne, and the German provinces, the principal agricultural regions were located in south-central Sweden, in southwestern Finland; and around Oslo and Trondheim Fjords in Norway. Most of Finland and Sweden, and much of Norway, is covered by coniferous forests, which here reach more northerly latitudes than anywhere else in the world, while hardwood forest extends from Denmark into parts of central Sweden and southern Finland and Norway. Today forests cover some 67 percent of Finland, 56 percent of Sweden, 25 percent of Norway, and 8 percent of Denmark.[2] Everywhere they provided vital resources: fuel; material for buildings, ships, furnishings, and implements; products for export; rough grazing for livestock; game, fish, and wild berries; reserves of land—especially in Sweden and Finland—for an on-going process of internal colonization. In addition to lakes and rivers, the Baltic, North Sea, and Atlantic provide valuable fishing grounds. Sweden possessed plentiful iron ore, some copper, and even silver, as did Norway in smaller amounts.

Within its vast latitudinal and longitudinal range, the climate of Scandinavia varies greatly, from comparatively mild in Denmark and the German territories to sub-Arctic beyond the Polar Circle. The Gulf Stream, passing between the British Isles and Iceland, sweeps along the Norwegian coast toward the Barents Sea, which gives the entire region milder temperatures than elsewhere in the world at comparable latitudes. Except in the interior of Iceland, and in limited mountainous areas in Norway and northernmost Sweden, there are neither glaciers nor permafrost. Yet the effects of the Gulf Stream are considerably modified by both terrain and longitude. Denmark and the lower-lying coastal regions of southwestern Norway have the most temperate climates in Scandinavia. In much of Norway and Iceland, however, altitude lowers temperatures, whereas the mountain barrier of the "Keel" shields most of Sweden from the milder maritime climate on the Norwegian side. Both winter and summer temperatures are generally more extreme in Sweden than in coastal Norway, and Finland, lying nearer the Eurasian land mass, shows still greater variations. Much of northern Scandinavia lies beyond the climatic frontier for settled agriculture.

At such high latitudes there are considerable seasonable variations in hours of daylight and darkness. At 60 degrees north latitude, approximately that of Oslo, Stockholm, and Helsinki, the sun is below the horizon for some nineteen hours at midwinter and above it the same number of hours at midsummer. At Hammerfest, Norway, at approximately 70 degrees, the sun never rises for some two and a half months in winter and never sets for the same length of time in summer.[3] Winters in Scandinavia are proverbially long and dreary, summers short and intense, when long hours of daylight compensate for the brevity of the growing season.

There have been long-term climatic fluctuations in Scandinavia. Winters, especially during the second half of the eighteenth and early nineteenth centuries, tended to be more severe than they have since become. Continuous meteorological records kept in Sweden since 1760 indicate a substantial moderation of winter temperatures over the past two centuries.[4]

Seasonal change profoundly affected the pattern of communications before the railroad age. Water was everywhere the chief medium of transport, both internally, via lakes, rivers, and coastlines, and externally, between areas separated by seas. Sweden had better communications with Finland across the Baltic than with Norway over the "Keel." Mountainous Norway was united above all by its coastal seaways and by easy communications with Denmark across the Skagerrak. Winter, however, largely changed this picture, for while Norway's harbors remained generally ice-free, Sweden's and Finland's Baltic seaports were frozen, and the Sound was blocked by ice floes for varying periods. Snow and ice, meanwhile, greatly improved transport overland on sledges, which could carry heavier loads than could be moved over rutted and often muddy roads during warmer times of year. Regulated systems of relay stations and inns provided for the movement of government officials, travelers, and mail.

At present the combined population of the five Nordic countries comes to about twenty-two million. By way of contrast, the Netherlands and Belgium, occupying a total area less than one-eighteenth as large, have a combined population slightly exceeding Scandinavia's, the last-named, taken as a whole, being Europe's most sparsely inhabited region. Except in Denmark, population density per square mile is markedly below the European average. In the eighteenth century Scandinavia's population was far smaller. In 1735 the Danish-Norwegian monarchy had some 1.4 million inhabitants; in 1749 the first regular census to be taken in any European country showed Sweden-Finland to have around 2.2 million. Thus in 1750 Scandinavia still had something under four million inhabitants, or less than one-fifth of its present population.[5]

Latitude, terrain, resources, climate—all played their part in determining both the numbers and distribution of Scandinavia's population. It was concentrated most densely where arable soil was most plentiful and the climate within tolerable margins: in Denmark, Skåne, and the German territories; in the fertile regions around the great lakes in south-central Sweden and in southwestern Finland; along Oslo Fjord and the valleys leading down to it, and around Trondheim Fjord; in scattered river valleys, coastlands, fjords, and islands, closed in by sea, mountain, or forest. Much of Norway's rugged mountainous interior remained unpopulated, except for herdsmen on their upland pastures in summer; the greater part of the country's population lived close to the long shoreline. Except for scattered settlements along the coasts, the northern two-thirds of Sweden, northern Finland, and Norwegian Finnmark were still practically uninhabited, aside from a handful of nomadic Lapps grazing their herds of reindeer and the occasional wandering fur-trapper. Throughout the century Iceland had only some 50,000 inhabitants, and often fewer, in scattered farmsteads around the coast.[6]

At such northerly latitudes the human ecology was extraordinarily sensitive to small variations in climate. Throughout Scandinavia frequent crop failures exercised a periodic check on population growth. For Europe as a whole it has been estimated that during the eighteenth century each decade included, normally, one year of crop failure, two bad years, five average, and two good. For Finland during the same period there were on the average two years of crop failure, three bad years, four normal, and not always one good year per decade. Iceland, on the sub-Arctic margin of habitable Europe, represents the extreme example. In 1808 the Icelandic scholar Magnus Stephensen counted no fewer than forty-three bad years on the island during the eighteenth century; fourteen of these years brought serious losses of population and livestock. It will be noted in what follows how periods of social and political unrest coincided with crop failures and famine.[7]

Diseases took their toll. Tuberculosis seems to have been almost endemic. Periodic epidemics carried off large numbers of persons weakened by hunger in times of shortage. Stockholm lost one-third of its population from the plague in 1711–12. Smallpox carried off a third of Iceland's population in 1707. Livestock was also affected. Beginning in 1745 Denmark in particular was ravaged by murrain, which within three years killed some 300,000 cattle.[8]

Famine and disease typically followed the ravages of war. Finland, as Sweden's borderland against its archenemy, Russia, was particularly exposed. By the end of the Great Northern War in 1721 Finland's population had been reduced by about one-quarter through death, emigration, and the loss of part of Karelia.[9]

Restrictive government policies, forbidding the division of farms, suppressing trade or seafaring among the peasantry, and establishing the monopolies of privileged towns or corporations over the commerce of entire regions, often tended to keep conditions depressed.

Nonetheless, the population of Scandinavia grew fairly steadily from the end of the Great Northern War. By mid-century it became evident that famine, disease, and war were no longer as destructive as they had formerly been, while agrarian reforms and humanitarian efforts in the later eighteenth century stimulated further growth. By the beginning of the nineteenth, Scandinavia's population had increased by over a quarter since mid-century, from under four to over five million. Within the two states it was especially noteworthy that Finland's population had more than doubled since 1749 and increased its share within the Swedish monarchy from 17 percent to 26 percent, while Norway's was half again as large as at the beginning of the century and now only 5 percent smaller than that of Denmark proper.[10]

During the eighteenth century the Scandinavians still provided for their material needs in ways generally closer to those of their medieval ancestors than of their present descendants. More than four out of five supported themselves by cultivating the soil or in related rural occupations. Peasant farming followed immemorial ways, providing for the cultivators' subsistence, and little else.

What necessities the household could not fashion for itself out of wood, birch-bark, wool, linen, or leather, could most often be obtained from rural craftsmen, themselves small cultivators, in exchange for products of the land. Rents and dues, tithes, and taxes were payable largely in grain, timber, or days of labor. Local officials of the crown, pastors of the Lutheran state churches, even much of the military and naval establishments were compensated through the tenure of house or cottage with land in specified amounts, which the occupant culti-vated or leased out for his support.

In such a society relatively little money changed hands. Artisans in provincial market towns exchanged their wares and services largely in barter for foodstuffs and raw materials, and local merchants, often themselves landowners in the sur-rounding countryside, were much occupied with trade in grain, cattle, fish, or timber.

The level of development in Scandinavia was not unlike that of Europe as a whole. Still, it would have to be reckoned among its less dynamic regions. In-deed, mechanisms for exchange, compensation, and the support of public func-tions without recourse to money were surely more elaborately developed there than in most parts of Europe by the beginning of the eighteenth century. Only limited areas of activity had risen—or were rising—above the basic subsistence and barter level, into the market economy and the cash nexus. In agriculture, the cultivation of manorial demesne lands created in places islands of capitalist enterprise in the traditional countryside, as did iron works, especially in Swe-den, and timber exploitation, particularly in Norway.

The governments, eager to increase their revenues in specie, encouraged and protected those activities most closely geared to cash profits in a market econ-omy, above all those that could provide directly for the needs of armies and navies, increase exports, and reduce imports. These included in particular min-ing and other extractive industries, manufactures, and overseas trade. The larger cities with their merchant oligarchies, especially the capitals, Copenhagen and Stockholm, were treated with particular solicitude. From the 1730s both Den-mark-Norway and Sweden-Finland followed strongly mercantilistic policies.

Agriculture was everywhere the basic activity, occupying the great mass of the population. Forms of landholding varied widely. In Denmark at mid-century about 84 percent of the land was held by some 750 manors belonging to private proprietors, or in some cases municipalities or foundations such as the Univer-sity of Copenhagen. The rest was the property of the crown, was attached to parish churches, occupied by towns, or held by a small number of peasant free-holders. Most land in the German provinces likewise fell under manorial con-trol. In Sweden the land was divided roughly equally at the beginning of the cen-tury between the crown domain, manorial (frälse) land, and peasant freeholds. Only around 9 percent of Finland belonged to private manors, located mainly in the southern coastal districts. They were likewise relatively few in Norway.[11] Throughout the northern two-thirds of Sweden, most of Finland, and northernmost Norway they were practically nonexistent, as they also were on Iceland and the Færøes.

In Denmark and the German provinces, as well as in Skåne and parts of south-central Sweden, extensive tracts of good arable land permitted demesne farming on some scale, utilizing labor from tenant farms and crofts. Such cultivation could employ more rational and productive methods than the peasant farms; it thus produced most of the necessary surplus for the towns and, in Denmark, for the needs of Norway, the Atlantic islands, and overseas colonies.[12]

Yet only a small part of the land consisted of demesne; even in Denmark, it amounted to only some 13 percent around the middle of the century. The rest consisted of peasant tenancies. Much demesne land in Scandinavia was moreover leased out. The wide dispersal of arable land frequently made demesne farming impracticable; many manors consisted of widely scattered tenant farms, whose proprietors were essentially rural *rentiers*.

By far the greater part of the land was thus everywhere held in the form of peasant farms, whether under tenancy or freehold. Only relatively small amounts of their produce, collected as land rents, tithes, or taxes, or bartered or sold in a nearby market town, were available for consumption outside the immediate area. Their principal arable crops were grain—mainly rye, oats, and barley—cultivated in rotation, generally leaving each field fallow every second or third year. Yields were meager, even in Denmark usually only around four times the seed planted on good peasant land.[13]

In most regions livestock raising was as important, or more so, than arable farming. Extensive areas beyond the cultivated fields provided wild hay and rough grazing for cattle, sheep, and goats, which in summer were often taken to summer pastures far from their home farms. In northernmost Norway, Iceland, and the Færøes, the climate made grain culture virtually impossible and the only field crop was hay for the winter feeding of sheep, cattle, and horses. In much of Scandinavia the available fodder was nonetheless insufficient to maintain more than a limited number of animals through the long winter. Little selective breeding was possible, and domestic animals were small and unproductive by later standards.

In common with most of Europe, much of Scandinavia practiced age-old systems of communal land allocation, in which the holdings of farms were intermixed. In Denmark, the German provinces, and much of Sweden and Finland, most peasants lived in compact villages, surrounded by open fields in which each farm held one or more strips of plowland, beyond which lay meadows, pastures, forests, wastelands, and fishing waters held in common. In Norway the compact village was practically unknown. The peasants lived on scattered farmsteads, often amounting to hamlets with their clusters of dwelling houses and outbuildings; yet especially in the poorer districts of the west, their arable lands were likewise often intermingled.

Otherwise, Scandinavia was notable for a degree of individual landholding unparalleled in most of Europe. In parts of the German provinces, such as the Ditmarschen in Holstein and the North Friesian Islands, as well as in much of Sweden, Finland, Norway, Iceland, and the Færøes, the individual farm with more or less compact holdings was the rule rather than the exception. Even within a particular district there could be much variation in this respect. Individual holdings were most common where arable land was widely scattered and where wastelands had most recently been settled.

Whereas European mercantilist thought was typically concerned with mining, manufacture, and trade, the Scandinavian governments were ever mindful of the importance of agriculture. Laws and ordinances throughout the century sought to ensure adequate labor for cultivation, to prevent or permit transfer of land from one legal category to another, to encourage productive or discourage wasteful use of resources, to promote the internal colonization of reclaimable wastelands. In 1735, at a time of depressed agricultural prices, the Danish government banned the import of foreign grain into Denmark and southern Norway, establishing a virtual monopoly for the Danish manorial proprietors. It also took vigorous action to end the cattle epidemic of the 1740s and 1750s. In Sweden-Finland attempts were made to overcome excessive fragmentation of village holdings through the enclosure ordinances of 1757 and 1762 (*Storskifte*), which, if they failed to have very much effect in the following decades, aroused much interest throughout northern Europe and provided an important precedent in the future.[14]

Despite the best efforts of the government in Stockholm, however, Sweden and Finland could no longer produce enough grain for their own growing needs as early as the 1680s, and thus had to import some grain, mainly from Russia, throughout the century.[15] Norway raised an even smaller part of its grain supply, whereas Iceland and the Færøes produced no grain at all. Denmark and Schleswig-Holstein could, however, normally produce enough to fill these needs, while leaving some surplus for export abroad. But bad crop years often affected the entire region, in which case Norway and the Atlantic islands in particular suffered serious deprivation.

Except in some of the richer agricultural areas, the Scandinavian peasant was seldom only a farmer. His environment provided both pressures and inducements to work at a variety of supplementary occupations as well. The forest gave numerous opportunities: for felling and floating timber, for burning charcoal, for hunting, fishing, and berry picking. Haulage by cart, sledge, and boat, for local ironmasters, grain merchants, and sawmill owners provided much part-time employment. On the coasts fishing was everywhere a vital supplement to farming. Some peasants along the main roads kept licensed inns and posting stations. In certain districts textile and other manufacturers employed peasants in cottage industries. Otherwise they everywhere practiced a wide variety of traditional crafts, most notably in the forest districts. Despite the governments' repeated efforts to prevent or at least limit it, peasants in many areas carried on a lively trade in the products of their handicrafts, often ranging far afield. In places, peasant seafarers carried on a good deal of trade on their own account. Manors provided much part-time work. From certain of the poorer regions, there was a seasonal migration of peasants to towns, to work at various menial occupations.

In large parts of Sweden, Finland, and southeastern Norway, the characteristic combination was farmer and woodsman, and often craftsman as well. In the coastal districts throughout Scandinavia, it was farmer and fisherman, and sometimes seaman.

Outside of agriculture, forests provided Scandinavia's most important products: sawn timber, ship's masts and spars, Stockholm tar for ships' rigging, charcoal for ironworking. Most of these commodities were consumed at home; Norway provided for most of Denmark's and virtually all of Iceland's and the Færøes' needs for timber. Forest products, however, also provided valuable exports abroad. Thanks to ice-free Oslo Fjord and the long North Sea sailing season, southeastern Norway (Østlandet) was the principal timber-exporting region. Here lumbering was organized on a large scale, with the sawmill owners of the coastal towns employing peasants in the hinterland to cut and transport timber. In Sweden and Finland, naval stores—masts, spars, and Stockholm tar—were the principal forest exports.

Fishing was carried on everywhere, in inland lakes and rivers as well as at sea, providing an important part of the domestic diet. There was a good market for dried and salted fish abroad, particularly in Catholic southern Europe. Cod from the great fishing banks off northern Norway constituted by far the greatest part of Scandinavia's export, whereas herring from both the North Sea and Baltic provided for much of the domestic consumption. The Danish government gave considerable attention to the Norwegian fisheries. Because of monopolistic trade policies, however, Iceland and the Færøes were unable to exploit their rich fishing grounds for direct export.

Iron mining and processing was an important industry in Sweden; to a lesser degree also in Norway. Ironworks were widely distributed throughout south-central Sweden, wherever they had access to both ore and charcoal; in Norway they were almost all located in forest-rich Østlandet in the southeast. The ironworks comprised small rural industrial communities providing much part-time employment for peasant charcoal-burners and carters within a wide radius.

Sweden was one of Europe's largest iron exporters and Swedish bar iron enjoyed a high reputation for quality. Between 1735 and 1780 Sweden exported between forty and forty-five thousand tons annually, almost all of it through Stockholm and Gothenburg (Göteborg). The greater part went to Great Britain, which up to mid-century received 75 to 90 percent of its imported bar iron from Sweden. Thereafter Russia gained an increasing share of the British market, but because this market was expanding rapidly Swedish exports there did not decrease until after 1800. The Stockholm government carefully regulated the iron industry to keep down the consumption and cost of fuel and to limit supply to hold up prices on the European market.[16]

The smaller Norwegian iron industry could not compete abroad with Sweden. In 1730 the government in Copenhagen granted it a monopoly in Denmark and in Norway itself. It thus provided for the needs of the domestic market.

Copper was produced at the great Swedish mine at Falun and in smaller amounts at Røros in Norway, although by the eighteenth century the yields of both were falling off from earlier levels. At Sala in Sweden and Kongsberg in Norway small amounts of silver were also mined.

Mercantilist theory drew rigid distinctions between rural handicrafts, the production of urban artisans, and manufactures. Of the three forms of production, the first was unquestionably of greatest importance in supplying the needs of the population. The governments sought, however, to keep rural handiwork out of trade, in favor of the urban artisans and especially the manufacturers who produced for the market.

Town craftsmen produced a wide variety of wares, including most of those luxury or semi-luxury items intended for the small middle- and upper-class market. Characteristically they were organized into guilds, with strict qualifications for entry and limited numbers of masterships. Guild craftsmen often felt hard pressed by the competition of rural crafts, foreign imports, and, not least, domestic manufacturers, and sought vigorously to protect their interests.

The term manufacture applied not so much to methods of production as to a form of entrepreneurial organization outside the guild system. Numbers of skilled workers—still employing basically handicraft techniques—worked with tools and materials, and in buildings, provided by the entrepreneur. Products included above all textiles, also glass, metalwares, munitions, and processed sugar and tobacco. Preliminary stages of production, particularly of textiles, were often carried out by cottage workers in the countryside.

Manufactures enjoyed the particular favor of the governments for the production of military necessities and substitutes for costly foreign imports. They were protected by high tariffs, granted monopolies and tax benefits, supported by subsidies and loans, and foreign entrepreneurs and skilled workers were encouraged to settle in the Nordic lands. Yet their position was precarious in competition with both rural and urban handicrafts, and foreign wares usually of better quality. Tariffs and import bans had little effect, since widespread smuggling could not be prevented. Manufactures, in the strict eighteenth-century sense, never came to employ more than a tiny fraction of the population—in Sweden not over 1 percent at its height around 1760—nor to produce more than a small part of the total goods consumed. During the last decades of the century Scandinavian manufactures largely languished.[17]

The greatest profits were to be gained through trade, which in keeping with mercantilist principles was strictly regulated in the interests of the towns and royal treasuries. Towns were categorized according to their trading privileges: from the staple town, which enjoyed monopolies on the most important commodities of foreign trade, to the provincial market town, privileged to trade with the surrounding countryside, to the secondary market town, which could only conduct business for merchants in the local market town.

The most lucrative forms of commerce were reserved for the great merchant houses and privileged trading companies of the two capitals. Copenhagen monopolized trade with the Danish overseas colonies; as home of the Danish East India Company, founded in 1732, with Canton in China; and with Finnmark in northernmost Norway, Iceland, the Færøes, and Greenland. The Danish government strove to make Copenhagen the commercial emporium of the North, from which valuable colonial wares, such as sugar, tobacco, tea, and Chinese porcelain, were reexported to other European destinations. It enjoyed special tariff privileges for foreign goods in transit. Stockholm held staple rights for the foreign trade of all of northern Sweden and Finland lying around the Bay of Bothnia, thus controlling the export of nearly two-thirds of Sweden's bar iron and almost all of the Stockholm tar, which came mainly from western Finland.

After the capitals, certain leading provincial towns enjoyed favored status. Gothenburg handled most of the remainder of Sweden's iron exports and was the home of the profitable Swedish East India Company, established in 1731, which like the Danish company traded with Canton. In Norway, Christiania (Oslo), Bergen, Trondheim, and Christiansand carried on a lively export of fish and timber. Flensburg was the leading trade center for the duchies of Schleswig and Holstein, and Altona, on the Elbe, enjoyed free-port status to compete with neighboring Hamburg. Stralsund, in Swedish Pomerania, and the Swedish port of Wismar, on the Mecklenburg coast, held special privileges for their areas.

None of the provincial towns in Denmark proper or in Finland enjoyed such favored status or prosperity. They were simply market towns, as were most of those in Norway, Sweden, and the German provinces. On Iceland, the Færøes, and Greenland, which had no real towns, all trade was carried on by factors for Copenhagen merchants.[18]

Within the Swedish monarchy there was relatively little exchange of domestic goods between Sweden and Finland, since both produced largely the same things. Within the Danish monarchy there existed a more complex balance. Denmark exported most of its grain surplus to Norway, for which Norwegian timber, iron, copper, glass, and fish covered only a part of the balance; the rest was made up through the export abroad of Norwegian timber and fish, and the freight services of Norwegian shipping. Thus whereas Norway provided the main market for Denmark's products, Denmark could offer only a limited outlet for Norway's, which therefore comprised the monarchy's principal native exports. Iceland and the Færøes meanwhile exchanged their raw wool, knitwares, eider down, and fish for Danish grain and Norwegian timber. Schleswig and Holstein formed their own separate tariff area within the monarchy—except for a few enclaves, of which Altona was the most important—and were largely oriented toward the Hamburg market.

Scandinavian trade, both domestic and foreign, was mainly waterborne, hence the vital importance of shipping. Norwegian shippers enjoyed a particular advantage over those in Baltic ports because of their longer sailing season from ice-free harbors and the shorter distances to western Europe, especially Great Britain, Scandinavia's principal trade partner. Norwegian ships could thus normally make at least two round trips to Britain during the season.[19] The same factors also largely account for Gothenburg's importance in Sweden's trade. Both governments sought to protect native shipping. The Swedish *Produktplakat* of 1724, modeled on the British Navigation Acts, required that foreign ships carry to Sweden only products of their countries of origin. The Danish trade monopolies largely served the same purpose. Meanwhile the wars of the late seventeenth and eighteenth centuries gave a great stimulus to neutral Scandinavian shipping.

The greatest weakness of the Scandinavian economies lay in the area of money and finance. Although they produced some copper and small amounts of silver, they lacked sufficient bullion for a wide metallic base, as well as trade balances that could accumulate it from abroad. Hence the extensive use of barter, payment in kind, and compensation for public services *in natura* and through crown tenancies. Hence also the regular issue of paper money in both states by the middle of the eighteenth century, to supplement specie.

Already in 1668 the Swedish state took over a private banking house that had failed, thus founding Europe's first national bank. A central bank for the Danish monarchy was established in Copenhagen in 1736. Credit remained in short supply, however. The banks in Stockholm and Copenhagen tended to compound the problem by favoring the large merchant houses of the capitals at the expense of the provinces. It was in particular a recurrent source of irritation to Norwegian merchants that Copenhagen, in keeping with its centralizing, mercantilistic policies, repeatedly refused to allow a separate bank for Norway. Swedish iron and Norwegian timber exporters commonly operated on credit extended to them by their foreign trade partners.

Worse than the tightness of credit was the instability of the currencies, particularly after 1760. Under the financial strains of the Seven Years' War both governments issued quantities of unbacked paper money. The same device would be employed again on various occasions down to the end of our period, wreaking periodic havoc in economic life.

As the Nordic lands were increasingly drawn into an international market economy fraught with financial hazards, there was a growing tendency by the later eighteenth century toward the concentration of wealth in the hands of the greater entrepreneurs, both rural and urban.

Just as the Danish monarchy presented western Europe's widest contrasts of topography and climate, it also offered its broadest spectrum of social conditions, from the highly corporatistic society, of the central European type, in Schleswig-Holstein, through the less elaborate structure of Denmark, to the sturdy peasant societies of Norway, Iceland, and the Færøes. Yet friction between these diverse elements was dampened by a royal absolutism which allowed no corporate role in the government of the realm to any of them. In Sweden-Finland circumstances were more uniform and contrasts less extreme. The political representation of the Estates, however, gave social distinctions a more immediate significance and led earlier to social conflict. Although conditions in Sweden's small German territories in Pomerania and Wismar resembled those in Denmark's German lands, their populations were far smaller.

Following the introduction of Christianity, a nobility of the European type had evolved in the Scandinavian North during the High Middle Ages. Its representatives in the eighteenth century were unevenly distributed. They were most heavily concentrated in the German provinces, Denmark, Skåne, and the fertile south-central provinces of Sweden; more thinly spread in the rest of the southern one-third of Sweden (the regions of Götaland and Svealand) and in southern Finland; and virtually absent—except in certain official posts—throughout Sweden's northern two-thirds (Norrland), most of Finland, and all of Norway, Iceland, and the Færøes.

Outside the German territories, nobility in Scandinavia showed certain distinctive features. Monarchical power had been relatively strong during the Middle Ages, and a free peasantry had remained the direct subjects of their kings. Thus apart from some of its trappings, feudalism never really developed in Scandinavia. Nobles might be powerful on the basis of their own alodial lands, but the holding of service fiefs never became hereditary and a pattern of subinfeudation never developed.

Although the Danish and Swedish nobilities had wielded great political power during the sixteenth and seventeenth centuries, they had been curbed in the later seventeenth century by their monarchs, with the support of the nonnoble orders, and largely replaced or diluted by new service nobilities. The process was not unlike that which transformed the Russian nobility around the same period and indeed provided inspiration for it.

The era of noble dominance (*"Adelsvældet"*) came to an end in Denmark when the Estates of the Clergy and Burghers combined at the Diet of 1660 to give Frederik III and his posterity full and undivided sovereignty. The king and his immediate successors mistrusted the old nobility of Denmark and Schleswig-Holstein, which was excluded from power and responsibility, and thereafter declined rapidly. Already by 1700 most of its lands had passed into other hands and many of the old families were impoverished. In Norway the last remnants of the proud medieval nobility sank into the peasant class.

The old Danish and Norwegian nobility had recognized no internal distinctions. In 1671, however, Christian V created a new high nobility of counts and barons (lensgreve and lensbaroner), to serve largely as an ornamental court noblesse as at Louis XIV's Versailles and endowed with special privileges on their manorial domains (lensgrevskaber and lensbaronier) of requisite size. In the same year there was established a table of ranks for the civil and military establishments, conferring personal or hereditary nobility upon the highest categories of officials. Both the small high nobility of counts and barons and the larger nobility of rank (rangadel) contained few persons from the older nobility and consisted almost entirely of persons drawn from the burgher and clerical classes, and of foreigners, above all Germans.[20]

In the Swedish monarchy, events followed a similar course in 1680, when the Clerical, Burgher, and Peasant Estates of the Riksdag conferred absolute sovereignty upon Karl XI, thus breaking the power of the nobility. The government thereupon reclaimed those crown lands that had been lost to the nobility since the beginning of the century, thereby reducing the total effective landholdings of the nobility by about half in Sweden and Finland. Although the older nobility remained active in state service, they could not fill heavy demands, especially for military officers, during the wars of Karl XII. Following the warrior-king's death and the end of royal absolutism in 1718, large numbers of nonnoble officers and bureaucrats were ennobled by the crown and accepted or "introduced" into the House of the Nobility (Riddarhus), the Noble Estate of the Riksdag. In the conflict within that Estate between the older and the newer, service nobility, the latter gained the upper hand by the 1730s. In Sweden, as in Denmark, the leading aristocrats of the eighteenth century were thus relatively new men and likewise often of foreign extraction.[21]

In both monarchies the nobility supported itself partly through landownership, partly through state service, which in turn was frequently rewarded, especially in Sweden-Finland, through the holding of service tenures of house and land on the crown domain. Those who were owners of manors (hovedgårde, säterier) enjoyed certain privileges, which, however, were attached to the land rather than the person. The most important of these were exemptions, under certain conditions, from the land taxes on the manorial demesne itself.

Throughout the century there was growing pressure from the nonnoble classes upon these traditional noble preserves. Manorial lands with their tax privileges fell increasingly into the hands of nonnoble proprietors. Axel Linvald noted that between 1730 and 1766 the number of farmsteads in Denmark owned by bourgeois proprietors increased from 33.5 to 42.5 percent, their total share of the assessed agricultural land grew from 22.9 to 30.9 percent, while roughly half of the land in noble ownership was held by members of the new nobility of recent burgher or foreign origin. One-third of Sweden and about 9 percent of Finland consisted of privileged manorial (*frälse*) land of various types, to which, at the beginning of the century, the nobility had exclusive legal right. In practice, however, they had already lost some of this land by 1723, when other persons of quality (*ståndspersoner*)—excluding the peasantry—were formally allowed to purchase most forms of manorial land. By 1760 some 15 percent of it in Sweden had passed into nonnoble ownership, and much of the remainder belonged to nobles of recent origin.[22]

In both monarchies at mid-century the top positions in administration, in the officer and diplomatic corps, and at court were monopolized by the nobility. No commoners sat on state councils or held rank in royal entourages. But below this level men of nonnoble status vied vigorously and generally successfully with the lower nobility. The Scandinavian kingdoms were no longer expansive European powers. Their aristocracies were now faced with mounting competition for land and state employment from the nonnoble orders, while custom made it difficult for them to enter other walks of life.

By around 1760 there were signs in Scandinavia, as elsewhere in Europe, of a growing aristocratic reaction in defense of noble exclusivity and status. In both the Danish and Swedish monarchies old traditions of hostility toward the nobility meanwhile lingered on from the conflicts of the seventeenth century and earlier. Characteristically the nonnoble classes, and particularly the peasantry, looked to their kings as their guardians against the pretentions of the nobility. According to a contemporary, meanwhile, Frederik V's failure in October 1760 to celebrate the centennial of royal absolutism was taken by the burghers of Copenhagen as confirmation "that we no longer have any king and that the nobles twist and turn him as they will."[23]

Both monarchies had their state Lutheran churches, whose clergy enjoyed corporate status and in effect comprised an element of the bureaucracy. In Sweden-Finland it was represented by its own Estate in the *Riksdag*. Although open to outside recruitment, the clergy tended to consist largely of an oligarchy of established clerical families. Few nobles or burghers sought ordination, while peasants' sons who did so seldom rose to the higher levels of preferment.[24]

Non-Lutherans were few and only gradually came to enjoy some measure of tolerance, largely because of the economic advantages to be gained by allowing the immigration of skilled foreigners. Religious freedom was permitted in the free port of Altona in Holstein, for instance, and a colony of Moravian Brethren would be established at Christiansfeld in Schleswig in 1772. By this time Moravians were already distinguishing themselves as missionaries in Denmark's overseas colonies. More important than the small numbers of non-Lutherans were widespread pietistic influences among the clergy and laity of the state churches themselves.

To the burgher estate belonged all who held citizenship rights in chartered towns, including merchants, municipal officers, and master craftsmen. Its members enjoyed privileged monopolies on most forms of trade and production for trade within their specified areas.

The estate had its own internal hierarchy. First came the powerful and wealthy merchant oligarchies of the capitals, Copenhagen and Stockholm, which controlled the lion's share of overseas trade and of finance, followed by the smaller elites of the main provincial centers also engaged in foreign trade: Gothenburg, Christiania, Bergen, Trondheim, Flensburg, Altona. Closely associated with and largely deriving from them were the magistratures of these towns. Below these levels were the mass of middling and smaller merchants, in both the larger centers and the smaller provincial towns, and the manufacturers, who generally operated on a modest scale. At the bottom were the craft masters, generally organized into guilds.

While the burghers tended to be socially ambitious, they were also jealous of their own distinctions and privileges, which they everywhere defended against encroachment. The great merchant families of the leading towns were closely knit through ties of business, blood, and marriage, and were often of foreign extraction. The wealthiest of them could rival the high nobility in opulence and style of living. Many owned manors in the countryside, and in Denmark-Norway, they indulged their vanity by purchasing honorific personal titles of the German type, such as *etatsråd* or *justitsråd*.

Within the burgher estate there were cleavages between different categories of merchant, between merchant and artisan, and between merchant and magistrate. In smaller provincial towns, however, they lost much of their import. Here the distinctions between merchant, artisan, and town official were less clear-cut. No guilds existed in many of the smaller localities, although their craftsmen might sometimes be affiliated with those in larger centers.[25]

Aside from those who enjoyed actual burgher status, there were elements, both urban and rural, that in a terminology soon to evolve would be recognized as "middle-class" and which included a variety of persons not legally belonging to any of the traditional estates. In Sweden they were referred to as *ofrälse ståndspersoner*, "nonnoble persons of quality," and included many landowners, ironmasters, manufacturers, and government officials. Here they were of particular significance, since they were prominent in the economy, administration, and society, yet were excluded from political representation in the *Riksdag*.[26]

During the century there were signs of an emerging sense of middle-class identity, encompassing not only the old burgher estate, but also a variety of non-noble persons of quality and, to a degree, certain elements of the clergy and even of the lower bureaucratic nobility which shared similar interests and outlooks. This development first manifested itself clearly in Norway, where in the virtual absence of a native nobility, the town merchants, manufacturers, civil and military officials, and clergy formed a common upper class—*"de konditionerte"* or "persons of condition"—as distinguished from the urban and rural masses. By the 1760s middle-class awareness was developing markedly in Sweden and Finland.[27]

The towns contained only a small part of the population. In Denmark this amounted as late as 1801 to about a fifth, in Sweden in 1805 to less than a tenth of the total; on Iceland, the largest community, Reykjavík, had at that time only some 300 inhabitants.[28] Within the towns, only a minority belonged to the burgher estate, or even the more broadly defined middle classes. The rest consisted of apprentices and journeymen, domestic servants, unskilled laborers, seamen, and enlisted military personnel, as well as paupers, orphans, and criminals, for whom the municipalities made some minimal provision. There were also migrant laborers from the countryside and in places a certain number of unnaturalized foreigners, among them Jews or other non-Lutherans, especially in Holstein.

Everywhere, however, the peasantry comprised the great mass of the population, and the greatest cleavages within Nordic society were those separating the peasants from those above them in the existing hierarchies. Of no less significance, Sten Carlsson has shown that the conditions of the peasantry—legal, economic, and political—were never farther apart in the different Scandinavian lands than they were by the middle of the eighteenth century.[29]

In the mid-eighteenth century conditions were probably worst for much of the peasantry of the German provinces, who were serfs, *Leibeigne* of the East Elbian type. In Denmark male peasants were bound to the manors through a form of virtual serfdom, in fact if not in name. In Norway, Iceland, and the Færøes, they were both juridically free and largely freeholders. The same was true in Sweden and Finland, where the peasant freeholders were also represented by their own Estate in the *Riksdag*.

Once again, it is the Danish monarchy that offers the greatest contrasts. In Denmark proper, the peasantry had been free—as it was in the other Scandinavian lands—until the agricultural depression of the fifteenth century, when the practice of *vornedskab* developed on the islands of Sjælland (Zealand), Møn, Falster, and Lolland. Under this system, a male peasant could not leave a manor without his lord's consent and was obliged to take over a vacant tenant farm at the lord's demand. From the same time there also took place a constant expansion of manors at the expense of peasant freeholds, so that by the mid-eighteenth century only about 3 percent of the peasants were freeholders.[30]

The Danish government showed a certain paternalistic concern for the peasantry, not least since it payed the land tax. The crown prohibited, in 1682, further incorporation of tenant farms into manorial demesnes, an injunction periodically repeated, though frequently enough circumvented, during the eighteenth century. In 1702 Frederik IV took the unprecedented step of abolishing *vornedskab* for peasants born in the affected area after 1701, the first real attempt at peasant emancipation in Europe.[31]

This reform proved immature, however, since the real root of the peasant problem was the manors' near monopoly of agricultural land, which reduced the peasantry to a dependent class of tenant farmers and hired laborers, even without *vornedskab* or where it had never existed. In return for their tenancies, most peasant tenants paid an initial fee (*indfæstning*) upon assuming their leases, as well as an annual quitrent *in natura* or in money, and generally provided varying amounts of labor (*hoveri*) to the proprietor's demesne (*hovedgård*).

The situation for both proprietors and peasants worsened with the severe agricultural depression of the 1720s and early 1730s. Proprietors had difficulty in filling vacant tenant farms and were much concerned over loss of labor through free migration. This led to the establishment of the *stavnsbånd* in 1733 by Christian VI: the male peasant was *stavnsbunden*, or "place-bound," forbidden to leave the manor where he resided from his fourteenth to his thirty-sixth year without the proprietor's permission. Its official purpose was to keep men of military age within their districts throughout their period of liability for conscription into the militia.

Militarily the *stavnsbånd* made little difference, for the regular Danish units—as opposed to the Norwegian—consisted of recruited, mercenary troops and relatively few peasants were called up for militia service. It was far more significant for the manorial proprietors, whose interests it clearly served. As they were empowered to designate men for conscription on their manors, they could use this threat to pressure peasants into accepting vacant tenancies, often on onerous terms; although militia service normally involved only brief training on Sundays, it was feared and hated by the peasantry.

Unlike the old *vornedskab*, the *stavnsbånd* applied to all of Denmark, except the islands of Bornholm and Amager. Proprietors continuously urged its extension. Already by 1746 it was extended from the ninth to the fortieth year; in 1762 its lower limit was set at four years. There were even attempts to include women under it, but this was hardly necessary for their mobility was effectively limited by the restrictions on male peasants.[32]

The *stavnsbånd* was a characteristically mercantilistic measure in its concern for the wealth of the state and view of the individual as a cog in the economic machine. The state's immediate concern was the agricultural depression; thus the *stavnsbånd* must be seen in connection with the closing of Denmark and southern Norway to foreign grain imports in 1735 and a temporary lowering of the land tax. Under the conditions of that time, increased agricultural production for the market was expected only from a more intensive cultivation of the manorial demesne lands. Within a few years production and prices did indeed rise, although it remains a matter of dispute to what extent this was due to the government's drastic measures in the early 1730s or to rising population and generally improved conditions throughout Europe.[33]

At the same time, the *stavnsbånd* is a sign of the government's administrative weakness. Despite the king's theoretical absolutism, the bureaucratic machine was still so undeveloped that it had to make use of the proprietor class to fulfill basic public functions at the local level, and was thus bound to accommodate its interests. The proprietor's responsibilities included providing candidates for conscription into the militia and collecting the land tax for all the peasant tenant farms on the manor. If these tenancies comprised at least 200 *tønder hartkorn*—the basic fiscal unit of land—the manor was designated as "complete," which exempted its demesne from the land tax. (For countships and baronies, much of the land in peasant tenancies was also exempt.) If his tenant farms fell vacant, the proprietor remained personally liable for their taxes. He was meanwhile forbidden to incorporate them into the demesne or to reduce their number. Noble proprietors and those with special royal dispensations were authorized to maintain their own manorial courts and to appoint the pastors of local churches under their patronage.[34]

The Danish peasants' lot in the mid-eighteenth century was unenviable. Manorial tenancies were normally granted for life, which was binding on the tenant, although his landlord could find reasons enough to evict him for real or alleged violations of his lease. When a tenant died, the landlord had first claim upon his estate to compensate himself for outstanding debts or for deterioration—real or alleged—of the tenancy, and his widow and children could be evicted to make room for a new tenant. Peasant families could thus be bound to poverty, generation after generation.

Labor services varied greatly in nature and extent, but they tended generally to become increasingly onerous up to the final decades of the century. The spread of market-oriented agriculture encouraged the establishment of new manors and the enlargement of existing ones, together with widespread, often complex transactions to consolidate scattered demesne lands and to cluster close around them the peasant tenancies providing labor for their cultivation. This labor increased in amount as landlords brought under the plow previously untilled demesne holdings. The burden became greater still as the crown confiscated many remaining peasant freeholds for tax defaults, then sold them to private proprietors, enlarging their demesnes while reducing the numbers of peasant farms paying taxes and supplying labor. Unspecified and unlimited labor obligations frequently compelled peasant farmers to keep hired hands and extra horses they could ill afford, while they themselves might be hard pressed to work their own holdings, especially in the busiest seasons. When laboring on the demesne, peasants could be subjected to degrading corporal punishment by the landlord's bailiff.

To be sure, conditions were seldom as bad in every respect as they could be. The proprietor's need to keep his tenancies filled with reliable tenants provided a strong, practical motive for moderation.[35] A certain number of peasants were, moreover, able to obtain so-called free passes from their landlords, usually for payment; some, indeed, eventually became proprietors themselves, in which case they were often reputed to be hard taskmasters. Yet abuses were all too common, and it is not surprising that the Danish peasantry, especially on Sjæl-land, had a reputation for listlessness and irresponsibility.

The island of Bornholm was unique because by 1744 all its peasant farmers were freeholders. Noble manorialism had indeed never existed there. Aside from Bornholm's approximately 1,100 peasant freeholds, there were only some 600 freehold farms in the rest of Denmark at mid-century. Yet the meaning of freehold (*selveje*) could vary considerably and at this time was often more or less synonymous with hereditary tenancy (*arvefæste*). The peasant freeholder could still be subject to the local manorial court and pay a perpetual annual fee or render labor services to a former manorial landlord for his holding. Outside Bornholm and Amager, he was also bound to his district—although not to a land-lord—by the *stavnsbånd*.[36]

In addition to the peasant farmers (*gårdmænd*) and their families, the peas-antry included various other categories. Farms and manors employed numerous hired hands, both male and female, who were generally lodged and fed by their masters. Cotters (*husmænd*) were provided with a cottage, with or without a plot of land, on a terminable lease, in exchange for at least part-time work on the farm or manor. *Inderster* rented lodgings on a farm, taking such occasional work as the neighborhood provided. Rural paupers received some minimal support from the parish. Under the *stavnsbånd* the demands upon the tenant farmer were often so great that many peasants did their best to avoid having tenancies forced upon them. Peasants frequently circulated from one category to another during the course of their lives.[37]

In the duchies, Schleswig and Holstein, conditions varied more widely. In eastern Holstein and southeastern Schleswig, serfdom (*Leibeigenschaft*) pre-vailed. The serfs were legal dependents of their lords, without codified rights under the law. They held tenancies at the lord's pleasure and performed heavy and arbitrary labor services (*Frohndienst*). Tenant farms did not enjoy the same protection as in Denmark, and their absorption into the demesne lands proceeded much further, resulting in large latifundia.

In western Holstein and most of Schleswig, however, the great majority of the peasantry was free and in some areas peasant freeholders were numerous. Meanwhile much of the peasant population consisted of cotters and landless laborers, especially in the areas with serfdom and large estates.[38]

The peasantry of Norway was juridically free and consisted largely of free-holders. The early eighteenth century was a good time for the Norwegian peasantry, in contrast to the Danish. During the 1660s the government had sold off much crown property, principally to merchants, officials, and other nonpeasants. After the end of the Great Northern War, it sold off most of its remaining landholdings in Norway, this time largely to peasants. During the agricultural depression of the second quarter of the century much of the former crown land purchased earlier by persons outside the peasant class was sold off to peasant buyers, who took advantage of depressed land prices. Thus, whereas the sale of crown lands in Denmark and the Duchies at this time profited mainly the manorial proprietors, the number of Norwegian peasant farmers who owned their land increased from around one quarter in the mid-seventeenth to three-quarters in the mid-eighteenth century, by which time about two-thirds of the land belonged to those who cultivated it. Whether this was mainly due to government policy in selling off crown lands or to low land prices during the agricultural slump has been argued by Norwegian historians.[39]

It was the pride of the Norwegian peasant freeholder that his farm, if hereditary property, was protected by *odel* right, according to which it could not be sold outside the family without its common consent, and could be repurchased from an outside buyer upon demand of a family member at the buyer's purchase price within twenty years. Under the *åsetesret*, the farm passed undivided to the nearest heir, who in turn provided compensation or support to the others. These ancient rights preserved peasant land in peasant hands, providing a protection without parallel outside Scandinavia, but could cause economic problems by obstructing the circulation of property on an open market and the raising of credit against collateral.

Peasant freeholding was most widespread in the richer and more populous Østlandet and Trøndelag regions, whereas tenancy remained common in the poorer districts in the west and north, as well as in Norway's only entailed noble manors, the countships of Laurvig and Jarlsberg, and the barony of Rosendal. Since 1687 life tenancy was mandatory in Norway. Rents remained fixed at relatively low levels, while only the fee payable upon assuming a tenancy could be raised, providing the landowner with his principal return. In the absence of manorial demesne farming, the tenant (*leilending*) usually owed no labor service and could devote himself entirely to his own farm. Most worked farms occupied by their families for generations, some leased large and profitable holdings, and many held land under both leasehold and freehold. Indeed, before the division of farms among heirs was legally permitted in 1769, and even thereafter, the ownership of a single farm was often shared by several persons, who were entitled to portions of its produce and responsible for parts of its land tax. The status of the cultivator was thus determined more by the size and prosperity of the farm he tilled, rather than by the terms of his occupancy.[40] Below the peasant farmers, both freeholders and tenants, there were numerous cotters, hired hands, day laborers, and paupers.[41]

The proud Norwegian hereditary freeholder—the *odelbonde*, whose family farm was protected by law and custom—was the ideal of eighteenth-century Danish agrarian reformers, just as the oppressed Holstein serf was its opposite. Yet among the landless elements of the peasantry in Norway the same ideal freedom did not apply. Unlike in Denmark, the backbone of the Norwegian part of the army was the territorial militia, while Norwegian farmers, like Danish landlords, feared a dearth of farm laborers during the first half of the century. An ordinance in 1754 therefore required that young, unmarried men who did not cultivate land take service for not less than a year at a time within their own parishes, which they were forbidden to leave without permission from the royal bailiff to ensure recruitment for the army.[42]

Within the peasantry there were thus marked social distinctions between a kind of "peasant aristocracy" of old, prosperous, and respected families and the mass of small farmers, cotters, and landless laborers. The greatest cleavage within Norwegian society was, however, that which separated the peasantry as a whole from the upper class of merchants, officials, and clergy, which was largely of Danish, German, or other foreign derivation. Toward them, the Norwegian peasants felt a hostility and suspicion that in Denmark, the duchies, and Sweden-Finland was reserved largely for the nobility. The peasantry in their often remote settlements lived as much as possible within their own world: their basically self-sufficient economy, the communal management of their own affairs according to custom, their ancient and elaborate culture. The attitude of their own leaders was well expressed by the peasant chieftan Trond Laurpak, who proudly claimed, "Frederik is king in Denmark, but I am king in Bjerkreim!"[43]

On Iceland and the Færøes the peasants were likewise free, although a much larger proportion were tenants than in Norway, and, on Iceland at least, under harder terms. Slightly over half the Icelandic farms were peasant freeholds; the remainder belonged to the crown, the bishoprics of Skálholt and Hólar, the parish churches, and charitable funds. Rents were fixed, but during bad years tenants were frequently evicted for nonpayment, and they were often heavily burdened with labor services to the landlord or bailiff. Extensive subleasing of landholdings frequently increased the tenants' obligations.[44]

Conditions for the peasantry in Sweden and Finland were basically uniform, and lay somewhere between those prevailing in Norway and in Denmark. The peasantry was juridically free, but many peasant farmers were tenants, on either limited or lifetime leases, on noble manors, which comprised about one-third of the land. Tenant farmers paid a fee upon assuming their tenancies and a yearly rent, usually in produce. Those close to the manorial seat could also be required to perform labor services. The situation was worse in this respect in the south-ernmost Swedish provinces of Skåne and Halland, which had been part of Den-mark until 1658, than elsewhere in Sweden and Finland. Here labor service pro-vided almost entirely for the cultivation of extensive manorial demesnes; it was not clearly fixed in amount, as elsewhere in the kingdom, and was often arbi-trarily increased and harshly enforced. Much of the manorial tenantry in Sweden and Finland meanwhile lived on widely scattered tenancies, unaffected by labor services, which were commuted to fees. Such tenants were often prosperous, and after it became legally possible in 1789, many bought their farms to become freeholders.[45]

About a third of the land belonged to the crown, following the *reduktion* or repossession of previously alienated domain in the 1680s. Peasant tenants on crown lands paid their rent directly to the treasury. During much of the century they were permitted to purchase their tenancies, which they did in large numbers.

The remaining third of Sweden at the beginning of the century belonged to peasant freeholders, who paid the land tax and, like crown tenants, could be called upon to perform limited labor service on roads and other public projects. Peasant freeholders and crown tenants were represented in the *Riksdag* by their own Peasant Estate. As elsewhere in Scandinavia, there were nonetheless limits to the peasant freeholder's rights of ownership, which did not apply to land-owners of other classes. These included restrictions on their hunting and forest rights, and until 1747 on their right to divide their farms. Although other com-moners were permitted to acquire outlying manorial lands in 1724, this privilege would not be extended to the peasantry until 1789. At times they were debarred from purchasing crown land. The most serious encroachment upon their free-dom was the regulations limiting the number of farm laborers they might em-ploy. According to a statute in force until 1747, these went so far that a peasant farmer was forbidden to keep his own grown or half-grown children at home if their number exceeded by more than one the number of hired hands allowed for his farm. Not until 1789 could the peasant farmer hire as many hands as he wished. The peasants nonetheless widely circumvented the legal restrictions on their freedom, so that their eventual abolition largely followed the actual state of affairs.[46]

Population growth was reflected most strongly in the relative increase of the cotter (*torpare*) and landless elements of the peasantry. Throughout the century, and beyond, unemployed, landless peasants could be compelled by statute to take work with local farmers under year-long contracts, on pain of being placed in workhouses. Their maximum wages were strictly limited, and in upper Norr-land and Finland laborers were forbidden until 1766 to leave their districts (*län*) to seek employment elsewhere. The master was allowed to administer "moderate corporal punishment" to his hired folk. Here, as elsewhere in Scandinavia, fear

of a lack of agricultural labor and military manpower during the century expressed itself in oppressive mercantilistic legislation and a growing gap between
the propertied and unpropertied elements of the peasantry.[47]

Swedish Pomerania, together with Wismar, had a population of around
90,000 in 1721 and 100,000 in 1800, most of which consisted of peasants. Like
Holstein, it remained a fief under the Holy Roman Empire, which perpetuated
its existing social structure. The Pomeranian peasants were serfs, under conditions evidently more oppressive than in Holstein. They were bound to their
manors, although their lords could move, exchange or even sell them at will.
They could marry only with their lords' consent and were under the jurisdiction
of manorial courts in all civil and criminal matters. Peasant tenants were burdened with heavy labor services, amounting usually to four days' work per
week, sometimes more, on the demesne. They could be evicted at any time from
their tenancies, which occurred frequently with the growing practice, throughout northern Germany, of expanding the demesne by incorporating tenant farms.
Increasing numbers of Pomeranian peasants were thus reduced to landless
laborers.[48]

In comparing peasant conditions in the North, we must beware of overly
facile generalizations. Manifest contrasts at the level of the farmholders, freehold or tenant, should not distract from a high degree of similarity in the status
of the landless classes, everywhere subject to legal restraints.

We should also realize that it is all too easy to judge peasant conditions from
a Western liberal perspective, simply equating personal liberty and freehold
property with overall well-being. A tenant farmer with a sizable, indivisible
tenancy, even if bound to the manor, was often more prosperous than the owner
of a small, unproductive freehold, subject to divided inheritances.[49] Johannes
Steenstrup argued in 1888 that the Danish peasant enjoyed greater protection
under the law than his English counterpart in the eighteenth century; more
recently Olaf Klose described the peasants under the juridically more onerous
Leibeigenschaft in Schleswig-Holstein as less oppressed and more independent
in their behavior than the Danish peasants under the stavnsbånd. Jerome Blum
estimated manorial labor services in Denmark and especially Holstein to be the
heaviest in any of Europe's "servile lands." Fridlev Skrubbeltrang holds, meanwhile, that a more productive agriculture protected the rural population against
famine better in Denmark than elsewhere in Scandinavia, and Eli F. Heckscher
recognized that a meager and insecure food supply was the price Sweden-Finland paid for the freedom of its peasantry.[50]

Scandinavian society—outside the German provinces—presented a distinctive
profile. For all its local differences, this was at once more archaic and more
"modern" than that of continental Europe as a whole. It was distinguished by a
small nobility, never really feudalized and virtually absent from entire regions,
where it was replaced at the top of society by essentially middle-class elites; an

urban element weak in numbers and in corporate organization outside the two capitals: above all by a peasantry with ancient traditions of freedom, which remained the direct subjects of their monarchs under the protection of the laws, despite varying limitations on their actual freedom by the mid-eighteenth century.

Neither of the two Scandinavian states was a fully unified, national state in the eighteenth century. The Danish monarchy, or rather the lands of the Olden-burg house, was indeed something of a showcase for early modern European dynasticism and colonialism, comprising a conglomeration of territories held under differing titles and historic claims, governed by different administrative structures and laws. Sweden-Finland formed a juridical and administrative unity, but this did not include the German territories of Swedish Pomerania and Wismar.

The complexity of the Danish state was reflected in the terminology applied to it. "The Monarchy" (*Riget*) referred to the state in its entirety; "the Duchies" (*Hertugdømmerne* or *die Herzogtümer*) to Schleswig and Holstein, although not to Oldenburg and Delmenhorst, which were geographically separate; and "the Kingdom" (*Kongeriget*) to Denmark and Norway, including the old Norwegian tributary lands of Iceland, the Færøes, and Greenland; there were also "the Colonies" in India, West Africa, and the West Indies.

In October 1660, when the three Danish Estates convened in Copenhagen, the Clergy and Burghers combined against the Nobility to declare the king hereditary and in effect to vest him with full sovereign power. The Norwegian Estates followed suit in 1661. Thus ended the long period of noble domination in the kingdom since the sixteenth century, and the Danish and Norwegian Estates consigned themselves to oblivion. The change in regime was confirmed by the Royal Law (*Kongelov* or *Lex Regia*) of 1665, the most uncompromising statement of royal absolutism of its time, which proclaimed the monarch respon-sible to God alone. Thus, from one of Europe's weakest rulers, the Danish-Norwegian king became its theoretically most absolute, at least within the King-dom proper.[51]

The basic features of Danish absolutism were concentration and uniformity. All authority emanated from the king, through the central administration in Copenhagen. This was organized collegially and largely staffed with foreigners to prevent any individual from gaining undue influence over the monarch or the old nobility from recovering its power. Local administration was standardized, and the laws were codified in Denmark and Norway.

Personal absolutism reached its height under Frederik IV (1699–1730). His immediate successors were, however, no longer up to the burden it imposed. Christian VI (1730–46) was well-meaning and industrious, but physically weak and prone to lose himself in detail. Increasingly the business of government devolved upon the government bureaus, or *kollegier*, where *de facto* heads emerged to take control. The more important of these sat on – or were eventually taken into – the royal council (*konsejl*), which became the real locus of power, with the king giving his more or less automatic consent to its proposals. This transformation from a personal to a bureaucratic absolutism was completed under Frederik V (1746–66), who, though handsome and popular, was lazy and debauched, and after the first few years degenerated into a hopeless alcoholic.

Both kings continued to fill the council and top administrative posts with foreigners, above all with Germans from outside the duchies. This became in time less a matter of principle than of convenience and personal connections, as Germans already in Danish service secured appointments for their relatives and friends. The language of the court, the army, and much of the administration was German under Christian VI and Frederik V. During Frederik V's entire reign only one Dane and one Holsteiner sat on the royal council.

Nationality as such meant little to cosmopolitan eighteenth-century statesmen, and the Germans were on the whole well chosen, capable, and dedicated. Denmark-Norway thus drew upon a greater reservoir of abilities than it itself could provide, while offering—together with much of the rest of Europe—a welcome field for underemployed talents from the smaller German principalities. After 1751 the dominating figure on the council was the Hanoverian Baron (later Count) Johan Hartwig Ernst Bernstorff, the foreign minister, who worked smoothly with the Mecklenburger Count Adam Gottlob Moltke, Frederik V's favorite, a conscientious and astute "gray eminence." They and their peers were representatives of an aristocratic bureaucratism, which stressed the monarch's need for stable institutions, dependable councillors, and the nobility as intermediaries between himself and the mass of his subjects.[52] In R. R. Palmer's terms, the Danish council—even though composed mainly of foreigners—was evolving into a kind of "quasi-constituted body," essentially self-recruiting, noble in origin, and imbued with an appropriate philosophy to justify its position.[53] It performed conscientiously and with all due deliberation, keeping the ponderous wheels of administration turning. It was not, however, given to rapid and decisive action or to daring innovation.

The king and council ruled over the entire monarchy. Immediately under them, the *kollegier* had both regional and functional responsibilities. The Danish Chancellery was charged with administrative and judicial matters in the kingdom, that is to say, the whole monarchy except for the German provinces, for which the German Chancellery fulfilled the same functions. The president of the German Chancellery also served *ex officio* as foreign minister until 1770, and in fact most of the time until 1797. The other government departments, such as the Exchequer (*Rentekammer*), the Board of Trade (*Kommerskollegium*), and the Army and Navy Boards, had jurisdiction in their fields over the monarchy as a whole.

The kingdom and the duchies were divided into administrative districts, *stifter*, further divided into *amter*, under *stiftamtmænd* and *amtmænd*, respectively, the latter represented in subdistricts by royal bailiffs and clerks. The parish clergy, in the Danish monarchy as elsewhere, also fulfilled public functions, especially with respect to education and the gathering and dissemination of information. In Denmark and the duchies, manorial proprietors handled basic administrative and often judicial matters on their own estates. Especially in Norway and among the free peasantry in the duchies, there was a certain amount of parish self-rule; here too, peasant *lensmænd* were entrusted with keeping the peace and enforcing the government's edicts.

During the century there was a tendency for the government to replace the traditional magistracies of the towns with appointed mayors (*byfogder*), and even where older municipal forms persisted, the burgomaster (*borgmester*) and councillors (*rådmænd*) were responsible to the local *amtmand*. Still, the towns retained some vestiges of their old liberties, even where the magistracies had disappeared, through their "elected men" (*eligerede mænd*), who represented the citizenry and reviewed administration and finances in their municipalities.

If the king's theoretical power was limited by God alone, his effective power depended upon the quality of his officials. Until well into the century this often left much to be desired. Influence and connections played their role in appointments; many offices or "expectancies" were simply sold to the highest bidder; and there was much "lackeyism," the practice whereby bureaucrats rewarded their own personal retainers with minor government posts. Salaries were generally pitifully inadequate for the lower functionaries, who were often dependent for their compensation upon fees for their various duties. There could thus be a fair amount of corruption. This was a particular problem in Norway, partly because the local officials were far from the central government, partly because the proud Norwegian peasantry were quick to remonstrate, often by sending delegations to the king in Copenhagen. Yet the situation was improving. Christian VI required that no one be appointed to a judicial post without examination by the faculty of law at the University of Copenhagen. Conditions of service gradually improved, and the worst abuses were gradually being eliminated.

The position of Norway within the kingdom was somewhat ambiguous. From 1380 until 1536, it was clearly a separate realm, in dynastic union with Denmark (and much of that time, with Sweden-Finland as well). In the latter year, however, the Danish royal council decreed that henceforth Norway should "neither be nor be called a kingdom in itself" and that it formed an integral part of the Danish realm. Yet this policy had not been publicly stated nor was it consistently carried out.[54] The Norwegians themselves never ceased to consider their land a separate kingdom under the Oldenburg house. The Norwegian Estates accepted absolutism separately for Norway in 1661, at the same time urging unsuccessfully the establishment of various special Norwegian institutions. Thereafter Norway was increasingly welded into a unitary administrative system with Denmark. The position of *statholder*, or viceroy, for Norway, still important at the beginning of the eighteenth century, sank into insignificance and remained unfilled much of the time. Many of the top positions were held by Danes, Holsteiners, and Germans, whereas few Norwegians advanced into the higher posts of the central government in Denmark.[55]

Yet there still remained some differences. Great disparities in physical conditions, economy, and above all, social structure led to the establishment of similar but nonetheless separate law codes for Denmark in 1683 and Norway in 1687. During the eighteenth century the Norwegian bureaucracy developed an increasing corporate sense, and even those of its members who were not themselves Norwegians by origin often identified enthusiastically with specifically Norwegian interests. The Norwegian army remained administratively separate from the Danish and thus, particularly during wartime, a focus for Norwegian sentiment.

The only part of the kingdom to have a bureaucracy and clergy that were virtually all native-born, except for the *stiftamtmand* himself, was Iceland. Few outsiders had any desire to be posted there, and few could understand the language.[56]

In the duchies the administrative situation was more complex. Here the Danish Royal Law of 1665 did not expressly or in practice fully apply because of Holstein's connection with the Holy Roman Empire and Schleswig's ''indissoluble union'' with Holstein, and since only parts of both duchies were under the Danish crown at that time; most of the remainder belonged to a younger, rival line of the Oldenburg house, the dukes of Holstein-Gottorp. The Danish kings were thus constrained to tread lightly in matters of local privilege.

In the Great Northern War, Denmark gained complete control of Schleswig by 1720. Frederik IV evidently wished to incorporate the duchy outright into the kingdom but was prudent enough to settle for a local administration for Schleswig, separate from his holdings in Holstein.

Between 1720 and 1773 Holstein was divided among the ''royal portion'' (Holstein-Glückstadt), the lands of the duke of Holstein-Gottorp, mainly in the southeast around the ducal capital at Kiel, certain territories administered jointly by the king and the duke, and a couple of small autonomous enclaves acquired by the king by mid-century.

Schleswig and the royal parts of Holstein—like Oldenburg-Delmenhorst—had their own governing institutions under the German Chancellery in Copenhagen; at times the duchies also had their own *statholder*, who nonetheless played a relatively minor role. They had their own systems of law, Jutlandic in Schleswig, Germanic in Holstein. They maintained their own regiments, and Holstein was obligated to provide forty cavalrymen and eighty infantrymen to the *Reichsarmee* in the event the Holy Roman Empire went to war. Except for the free port of Altona, the Duchies formed their own tariff area, separate from the kingdom.

The old Schleswig-Holstein Estates, which had been powerful in the sixteenth century, fell into abeyance during the seventeenth; a last rump session of the Prelates and Nobility was held in 1711. The Schleswig-Holstein *Ritterschaft*, consisting of the old, established nobility throughout both duchies, nonetheless maintained its corporate existence throughout the century and beyond, holding periodic convocations and addressing repeated petitions for the preservation or increase of its privileges to the king in Copenhagen. In the absence of the defunct Estates, the *Ritterschaft* considered itself the guardian of the ancient rights and privileges of the duchies.[57]

There were, as seen, separate military establishments for Denmark, Norway, and the duchies. In all three territories peasants were conscripted on the basis of one man per designated area of farmland (*lægd*) to serve in the territorial militia. The difference was that whereas in Norway and the duchies the armies consisted principally of the militia regiments, in Denmark its core was composed of recruited, regular units, composed mainly of German mercenaries from outside the monarchy. Whereas the territorial troops lived on the land in their respective districts, meeting periodically for regimental training, the regular troops were permanently garrisoned in the capital and other towns and fortresses. The navy was a common institution, with regular cadres that could be filled out through maritime conscription in certain towns and districts, especially in Norway; the greater part of its personnel was indeed Norwegian.

Finance was always the greatest weakness of the Danish state, as it was in most of Europe. Its principal revenues derived from the regular land taxes, excise duties, tolls, tariffs, and income from the royal domain. At times these were augmented by extraordinary levies. Denmark bore the heaviest fiscal burden. It was lighter in Norway, which raised and maintained its own territorial troops; the government in Copenhagen was moreover always wary of stirring up discontent among the free Norwegian peasantry, whose loyalty was essential to defend their land against Sweden. Norway provided about one-sixth of the state revenue. In the duchies taxes were also generally lighter, owing to local privileges. Yet even in Norway and the duchies the burden could be onerous enough, considering the multitude of local levies and separate fees for the services of local officials, as well as the scarcity of money and credit.

From around 1730 until the early 1750s, the state budget varied between four and four and a half million *rigsdaler* annually, of which about half a million went to the king's privy purse. Altogether about a million *rigsdaler* went to the support of the royal family and court establishment; military and naval expenditures were the next largest item, followed by the civil administration, and thereafter by subsidies to economic and cultural enterprises.

Frederik IV had retrenched administrative costs and sold off crown lands to pay off the national debt following the Great Northern War. Sale of crown properties continued to reduce the standing debt until as late as 1754, but both Christian VI and Frederik V were lavish in their tastes, as attested by numerous monumental buildings and royal residences in and around Copenhagen. Christiansborg palace, begun in 1733, is estimated to have cost as much as all the landed property on Sjælland was worth during the years of its construction. Such luxury expenditures could be justified in mercantilist thought on grounds that they stimulated the circulation of money within the realm. But not surprisingly, the standing debt rose rapidly after 1754.[58]

Sweden and Finland comprised a single, unitary kingdom. Here too a royal absolutism was established, under Karl XI in 1680, a generation later than in Denmark-Norway. At the *Riksdag* of that year, mounting social conflicts led to the lower nobility combining with the Clerical, Burgher, and Peasant Estates to overwhelm the high nobility which had dominated the state council (*råd*). The *Riksdag* declared the king's authority limited by no law. There followed, as noted, a large-scale reappropriation (*reduktion*) from the nobility of previously alienated crown lands. The civil and military establishments were rationalized, the bureaucracy strengthened, and its higher functionaries ennobled. Yet just as the Swedish king had never been as limited in power during the seventeenth century as the Danish, "Caroline autocracy" was never as complete in practice as Danish absolutism. Karl XI preferred to work with, rather than abolish, the *Riksdag*, which had played a far more active role in the past than the Danish or Norwegian Estates. It retained the right to approve taxes under normal circumstances and gradually expanded its limited sphere of action.[59]

The ruinous Great Northern War and the sudden death of Karl XII without a direct heir in 1718 brought an end to Swedish absolutism and a powerful reaction against it. The *Riksdag* seized the initiative. In 1719–20 it accepted the late king's younger sister, Ulrika Eleanora, and her consort, Fredrik of Hesse, as reigning monarchs, subject to their acceptance of a new constitution ostensibly intended to restore an earlier, traditional balanced polity of crown, council, and estates. In actuality, the royalists soon had cause to complain that the king was reduced to a kind of "Venetian doge." He could administer the kingdom only through the council, which was set at sixteen members, where he could cast two votes in case of an even split; he was otherwise bound to the majority decision. Under such circumstances he could hardly play an independent role.

Until the 1730s it appeared that the council had regained its old and powerful role in government. It governed with wide discretionary powers between *riksdagar*, and its members were in principle appointed for life. Yet from the beginning its membership represented the dominant faction in the Estates. This principle was firmly established by 1738, when a new faction, which called itself the "Hats," gained ascendancy. The Hats arraigned most of the old "Cap" councillors on charges of misuse of power under the constitution before a *Riksdag* commission, which dismissed them, after which they were replaced by leading Hats. This process of *licentiering* would be repeated as *Riksdag* majorities changed in 1765, 1769, and 1771. Despite the legal fiction of dismissal for cause, former councillors normally retained the title and pension of the position and could be reappointed to the council with later changes of regime. There thus evolved a kind of parliamentarianism in Sweden, without parallel outside Great Britain.[60]

The ultimate power during Sweden's "Era of Liberty" (1718–72) thus resided in the *Riksdag*, which continually widened its jurisdiction. It legislated and had complete control of state finances. A flourishing system of *Riksdag* committees formulated policy and reviewed in minutest detail the performance of the council and government departments. Of central importance was the so-called Secret Committee (*Sekreta utskottet*), which concerned itself with vital matters of state security and finance, and evolved into a kind of "shadow cabinet" behind the council. Standing deputations watched over the administration between *riksdagar*, normally held every three years. On repeated occasions, special *Riksdag* commissions intervened directly in administrative matters or held inquests on politically suspect persons. The *Riksdag* determined the royal succession in 1719–20 and 1743.

The *Riksdag* was composed of four Estates: the Nobility (*Riddarskap och Adel*), the Clergy (*Prästestånd*), the Burghers (*Borgarstånd*), and—unique in Europe—the Peasants (*Bondestånd*). Of these, the Noble Estate was by far the largest and most influential, with proud constitutional traditions tracing back to the Middle Ages.[61] It consisted of the headmen of each of the "introduced" noble families in the kingdom, or their authorized proxies, altogether well over a thousand in number, although attendance was usually much smaller. In the seventeenth century it had been divided into three classes, each with one vote within the Estate, giving predominant power to a small high aristocracy of counts and barons, which had likewise dominated the council. This class division was abolished in 1719, allowing each member his individual vote, while the mass ennoblement of nonnoble officers and bureaucrats from the preceding war years soon flooded the *Riddarhus*, or House of the Nobility, with new men. The old "noble aristocracy" was thus overwhelmed by the new "noble democracy," to use Hugo Valentin's terms, most decisively with the Hat victory of 1738.[62] Indeed, one may carry Valentin's insight further and perceive the beginning of the dissolution of an aristocratic order in Sweden within the Noble Estate itself. The Nobility elected its *lantmarskalk*, or speaker, at each *Riksdag*. It provided half of the 100-man Secret Committee—which nonetheless voted by Estate—the other half being divided between the Clergy and the Burghers.

The Clerical Estate consisted of the bishops and elected members for each diocese, normally fifty-one in all, presided over by the archbishop of Uppsala. Although curates without parishes of their own were permitted to elect representatives, few of them ever sat in the Estate.

The Burgher Estate comprised the representatives of Sweden's and Finland's 101 towns, of which Stockholm sent ten—among whom the speaker, or *talman*, of the Estate was traditionally elected—Gothenburg sent three, and the remainder one or two each. Because smaller towns often combined to send a common representative, the Estate usually numbered between eighty and ninety members. In Stockholm, which by the 1760s had some 40 percent of Sweden's entire urban population, elections to the Burgher Estate were indirect, within a number of separate occupational groups; in other towns they were usually direct. Graduated voting rights favored the wealthier burghers.

Members of the Peasant Estate were elected, usually indirectly, by all peasant freeholders and crown tenants. They generally numbered some 150. Although they elected their own speaker, the influential secretary was appointed by all four Estates together, and the Peasants did not sit on the Secret Committee or participate in the selection of state councillors. It was argued that they lacked the judgment and experience necessary for such matters of state, but their leaders had acquired much of both by the 1760s.

Legislative proposals could be presented to the *Riksdag* either by the council or by its own committees. Usually after considerable lobbying between the Estates, each of them would vote internally, then cast its corporate vote. For ordinary legislation, a majority of three Estates was required; in matters of corporate privilege and, from 1766, constitutional amendments, the unanimous vote of all four Estates, provisions that anticipated the proposals of Louis XVI's government at the royal session of 23 June 1789, the cornerstone of the political program of the French Counterrevolution in the years that followed. Although much admired by the European political thinkers of the day, the Swedish system was unwieldly, even less adapted than the Danish bureaucratic absolutism to rapid, decisive, or innovative action.[63]

It has often been held that the *Riksdag*, in its turn, was essentially the organ of the bureaucracy, taken in the widest sense. Officeholders were prominently represented in the Estates: the Clergy were all public officials by definition; a large part of the Nobility, generally around 80 percent, were officers or bureaucrats; and the Burgher Estate regularly consisted largely of magistrates, usually the majority before 1756. The Peasant Estate meanwhile consistently excluded all but bona fide peasants from its membership. Yet clergymen and military officers, who were compensated with rural service tenures, were as much agriculturalists as officials, and urban magistrates were generally directly involved in the economic life of their towns or closely associated with it through family connections. No common bureaucratic esprit de corps developed across class lines and officeholders within different Estates often counteracted each others' interests. A growing concern over bureaucratic influence nonetheless began to make itself felt in the *Riksdag* by mid-century, most notably in the Burgher Estate, which would play an important role in the political conflicts of the 1760s.[64]

Since the 1680s the Swedish central administration, like the Danish, was collegially organized. The *Kanslikollegium*, or chancellery, dealt both with foreign affairs and with a wide range of administrative, judicial, and ecclesiastical matters. Other *kollegier* were charged with finance, commerce, and the armed forces. The kingdom was divided into *län*, or administrative districts, each under a *landshövding* appointed by the central government, served by various local functionaries. Manorial proprietors possessed no civil authority. Local affairs in the countryside were largely managed by village and parish councils, and peasant jurymen served at the sessions of the district court. The towns were administered by elected burgomasters and councilmen. Except at the higher levels, the purchase of civil and military posts was common: under the informal *ackord* system, practiced mainly in the military, the government appointed to the position, but the appointee compensated his predecessor for it, providing a kind of primitive pension system. Regular pensions were first instigated for the military in 1756 and for the civil service in 1778. Under the vigilance of a free political system there appears to have been relatively little corruption among the bureaucracy, in contrast to the *Riksdag*, where bribery and influence-mongering, especially by foreign powers, was all too common in the Era of Freedom.

Administrative complaints were most frequent in Finland, owing mainly to relative isolation from the capital, excessively large districts, and many officials' ignorance of the Finnish language. The central government held firmly to the ideals of centralization and uniformity, but it could not disregard special Finnish circumstances, in particular Finland's exposure to attack by Russia and the devastation caused by the Russian wars of 1700–21 and 1741–43. Special *Riksdag* commissions deliberated on Finland's defense and economic development, and the Finnish *riksdagsmän* frequently banded together in matters affecting their part of the kingdom. Both the Finnish regiments and the Finnish civil administration were staffed mainly by Finns, who developed a growing corporate sense throughout the century. Finland's position within the Swedish monarchy is strongly reminiscent of Norway's in the Danish, with the notable difference that Finns were often found in the highest positions in government and at court in Stockholm.[65]

Aside from a few recruited, regular units, the army was composed of national territorial regiments, which were quartered in their rural districts and met periodically for training. Under Karl XI's military organization of the 1680s, officers lived on landed service tenures, cavalrymen were allotted the taxes from certain farms, infantrymen and naval ratings were provided with cottages and small plots of land by groups of farms for their maintenance. The navy was

divided into the high seas fleet and the ''army,'' or skerry, fleet, the latter composed of oared galleys for operations among the Baltic islands and inlets.

As in Denmark, state finances were a weak point. Revenues derived from the
same sources, especially the regular land tax, which the *Riksdag* could supplement with extraordinary levies when required. Despite the construction of the
present royal palace in Stockholm, completed in the 1750s, expenditures on the
royal family and court were relatively modest compared with Denmark. The
greatest expenses were military, for whereas Denmark kept out of war after
1720, Sweden was twice drawn into armed conflict in the middle decades of the
century.

Swedish Pomerania and Wismar were not parts of the kingdom proper but
fiefs of the Holy Roman Empire. The king of Sweden was represented by a
governor-general in Stralsund, local interests by a council (*Landrat*) and the
provincial Estates (*Stände*), consisting of delegates of the nobility and the chartered towns.[66] As in Holstein and Oldenburg-Delmenhorst, the connection with
the empire perpetuated local and corporate privileges and immunities, with a
considerable measure of self-government.

International relations in the Nordic world were dominated in the eighteenth
century by rivalry between the two Scandinavian states and the interests of the
greater European powers, particularly Russia. Since the breakdown of the
Kalmar Union in 1520, Denmark and Sweden fought repeated wars, in which
Sweden had succeeded by 1658 in expanding to its present natural frontiers to
the south and west—the ''Keel'' and the coast—through the conquest of several
old Danish and Norwegian provinces. In its struggle Sweden found useful support from the dukes of Holstein-Gottorp, whose territories in the duchies provided a bridgehead from which to attack Denmark from the rear. Denmark in
turn found willing allies in the Russian tsars, who could attack Sweden in Finland. Similarly, Sweden could attack Denmark in Norway—or itself be attacked
from there.

Denmark accepted the role of a second-class power after failing to regain the
lost provinces in Sweden while holding Norway and gaining the Holstein-Gottorp lands in Schleswig during the Great Northern War. Henceforward its policy
was devoted to maintaining peace, acquiring the ducal portions of Holstein, and
securing Norway against future Swedish designs.

Although Sweden, too, was no longer a major European power following the
Great Northern War, much of the aristocracy was unprepared to recognize this
change. The Hat party, which arose during the 1730s, followed a belligerent
policy of expansion with French support, involving Sweden in unfortunate wars
with Russia in 1741–43 and with Prussia in 1757–62.

The dukes of Holstein-Gottorp meanwhile sought support against Denmark
from both Sweden and Russia. Their grievances provided St. Petersburg with

a welcome issue to keep Scandinavia divided and therefore weak, ensuring Russia's newly won dominance in the Baltic. In 1743 the empress Elizabeth named Duke Peter Ulric of Holstein-Gottorp her heir on the Russian throne, and as the condition of a lenient peace, involving the loss of only a small part of Finnish Karelia, she prevailed upon the Swedish *Riksdag* to elect the duke's cousin, Adolf Fredrik, as successor to the childless Fredrik I. Russia thereafter strove repeatedly, through both bribery and threat, to oust the Hats from power and replace them with the Caps, who favored good relations with St. Petersburg.

Faced with a Holstein-Gottorp succession in both Russia and Sweden, Bernstorff turned for support to France, but following the accession of Catherine II in 1762, Denmark would again be drawn into the Russian orbit, in hopes of negotiating a solution to the Holstein-Gottorp problem in the duchies and of securing Norway against Sweden. By the 1760s both Scandinavian monarchies were thus highly susceptible to Russian manipulation.[67]

Although the two Scandinavian monarchies were ruled by very different political regimes and had long been rivals in the international arena, they had never ceased to form a closely related cultural community. Their elites of power, wealth, and learning shared the cosmopolitan culture of their peers throughout the Western world. At a more fundamental level, the more distinctive traditions of their cultures were the products of an ancient, common Nordic heritage.

Danes, Norwegians, and Swedes spoke mutually comprehensible languages which had evolved from a common Old Nordic tongue. Beneath the level of the official languages, the peasantry spoke local dialects which shaded, almost imperceptibly, from one linguistic region into another.

Danish and Swedish were the official languages, except in the German provinces. Danish was spoken throughout Denmark, as well as in northern and central Schleswig. It was also the language of the upper classes in Norway, and to a degree in Iceland and the Færøes. The Norwegian peasantry continued to speak distinctive Norwegian dialects, whereas distance and isolation had preserved Icelandic and Færøese as archaic variants of Old Norse.

Swedish was spoken throughout Sweden. It was also the language of close to one-fifth of Finland's population, including both the upper classes throughout the country and the peasantry in extensive coastal districts. The majority of the Finns meanwhile spoke Finnish, a tongue entirely unrelated to the Indo-European languages, which was also still spoken by the descendants of Finnish settlers in scattered forest regions in both Sweden and Norway.[68]

In southern Schleswig and throughout Holstein, Oldenburg-Delmenhorst, Wismar and Swedish Pomerania, the population spoke German, generally the Low German (*Plattdeutsch*) dialect, except along the North Sea coast of the duchies, where the inhabitants were largely Frisian in speech.[69] Colonies of

Swabians were established in the early 1760s to cultivate the heathlands of Schleswig and Jutland. There was a sizable German-speaking element in many towns both in northern Schleswig and in Denmark itself, not least in Copenhagen.

The Lapps of northern Norway, Sweden, and Finland spoke their own tongue, remotely related to Finnish. In the colonies, a variety of languages were used. In the Danish West Indies, only a minority of the white population was Danish or Norwegian, and the most common tongue was English.

Language usage was closely connected with social class. French was widely used by the aristocracy everywhere. It dominated at the Swedish court, whereas in Denmark High German was during most of the century the language of the court, the army, and much of the administration, owing largely to the prominence of German bureaucrats, officers, and courtiers. In Norway, Finland, and the Danish-speaking parts of Schleswig, social mobility implied language mobility: those who rose out of the peasant masses abandoned Norwegian or South Jutish dialects, or the Finnish tongue, in favor of Danish, High German, and Swedish, respectively. Such vestiges of the old local speech as still survived among the upper classes at the beginning of the century gradually disappeared. There were, however, certain exceptions. The clergy in the Finnish-speaking parts of Finland naturally had to keep their command of the language of their parishioners. Icelandic literature had been the glory of medieval Scandinavia, and Icelandic, although spoken by only a tiny folk group, remained a literary as well as an ecclesiastical language.

Since the sixteenth century the Protestant faith placed a strong emphasis upon literacy, which early became widespread by European standards. As early as 1631, Anders Bure wrote of the inhabitants of Swedish Norrland that they were so fond of letters that although schools were few, "the literate instruct the others with such enthusiasm that the greatest part of the common people and even the peasants are literate." In 1741 a Norwegian bishop claimed to find no peasant in remote Nordland *Amt* "who has not learned to read in a book," and that "indeed, most of the peasants are well-read." An English visitor was deeply impressed in 1811 by the literacy and "mental culture" of the Icelanders, even though "the transmission of knowledge can take place only through the private and domestic habits of the people."[70]

As these quotations suggest, widespread literacy was only to a limited extent the result of schooling. Yet sporadic efforts were made in this direction. In 1721 Frederik IV established 240 rural schools (*"rytterskoler"*) on his domain lands in Denmark. A Swedish ordinance of 1723 held parents or guardians responsible for teaching their children to "read in a book" and their articles of faith, but made no provision for schools. In 1739 the Danish government required the establishment of a school in each parish, but because implementation was left to landowners in Denmark and to peasant parish councils in Norway, little was accomplished. Only here and there in Scandinavia were modest peasant schools established and kept alive by persuasive parish pastors or enlightened landlords. Many of them consisted of no more than an ambulatory schoolmaster, and they imparted only a bare minimum of literacy and religious instruction. The peasantry showed little desire for parish schools, especially where they themselves had to pay for them, on top of all their other obligations to the state. Yet this did not imply hostility toward literacy or even a certain degree of learning as such, as the high level of home instruction indicates. And despite everything, the numbers of rural schools did increase throughout the century.[71]

The towns had their own elementary, or "trivial," schools for the burgher class and often schools for poor children, maintained by charity or connected with orphanages and workhouses, and oriented toward teaching useful handicrafts. In addition, various individuals, including regular schoolteachers in their free hours, kept private schools for paying pupils.

Latin schools, primarily for boys preparing for clerical careers, were located in cathedral towns, and were small in both staff and enrollment. In the Danish monarchy several moribund Latin schools were closed or amalgamated in the 1750s, leaving twenty in Denmark but only four in Norway. Iceland's two cathedral schools were combined by the end of the century into one, where in 1811 an English visitor found only three masters and "twenty-three or twenty-four" scholars. Sweden had eleven Latin schools, or *gymnasia*, Finland only one.[72] The primary concentration of cultural life in the metropolitan lands, Denmark and Sweden, and especially in the capitals is evident. Wealthier noble and burgher families were often instructed by private tutors, and where possible the Grand Tour through Europe's capitals with his tutor was the climax of a young nobleman's education.

In the Swedish kingdom there were universities at Uppsala, Lund, and Åbo (Turku), the last in Finland. Educational policy was more centralized in the Danish state, where the University of Copenhagen served the entire kingdom. Lack of a university of their own was a growing grievance among the Norwegian upper classes, first voiced already at the last meeting of the Norwegian Estates in 1661. The German provinces had their own universities, at Kiel (which until 1773 lay in Holstein-Gottorp territory) and in Greifswald in Swedish Pomerania.

All were small, and only Uppsala achieved any European prominence, above all thanks to the work of the great Carl Linnæus and his circle of young naturalists. Linnæus's ennoblement under the name von Linné in 1757 was symptomatic of the governments' mercantilistic interest in forms of learning useful to their national economies. The natural sciences were especially favored, an area in which several other Swedes, such as Carl Wilhelm Scheele, Anders Celsius, and even Emanuel Swedenborg, also distinguished themselves. Increasingly the universities prepared young men for bureaucratic, as well as clerical, careers. In both monarchies there were schools for military and naval cadets, and a school of mining technology was established at Kongsberg in Norway in 1757. The old *Rytterakademi* at Sorø, near Copenhagen, supported after 1747 by a legacy from Ludvig Holberg, was an aristocratic finishing school for young gentlemen and provided sinecures for several historians and political thinkers of stature. Many young Scandinavians meanwhile studied for a time abroad.

As elsewhere in Europe at this time, the most significant thought and scholarship took place largely outside the schools and universities. The royal courts played a central role in patronizing the sciences as well as the arts, in Copenhagen up to the 1770s, in Stockholm until the 1790s. Numerous academies, learned societies, and reading circles were established, characteristically much concerned with the utility of learning. In Sweden, the Royal Academy of Sciences was founded in 1739 and the Royal Academy of Letters (*Vitterhetsakademien*) in 1753. Both have played a prominent cultural role since that time, as has the Danish Royal Agricultural Society (*Det kongelige Landhusholdningsselskab*), organized in 1769. The Trondheim Scientific Society, established in 1760 and renamed the Royal Norwegian Scientific Society seven years later, served as the real center for intellectual life in Norway until the University of Christiania finally came into being in 1811. The Aurora Society was founded in 1771 by academics at Åbo University and followed in 1797 by the Finnish Economic Society (*Finska hushållningssällskapet*). Even remote Iceland had its literary and scientific societies.[73] Most members of these and similar organizations were gentlemen in private circumstances, among whom many rural landowners and clergymen distinguished themselves by carrying enlightenment and new ideas to their neighborhoods.

Architecture, sculpture, painting, the decorative crafts, and the performing arts had formerly been the preserve mainly of foreign artists and artisans, working in international European styles. The eighteenth century represents a new and important stage in Nordic cultural development. Mercantilism fostered native talent, and the arts now came to be practiced mainly by Scandinavians, although they still continued to follow cosmopolitan fashions—baroque, rococo, neoclassical—and often received some of their training abroad. Certain of them indeed achieved international renown, such as the Swedish rococo painters Alexander Roslin and Nils Lafrensen (Lavreince) the younger, who were as well known in Paris as in Stockholm, and later the Danish-Icelandic sculptor Bertel Thorvaldsen, who was recognized as one of the leading European neoclassicists. By the later decades of the century, certain artists, like the Swedes Elias Martin and Per Hilleström the elder, and the Danes Jens Juel and Erik Pauelson, would begin to reveal a growing interest in the characteristic landscapes and folklife of their native lands, foreshadowing the distinctively national cultural forms of the nineteenth century.[74]

Literature likewise reflected the cosmopolitan impulses of the time. From France emanated the influences of classicism and rationalism, from England,

Germany, and Switzerland those of preromantic sensibility. Their impact was generally felt a decade or more after their first appearance in the lands of their origin, but once introduced they could spread rapidly within the small and closely knit Scandinavian literary and artistic circles. French influences clearly dominated in Sweden-Finland and were relatively stronger in Norway, with its close maritime connections with the West, than in Denmark, where Germanic impulses were particularly prominent, especially after mid-century. English ideas gained currency largely through French or German translations or popular writings. Upon each other, the Scandinavian countries meanwhile exercised less cultural influence, although Ludvig Holberg was widely enough read in Sweden-Finland and Swedish science and technology were followed with some interest in Denmark-Norway.[75]

The Norwegian-born Holberg, who spent most of his life in Denmark and was made a baron in 1747, occupies a position in Scandinavian letters in the eighteenth century comparable only to that of the Swede Linné in natural science. Although he was also a historian, political thinker, moral philosopher, and even metaphysician, he is chiefly remembered for his spritely satirical comedies, in a style reminiscent of Molière, on the pretentions of the "powdered wigs" ("Parykkerne") and the lighthearted insouciance of the lower classes. For all his classicism, his characters embody much of the specifically Danish national psyche.

German-language literature also had its place in eighteenth-century Scandinavia, inspiring a growing preromantic moral earnestness. Friedrich Klopstock came to Copenhagen in 1751 and stayed for nineteen years as a pensioner of the Danish king, dominating the literary scene following Holberg's death in 1754. The Schleswiger, H. W. Gerstenberg aroused the interest of the Germanic world in Old Norse mythology.[76]

"How innocent, indeed naive, was not all of literary life, if we compare the time of my youth with the present," wrote the Dane Henrik Steffens in the 1830s; "The general trend of the popular writers was, however, to improve morality."[77] The didactic tone dominates, whether in the satiric or the sentimental genre. The spirit of the times stressed reason, progress, the general good, and Scandinavian literati were well acquainted with the European literature of the enlightenment. Addison and Steele with their *Spectator*, Montesquieu with his *Lettres persanes*, Voltaire with his philosophic tales and histories, Rousseau with his glorification of nature and the common man—all found their admirers and imitators. Nor, as we have seen, can the Germans, such as Gellert, Lessing, and later, Kant, be left out of account.

Characteristically for the times, however, *belles-lettres* comprised only a small part of what was published. Aside from devotional literature, which always accounted for the largest share, works on practical topics constituted the greater part, of both what came out in print and what was usually to be found in private libraries. In addition to practical handbooks of all kinds, there were numerous works dealing with economic, social, and political questions.[78]

Such works appeared in considerable numbers in Sweden-Finland after 1718, although until mid-century government censorship generally restricted the political opinions published to those acceptable to the party in power, and opposing views often circulated in handwritten manuscripts. After 1746 censorship was relaxed.[79] Under Danish-Norwegian absolutism, censorship was stricter still, although those who praised and justified the regime, such as Holberg and the political theorists of the "Sorø Enlightenment," Jens Schjelderup Sneedorff and Andreas Schytte, were free enough to publish their views.[80] Danish censorship became more liberal under Frederik V, and in 1755 the king, prompted by his favorite, Count A. G. Moltke, went so far as to solicit writings on projects useful for "the flourishing of the land," to be printed in *Danmarks og Norges Oeconomiske Magazin*. The results contained, in addition to purely economic ideas, much with social and even political implications.

Public debate, especially after mid-century, is pervaded with the thought of the Enlightenment and makes frequent and specific reference to the works of the *philosophes*. Locke, Bolingbroke, Montesquieu, Voltaire, Helvétius, Rousseau, Pufendorf, Justi and the German cameralists, Quesnay, the elder Mirabeau, Le Mercier de la Rivière and the physiocrats, Didérot and the encyclopedists, Adam Smith, Arthur Young and the English agricultural reformers—all these and a host of others are constantly called to mind in the writings of Danes like Sneedorff, Schytte, Tyge Rothe, Peter Frederik Suhm, Norwegians like Holberg and Gerhard Schøning, Swedes like Olof Dalin, Anders Nordencrantz, and Carl Fredrik Scheffer, Finns like Anders Chydenius and Gustaf Filip Creutz, even Icelanders like Magnus Stephensen and Hans Finsen. Natural right and social contract, the balance of public powers and social classes, the security of person and property, legal despotism, the public good, the general will, the war against ignorance and superstition, resistance to tyranny—all are to be found among their writings. As elsewhere, the "party of Enlightenment" was best represented among the most influential and best educated elements of society, among which it often lost something of its critical edge. But intense pamphleteering during periods of relative press freedom and of social and political ferment in both monarchies showed that its fundamental ideas—generally passed on at second or third hand—had not failed to penetrate deeply among the literate middle classes, and even among some of the artisans and better-informed peasants, as will be seen.

In contrast to the Enlightenment in France and to Catholic Europe generally, that in Scandinavia gave rise to little anticlericalism. Rather, it largely carried the bastions of the church itself with the breakthrough of rationalism in theology, especially at the University of Copenhagen, where the entire Danish-Norwegian clergy was trained. This involved the explication of the faith in terms comprehensible to human reason. Henrik Steffens later called it "an unbearable, raw mixture of rigid orthodoxy and insipid rationalism."[81] Yet at a more practical level, rationalism emphasized the role of the pastor as the public enlightener. Bishops and clergymen were in the vanguard of practical efforts to improve farming methods, popular literacy, public health, and the maintenance of the poor and helpless. They became characteristically more concerned with small-pox vaccination or proper ditching and draining than with the mysteries of the incarnation. In Norway such pastors were called "potato-priests" (*Potetpræster*), thanks to their enthusiasm for this useful plant.[82] In Sweden the Clerical Estate of the *Riksdag* was much concerned with economic questions. Throughout the North clergymen were the principal contributors to that wealth of detailed topographical descriptions of individual parishes and districts so characteristic of their time, with its emphasis upon the rational exploitation of resources.[83]

By the 1760s the European Enlightenment seemed to reign triumphant among Scandinavia's educated classes. Yet at that very time there were signs of a growing reaction against its rationalism and cosmopolitanism. This assumed various guises. Pietism, originally of German inspiration, had remained an undercurrent within the church, and as the century wore on it gathered renewed vigor in urban circles in reaction to religious rationalism and through the edifying example of the Moravian Brethren.[84]

At the same time, the Rousseauian exaltation of the simple life reinforced the old Nordic ideal of *nøjsomhed* (or *förnöjsomhet*), that untranslatable term which means contentedness in frugal but adequate circumstances. Throughout the Nordic world by the 1760s there was a growing reaction, especially within the middle classes, against vain ostentation and foreign luxury, together with a senti-mental idealization of the sturdy peasant freeholder.[85] This cult of virtuous sim-plicity thus opposed the pleasure-pain principle and the materialistic concept of human felicity of the rationalistic and progressive High Enlightenment. It could be sternly puritanical, not to say downright philistine, in tone, as when the Swedish diarist, Rutger Fredrik Hochschild dourly blamed the court for encour-aging "arts and sciences which a poor land could better do without."[86]

National feeling was likewise on the rise by the 1760s. It expressed itself in part through the flourishing of societies devoted to national development and in a rich topographical literature. Much of the regional feeling in Finland, Norway, and Iceland found its outlet in such activities. Thus, for instance, while many upper-class Finns were concerned about Sweden's ability to defend their part of the kingdom against Russia, the scholars in Åbo who devoted themselves to Fin-nish language and folklore remained unaffected in their loyalty to the Swedish state. In Norway the middle classes felt increasing frustration over their coun-try's provincial status within the kingdom, while the peasantry tended more than ever to regard the same classes as an alien element in their midst, yet neither showed hostility to Denmark as such. National feeling was aroused in reaction to the prevailing cosmopolitanism and through friction with other national groups and cultures. In Sweden-Finland this took the form of a growing reaction against the French cultural affectations of the court and the higher aristocracy. Meanwhile, at the same time that the Germans—including those in the Scandinavian monarchies—were awakened to a new pride by the exploits of, ironically, the gallophile Frederick the Great and of Prussia in the Seven Years' War, the Danish and Norwegian middle classes became aroused over the preeminence of the Germans in government, the economy, high society, and culture, especially in Copenhagen itself. Although many native Danish nobles also reacted against the German ascendancy and feeling often ran high between Danish and German artisans, national and class conflict tended to become associated, as "German" came to be identified in the popular mind with "aristocrat" and "Danish" with "bourgeois."[87] When Danish-Russian diplomacy held out the prospect of the final unification of all of Holstein under the Danish crown by the later 1760s, the *Ritterschaft* in the duchies was revivified by concern for the maintenance of their surviving Germanic rights and liberties.[88]

National feeling stimulated, and was stimulated by, the rediscovery of Nordic antiquity by the 1760s. It had, to be sure, never ceased to be cultivated by Scandinavian scholars, but widespread enthusiasm for the subject was inspired, characteristically in this cosmopolitan age, by outside impulses. Montesquieu invoked both Jordanes and the earlier Swedish scholar Olof Rudbeck in 1748, proclaiming the Scandinavian North to be the home of European liberties, the "factory of those instruments which break the shackles forged in the South."[89] The Swiss Paul Henri Mallet, who lived for several years in Copenhagen, captured the imagination of Europe in the 1750s with his works on Denmark's early history and on Old Norse literature. The "bardic" verse of Edward Gray and the Ossian poems of James Macpherson meanwhile excited preromantic sensibilities in Scandinavia. The German Schleswiger Gerstenberg inspired both the German Klopstock and the Dane Johannes Ewald to turn to ancient Scandinavian motifs. Around 1760, too, the Norwegian Gerhard Schøning, and the Dane P. F. Suhm, founders of the Trondheim Scientific Society in that year, devoted themselves to the early history of their respective lands, while in Sweden Sven Lagerbring continued his work on the origins of the Swedish kingdom. In Finland a small group of scholars around Henrik Gabriel Porthan in Åbo began the first systematic and critical study of the Finnish language and folk culture.[90]

Interest in Nordic antiquity led to an increasing sense of a shared heritage and community of interests among the Scandinavian lands, especially in the face of mounting outside pressures: the German challenge to Danish culture and the Russian threat to the security of both Scandinavian states.

Literature and learning were naturally the preserve of a small cultivated elite. Something of its extent and interests in Scandinavia is revealed by studies of the book trade and the contents of private libraries during the eighteenth century. Most preserved estate inventories contain some books. They were usually few and, where specified by title, mainly devotional works and practical handbooks. Yet noblemen, bureaucrats, merchants, and clergymen often had well-stocked libraries, some indeed of a magnitude rarely surpassed since the founding of public libraries, including the most significant works of contemporary European literature and scholarship, both in translation and in the original languages. Their proud owners were usually liberal in allowing access to others and frequently bequeathed them to form the nuclei of important public libraries. P. F. Suhm's estimated 100,000 volumes, for instance, played an inestimable cultural role during his lifetime, first in Trondheim and later in Copenhagen, and were donated upon his death to the Danish Royal Library. In the later eighteenth century private library societies and lending libraries were founded. The ideas of the time were meanwhile disseminated largely through a growing variety of periodicals and pamphlets, the latter often anonymous, clandestinely printed, or even copied out by hand. Although their circulation figures were limited, each copy was usually read by several persons and its contents passed on to wider circles in conversation and argument.[91]

The lower classes of the towns tended, within their means, to emulate, if not to parody, the manners and customs of their social betters.[92] The great mass of the peasantry, meanwhile, lived a life apart. Its relative isolation from the rest of society was partly geographical, as in much of northern Scandinavia, including the Atlantic islands. The entire central Finnish province of Savolaks (Savo), for instance, did not contain a single town before the 1770s; the nearest was 600–700 kilometers away.[93] More significant, however, were the social barriers of a still largely corporate society and the policies of governments determined to prevent the decimation of the "producing" by the "consuming" classes. Practical and, in varying degree, legal restrictions hindered occupational mobility out of peasant status. Although literacy in the printed word was widespread, few peasants read any but devotional books and few possessed the means to educate their sons for nonpeasant occupations. Relatively few, moreover, showed any desire to see them leave their own social class, except perhaps for a clerical career, for the peasants, too, particularly the more prosperous farmers, had their class pride and traditional suspicion toward other social groups. The Peasant Estate of the Swedish *Riksdag*, for example, jealously excluded from membership farmers of nonpeasant origin and those who lived like gentlemen. Language also limited the peasants' horizons, for they generally spoke vernaculars different from those of the educated classes, or even a different language altogether, as in much of Finland. Local dialects even made communication difficult between peasants from various parts of the same country, especially in Norway.

Yet the peasants' isolation was never by any means total. In the more densely settled areas they lived close to towns, officers' residences, parsonages, and often manor houses, with all of which they had numerous contacts. Timber haulage, periodic fairs and markets, seasonal labor migration, fishing, seafaring, military service—all brought peasants from remoter areas, where parishes could be the size of English counties, into touch with the wider world beyond. Peasant culture thus reflected much in upper-class life: impulses that were usually modified through naiveté and older traditions, and preserved long after upper-class fashions had changed. Such influences are still evident in the construction and decorating of houses and furnishings, in folk dress, music, and dance. Emulation of the upper classes indeed was a matter of concern to the governments, which repeatedly resorted to sumptuary ordinances to keep peasant christenings, betrothals, weddings, and funerals from becoming displays of opulence unbefitting the peasants' station in life. But such restrictions met with only indifferent success, for these occasions were traditionally the high points of peasant social life.

There were indeed wealthy peasants, particularly in Norway and Sweden, who lived in some style. There were those in Norway who read their law book, Snorre Sturlason's sagas in Peder Claussøn Friis's sixteenth-century Norwegian translation, and even Holberg. In Simen Fougner in Gudbrandsdalen, Norway had a peasant poet of modest pretentions.[94] The leading peasant politicians in the Swedish *Riksdag* developed considerable worldly sophistication, both politically and otherwise. An occasional peasant was even said to drink coffee and wear a wig.

Yet the peasantry on the whole lived its own way of life, passed on through countless generations. Theirs was not a literary culture in a bookish sense, yet oral tradition preserved an immense body of ancient lore, such as the Finnish folk epics and the Danish medieval folk ballads. Peasant wisdom was embodied in innumerable proverbs, rhymes, and songs. The peasants had their own styles in building and decoration, in music, dance, and games, which clearly trace back to the Viking age, and beyond. Theirs was a culture rich in weaving and embroidery, in woodcarving, ironwork, and decorative floral painting, in the ingenious use of straw, birchbark, and pine shavings. In the peasant world the Christian God and Devil coexisted with their predecessors, a host of supernatural beings—trolls, elves, watersprites, fairies, ghosts—and ultimate concern for salvation through the church was balanced by immediate needs to propitiate the spirits of farm, forest, and stream. "Wise" old men and women were charged with the cure of man and beast, and undertook a variety of other transactions with the unseen world.

CHAPTER 2

# The Winds of Change
# 1760–70

In June 1756 Great Britain and France once again went to war. The global conflict that followed profoundly affected developments throughout Europe, not least in the Nordic lands.

As before, war between the maritime powers brought lucrative opportunities for neutral Scandinavia. Both Britain and France needed imports of naval stores and iron; the latter, being the weaker power at sea, was largely dependent upon the shipping provided by neutral states. During the war years Denmark-Norway enjoyed a near-monopoly of European trade in the Mediterranean, and the Danish colonies in the West Indies, West Africa, and India flourished as neutral emporia. With French encouragement, the two Nordic states in July 1756 concluded an armed neutrality convention, for the mutual protection of their shipping against encroachments by the belligerents, and outfitted naval squadrons to uphold it.

The convention was, however, soon overshadowed by the outbreak of war on the Continent, with Frederick II's invasion of Saxony in August 1756. Prussia was opposed by a coalition of Austria, France, Russia, and Saxony, joined by Sweden in June 1757. Formally, Sweden acted as a guarantor of the Peace of Westphalia of 1648; behind this lay the Hats' determination to maintain close relations with France and their desire to revive Sweden's past glory through territorial expansion in northern Germany. For the allies, Swedish Pomerania offered a strategic bridgehead. In September Sweden attacked Prussia with 20,000 men.

Sweden was ill prepared for the so-called Pomeranian War. As during the Hats' war with Russia in 1741–43, the army made a mediocre showing, plagued by problems of command and supply. Casualties were heavy. Despite the efforts of Hat propagandists, the war never aroused public enthusiasm at home. State finances and the monetary system, already disordered since the earlier war, were thrown into further disarray, especially as promised subsidies from France were never paid in full.

Denmark, under the guiding hand of Baron Bernstorff, remained neutral in the continental struggle, as in the maritime war. Yet neutrality too exacted its price. In addition to naval units, a field army of some 25,000 men was assembled and maintained in Holstein to cover the southern frontier. As the mobilization revealed shortcomings in the army, Bernstorff secured the services of the Comte de Saint-Germain, probably the ablest French general of the war, who had fallen out of favor at Versailles and in 1760 was commissioned a field marshal by Frederik V. To strengthen the state finances, already badly weakened by court extravagance, Bernstorff the following year called in Heinrich Carl Schimmelmann, a Hamburg financier regarded as a financial wizard.

Thus reinforced, Bernstorff sought to exert diplomatic pressure on Russia to bring about a solution of the Holstein-Gottorp problem. St. Petersburg made no positive response. But in January 1762 the empress Elizabeth died and her adopted heir, the duke of Holstein-Gottorp, became Tsar Peter III, confronting Scandinavia with an entirely new situation.

The new tsar was inspired by an intense admiration for Russia's enemy, Frederick II of Prussia, and by an inherited hatred for Denmark which Bernstorff's diplomatic maneuvers had done nothing to assuage. During the next few months he made peace with Prussia and prepared to attack Denmark to seize Schleswig and humble the old enemy of his house. To gain Sweden's support he held out enticing prospects of strengthening monarchical power there and Sweden's acquisition of Norway.

For Denmark the situation appeared perilous in the extreme. Although its navy was superior, its army was hardly a match for the Russians. Saint-Germain nevertheless resolved to fight an aggressive campaign and advanced into Mecklenburg. His advance posts had just made contact with the Russians when news arrived from St. Petersburg that the tsar had been deposed through a palace revolution on 9 July. He was murdered soon thereafter.[1]

The empress Catherine now assumed power and quickly liquidated the quarrel with Denmark. She was soon prepared to negotiate over the future of Holstein-Gottorp. In the meantime she showed a particular interest in the little duchy, practicing there, through her principal ducal minister, Casper von Saldern, the kind of enlightened despotism that circumstances so greatly impeded in Russia itself. For the next decade the Holstein-Gottorp model state inspired reforms in both the royal and jointly administered parts of Holstein, as well as elsewhere in the German world.[2]

The crisis of 1762 badly shook the Danish council, impressing it with the need for basic financial and military reforms. As finance minister, H. C. Schimmelmann tried to stabilize the inflated currency and to reduce the heavy national debt through the sale of state property, foreign loans, and in September 1762 the imposition of a special levy, the poll tax (*ekstraskatt*) of one *rigsdaler* annually per person, regardless of means, throughout the monarchy, except for the peasants in Finnmark, Iceland, and the Færøes.

The new tax reveals the government's remarkable ignorance of local conditions. It had no more grasp of what the total burden of taxes, tithes, tolls, fees, and local contributions amounted to in different parts of the monarchy than it is possible for us to have today; it knew only of its needs and what actually came into the treasury. In Denmark and the duchies the poll tax imposed a heavy additional load and led in places to disturbances; on Bornholm with its free peasantry, these were so serious that in 1763 its assessment was reduced by half and in 1770 its special privileges were clarified and confirmed.[3]

In Norway the situation was far more serious. Here previous special levies had never affected the peasants. Money was in much shorter supply, and many farm laborers scarcely earned as much as one *rigsdaler* in cash in a year. Whereas in Denmark the proprietor was held responsible for the taxes of those on his manor who were too poor to pay them, in Norway this obligation rested on the peasant farmers, most of whom worked poor holdings and saw little cash. Times were bad. Fishing was poor and crops were scanty in 1762 and 1763, forcing the peasants to buy more Danish grain than usual. During the first two years the tax was collected with little difficulty, as it was understood to be "the king's will." By the third year economic hardships reduced the intake, collection was resisted in some localities, and the government exempted certain categories of persons from the tax. Unfortunately these relief measures were piecemeal, complicated, and inadequately publicized. They moreover tended to favor the dependents of freeholders as opposed to tenant farmers, which caused particular bitterness in the poorer districts of western Norway, where freeholders were still relatively few.

Under Frederik V the bureaucracy in Norway was less controlled than previously from Copenhagen, and complaints mounted against various local officials. Their forcible confiscation of livestock, tools, and household goods for nonpayment of the poll tax aroused particular resentments. The peasants tended to believe the officials were interpreting the tax stipulations to enrich themselves and without the king's knowledge. In time-honored fashion groups of Norwegian peasants went to Copenhagen to present their grievances to the king, but such deputations seemed more coldly received by haughty bureaucrats than in the past.

In the meantime, the poll tax led to open rebellion in the poor but populous Nordhordland district around Bergen. In February 1765 about a hundred "Striler," as the peasants of the area were called, visited the *stiftamtmand*, or provincial governor, in Bergen, U. F. Cicignon, and demanded to see the king's orders regarding the tax. Cicignon could only try to explain them, but he promised that confiscations would be suspended and forwarded the peasants' complaints to the capital. When it became known, however, that confiscations would be resumed, over a thousand peasants marched on Bergen in April, joined by the poorer classes of the town. In the resulting tumult the crowd mishandled the *stiftamtmand*, who in the heat of the moment promised that the poll taxes thus far collected would be refunded. Next day some 9,000 *rigsdaler* were paid out and the peasants went home. News of the tumult quickly spread, particularly in western Norway, resulting in confrontations with frightened local officials and a virtual tax strike.

By that time, the government in Copenhagen had already backed down. On 9 April it exempted the children and hired hands of both freehold and tenant farmers. But it was too late. From then on, until the final abolition of the poll tax for Norway in 1772—in Denmark it remained in effect until 1812—the sums collected varied from 80 percent of the amounts levied in parts of Østlandet to no more than 10 percent in Sunnfjord and Nordfjord in the west. A government commission in Bergen, backed by 350 Danish mercenary troops, meted out death sentences to four peasants; one had already died, and the others had their sentences commuted to prison terms. The real instigators were never found. Cicignon and several other officials were dismissed or transferred, and confiscations virtually ended.[4]

The so-called *Stril* War was a sobering experience for the government, the first actual peasant insurrection against royal authority. The loyalty of the Norwegian peasantry to their king had been taken as axiomatic. It now became clear that this by no means meant unquestioning obedience to the policies of his ministers. Uniting for the first time in a movement extending beyond their parishes and districts, the peasants became aware of their strength and the government's weakness. Too much should not be made of this initial clash, as some historians, like Halvdan Koht, have been inclined to do. It was far from national in scope, and nationalism as such played no part in it. Yet it formed the background for more serious confrontations later on. From the later 1760s forward, the government's policy toward Norway seems, in retrospect, increasingly defensive.[5]

The Comte de Saint-Germain meanwhile addressed himself to military reform. He was convinced of the ineffectiveness of both the foreign mercenary troops and of the Danish territorial militia in its existing form, and proposed that an increasing proportion of native conscripts be integrated into the regular regiments for periods long enough for proper training and discipline, before transfer to the reserve. He thus hoped to build up a wartime strength of fully 100,000 men, in ways reminiscent both of the contemporary Prussian cantonment system and the later French *amalgame* of 1792. Under Turgot's ministry in France he would likewise seek to implement reforms *à la prusse*, and he is since regarded as one of the pioneers of modern military theory. Around him Saint-Germain gathered a circle of military men including General W. F. von Schmettau,

Colonel Karl Görtz, Lieutenant-General P. E. Gähler, and Count Schack Carl Rantzau-Ascheberg. Loosely associated with them in certain respects were Count Frederik Danneskiold-Samsøe and Crown Prince Christian's influential tutor, the Swiss E. S. F. Reverdil.[6]

The new, national army, however, could only be the cutting edge of a whole substructure of administrative reorganization. Like many others in Europe at the time, Saint-Germain and his friends looked for their ideal to Frederick the Great and his efficient *Kabinettsregiment* in Prussia. From their correspondence the broad outlines of a reform program emerge, involving above all the personal exercise of power by the monarch, the replacement of the high aristocratic, semi-autonomous, and slow-moving council by a small group of "honest" and enlightened friends of reform close to the king's person, the opening of higher offices to talented men regardless of birth, the improvement of state finances, the clarification and consistent application of the laws. The bases of the new system were to be simplicity and effectiveness.[7]

But administrative reform would in turn ultimately have to depend upon a restructuring of society itself to break the resurgent power of the aristocracy. As Saint-Germain put it (according to Reverdil):

> Aristocratic rule has been eradicated only in appearance. The nobility still dominate and out of fear that the king might make himself all-powerful within the realm if he were to win consideration outside of it, they oppose his acquiring an army. The present army is only a sham. The nobles' dominance within the state is based upon the power they have retained on their manors. The noblemen are petty despots and are more to be considered taxable vassals than subjects. How has this power come about? Through the stipulations concerning the militia. But this militia, which is useless for defending the realm, is at once a means to oppress the common man and a hindrance to a good composition for the army. This is the real reason why the infantry is recruited at great cost abroad, among the dregs of Germany.[8]

Here the field marshal and his friends joined hands with growing numbers of critics of the *stavnsbånd* and the oppressive condition of the Danish peasantry. Behind both of these circles there was an awakening public opinion within broad middle-class strata in Denmark and Norway, which was increasingly alienated by the rule of the high aristocratic "Excellencies" and by the German dominance in government and at court.

Bernstorff, Moltke, and their fellow councillors were humane and well-meaning men, amenable to cautious and well-considered reforms. But in the "party of Sant-Germain" they saw a serious threat, not only to the existing order, over which they presided, but to their very political philosophy, which stressed peace, prosperity, stability, and *noblesse oblige*.

During 1763 Saint-Germain and his friends prepared an ambitious program of military reforms, and in October of that year the old *Krigskancelli*, or war office, was transformed into a *Generalkrigsdirektorium* on the Prussian model, giving its president, Saint-Germain, direct access to the king. But through Count Moltke's influence with Frederik V, the council remained unassailable. In the end the plan of 1763 was quietly shelved, although the separate militia regiments were liquidated in 1764 and peasant conscripts began to train with regular army units from 1767. Meanwhile, Bernstorff's improvement of relations with Russia further strengthened the civilian council against the military clique.

The "Excellencies" were thus as firmly in power as ever when Frederik V, worn out by his debaucheries, died at the age of forty-two, on 14 January 1766. The hopes of the reformers focused immediately upon his sixteen-year-old son, who now ascended the throne as Christian VII.

Russia's sudden withdrawal from the war with Prussia in January 1762 gave Sweden a welcome opportunity to follow suit. Queen Lovisa Ulrika used her good offices with her brother, Frederick II, resulting in the Peace of Hamburg on 22 May 1762, based on the *status quo ante bellum*.

The war, which the Cap bishop Jacob Serenius later proclaimed to have been begun "with Saul's foolishness and the boastfulness of the Moabites," badly undermined the Hat party.[9] In power uninterruptedly since 1738, the Hats had been at the peak of their power during the 1750s. Their principal strength lay in the bureaucracy and officer corps, and among the larger export merchants and manufacturers. They upheld officialdom both against king and council, and against public opinion, and inclined toward the doctrine, expressed by B. Frondin in 1747, that the *Riksdag* was responsible only to itself, not to its electors.[10] Their economic policy was rigidly mercantilistic, considering necessary both a small, favored entrepreneurial elite, concentrated mainly in the capital, and a large and growing population, strictly regulated in its economic pursuits and held close to the poverty line to provide cheap labor. Their system of subsidies, protective tariffs, and monetary inflation favored the larger exporters and manufacturers. As war and expansion held out tempting opportunities for officers, bureaucrats, and entrepreneurs alike, the Hats favored alliance with France, the only European power that would encourage Sweden to follow an aggressive foreign policy. To stifle criticism, they held strongly to secrecy in *Riksdag* transactions and to press censorship.

The Hats had owed their virtually unassailable position in the 1750s partly to their strength in the Noble and Burgher Estates, partly to the lack of a viable rival party. The faction turned out of power in 1738, which came to be called the Caps, was in disarray, and certain of its leaders were discredited through unseemly intrigues with the Russians to overthrow their rivals.

Sweden's inglorious participation in the Seven Years' War proved the rock upon which this increasingly heterogeneous party foundered. The Hat council involved Sweden in the conflict, and politically appointed Hat commanders bungled the campaigning in the field. Inflation increased rapidly through the issue of unbacked paper currency, which declined to about one-third of its prewar value, benefiting large exporters and manufacturers holding loans from the state bank while hurting creditors and importers.

When the *Riksdag* convened in 1760, the Hats retained a clear majority only in the Burgher Estate, and only the support of the small Court party prevented their losing control of the Nobility. During the twenty-month session that followed, various splinter groups formed briefly on specific issues. In this unstable situation the Cap party coalesced as a powerful opposition, drawing to itself discontented elements from the rival camp.

A sign of things to come was mounting friction between the Estates. The prestige of the Nobility suffered when over 200 noble officers left the front in Pomerania to take their places in the House of the Nobility. The nonnoble Estates voiced demands that would weaken the position of the nobility in state service, while the Burghers even suggested appointing commoners to the state council itself. "The croft is as rich in genius as the noble household," one speaker proclaimed rhetorically.[11]

The nobility—consisting, as seen, largely of men of relatively recent title—closed ranks. In 1761–62 the council sharpened restrictions against the acquisition of manors by persons not already nobles; in 1763 it ended the sale of crown lands to the peasantry and sought to limit the latter's hunting and fishing rights. Most significant, the Noble Estate resolved in 1762 to introduce no new nobles into its number until this fell below 800. Since there were then some 1,250 introduced noble families, with normal attrition it would take a good half-century before any new ones might join the charmed circle. This aroused great bitterness among the Burghers and Clergy. Yet it also produced a more forward-looking reaction among many leading commoners, who now felt a new pride at remaining within and identifying with their own Estates.[12]

The Caps drew support from various sources. During the 1750s what remained of the party was still generally aristocratic and conservative, deriving largely from the old nobility which had lost control of the Noble Estate by 1738. Most of the clergy and much of the bourgeoisie were meanwhile repelled by the opulence and luxury in leading Hat circles. By the early 1760s the Cap party shifted character, reflecting an accumulation of new grievances and demands. The "Younger Caps" built their following upon opposition to the war and to the militaristic, expansionist stance behind it; to the government's extravagance and inflationary policy; to its favoritism toward exports and manufactures to the neglect of agriculture, extractive industries, imports, and internal trade, and toward the capital as opposed to the provinces; to the monopolistic rights of staple towns and indeed of towns as such in relation to the countryside in local commerce; to the relative neglect of Finland's particular interests; to restrictions in peasant land acquisition and freehold rights; to the favored position of the bureaucracy in both municipal and national government; to secrecy in official matters and to press censorship; to aristocratic preference in state appointments and promotions; and, not least, to the concept that neither officials nor even *riksdagsmän* were accountable to the governed. Faced with this rapid shift, the Hats reacted by holding even more inflexibly than ever to their established positions.[13]

It is clear that the grievances of the Younger Caps derived from existing circumstances in Sweden and Finland. Yet mercantilism and the aristocratic ideal reflected conditions throughout the European world of the time, as well as the thought of the earlier Enlightenment, which was above all a movement of secularization and did not yet call into question absolutism, mercantilism, privilege, or individual libertinism. By mid-century, meanwhile, a new intellectual climate was emerging with Rousseau, Helvétius, the encyclopedists, and the physiocrats, stressing the legitimate needs of the individual and holding the state to be the means to the "general good," rather than an end in itself. Such a view implied a new social ethos, a concern for the common man and for agriculture which provided his principal sustenance, opposition to militarism and war, to special privileges and monopolies, and to vain ostentation. The later Enlightenment combined rationalism with the new moral fervor of the preromantic awakening.[14]

In Sweden, such ideas fell on fertile ground from the 1750s on, attracting many of the better minds, which by the following decade generally aligned themselves with the Younger Caps, helped to articulate their program, and provided them with their ideology. That the Caps should come to represent the new intellectual climate was at first by no means ensured. A number of Hat thinkers were likewise beginning to question mercantilist dogmas. But the economic problems created by the Hat party and its generally hardening conservatism in the face of criticism by the early 1760s cemented the union between the leading intellectuals and the Younger Caps.[15] Of particular importance was the influence of Anders Bachmansson Nordencrantz.

Anders Bachmansson, born in 1697, the son of a Sundsvall merchant and burgomaster, lived for a time in England and served as consul in Lisbon before being ennobled under the name Nordencrantz in 1743 and serving on the *Kammerkollegium*. His first writings, in the 1730s, were on economic subjects and traditionally mercantilistic in tone; in the *Riksdag* he was originally aligned with the Hats. As the owner of ironworks in Sweden and Finland, however, he fell afoul of the Hats' economic policy and was forced to sell out in 1756. Because of inflation, Nordencrantz took a serious loss on the sale, directing his vast indignation against the Hats' monetary and banking policy. From the mid-1750s he resumed his writing, now attacking the Hats. By the early 1760s he was acclaimed as the political and economic oracle of the Younger Caps. ·

Nordencrantz was a passionate polemicist rather than a speculative philosopher. His numerous writings are long-winded, disorganized, and at times ambiguous and contradictory. As a theorist, perhaps especially in the economic sphere, he was easily outclassed by several of his contemporaries. Yet none were more widely read or profoundly influential among both intellectuals and *riksdagsmän*. Taken as a whole, they embody the new criticism of the existing state and society.

He was a true son of the Enlightenment in his basic rationalism and enormous reading in the works of the *philosophes*, to whom he made constant reference. There is an underlying pessimism regarding human weakness behind his pervasive fear of the abuse of unrestrained power, either political or economic. He was nonetheless confident of the power of human reason and enlightened legislation to rectify human errors.

In Nordencrantz's view, all power derived from the people, not from its government. There must therefore be checks and balances. Public officials must be accountable to the public, elected for limited terms by those they served, who could thus watch over their performance. Those officials with judicial functions must share these with elected juries. Neither such "judges" nor the representatives of special economic interests should be eligible to serve in the national legislative body, which Nordencrantz envisioned as a single chamber, elected by and composed of men of adequate, independent means, without reference to Estate, incorruptible by threat or bribery, and fearing only "God and the law." The exercise of the people's will required public enlightenment and the free exchange of ideas, hence popular education and freedom of the press. In his bitterness against suspected, highly placed financial speculators, whom he rather wildly imagined to have the state and its bureaucracy in their power, Nordencrantz even asserted in the early 1760s the right of rebellion against tyranny. It follows that he opposed special privilege of all kinds, yet he did not reject Montesquieu's concept of an aristocracy to serve as guardians of public freedom. In economic matters Nordencrantz continued through the 1760s to attack the established mercantilist system, in which bureaucratic decisions rather than the individual's free choice determined who should be rich and who poor.[16]

These basic ideas are echoed by other Cap publicists during the 1760s. Their rivals in the Hat camp most generally based their defense of the existing and, in their view, natural balance of powers within state and society upon Montesquieu.[17]

In the fall of 1764 elections were held for a *riksdag* to meet the following winter. Campaigning was livelier than ever before, revealing that both parties— especially the Caps—had been marshaling their forces. Foreign diplomats in

Stockholm distributed money with unaccustomed largesse, with France backing the Hats, Russia and Britain the Caps.[18] The result was a resounding defeat for the Hats; the Caps gained majorities in all four Estates, by a narrow margin in the Nobility, by substantial ones in the other three.

Far more significant than foreign influence, which was largely self-canceling, were important changes in the social bases of the nonnoble Estates. Among the Clergy, which had never been more than lukewarm toward the Hats, leadership shifted increasingly from the bishops to the parish pastors. In 1766 the Estate even formally excluded from future *riksdagar* any of its members who had accepted ennoblement for themselves or their children, which removed the archbishop and several bishops.

More important still was the striking Cap victory in the Burgher Estate, based on a new coalition of middling and smaller merchants, mainly engaged in import and internal trade, and well-to-do artisans, now increasingly activated politically in a manner recalling Britain in the same years. The larger merchants, manufacturers, and municipal magistrates who had traditionally dominated the Estate meanwhile remained Hats. This shift was most notable in Stockholm, where social cleavages within the bourgeoisie were greatest and where the Hats now lost all but one of the city's ten seats in the Burgher Estate. In the provincial towns the lines were generally less sharply drawn and the elections were often determined by personalities and local economic issues. During the *Riksdag* that followed, the social reorientation of the Estate was further consolidated through the removal of regulations from the 1750s affording government officials a voice in the election of town magistrates and restricting the burghers' freedom of assembly. In 1766 anyone who had previously had the "character" of a government official was moreover barred from membership in the Estate.

The peasantry were repelled by the Hat council's recent limitations on peasant land acquisition and property rights, while being attracted by the Caps' concern for agriculture and liberalism with regard to rural trading. It is not coincidental that several of the new Cap leaders in the Peasant Estate were rural entrepreneurs as well as farmers.[19]

After the *Riksdag* convened in January 1765 it dismissed most members of the state council and replaced them with Caps. A number of new leaders appeared, many of them younger men making their political debut. Of them, the most outstanding was Anders Chydenius, representative in the Clerical Estate of the chaplains of Österbotten in Finland.

While he freely acknowledged his debt to Anders Nordencrantz, Chydenius was at once more consistently radical and the master of a far more lucid and compelling literary style. With unbounded energy he crusaded in the *Riksdag* and in numerous writings for the freedom of the individual from all forms of wardship and constraint. He thus led the fight for freedom of the press and against restraints to free trade, in particular Stockholm's staple rights over the

Bothnian ports in Sweden and Finland. He would later campaign against the monopolistic rights of craft guilds, restrictions on the grain trade, the oppressive authority of masters over their servants, and religious intolerance. Over a decade before Adam Smith, he argued that "each individual voluntarily seeks out the position and the economic pursuit in which he best increases the national profit."[20] Beyond the destruction of special privileges and monopolies, Chydenius envisioned a kind of rough economic democracy, without poverty and dependence on the one hand, and idleness and luxury on the other. As a clergyman, he took his duties seriously, holding to Lutheran orthodoxy and enforcing his parishioners' religious obligations. Like Rousseau—and later Robespierre— he was impressed with the concept that the exercise of freedom required the virtue that only a shared faith could impart.[21]

The Caps' program during the *Riksdag* largely bears the impress of Nordencrantz and Chydenius, although often attenuated by political give-and-take. A landmark was the abolition of press censorship for all nontheological writings in 1766, providing a freedom of expression unmatched outside Great Britain and the Dutch Netherlands and stimulating a torrent of political pamphleteering. An inquest was held into the previous Hat financial administration, and stiff penalties were meted out. Stockholm's monopoly on Bothnian exports was abolished. Rural trade became freer, and peasants were permitted to ship their wares directly to their destinations. Many now took them to Stockholm, bypassing their local market towns. Peasants were again permitted to buy crown land.

The Caps meanwhile sought to practice thrift in government. Special subsidies to manufacturing were cut back. To reduce the national debt and improve the trade balance, they prohibited the import of a number of foreign luxuries and semi-luxuries, and imposed sumptuary ordinances. Some steps were also taken to exercise a stricter control over public officials. They sought to develop peaceful and friendly relations with Russia, Denmark, and Britain, while economizing on defense, thus suspending the construction of fortifications in Finland.

The Hats eventually regained control in the House of the Nobility through an alliance with the small Court party, adding a growing element of class strife to the political conflict. Alarmed at the new radicalism within their party, some Caps, especially among the nobility, crossed over to the Hat camp. The poet and nobleman G. F. Gyllenborg later recalled his repugnance toward the "violent regime" of the "democrats," similar in character to "the beginning of the French Revolution."[22]

Across the Sound in Copenhagen, the accession of the sixteen-year-old Christian VII in January 1766 was followed by a complex and confused struggle for dominance between the rival factions of recent years. The council persuaded the young king to dismiss Field Marshal Saint-Germain within a few days of his accession; Saint-Germain was replaced by twenty-two-year-old Prince Carl of

Hesse, who shortly thereafter married one of Christian's sisters. But Christian soon gave ear to the council's opponents. He dismissed his father's favorite, Count Moltke, from the council, replacing him with Count Frederik Danne-skjold-Samsøe, a Dane and the implacable foe of the German "Excellencies." Around him gathered other opponents of the existing regime, including Colonel Görtz, Count Rantzau-Ascheberg, and the Prussian minister, Baron H. H. Borck. By August 1766 Danneskjold-Samsøe had Christian on the point of dismissing Count Bernstorff himself, which was apparently only forestalled by Reverdil's energetic intervention. By March 1767 the king had tired of Carl of Hesse and recalled Saint-Germain.

The old "Excellencies" still had one strong suit. Following the crisis of 1762, Bernstorff had worked with notable success to improve relations with St. Petersburg. A Danish-Russian Treaty of Friendship, signed in March 1765, contained a secret article providing for negotiations to settle the Holstein-Gottorp question. Bernstorff thus appeared indispensable for the success of this vital enterprise and by March 1767 the Russians pointedly warned the king to stay away from intrigues against the existing council.

The tide turned. In October Danneskjold-Samsøe was dismissed from the council, followed by Saint-Germain in November. Both were banished from the capital, as was Rantzau-Ascheberg, and even Reverdil, who had striven to remain neutral. By February 1768 Moltke was back on the council. Two years after the beginning of the new reign the old council had apparently weathered the storm. As Rantzau-Ascheberg now rightly predicted, it would take some unforeseen turn of events to break its grip.[23]

Although it represented more rational concepts of administrative efficiency, the antiministerial faction suffered serious handicaps. It was united mainly by opposition to the "Excellencies"; among its adherents personal ambitions caused much rivalry and suspicion. More important surely was the widespread fear in government circles, expressed by the influential *generalprokurør* (chief legal expert) for the Danish Chancellery, Henrik Stampe, that a "military government" would be inimical to Denmark's basic constitution.[24] Only a strong-willed monarch could thus have seized the opportunity provided by the French field marshal and his friends and turned it to account.

Unfortunately, Christian VII was altogether unequal to such a challenge. The young king was not unintelligent, and Reverdil had done his best to instill in him some sense of responsibility with the aid of Fénélon's *Télémaque* and Montesquieu's *L'Esprit des lois*. Yet he showed little inclination for effort or concentration. Had he been prepared to leave governing to the council, as his father had done, this too would have decided the contest for power. But Christian took a childish, malicious delight in unexpectedly dismissing and appointing officials, and in playing one faction off against the other. At the same time, he was easily swayed. Hence much of the administrative confusion and insecurity of his early reign.

Christian quickly revealed a restless passion for distraction. To his court surgeon he declared his intention to "rage for two years."[25] Bernstorff, hoping to settle him down, hastened the king's marriage to sixteen-year-old Caroline Mathilde, sister of George III of England, in the fall of 1766. Christian soon tired of the restraints of married life and with his boon companions made nocturnal rounds of Copenhagen's taverns and brothels, often brawling with the abashed guardians of the peace.

In 1768 the king announced his intention to travel abroad for two years, causing Bernstorff and his associates the gravest apprehensions for Denmark's international prestige. With the reluctant Bernstorff as cicerone, the royal party set off in July on a tour that fortunately lasted only eight months. Christian visited London and Paris, where he behaved himself with unexpected probity. But for those closest to the royal person there could now be little doubt of what Reverdil had suspected in his pupil: that Christian VII was touched with insanity.[26]

This appalling circumstance would long remain a well-kept secret; that the public tended to take a broad view of the king's pleasure was clear from the dissolute but amiable Frederik V's unfailing popularity. Thus the first years of Christian's reign were a time of sanguine hopes and numerous projects for useful reform. Of these, none aroused as much interest and debate as those concerning the agrarian question.

The steady rise of agricultural prices since the low of the 1730s had encouraged increasing numbers of middle-class entrepreneurs to invest in manorial lands and ensure their profitability through the strictest interpretation of their proprietary rights. There thus occurred here, as elsewhere in Europe, "a seigneurial reaction connected with the development of the capitalist spirit," as Kåre D. Tønnesson has observed.[27] By the 1750s, however, Denmark's agrarian structure was reaching the evident limits of productivity under its archaic forms of cultivation and its wasteful and unjust social organization. To many it was increasingly clear that dispersal of village landholdings into scattered strips kept cultivating practices primitive and productivity low, and that insecurity of tenure and tenant rights, mounting labor obligations, lack of personal freedom, and the degrading treatment that frequently resulted, left the Danish peasants apathetic and ineffectual, both as cultivators of their own land and as laborers on the landlord's, while they still remained a charge on the latter's resources, particularly with respect to responsibility for the tenants' land tax.

Inspiration for specific agrarian reforms was both practical and humanitarian. Early in the century new fodder crops and crop rotations, inspired by north German, Dutch, and English practice, increased productivity on manorial demesnes in the duchies. Beginning in 1739, Count Hans Rantzau-Ascheberg experimented with enclosures and the commutation of labor obligations on his Holstein manor. By 1761 he had created some twenty compact peasant leaseholds out of his demesne, from which the rents compensated for the loss of labor service. The results were widely publicized and aroused great interest within the kingdom.[28]

Count Moltke had called attention to the unsatisfactory state of Danish agriculture at the beginning of Frederik V's reign in 1746 and had himself experimented with enclosures and an eleven-field rotation on his Bregentved Manor. In 1757 an Agricultural Commission was set up under Moltke, which concerned itself mainly with separating out the lands of different villages and estates. In 1764, meanwhile, the *stavnsbånd* reached its furthest development when it was extended from the male peasant's fourth to fortieth year.

The Holsteiner Count Christian Günther Stolberg experimented along the lines suggested by Rantzau-Ascheberg on his own estate at Branstedt and, from 1751 on, as *overhofmester* for the dowager queen Sophia Magdalene on her manor at Hirschholm (Hørsholm) on north Sjælland. Count J. H. E. Bernstorff's nephew, Andreas Peter Bernstorff, was an intimate of the Stolberg household, where he mixed with such articulate proponents of agrarian reform as J. S. Sneedorff, Tyge Rothe, Reverdil, and the German G. C. Oeder. When the elder Bernstorff acquired lands for a new manor just north of Copenhagen, his nephew, with a capable estate manager, Torkel Baden, carried out ambitious reforms, beginning in 1764.

While Stolberg had divided the Hirschholm lands into compact farms and moved their tenants onto them, the Bernstorffs also granted hereditary leaseholds and commuted labor obligations. The peasants at first resisted being uprooted from the comforting security of their old villages and vainly petitioned the king to prevent it. An enterprising peasant, Hans Jensen Bjerregaard, who was idealized by the enthusiastic Sneedorff in his influential journal, *Den danske Tilskuer*, took the lead, however, and by 1767 both the Bernstorffs and their tenantry were highly satisfied with the changes. Torkel Baden described them in a widely read account and the Bernstorff manor, being on the outskirts of the capital, was much in the public eye.[29] Similar reforms were carried out at Bistrup, a manor belonging to the Copenhagen magistrature.

Separately, a grass-roots movement toward peasant freeholding was getting under way in west Jutland, where from the later 1750s peasants on occasion purchased their tenancies. When Grubbesholm Manor went up for sale in 1761, it was bought in its entirety by its tenants, who divided it up into individual farms. After the Seven Years' War, the government, to help restore state finances, sold off much crown property between 1764 and 1769. In Denmark crown estates were usually sold intact, creating dozens of new manors, although in some areas, mainly in Jutland, peasants were able to buy their own farms; in the duchies policy favored the extensive parceling out of crown land to peasant purchasers, who thereupon became free if they had formerly been serfs.[30]

All aspects of agrarian reform were discussed and debated in great detail. In Norway there was the inspiring example of the free *odelbonde*, made much of by the friends of reform; perhaps at a more immediately practical level there was that of the numerous small freeholders and hereditary leaseholders in the duchies. From England, France, Germany, even Sweden, came examples of specific, useful reforms, while English economic thought, French physiocracy, and German cameralism alike stressed the primacy of agriculture, the blessings of individual ownership, and the freedom and dignity of the cultivator. Whereas English and French thinkers tended to emphasize the free play of market forces and thus to favor large-scale, economically profitable exploitation, the German cameralists, notably J. H. von Justi, who himself spent some time in Denmark, placed greater weight upon the responsibility of the state to protect the economically weak against the strong, and hence upon the creation and preservation of small, independent farms.[31]

Much of the voluminous agricultural literature in Denmark during the 1750s and 1760s dealt with technical, thus relatively noncontroversial matters, but reform-minded men were not slow to attack the roots of the agrarian problem: the peasants' lack of freedom and their burden of labor obligations. Niels Schelde, himself born a peasant, called for the end of the *stavnsbånd* and was joined by Sneedorff and others. They argued not only that existing conditions offended against both justice and humanity, but that freedom alone could give peasants the self-respect and initiative necessary to make them responsible and truly productive members of society. Their arguments recalled those that had justified Frederik IV's abolition of *vornedskab* in 1701. Their opponents maintained that peasants were by nature so shiftless and improvident that to abolish the *stavnsbåand* would unfailingly bring ruin both to the state and to the peasants themselves.

Supporters of emancipation were meanwhile divided over the question of the landlord's property rights. Enlightened proprietors, such as Tyge Rothe, who saw the need to free the peasantry, also generally favored an end to paternalism and the full right of the proprietor to dispose of his property as he saw fit. The Fyn landowner Baron Poul Abraham Lehn maintained in this regard:

> A peasant is a man, neither more nor less. Give him all the rights the state may bestow upon every citizen, but give him nothing that belongs to anyone else. . . . When he thus becomes his own master, he becomes a *farmer*, as in England. The landlord is bound to uphold his side of the contract and he [the tenant] his.

Discussion of agrarian questions received a further, important stimulus with the founding in 1769 of the Royal Agricultural Society (*Det kongelige Landhusholdningsselskab*), based on British models.[32]

Both Reverdil and Saint-Germain were opponents of the *stavnsbånd*. Whereas the former's motives were philosophical and humanitarian, the latter's were essentially military and political. Reverdil had long impressed the young king with the need for peasant emancipation, to be accomplished gradually through example and persuasion, and without violating property rights. Christian showed keen but sporadic interest. In 1767, for instance, he granted hereditary leases to his crown tenants in Kronborg and Frederiksberg *Amter* in north Sjælland.[33]

At the prompting of Saint-Germain, meanwhile, the king decreed in October 1767 the establishment of a commission to consider the improvement of agriculture and particularly of conditions among the peasantry. Apparently sensing a political coup by the "party of Saint-Germain" and fearing the reaction this would surely create, Reverdil prevailed upon Christian to appoint to it men commanding general respect, including both supporters and opponents of emancipation. The case for the former was stated by the Copenhagen magistrate Oluf Bruun:

> No subject of a realm, however great, powerful, and respected he may be, should or can be said to own another subject, of however humble estate and condition, and least of all in this kingdom, which is ruled by a king, of sovereign and unlimited power, whose law is equally just for all subjects.

The opposing view may best be represented by Baron Holger Rosenkrantz, known to be a humane landlord, who stated:

> The peasantry is and remains the foundation of all other estates, and its welfare is certainly in the true interests of its masters. Whatever may be devised to improve the peasant's lot is to the advantage of the proprietor, who stands in the same relationship to His Royal Majesty as the peasant does to the proprietor. . . . That the peasants would be helped if they were given freedom to move in their younger years from one manor to another . . . I cannot but [doubt and] fear that they would misuse such freedom and leave the manors. . . . The landlord and peasant are in constant need of each other and should comprise a common economy for their mutual benefit.

He later quoted an unidentified French authority on the peasantry: "One must support, direct, and occupy them without crushing them." Another landlord put it more bluntly: "All peasant labor is so onerous that a certain compulsion is necessary lest it cease altogether." Fears were expressed that peasants would abandon the poorer regions for more prosperous ones and crowd into the towns to become lackeys and idlers, rather than staying on the land where they belonged.[34]

Reverdil condemned servitude as "barbarous," yet like Bruun he proposed that it be abolished in stages, to avoid disruption. Saint-Germain's new *Generalkrigsdirektorium* was more imperious: it demanded immediate abolition of the existing militia and of the *stavnsbånd*, retroactively for all male peasants born since October 1760 and by degree for others, as well as land enclosures, hereditary tenure, and limitation or commutation of labor services. In Reverdil's view, this brash proposal spoiled everything. Both he and Saint-Germain had long been regarded with ill will in high and distinguished circles, and within a few days both were dismissed from the commission and banished from the kingdom. In February 1768 new appointments were made, including Moltke and Schimmelmann, whose attitudes toward reform were anything but radical, and in March the commission was further domesticated by converting it into a regular government department.[35]

All was not lost, however. Henrik Stampe, who had written the commission's original instruction, took the initiative in his cautious and undramatic manner, and by 1769 prepared several well-intended ordinances: for encouraging enclosures, fixing labor obligations, sharpening penalties against engrossment of peasant tenancies into manorial demesne, and, most notably, encouraging freehold purchases and protecting peasant freeholders against encroachment from neighboring manors. Although they accomplished relatively little at the time, the Stampe reforms point the way toward the specific character of the great Danish agrarian reforms a generation later.[36]

In the Swedish monarchy, the Younger Cap regime did not long survive its impressive victory. Already before the end of the long *Riksdag* of 1765–66 a growing reaction was evident against much of its program. Its deflationary policy proved too sudden and drastic, particularly because the economy was still depressed by the international postwar slump. Sweden's monetary system was badly deranged, and numerous bankruptcies followed, not least among manufacturers dependent upon government support, which the Caps now reduced or eliminated. Their import restrictions and sumptuary regulations were unpopular and widely evaded. The government suffered a serious loss of revenue, compounded when France ceased to pay subsidies, which Russia, Britain, and Denmark failed to make good.

The Caps' partisan intolerance toward dissent likewise alienated many. Various *riksdagsmän* suffered persecution for opposition to the majority; even Anders Chydenius was expelled from his seat in the Clerical Estate for criticizing the party's monetary plan. In addition to merchants in foreign trade, manufacturers, and debtors, many others had reason to feel apprehensive about the Younger Caps' challenge to the old order: noblemen were concerned about their sons' futures; bureaucrats and magistrates about their jurisdictions, promotions, and compensation; officers about neglect of the military establishment; small-town merchants about increased peasant trading; craft masters about the traditional monopolies of their guilds; and many in different walks of life about unabashed partisanship and an uncensored press. As in Denmark, there was also growing apprehension over increasing subservience toward the Russian colossus.

Under such circumstances, the small Court party, which aspired to increase royal authority, held the balance in the Noble Estate. Although Queen Lovisa Ulrika despised the rule of the Estates and had intrigued repeatedly to overcome it, her husband, Adolf Fredrik, showed little stomach for political infighting. The hopes of the monarchists—and of France, now disillusioned with the Hats—thus focused increasingly upon Crown Prince Gustav.

The leading figure among the Court faction was Count Carl Fredrik Scheffer, a former Hat councillor and Swedish minister to Paris, where he was well known in philosophic circles and by the 1750s was much impressed by the Physiocratic school. In 1756 he was appointed Prince Gustav's governor. It was Scheffer who in 1767 called Gustav's attention to P. F. J. H. Le Mercier de la Rivière's *L'Ordre naturel et essentiel des sociétés politiques*, published that year in London, with its ideal of a "legal despotism," based upon the natural order, as opposed to the "arbitrary" despotisms of the past or those necessarily resulting from "aristocratic" or "democratic" rule. Gustav was profoundly impressed, and Le Mercier's concept of enlightened despotism would hereafter remain one of the poles of his political thinking.[37]

The Hat leaders, most notably Count Frederik Axel von Fersen, were prepared to support some increase in royal authority as the price of an alliance with the Court faction. They now placed their hopes in an extraordinary *Riksdag*, to profit from dissatisfaction with the new regime. The opportunity was provided by the Cap council in December 1768, when it initiated an inquest on the *Kammerskollegium*, causing alarm among the higher bureaucracy. At the instigation of Prince Gustav, Adolf Fredrik declared his intention to abdicate unless the Estates were convened; in the meantime he refused to sign state papers, backed by a kind of general strike by most of the bureaucracy, foreshadowing that which in the summer of 1788 would compel Louis XVI to call the French Estates-General. When state business practically ground to a halt, the council gave way and elections were proclaimed. Prince Gustav prepared two successive drafts for a more monarchical constitution.

The Court party and its Hat allies had chosen their moment well. After vigorous electioneering in the spring of 1769, showing the rapid development of party organization and propaganda in recent years, the Hats won an electoral victory hardly less striking than the Caps' four years earlier, gaining control of all four Estates. Ten members of the council were promptly replaced with Hats, and the *Riksdag*, meeting in Norrköping, confronted its two main tasks: the monetary problem and constitutional revision to increase royal power.

No real solutions were reached during the next nine months. The monetary issue bogged down in partisan strife, and the defection of a group of Hats to the Caps in the Noble Estate, led by Carl Fredrik Pechlin, broke the common front necessary for constitutional change, thereby missing, as Michael Roberts argues, what would be the last chance to convert the existing regime into a balanced and viable constitutional monarchy.[38]

Class antagonisms resurfaced at the *Riksdag*. Both parties roundly accused each other of "aristocracy," meaning thereby domination by a small, exclusive clique.[39] The Hat council again limited the purchase of crown lands by the peasantry. In January 1770 class conflict assumed a new prominence when the burgomaster of Borgå (Porvoo) in Finland, Alexander Kepplerus, presented to the Burgher Estate an appeal for guaranteed equality in rights and honor for noble and commoner alike, for the unenfranchised masses as well as those groups represented by the traditional Estates. Although it could at this point hardly affect the course of the current *Riksdag*, which expired at the end of the month, it pointed unmistakably to privilege as the central issue the next time it convened.[40]

Soon thereafter, in May 1770, the appointment of a new vice-president for the appellate court (*hovrätt*) in Åbo, Finland, brought this issue to a head. The Hat council proposed three candidates, all noblemen, deliberately bypassing two admittedly better-qualified aspirants, one a commoner, the other a man ennobled by the king but excluded from the House of the Nobility by its resolution of 1762. As vice-presidencies of government *kollegier* had not previously been reckoned among the high offices reserved for men of noble status by the Statute of Privileges of 1723, the council's action seemed to presage a further advance of noble pretentions, against which not even the king's patent of nobility might now prevail. In retrospect, Baron Adolf Ludvig Hamilton later recognized in the reaction this created "the first spark of a Jacobinism not yet named."[41] The battle lines were drawn.

While the *Riksdag* of 1769–70 ultimately failed to fulfill the hopes of those who sought to strengthen the Swedish crown, it caused alarm in Russia and Denmark. The Danish-Russian Treaty of 1765, which had initiated negotiations over Holstein-Gottorp, also affirmed the interest of both powers in preserving Sweden's constitution. In 1769 Russia negotiated closer alliances with both Denmark and Prussia; the convention with Denmark now specified that both powers consider as a casus belli against Sweden the slightest modification of its existing form of government. At that very time Russia was negotiating with Prussia and Austria over the first partition of Poland; it is evident that a similar partition of Sweden's territories was under consideration in St. Petersburg, Copenhagen, and Berlin, in the event of a war to rescue Swedish liberties.[42]

The Seven Years' War aroused a growing public opinion in the Scandinavian lands to a new concern for public issues and to a heightened awareness of the outside world, while the military and financial burdens it imposed clearly demonstrated the need for practical reforms. The ideas of the later Enlightenment meanwhile gained ground rapidly in the North, stimulating a growing demand for greater justice and humanity. In Sweden-Finland their influence was basically political, leading toward the early development of the concept of popular sovereignty; in Denmark-Norway, essentially social, concerned with improving the conditions of the most oppressed class. In both, reforming thought aspired toward the equality of citizens under the law.

New regimes came to power in both Nordic states in 1765-66, initially holding forth the promise of far-reaching reform programs. Respectable efforts were indeed made in both during the later 1760s. Still, it remained to be seen just how far Denmark's absolute and Sweden's constitutional monarchies could go, at this stage, in challenging the old order.

CHAPTER 3

# The First Assault on Privilege
# 1770–72

During 1770–71 the way opened unexpectedly for a headlong assault on the old order in both the Nordic states. By the summer of 1772, however, this assault had seemingly been contained on both sides of the Sound. Yet it left behind ideals and programs for change which it would be the work of the next two generations to fulfill.

The unforeseen development that Count Rantzau-Ascheberg had predicted would be needed to change the regime in Denmark turned out to be the astonishing rise in royal favor of an obscure and low-born German physician, Johann Friedrich Struensee. Born in Halle in 1737, the son of a strongly pietistic Lutheran pastor and theologian, he attended the university there, where he rebelled against his strict religious background and was attracted by the materialistic world view of the French *philosophes*. He became a doctor of medicine already at the age of nineteen and moved the following year, in 1757, to Altona in Holstein, where he became the public physician for both the town and the districts of Pinneburg and Rantzau.

Struensee was ambitious and found his way into the society of the local nobility, several of whom had close connections with the court and government in Copenhagen. He thus became closely associated with Enevold Brandt, Colonel S. O. Falkenskjold, and Count Rantzau-Ascheberg. The count found in the young physician an enthusiastic disciple of the French Enlightenment, above all of Voltaire, Rousseau, and Helvétius, and generally of the ideas of the "party of Saint-Germain," to which Rantzau passionately adhered. Together, Rantzau, Falkenskjold, and Struensee read political treatises and fantasized over sweeping social reforms.

During the summer of 1767 Christian VII toured the duchies. In Altona and

67

later while visiting Rantzau's father, the pioneer agrarian reformer, at Asche-
berg, he met Struensee, who well impressed both the king and Reverdil. That
autumn both the younger Count Rantzau and Reverdil fell out of favor, together
with Saint-Germain. When Christian VII set off on his foreign tour in July 1768,
Struensee nonetheless secured appointment as his traveling physician. He
proved effective in soothing the king's overwrought emotions. By the time he
returned to Copenhagen in January 1769, Christian found Struensee indispensable and he was permanently attached to the royal household.[1]

The young queen, Caroline Mathilde, had suffered repeated humiliation, both
from her capricious husband and from a succession of his favorites, which not
even the birth of an heir, Crown Prince Frederik, in 1767, had prevented.
Struensee's favor with the king thus made him suspect in her eyes, all the more
as she heard of his reputation as a libertine. During the summer of 1769, however, she was seriously stricken with a malady, which in retrospect seems to
have been a long-overdue nervous breakdown. Christian at last persuaded the
queen to let his physician attend her. With his sympathetic and tactful manner
he soon gained her grateful confidence and she quickly recovered. In January
1770 Struensee was lodged in Christiansborg palace. Soon the doctor could do
no wrong in the eyes of his royal patrons. He was made the king's reader and
the queen's cabinet secretary, with the title of *konferensråd*. By late spring, if
not before, the thirty-three-year-old physician and the eighteen-year-old queen
had become lovers.[2]

Passionately in love for the first time, Caroline Mathilde behaved with a
remarkable lack of discretion and Struensee was hard put to preserve appearances. Despite rumors, the exact nature of their relationship remained a secret—of sorts—for some months to come. That the doctor enjoyed the royal
couple's unbounded confidence and that the queen was gaining a growing dominance over her husband was, however, obvious by the summer of 1770.

In Altona, Count Rantzau saw the rise of Struensee's fortunes as the prelude
to his own. Although the old reform party led by a field marshal, Saint-Germain,
had failed, Rantzau now envisioned its revival under an even more powerful
"colonel in a long skirt." "The queen's party," he hoped, would at last break the
influence of the despised Bernstorff on the young monarch.[3]

As for Struensee, it is unclear when he began seriously to conceive of playing
a political role. During his Altona years he had been both ambitious and critical
of existing conditions. Yet he could hardly have anticipated the opportunities
that opened before him by mid-1770, and which his dangerous relationship with
the queen compelled him to seize. His rise to power reveals the interplay of circumstance and personality.

During the summer of 1770, Struensee was able to restore his friends Rantzau
and Brandt to royal favor. They were soon understood to form a "triumvirate,"
and Bernstorff saw the handwriting on the wall. On 4 September the king issued

three edicts: ordering an inquiry into an unsuccessful naval expedition against the Algerine pirates, limiting the grant of honorary titles to persons of demonstrated merit, and permitting freedom of the press. All three implied criticism of Bernstorff's foreign and internal policies; significantly, too, they were promulgated as cabinet orders, thus bypassing both *kollegier* and council. The same day Rantzau and General P. E. Gähler were made state councillors. On 14 September, Bernstorff, having resisted all pressure to resign, was dismissed. "If the king holds to what he has begun," Gähler wrote enthusiastically to Saint-Germain in France, "you will once again see a philosophical, beloved prince, who seeks only what is good and what is right."[4]

For the time being it remained unclear who would be the real power behind the throne. Clearly Rantzau pictured himself in the leading role. He saw foreign policy and military affairs as his special competency and was prepared to leave internal matters to Struensee, who kept himself in the background. Europe was meanwhile thunderstruck by the fall of the venerable Bernstorff after two decades in office. "In Denmark they change officials as the queen changes her chemise—if for that matter she still uses such a garment," wrote Catherine II.[5] To make matters worse, Rantzau had earlier made himself *persona non grata* in St. Petersburg. Catherine suspended the provisional treaty for settlement of the Holstein-Gottorp problem which Bernstorff had negotiated in 1767. Relations with Russia deteriorated to the point that Struensee was compelled to reduce Rantzau to a secondary role. On 18 December 1770 Struensee was made *maître de requêtes*, through whom all state business would henceforth be conveyed to the king. On 27 December the council itself was suspended. Count A. S. von der Osten, a former envoy to Russia acceptable to the empress, was made foreign minister. Now clearly the most powerful man in the realm, Dr. Struensee could embark upon its internal transformation.

The instrument of his rule was the cabinet order. Beginning already in 1768, Christian VII had made occasional use of this procedure, at first in relatively minor matters. Of some 2,200 cabinet orders issued from that time through January 1772, however, fully 1,880 date from the period beginning in September 1770. Emanating ostensibly from the king himself, they were now written and almost invariably composed by Struensee. They were in German, brief, and to the point, seldom providing any rationale or justification.[6]

With tireless energy Struensee dealt simultaneously with a bewildering variety of subjects. He never prepared a clear statement of his overall program and objectives, which doubtless evolved with circumstances. Still, certain basic features emerge. Struensee's world view was that of the later French Enlightenment, and from the "party of Saint-Germain" of the preceding decade he received many of his ideas for specific reforms.[7] The inspiration of Prussia is likewise evident.

Struensee's greatest efforts were concentrated upon administrative reorganization. By the end of 1770 the council was suspended, as seen, and the large, semi-autonomous *kollegier* were broken down into smaller departments with more limited functions, directly subordinate to the king—that is, to Struensee. This was accompanied by the wholesale dismissal of the heads of the former *kollegier*, who were nobles, permitting their subordinates of common origin to rise to the top of the new departments on the basis of merit. Struensee now combined certain functions, most significantly those of the old *Rentekammer* (Exchequer), *Kommerskollegium* (Board of Trade), and *Tollkammer* (Customs Office) into a new *Finanskollegium*, the heart of his administrative system, under his elder brother, Karl August Struensee.

Both the new *Finanskollegium* and the Danish and German Chancelleries, responsible for internal affairs, were subdivided into regional departments for Denmark, Norway and the Atlantic islands, and the duchies. Foreign affairs were removed from the German Chancellery and entrusted to a new department under Count von der Osten.

Struensee undertook to reorganize the judicial system, establishing a new superior court in Copenhagen, and worked for the consistent application of the laws by eliminating various immunities and special tribunals.

Count U. A. Holstein, one of the few nobles Struensee appointed to office, was made *overpresident* for Copenhagen. The old town government, while it preserved some vestige of burgher representation, was lax and corrupt. The magistrature and the burgher assembly, "the Thirty-Two Men," were replaced by a town council appointed by the crown.

In matters of procedure, Struensee stressed speed, simplicity, and strict subordination. He insisted that reports be brief and concise, as were his own directives. He strove to introduce the strictest economies in government—although not always at court. This led to the reduction of excessive salaries and emoluments, and to the dismissal of unnecessary functionaries, many of whom were nobles, often without pension. Struensee likewise undertook to cut back the overgrown military establishment by as much as one half, beginning with the dissolution of the elite Mounted Guards' Regiment in May 1771.

There were understandable reasons for Struensee's concentration upon administrative reform. He knew that as a foreign *parvenu* of common origin his position was a precarious one, which only an efficient administrative machine staffed by trustworthy men could secure. This was the necessary precondition to fundamental social and economic reforms which were certain to arouse widespread opposition. Temperamentally he was inclined to put great faith in logic, consistency, and oganization.

Still, Struensee did not wait to begin reforming society. Thus there emerges a second characteristic of his efforts: his essential liberalism. With the physiocrats, he clearly believed that the state should use its absolute authority to create the greatest possible sphere of personal freedom and opportunity for its subjects.

As seen, he opened careers to talent in the service of the state; he even admitted notables of common birth to court. Personal morality he held to be a private matter, provided it did not harm others, and he abolished numerous police regulations for its surveillance and control. By establishing press freedom in September 1770, Struensee invited public opinion to play its part in public affairs. Being a freethinker himself, he favored religious tolerance and encouraged the Moravian Brethren to settle in Schleswig.

His liberalism is also evident in his economic policies. He removed the tariff barrier between the duchies and the kingdom, deprived Copenhagen of its favored status in foreign trade, and ended government subsidies to manufactures and the arts. He reduced the monopolistic privileges of the artisan guilds and encouraged free masterships. In December 1771 he ended the Danish grain monopoly in southern Norway.

Struensee likewise set out to deal with Denmark's greatest social problem, that of the peasantry, and already in November 1770 established a new agrarian commission composed of known proponents of reform. Its main accomplishment was the limitation in February 1771 of manorial labor obligations, based on the size of the tenant's holding rather than the manor's need for labor; for a tenancy of average size (six *tønder hartkorn*), these were now restricted to 144 days a year. In contrast, some tenant farms on Sjælland had, by 1770, become liable for as many as 265 days annually. In August the commission submitted its proposal for the gradual abolition of the *stavnsbånd*. It also favored a free contractual relationship between landlord and tenant.[8] A loan fund was established to encourage peasant freehold purchases. The commission's measures were not yet implemented when Struensee fell from power the following winter. In January 1771, meanwhile, *odel* protection of freehold farms in Norway was reduced from twenty to fifteen years to allow a greater mobility of wealth there.

Finally, Struensee's reforms reveal his humanitarianism, in the spirit of the later Enlightenment. He abolished various Draconian punishments and improved conditions in prisons and workhouses. As a physician, he was much concerned with public hygiene, opened Copenhagen's hospitals to the poor, established a foundling home to discourage infanticide by unwed mothers, and provided medical control over brothels.[9] He likewise unified and improved the system of poor relief in the capital.

Struensee reached the height of his power in July 1771, when he was made a count, together with his friend Enevold Brandt, the master of the king's pleasures. The king appointed Struensee to the newly created post of *Gehejmekabinettsminister*, with the unprecedented authority to sign cabinet orders without the royal countersignature.

But at this point his most active and creative period was over. He spent most of the summer and fall with the royal family at Hirschholm, increasingly absorbed with the amusements of the court and his relationship with the queen, which by now was common knowledge and was accepted with apathetic equanimity by the king. Christian VII's condition deteriorated rapidly. In September Reverdil was recalled from Switzerland to distract him and was appalled.[10] Under such conditions discontent bred rapidly throughout the monarchy, especially in the capital.

Struensee's change of regime had naturally made enemies of those he had driven out of power, the old ministerial party, who looked to Count Bernstorff, now in exile in Mecklenburg, as their leader. Behind them was the nobility as a whole, alarmed at the large-scale dismissal of their peers from civil and military employments and sinecures, the loss of their traditional preference in the higher offices of state, the limitation of their tenants' labor obligations, the loss of the protected grain market in southern Norway, and the impending abolition of the *stavnsbånd*. They were outraged by Struensee's common birth, and more so when he was made a count.

Struensee attacked all forms of privilege and vested interest simultaneously. The lackeys of the high and mighty were deprived of what they regarded as their right to reward through government sinecures. Bureaucrats felt insecure over tenure and compensation, and frustrated by the loss of accustomed discretionary powers. Military and naval personnel, including rank and file, were apprehensive about their future prospects. The Copenhageners were offended by the suppression of their municipal liberties, which had been reconfirmed as recently as 1760. Bourgeois social climbers were indignant at no longer being able to indulge their "title sickness" by being made *etatsråder* or *kommersråder*.

Artisans were fearful for their guild privileges. Merchants in the capital were concerned about Copenhagen's foreign and colonial trade and those in the provinces about diminished grain exports to Norway. Manufacturers faced ruin through the ending of subsidies and competition from the duchies. Unemployment rose rapidly, and during 1771 more than 4,000 persons left the capital. Poor harvests between 1770 and 1772 meanwhile caused widespread distress. Struensee's efforts to provision the capital were insufficient, and the repeal of the grain monopoly came too late to save his popularity in Norway.

Struensee at the same time offended the nation's pride and moral sensibilities. He was clearly not opposed to nobility as such, provided it were an elite open to merit as it had been under the earlier Danish absolutism. But his own elevation to the highest rank of the nobility seemed cynical and hypocritical in view of his manifestly democratic tendencies heretofore, just as the emolument of 60,000 *rigsdaler* which accompanied it seemed indefensible when his strict economies in government had deprived many officials of their posts and pensions. His habitual use of German in the administration and continued ignorance of the Danish language offended a Danish national sentiment which was already on the rise. Clergy and laity alike were scandalized by his apparent godlessness and immorality, as evidenced by his relaxation of controls over private behavior.

Above all, the nation could not accept the manner in which Struensee had risen to royal favor and his domination of the king and queen.

Struensee's proclamation of press freedom in September 1770 released a flood of pamphleteering, as had the Swedish law four years earlier. Although much of it was scurrilous and irresponsible, taken as a whole it gave vent to accumulated hopes and frustrations throughout the monarchy and dealt with almost all contemporary conditions.[11] In Denmark this meant much discussion of agrarian questions.

Similarly, press freedom aroused high hopes for important reforms in Norway. Local sentiment was on the rise, spurred by the growing feeling that Denmark consumed what Norway produced. The appearance in 1771 of the first volume of Gerhard Schøning's history of ancient Norway produced a surge of local patriotism, while in Denmark such influential opinion makers as P. F. Suhm, Tyge Rothe, and G. C. Oeder vocally supported Norway's claims to more equitable treatment.[12]

In particular, the Norwegian writings called for a separate bank, university, and board of trade, and for the repeal of the Danish grain monopoly in southern Norway, all old demands now restated more forcefully than ever. In June 1771 Struensee summoned to Copenhagen the bishop of Trondheim, Johan Ernst Gunnerus, co-founder with Schøning and Suhm of the Trondheim Scientific Society in 1760, to discuss the reform of the University of Copenhagen. Here the bishop presented his own plan for a Norwegian university, to be supported by the endowment his compatriot Holberg had given to Sorø Academy in 1747. Nothing came of it, however. Copenhagen feared that abandonment of the monarchy's traditional centralism would ultimately threaten its unity. Although Struensee's administrative reorganization had provided for greater attention to local interests than heretofore, he could ill afford by the fall of 1771 to sacrifice what support he might still hope for in Denmark through concessions to Norway. Thus, like the proponents of agrarian reform in Denmark, the leaders of opinion in Norway found their hopes first encouraged, then discouraged.

In establishing press freedom in 1770, Struensee had hoped not only to open channels between the governor and the governed, but to gain popular support for his attack on privilege and administrative inefficiency. At first such support seemed forthcoming. But as Struensee's dictatorial manner and refusal to consider the views of others made ever more enemies, the press turned against him. Personal attacks in the press became so bitter that he felt compelled to limit its freedom, one of his most cherished reforms, in October 1771. Meanwhile, disaffection reached the point where implied criticism was directed against the absolutistic form of government itself: it was suggested that an assembly of Estates be established to watch over and control the government, that the monarch should be the representative of the nation, responsible to it and replaceable by it.[13] Count A. P. Bernstorff was sufficiently alarmed by the prevailing tone that he wrote to his uncle on 23 September: "If there should be a popular uprising, it could well lead to the overthrow of the monarchical system. I see nothing more clearly than that thoughts in that direction are becoming quite common. I can perceive them in all the writings that are coming out . . . ."[14]

In September a crowd of Norwegian seamen from the naval dockyard in Copenhagen marched out to Hirschholm to demand their back pay. Struensee's weak handling of the situation encouraged further insubordination. The following month placards appeared in the capital calling for the assassination of the "tyrant." In December Struensee's order to disband the last remaining guards' battalion, composed mostly of Norwegians, led to a full-scale mutiny, which was only ended by damaging concessions. Rumors were now circulating that Struensee intended to do away with the king and even the crown prince, marry the queen, and make himself master of the realm, as a new "Cromwell" or even as usurper of the crown itself.[15]

Struensee was, however, brought down not by popular insurrection but by a palace revolution. By the end of 1771 his reforms and manner had alienated even most of his former supporters. Enevold Brandt, the one man he still really trusted, was plotting his overthrow when it became known that he himself had physically chastised the king, allegedly with Struensee's approval, which thereby cut off his own retreat.

Count Rantzau now despised Struensee as a lowborn upstart. With Magnus Beringskjold, a bitter opponent of peasant emancipation, he conspired to bring about the favorite's downfall. They came in contact with the dowager queen, Juliane Marie, and her son, Hereditary Prince (*Arveprins*) Frederik, who had been repeatedly slighted by Struensee and Caroline Mathilde. As the king's nearest relatives, his stepmother and half-brother gave the conspiracy a certain legitimacy, while their astute confidant, Ove Guldberg, the hereditary prince's former preceptor, may have been the real mastermind behind the plot.[16] The conspirators ensured the support of the military by recruiting Generals H. H. Eickstedt and G. L. Köller.

Following a masquerade ball at Christiansborg Palace on the night of 17 January 1772, a party led by Guldberg gained access to the king's bedchamber, where the bewildered monarch was inveigled into signing orders for the arrest of the queen, Struensee, Brandt, and certain others. Rantzau then seized the queen while Köller secured Struensee. Brandt, Gähler, Karl August Struensee, and several others were likewise arrested. The following day Christian VII was driven through the streets of the capital to show he had been freed from the tyrant. The author, Charlotta Dorothea Biehl, who remained ever sympathetic toward Struensee and the unfortunate queen, remembered the king as "pale as a corpse and with the greatest anguish in his face, drawn by eight white horses in the magnificent coach . . . surrounded by the shrieking, howling populace, which knew not what it was cheering for."[17] The coup was welcomed throughout the monarchy with rejoicing, which in Copenhagen degenerated into the pillaging of brothels—which Struensee was accused of having encouraged—and the property of local Germans. Juliane Marie, Hereditary Prince Frederik, and their associates were heaped with fulsome praise.

Caroline Mathilde was confined to Kronborg Castle in Helsingør (Elsinore). Struensee and Brandt were held in chains in Copenhagen's citadel, and a special tribunal was appointed for their trial. When a search of the prisoners' papers failed to reveal evidence of a plot against the king, the tribunal concentrated on Struensee's relationship with the queen and usurpation of the monarch's authority, and Brandt's violence against the king's person. After long questioning— and very likely the threat of torture, which he himself had abolished—Struensee admitted to adulterous relations with the queen. Confronted with this confession, Caroline Mathilde admitted her guilt. Struensee and Brandt were condemned for having violated the king's honor and authority under the *Lex Regia* of 1665.[18]

This fundamental law made no provision for the monarch's insanity, and its stipulations regarding *lèse-majesté* were vague. The legality of the verdict thus remains disputable.[19] The persons now in power, however, needed to justify their own seizure of the state, and they feared that once the initial enthusiasm wore off, a popular reaction in favor of Struensee and the unfortunate queen would take place.

On 25 February Struensee and Brandt were declared forfeit of life, honor, and goods, and condemned to death. Both long remained confident—as did many others—of their eventual pardon or reprieve. Catherine II, despite her earlier antipathy, sought to intercede. But the new regime dared not show clemency. On 28 February, before an immense crowd, they were beheaded, after their right hands were struck off. Their bodies, drawn and quartered, remained on public display on the edge of Copenhagen for the next four years. Europe was aghast at this savage display of medieval barbarism toward persons of such standing and prominence.

A separate tribunal divorced Caroline Mathilde from Christian VII. Thanks to British intervention, George III's sister was spared from life imprisonment and granted asylum in Hanover.

Thus ended the most dramatic and tragic episode in the history of European enlightened despotism. More strikingly even than Emperor Joseph II, the German physician demonstrates its ethos, goals—and limitations. The Danish-Norwegian monarchy offered in many ways an ideal laboratory for the experiment he undertook. Royal power was in principle unlimited. With the partial exception of the duchies, the state formed an administrative and economic unity, and possessed by European standards a loyal and relatively efficient bureaucracy. It was not burdened with militarist and expansionist ambitions.[20] It is indeed notable how far the experiment was able to proceed before an effective opposition mobilized against it.

Yet these advantages were largely neutralized by Struensee's personal short-comings: his self-righteous dogmatism, his lack of political common sense, his insensitivity to historic traditions and prejudices, his imperious manner, his frequent superficiality and inconsistency. In his cold devotion to principle, he seems a more humane and self-indulgent Robespierre.

Struensee always remained an outsider, without attachment to the native traditions or ruling class of his adopted country. He was thus prepared to ride roughshod over both. No regime in Europe attempted so many and such radical changes in so brief a period. Henry Steele Commager has claimed that while elsewhere in Europe there emerged a "blueprint" for a new social order, in Denmark "we have—briefly at least—the new order itself."[21]

Struensee's position as an outsider was, however, also his basic weakness. He had little understanding for the state he sought to transform. "He seemed to believe," wrote Reverdil, who was not unsympathetic, "that a minister who stood behind a curtain and set a royal puppet in motion had as much power as an absolute and enlightened king."[22] Perhaps this is unfair. But in his position, Struensee could only gain mastery over the state through exceptional circumstances and irregular means, which in turn could only weaken the royal authority upon which he ultimately depended. Well-prepared reforms that Denmark-Norway could and did accept later, when enacted by its legitimate crown prince over a period of years, it could not tolerate as an all-out attack on the existing order by a foreigner of common birth within a few months in 1770–71. It seems inconceivable that Struensee could have remained in power much longer than he did, when even Joseph II was ultimately compelled to retreat from his more careful—but no more radical—program a generation later.

Yet Struensee's efforts were not lost. The period of reaction that followed his regime made manifest the need for the fundamental and lasting reforms that followed after 1784 and that made unacknowledged but unmistakable use of Struensee's blueprint.

The unforeseen occurred in Sweden when King Adolf Fredrik died on 12 February 1771 and was succeeded by his twenty-five-year-old son, Gustav III. The beginning of a new reign required the prompt convening of the Estates to receive the new monarch's coronation oath and to swear allegiance to him. The oath was to guarantee the constitution and the privileges of the Estates. Because feeling remained high on both scores since the recent *Riksdag* of 1769–70 and because it was already evident that the new king was both ambitious and astute, it was clear that a stormy session lay ahead.

News of his father's death reached Crown Prince Gustav in Paris. As seen, he had concerned himself with projects for a coup to strengthen royal power since at least 1768. He now visited the French capital to arrange for French support with the Duc de Choiseul. En route, however, Gustav learned that Choiseul had just been dismissed. The French ministry now proved to be cool toward any precipitous action.

In the meantime, Gustav, who had grown up on the writings of the French *philosophes*, frequented the intellectual salons of Paris. Here he was received with great adulation, reflecting a long-standing interest in Sweden, which Voltaire had called "the freest kingdom on earth" in 1756, and not least its constitution of 1720, which Mably considered the "masterpiece of modern legislation" in its provisions for "the rights of humanity and equality." To his mother, Gustav admitted to the "frightful blasphemy" that the *philosophes* were "more amiable to read than to see."[23]

Before he departed Paris, the French ministry granted a subsidy to Sweden but cautioned Gustav against attempting a coup; he received a similar warning from his uncle, Frederick II, in Potsdam on his way home. On 30 May he entered Stockholm, where the Estates were already summoned to meet the following month.

The Hat and the Cap parties organized their election campaigns to a hitherto unparalleled degree, and both Hat local officials and foreign envoys sought vigorously to affect the outcome. In their campaigning for the nonnoble Estates, the Caps above all exploited the burning issue of privilege, both on principle and for the tactical advantage it now offered. The atmosphere within these three Estates when they convened in June has been compared by P. J. Edler to that within the French Third Estate in May 1789 and the instructions prepared by the electoral assemblies to the *cahiers de doléances*.[24]

The leaders of the Noble Estate had serious cause for alarm. The Hats feared a vindictive purge of the council, which they had controlled since 1769; the noble Caps that the triumph of their party in the nonnoble Estates would lead to a general attack on noble privileges. On the eve of the *Riksdag*, three noblemen from each party thus worked out a compromise agreement, or "composition," under Gustav III's mediation, allocating places on the council and on *Riksdag* committees, and stipulating that the coronation oath remain the same as at Adolf Fredrik's accession in 1751.

When the *Riksdag* convened, the Caps commanded strong majorities in the Burgher and Peasant Estates, and initially a majority of one in the Clergy. Only the Nobility was dominated by the Hats, with support from the Court party.

On 25 June Gustav III opened the *Riksdag* with an eloquent appeal for concord and patriotism, and declared it his greatest glory to be "the first citizen of a free people."[25] Despite his earlier speculations and developments later in his reign, there seems to be good reason to take him at his word at this point. Not only had he been warned, in Paris and Potsdam, against attempting a coup, but he evidently returned from Paris not unaffected by the libertarian and anglophile influences he had encountered there. He seems to have hoped that in mediating between factions and classes he could strengthen his own position by building up his own following. Already in July he was hailed by a pamphleteer as a "patriot king," with clear reference to George III and the "king's friends" in Great Britain.[26]

Just as Gustav was impressed with the importance of willing subjects, so too was he convinced, as his earlier papers reveal, of Montesquieu's axiom that a true monarchy must rest upon a social hierarchy headed by a healthy aristocracy. He was no less proud to be the first gentleman than the first citizen of the realm. Thus both principle and temperament committed him inwardly to the defense of the nobility.[27]

The Caps in the nonnoble Estates disregarded the composition arranged by the party leaders in the House of the Nobility by packing their places on the *Riksdag* committees with their own adherents. The Nobility could only respond by filling their places with Hats. By now class conflict overshadowed party. To consolidate their position, the nonnoble Estates resolved that an act passed by three Estates should immediately become law, even if the fourth delayed in passing it.

The main issue was now the coronation oath. If it remained as in 1751, the monarch would be committed to preserve all existing rights and privileges. The nonnoble Estates therefore strove to change it. Whereas the Peasants were particularly concerned with property rights and the equality of their Estate within the *Riksdag*, the Burghers concentrated on equal access to the higher offices of state. Both Estates busied themselves with preparing statements of their corporate privileges and with the Clerical Estate considered drafts, based principally upon Alexander Kepplerus's memorial of January 1770, for a common charter of privileges for the nonnoble orders, to become a constitutional statute corresponding to the Nobility's charter of 1723.[28] The nobles came under increasing attack in a spate of pamphleteering. "The inferior orders," the French ambassador, the Comte de Vergennes, reported in August, "breathe nothing but democracy."[29]

The Noble Estate clung determinedly to the coronation oath of 1751. In actuality, the rights it defended were modest enough by European criteria, although they could still provide that margin of security which might permit noble families to maintain themselves as befitted their station—however frugally—in the employment of the state or on protected manorial lands. The Estate was sorely offended by the attacks against it and responded with much golden oratory on the valor and sacrifices of its ancestors in the service of the fatherland. Its apologists invoked Montesquieu in arguing that the nobility provided the necessary bulwark for the liberties of all, and pointed to the example of Denmark, where the degradation of the nobility formed the basis for absolutism. Most fundamental to the nobility was, however, the principle that three Estates could not interpret or change the privileges of the fourth without its own concurrence: nobles were not prepared to "take law" from commoners.[30]

In vain Gustav III harangued the speakers of the four Estates on 28 November, urging a compromise, which served largely to arouse the suspicion of the nonnoble Estates. The same day, the burgher Aron Westén wrote in his diary, "This meeting became immediately known, and it was said everywhere that the king has now removed his mask, and that . . . he is entirely devoted to the nobility."[31] It appeared the *Riksdag* might break down into two hostile confederations, each with its own coronation oath, which would compel Gustav to choose sides. "Gustav III, it seemed, would be faced with the same choice between the ancient regime and the new era as Louis XVI a couple of decades later," Fredrik Lagerroth has asserted.[32] To his mother, Gustav wrote on 11 February 1772: "We have reached the point where shortly real anarchy, a civil war, or perfect order will be born out of all these disorders. . . . There are no longer Caps or Hats; there is the Nobility on the one side and the other three orders on the other.[33]

The Estates, however, stopped short of the brink. On 4 March Gustav III signed a revised coronation oath binding him to appoint and promote in state service without consideration of "favor, official character, estate, or standing," on the basis "only"—rather than "preeminently," as in the past—of skill and merit. In return, the nonnoble Estates offered a rather meaningless joint statement that the privileges of no Estate should be prejudiced by the new oath.[34]

Why had the nonnoble Estates not pressed their advantage to the full? Traditional respect for the law had doubtless restrained many *riksdagsmän* from extreme measures. The debates over a charter of nonnoble privileges meanwhile reveal a significant cleavage between the liberal individualism of a few advanced thinkers, such as Chydenius, and the traditional corporatist mentality of the majority. For most, the way to social equality was naturally to increase and guarantee the rights of the three nonnoble Estates, rather than to destroy special privileges as such. They envisioned a kind of balance between separate but equal states within the state. Cooperation between Burghers and Peasants tended in practice to break down over specific economic privileges involving the protectionism of the towns versus free trade in the countryside. Thus in the end no charter emerged from the *Riksdag*.[35] The time and circumstances were still far from ripe for a Declaration of the Rights of Man and the Citizen.

At the same time there were signs that the bitter clash of class and faction had gone beyond the political nation as a whole, leading to a growing weariness with politics.[36] Disheartened, many Hat nobles now left the *Riksdag*, as much of the Danish nobility had withdrawn from Struensee's Copenhagen the year before, weakening the remaining defense against the Cap onslaught. But many others throughout the kingdom were likewise disillusioned. During the poor crop years 1771–72, *Riksdag* politics seemed increasingly remote from immediate concerns. Since 1760 politicization had proceeded too rapidly. There were still relatively few who were prepared to agree wholeheartedly with Jacob Wallenberg when he proclaimed in 1770 that

> Once Rome had ceased to wrangle,
> She saw her power declining;
> And England rules the world,
> 'Mid parliamentary strife.
> From party, freedom draws its life.

To most, the concept of party was still disturbing and the idea of a loyal opposition a contradiction in terms, as amply confirmed by the rising factiousness and declining efficiency of the current *Riksdag*.[37] Finally, too, many feared the further exploitation of a divided Sweden by foreign powers, especially the old enemy, Russia. Increasingly both the nobility and much of the rest of the nation looked to the young king for inspiration and leadership.

The later course of the *Riksdag*, after the king's oath and his coronation in May, was not calculated to restore social peace or public tranquillity. The council was now purged of its Hat members, and various Hat local officials were brought to trial for interfering in the elections of the preceding year. The *Riksdag* condemned the previous council's filling of the vice-presidency of the Åbo superior court in 1770 as "a measure insulting to nonnoble men and contrary to law."[38] The three Estates resolved in early August that nonnobles should be eligible on an equal basis with nobles to the highest offices of the realm, meaning above all to the council, while the Peasants, supported by the Clergy and Burghers, demanded representation on the powerful Secret Committee of the *Riksdag*. The same month the *Riksdag* considered an alliance with Russia, at the very time when that power was arranging with Prussia and Austria to partition Poland.

By this time Gustav III had determined to take matters into his own hands, prodded by France, which secretly threatened to suspend subsidies unless he took firm action. Since he had learned early in life to keep his intentions well disguised, it is not certain exactly when he decided upon a coup d'etat.[39] His letter of 11 February 1772 to his mother—already quoted above—may, however, give some indication:

> They did not want a well-regulated liberty in 1769; they shall have it in 1772—my dear mother may guess. . . . There have been certain members of the other [i.e. nonnoble] orders who have responded that if they cannot enjoy those rights and liberties which every man ought justly to claim in a free country, they would prefer to have one master, rather than a hundred tyrants.[40]

To his Parisian friend, the Comtesse de Boufflers, he wrote in June of the "onslaught of Democracy against the expiring Aristocracy, the latter preferring to submit to Democracy rather than be protected by the Monarchy, which opens its arms to it."[41] This was, however, no longer true. Already in May 1766 J. H. E. Bernstorff in Copenhagen had predicted that when the Swedish nobility became sufficiently hard pressed by the other Estates, it would prefer "sovereign power" to "democracy." Confronted with a rout in the *Riksdag*, the nobility turned increasingly to the king as their last resort. The Hat chieftain, Count Fredrik Axel von Fersen, sounded out the king over the possibility of a "revolution" to "draw Sweden out of her degradation."[42]

Gustav indeed felt much sympathy for the Hats, while despising the Caps, but he was not anxious to be beholden to the leaders of either party. He preferred to use new men, dependent upon himself. Such a one was the Finnish colonel Jacob Magnus Sprengtporten, a Hat nobleman who organized a royalist club in Stockholm during the *Riksdag*; his "main purpose," he later candidly declared, was "to defend the privileges of the nobility . . . and if possible give greater authority to the king." Sprengtporten prepared a plan for a military insurrection in Finland.[43] A similar uprising was planned for Skåne, to be led by Johan Christopher Toll, likewise a noble.

The time was right, but there was none to lose. Russia, the most implacable opponent to constitutional change in Sweden, was embroiled in war with Turkey and the first partition of Poland, a fate which Gustav alleged lay in store for Sweden itself.[44] Prussia, Britain, and Denmark seemed indisposed to act against Sweden without Russian support.

At the last moment plans for the royalist coup leaked out to the British minister in Stockholm, who reported them to his Russian colleague. But already on 12 August Toll raised the standard of revolt among the garrison at Kristianstad in Skåne, and two days later Sprengtporten raised the troops in Borgå (Porvoo), who were quickly joined by those in Helsingfors (Helsinki) and at Sveaborg fortress.

Sprengtporten's force was now to sail for Stockholm but was delayed by contrary winds. News of the Kristianstad uprising meanwhile reached Stockholm on 17 August. Realizing that the council would commandeer loyal troops to the capital, Gustav III saw that he could not wait for Sprengtporten and his Finns. Assured of funds by the French ambassador, Vergennes, he appealed to the officers of the Life Guards' Regiment for their support on 19 August. After some hesitation, they agreed. They seized and briefly detained the council while they took control of Stockholm. No blood was shed. Riding through the streets to reassure the inhabitants, Gustav III was received with jubilation. As word spread to the provinces, no effort was made to defend the old order.[45]

Two days later Gustav III summoned the *Riksdag* to the royal palace, where troops and loaded cannon were much in evidence. Addressing the assembled Estates, the king justified his revolution by asserting that "a small number of persons" had brought the kingdom to the verge of ruin. Liberty had "degenerated into an aristocratic yoke, odious to all Swedish citizens."[46]

Gustav's rhetorical condemnation of "aristocracy" deserves some comment. Count Fersen, whose relationship with the king would undergo various vicissitudes, later wrote of it in his memoirs:

> That word, aristocracy, although without any meaning with regard to the existing constitution of that time, which was democratic in principle and which had degenerated into the rule of the rabble and anarchy, was of great help; harsh and jarring in sound, the people acquired a strange conception of its meaning and cried out against "aristocrats" as against werewolves.[47]

The king of course applied the word as it had long been used in Swedish poltical polemics: in the sense of the engrossing of power by a small oligarchy, without reference to estate. During the 1760s Hats and Caps exchanged the epithet—although this did not prevent the Hats from sometimes accusing their opponents of "democracy"—just as during the 1720s and 1730s the so-called younger nobility had castigated the "older" nobility for "aristocracy." Yet Count Fersen's comments suggest that the term by now contained a certain ambiguity which the king exploited demagogically to ensure the support of the nonnoble orders.[48] The nobility as a whole meanwhile realized full well that Gustav's revolution was anything but "democratic" and that it had indeed rescued them in the eleventh hour. "Far from violating liberty [the king now continued], I wish only to abolish license and to replace that arbitrariness which heretofore has governed the realm with a wise and regulated form of government, such as the ancient laws of Sweden prescribe and was established under my glorious ancestors."[49]

His project for a new constitution was read to the *Riksdag*. It was immediately accepted by acclaim and signed by the four speakers for their respective Estates. Henceforth the king forbade further use of the old party names: the past should be forgotten and concord now prevail. On 9 September the *Riksdag* was dissolved with the assurance that the next one would be called six years hence. Thus, after fifty-three years, Sweden's "Era of Freedom" expired without a struggle.

The new constitution represented a compromise between new concepts of enlightened absolutism and old Swedish parliamentary traditions. Count Scheffer and Vergennes had strongly urged a royal absolutism whereas Sprengtporten had pointedly reminded the king of "the rights of the nation." Gustav was anxious for his constitution to be unanimously accepted by the Estates, thus gaining the widest popular backing. Moreover, Russia and its allies should not be too flagrantly provoked by the new regime.[50]

Gustav's constitution provided a certain balance of powers, revealing something of Montesquieu's influence. Executive power was vested in the king. Whereas the council was made responsible to him alone, he was obliged to consult it on administration of justice, proposed legislation, war, peace, and foreign alliances, and his own travels abroad. On certain points his will could be overruled by its unanimous vote. Legislative power was shared between the king and the Estates, and each was empowered to propose or reject legislation. The Estates meanwhile retained control over taxation, and the king was accountable to them for state expenditures. He was expressly forbidden to wage an offensive war without their consent. The *Riksdag* would, however, meet and dissolve at the king's pleasure. On the sensitive issue of appointment and promotion in state service, all "commissions of the crown" in both the "civil" and "military states," except for court positions, were to be awarded on the basis of "ability and experience . . . without regard to favor or birth when not accompanied by merit."[51] To his mother, Gustav wrote on 22 August:

> I had absolute power in my hands through the voluntary submission, separately, of each of the Estates, but I considered it nobler, grander, more conformable to all I had said previously, and certainly surer for my future government, myself to limit the royal authority, leaving to the nation the essential rights of liberty and keeping for myself only what is necessary to prevent license.[52]

The constitution was meanwhile complex and, on important points, vague. Gustav declared repeatedly that he intended to restore the "constitution of Gustav Adolf." To the French foreign minister he had written already in 1768 that "since Sweden has never had a fixed constitution, nothing is more indefinite than the promise of restoring the old laws." What he envisioned then and in August 1772 was the benevolent reign of a royal patriarch, whose broad powers were not too closely confined by petty limitations, over a trusting and harmonious hierarchical society. Although this ideal of kingship now had to be expressed in a written constitution, such as the nation had become accustomed to since 1720, it was, as Folke Almén has pointed out, essentially "heroic" and "preromantic," in contrast to "the striving of the Enlightenment to regulate society through definite legal requirements."[53] The ambiguities of the constitution were such that it could later be interpreted in the direction either of a more independent *Riksdag* or of a more powerful monarch. Not surprisingly, they gave rise to varying views even at the time the constitution was written. In a speech in October 1772, Count Scheffer argued that the new constitution provided for

> . . . a king, armed with power to govern, shelter, and defend, without power to disturb, oppress, attack, or offend . . . subjects bound to obey

in matters of general concern but free and secure in all that pertains to them personally . . . the leader and the led bound together through an inseparable interest in preserving the law and powerless unilaterally to decide its abrogation.[54]

Yet others were not convinced. In her chagrin, Catherine II predicted that Gustav would become "as despotic as the sultan, my neighbor." In London, Jean Louis de Lolme, discounting fears of a similar royalist coup in Britain, described the former Swedish government as "an aristocratical yoke" under the nobility, but considered Gustav III now "as absolute as any monarch in Europe." In Paris, Mably and Abbé Raynal were especially critical. Even his friend, the comtesse de Boufflers, forthrightly wrote to Gustav that she could not regard him as other than an "absolute king" and warned him that autocracy was "incontestably" a "mortal malady."[55]

Later historians, too, have remained divided over the nature and original intent of Gustav III's constitution of 1772.[56] But to contemporaries, only time and circumstances would reveal the directions in which it would ultimately evolve.

Gustav's coup raises fundamental questions about the regime it replaced: in particular, how far Sweden had advanced during its "Era of Freedom" toward a modern form of parliamentary rule and party politics, and how viable this government proved to be in coping with the problems of the realm. Critics, beginning with Gustav III himself, have traditionally stressed the regime's inadequacies in this latter respect, and it seems apparent, as Michael Roberts recently reiterated, that, never very efficient to begin with, the rule of the all-powerful *Riksdag* became unwieldly to the point of impotence amid the very class and partisan conflict that in its final tumultuous years carried it furthest in the direction of parliamentarism and a party system. At the same time, as others have maintained, from Fredrik Lagerroth in 1915 to Michael F. Metcalf in recent years, this development was by 1772 probably more advanced in structure and procedure than were similar developments anywhere else in the Western world, even including Great Britain, to which it offers the closest parallels.[57]

The immediate result of the Swedish "revolution" of August 1772 was a threatening international crisis. For Catherine II, Gustav's coup represented the greatest diplomatic setback she had thus far encountered, but Russia was still at war with Turkey, involved in Poland, and the following year shaken by Pugachev's uprising. Copenhagen, fearful over Norway, was if anything even more alarmed, and Count von der Osten urged an immediate attack on Sweden, even without Russian support. Despite their rivalry, however, both France and Britain were opposed to any disturbance to tranquillity in the North, and their separate diplomatic representations and naval preparations to maintain it evidently helped cool the crisis by the spring of 1773.[58]

Throughout the period 1760-72, there is a notable correspondence between developments in the two Nordic states. In the early 1760s practical pressures for reform coincided with the breakthrough of the radical and humanitarian later Enlightenment. In 1765-66 the victory of the Younger Caps in Sweden and the accession of Christian VII in Denmark held forth prospects for far-reaching changes, which were temporarily checked by 1769, when the old council reconsolidated its position in Denmark and the Hats returned to power in Sweden. Finally, the years 1770-72 witnessed a serious challenge to the old order from Struensee and the Caps at the *Riksdag* of 1771-72.

These developments fall into a larger Western context. The efforts of Struensee and others in Denmark took place against the background of numerous experiments in enlightened absolutism following the Seven Years' War, including the reconstruction of Prussia under Frederick II, who provided a model throughout Europe, and of Austria, where Joseph II joined his mother, Maria Theresia, as co-regent in 1765, the same year in which his brother Leopold commenced his reforming reign as grand duke of Tuscany. In 1767, when Christian VII appointed his new Agrarian Commission, Catherine II summoned her Legislative Commission—which in the end proved no more effective. Duke Charles Emanuel of Savoy was the first European ruler to abolish serfdom, in 1771, the year in which Louis XV at last suspended the aristocratic *parlements* in France.

Other developments during the same period recall the striving of the Younger Caps in Sweden for a more egalitarian society and representative government. John Wilkes began his stormy career as a political gadfly in 1763, leading by the end of the decade to the beginnings of the British parliamentary reform movement. In 1765, when the Younger Caps came to power—and the Norwegian *Striler* rebelled against Schimmelmann's new poll tax—the American colonists protested the Stamp Act on the principle of no taxation without representation. In 1768 the lower bourgeoisie staged a brief revolution against the ruling oligarchy in the republic of Geneva.

Against this background one cannot but be impressed by the force and radicalism of the first assault upon the old order in Scandinavia during this decade. Indeed, one would search in vain elsewhere in the Western world for persons active in affairs of state with social, economic, or political ideals more advanced in the context of their time than Nordencrantz, Chydenius, Kepplerus, Reverdil, Saint-Germain, or Gähler, or for programs of reform more ambitious and far-reaching than those evolved by the Younger Caps or by Struensee, as Scandinavian historians have on occasion pointed out, or at least implied, albeit rather cautiously.[59]

In both Nordic states there nonetheless proved by 1772 to be practical limits to radical reform. In Denmark these derived above all from the monarch's disability and the fundamental weakness of Struensee's personal position in the face of established vested interests. Both in Denmark and in Sweden, the old corporatist spirit proved strongly resistant to the inroads of newer, individualistic doctrines. This was particularly evident in Sweden, where efforts to level social distinctions focused mainly upon building up the privileges of the nonnoble orders, rather than upon destroying privilege as such, and where attempts to construct a common charter of nonnoble rights came to nought owing to conflicts between Estates over specific economic advantages.

In both Nordic states—as elsewhere—the main objects of solicitude were meanwhile those elements of society that owned or at least disposed of property: merchants, entrepreneurs, tradesmen, farm-holding peasants. The unpropertied classes—cotters, farm laborers, the urban poor, and paupers—remained under an authoritarian, if at best humane, paternalism.

Whereas in Finland local grievances found their natural outlet in the *Riksdag*, where Finnish representatives played a leading role in formulating the Younger Cap program, in Norway reforms or the prospect of reforms stimulated the rapid rise of separatist feeling, which threatened eventually to undermine the authority of the unitary Danish state itself.

In both Nordic realms the radical offensive of the early 1770s set agendas for future social and political reforms, yet by its very vehemence it postponed their realization for at least the decade and a half that followed.

# CHAPTER 4

# The Rallying of the Old Order 1772–76

The shocks of the preceding two years had placed the existing society and institutions of the Nordic lands under heavy strain. Through the coups of January and August 1772, however, the assault on the old order was routed, allowing a last respite before the more thoroughgoing and lasting transformations of the following decade.

In the Danish monarchy Struensee's overthrow on 17 January 1772 brought to power a miscellaneous group of persons united only by their detestation of the German physician. Because the autocrat himself, Christian VII, was by now altogether incapacitated by insanity—although any public acknowledgment of this fact was scrupulously avoided—and because his son was still a child of four, the legitimacy of the new regime necessarily depended upon the continued participation of his nearest relatives.

Thanks to the romantic legend surrounding the unfortunate Caroline Mathilde, posterity has not dealt kindly with the king's stepmother, the dowager queen Juliane Marie, or with his half-brother, the hereditary prince (*arveprins*) Frederik. At forty-three, the dowager queen was an intelligent and strong-willed woman, now faced with an unanticipated opportunity that whetted new ambitions. Once she held real power in her hands, she had no wish to relinquish it. She was realistic and tactful enough not to seek to exercise it directly and publicly, but what happened in the monarchy took place with her concurrence. She generally acted through her beloved son, Frederik, a young man of eighteen, whose lack of any real abilities was matched only by his inflated and touchy sense of self-importance. The dowager queen was meanwhile sensibly aware of her own lack of practical experience and was prepared to profit from the counsel of persons whose judgment she respected. Regarding international affairs, her own particular interest, she corresponded with her revered brother-in-law, Frederick II of Prussia. In internal matters she had implicit faith in her son's former preceptor, now his cabinet secretary, Ove Guldberg.[1]

Guldberg, the son of a small merchant in Horsens, had followed a scholarly career as a historian and as *professor eloquentiæ* at Sorø Academy before becoming a part of the dowager queen's household. He was a man of modest, even humble demeanor, unfailingly deferential to his royal patrons and respectful toward his social superiors. Yet his unprepossessing exterior concealed a powerful ambition to implement a firmly held social, economic, and political philosophy. He was above all dedicated to the royal house and to unrestricted royal absolutism; his son would later call him a "product of the spirit of 1660." Throughout the years that followed, down to 1784, there is no sign of any fundamental disagreement between Guldberg and his patrons. To initiates, it soon became evident that Denmark was governed by a triumvirate. Of the three, the hereditary prince, nominally the leading figure, was the least significant, whereas the ideas he represented emanated from his mother and, increasingly, from Guldberg.[2]

Those who had overthrown Struensee were determined that there should henceforth be no single, all-powerful minister, capable of dominating through cabinet rule. A royal decree of 13 February 1772 thus reestablished the council under the new title of *Gehejmestatsråd*. It was charged with preparing all royal ordinances for the king's signature, and all government *kollegier* were made subordinate to it. Ostensibly the council was granted wider powers than it had exercised before Struensee's time. Yet the question of what to do about Count J. H. E. Bernstorff, waiting expectantly on his estate in Mecklenburg, soon revealed that the new masters intended no total restoration of the old regime. Conveniently, Bernstorff died on 18 February. The new council included Hereditary Prince Fredrik and the former conspirators Count Rantzau and General Eickstedt, as well as Count A. S. von der Osten, who remained on as foreign minister. Its most outstanding member was at first Count Joachim Otto Schack-Rathlou.

The hapless Christian VII attended the council and signed whatever it placed before him. At first, Juliane Marie also sat in to keep an eye on him while her son represented the views of the court. The dowager queen became de facto guardian of the insane king and of his two children.

The decree of 13 February did not, meanwhile, renounce the use of cabinet orders, which continued to be issued, especially on matters of appointment, promotion, and honors. This type of patronage was particularly attractive to Juliane Marie, her son, and Guldberg, and the court exercised it with a lavish hand. This frequently caused consternation in the council and *kollegier*, which sought with indifferent success to keep control over personnel matters. Yet behind the court's apparent capriciousness lay Juliane Marie's and Guldberg's determination that the crown remain the source of all favor and advancement to build a solid foundation of obligation and support. In March 1773 Guldberg became cabinet secretary to the king as well as to the hereditary prince, now allowing him to compose all cabinet orders. By the summer of that year Osten complained that Guldberg was "the way to all grace and favor, and disposes over rain and sunshine."[3]

The position of the court was meanwhile enhanced by discord among the men who had overthrown Struensee and by a lack of any concerted resistance by the new council. Beringskiold and General Köller soon disappeared from public life. Saint-Germain, who had returned expectantly to Denmark, departed after a few months. Rantzau resigned from the council already in July 1772 and retired with a pension to France, where he is later recalled to have been a humane and enlightened manorial landlord. Early in 1773, H. C. Schimmelmann and Count Andreas Peter Bernstorff, the old count's nephew, were recalled to Copenhagen to take in hand the tangled state finances. In April that year the younger Bernstorff was appointed foreign minister to succeed Osten. Thus there now appeared in the council chamber the man who more than any other would dominate the course of Danish public life during the next quarter-century.

Shortly after 17 January 1772, J. H. E. Bernstorff had written to a friend that while many changes would surely be made, he hoped the new regime would not "throw the baby out with the bathwater" and reject all the recent innovations simply because they had been made by "hateful men." Those now in power felt little inclination, however, to see any good in Struensee's reforms. A commission was appointed to consider all his cabinet orders, most of which were now revoked.[4]

Whereas Struensee had concentrated upon reorganizing the administrative structure to weaken the internal autonomy of the *kollegier* and make them instruments of cabinet rule, the new regime restored the earlier organization almost entirely, seeing in collegial decision-making and accountability a proven bulwark against the rise of another overmighty minister. Copenhagen's traditional town government was restored. Numerous officials who had served under Struensee were dismissed or relegated to minor provincial posts. Several of Struensee's judicial reforms were retained, although some use of pretrial torture was again permitted and the police were once more charged with the surveillance of private morals. A number of humanitarian reforms dealing with the care of the sick and indigent were kept on.[5]

In the economic sphere the new regime returned wholeheartedly to the mercantilist system Struensee had sought to dismantle. The tariff barrier was restored between the kingdom and the duchies. In March 1774 the Danish grain monopoly was reestablished in southern Norway. Copenhagen again enjoyed favored status, and foreign entrepreneurs were offered special inducements as before. Government subsidies for manufactures and foreign trade soon reached even higher levels than in the elder Bernstorff's time. The economic life of the towns and particularly of the capital soon recovered from the disarray wrought by Struensee's headlong drive to liberalize it, and the return of good harvests by 1773 further eased the situation.

While the new regime focused much of its attention upon commerce and manufactures, its attitudes toward agriculture were similarly mercantilistic: it was above all concerned with increasing production to improve the foreign trade balance, provide for domestic needs, and strengthen the tax base. It thus favored the interests of the manorial proprietors who produced for the market, and large landlords, such as Schack-Rathlou, played a leading part in determining its agrarian policy. The sale of crown lands, undertaken on a large scale in the later 1760s, resumed in 1774 under provisions even more favorable to the formation of new manors and the expansion of existing ones, both of which now proceeded apace. Peasant freehold purchases dwindled, and in some areas peasants had to relinquish properties they were buying.

The proprietor's control over his peasant tenants was meanwhile strengthened. Whereas Struensee in February 1771 had limited labor obligations throughout Denmark on the basis of 144 days per year for a tenancy of average size, a new ordinance of 12 August 1773 decreed that the obligations were to be determined by "the custom and usage of each province or region," i.e., as much labor as each manor might require.[6] In September 1774 a new militia ordinance increased the quota of recruits to be provided under the *stavnsbånd*; at the same time manorial proprietors were allowed to extend a soldier's service by six years, following his twelve-year term, if he would not accept a lease on his home manor. The Danish peasantry had reached the nadir of its subjection and exploitation. In the government's view, each estate had its function; that of the peasantry was to perform the menial labor upon which the very existence of society depended. "The peasant's yoke could not be cast off," Guldberg wrote to Suhm in 1776, "without shaking the state to its foundation."[7]

At the same time, the government continued to promote that aspect of agrarian reform which promised to increase productivity without upsetting proprietorial prerogatives: the consolidation and enclosure of scattered landholdings, as will be seen in the following chapter.

The freedom of the press proclaimed by Struensee in September 1770 allowed for an outpouring of pamphleteering celebrating his fall in terms of the coarsest abuse while praising those who had brought it about and protesting loyalty to the royal house. But before long the government felt less inclined to indulge the press, as a softening of its tone toward the unhappy Queen Caroline Mathilde became discernible. Although the latter had no plans to avenge her degradation, there were others who sympathized with her and hoped for their own reasons to restore her to power; these included Count U. A. Holstein,

Struensee's former *overpresident* for Copenhagen, Count Ernst Schimmelmann, the finance minister's young and impressionable son, and an English adventurer, Nathanael Wraxall. Caroline Mathilde, in exile in Celle, allowed herself to be drawn into their speculations. Juliane Marie and the new men in Copenhagen meanwhile feared that when the crown prince came of age he might recall his mother. Such fears ended only when Caroline Mathilde died in May 1775, at the age of twenty-four.[8]

In time some sympathy was expressed for Struensee as well. A Jutland peasant described him to a visiting Copenhagener as "a brave man, who gave us the former ordinance establishing labor obligations, and, I can well believe, that is why they cut off his head in Copenhagen." As late as 1777, a man was banished from the capital for being "confused in his mind, full of political fancies, and enthusiastic for the Struensee party."[9]

A more serious challenge to the regime came, however, from ideas that called into question the principles of royal absolutism itself. Even before 17 January 1772, P. F. Suhm prepared a draft constitution, limiting royal power through a parliament of forty-eight members from the entire monarchy, whose approval would be required for all taxation and for major economic or internal administrative policies, and protecting officials against arbitrary dismissal. On the very day of the coup he gave his draft to Guldberg, but the latter, accustomed, Suhm complained, "to slavery," rejected it. Suhm thereupon published a celebrated open letter to the king (*Brev til Kongen*), proclaiming, "An awesome power is autocracy! The greater the power, the greater the responsibility." The same theme was reflected in other writings in the months that followed. In October 1772, a young visionary, Kristian Thura, was imprisoned for rejecting passive obedience; he had suggested that sovereign authority could in certain cases become "harmful" and had proposed that the *Lex Regia* be amended to provide for the possibility that the king might be "deprived of his reason."[10]

Criticism of specific government policies reached such a pitch in Norway by the fall of 1772 that the *stiftamtmand* in Christiania began to introduce a de facto censorship on his own authority. A year later, on 20 October 1773, the government in Copenhagen decreed limitations on press freedom throughout the monarchy. Hereafter it intervened constantly in press matters. Even though the new regulations were not extreme and indeed allowed for some criticism of corrupt or negligent officials, the threat of intervention effectively muzzled the press for the next decade.

The government was all the more gratified by publications upholding the absolutist principle. Of these, the most influential by far was Andreas Schytte's *Staternes indvortes Regering* (On the Internal Government of States), printed in 1773. Schytte drew heavily—albeit selectively—upon his revered master, Montesquieu. He classified governments as "republics," "monarchies," "aristocracies," and "despotisms." The latter two he considered oppressive corruptions of the former. Republics, though admirable in theory, made impossible demands upon the virtue of their citizens. Thus monarchy provided the surest practical guarantees for the basic rights and felicity of its subjects. While the monarch must in principle possess absolute power for the public good, he was distinguished from the "despot" by voluntarily accepting the civil laws of the land. "The most unlimited monarch," he wrote, "represents a double personage within the state, that of a prince and that of a citizen. As a prince he commands, as a citizen he obeys." Schytte's presentation culminates in praise of the Danish-Norwegian monarchy since the council had been restored and the *kollegier* had regained their rightful place. "To abolish *kollegier* in a monarchical state is the same as to make the regent blind and to turn the regime into a despotism." Here was a political philosophy in the tradition of Holberg and Sneedorff, admirably suited to the circumstances, which would long provide a theoretical foundation for the specifically Danish-Norwegian form of absolutism.[11]

The new regime reacted not only against Struensee's reforms but against the whole free-thinking and innovative spirit that underlay them. This reaction is apparent in its policies toward religion and education, both areas of special concern to Guldberg. Lutheran orthodoxy was strongly upheld, buttressed by the return to censorship and the regulation of private morality. Education was conceived in narrowly utilitarian terms. Such an attitude allowed little place for the instruction of the broader masses. As Guldberg later expressed it:

> Peasant children ought perhaps to learn their Christian principles and their duties, learn to read, and to acquaint themselves with the Bible, learn to write, and also, if need be, to reckon a little . . . More knowledge here makes the peasant's lot unbearable to him and produces only boredom and disgust with the hard and monotonous work in which his days must be spent and the state must and shall use his days. . . . For nothing in the world [should we adopt] any German projects, any ingenious Copenhagen improvements, but simply what produces the result that can be obtained, in accordance with the small resources the state and land possess.

The last sentence well summarizes Guldberg's mercantilistic philosophy in general. Regarding popular education, he put the matter more succinctly on another occasion: "The peasant must not be enlightened, otherwise he will rebel."[12]

The government did, however, initiate a new cultural policy in one important area: in its strong assertion of *danskhed*—Danish nationality and language. Although originally a Brunswick princess, Juliane Marie identified strongly with her adopted land and its culture. Breaking precedent, she had given her son, Hereditary Prince Frederik, a Danish, rather than a German, upbringing. Their confidant, Guldberg, a Dane of modest background, thoroughly shared the growing animosity of his compatriots toward the German cultural domination of the past, a reaction exacerbated throughout Denmark and Norway by Struensee's high-handed disregard for Danish sensibilities. In striking contrast to earlier practice, the restored council consisted entirely of Danes, except at first for Rantzau, a Holsteiner, and after 1773 Bernstorff, a German from outside the monarchy. It too contained its strong advocates of *danskhed*, most notably Count Schack-Rathlou.

In its appointments and promotions, the court and government showed a distinct preference for Danes and Norwegians. On 13 February it was decreed that henceforth all state business, except that pertaining to the German provinces, be transacted in Danish. Soon after, Danish was made the language of command in the army—it had never ceased to be in the navy—as an aspect of the progressive nationalization of the military forces. Recruits were now drawn increasingly from the native peasantry, and with the new militia ordinance of 1774, the enrollment of foreign mercenaries was ended in principle, although in practice it continued on a diminishing scale until after the turn of the century.[13]

The Danish national reaction had clearly antiaristocratic overtones. The court strove to build its base of support with the Danish middle classes. Inspired by Guldberg, it tended—particularly at first—to favor commoners in its appointments to government posts. It was lavish with the honorific titles and distinctions Struensee had abolished in 1770, without regard to estate, and prominent commoners were received at court.[14]

The government's policy of *danskhed* and the court's evident disregard for the distinctions of birth caused complications for the solution of the monarchy's greatest international problem, that of the southern frontier. Following the war scare of 1762, J. H. E. Bernstorff had worked tirelessly to induce Catherine II of Russia to exchange her minor son Paul's hereditary duchy of Holstein-Gottorp for the nonadjoining counties of Oldenburg and Delmenhorst in northwestern Germany. Formal negotiations were begun in 1766 and continued fitfully until the dismissal of the elder Bernstorff in 1770. They remained in obeyance throughout the Struensee period. Gustav III's coup of August 1772 in Sweden, however, impressed both St. Petersburg and Copenhagen with the need for a closer alliance, and the matter was taken up again in April 1773, following Count Andreas Peter Bernstorff's appointment as foreign minister.

Negotiations were quickly concluded, and the exchange treaty was signed already on 1 June 1773. A secret clause held that since the *casus fœderis* under the secret stipulations of the Danish-Russian alliance of 1769 had already occurred through Gustav III's coup d'etat, the allies were to strengthen themselves by land and sea, and, following Russia's ongoing war with Turkey, to seek a favorable opportunity for reimposing Sweden's former constitution.

Even though the exchange at last removed ducal Holstein as a bridgehead for possible attack by hostile monarchs of the house of Gottorp in Russia or even Sweden, it created new problems. The leading inhabitants of Holstein-Gottorp had long regarded the Danish monarchy as their archenemy. During her regency over the duchy, Catherine II—herself of Gottorp blood—had taken much pride and interest in its affairs. Yet St. Petersburg, unlike Copenhagen, was comfortably far away, and the duchy had been governed by its own administration under its own laws. Practical reforms in recent years had, moreover, scrupulously respected the established rights and privileges of the burghers of Kiel and other chartered towns, and above all of the powerful landed nobility.

The politically influential classes in Holstein-Gottorp were meanwhile all too aware of the anti-German and, to a degree, antiaristocratic stance of the new Copenhagen government. Since Struensee's fall, the affairs of the duchies once again came under the German Chancellery. The four members of this *kollegium* were all commoners. While all shared equal status, the leading figure was Christian Ludwig Stemann, who notwithstanding his Holstein background was intimately associated with Danish circles in the capital; as a close friend of Guldberg's, he was clearly the court's chosen instrument and thus the focus of suspicion and ill will in Holstein-Gottorp.

Formerly Copenhagen had intervened little in the internal affairs of Schleswig and the royal portion of Holstein. During his long years as *oversekretær* of the German Chancellery, the elder Bernstorff had carefully avoided offending local sensibilities in the hope of reconciling the inhabitants of the ducal portion to eventual annexation. With the duchies now reunited under the Danish crown, such restraints would appear to have been removed. During 1773 there emerged a so-called Swedish party, with reference to the traditional anti-Danish alliance of the seventeenth century, and the malcontents were quick to assert the interests of the duchies as a whole.

The situation appeared so ominous that the Holsteiner Casper von Saldern, Catherine II's right-hand man in Kiel and principal negotiator for the exchange treaty, intervened with the Danish council. He insisted that the German Chancellery be headed, as before 1770, by an *oversekretær* with full authority in his field, and that he be a high German noble personally associated with the duchies. The obvious candidate was Count A. P. Bernstorff, whose uncle's memory was revered in the duchies and who was the proprietor of Borstel manor in Holstein. Such demands ran counter to the principles of administrative uniformity, collegial responsibility, disregard for birth and privilege, and Danish cultural predominance cherished by the court. But the exchange treaty was too important to hazard and Saldern did not hesitate to threaten its suspension.

The Danish council thus felt compelled to back down. In November 1773 Bernstorff was appointed head of the German Chancellery while remaining foreign minister, once again combining the functions his uncle had held. The appointment was made palatable to the court by providing that he should not be titled *oversekretær* but simply *direktør*, which ostensibly assured some role in decision-making to the other members of the German Chancellery. It was meanwhile arranged that Bernstorff be received into the Schleswig-Holstein *Ritter-schaft*, to reinforce his personal ties with the nobility of the duchies.

No better man could have been found to fill this difficult position. Bernstorff satisfied himself with the substance, if not all the outward attributes, of power within the German Chancellery. He was respected by the German inhabitants of the duchies and strove with patience and tact to bridge the chasm of suspicion and ill will that separated Copenhagen from the former Holstein-Gottorp nobility.

Bernstorff understood both viewpoints and sought constantly to balance the conflicting claims of Danish absolutism and the traditional German liberties of the duchies. Whereas he fully accepted the *Lex Regia* of 1665 where the kingdom was concerned, he respected the historic rights of the duchies, as long as they did not affect the vital interests of the monarchy as a whole. While maintaining the distinctions between the kingdom and the duchies, he also worked to amalgamate Schleswig and the reunified Holstein into a single entity within the state.

Bernstorff was soon put to the test. Although the Danish crown, upon acquiring Holstein-Gottorp, had formally guaranteed the existing rights of the *Ritter-schaft*, the latter was not slow to assert itself and to seek to extend its privileges. In 1774 its convocation in Kiel considered petitioning the king to revive the old Schleswig-Holstein *Landtag*, or diet. The majority, however, considered this too overt a challenge to Copenhagen and preferred a less direct approach. A deputation was sent to the capital to demonstrate the loyalty of the *Ritterschaft* to the sovereign and, at the same time, to present a memorandum on its particular desires. Alluding pointedly to the old *Landtag*, "never abolished but only postponed during the time that has elapsed," it proposed the establishment of a "perpetual select committee" of the *Ritterschaft* that would present to the crown "valid [*unvorgreifliche*] ideas and proposals for the true benefit of the religious foundations and noble manors," and which the government should consult about any ordinances that might affect their domains.[15] If these demands appear both modest and imprecise, they were an entering wedge, behind which loomed the ideal of a corporate representative body sharing power with the monarch throughout the duchies.

The deputation submitted its memorandum to Bernstorff, who was quick to recognize that any allusion to provincial estates, however indirect, would unfailingly arouse both the court and his Danish colleagues on the council. He let the memorandum go no farther and impressed upon the *Ritterschaft* the recklessness of its action. Half a year later, its leading moderates prepared a new project for a standing committee with more modest pretentions, which at the same time would weaken the influence of the more intransigent Holstein-Gottorp cabal, led by Count Cai Rantzau. It made no mention of the old *Landtag* or of any role in legislation affecting the duchies and was thus innocuous enough for Bernstorff to present to the council.

At this point, however, the Militia Ordinance of September 1774 created fresh complications. In the duchies it increased the number of recruits a land-owner had to provide per unit of land (*Plovtal* or *Pflugzahl*) by one-sixth. Thus, whereas their population was over half as large as the kingdom's, they would supply one quarter of the troops; for Denmark the number of recruits per *Plovtal* was increased by fully two-thirds. Yet to Cai Rantzau and his friends, what was involved was a matter of principle: an attempt by the Copenhagen government to subvert the established privileges of the Schleswig-Holstein nobility. Their bitter attacks on the new ordinance aroused indignant opposition on the council to the new proposal for a standing committee of the *Ritterschaft*. Bernstorff had to warn the *Ritterschaft* to quiet down its opposition before its new *Fortwäh-rende Deputation* could at last receive royal approval in March 1775. Its functions were, in effect, limited to preparing matters for discussion by the *Ritterschaft* itself and to conveying to it the government's decrees. Yet its mere existence had symbolic significance in keeping alive ideals inimical to Danish absolutism, and the time would come when the *Ritterschaft* would seek to expand its role.[16]

In Norway, Struensee's fall was celebrated as jubilantly as in Denmark and the duchies, although this had its paradoxical aspects. Struensee had indeed shown no small interest in Norway. Yet tangible results had been disappointing when compared with the hopes aroused, and Norway was particularly hard-pressed economically in 1770-72. As noted, Norwegian sailors and guardsmen were conspicuous in the disturbances in Copenhagen preceding Struensee's overthrow.

The new regime meanwhile showed no sympathy for Norwegian particularist aspirations. Although compelled by circumstances to accept a special status for the duchies following their reunification in 1773, it was strongly centralist in its views. Struensee's special administrative sections for different regions were quickly abolished, and Copenhagen was restored to its dominating position in all aspects of the life of the kingdom, reducing provincial Denmark together with Norway to their previous subordinate status.

Norwegians had shared in the mounting reaction against German predomi-nance. In Copenhagen it was the Norwegian literary society, *Det norske Sels-kab*, established in late 1771, that took the lead in attacking German influences in Danish literature. Yet the new government's policy of *danskhed* implied a concept of cultural unity throughout the kingdom that allowed no place for the growing sense of a separate Norwegian identity, now greatly enhanced since the abolition of press censorship in 1770. During the Struensee period, while Nor-wegian pamphleteers like "Philonorvagus" had argued vigorously for the estab-lishment of specifically Norwegian institutions—above all a university and a bank—Guldberg, under the pseudonym "Philodanus," had polemicized against their particularist demands. His oft-quoted admonition to Suhm in 1776 summarizes his consistent attitude: "There are no Norwegians. We are all citizens of the Danish state. Don't write for the contemptible Christiania *raisonneurs!*"[17]

Norwegian *"raisonneurs"* continued to belabor the inequities of the existing system. Their writings reflect the curious ambivalance of a still only half-awakened sense of nationality. Their accusations of Norway's exploitation by Denmark and the willful denial of its legitimate interests could be bitter in the extreme, yet were characteristically combined with fervent protestations of loyalty to the crown and the brotherhood of the Norwegian and Danish peoples. In actuality, they expressed the particular grievances of a small but articulate upper bourgeoisie, especially in Christiania and its hinterland, against the overpowering administrative, commercial, and cultural dominance of Copenhagen. Their silence regarding the distinctly favored status within the kingdom of the great majority of their countrymen—the peasantry—as compared with their opposite numbers in Denmark, is indicative.[18]

The government might have paid little heed to these complaints, were it not for Gustav III. Since the last century the Swedes had repeatedly shown an interest in acquiring Norway from Denmark. That the idea was fairly widespread is suggested by verses in a popular travel account by Jacob Wallenberg, which appeared in 1770:

> Slavish in their ways of thought,
> Raised in shackles from their birth,
> Norway's folk toil 'neath the lash,
> Enjoying nought but the rights of oxen.
>
> . . .
>
> Brother Northmen, join us now
> In the Swedish kingdom.
> Your kings shall in your place
> Receive our Pomeranians.[19]

Gustav III had long been interested in Norway and in August 1772, shortly before his coup d'etat, he wrote lengthy "reflections" on its possible acquisition. Whereas in Sweden, he maintained, an excess of freedom had degenerated to a "license" that threatened with the fate of Poland, in Denmark "despotism in the hands of a child" had fallen prey to "magnates" and "favorites," and after Struensee's fall it was "the aristocrats who rule[d]." This had aroused the Norwegians, who "have had to feed greedy masters without sharing their booty." Gustav thus hoped for an insurrection in Norway, which he could then hasten to support, winning him esteem both at home and abroad.[20] Implicit in his speculations was the old aim—analogous to Denmark's long-standing designs on Holstein-Gottorp—of breaking the Danish-Russian encirclement by securing Sweden's long western frontier.

Copenhagen immediately perceived Gustav III's coup of 19 August as a threat to Norway. Foreign Minister von der Osten was so aroused that he urged a prompt attack on Sweden, even without Russian support.[21]

Gustav III was meanwhile investigating the possibilities. He conferred privately with Carsten Anker, a prominent Christiania merchant in Stockholm on business, until the Danish government became alarmed and called him home. Swedish agents circulated in Norway to gauge opinion. In November Gustav visited Sweden's southwestern border region, where he received a group of Norwegian peasants. Rumors were afoot in Stockholm of some impending design against Norway.[22]

The Danish government strengthened its defenses, wisely relying upon Norway's own military forces and thereby expressing a greater confidence than all of its leading figures privately shared. In September 1772 the Norwegian viceregency was reestablished, and Prince Carl of Hesse, the king's brother-in-law, was appointed *statholder*, although not without some misgivings on the council. Osten feared he might seek to make himself king in Norway—as another prince of the royal house, Christian Frederik, would do nearly half a century later, in 1814. Prince Carl arrived in Christiania in November and was received with jubilant manifestations of loyalty.

The crisis soon passed. Wiser counsels than Osten's prevailed in Copenhagen, while Gustav III's sanguine hopes were cooled by unmistakable signs of Norwegian loyalty to the Oldenburg house. The Danish court and council made a few small gestures of solicitude for Norwegian concerns: Hereditary Prince Frederik, for instance, donated 500 *rigsdaler* to the Royal Norwegian Scientific Society. In November 1772 the government rescinded for all of Norway the hated poll tax of 1762, which meanwhile remained in effect in Denmark. In actuality, the tax had been largely uncollected in Norway since it had set off the *Stril* War of 1765. But to the Norwegian peasantry it could appear as confirmation of their traditional exemption from special levies, hence of their favored status within the monarchy. Although times remained hard through the winter, harvests and fishing improved in 1773, allaying the unrest in the countryside of the past three years.

The government had handled the situation adroitly. Its display of confidence in Norwegian loyalty had paid off handsomely, and with the peasant masses placated, there was no need for substantial concessions to middle-class demands. As seen, de facto censorship began to silence its critics in Christiania already by the fall of 1772. A year later the curtain fell on the free debate of public affairs throughout the monarchy. Prince Carl returned to Denmark in the fall of 1773. Even the reimposition of the Danish grain monopoly in southern Norway in March 1774 failed to arouse any public reaction. But the ideas that had been ventilated during the preceding years did not disappear. Nor did the government's apprehensions about Norway.

In Sweden-Finland Gustav III's coup d'etat of 19 August 1772 likewise marked the rallying of the old order. His writings show the young king to have been much concerned with the concept of a traditional balance in state and society, clearly under the influence of Montesquieu. This idea had come to the fore already during the abdication crisis of late 1768, when Crown Prince Gustav had prepared two draft constitutions. In one he wrote:

> Despotism is each and every government in which the executive and legislative powers are united, either in one person, or in certain families, or in an assembly of all the citizens. Sweden has fallen into such a state of disorder. Its government, from having been monarchical, has become aristocratic, and from aristocratic, democratic. The confusions of fifty years have proven this.[23]

In his public statements following the coup of 1772, Gustav constantly reiterated that the just polity of the Vasa kings, especially Gustav I Vasa and Gustav II Adolf, had been destroyed, and with it Sweden's power and prosperity, first by the "sovereignty" or royal despotism established by Karl XI in 1680, then by an egotistical and ineffectual "aristocracy" following Karl XII's death in 1718. Stressing his own rather remote descent from the house of Vasa, Gustav presented himself as the champion of its traditional balance between king, council, and estates, and the restorer of the nation's greatness.[24]

In Gustav's mind the balance of political forces must rest firmly upon a hierarchical social order. He thus regarded the close alliance between the king and his nobility as essential to Sweden's social and political stability. This ideal was perhaps best expressed in a letter to Madame de Boufflers written at the time of the 1778 *Riksdag*:

> It is so difficult to judge properly each country's internal arrangements: climate, fundamental principles differ so greatly from one nation to the next that what suits the one is harmful to the other. There are certain parties which seek to gain too great an ascendancy over the others and which must be repressed; it is the true science of sovereigns to balance them, and to hold this balance in just equilibrium. If this equilibrium is ever lost, harmful consequences follow: with us it is democracy which seeks to gain the upper hand and all my efforts are aimed at reestablishing the old high nobility. With you [in France] perhaps the people are too oppressed and count for too little, the nobility too favored.[25]

Gustav's astute manipulation of the ambiguous term "aristocracy" during the change of regime in 1772 proved effective propaganda, obscuring for the time being his strong attachment, both in principle and in sentiment, to the nobility. As Tom Söderberg has put it, his revolution saved the social order at the expense of the political.[26]

While defending the aristocratic principle, Gustav largely disarmed opposition by co-opting many of its potential leaders into the nobility, in a manner that recalls the stabilization of Swedish society a half century earlier, following the Great Northern War. In his new constitution the king reaffirmed his right to ennoble those who distinguished themselves through loyalty, virtue, valor, or learning, although he was prepared to limit himself to 150, who could not be denied introduction into the Noble Estate. In September 1772 he created forty new nobles, largely for loyalty in his revolution; in December he granted patents of nobility to all whom Adolf Fredrik had resolved to ennoble, but to whom the Noble Estate had refused introduction since 1762. Thereafter ennoblements dropped off to an average of three per year until the end of his reign. In all, Gustav III created about a hundred new nobles.[27] Other prominent commoners were awarded a variety of distinctions, including Gustav's Order of Vasa, established after his coup to recognize accomplishment in agriculture, mining, manufactures, commerce, and the arts.

Gustav's sympathies meanwhile lay with the old high nobilty. He created an elaborate court ceremonial, inspired by the Versailles of Louis XIV, which reserved for them a prominent role, although this ill accorded with Sweden's slender resources or its political traditions. The wording of the new constitution enabled him to favor nobles over commoners in appointments and promotions in state service. During the 1770s the number of nonnoble students in the universities preparing for civil appointments declined whereas those studying for clerical careers increased.[28]

Gustav III's revolution of 1772 was greeted with relief and jubilation by most of his subjects. Yet his efforts to arouse the hopes of all classes while actually favoring the nobility could not but be risky. This first became evident among the hard-pressed peasant tenantry of the former Danish provinces in southern Sweden. Here, as elsewhere in Scandinavia and throughout much of Europe, the lean years from 1770 to 1772 made manorial obligations particularly burdensome. Their hopes aroused, it was believed, by Gustav's polemical attacks on "aristocracy," tenants in southern Halland petitioned the king in the spring of 1773 to limit the unregulated labor services they owed their landlords, and defied the latters' unreasonable demands. Similar movements developed in neighboring Skåne and in southeastern Finland, close to the Russian border. Except for a clash between rebellious peasants and government troops near Värälä in Finland, there was little lawlessness or violence. The dispute dragged on in the courts until 1779.

In the tense international situation following his coup, Gustav III feared that peasant discontent in border regions might invite Danish or Russian collusion and suspected that disgruntled former Cap leaders were secretly behind it. Worse still, it threatened the social harmony he was striving to restore. A lengthy statement to the council in February 1774 reveals his uncomfortable dilemma. No one, he held, possessed the right to establish a serfdom resembling slavery in conflict with Sweden's fundamental laws. He recognized the justice of the peasant tenants' complaints. Yet to make any public pronouncement against the proprietors would be politically dangerous, since it would offend the nobility and encourage the peasants to become "more obstinate." "If they themselves do not fear," he stated "they will seek to make themselves feared." A direct pronouncement against them could, however, shake their traditional loyalty to the crown. Gustav thus limited himself to urging proprietors privately to treat their tenants fairly and left the settlement of disputes to the courts, which consistently rejected the peasants' appeals, imposed fines, imprisonment, and the lash, and upheld forcible evictions. It was in line with Gustav's social policy that he suspended further sales of crown lands to the peasantry in 1773. As in Norway and Denmark, however, peasant unrest gradually subsided with the return of good harvests after 1773.[29]

No sooner had the king dismissed the *Riksdag* in August 1772 than he embarked upon an impressive program of reforms, in keeping with his sanguine and ambitious spirit.[30] Not unlike Charles I of England after 1629, he set out to validate his new regime through justice, administrative efficiency, and prosperity, thereby healing the political and social conflicts that rent the country. He was meanwhile eager to win goodwill and esteem abroad, not least among the opinion makers of the "philosophic party."

The peasant unrest beginning in 1773 revealed much administrative inefficiency and corruption. While Gustav avoided offending the proprietorial class, he instigated in 1773 a wide-ranging inquest on the provincial bureaucracy, leading to numerous transferals, censures, and dismissals. The king himself severely reprimanded the Göta Court of Appeals in Jönköping; five of its members were dismissed, others were suspended or fined. The following year the bureaucratic structure was reviewed; a number of positions and pensions were found superfluous and eliminated. Special commissions were appointed to study specific problems and recommend administrative action. Plans were meanwhile prepared to improve conditions of employment in state service, and these plans would be put into effect in 1778.

The new constitution enabled Gustav to abolish judicial torture already in 1772, and he thereafter made the penalties for many offenses more humane; he not only wished to conserve usable labor but was ahead of his time in his concern for the social rehabilitation of the wrongdoer.[31]

The king's visit to Finland in 1775 led to several useful administrative improvements. Four new towns were laid out, beginning with Tammerfors (Tampere) that year. The administrative provinces (*län*) were increased from four to six in 1776, when northern Finland also received its own court of appeal in Vasa (Vaasa).

While Gustav himself lacked any deep understanding of economic matters, he was impressed by the French physiocrats—largely because of their views on strong royal authority—describing himself to the elder Mirabeau as their "disciple'' in 1772.[32] His two principal economic advisers, his former governor, Count Carl Fredrik Scheffer, and his de facto finance minister from 1773, Johan Liljencrantz, were highly receptive to physiocratic ideas. The new regime in Sweden thus pursued a policy of relative economic liberalism, largely set forth in a comprehensive plan presented by Liljencrantz in January 1774, which stands in marked contrast to the revived mercantilism of the Danish regime after January 1772. During the first year following the coup, the Swedish government meanwhile strove to relieve the shortages caused by recent crop failures.

Gustav and his advisers were keenly interested in agriculture, which, the king stated in 1772, ''this enlightened age'' must recognize as the ''primary and essential basis for all prosperity.''[33] They promoted the ongoing process of partial land consolidation (*storskifte*), which had been initiated in 1757 but still affected less than a third of the kingdom. This was particularly true in Finland. An ordinance in 1775 divided extensive forest lands, which the Finnish peasantry had heretofore regarded as unrestricted commons, between the villages – on the basis of set allotments per farmstead (*hemman*) – and the crown. This aroused some discontent in areas where the inhabitants were accustomed to making extensive but wasteful use of large tracts of forest. But although peasant forest holdings were later increased in places, the new arrangement promoted more intensive, efficient, and economical forms of farming and forest use, while the crown opened up its enlarged domain to new settlement and development. Gustav III's agrarian reforms in Finland are thus rightly considered a landmark in its economic development.[34] At the same time, the suspension of the sale of crown land to the Swedish and Finnish peasantry in 1773 may be seen as a means to encourage more productive forms of agriculture on manors and the royal domain. Later, in 1779, tenants on well-tended crown tenancies were granted twenty-five- to fifty-year leases.

Productivity was likewise encouraged by the peasants' right, since 1766, to transport their own products by sea within the kingdom, which Gustav III confirmed. In 1775 he freed the grain trade from old restrictions in the more fertile provinces, inspired largely by Turgot in France, a reform extended to the rest of the kingdom in 1780. In numerous locations the government established depots for storing grain reserves against future crop failures, a measure corresponding to its efforts to improve public health through provincial physicians, trained midwives, and better infirmaries.

Marstrand, on Sweden's west coast, was made a free port in 1775, and the following year staple rights were granted to a number of towns around the Gulf of Bothnia which had not received them in 1766. Although tariffs still protected native manufacturers, a new schedule in 1776 removed various import restrictions and lowered several import duties. In 1773 artisan guilds were prohibited from imposing unreasonable demands to prevent journeymen from establishing themselves as masters, and thereafter a number of new municipal charters allowed for "free masters," unattached to guilds. For the benefit of the treasury, distillation of spirits was made a crown monopoly in 1775, partly farmed out to concessionaires at substantial fees.

These reforms were not uniformly popular. Town merchants were alarmed over peasant navigation, free trade in grain, and the grant of new staple rights, which bypassed old, established monopolies. Craft masters protested that not all apprentices "should necessarily become masters" but that it should be the lot of some to "live and die as journeymen."[35] Not only merchants but peasant farmers resented the ban on private distilling, and the clergy was concerned that the government-licensed distilleries encouraged drunkenness.

The greatest economic problem was that of Sweden's currency, badly inflated through the constant issue of unbacked paper money during Sweden's wars after 1738, and correspondingly devalued on the international money market. All of Gustav's early economic reforms were aimed largely at improving productivity and the kingdom's foreign trade balance, as well as increasing state revenues. In addition, a number of superfluous religious holidays were abolished, a state lottery was set up, as well as discount banks for private borrowers and an office for the management of the national debt. Most important, Johan Liljencrantz devised a plan for stabilizing the national currency. International economic conditions compelled Gustav III and Liljencrantz to bide their time until 1776, and the conversion was carried out the following year, as will be seen.

Just as Gustav III's conservative social ideal found support in Montesquieu, so too do his practical and humanitarian reforms bear the unmistakable imprint of the Enlightenment. No contemporary European monarch was better read in the works of the *philosophes* than he; nor was any initially more enthusiastic. His record as an enlightened reformer bears favorable comparison with any of his time.

Unlike the autocrats of central and eastern Europe, however, Gustav III had to labor under certain limitations. Although his coup of 1772 greatly strengthened his hand, his power was not absolute, either in theory or in practice. He remained dependent upon the Estates for the grant of any extraordinary revenues, yet to consolidate his new regime he was anxious to put off the convening of another *Riksdag*. Given Sweden's old constitutional traditions, he could not proceed without regard for public opinion. Deeply as he might be influenced by the thought of the Enlightenment, Gustav also saw his reforms as essential to the very survival and revival of the state, riven internally by recent, bitter contentions and encircled by watchful, hostile powers.[36] He naturally tempered philosophic idealism with practical raison d'etat.

Nowhere is Gustav III's mixture of motives more evident than with regard to freedom of the press. This was a central tenet of the *philosophes*, not least of the physiocrats, who found therein the essential bulwark against abuse of that strong public authority necessary for effective reform. The Swedish law of 1766 on press freedom was therefore widely admired in European philosophic circles. Gustav III himself loved the free exchange of ideas on the theoretical level in select company. Yet it was apparent to him that free public debate on national issues could keep alive in Sweden the conflicts of a bygone era and compromise the success of his reform program. As his new constitution abrogated all fundamental laws back to 1680, he was in a position to redefine freedom of the press to suit the circumstances.

The matter was widely discussed in the press itself following the trial of an editor for libel in late 1773. The historian, Anders Schönberg, for instance, urged revocation of the law of 1766, pointing to the abuse of press freedom both in Sweden since that time and in Britain by John Wilkes and his following. Per Johan Höppener retorted by accusing the old "aristocratic-bureaucratic league" of seeking to suppress press freedom to hide its own abuse of power. The council of state strongly favored the abolition of press freedom.[37]

The result was Gustav III's ordinance of April 1774, a masterpiece of studied ambiguity. In a lengthy preamble the king stated that the press law of 1766 had appeared during a "period of anarchy," when men's rights had been trampled underfoot by "violence and self-interest," whereas the present constitution was based on "liberty, security, and property"—a formula deriving from Le Mercier de la Rivière. "Under such a government, all should have the right to think, speak, and write on anything that is not contrary to the tranquillity of the realm." To avoid the ills of the past, it was essential that "freedom of the press, maintained and protected, be used to enlighten the public as to its own best interests and to reveal to the sovereign the opinion of the nation." Persuaded of these "verities," the king deemed it necessary to revise the law of 1766 in only a few particulars to conform to the constitution of 1772 and "the new type of administration."[38]

In truth, these revisions were not inconsequential, since they declared treasonable any statement that "touches upon or offends" the majesty of the king, realm, or constitution, and held authors and printers jointly accountable, as also in cases of libel and fraud. Publication of the proceedings of the council and the *Riksdag* was now prohibited, as was discussion in the press of relations with foreign powers. A basic physiocratic function was still served by permitting criticism of public officials and the publication of bureaucratic and judicial records as a check on their performance.[39]

In the context of its time, the ordinance was not illiberal. The concerned public, aware of the council's intransigent position and fearing a reversion to the old press controls from before 1766, expressed both relief and satisfaction. Yet the danger zone of treasonable statements was broadly enough defined to permit an increasingly rigorous application, as would indeed be the case, and holding printers jointly responsible subjected authors to their effective and generally cautious censorship. Most important, press freedom was now governed by administrative fiat. If the new ordinance nevertheless failed to muzzle public debate to the same extent as the Danish decree of 1773, this was surely due to Sweden's more pugnacious political traditions. It might be noted that between 1774 and 1776 Gustav also established a secret police on the French model, to keep himself informed.[40]

It is tempting to take Gustav III's handling of press freedom as the key to his character and reign. To Stig Boberg, it simply demonstrates the king's basic hypocrisy and cynicism.[41] Yet one may wonder if Gustav would really have been so naive as to send his preamble to Voltaire for approbation, claiming that Sweden still enjoyed a greater freedom of expression than any country in Europe including Great Britain, had he not believed that he had found a reasonable means to protect "true freedom" against degenerating into harmful "license." Perhaps his search at this time for a middle way between idealism and realism was best expressed four years later, in 1778, when he proclaimed:

> It is philosophy itself which I call to my aid; not that dangerous philosophy which teaches one to despise everything, to deliver up good sense to ridicule, which creates sects, and which, to dominate alone, overturns all that is respectable; I call upon that benevolent philosophy which clears away all harmful prejudices, all those petty considerations which are opposed to the execution of the most important projects, [which] delights in conceiving or encouraging every bold enterprise that tends to the general good.[42]

It was, after all, a king, rather than a philosopher, who spoke. On the whole, the *philosophes* themselves were well impressed.[43]

At the time of his revolution, Gustav III banned further reference to the former Hat or Cap parties, yet both contributed to the character of his new regime. Gustav had despised the Caps, not least for their unheroic stance in the international arena, and he perpetuated the Hat tradition of seeking to revive Sweden's past greatness through an aggressive foreign policy and a strong defense. This notwithstanding, Gustav was more Cap than Hat in his internal policies, as shown by his vigorous campaign against bureaucratic abuse, his economic liberalism, and his monetary reform.[44] Former Caps played important roles in his internal administration; others, such as Anders Chydenius in Finnish Österbotten, expressed their warm satisfaction with the new regime, which among other things gave much special attention to Finland's particular problems.[45] At the same time, however, neither Hat ideals of constitutional liberty nor Cap traditions of social leveling had disappeared, as would later become evident.

Like the new rulers in Copenhagen, Gustav III had despised Struensee as an insolent upstart.[46] Yet he and his advisers must surely have followed the latter's experiment in enlightened despotism with close attention, and evident similarities in Gustav's own reform program during the mid-1770s were surely more than coincidental.

In both the Scandinavian kingdoms the first years following the changes of regime in 1772 were a period of social and political consolidation, in which the old order was largely reconfirmed. Yet it became evident, especially in Sweden-Finland, that social conservatism did not preclude practical and humanitarian reforms.

The continued European peace made such a combination of conservatism and reform possible. Both kingdoms devoted themselves to the development of their economies, although along opposite lines: mercantilistic in Denmark-Norway, liberal in Sweden-Finland. Regarding the most basic sector, agriculture, there is meanwhile greater similarity in their attempts to maintain control over peasant tenants, while encouraging manorial demesne farming and land reallocations.

It was a time of blossoming national consciousness throughout the Nordic world. In Denmark the new regime frankly displayed its *danskhed*, whereas in Sweden Gustav III invoked past traditions of Sweden's grandeur. Yet these developments themselves aroused reactions. Danish cultural centralism left little place for a reviving sense of Norwegian identity and could not but clash with the proud *Deutschtum* of the newly reunified duchies. It would soon also be evident that Gustav III's Swedish chauvinism (*"storsvenskhet"*) produced similarly ambiguous reactions in Finland.

The new hopes and aspirations aroused by the Younger Caps in Sweden-Finland and by the Struensee regime in Denmark-Norway lay dormant until once again revived by the outbreak of a new war, on the field of battle and in the minds of men.

# CHAPTER 5

# The Clash of Arms and Ideas 1776–83

During April 1775 the long-smoldering dispute between Great Britain and its North American colonies led to open conflict. News of the American insurrection soon reached Scandinavia, where as elsewhere throughout Europe it caused a considerable stir. It was before long a leading topic of conversation in salons, coffeehouses, and taverns. The Swedish poet and balladeer Carl Michael Bellman described his friends of the Society *Pro Vino*, "as usual . . . sitting with long Holland pipes and wise perukes by their glittering pear glasses, constantly arguing about the good of the city, about the English colonies, Washington, the price of hay, the scarcity of money and similar subjects."[1]

In Sweden-Finland, where the press remained relatively free, the newspapers devoted much attention to events in America. In the Danish monarchy, where it was more tightly controlled, American affairs apparently received somewhat less prominence, although the *Altonaischer Mercurius* in Altona and the *Kiøbenhavnske Tidender* in Copenhagen printed edited translations of the American Declaration of Independence in the fall of 1776, prudently omitting mention of the "King of Great Britain" and his intended "absolute Tyranny over these States." In October 1776, Gustav III himself privately expressed an interest in the Americans, predicting that, like a new Rome, they might someday "place Europe under tribute."[2]

Reactions to the American insurrection were nonetheless mixed and remain difficult to assess. Gustav III's apparent interest quickly turned to a marked aversion. While some of the younger members of his circle in Copenhagen, such as Count Ernst Schimmelmann, felt at first a romantic fascination for the intrepid colonists, Count A. P. Bernstorff set forth his own view in a letter dated October 1776:

The public here is extremely enthusiastic for the rebels, not through knowledge of the circumstances but because the mania for independence has actually infected the popular imagination, and because this poison gradually spreads from the works of the philosophers down even to the village schools.[3]

The Swedish newspapers were by no means in agreement about the revolution. Some, such as Johan Pfeiffer's *Dagligt Allehanda*, were clearly hostile, drawing their material largely from English journals or the anti-American publicist August Ludwig Schlözer of Göttingen. Others, like the various journals published by Carl Christoffer Gjörwell, while not partial toward Britain, regarded the revolution as the usurpation of legitimate authority. *Stockholms-Posten*, the organ of Johan Henrik Kellgren, expressed in the philosophical language of the day approval of the American revolution as a warning to "tyrants," but in general terms and without application, expressed or implied, to conditions in Sweden. Finally, as will be noted, certain small journals, published toward the end of the war, enthusiastically backed the American cause, borrowing from the Abbé Raynal as liberally as *Dagligt Allehanda* made use of Schlözer.[4]

It is evident that much of the apparent enthusiasm in Scandinavia had little to do with the Americans. Of greater importance was surely the old resentment against British high-handedness in matters of trade and maritime rights, recently revived during the Seven Years' War, combined with prospects for lucrative trade with the belligerents, especially with Britain's enemies, who were largely dependent upon neutral shipping. An observer in Altona commented wryly that if Washington's and Franklin's actions had impaired commerce, there would have been nothing but scorn for American independence.[5]

As the Americans took their stand on the principle of "no taxation without representation," a curiously analogous conflict developed in the newly reunified duchies of Schleswig and Holstein, between the virtually closed corporation of the *Ritterschaft* and the more numerous nobles of more recent origin in the duchies—the so-called *non recepti* or *Nichtrezipierte*—who remained excluded from it. The dispute arose over the assessment of local levies upon all manors by the *Ritterschaft*, which certain *non recepti* now refused to pay on the grounds that they were not represented in that body. Already in 1774 the *Ritterschaft* felt compelled to appeal to Copenhagen, and a royal commission was set up to study the matter.

In defending the status quo, the *Ritterschaft* appealed to tradition and historic rights. Its adversaries, like the America Patriots, invoked the principle of natural right, while stressing the claims of personal merit over those of birth.[6]

The implications led, in this instance, not to political democracy but to enlightened despotism. All privileges, the *non recepti* emphasized, emanated from the monarch alone. In October 1777 *Landräte* von Hedemann and von Schilden appealed to the king:

> Your Majesty will know how to vindicate your sovereign rights over your subjects. . . . When such a corporation [as the *Ritterschaft*] arrogate to themselves great preferential advantages within the State, when they play the part of a co-regent, when they comprise a state within the State, when they command others, when in actions concerning reception they exercise the rights of majesty, levy contributions, and seek unlawfully to compel others, unconsulted and unheard, to contribute to and to submit themselves to their power, not only does common sense rebel but no prince can or will suffer such impertinence.[7]

Above all, not the king of Denmark, "the most sovereign monarch of Europe," they added pointedly.

It again fell to Bernstorff to dampen the conflict. He remained all too aware of the danger of turning the *Ritterschaft* into a center of opposition to the government. At the same time his own aristocratic sensibilities were offended by the clamorous attack of the *non recepti* upon the very principle of hereditary nobility. To strengthen the aristocratic element, he would have preferred if possible to fuse both *recepti* and *non recepti* into a single body.[8] The royal commission's recommendation, approved by the king in 1778, nonetheless approved the *Ritterschaft*'s own compromise proposal: *non recepti* proprietors of manors were to be represented in matters concerning the disputed levies, but were denied equal status with the *recepti*. The *Ritterschaft*'s solution also provided that non-noble manorial proprietors be included in this representation, doubtless to undercut the noble *non recepti*; such nonnoble proprietors, who were especially numerous in Schleswig, had thus far remained outside the fray. At Bernstorff's prompting, the *Ritterschaft* displayed its gratitude and loyalty to the crown by donating 10,000 *Taler* to establish a teachers' seminary in Kiel.

Pasch von Cossel sought to hold together the remnants of the *non recepti* movement, hoped to arouse European sympathies, and spoke of appealing to the court of appeals (*Reichskammergericht*) of the Holy Roman Empire in Wetzlar. They drew a sharp royal reprimand in January 1780, and their efforts came to naught. But tensions would remain within the divided aristocracy in the duchies until the disasters of the Napoleonic wars would draw them together.[9]

There seems to be no direct evidence of American influences at work among the *non recepti*, though Bernstorff may not have been unmindful of the duchies when he complained in October 1776 of the "mania for independence" that aroused sympathy for the American rebels. Nor is the possibility of inspiration from across the Atlantic to be excluded as the conflict wore on. More significant, however, was surely the widespread correspondence of political and social ideas throughout the Western world by the mid-1770s.

As Bernstorff was striving to reconcile competing factions in the duchies, he found both his position and his principles seriously challenged in the capital. On 15 January 1776, the government promulgated a Law on Indigenous Rights—the *Indfødsretslov*—henceforward barring any but subjects of the realm from entering the service of the state. This measure represented the culmination of the nationalist reaction following Struensee's fall and met with widespread acclaim. Like the English Act of Settlement of 1701, it ensured that the nation would develop on the basis of its own human resources. Edvard Holm has described it as mercantilism applied to state employment.[10]

At the same time, the new law was an adroit political maneuver by the court. It had been prepared in secrecy by Guldberg with the help of Count Schack-Rathlou and was promulgated as a cabinet order, without being considered by the council; this notwithstanding, it was proclaimed as an irrepealable "fundamental law"—in violation of the *Lex Regia*. The *Indfødsretslov* thus set an important precedent, in a highly popular cause, for a return to cabinet rule, by-passing the council, which in turn was weakened by driving a wedge between the strongly Danish Schack-Rathlou and Bernstorff, its two leading figures.

Predictably Bernstorff reacted strongly. In his view, Denmark remained a backward nation in need of all the talent it could muster, of which little was available within its own frontiers. It was painful, he wrote, to see Denmark adopt an unjust and narrow-minded policy, "which may cause it to fall back into that barbarism out of which it has been raised up by thirty years of careful government and fatherly concern"—an obvious reference to both his uncle's and his own efforts.[11]

Bernstorff held steadfastly to the central role of the council and hence of the noble order in government. He was a staunch upholder of Danish royal absolutism and expressed little sympathy for "aristocratic" government, of which he considered Sweden during the Era of Liberty a notorious example. Yet since neither Frederik V nor Christian VII ruled personally, he, like his uncle, considered it essential that the state council govern in their place, and that the council in turn be composed of noblemen. While all should enjoy the equal protection of the laws, it was the specific purpose of the noble order to serve the crown; thus, in Bernstorff's view, it was proper that noblemen should enjoy preference in state service, that they alone should have access to the king's council, and that the highest titles and distinctions be reserved for them. While he opposed the preferential treatment of undeserving nobles, he was also indignant during this period when the court bestowed upon commoners honors he considered appropriate only for noblemen.[12]

Thus Bernstorff, the cosmopolitan German *grand seigneur*, stood in direct conflict with the Danish bourgeois vizier, Guldberg. Bernstorff fought at every turn to uphold the council's authority but lacked the firm backing of his colleagues. Especially after the *Indfødsretslov* in January 1776, he found himself increasingly isolated as the only non-Dane on the council. His basically pro-British sympathies during the American War contrasted with Juliane Marie's and Guldberg's anglophobia, stemming back to Caroline Mathilde's days.

Bernstorff's home was the favored gathering place for a crowd of young aristocrats from the duchies and the empire—most of them relatives by blood or marriage—with strongly German sentiments, which often found an outlet in tactless contempt for both Danish culture and Danish absolutism. While Bernstorff himself maintained the strictest propriety, his young kinsmen from Holstein, Counts Christian and Friedrich Leopold Stolberg, inspired by the German national romanticism of the Göttingen *Hainbund* and the Americans' fight against royal despotism, caused him no small embarrassment. From the perspective of Christiansborg palace, Bernstorff's manor outside Copenhagen could appear increasingly to be a rival court. Yet for the time being, Bernstorff remained indispensable in his dual role as foreign minister and director of the German Chancellery.[13]

To return to the *Indfødsretslov*, it has been variously interpreted, as a clever piece of propaganda and a political maneuver to strengthen Guldberg and the court, and as a statesmanlike break with the monarchy's dependence upon foreign personnel, essential to the future development of its own potentialities. Both viewpoints contain their element of truth. The law was widely acclaimed throughout the realm, which events would prove was now indeed capable of providing its own leadership. Guldberg and the court meanwhile sought to exploit its propaganda value from a specifically Danish-national perspective. Nonetheless, while the frontier for recruitment might now be closed at the Elbe, as long as it remained open at the Eider the German element in the bureaucracy and military would remain prominent. The "foreign" Germans had been cosmopolitan in outlook and thus dedicated servants of the crown, as Christian Degn has observed, whereas the aristocrats from the duchies who largely replaced them after 1776 were often divided in their loyalties to Danish absolutism and to Schleswig-Holstein particularism. Although the *Indfødsretslov* was intended to strengthen the monarchy, in important respects it increased its internal tensions.[14]

In Sweden-Finland, Gustav III's reform program meanwhile continued. By 1776 economic conditions were sufficiently improved to implement Johan Liljencrantz's plan for currency reform, which went into effect on 1 January 1777. A new silver-based *riksdaler* was established, and the crown redeemed the existing paper currency in silver at half its nominal value. New convertible banknotes were also issued. The plan restored confidence in Sweden's currency at home and abroad, enabling the government to raise loans to cover the conversion. In 1778 the king established a "national dress" for the nobility and burgher class, to encourage native manufactures and reduce luxury imports. In 1778 a reformed salary schedule was adopted for the state service, and officials were permitted to retire on pension at the age of seventy.

The defense of the realm received a high priority. Mobilization against the threat of war in 1772-73 had revealed serious deficiencies. A third of the billets in the army remained unfilled, munitions and supplies were inadequate, naval vessels were run-down and obsolete, the officer corps was inexperienced, demoralized, and strongly politicized. In 1774 a commission was established to review the entire defense establishment, which from 1776 on carried out numerous improvements.

In September 1778 Gustav summoned a *riksdag* to convene within twelve days in Stockholm. In so doing, he fulfilled his promise to the Estates in 1772; moreover he needed their approval for certain details of his monetary conversion and bank policy, as well as for the renewal of existing revenues. The time was propitious. The economy was thriving. In 1777 Gustav had paid a conciliatory visit to Catherine II in St. Petersburg, and in the fall of 1778 he concluded a new subsidy convention with France. By allowing the shortest possible time for elections, Gustav sought to keep political agitation and foreign interference to a minimum.

The king placed high hopes in the popularity of his reform program. He opened the *Riksdag* with a glowing report on his accomplishments. On the whole it proceeded satisfactorily. The royal proposals on monetary matters were approved, and the tax subvention was renewed until the next *Riksdag*. The criminal code was made more humane in important respects.

In the Clerical Estate, Anders Chydenius proposed, with the king's support, freedom of religion for residents of foreign origin. His clerical brethren vehemently rejected his proposal, but a similar motion in the House of the Nobility was adopted by the three secular Estates. This formed the basis for Gustav III's ordinance of 24 January 1781, which allowed foreign denominations, even including Roman Catholics, to carry on their own organized religious life, as well as his ordinance of 1782, which permitted Jews to settle in Stockholm, Gothenburg, and Norrköping, subject to certain restrictions; these foreign religions were nonetheless forbidden to proselytize, and members of the state church remained subject to severe penalties if they sought to leave it.[15]

The Clergy proposed the establishment of fixed schools in each parish, to be linked to the extension of confirmation throughout the kingdom. Gustav III turned these matters over to State Councillor A. J. von Höpken, who reported in June 1779—after the end of the *Riksdag*—that he could see in the proposal nothing but a "hierarchical" scheme for clerical domination over the peasantry, that it would require great sacrifices without spreading "true enlightenment," that it was ill prepared and "harmful to the political regime." Gustav found these considerations "quite justified," upon which both proposals fell through. A comprehensive system of popular education in Sweden would have to wait for another half century, until 1842.[16]

Outside the *Riksdag*, Anders Chydenius resumed his fight for personal freedom in his *Tankar om husbönders och tjänstehjons naturliga rätt* (Thoughts on the Natural Rights of Masters and Servants), which appeared in Stockholm in late 1778. It attacked existing requirements that landless farm laborers take service for a year at a time at controlled wages as a flagrant violation of their rights under both natural and Swedish law.[17]

The *Riksdag*, meanwhile, did not pass without political remonstrance, as Gustav had hoped. The constitution of 1772 left unanswered significant questions of parliamentary procedure, and the king's determined efforts to solve them in ways strengthening his control over the Estates led to mounting opposition, particularly in the House of the Nobility, with its ancient traditions as the guardian of Swedish liberty. In summoning the *Riksdag*, the king decreed the reestablishment of the old division of the Noble Estate into three classes, each with one vote in internal deliberations, which had been abolished in 1720. The division, he wrote, would "bring to an end that democracy which prevailed within the House of the Nobility, and which caused the first Estate of the realm to resemble an undisciplined mob, ignorant of its rights and its interests."[18] This was hardly calculated to be popular with the majority of the nobility, lumped into the third class; it moreover gave the king the means of packing the first class by creating counts and barons, and the second class through the awarding of certain royal orders. The king's appointment of the speakers of the Estates and his efforts initially to limit their deliberations to royal proposals only and to have important matters handled by joint committees, often in secrecy, rather than by the *Riksdag* as a whole, likewise seemed manifest encroachments on the political role of the Estates, and gave rise to mounting dissention, only partly dispelled by the birth of Crown Prince Gustav Adolf, in November.

It was thus with much relief that Gustav III dissolved the *Riksdag* in January 1779. A bit of anonymous doggerel cynically summarized its results:

> The Nobles received classification,
> The Clerics indifference in religion,
> Burghers, in their trade, systematic confusion,
> The Peasants all the proposed contribution,
> And Harlequin dress, the entire nation.

The joyous honeymoon between the young king and his subjects was over. Count Ulrik Scheffer, himself a staunch royalist, commented privately that

> the Estates of the realm had found the form of government different in its application than they had believed it to be in its letter. The old spirit of

party has been aroused rather than slaked. The nation has learned to cabal against the crown, since the crown began to cabal against the nation.[19]

Criticism of his regime and of penal reform and religious tolerance at the *Riksdag* of 1778–79 was deeply disillusioning for Gustav III. No less distressing was the bitter conflict with his mother, which, long submerged, came to the surface in 1778, when Lovisa Ulrika accepted and even spread the rumor that the newborn crown prince was not Gustav's son and which lasted until her death in 1782.

Gustav lost much of his earlier enthusiasm for internal reform, which continued rather fitfully in the years that followed. A marked cooling of his attitude toward the *philosophes* and their ideas became discernible, and he was for a time drawn to the mysticisms of Swedenborgianism and Freemasonry.[20] Increasingly he sought distraction in the amusements of the court, particularly its theater, in which he was active as impressario, actor, and even playwright—to the dismay of many both inside and outside the court. It was at this time, too, that he revealed a growing fascination for *la grande politique* in the international arena.

The American revolt turned into a European conflict when France went to war with Great Britain in June 1778, followed by Spain in 1779 and the United Netherlands in 1780; during 1778–79 the inconclusive War of Bavarian Succession threatened moreover to merge continental with colonial conflict. While Bernstorff in Copenhagen strove above all to preserve Danish neutrality and uphold neutral shipping rights, Gustav III in Stockholm speculated about exploiting a general European conflagration to seize Norway from Denmark and the overseas struggle to acquire a colony in the New World, preferably a West Indian island.[21]

The American war provided a welcome opportunity for Swedish officers to acquire combat experience as volunteers abroad. Over 100 Swedes and Finns served in the French forces, 116 with the Dutch, and at least 30 in the Continental navy or on America privateers. After France entered the war, Swedish officers turned up in Paris in such numbers that the Swedish ambassador hardly knew what to do with them. Most, seeking army commissions, were turned away, although a few seem to have later found places in the Continental forces. Naval officers were in greater demand. Gustav III encouraged his officers to serve in the allied forces to enhance his good relations with France. Numerous Danish subjects seem also to have taken part, although less is known about them. Guldberg noted in September 1781 that in their most recent naval action the Dutch crews had included 155 Danes (most of whom were probably Norwegians), a reduction, he claimed, from the usual one-third of Holland's seamen.[22]

Guldberg once expressed the view that one could safely count on there being six to eight European wars in each century.[23] It was precisely at such times that neutral Scandinavian merchants and shippers saw their most brilliant prospects for profit, through which they could make up for the lean years of European peace. According to official statistics, Swedish exports to the "West Indies," i.e., the whole of the New World, increased in value from 6,107 to 153,005 *riksdaler* between 1777 and 1783, while during the same period the Swedish East India Company, profiting from the war in the eastern seas, recorded annual gains of up to 300 percent. The free port of Marstrand on Sweden's west coast was open to vessels of all nations and served as a center for the sale of prize ships and the transshipment of goods to other European and American destinations. From 1780 on, "West Indian" trade was encouraged through favorable tariff and bonding privileges. The overall value of Swedish-Finnish exports increased from 3.9 million *riksdaler* in 1774 to 5.8 million by 1782, producing a favorable balance of trade and a considerable accumulation of silver.[24]

Even before the war was over, the Swedish ambassador in Paris, Count Gustaf Philip Creutz, negotiated with Benjamin Franklin for a treaty of amity and commerce, signed in April 1783. Creutz hoped it might be remembered that Sweden was the first power to offer unsolicited its friendship to the new republic.[25]

The wartime trade of the Danish monarchy was even greater than Sweden-Finland's, owing to its larger merchant marine, its overseas colonies, and Copenhagen's preeminence as the emporium of the North. For Denmark alone, European imports—not counting goods reexported—increased in value from 1,461,000 *rigsdaler* in 1775 to 3,441,000 in 1782, while exports grew from 1,211,000 to 3,476,000 *rigsdaler*. Comparable figures are lacking for the other parts of the monarchy. Between 1777 and 1783, merchant shipping increased correspondingly, quadrupling in tonnage in Altona, tripling in Copenhagen, and doubling in Norway.[26]

This commerce consisted overwhelmingly in the transit of foreign goods, rather than in the sale of products from the monarchy itself. Much of the shipment of noncontraband cargoes within Europe, particularly to the anti-British allies, fell into Scandinavian, mainly Danish and Norwegian, hands. As during the Seven Years' War, the Mediterranean trade became once again a largely Danish enterprise, and the Danes largely replaced the Dutch in the Baltic.

The Danish West Indies provided a thriving entrepôt for goods of varying nationality, especially after the British attack on Dutch St. Eustatius in February 1781, when many American, European—and even some British—merchants and skippers shifted operations to St. Thomas. The Danish government officially forbade its subjects to ship arms to the Americans, but such traffic was too profitable for Copenhagen to seek actively to restrain it. American wares, carried to the Danish islands by American or sometimes by Danish ships, were reexported to Copenhagen and thence to other European destinations. American skippers were occasionally "naturalized" as Copenhagen merchants or their vessels sailed under the nominal command or ownership of Danish subjects, permitting them to fly the Danish flag. A large part of the sugar and rum exported from St. Thomas and St. Croix came from the French islands, to enjoy the protection of neutral shipping. To Guldberg, trade with the French colonies was "one of our richest goldmines."[27]

The heaviest investments went into the East Indian trade, which produced the most spectacular profits. Since the early 1770s, Danish merchants at Tranquebar on the Coromandel Coast and Fredriksnagore in Bengal had carried on a lucrative trade financed by British sources in India. Employees of the British East India Company accumulated fortunes, largely through abuses prohibited by the company. To avoid problems in transferring their gains back to their homeland, they made extensive loans at low interest to foreign, including Danish, traders, who used them to purchase Indian goods for export to Europe, and eventually repaid the creditors' accounts in London. This trade increased considerably during the American war as first the French, then the Dutch, were eliminated from the India trade. Danish vessels now began to carry cargoes from Isle de France and Batavia, where they had not previously traded. On occasion ships belonging to nationals of the belligerent powers sailed under the Danish flag. The Canton trade with China likewise thrived.[28]

The war years brought unprecedented prosperity to Copenhagen, especially to its great merchant houses. Outside the capital and, to an extent, the colonies, the benefits of the war were far more modest. Altona and Flensburg in the duchies did well, as did Bergen, and some of the smaller seaports in southern Norway (Sørlandet), especially Christiansand. In this part of Norway opportunities offered by shipping and shipbuilding led to a rapid spread of the market and money economy, at the expense of the old rural self-sufficiency, leading to heightened social tensions during the years that followed. Many peasants from the countryside became involved in activities traditionally monopolized by the towns; some built and operated their own vessels. Eastern Norway (Østlandet) fared less well, for its economy was based mainly upon timber export, which languished.[29]

One remote outpost of the Danish monarchy deserves more than passing notice: the port of Tórshavn in the Færø Islands. Here Niels Ryberg, an enterprising Copenhagen merchant of peasant origin, had established a trading depot in 1767, which soon supplanted the Isle of Man as a center of the smuggling trade into Great Britain. During the American war large quantities of colonial wares from both the East and the West Indies were brought to Ryberg's depot, in part in American vessels, where they were picked up by smugglers, mainly from Scotland and Ireland. All this activity provided new employments and developed new skills among the local population, bringing them for the first time into close contact with the outside world. It provided an essential impetus to the process of change in an isolated and almost timeless society.[30]

In their pursuit of wartime profits, the Nordic courts steered as close to the wind as they could and still remain neutral. Yet despite their attempts to observe the proper forms—or preserve appearances—conflicts of interest arose with the belligerent powers, particularly Great Britain. Individual merchants and skippers obviously violated the established rules of neutrality, even if usually under legalistic pretexts. More important, however, were varying interpretations of what constituted contraband, which neutral vessels might not carry to belligerent powers and which their enemies could rightfully confiscate on the high seas. Great Britain, as the dominant naval power, long held and sought to enforce a broad concept of contraband; after 1778 it faced a life-and-death struggle against a growing combination of European and American naval forces, which the British naturally sought to deprive of needful supplies. The anti-British allies maintained a narrow interpretation of contraband, limited essentially to arms and munitions, as did the neutral maritime nations, for which large profits were at stake.

Individually the Northern kingdoms were too weak to assert their interests, but by combining forces they might hope to compel respect. Such a solution had been tried with some success during earlier European wars, in 1666, in 1691, and, as noted, in 1756. On 25 August 1778, Count Bernstorff sent to St. Petersburg a proposal for a common defense of maritime rights, based upon an influential treatise, *De la saisie des bâtimens neutres* (1759), by the Danish jurist Martin Hübner; quite by coincidence, the Russian court dispatched a similar proposal to Copenhagen the same day. In their mutual mistrust of Sweden, Denmark and Russia at first considered only a bilateral arrangement. The following month, however, France strongly urged Scandinavian cooperation in defense of neutral rights in Stockholm and Copenhagen. In October and November, Gustav III invited Russia and Denmark to undertake joint measures.

Agreement was delayed for over a year, owing mainly to the vagaries of Russian policy, but also to mutual suspicion between the Scandinavian governments; indeed during 1779 Gustav III again began to speculate about the possibility of seizing Norway.[31] Meanwhile, numerous Scandinavian vessels were seized by the belligerent powers, condemned in admiralty courts, and sold with their cargoes as lawful prizes. During 1779 Sweden organized a naval escort for its merchantmen as far as the Mediterranean; soon after, Denmark began convoying its East Indiamen. By March 1780 Catherine II's policy took an anti-British turn, and she proposed a League of Armed Neutrality, obviously based on Bernstorff's draft of August 1778. Denmark joined in July and Sweden in September, to be followed in due course by Prussia, Austria, Portugal, and the Kingdom of the Two Sicilies.

Lord North is supposed to have asked in 1779, "Who then is to escort the Swedish war vessels?"[32] In practice, however, the Scandinavian convoys and the League of Armed Neutrality compelled greater respect from the belligerent powers and privateering declined. Scandinavian maritime trade reached its high point between 1780 and 1782.[33]

The league was, however, compromised from the start by conflicts of interest, which led to a political crisis in Copenhagen. Sweden-Finland was Europe's principal source of naval stores—ship's timber, masts and spars, sailcloth, pitch, tar, hemp, and cordage—which provided its greatest source of profit, especially in western Finland, but which the British held to be contraband. The Swedish government therefore pressed for the narrowest interpretation of contraband within the league and for solidarity among its members in upholding it. Denmark-Norway's wartime prosperity was much more dependent upon its far-flung transit trade in foreign commodities than upon its own products. The Danish colonies lay exposed to the British fleet. Count Bernstorff, though concerned with neutral rights and balance of power, was basically an anglophile and disapproved of Russia's and Sweden's anti-British bias. Thus, while negotiating Denmark's entry into the league, he secretly bargained with London, resulting in the Explanatory Article of 4 July 1780, by which Denmark undertook not to ship contraband, specifically including naval stores, although not Norwegian pine lumber. Five days later, on 9 July, the armed neutrality pact concluded with Russia accepting all prior commitments of the contracting parties to both Britain and France.

The Russian government was outraged when it learned of Denmark's private deal with Britain; the reaction in Stockholm may well be imagined. Guldberg and the Danish court, strongly anglophobe, were no less mortified and seized the opportunity to compel Bernstorff's resignation on 10 November 1780, the culmination of a long and intense rivalry, based on political principles but with social, cultural, ethnic, and personal overtones.

Although Bernstorff's resignation took place under honorable forms, it caused a sensation both at home and abroad. There was panic on the Copenhagen stock exchange and widespread dismay in the duchies. Even Catherine II was taken aback and protested Bernstorff's removal. Withdrawing to his estate in Mecklenburg, the ex-minister remained the focus of the hopes of those within the monarchy dissatisfied with the existing regime, in a way recalling the Duc de Choiseul at Chanteloup after 1770.

General histories often call the entire period from 1772 to 1784 in the Danish monarchy the "Guldberg era." However, this began, properly speaking, only after Bernstorff's dismissal in November 1780 removed the last real obstacle to a cabinet rule that would reduce the state council to an empty formality. The German Chancellery was now managed collegially by its members, and the new foreign minister, the Norwegian-born Marcus Gerhard Rosencrone, was a nonentity without a seat on the council.

In foreign policy, as in virtually everything else, Ove Guldberg now became the monarchy's all-powerful vizier. Slowly but surely he had increased his power behind the scenes. In 1776 he was appointed state and secret cabinet secretary (*stats- og gehejme-kabinettssekretær*). In 1777 he was ennobled under the name Høegh-Guldberg. At the end of 1780, after Bernstorff's dismissal, he was made a titular state councillor (*gehejmråd*), assured of an eventual seat on the council. Nothing now stood in his way.[34]

The regime meanwhile continued along its earlier lines of development: cabinet rule, based upon close agreement between Guldberg, the dowager queen Juliane Marie, and her son, Hereditary Prince Frederik; centralized direction of all areas of national life; a conservative stance in social, religious, educational, and cultural matters, combined with a policy of *danskhed*. Although Guldberg's ennoblement in 1777 was in keeping with Danish absolutism and its nobility of rank, the regime tended to lose some of the ''bourgeois'' quality that had characterized its early years, since 1772.[35] As before, Guldberg kept himself out of the limelight.

In no sphere was the *étatisme* of the Guldberg era more evident than in its ambitious mercantilism. In response to the opportunities of the American war, the government, led by Guldberg and H. C. Schimmelmann, embarked on far-reaching commercial ventures. Already in 1777 it took over the Danish East India Company's establishments in India and those of the Guinea Company in West Africa. In 1778 it chartered a West Indian Company, with the intention of making St. Thomas a competitor to Dutch St. Eustatius as an entrepôt for European trade with America. A Baltic and Guinea Company was decreed in 1781. Most grandiose in conception was the Trading and Canal Company of 1782, for worldwide commercial operations, as well as fishing and whaling in the North Sea and the Arctic. Its title likewise refers to the Schleswig-Holstein Canal between the Bay of Kiel and the Elbe estuary, begun in 1777 and opened in 1784, which reduced the water route between the Baltic and North Seas by 300 sea miles and which up to 1830 was the most heavily trafficked canal in Europe. While the main focus of the government's interest during the war years was upon trade and seafaring, it also encouraged and supported numerous other enterprises, not least of all shipbuilding.[36]

It is worth considering the *Indfødsretslov* of 1776 once again in the light of the monarchy's economy. Although it barred the future employment of foreigners in the state service, in the interests of the Danish *noblesse de la robe*, it did not interfere with the immigration of foreign entrepreneurs and artisans with capital and skills still essential to national economic development. Later research shows that there was little change in the numbers of foreigners receiving burgher rights in Danish towns before and after 1776. Albert Olsen has characterized the outlook of Guldberg and his associates as fundamentally more mercantilistic than nationalistic.[37] Looked at in another way, the indigenous potentialities of the monarchy had developed further in the administrative than in the economic sphere.

If, as seen, the period after 1772 saw the reversal of earlier efforts—since 1766—to secure greater personal freedom and property for the peasantry, it also saw the culmination of the trend toward land reallocation and consolidation in the interests of more rational and productive cultivation, through ordinances in May 1776 and April 1781. The latter in particular was of epochal importance for Danish agriculture, since it permitted the individual landowner to have his holdings consolidated, upon demand, into one, two, or at most three parcels. The similarities to contemporary British and Swedish practice are unmistakable. Henceforth enclosures and the movement of peasant farmers out of the old compact villages onto new consolidated farms proceeded at an ever increasing pace, transforming the very appearance of the countryside, and leading before long to increased production and greater peasant initiative.

Across the Atlantic, the Americans continued their struggle for independence. In 1779, the American Francis Dana wrote from St. Petersburg, "Britain has not a single friend among all the powers of Europe."[38] As seen, the Scandinavian lands—directly and indirectly—gave support to the Americans: Scandinavian volunteers fought in the allied forces against Britain, while neutral Scandinavia permitted an ongoing exchange of products between Europe and the rebellious colonies. Behind this situation lay calculations of power and profit, but certainly no sympathy for the American cause on the part of those who determined policy in the Northern courts.

Bernstorff set forth his views in a letter dated 27 December 1777. If North American independence had no other consequence than to prevent Britain from henceforth "usurping a tyrannical domination of the seas," he would consider it beneficial. But he feared not only that this would strengthen France—Sweden's ally—in the European balance, but also that an independent America would become a serious competitor in the markets for the Danish Monarchy's principal exports—timber, fish, and grain—and could in time usurp the Greenland fisheries and the Danish West Indian islands. "The rebellion," he wrote in June 1779, was "hardly excusable and the most pernicious example that could exist."[39] Under the circumstances, however, he strove to maintain Denmark's neutrality in the war, while drawing the greatest commercial benefits from it, in ways not directly inimical to British interests.

In April 1779, the French ambassador in Stockholm wrote to Paris, "In general, the cause of the Americans is not that of sovereigns; Gustav III has not, as of the present moment, shown himself favorable to them."[40] When in 1780 the king further tightened control of the press under his ordinance of 1774, one of the first victims was the Abbé Raynal's popular *Histoire des Deux Indes*. As the events of the war called for some commitment on his part, Gustav III turned steadily against the Americans. His letter of 19 August 1778 to Creutz in Paris foreshadows that fear of revolution which he was to show so strongly for the rest of his life: "I cannot admit that it is right to support rebels against their king. The example will find only too many imitators in an age when it is the fashion to overthrow every bulwark of authority." In December 1782 he wrote: "This is the cause of kings. I have always considered it so; either this is a prejudice belonging to my position, or it derives from the relationship in which at the beginning of my reign I stood with regard to my own subjects, the impression of which is hard to efface."[41]

The clear analogy Gustav perceived between the American Revolution and earlier developments in Sweden is again reflected in 1784, when he forbade two Swedish officers, Baron Curt von Stedingk and Count Axel von Fersen, the younger, to accept the new American Order of the Cincinnati. "I do not despise the nomination," the king wrote to Stedingk, "but too recently having ourselves escaped from our troubles that there should not exist, no doubt, some germs of our former divisions, it is my duty to avert anything which could reawaken such ideas." George Washington came close to the truth when he wrote to General Rochambeau in August that year, "Considering how recently the King of Sweden has changed the form of the constitution of that Country, it is not much to be wondered at that his fears should get the better of his liberality at anything which might have the semblance of republicanism.[42]

Swedish-American historians in particular, anxious to stress their country-men's contributions to American liberty, have gone to some pains to demon-strate a natural affinity and wide popular support for the American cause among their ancestors. Above all, they have emphasized the participation in the war of a striking number of Swedish and Finnish volunteers.[43] Here too, however, a more sober examination reveals little overt enthusiasm for American ideals as such. Only after France entered the war in 1778 is there clear evidence that any Swedish subjects took part in it. There was no Swedish Kosciusko or Lafayette, or indeed any Swedish counterpart to the Danish-born brigadier-general in the Continental Army, Hans Christian Fibiger, who had arrived from St. Croix and was familiarly known as "Old Denmark." The great majority of the Swedish officers were noblemen and officers in Swedish or French service when the war began. Most were dependent upon military employment, and, like other foreign officers who sought to serve, they were in straitened circumstances following a long period of peace in Europe. Stedingk wrote indignantly that the importu-nate demands of many of his countrymen for French commissions were "nothing more than disguised begging." The largest number of Swedish officers served in the Dutch navy, which offered the greatest opportunities for foreigners. Meanwhile some fifty Swedes held commissions in the British navy, into which over 370 Swedish seamen were either enlisted or impressed. Apparently none of the Swedish officers remained in America or ever returned there. In general, they distinguished themselves in later life through loyal service to their king. As for Swedes below officer rank, their part in the war may on the whole be attributed to the vagaries of life at sea.[44]

Few of the Swedish volunteers served ashore in the American colonies, and of those who did, only two, Curt von Stedingk and Axel von Fersen, left any very revealing impressions of the American Revolution. Claims have been made that both served out of enthusiasm for the American cause, but their preserved letters make it clear that such considerations were far from their minds. Both desired active military service, while Fersen, whose name was already linked romantically to that of Queen Marie Antoinette of France, considered it prudent to leave Paris. Stedingk wrote to a friend in Sweden, "the desire to go to America has become so great and fashionable since Lafayette received such a favorable reception from the whole [French] nation, that it can be compared with nothing less than what the Crusaders of old experienced when they made their way to the Holy Land." However, "As far as I am concerned, who sadly enough cannot be reckoned among their number, it is reason and calculation which have determined the matter."[45]

While enthusiastic at the prospect of French success, Stedingk and Fersen regarded their British adversaries with professional admiration and had little but contempt for the ragged American forces. They noted the existence of large and influential loyalist elements. Although at first well impressed with America, Fersen became disillusioned with the mercenary nature of the Americans, who sold as willingly to the enemy as to their French allies. Both he and Stedingk considered it likely for a time that Britain would partition America, keeping the more desirable southern provinces. Fersen, later noting that the Virginians possessed "all the aristocratic principles," expressed surprise that they should have been able to "enter into the general confederation and to accept a government based upon a perfect equality of condition." Indeed, he expected that "the same spirit which has brought them to free themselves from the English yoke" would lead the Virginians to detach themselves from the other states and that the American government might in time degenerate into "a perfect aristocracy," presumably on the same disjointed and licentious model as Poland or Sweden before Gustav III's coup of 1772.[46]

Harald Elovson has maintained that Stedingk's and Fersen's attitude toward the conflict may be taken as representative of the Swedish officers who took part. More recent studies have nonetheless shown that certain of the volunteers, enthusiastic over the ideals of the Enlightenment, were genuinely inspired by the revolution in America and were later involved in opposition to Gustav III. Among these were the three brothers of Hans Järta, one of the principal authors of the Swedish constitution of 1809; Adolf Ludvig Ribbing, who in 1792 took part in the assassination of Gustav III; and Göran Magnus Sprengtporten, leader of the movement for Finnish autonomy in the later 1780s, who held a temporary commission in the French army for a few months in 1780–81. These are names we shall encounter again.[47]

The American Revolution and War of Independence lasted for more than eight years, during which Swedish political opinion underwent a considerable transformation. In 1772 most Swedes of all classes had welcomed Gustav III's coup d'etat. At first the American Revolution aroused little political response among a people still basically satisfied with their regime and strongly attached to their king. The *Riksdag* of 1778–79, however, revealed signs of discontent, which in some circles found an outlet in an increasing idealization of the Americans and their struggle for liberty. Already in 1777 the poet Bengt Lidner wrote his dissertation at the University of Greifswald defending the legitimacy of the American Revolution. Around 1780 there appeared certain small journals expressing opposition to royal policy, such as Josias Carl Cederhjelm's *Sanning och Nöje* and the publications of Major Pehr af Lund, which enthusiastically espoused the American cause as a means to belabor the government in Sweden. Lund, for instance, wrote in his *Tryck-Friheten den Wälsignade* for 28 April 1783, that the knowledge that "there is one place on earth where man can be free from his chains" should "frighten the despots and hold them in rein."[48]

As opposition increased during the years following the war, important segments of Swedish opinion tended to idealize the American Revolution in retrospect. This is apparent in literature, especially in poetry. In his *Året 1783* (written in 1784), Bengt Lidner sang the praises of a "Brutian Washington" who "snatches a bloody scepter from the tyrant's hand," and several years later, Bishop Johan Olof Wallin lauded "the first American" in his *George Washington*. During the mid-1780s the young noble malcontents in Finland regarded their leader, Göran Magnus Sprengtporten, as "a second Washington, the savior of his oppressed fatherland, and the founder of its freedom and felicity."[49] In 1790 the editor of the radical journal, *Medborgaren*—"The Citizen"—Carl Fredrik Nordenskiöld, proclaimed, in looking back, that

> the independence of America for all time shall cause wise rulers to govern their subjects under the banner of freedom, for America has taught Nations to know their rights and the equal protection which a benevolent nature affords to all. All men are born free and equal; this was the first meaning of the actions of the American states. These words were made the fundament of their form of government. The virtuous Americans will soon teach all nationalities the meaning of the Majesty of Nations: the Majesty of Man! . . . Philosophers, Friends of Mankind, Citizens, what a magnificent prospect for you!

Gustav III was, in effect, saying the same thing, although in a very different spirit, when he denounced, early in 1791, the "epidemic of popular disturbances'' which had ''spread from the soil of America to France'' and which threatened all thrones.[50] Even when in later years, members of the old opposition against Gustav III became disillusioned with the excesses of the French Revolution, they tended to retain their admiration for America.[51]

Aside from Bernstorff's intriguing remark from October 1776 about popular enthusiasm for the ''rebels,'' based upon the ''mania for independence,'' contemporary testimony is notably sparse regarding the impact of the American Revolution upon opinion in the Danish monarchy. Censorship was more effective—or the press simply more cautious—than in Sweden-Finland, and preserved letters and diaries seldom discuss American affairs. Surely for this reason the topic remains neglected by scholarship.[52]

Later references, however, help to confirm that the revolution in America left a considerable impression in Denmark, Norway, and the duchies, as it did elsewhere in Europe. Lecturing on ''the most important revolutions of the past three centuries'' at Copenhagen University in the mid 1790s, the young historian Frederik Sneedorff said of the ''North American Revolution'':

> It was not only against vigorous armies that they [the British] had to fight, but there was a whole nation, inspired by that spirit of freedom and hatred for tyranny that made a soldier of every man; they were their own compatriots, who had with them from England laws, customs, and concepts of liberty. And finally France entered the fray and the spark which was struck in North America burst out into the flame that has swept over the whole world.[53]

''Franklin was ever my ideal,'' wrote a contributor to the Copenhagen journal *Minerva* in 1798; ''Franklin . . . who made something of himself through honesty, ambition, and work. His example is worth more than all of Plutarch's heroes.'' After describing the ''spirit of submissiveness, of the prevailing deference to mere rank and title'' in the Altona of his youth, the Holstein schoolmaster Georg Friedrich Schumacher recalled how Washington and Franklin,

> the idols of the day, expressed principles we had not been used to hearing, and even if no one in our land actually considered offending against the king's authority, we nonetheless became familiar in theory with the idea that in certain circumstances it could be just and honorable to defy the arbitrary will of a ruler.[54]

It was, finally, a Dane, Henrik Steffens, who has left one of the most revealing pictures that has been preserved of the impact of the American Revolution in Europe. The peaceful island of Sjælland seemed in his childhood remote from the great events of the time, such as ''the earthquake in Calabria'' or the war in America: ''That the flat land which we inhabited might quake, that the civil order in which we lived might be destroyed, was a fear unknown to us." Yet he described his father, a regimental surgeon who "admired Rousseau," in terms that would be familiar elsewhere in Europe:

Talented, spirited, dissatisfied with his situation, he felt himself, often not without reason, called upon to decry the oppression of the powerful, and did so not infrequently with the vehemence that belonged to his nature. His complaints thereupon often took a more general turn: it was then that I first heard of the caprice of the higher authorities and the pride of the nobility, of the arrogance of the rich and the reward of the undeserving, of the oppressed condition of the burgher and the burden of the great standing armies, all those expressions of discontent which later, often justifiably enough, would move the world and myself with it, and dark intimations of these [evils] mingled with fiery resolves for future action.

"I too," Steffens reminisced, "was well enough informed of the significance of the North American war to sympathize heart and soul with a nation which so courageously fought for its freedom . . . The attitude of my father spurred the enthusiasm of his sons, indeed first aroused it." Steffens's boyhood heroes were Washington and Franklin, especially the latter who rose to eminence "from a simple burgher background." He adds, "Surely there were few young men of spirit in that peaceful land who did not support the cause of the North Americans."

At length news of the Peace of Paris in April 1783 reached Helsingør on the Sound, where the family lived. It was a brilliant day; ships of all nations lay at anchor in the roadstead, decked out with flags and pennants; the crews cheered; the war vessels—"even every merchantman that carried a couple of cannon"— fired salutes. The elder Steffens assembled his friends around a punchbowl, and "the victory of the Americans, the cause of the freedom of nations, was enthusiastically discussed." Eager to nurture in his sons a "sense of civic liberty," he summoned them and "sought to make clear to us the meaning of this festive occasion, and as a toast was drunk to the fortunes of the new republic, a Danish and an American flag flew in our garden."

Looking back in the 1830s, Steffens saw in this unforgettable occasion "an intimation of the great events that would arise out of this victory." Behind the striking growth of public concern for the general good and mounting social friction in the Nordic lands during the years immediately following, it is difficult not to recognize the powerful influence of the revolution across the sea. To Steffens in his later years, it was "the amicable dawn of the bloody day of history."[55]

# CHAPTER 6

# Changing Bearings
# 1783–86

The end of the American war ushered in a depressed and troubled period throughout the Nordic world. Economic distress fed social and local discontents, leading to political crisis and new lines of development.

Most dramatically, remote Iceland was struck by one of the worst natural catastrophes of its long history of disasters when volcanic eruptions in the Skaptarjökull massif in the southeast devastated one of its most developed and populated regions in June 1783. Two churches and numerous farms were destroyed. A thick pall of smoke long obscured the sun, spreading sickness and death. According to one witness, scarcely anyone remained living to bury the dead. Meadowlands were covered by lava and volcanic ash, and two parishes remained uninhabitable for the next two years. Iceland had hardly begun to recover when the southern part of the island was visited by a series of earthquakes which destroyed hundreds of farmsteads during the summer of 1784. Some 9,000 persons lost their lives, about one-fifth of Iceland's sparse population, together with a large part of its livestock, between 1783 and 1785. The government in Copenhagen did what it could to provide relief, although with little immediate effect.[1]

Scandinavia as a whole meanwhile fell victim to the economic slump following the American war. The loss of opportunities in the foreign carrying and transit trade made itself felt before the end of 1782, above all in Copenhagen. Especially hard-hit were the great trading companies established or reorganized by Guldberg and his associates during the prosperous war years. Even at best, these had been buoyed up through government subventions, which now rapidly increased as foreign trade fell off.

The Danish government had failed to capitalize on the windfall profits of the

126

war to put its financial house in order. Taxes rose, but state and court expenditures increased more rapidly. The national debt grew by over one-half between 1772 and 1784. The government sought to cover its deficits by issuing unbacked paper currency, which increased three times over during the same period. Inflation set in by 1781, as confidence in the currency suffered at home and abroad. Paper money fell off one-fifth in value during 1783–84. To shore up the monarchy's sagging trade balance, the government imposed a sumptuary ordinance in January 1783; this severely restricted the use of numerous luxuries or semi-luxuries of foreign origin, and aroused widespread resentment, even among the peasantry—especially in Norway—for whom the lavish celebration of christenings, weddings, and funerals provided life's traditional high points.[2]

Aside from the Danish overseas colonies, the rest of the Scandinavian world, being more dependent upon the export of native products, was rather less affected by changing trade conditions. Northern Europe as a whole, however, suffered a series of bad crop years between 1781 and 1785. These caused particular distress in southern Norway—Akershus and Christiansand *Stifter*—where the Danish grain monopoly had been reimposed in 1774.[3]

In the Danish monarchy, economic hardship pointed up Ove Høegh-Guldberg's shortcomings as a statesman, especially after 1782, when Baron H. C. Schimmelmann's death left him saddled with sole responsibility for their economic policy. It likewise gave an impetus to intellectual currents, which the regime had sought to hold in check.

A sign of the times were the numerous clubs and societies, which from the early 1770s began to appear in Copenhagen, setting their stamp upon bourgeois life in the capital. Although devoted to conviviality, they represent a considerable advance in refinement over the boisterous tavern life of Holberg's day. The new clubs had rules and selected their members with care. The steaming punch-bowl provided the centerpiece for their gatherings, inspiring elaborate toasts and verses, and ushering in the golden age of the drinking song in Denmark. "The wine we enjoyed," Henrik Steffens later reminisced, "was more sung about than drunk."[4] Characteristically, too, the clubs aspired to some higher purpose. Several were devoted to the cultivation of literature; the Norwegian Society (*Det norske Selskab*), one of the first such groups, indeed played a significant role in the evolution of a specifically Norwegian literature. Others interested themselves in the theater, natural science, or, not least, in philanthropic projects.

All of this sounds innocent enough. Yet for the government there were disquieting undertones. The English word *club*, which came into use in the 1770s, reflected an "Anglomania" characteristic of the time, which could be taken to imply an affinity for English ideas and even sympathy for the unfortunate Caroline Mathilde.[5] From the discussion of literature it was only a short step to the consideration of public affairs.

In May 1780 a cabinet order, drafted by Guldberg, was issued, for the regulation of the "so-called clubs." Although not harmful in themselves, these societies, the order explained, could lead young men astray into "idleness, neglect of their high duties, and the waste of their time, which is nonetheless valuable for the state," and in the long run to "even more dangerous excesses." The Copenhagen police were instructed to keep the clubs under surveillance. Their leaders were to be public officials, or at least "men of respected age and settled ways, known for good behavior." In brief: "Anything that virtue, law, and decency condemn, will not be tolerated." Meetings were to end promptly at 11:00 p.m.[6]

The cabinet order meanwhile required each club to prepare regulations, thus to reflect carefully upon its philosophy and raison d'être. Their outlook was perhaps best expressed by Drejer's Club, the most notable of them, established in 1775, which by 1780 counted 130 members of Copenhagen's leading citizens. The club's purpose, its new constitution proclaimed that year, was "to promote all possible utility."[7]

By the early 1780s the peasant question was becoming urgent. Since 1772, Danish agricultural policy had again favored the manor as the primary unit of production for the market, at the expense of the peasantry. The poor crop years after 1781 seemed, however, to call into question the adequacy of this approach, even on practical, economic grounds. The landlord remained responsible to the government for the payment of his tenants' taxes. The peasant, bound to the manor, remained all too often a listless and inefficient worker, increasingly a burden rather than an asset to his landlord, who had to advance tax payments and other necessities to keep his tenancy filled. Both the cause and the effect of the peasant's lassitude were the heavy labor obligations to the manor, which often led to the relative neglect of their own holdings. In sum, efforts to obtain a somewhat better yield on a small part of the land impeded the effective cultivation of the rest.[8]

The solution of Guldberg and the conservative proprietors was constantly to strengthen the landlord's control over the peasant, which to a growing number of critics only compounded the problem. In their view, personal freedom could alone restore the peasant's self-respect and initiative, hence the productivity of agriculture as a whole. All the basic arguments of twenty years or more were once again aired, while increasingly the debate revealed fundamentally opposed concepts of human nature itself. Still, the would-be reformers now had behind them the added force of European advances in agrarian theory and practices in recent years, as well as the growing trend of enlightened thought in the Western world to regard the state as the instrument of individual human felicity, rather than as an end in itself.[9]

Discontent thus mounted, on both practical and ideal grounds, against the existing regime. Meanwhile, even persons in agreement with its conservative social and economic views could disapprove of its method of governing. In March 1784 Tønne Lüttichau, a Jutland proprietor and outspoken opponent of peasant emancipation, protested to the king the use of cabinet orders: "If these should have such force as to nullify, amend, and in all respects recast and strike down the privileged laws, you do not reign over a free people, but rather over a couple of million slaves, whose inheritances, lives, and goods are all confined to your Majesty's high cabinet."[10]

By this time the hopes and fears of the Danish monarchy were focusing increasingly upon Crown Prince Frederik, whose confirmation at the age of sixteen would mark his coming of age in the spring of 1784. The young prince remained something of an unknown quantity. His early upbringing had been largely neglected, for Struensee had held to the relaxed educational ideals of Rousseau's *Émile*, while the cold and imperious treatment he thereafter received from Juliane Marie and Hereditary Prince Frederik had made him withdrawn and taciturn. Those closest to him were two personal retainers, his *kammerjunker*, the scholarly Johan von Bülow, and particularly his Norwegian-born *kammerpage*, Theodor Georg Schlanbusch.

Already in August 1781, at the age of thirteen, the crown prince confided his dissatisfaction with the confining tutelage under which he was placed to Schlanbusch, with whom he began considering schemes to establish himself as de facto regent in place of his stepgrandmother and uncle. Schlanbusch saw in Count A. P. Bernstorff an indispensable ally, and tried to win him over. Bernstorff was clearly eager to return to power, but insisted that no action be taken until after the crown prince's confirmation in 1784.[11] Others were meanwhile initiated into the conspiracy; these included Count Ernst Schimmelmann, who in 1782 succeeded his deceased father as director of finances, Counts Christian Ditlev and Johan Ludwig Reventlow, and eventually Bülow and State Councillor Count Schack-Rathlou.

Guldberg and his royal patrons paid little heed to disturbing rumors but nonetheless took measures to strengthen their position in preparation for the crown prince's coming of age. On 4 April 1784, the day of his confirmation, Frederik received a letter from Juliane Marie, informing him that he might now "help" her and his uncle in the exercise of sovereign power and attend the council. Guldberg gave him a letter he had formulated in Christian VII's name, admonishing him: "Hold in all things to my mother and brother. Until now we three have been as one, and now we four shall be as one." "Guldberg," the letter added, "will see to it that you learn daily what I decide."[12] The confirmation was marked by the bestowal of numerous honors to faithful supporters of the regime.

Two days later, the pro-government element on the council was reinforced when Guldberg at last took his place on it, together with two of his close associates. The real locus of power was still to remain the cabinet, thereby bypassing the crown prince. All state papers destined for the council were meanwhile to be sent first to Hereditary Prince Frederik, so that he could bring his influence to bear on his young nephew.

On 14 April Crown Prince Frederik attended his first meeting of the council. The agenda was to open with the swearing in of the three new state councillors, but the crown prince interrupted and obtained Christian VII's permission to read a document he had with him. This called for an end to cabinet rule and a return to the principles of collegial government formally reestablished by the ordinance of 18 February 1772, following Struensee's fall, as well as the appointment to the council of Count Bernstorff and three of his supporters. He requested the king's immediate acceptance of the document. Despite the hereditary prince's desperate protests, the demented king signed it, then fled the room. The crown prince thereupon dismissed the dumfounded, unsworn councillors. The coup was thus carried off with astonishing ease, although the conspirators had been prepared to use force.

Unlike in 1772, in 1784 there were no reprisals. Juliane Marie and her son were allowed to sink back into decent obscurity. Guldberg was appointed *stift-amtmand* in Aarhus, a position he thereafter filled both loyally and with greater competence than he had shown in guiding the destinies of the state.

Looking back, we can see that the fallen regime had been compromised both by its origins and by its manifest inner contradictions. The coup that brought it to power recalls the bloody palace revolutions of eighteenth-century St. Petersburg, and its shadow lingered on. Ostensibly it freed Christian VII from domination; in actuality Juliane Marie and Guldberg replaced Caroline Mathilde and Struensee as custodians of the royal will. Government by council was formally reinstated in 1772, with the regular bureaucratic procedures of the past; in fact cabinet rule suffered little interruption, and its constant intervention created bureaucratic confusion and insecurity.

The men of 1772 had sought to prevent the rise of another all-powerful minister. In effect, they succeeded both too well and not well enough. Lacking a monarch capable of ruling in person, government remained hamstrung and inefficient. Guldberg ultimately came closest to dominating the regime, yet his progress was slow and necessarily roundabout, and his official position remained ambiguous. He was loyal, honest, and industrious: altogether he drafted four to five thousand cabinet orders, often even writing them out himself in clear copy.[13] His views set their stamp upon the era. But he lacked the vision and initiative of real leadership.

Guldberg liked to think of himself as a hardheaded realist. Yet although he could be pragmatic enough in political maneuver, he was woefully lacking in practical experience in matters of state, and his viewpoint remained firmly grounded in the baroque world of early Danish absolutism, with its hierarchy, mercantilism, and authoritarian cultural and moral tutelage, which he strove against mounting odds to uphold.[14]

According to the ordinance of 14 April 1784, the crown prince was henceforth to countersign all royal decrees. In a formal sense, this provision limited the king's authority and was thus a violation of the *Lex Regia* comparable to Struensee's in 1771. Yet because Frederik was the legal heir to the throne, such a consideration scarcely came to mind. In actuality, his power was now essentially unlimited, a situation he would in due time exploit.

For the present the young prince was prepared to rely upon an impressive group of advisers. Among them, Count Bernstorff, now restored to the council, foreign ministry, and German Chancellery, was clearly the dominant figure. At forty-nine, he was at the height of his powers. His years of enforced idleness on his Mecklenburg estate had allowed him to reconsider his basic views on state and society. Up to 1780 his outlook had been strongly aristocratic. By February 1783 he wrote of the need for a "total reform"; what he might have meant at this point is not clear, but later developments would show that this was no idle remark and that his views had broadened considerably.[15]

His principal collaborators would be his younger colleagues Count Ernst Schimmelmann, now in charge of the treasury, and Count Christian Ditlev Reventlow, who among his various posts presided over the *Rentekammer*, or Exchequer, which served in part as a kind of ministry of agriculture. Both held views even more liberal than Bernstorff's. For the time being, neither was a member of the council, where Count Schack-Rathlou remained a force to be reckoned with.

This group stands in striking contrast to Guldberg and his friends. Its leading figures were high noblemen of ancient lineage. Although all were subjects of the Danish crown and landed magnates within the kingdom, all except Schack-Rathlou were German in background and culture. Bernstorff, Reventlow, and Schimmelmann were related by blood or marriage. Outwardly they recalled the old "Excellencies" of Frederik V's day. Yet they would carry out a sweeping program of reform, largely transforming Danish society and laying the foundations for its future revolution. Bernstorff and his younger associates were men of cosmopolitan outlook and generous principles, grounded in part in the humanitarianism of the Enlightenment, but even more in that of German preromantic idealism. Their high sense of *noblesse oblige* and their warm Lutheran piety – in Bernstorff's case including an element of mysticism – found their outlet in practical projects to improve the lot of their fellow men.[16] They represent that creative synthesis of sense and sensibility so characteristic of the 1780s.

The new regime lost little time in embarking upon needed reforms. In 1784 a commission was established under Ernst Schimmelmann to prepare a comprehensive plan for reviving national prosperity and restructuring the state finances.

A royal decree the following year called for reform of the monetary system. C. D. Reventlow was placed at the head of the so-called Smaller Agrarian Commission (*den Lille landbokommission*) in 1785 to improve conditions on the crown estates in north Sjælland—thus resuming the efforts of the 1760s—for the benefit of both the tenantry and the treasury.

The government meanwhile began investigating the status of the peasantry throughout Denmark. Count Reventlow proposed the establishment of a commission to deal with all aspects of the problem, which was officially decreed on 25 August 1786. Learning of the crown prince's approval, Reventlow wrote to his sister on 14 July:

> Joyously and with thanks to God, I hasten to write these lines to you. God's blessing, tidings of freedom, have come. . . . Hurrah, hurrah, hurrah! Cry out with me, that our voices may join together where great men in blue cordons sit and cross themselves over these strange happenings. . . . I shall not rest, either in body or soul, until the whole task is completed, until the temple of thralldom is destroyed and that of freedom is built.[17]

Although the coup of 14 April 1784—unlike that of January 1772—caused little immediate stir, the new spirit quickly became evident to the informed public. No formal change was made to the ordinance of 1773 on control of the press, yet a new freedom was understood to prevail, as reflected in the rapid appearance of new periodicals throughout the monarchy in the mid-1780s and the zest with which they addressed themselves to matters concerning the public weal. The heady new spirit was exemplified by the journal *Minerva* in Copenhagen, which in 1785 lightheartedly asked whether "general enlightenment is not a dangerous thing," replying tongue-in-cheek that almost any kind of learning must surely imperil society—especially in Denmark.[18]

The clubs entered their golden era, reflecting the new atmosphere of optimism and civic virtue. At the ten-year anniversary of Drejer's Club in 1785, Thomas Thaarup extolled its purposes as "noble" and "philosophically grounded," and its members as honored within its walls not according to those distinctions the service of the state required but to the extent each "served the general good," and "according to his qualities of mind and heart." Typical of many new societies was the Schleswig-Holsteinische Patriotische Gesellschaft, founded in Kiel in 1786 "for the advancement of agriculture and civic welfare."[19] A new epoch was at hand.

In the Swedish monarchy new ideas of agrarian reform were likewise making themselves felt in deed and word. In 1785 Baron Rutger Maclean, having inherited Svaneholm manor in Skåne, commenced the consolidation of his lands into compact model leasehold farms on the new Danish model, eventually inspiring a movement of fundamental significance. And in Swedish Pomerania *Kammerrat* J. D. von Reichenbach was the first, beginning in 1784, to condemn the absorption of peasant farms into manorial demesnes (*Bauernlegen*)—which the Swedish governor-general, the Prince von Hessenstein, was striving with indifferent success to limit—and above all serfdom, which he characterized as "a barbarous institution which no custom can exonerate, which arouses horror in every well-meaning citizen, which offends against the dignity of man, robbing him of all physical and moral strength, for the primeval right of all men is freedom and equality."[20]

In Stockholm Gustav III had been much occupied since 1779 with plans to seize Norway from Denmark. The Danish economic crisis at the end of the American war and renewed signs of discontent in Norway, resulting from crop failures and the Danish grain monopoly, seemed to augur well for such a venture. Plans were laid for a direct attack on Copenhagen, and the army and navy were prepared for action.[21]

Despite Gustav's amiable visit in St. Petersburg in 1777, the position of Russia in the event of an attack on Denmark remained disquieting. In the summer of 1783 Gustav accepted Catherine II's invitation to visit her in Fredrikshamn, in Russian Finland, where amid mutual amenities both sought to sound out the other's intentions. Gustav came to recognize that the Russian-Danish alliance remained undisturbed and put off his "Grand Design" until the following year.

He meanwhile hoped to allay suspicion by departing in September 1783 on a grand tour of Italy and France, which lasted until the following August. This brought him personal contacts with Emperor Joseph II, Grand Duke Leopold of Tuscany, their sister, Marie Antoinette, and Louis XVI of France, and it was to be of great cultural significance for the breakthrough in Sweden of the neoclassical late Gustavian style in architecture and the arts. At the same time it revealed Gustav's growing disenchantment with the French *philosophes*.[22]

From the political viewpoint, the grand tour gave little satisfaction. Gustav discerned no encouragement for his daring plans in any quarter. His hopes were aroused when Catherine II's annexation of the Crimea offered the prospect of Russia's becoming embroiled in a war with the Turks, leaving him a free hand in the North. Through his ambassador in Constantinople he did his best to rouse the Porte to action. When news of a Turkish-Russian settlement reached him in Naples in March 1784, however, it became clear that his "Grand Design" would have to be abandoned. British intelligence had meanwhile revealed his plans to St. Petersburg, which warned that Russia would stand by its Danish ally. In April the coup d'etat took place in Copenhagen, and Denmark-Norway's defenses were set in readiness.

Continuing to Paris and Versailles, Gustav had to content himself with a new defensive and subsidy treaty with France, concluded in July 1784, which also ceded to Sweden the small West Indian island of St. Barthélemy.[23]

With characteristic flexibility, Gustav III continued to explore possibilities in Denmark-Norway, including a farfetched scheme to stir up civil conflict through the cooperation of Juliane Marie—which she refused to consider—and intimations to the Danish court concerning a future Scandinavian dynastic union.[24] At this time, in July 1785, he wrote to his confidant, J. C. Toll:

> With Norway there does not seem much that can be done. It will be in Copenhagen that its crown will be taken. . . . To arouse a republican spirit there could easily take place; but who knows whether it might develop as we might wish, and I would then fear its contagion in Sweden, which so recently has been cured of it.[25]

While Gustav III speculated about intrigue and agitation in Denmark-Norway, Catherine II secretly instructed her ambassador to Stockholm in December 1784 to revive the old pro-Russian faction in preparation for a Russian attack, when circumstances permitted, to restore the constitution Gustav had overthrown in 1772.[26] The Danish minister to Stockholm received similar instructions soon thereafter.

In preparation for the *Riksdag* in 1778, the Russian and Danish envoys had sought to encourage opposition to the king.[27] But times had then been good, and Gustav III's regime still retained its early popularity. By the mid-1780s, however, discontent was rapidly mounting. Crop failures caused widespread misery. Military expenditures weighed down the depressed economy. By 1783 alarming rumors circulated that the king intended to attack Denmark.[28] Gustav's grand tour on the Continent in 1783–84 was condemned as frivolous and extravagant, especially at a time of want at home.

Hard times aggravated existing grievances. Many burghers, especially in Stockholm, fretted against the king's economic liberalism in such matters as free trade in grain and "free" masterships outside the guilds; they also feared a planned royal monopoly on tobacco, a particularly lucrative commodity. The peasantry in particular strongly opposed the ban on private distillation of spirits, on both practical and legal grounds. The clergy were increasingly indignant, not only over the decline of public morality and the unedifying example of the court itself, but also over the growing "sale" of pastorates, often mediated by the king's current favorites in return for substantial *douceurs*. In such manner, for instance, the bishop of Gothenburg, Johan Wingård, managed to engross the incomes from eleven pastorates and to have himself appointed dean of his own cathedral.[29]

Such grievances often concerned the aristocracy as well. But opposition within the noble order was based above all on constitutional considerations. Gustav III's high-handed management of the *Riksdag* in 1778–79 had not been forgotten. Press freedom was further limited by royal decree in 1780 and again in 1785.[30] Increasingly the king bypassed his council and the regular bureaucracy, and governed with the aid of a miscellaneous group of confidants, which by the early 1780s no longer included such respected figures from his earlier reign as Count Ulrik Scheffer or Johan Liljencrantz. Among the new men around the king were various young favorites—most notably the Finnish Baron Gustaf Mauritz Armfelt—who were despised as corrupt and unprincipled opportunists, and about whom scandalous stories circulated. Appointments and promotions became increasingly arbitrary. The king, it seemed apparent, was reducing his own constitution of 1772 to an empty form. To Armfelt, Gustav confided in November 1781 the principle that ''a king ought never to allow himself to be controlled by anyone in his projects.''[31]

Noble discontent was particularly acute in Finland. There the government's limitation of private forest holdings affected not only the freehold peasantry but also a nobility highly dependent upon income from its estates, which tended to be smaller and less profitable than in Sweden proper. The crown's confiscation of so-called excess forest lands at a time of ruinous harvests—perhaps the worst period economically for Sweden-Finland between 1720 and 1800—bore heavily upon the Finnish nobility, which tended to see Gustav III's land policy for their part of the kingdom as yet another alarming indication of his mounting despotism.

There meanwhile remained the longer-term problem of Finland's security against Russia. Occupation by the Russians in 1713–21 and 1741-43 had made the Finns painfully aware of Sweden's weaknesses and their own exposed position. Following the Peace of Nystad of 1721, Sweden made only sporadic efforts to strengthen its eastern frontier. Gustav III's more vigorous defense policy after 1772, however, had encouraged the Finnish nobility, many of whom held military commissions.

Within the Finnish officer corps, Colonel Göran Magnus Sprengtporten distinguished himself by organizing a flexible system of defense along the frontier. He also undertook to instruct young Finnish noblemen in military science, an initiative leading by 1781 to the establishment of a military academy at Haapaniemi. Visiting Stockholm in 1777–78, however, he became disillusioned with Gustav III, in part for what he considered ingratitude. Resentful and hardpressed economically, he left in 1780 for the Continent, where he sought a billet in the French army during the American war. At the same time, his elder halfbrother, Jacob Magnus—the king's devoted collaborator in the coup of 1772—addressed to Gustav a long and forthright statement of his profound disenchantment with the existing regime.[32]

Returning from France in 1782, G. M. Sprengtporten turned to new speculations. ''North America's independence,'' a contemporary later recalled, aroused in him the thought that ''Finland might also be separated from Sweden and become independent. He preached on this theme for all whom he believed to be his friends and devoted to him.''[33] The latter included many of the younger

Finnish officers, who tended to see in him a "true patriot, worthy of treading in the footsteps of a Washington."[34] In 1784 Sprengtporten sounded out Duke Carl of Södermanland—whose relations with his brother, Gustav III, were often known to be strained—over the prospect of his ruling an independent Finland, but the duke shied away.

The following year, Sprengtporten entered the service of the United Netherlands, at a time when that strife-ridden republic was, in Bruno Lesch's words, "the best school for revolutionaries Europe then had to offer," and quickly became involved with the "Patriot" party.[35] He prepared a draft constitution for a "Republic of the United Provinces of Finland," on a strongly federative model. Provincial diets, composed of the traditional four estates, were to meet annually, and a national Finnish *Riksdag* was to be convened every third year. The ongoing business of government would be conducted by a small standing "congress," consisting of representatives of both noble and nonnoble landowners—for which peasant freeholders might vote without themselves being eligible—as well as for each diocese and staple town, elected for three years but subject to recall by their electors. The congress would be presided over by a member elected for a three-month term, who officially represented the state. Executive functions would be handled by a state council composed of elected civil servants with life tenure. Within the Noble Estate, Gustav III's division into three classes was to be abolished, as were the titles of count and baron, making all noblemen equal in status. Voting in the congress was evidently to be by head rather than by estate, and any citizen might propose legislation to the *Riksdag* or congress. Social origin was to play no role in public appointments. Complete press freedom and considerable religious liberty were to be guaranteed.[36] The project thus contained a mixture of both aristocratic and democratic elements. It bears manifest similarities to the Swedish constitution of 1720, which Gustav III had overthrown, as well as those of the United Netherlands, the United States under the Articles of Confederation, and even of Poland, which Sprengtporten had visited in 1779.

To what extent such an arrangement might have corresponded to actual conditions in Finland, with its relatively primitive social structure and strong traditions of Swedish centralism, remains an open question. Clearly Sprengtporten was seeking a formula that might gain support from various constituencies in Finland, as well as from abroad. For under what conditions might Finland conceivably achieve its independence from Sweden? Only with support from Russia, which in turn would imply some kind of a protectorate such as the Russians seemed to favor in their borderlands—in Poland, Courland, and the Crimea—during the 1770s. The idea of an autonomous Finland under Russian protection had indeed first been openly proposed by Empress Elizabeth in a manifesto to the Finns in March 1742 during the war with Sweden. Thereafter such ideas did not entirely disappear, either in Finland or in St. Petersburg, which remained perilously close to the Swedish frontier.[37] In 1785 Sprengtporten presented his scheme to the Russian minister in The Hague; returning to Stockholm the following year, he took it up with the Russian ambassador there. Later in 1786 he accepted a commission as a Russian major-general and departed for St. Petersburg.

Years later, in 1809, Sprengtporten justified his actions on the basis of Sweden's basic inability to defend Finland: "Let us agree that security against a foreign enemy is the first condition of life within society, and that the contract upon which it is based is broken as soon as this condition is no longer fulfilled."[38] In the 1780s, however, only a few of Sprengtporten's more devoted followers were prepared to go so far as to break entirely with Sweden and accept the protection of the hereditary foe. Few could contemplate Finland's future "independence" except in terms of self-government under the Swedish crown, analogous to that of Ireland within the United Kingdom after 1782, which—it might be hoped—would allay Russian fears of Swedish aggression.

The Finnish autonomist movement of the 1780s thus included a small inner, and a wider outer circle, with differing concepts of self-rule; knowing the traditional Russophobia of most of their countrymen, the Sprengtportians kept their ultimate intentions to themselves.

The movement as a whole received moral reinforcement from the Valhalla Order, founded by Major Jan Anders Jägerhorn in 1780–81 among the younger officers at Sveaborg fortress, commanding the seaward approach to Helsingfors (Helsinki). Secret lodges on the Continental model, with graduated hierarchies and elaborate mystical rites, were as characteristic of Sweden-Finland during this period as were the convivial clubs of the English type in Danish society. Both, however, were inspired with an intense concern for the public good. The Valhalla Order combined patriotism to the "fatherland"—which ever more came to mean Finland rather than the monarchy as a whole—with a cult of antique virtue, largely inspired by "our forefathers' pure and simple customs." Both republican Rome and ancient Scandinavia provided its heroes. Increasingly its initiates came to see in the cynical and frivolous court of Gustav III the very antithesis of its lofty ideals and moral fervor.[39]

Finnish nationalist historians earlier in this century—in particular J. R. Danielson-Kalmari—tended to perceive the autonomists of the 1780s as precursors of Finnish ethnic nationalism and its struggle against Swedish language and cultural domination in the nineteenth and early twentieth centuries. More recent scholarship has dismissed such an interpretation as anachronistic.[40] The autonomists were almost exclusively noblemen, particularly from the exposed southeastern border districts. All were Swedish in language and culture, and although a few were affected by academic interest at Åbo University in native Finnish traditions and speech, many knew little of the indigenous language. Among the nonnoble classes, not least among the overwhelmingly Finnish-speaking peasantry, there was little sympathy either for the nobility or for its ideals.

After its first flush of enthusiasm, the autonomist movement wavered with the course of events. In 1783 Russia's outright annexation of its Crimean protectorate proved disillusioning to those who fixed their hopes upon St. Petersburg, as did the administrative Russification of the Baltic provinces and Russian Finland, overriding privileges guaranteed under the Peace Treaties of Nystad and Åbo, which began the same year. The freeze in Gustav III's relations with Catherine II in the spring of 1784, however, again aroused fears for Finland's security, as did word of a new defense plan in 1785, calling for an initial strategic retreat far to the west and north, until a counterattack could be mounted. A rumor circulated at this time, evidently inspired by St. Petersburg, that Gustav III was considering trading Finland for Norway. The *Riksdag* of 1786 in Stockholm further aroused noble resentments against the king, as will be seen. Yet Sprengtporten's departure for Russia that year left his followers leaderless, while a visit by the king to Finland in 1787 and further attention to its defenses apparently allayed—for the time being—some of the anxieties underlying the autonomist movement.

On 2 April 1786 Gustav III unexpectedly summoned a *Riksdag*, to convene a month later in Stockholm. Such short notice gave rise to suspicion and ill will from the beginning, since many provincial *riksdagsmän*, especially from Finland, could hardly reach the capital by the appointed date. There was little time for preparation, yet the political composition of the *Riksdag* reflected the rising tide of dissatisfaction with the king and his policies since its last meeting in 1778-79.

The Noble Estate was clearly dominated by the anti-royalist "Patriots," around the former Hat chieftain, Count Axel von Fersen, the elder, who called for a return to strict observance of the constitution of 1772. A more radical faction aspired to limit the king's constitutional powers; some of its adherents were prepared to revert to the practice of the "Era of Freedom" and seek covert support from the Russian and Danish envoys, but the latter, taken unawares, were unable to play a very effective role. A small but determined royalist minority was led by the king's confidant, Colonel J. C. Toll. Elections among the nonnoble Estates produced less clear-cut results: whereas the peasants strongly inclined toward opposition, the Clergy and Burghers were initially more closely divided.

Upon convening, the Noble Estate raised a basic procedural question still not clearly settled at the previous *Riksdag*: the reckoning of votes by house for the passage of legislation. It proposed that the votes of three estates be sufficient, except for revenue matters, in which each Estate would vote on its own share of proposed taxation, and questions of privilege, which would require the assent of all four estates. Gustav III accepted this solution, which was thereupon adopted by the other three estates.

The king looked forward to continued cooperation. He had given no explanation for his calling the Estates. In 1778–79 they had extended the regular grant of revenue until the king might see fit to reconvene them. It seemed clear that the king now sought to increase his revenues, even though the mounting burden of national debt remained a carefully kept secret. Among the opposition, it was rumored that he planned to seize greater power for himself.

The crown's principal proposal, inspired by Colonel Toll, called for commutation throughout the kingdom of the landowners' standing obligation to provision and transport the territorial troops maintained by their localities during annual regimental musters into a money payment, the *passevolans*. Such arrangements had been made by local agreement in Finland and parts of Sweden, resulting in improved military efficiency.

The opposition within the Noble Estate resolutely rejected the proposition on both practical and constitutional grounds. It saw in the commutation of specific local requirements *in natura* and in labor to money payments a disguised form of permanent taxation that would increase the king's freedom of action in the military sphere—in which he was known to have dangerously adventurous ideas. In vain Gustav sought to intimidate Count Fersen, threatening, according to the latter, that he had the means to uphold his "rightful authority" by force.[41] Finnish members of the Noble Estate, realizing its implications for the defense of their part of the realm, fought a losing battle for the *passevolans*. Although the royal proposition was passed by the Clergy and the Burghers, it was roundly defeated by the Nobles, followed by the Peasants. With the Estates thus evenly divided, it failed by default, in accordance with the voting procedure the king had just accepted.

Except for a project for local grain magazines, which passed in scaled-down form, the crown's remaining propositions were likewise defeated. The question of distillation provided further grist for the opposition. A royal proposition for licensing parish distilleries was defeated by all four Estates. When the king then offered to permit free household distillation in return for a standing tax, the "Patriots" among the Nobility declared household distillation a basic property right, in return for which the king could not legally demand a new permanent revenue. The Clergy, Burghers, and Peasants were prepared to compromise, but Gustav III refused to alter his proposition and it failed to pass. The Estates limited their regular grant of revenue to the next four years, virtually compelling the king to summon another *Riksdag* upon its expiration. As a further lesson to him it was reduced by a symbolic 1 percent.

The Estates, separately and in combination, also petitioned against numerous grievances in recent years, including royal monopolies and limitations on freedom of the press. To justify their actions before public opinion, the Noble, Burgher, and Peasant Estates published their proceedings.

After seven weeks, Gustav III dissolved the *Riksdag*. He deplored the "ill-founded suspicions'' that had disturbed its deliberations, and appealed to posterity to vindicate his devotion to his subjects' welfare.[42] He had convened the Estates, it would appear, partly as a means to sound opinion, which by 1786 was largely silenced in the press. But he was hardly prepared for the force of opposition he encountered in all four Estates. This proved a bitter blow for a monarch who had gloried in the adulation of his people.

Gustav III was, however, too astute a politician not to learn from the experience and to adapt himself accordingly. It was evident during the *Riksdag* that opposition among the nonnoble Estates was based upon specific, material grievances, which left essentially unshaken the traditional loyalty of the commonality to the crown, whereas among the nobility it bore the intransigeance of principle and challenged the very nature of the regime itself on constitutional grounds. The lesson was clear: locked in a struggle for power, the king must split the opposition and isolate the nobility.

To do so meant a return to an age-old principle of statecraft, even if this did not come easily to Gustav III with his aristocratic predilections. These had by no means changed by 1786. The year before he had still deplored "that spirit of democracy which brought about the fall of our former government, and which would have succeeded in its goal of annihilating the nobility if the revolution [of 1772] had not come in time to raise a barrier against it."[43] It was also in 1785 that Gustav had considered eliminating commoners altogether in his officer corps. Nor, as events would prove, did he abandon the ideal of a special relationship between the king and his nobility—provided the latter could be reduced to political submission. Eino Jutikkala has aptly described Gustav III's motto as "everything for the good of the nobility, but nothing through the efforts of the House of the Nobles."[44] For the time being, its realization required other allies.

Already by the end of the *Riksdag* in June 1786, Gustav made a play for peasant sympathies in particular by voluntarily renouncing the fourth year—one-quarter—of the tax revenue just granted him. Soon thereafter he abandoned the projected tobacco monopoly, to the relief of the burghers. A new ecclesiastical commission reformed the corrupt traffic in clerical appointments. Most important, in 1787 free household distillation was again permitted, for a fee based on the size of the farm involved. Although this arrangement was rejected on principle by some landowners, mainly noblemen, it was enthusiastically received by the great majority of the peasants. "The marriage between the peasantry and the high and mighty is now broken," Gustav III wrote to Toll, "and that alone is useful."[45]

Throughout Scandinavia, the period beginning in 1772 and lasting to the middle 1780s is characterized by a conservative reaction against the radical impulses of the years immediately preceding. There was a trend toward the concentration of political power: in Sweden this was the work of the king himself,

Gustav III; in Denmark of the monarch's self-appointed representatives, Guldberg and the court. In both kingdoms new regimes had come to power during a time of economic crisis, in 1772, which threatened the stability of the old society; in both renewed economic distress prepared the way for changes of direction in the mid-1780s.

Social and economic policy throughout Scandinavia during this period strengthened the position of the manorial proprietors—still predominantly noble in both kingdoms—while holding peasant interests in check, despite Guldberg's bourgeois tone and Gustav III's protestations of concern for the peasantry. One cannot but be struck by the similarity of Bernstorff's and Gustav III's aristocratic values during these years, as well as by the fact that both would take the lead in transforming society by the later 1780s. Both regimes sought to uphold the cultural values of earlier epochs, in the face of new impulses both at home and abroad. Whereas Gustav III romanticized the great age of the Vasa kings of the sixteenth and seventeenth centuries, Guldberg looked back to the regimented and docile society of early Danish absolutism in the later seventeenth and early eighteenth centuries.

This era in the Scandinavian kingdoms reflects developments throughout the Western world. In France the decade and a half following Louis XVI's accession in 1774 was marked by an aristocratic reaction which blocked repeated efforts at reform. British conservatism hardened in the face of the Americans, the Irish, and the would-be parliamentary reformers. Catherine II's Charter of the Nobility at last conferred corporate status upon the Russian aristocracy in 1785. Frederick II was at the time of his death in 1786 preparing the Prussian law code, adopted in 1794, which could be considered the culmination of the corporative ideal in Europe. A patrician counterrevolution took place in Geneva in 1782, while in the Habsburg lands there was determined resistance to reform, in the name of ancient privileges.[46]

Yet there were other forces at work that could not be denied. The later Enlightenment upheld the rights of the individual against the demands of the state, a principle vindicated in impressive fashion by the revolution in America. In Scandinavia itself a "middle class" was steadily evolving—the term itself first appears in the Swedish Academy's dictionary in 1792—borne up by the profits of trade, extractive industries, manufacture, and shipping, at a time when agriculture, the mainstay of the aristocracy, remained largely depressed, despite government efforts to encourage it.[47] Meanwhile in both kingdoms influential members of the nobility itself were prepared to envision a more open society, offering greater incentives to talent and ambition. In Copenhagen, government moved after 1784 in the direction of enlightened aristocracy; in Stockholm after 1786 toward Caesarian democracy. In both capitals it now began to respond to an evolving society.

CHAPTER 7

# Enlightened Despotism and Revolt
# 1786–89

During the period from 1772 to the mid-1780s, there was a growing tension in Scandinavia between social evolution and policies of state. In the years immediately following, this tension was dramatically released as epochal reforms and rebellion occurred in both Nordic kingdoms. The aspirations of the Scandinavian radicals of the 1760s and early 1770s came in large part to be realized in the climactic years 1786–89—on the eve of the great revolution in France.

In Copenhagen young Crown Prince Frederik showed from the beginning his conscientious concern for the affairs of state. Above all, he was fascinated by the military, in which he was encouraged by his uncle, Prince Carl of Hesse, who also managed to arouse in him a fleeting interest in mystical religion and Freemasonry. A contrary source of interest soon appeared with the arrival from Schleswig of the three sons of the Duke of Augustenburg, two of whom— Friedrich Christian and Christian August—would play important roles in his later reign. The Augustenburgs, a junior branch of the Oldenburg house, represented a strongly rationalistic outlook, thus appealing to Frederik's basically prosaic nature. Being gregarious and high-spirited young men, they overcame the crown prince's rather shy indifference to the amenities of social life. *Kammerjunker* Johan von Bülow, now also the crown prince's personal secretary, strove to hold his young master to the straight and narrow path.

Most of what was accomplished in the Danish monarchy during the first years following the coup of 14 April 1784 was the work of the council and government departments. The crown prince remained in the background, following with particular attention developments in those areas that interested him the most, such as military or agrarian matters. A. P. Bernstorff took the lead in the council, where he was joined in 1788 by Ernst Schimmelmann; outside the council C. D. Reventlow took in hand a variety of reform projects concerned mainly with agrarian questions. They could count on—and did not hesitate to cultivate—the enthusiastic support of progressive opinion throughout the monarchy, especially that of the pace-setting clubs and journals in the capital.

In 1785 Crown Prince Frederik established the so-called Smaller Agrarian Commission (*den Lille landbokommission*), headed by Reventlow, to resume the reform of the crown estates on north Sjælland begun during the first years of Christian VII's reign. The commission pursued a vigorous policy of land reallocation combined with hereditary leaseholds for the new consolidated farms. Labor services were virtually abolished, and crown tenants were relieved of the royal portion of the tithe, in return for reasonable yearly money payments. *Husmænd*, or cotters, who performed necessary seasonal labor, were provided small plots of land. Inspired largely by Count Ludvig Reventlow, who also served on the commission, attention was likewise given to improving the elementary schooling of the children of royal tenants.[1]

By mid-1788 these reforms were largely prepared. On 15 August C. D. Reventlow presented the first fifteen hereditary leasehold contracts to crown tenants from Frederiksborg and Kronborg *Amter*. In a speech for the occasion, printed in the influential progressive journal *Minerva*, in Copenhagen, he stressed the king's concern for his peasant subjects and painted a glowing picture of the future: enlightened cultivators would transform wastelands into lovingly tended gardens and orchards, rich fields, and useful woodlots; and both peasant and cotter would be satisfied with their lot, amid growing prosperity.[2]

In many ways the reforms of the Smaller Agrarian Commission in north Sjælland served as a kind of pilot project. In his speech Reventlow held that the good of the peasants, rather than revenues to the treasury, were the king's principal concern. Yet the financial interests of the crown could scarcely be overlooked. In April 1784 Tyge Rothe had written to Bülow, "What is essential [for the state] is not to save, but to earn." The government advanced considerable sums to reform the crown estates, but in the long run these investments would pay off in rents and taxes.[3]

Greater problems meanwhile awaited solution. In September 1783 a crown bailiff in Viborg had raised the question whether the government, rather than the manorial proprietor, should not appoint executors for the estates of deceased tenants, thus ending old abuses preventing peasant families from bettering their lot from generation to generation. His inquiry received little attention under the Guldberg regime, but it raised in concrete form the whole question of the peasant's dependent and exploited condition.[4]

In July 1786 C. D. Reventlow brought up this question with Crown Prince Frederik, who replied warmly that no time ought to be lost in dealing with so vital a matter. Reventlow prepared a memorandum from the *Rentekammer* to the council, proposing a royal commission to consider the whole question of the Danish peasant's legal status. The crown prince approved of this idea on 14 July, to Reventlow's boundless delight, as seen in the last chapter.

The Great Agrarian Commission (*den Store landbokommission*) was decreed on 25 August 1786. The government was solicitous to assemble a group of sixteen men that might command respect, not least among the proprietorial class, who were directed to consider "everything which can aid the improvement of peasant conditions, so far as is possible without interfering with any of the landlord's legal property rights and without hindering the landlord in the legal utilization of his manor."[5]

While the commission included proprietors of conservative views, its majority were government officials, who might be counted on to place national ahead of private considerations. Its published proceedings do not reveal the role played by its individual members. There is evidence of sharp conflicts and heated exchanges. It soon became apparent, however, that its dominating personalities were its chairman, C. D. Reventlow, and the *generalprokurør*, or juridical counselor of the Danish Chancellery, Christian Colbjørnsen, who served as its secretary. The latter, a Norwegian, represented his homeland's tradition of the proud yeoman farmer, and he brought to bear his fiery indignation against the degradation of the Danish peasant. They made a strange pair in many ways, the high-spirited and sanguine Danish-German *grand seigneur* and the often morose and pessimistic, but fiercely antiaristocratic Norwegian jurist; yet both were equally dedicated supporters of a benevolent despotism to improve the lot of the broader masses.

Largely through Colbjørnsen's efforts and legal expertise the initial question was solved by royal ordinance on 8 June 1787, which protected the estates of deceased manorial tenants through government appointed executors. It also provided for impartial outside inspectors to determine the condition of a tenant farm at the beginning of a lifetime lease and to confirm that it was sufficiently stocked with draft animals, implements, and seed grain to permit the tenant both to work his own tenancy and to fulfill his stipulated labor services on the demesne. Landlords were thereby prevented from making unsubstantiated claims against a deceased tenant's estate. The right of the proprietor or his agent to inflict corporal punishment upon peasants performing labor service was severely curtailed. A second ordinance, issued the same day, prohibited the landlord from reducing the size of a tenancy without the express consent of the tenant, except under certain limited circumstances.[6] By this time, the commission had meanwhile begun to confront the central question of the peasant's legal status: the *stavnsbånd*.

The royal instructions to the commission stated that landlord-tenant relations were to be "based upon the rights and duties which after the abolition of *vornedskab* ought to prevail between the proprietor and the peasant estate, and it shall therefore be incumbent upon the commission, upon determining whether these have not been modified or set aside by later decrees, to make recommendations as to how they may be put into effect."[7] The intention was evident enough. Frederik IV had abolished *vornedskab*, the earlier form of partial serfdom in eastern Denmark, in 1702. The "later decrees" could only refer to the *stavnsbånd*, established in 1733. The question was not whether it should be repealed, but how.

In this matter Reventlow took the lead and quickly stirred up controversy, both within the commission and beyond. The commission's published proceedings indeed reflect all the long-familiar controversies both for and against peasant emancipation. The essential question remained that of basic human nature: how would the common man use or abuse freedom?

For Bolle Luxdorph, an old friend of reform, "Freedom, like mental and physical faculties, is not a reward for previous accomplishment, but rather the means to make oneself deserving, after which one may expect one's reward." On the other side, his colleague on the commission, F. C. Rosenkrantz, was convinced that there was greater poverty in England, "whose subjects have wrested such freedom from their government," than in Denmark. Similarly, the diplomat Peter Schumacher wrote from abroad, "Experience clearly shows that there is far less poverty among peasants where they are unfree," and on the basis of his own observations compared Italy, with its crowds of free beggars, with Russia, where "sensible" landlords saw their peasants' welfare as essential to their own. The reformers, who "sit in their studies hatching projects," he dismissed as motivated solely by "lust for change, self-importance, and conceit." In Aarhus, Guldberg foresaw the ruin of both the peasantry and the state itself. He scoffed at "all the general principles of freedom argued by the *theoretici* in their government offices, sung about by the poets, shown on the stage, defended in the clubs," and warned darkly that "those same persons who now wish to release the peasantry from all constraints also . . . [portray] the discipline which princes impose upon their subjects as the bonds of slavery, which should be broken." To conservatives, the very fabric of society seemed imperiled.[8]

The whole issue of reform—particularly agrarian—created a rift within the government itself, discernible already by the end of 1784. On the council Bernstorff was its leading proponent. The opposing faction was headed by the formidable Schack-Rathlou, who had played a prominent part in agrarian affairs during the Guldberg years, and even more vehemently by F. C. Rosenkrantz; the presence of both on the council following the coup of April 1784 had indeed been intended to reassure conservative and Danish national sentiments. Behind the scenes, Guldberg sought to exercise an occult influence upon the crown prince through Bülow, whose earlier progressive views had quickly evaporated.

Conservatives were proud to identify themselves as the "Danish" and to label the reformers as the "German" party. They did not hesitate to attack the "foreign," and even the high-aristocratic, character of their rivals. Yet nationality and aristocratic ranking were only tactical expedients obscuring the real struggle for power. Prince Friedrich Christian of Augustenburg and his personal rival, Prince Carl of Hesse, great lords thoroughly German in culture, associated themselves with the "Danish" faction, whereas Henrik Stampe, Colbjørnsen, and enlightened opinion generally, both inside and outside the government, identified with the "Germans." The headstrong C. D. Reventlow became the particular bane of the conservatives, while F. C. Rosenkrantz was singled out by the friends of reform as their most implacable enemy. In December 1787 the funeral of the Copenhagen shipbuilder Henrik Gerner, an outspoken proponent of reform, was turned into a great demonstration against Rosenkrantz. Feelings ran high, and most of the capital's prominent intellectuals, including Christian Colbjørnsen, followed Gerner to his grave.[9]

The ultimate decisions lay with the young crown prince, who was already committed firmly to reform. The conservatives were thus reduced to a futile rear-guard action. By the end of April 1788 the Great Agrarian Commission completed its proposal for abolishing the *stavnsbånd*. By royal ordinance on 20 June 1788, the Danish peasantry was emancipated by stages. Male peasants under fourteen and over thirty-six years of age, as well as those who completed military service, were immediately free to leave their manors of origin; the old restrictions remained in force for the rest until 1 January 1800. Conscription, reduced from twelve to eight years, was to be handled by regimental recruiting districts (*lægde*), from which male peasants of military age might not move before completion of service except by permission of the local recruiting officer. Conscription was henceforth based on population, rather than productive farmland.[10]

Emancipation was thus to be carried out gradually, to avoid any sudden disruption of the military establishment or of agriculture. Yet its import could not be mistaken: Danish peasants were freed from their legal dependence upon the lord of the manor. The proprietor lost his most effective means of coercion, particularly for forcing tenancies on unfavorable terms upon reluctant tenants. Henceforth competition and free contract would govern relations between them. Revocation of the *stavnsbånd* of 1733 thus completed the task tenuously begun with Frederik IV's abolition of *vornedskab* in 1702, and may illustrate the degree to which the growth of bureaucratic government during the eighteenth century had strengthened the crown.[11]

The legal emancipation of the peasantry was widely recognized at the time, at home and abroad, as the decisive breach in the old order. It effectively broke the will of the opposition, allowing further reforms to follow in due course. Already on 1 June Schack-Rathlou resigned from the council, soon followed by Rosenkrantz. In February 1788 Guldberg had considered Denmark to be in a state of "veritable crisis" and had written Bülow that the only remaining hope lay in blocking implementation of the impending reforms; surely this was as close as this dedicated absolutist ever came to outright defiance. Yet a year later he expressed to Bülow "the greatest horror" at the thought of being a "*frondeur.*" "As a functionary," he continued, "it is now my duty to put into effect the commands of the government and to seek only to know what they are, rather than what I might wish them to be." He was gratified in October 1789 that the proprietors in his *stift* felt as he did, that

> when the king has once decreed a law, fundamental law is established, and thereafter no more prattle, no more outcry, no more intrigues. The *stavnsbånd* is now abolished: the most numerous estate has now regained from the Legislator its lost freedom, and woe to him who might seek secretly or openly to violate a right which Nature conferred and the Legislator has restored.[12]

A few additional reforms also belong to the first period of the Great Agrarian Commission's activity. Already in August 1786 a credit bank (*Kreditkasse*) was set up to encourage peasant freehold purchases throughout the monarchy. The export trade in cattle, which went mainly to Germany, previously the monopoly of the manorial proprietors, was opened up to all in June 1788, providing a potentially profitable market to peasant cultivators. In July the Danish grain monopoly in southern Norway was finally abolished for good. Court records meanwhile reveal a marked tendency toward judgments favorable to peasant interests during this period.[13]

The Great Agrarian Commission was inactive between May 1788 and February 1790. This was in part because the government was then faced with other concerns, especially in foreign affairs. But it also considered it prudent to see what results the changes already wrought would produce before proceeding further.

What had thus far been accomplished? Present-day historians, more keenly aware of the importance of economic factors, might find it difficult to accept V. Falbe-Hansen's view in 1889, that the later transformation of Danish agrarian life would have followed by itself from the abolition of the *stavnsbånd*.[14] Serious problems still remained after 20 June 1788, some of which affected rural life even more deeply than the *stavnsbånd* itself. The ownership of land remained virtually the monopoly of the manors, thus the overwhelming majority of peasant farmers could still only be manorial tenants, subject to heavy and variable labor services, and to the discipline of the landlord's bailiff. The tithe remained an onerous burden. Much of the peasantry consisted of cotters and landless laborers, largely dependent upon seasonable employment. In the duchies serfdom continued to exist. These were questions that would engage the agrarian reformers for years to come.

The government meanwhile embarked upon a variety of economic reforms. The Guldberg regime had left a heavy national debt and a badly inflated currency. An investigative commission appointed in 1784 presented its far-reaching proposals for financial reorganization and monetary reform, partially inspired by the recent Swedish example, set forth in a royal proclamation on 8 July 1785. Like the proceedings of the Great Agrarian Commission soon after, this was widely publicized by the government, recalling similar uses of publicity to win the support of enlightened opinion for intended reforms elsewhere in Europe during this decade.

In May 1787 a finance commission, headed by Ernst Schimmelmann, was appointed to carry out financial and monetary reform. Schimmelmann proposed to make a start within the duchies by making the Altona bank (*Altonaer Giro- und Leihbank*), established in 1776, the central bank of issue for a new, reformed currency for Schleswig and Holstein, which traded extensively with Hamburg. This was opposed by the "Danish" faction on the council and its friends, ever suspicious of any suggestion of special status. Guldberg, who complained that the Danes were perpetually the "king's stepchildren," feared that the duchies would become an economic "state within the state." But backed by Bernstorff and Reventlow, the crown prince approved the measure. The Altona bank was reconstituted in February 1788 with its own independent board of directors and adequate funding.[15] There now began a long period of economic stability and prosperity in the duchies, lasting until the later Napoleonic wars, which unfortunately came to contrast all too glaringly with conditions in the kingdom, where circumstances prevented the completion of the Finance Commission's ambitious plans and where the currency was never really stabilized before the later 1830s.

The government abandoned the strict mercantilism of Guldberg's day and adopted a more liberal stance reminiscent of Struensee's brief experiment. The term "liberal" is used here—for lack of a satisfactory alternative—simply in a relative sense, to denote greater freedom in economic enterprise, rather than the full-blown, classic *laissez-faire* Liberalism which came to prevail in the early nineteenth century, in Denmark following the state bankruptcy of 1813. Hans Chr. Johansen indeed argues that during this period economic policy in Denmark, as in Europe generally, is best described as "late mercantilism," with government continuing to play an active role, albeit now with greater emphasis upon population growth and public welfare.

No attempt was made to resuscitate Guldberg's great Copenhagen trading companies, or indeed to preserve the specially favored economic status of the capital. A royal ordinance on 18 August 1786 ended, as of the beginning of 1788, the Icelandic trade monopoly, held since 1602 by privileged companies of Copenhagen merchants or by the crown itself. Henceforth both trade with Iceland and fishing in Icelandic waters were opened up to all subjects of the monarchy and six localities on the island were designated staple towns, of which Reykjavík, with a population of some 300, was the largest. The Icelanders were, however, still forbidden to trade directly with foreign merchants.[16]

The trade monopoly for Finnmark in northern Norway, established in 1687, was abolished in September 1787, and staple towns were founded at Tromsø, Hammerfest, and Vardø, where both Swedes and Russians were also permitted to trade. Finnmark developed rapidly during the years that followed. Restrictions on trade with the West Indian, African, and East Indian colonies were likewise relaxed, and a special commission would eventually recommend the freeing of trade with the Færø Islands by 1796. The Greenland Commission, set up in 1788, nonetheless opposed opening up trade with that remote colony, which thus remained in royal hands to protect the native population.[17]

Basically pragmatic in its approach to reform, the government did not immediately withdraw subsidization to manufactures or remove tariff barriers against imports from the duchies or from abroad. It did, however, promote the wider dispersal of industry throughout the provinces. In Schleswig it encouraged the settlement of industrious Moravian Brethren from Germany by granting special privileges to their colony at Christiansfeld, near Haderslev, in 1788.[18]

While the new regime of Crown Prince Frederik was launching its ambitious reform program in Denmark, an explosive situation was developing across the Skagerrak in southern Norway, arising out of the fundamental conflict between an essentially self-contained peasant society, with age-old traditions of self-rule, and the encroachments upon its way of life by a steadily growing state bureaucracy and urban merchant class. Economically it reflected the clash between a peasantry, which by tradition and the limitations of its environment supported itself largely through nonagricultural pursuits, and a town middle class, which, backed by the mercantilist policies of recent regimes in the capital, progressively limited peasant economic activity.

This conflict was not new in Norway. It had already produced a frightening outburst in the *Stril* insurrection of 1765 in Vestlandet. Circumstances in the 1780s now once again brought it to a head. The American war produced a boom in seafaring and commerce, but lean conditions in farming and logging. To deepen the rift, there were poor harvests in 1781 and 1782. Even though the Guldberg government temporarily allowed some limited import of foreign grain into southern Norway, scarcity drove up prices to the profit of town merchants and the detriment of much of the peasantry. The latter normally bought at least a part of their grain supply even in good years, particularly in Sørlandet, where the contrast was greatest between urban prosperity and rural poverty during the war years. Here capable and ambitious peasants ventured into modest shipbuilding, trading, mining, and timber enterprises of their own. This violated the commercial privileges of the towns, but it did not immediately lead to confrontation.

The situation changed, however, with the end of the American war and the European economic crisis that followed. Faced with harder times, the town merchants became more jealous of their privileges and were backed by the Guldberg regime. The authorities strove to suppress trade and seafaring among the peasantry. The privileges of Christiansand and Arendal on the south coast were strengthened at the peasants' expense: the latter were forbidden to buy grain directly from importing vessels or to sell their timber except to licensed sawmills. The monopolies of privileged merchants led to growing indebtedness in the countryside and to perpetual complaints about poor merchandise at exorbitant prices. Having now become so largely integrated into a money and market economy through the pressures and opportunities of the recent war, much of the peasantry in Sørlandet—including some of its most able and venturesome members—neither could nor would return to their old subordinate economic role. To make matters worse, in 1784 and 1785 harvests were particularly bad. In 1785-86 mortality in Norway exceeded nativity.[19]

Economic hardship heightened old antagonisms between peasants and bureaucrats. The state official was of old regarded as an unwelcome intruder in the countryside, ever at odds with the traditional leadership within the peasant community itself. While bureaucrats complained of the lawlessness and intractability of the stiff-necked Norwegian peasants, they themselves were all too often self-willed, arbitrary, and arrogant. Still mainly dependent for their livelihoods on perquisites for their services, many officials were unscrupulous in their exactions. Hard times following the American war meanwhile put them in the position of driving in debts and taxes, which only added to their unpopularity. Thus, paradoxically, while in Denmark the state official was emerging as the champion of the peasantry, in Norway he still appeared as the self-serving henchman of an oppressive town patriciate.[20]

By tradition the Norwegian peasantry was staunchly loyal to its king and cherished its ancient right to present its grievances directly to him. The monarchs had encouraged this practice during the earlier years of absolutism as a means of breaking aristocratic influence, but by 1744 deputations of Norwegian peasants arrived in Copenhagen with such frequency that it was henceforth forbidden. This prohibition was, however, never strictly enforced, since it helped the central government keep an eye on its officials in Norway, and after 1784 word got out that the young crown prince was sympathetic to the plight of the common man.[21] Norwegian peasants could likewise count on the admiration and goodwill of reformist opinion in Copenhagen, where a sympathetic newspaper would write of them in 1790: "The king is their God here on earth. Nothing that is oppressive to the people can come from a king; it is the work of those hateful beings who stand between them."[22] The more absolute the monarch's power, the more absolute the Norwegian peasants' confidence that he could and would end their grievances. As Sverre Steen has put it, they "seized the doctrine of the king's unlimited power and used it as a weapon against the state itself."[23] The danger was that this naive, unquestioning confidence in the monarch's power and goodwill might suffer disillusionment, and thereby be undermined for the future.

By the mid-1780s peasant discontent found its natural leader. Christian Jensen Lofthuus was no ordinary peasant. He was born in Sørlandet, the illegitimate child of a socially prominent father and a local peasant woman. An enterprising farmer near Lillesand, he branched out during the American war into shipbuilding, navigation, and trade in grain, timber, and other wares. These activities took him as far as England and involved him in frequent unsuccessful litigation. In 1782 he was tried and fined for violating the commercial privileges of the town of Arendal; to meet his debts he was compelled to sell his farm. At every turn he found his path blocked by that commercial and official class to which he himself half belonged. His grievances made him the outspoken champion of the peasantry.[24] He was a classic case of the ambitious and frustrated outsider as insurrectionary leader. Lofthuus quickly gained a hearing among the peasantry in Sørlandet.

In June 1786 Lofthuus appeared in Copenhagen, where he personally presented to Crown Prince Frederik a complaint against the royal bailiff of Nedenes *Amt*, Andreas Dahl, his predecessor in office, and the burghers of Arendal, made "on behalf of the Fatherland" but signed only by himself. He thereupon returned to Sørlandet, implying that he was charged by the crown prince himself to gather further evidence. The following month he was back in the capital, but again more evidence was required. By early August he had ready two petitions signed by 532 persons in thirteen parishes, including both landowning farmers and rural poor, requesting a royal commission to investigate their grievances.[25] When Bailiff Dahl threatened to take action against them, the peasants became defiant. Lofthuus now traveled about armed and with a bodyguard. To accompany him to Copenhagen, he assembled representatives of each parish in Nedenes *Amt*, plus several from neighboring Bratsberg *Amt*. In so doing, he violated an ordinance from the time of the "*Stril* War" in 1765, forbidding public meetings without official approval. At the end of September Bailiff Dahl sent a detachment of soldiers to arrest Lofthuus, who managed to escape.

This touched off a general insurrection. On 2 October several hundred armed peasants marched into Lillesand, where they forced the bailiff to urge the *stiftamtmand* in Christiansand to guarantee Lofthuus immunity from arrest. Faced with this threatening situation, the latter granted Lofthuus and his deputation a pass to travel to Copenhagen. On 17 October they departed, thirty-eight strong. Informed of these developments, the state council resolved to arrest Lofthuus. Since national units appeared untrustworthy, the *stiftamtmand* in Christiansand was authorized to request regular troops from Denmark.

Lofthuus and his deputation made their way through Sweden, where word reached them of Lofthuus's impending arrest. His companions continued on to Copenhagen to arrange his safe passage. The government meanwhile had second thoughts. Unwilling to leave disgruntled Norwegian peasants in Sweden, where they might provide unwelcome opportunities to Gustav III, it cancelled the arrest order. But it was now too late, for Lofthuus had returned home. Fearing some collusion on his part with the Swedes, the authorities in Sørlandet were determined to hunt him down, while the peasants rallied to Lofthuus's cause in large numbers.

By the end of November he had an armed following of some 800 men. The burghers of Arendal and Christiansand, thrown into a near-panic, organized town militias to defend themselves. The moment of decision was at hand, but Lofthuus failed to provide resolute leadership: neither he nor his following could bring themselves to use force against constituted authority. Most of his men soon returned home, and the initiative passed to the other side.

In December the government appointed a commission to investigate peasant grievances. Beginning early in January 1787, it heard testimony from 350 peasants—including Lofthuus himself, under a temporary safe-conduct—and called to account a number of officials. Already by 13 February its report was ready. It found many of the peasants' complaints justified and made numerous recommendations to the council in Copenhagen. It meanwhile determined that as "the people's hero," Lofthuus himself must be gotten out of the way. "Guile is what must be resorted to in this case," it recommended. "We must seek to arrest Lofthuus quietly."[26]

Lofthuus's safe-conduct expired in February, and the authorities seized and imprisoned him the following month. A storm of indignation swept through the peasantry of Nedenes and Ovre Telemark, who once again mobilized; those who would not join were forced to contribute to their support. This peasant host seized Bailiff Dahl in Øyestad, as a hostage for Lofthuus's release, and here 800-900 armed peasants assembled. They nonetheless backed down and released the bailiff when confronted by 300 troops supported by cannon.

The threat of bloodshed thus passed during the spring of 1787, although this was not immediately evident. The peasants remained aroused throughout Sørlandet and much of Østlandet; ominous gatherings were reported as far afield as Østerdalen and Gudbrandsdalen. In Christiansand, the *stiftamtmand* called in a regiment of Danish troops. He was now no longer as much concerned about the farmers as about "the workers at the ironworks and mines, the seamen, the timber-cutters on the coast, folk who owned nothing and were accustomed to all kinds of excesses."[27] In May a three-man delegation went to Copenhagen to seek Lofthuus's release from prison, but was severely reprimanded by the council for its attempt.

By summer, the situation began to cool as a good harvest ripened in the fields and the government undertook to alleviate the causes of unrest. A number of officials were punished, transferred, or dismissed for abuse of power or for inept handling of the recent crisis. Various bureaucratic abuses were reformed locally, and in June 1788 a new ordinance regularized the entire system of official perquisites. Most important, the same month the Danish grain monopoly in southern Norway was abolished once and for all. Over the next few years the new regime's economic policy was reflected in relaxed restrictions upon rural trade, especially in timber.[28]

As for Lofthuus himself, he languished in the dungeon of Akershus fortress in Christiania, chained to a rock. While the government had no intention of releasing him, it was in no hurry to bring him to trial, lest this stir up fresh disorders. He was finally condemned to life imprisonment in 1792; the sentence was confirmed by the supreme court of appeal in Copenhagen in 1799—two years after his death. In 1800 twelve others imprisoned at the same time were finally released. The reflections of the wealthy Christiania merchant Bernt Anker in March 1787 give some idea of the fears and hatred Lofthuus aroused among his middle-class adversaries:

> If the rebellious mob is not punished, it can murder us in our homes and go scot-free. This is a base soul, a rascal in public affairs and a stupid rebel in political life. They come running to see this miserable fellow, who dares to appear important in his chains. Some call this rude butcher a second Washington, but if I should wish to see him it would be to spit in his face.[29]

In retrospect, the Lofthuus insurrection cannot be regarded as a national uprising. While protesting their traditional loyalty to their sovereign, the peasants reacted against men no less Norwegian—in sentiment, if not always by descent —than themselves, of the type who had been vocal in condemning Danish exploitation in the early 1770s and who would take the lead in the movement for Norwegian independence a generation later, in 1814. Nor had the time yet come in Norway when a peasant movement could encompass the entire country. At its height it remained limited to the South and Southeast. It is noteworthy that the *Stril* district in Vestlandet, the center of revolt in 1765, played no part in it.

The peasants' grievances in southern Norway were preeminently economic- —at least on the face of it—as were the reforms that placated them after the uprising. Yet the movement's significance in Norway's modern history is far broader. For all his shortcomings, Christian Jensen Lofthuus was the first Norwegian peasant leader in recent centuries with real ability to gather and lead a large following from a wide area. Had the government not tempered firmness with real concessions, the episode might have become far more serious than it did. Even more than the *Stril* War, it made the Norwegian peasantry aware of common interests beyond the confines of their local parishes and districts, and confident of their own capacity for leadership and effective action. Lofthuus was thus the first in an impressive line of peasant leaders who throughout the nineteenth and into the twentieth century have advanced the status of their class within Norwegian society—one of the dominating themes of their nation's recent history—as well as its martyr.

There nonetheless remains an underlying ambivalence about the Lofthuus movement. On the one hand, it was profoundly conservative, the attempt to protect an ancient way of life against outside encroachments. On the other, it sought to break out of the legal constraints that restricted the peasantry to that very way of life by denying them access to more dynamic and profitable fields of activity. This dichotomy, too, would remain characteristic of the Norwegian peasant movement of coming generations, as it surely is of peasant movements in general.

From Stockholm, Gustav III followed these developments with keen interest. A Swedish informant in Norway wrote to him early in 1787 that 3,000 Norwegian peasants were ready to put themselves at the disposal of the Swedish king. Similar rumors in official circles in Norway and in Copenhagen itself did nothing to still the fears of the Danish government. In May 1787 Gustav III established a Swedish consul general in Christiania; it was well understood that his real purpose was espionage and contact with malcontents in Norway.[30]

Gustav had, however, determined two years before that Norway would have to be taken "in Copenhagen," that is, through the military defeat of Denmark, which would prevent the "republican spirit" behind an anti-Danish uprising in Norway from contaminating Sweden itself.[31] But Denmark could only be beaten if detached from its ally, Russia.

By the spring of 1787 it was this which above all concerned Gustav III. Following his coup of 1772, he had concentrated upon winning his cousin Catherine II's goodwill, largely to wean her away from her Danish commitment. By 1784 this attempt had clearly failed. The alternative would be to weaken Russia through military defeat, removing the threat of Russian intervention in Sweden's internal affairs, and clearing the way for a showdown with Denmark and the annexation of Norway, thereby breaking Sweden's encirclement.

During the Crimean crisis of 1783–84, Gustav had vainly hoped for a new Russian war with Turkey. By 1787, such a conflict was clearly imminent. Gustav thus envisioned an opportunity to strike at Russia while the bulk of its forces were engaged against the Turks far to the south.

Gustav was no less mindful of internal considerations. The *Riksdag* of 1786 had revealed the extent of opposition among the Swedish and Finnish aristocracy. An audacious and successful campaign against the hereditary foe might once again rally the nobility around their king, while giving him the chance to increase his powers. To J. A. Ehrenström, Gustav complained in the fall of 1787 that he had been young and inexperienced when he had adopted the constitution of 1772, which now caused "embarrassments." His sister-in-law, Duchess

Hedvig Elisabeth Charlotta, reported him to say, about the same time: "The Swedes seem to have tired of a mild and peaceful regime and to long for stricter treatment. If we had a war, they might become more tractable. And who knows whether they may not someday have their way?"[32]

That fall the anticipated war broke out between Russia and Turkey. Gustav now sought support from France, Great Britain, Prussia, and the Ottoman Porte. France was strongly opposed to any Swedish aggression. Britain and Prussia, while not anxious to see Russia overwhelm Turkey, remained noncommittal. Only the Porte promised subsidies, which in the end were never paid.

Denmark-Norway was technically bound to its defensive alliance with Russia. Yet it seemed evident that Copenhagen, deeply involved in internal reform and still anxious about the volatile situation in Norway, would gladly avoid involvement. Bernstorff had, moreover, little desire to see Denmark's over-mighty ally strengthened still further. In October 1787, Gustav III paid a surprise visit to Copenhagen, where he sought a guarantee of Danish neutrality in the event of a Swedish-Russian conflict. It was to no avail: Bernstorff was prepared to do anything possible to improve relations with Sweden—anything that did not violate Denmark's treaty obligations to Russia.[33]

In another sense, Gustav's visit to Copenhagen was of greater import, for it revealed the extent to which old enmities had given way to a new sense of a common Scandinavian identity, especially within intellectual circles in the Danish capital. *Minerva* wrote:

Surely it is a joyful and captivating sight for every Scandinavian to see the peoples of the three kingdoms, represented by their monarchs, wander together in friendship, hand in hand. What more beautiful, what symbol more striking to the senses of the concord, friendship, and good understanding so longed-for between these nations, which proximity, common origins, common interests, language, customs, which everything unites![34]

Thus although Gustav did not obtain the assurance he sought, he felt little threat from Denmark-Norway. He was determined to seize the opportunity to attack Russia and meanwhile turned to other expedients. In 1783 Russian administrative and judicial reforms in the Baltic provinces had aroused much resentment among the Baltic German nobility, a situation Gustav instructed his minister in St. Petersburg to watch closely already in the fall of 1786. Now in the fall of 1787 he sent J. A. Ehrenström on an ostensibly private visit to Livonia and Estonia, not only to sound opinion but to seek to stir up a noble revolt. Both Ehrenström and the Swedish minister in St. Petersburg reported much discontent among the Baltic nobility but put no faith in their support, since they were too dependent upon Russian state service and paralyzed by the fear of their own serfs, whom Ehrenström believed to be "devoted heart and soul to Sweden." At the appearance of the first Swedish troops, he reported, the latter would rise in rebellion, as much against their own masters as against Russian overlordship, in expectation of their freedom. Nonetheless, during the war that followed, Gustav never attempted to strike at Russia by this means, damaging as it might have been. Other strategic considerations aside, he was apparently no more prepared to stir up the peasantry of the Baltic provinces—close to his own domains —than he was in Norway, for fear of repercussions in Sweden and Finland.[35]

At the end of 1787 Gustav also sent Lars von Engeström to Warsaw to seek to mobilize Polish support against the Russians and to encourage rebellion in the former Polish lands lost to Russia in 1772.[36] He thus pursued the time-honored ideal of a Swedish-Polish-Turkish common front against the Muscovite.

Thanks largely to reforms since 1772, Gustav was meanwhile able to raise forces totaling some 40,000 men, the largest thus far assembled by the Swedish monarchy. Colonel Toll worked out a plan of attack. Following the spring thaw, the Russian Baltic fleet was expected to depart for operations against the Turks in the Mediterranean. The Swedes would then land their main force near St. Petersburg, which it would seize before that city's defenses could be organized.[37] The king justified his warlike preparations by claiming a threat from Russia, but the Russians avoided provocation and few, at home or abroad, were misled by Gustav's allegations. Disquieting reports meanwhile came in regarding the inadequacies of the Swedish military dispositions, particularly in munitions and supplies.

Gustav III embarked for Finland with his fleet in mid-June 1788, "as though leaving for a festivity," as the younger Fersen described it. "In a word," the king wrote to Baron Armfelt, "it is like 1772," sanguine in the belief that his great enterprise was restoring social harmony and devotion to the crown. It was meanwhile essential to Gustav that Russia appear the aggressor, since his constitution of 1772 prohibited a war of aggression without the consent of the Estates, and since this might also provide Denmark with a pretext for remaining neutral.[38] On 28 June a border incident at Puumala provided the necessary provocation; later it was claimed that it had been staged by Finnish soldiers disguised as Russians. Gustav thereupon sent off an impossible ultimatum to St. Petersburg, demanding the return "for ever" of those parts of Finnish Karelia ceded to Russia in 1721 and 1743, the dismantling of the Russian Baltic fleet, and Swedish mediation in the Turkish war. It was also rumored that Gustav hoped to regain the Baltic provinces, even including St. Petersburg itself, and round out Finland to the White Sea.[39] The ultimatum was delivered on 12 July; already on 19 June the Swedes attacked Nyslott (Savonlinna) in Russian Finland.

The success of the Swedish war plan depended upon surprise and speed. Gustav opened the campaign with some 25,000 troops in Finland, as opposed to an enemy force of only about 15,000 in Ingria and Russian Finland.[40] The attack caused great alarm in St. Petersburg. Most of the Russian Baltic fleet, however, was still at Kronstadt, barring a landing near the Russian capital. On

17 July, the two fleets met near the island of Hogland (Suursaari) in the Finnish Gulf. The Swedes, under Duke Carl of Södermanland, might have won a decisive victory had they not run short of ammunition. As it was, the battle ended in a draw, and the landing on the Ingrian coast had to be abandoned.

The only alternative was now to advance overland against the Russian capital. The Karelian Isthmus was as yet only lightly defended, but the terrain was rugged and Swedish logistical deficiencies began to make themselves felt. At the beginning of August, Gustav attacked the Russian border fortress of Fredrikshamn (Hamina), but the operations were ineptly handled and soon broken off.[41] The campaign thus seemed to have reached a stalemate when events took a new and alarming turn: Gustav was confronted by the mutiny of a large part of his Finnish officer corps.

For months prospects of war had caused growing concern in Sweden and Finland. Although the council had gone along with the king's demand for defensive measures, it was strongly opposed to any thought of an offensive war. Yet through the boastful indiscretion of Gustav's favorites, his true intentions soon became an open secret.

It was widely feared that the time was now long past when Sweden could hope to stand up against the Russian colossus, even together with the Turks. Moreover, to those in the know it was evident that military preparedness was inadequate, despite recent reforms. There was meanwhile widespread mistrust in aristocratic circles of the king's despotic intentions. In his memoirs, the elder Count Fersen would later write: "The preparations for this monstrous war plan were not undertaken against Russia alone, but equally against the Estates of the realm, against the constitution, and council; in short, for the furtherance of absolutism." It was rumored that Gustav planned, upon arrival with his army in Finland, to hold a surprise *Riksdag* in Åbo to change the constitution. Duchess Charlotta was shocked in June to hear it suggested in society that the king's death would be the nation's only salvation. Like others, she feared "the greatest misfortunes."[42] Gustav's pretense of Russian aggression seemed a clumsy and cynical charade; there could be no mistaking the king's deliberate violation of his own constitution of 1772.

Opposition and alarm were greatest among the Finnish nobility, particularly those from the manorial region in the southeast, adjoining the Russian border, who were strongly represented in the officer corps. As noblemen, officers, and Finns, they had long held mounting grievances against the king for economic, constitutional, and military reasons, as has been seen. Although the rather vague and ambiguous autonomist movement seems to have declined somewhat following G. M. Sprengtporten's departure for Russia in 1786, it quickly revived with the outbreak of Gustav III's unconstitutional and poorly prepared war, and the peril to which it exposed Finland. Numerous officers resigned their commissions and went home even before the fiasco at Fredrikshamn.

On 9 August, a group of officers from the Finnish army corps met at Liikala, near the front, where they drafted a note to Empress Catherine II. In it, they declared the attack on Russia to be "in conflict with the rights of the nation, which we consider it no less incumbent upon us as citizens to protect than to fulfill our military duties," and proclaimed it the sincere wish of "the whole nation, and especially of the Finnish [nation]," that "eternal peace and neighborly relations" with Russia be established. As its "surest guarantee," they made bold to suggest that Russia return those parts of Finland that had been lost in 1721 and 1743. They thereupon requested the empress's "gracious views on how negotiations may properly be carried out with the representatives of the nation." The nature of her reply would determine whether they could "lay down their arms and return to that tranquillity upon which the well-being of the realm depends," or continue to bear them in a manner worthy of "honorable Swedish men when they know with certainty that it is for their fatherland that they defy perils and death." The note was signed by seven officers, including General Carl Gustaf Armfelt, the elderly commander of the Finnish army corps.[43]

While taking a desperate measure in the face of what appeared a dire threat, the authors of the Liikala note sought to use this very threat to turn the tables on their own king. Just as he was suspected of seeking to use the war to justify an increase of his autocratic powers, they hoped, with the backing of the Russian empress, to force Gustav back within the bounds of his own constitution or, better yet, to restrict even further the authority it allowed him.

Such an appeal was not without ample precedent in past decades, even in time of hostilities. Repeatedly during the Era of Freedom, Swedish factions—generally the Caps—had called upon Russia to bring pressures to bear against their domestic rivals. During the unfortunate war of 1741–43 the army in the field had on its own initiative sent an officer to Moscow to negotiate for peace, who may have suggested to Empress Elizabeth the idea of appealing to the Finns in 1742 to establish their autonomy under Russian protection. The concept of the social contract and its violation by the monarch is implicit in the words and actions of the insurgents, who included a number of G. M. Sprengtporten's disciples in the "independence" movement of recent years.[44] It was one of the leading separatists, Major Jan Anders Jägerhorn, who departed the same day to deliver the Liikala note to Empress Catherine in St. Petersburg.

When disquieting rumors reached Gustav III at Kymmenegård, he demanded that his officers swear an oath of allegiance. In response, the insurgents, now encamped at Anjala manor, prepared a declaration on 12–13 August, signed by 112 officers. "Concerned as citizens for the sanctity of the form of government to which we have sworn allegiance, the nation reserves to itself the right to judge the necessity of offensive war," it stated. "The conviction of the necessity of war, which, among a people intended by Nature for freedom, creates fighting men who cannot be defeated, has vanished." The military situation was hopeless: "the whole land is exposed and we have nothing but the generosity and humanity of the victors to rely upon." The insurgents protested their basic loyalty to the king in seeking themselves to mediate peace between him and the Russian empress, which function they could more advantageously fulfill than any foreign power. If the empress should refuse to make peace, they would "not leave their weapons while alive until the peace and security of the fatherland were assured."[45]

An unsigned copy of the declaration was sent to Gustav while it was widely circulated to other Finnish and Swedish military units and among the nobility at large. Thus was born the so-called Anjala Confederation, the cutting edge of the aristocratic resurgence throughout the monarchy.[46]

Arriving in the Russian capital, Major Jägerhorn delivered the Liikala note and conferred with the empress, with Russian officials, and with Sprengtporten. All quickly seized upon the opportunity the Finnish officers' mutiny and its appeal to St. Petersburg seemed to offer for separating Finland from Sweden and making it a Russian protectorate, encouraged by Jägerhorn on his own initiative.[47] Catherine II at length gave Jägerhorn a reply to take back to his confederates. Vaguely formulated and prudently unsigned, it urged the Finns to convene a "representative body" of their own, which could give "lawful sanction" to their decisions and which the Russian commanding general would aid and support. Only then might the empress be able to give expression to the "noble and benevolent sentiments she holds for the Finnish nation." These sentiments are set forth more clearly in her instructions to General Musin-Pushkin in Viborg, in which she spoke of an autonomous Finland under her own protection.[48] Like Empress Elizabeth's manifesto of 1742, Catherine II's reply to the Liikala note seems intended as a trial balloon to determine exactly how far the Finns themselves were prepared to go in breaking with Sweden.

With his army paralyzed by mutiny and his fleet now blockaded by the Russians at Sveaborg, Gustav III was in desperate straits. He appealed secretly to France, but also to Britain, Prussia, and even Denmark to mediate peace with Catherine II. He even contemplated abdication. In the midst of this situation, he received what should have been the crowning blow, the news that Denmark intended to intervene militarily in support of its Russian ally. It produced just the opposite effect, and Gustav is supposed to have exclaimed, "I am saved!"[49] The Danish declaration gave him the opportunity to leave Finland and appeal to the broader masses of his subjects to rally against the nation's enemies, external and internal. By late August he was back in Stockholm.

Nothing could have been less welcome to Copenhagen than a war between Sweden and Russia. Count Bernstorff had hoped that Gustav III might be restrained by his constitution, but once he attacked Russia there was no question that Denmark would have to come to its aid. Only the Russian alliance could prevent the eventual loss of Norway to the Swedes. Yet Russia's very success against Sweden could force Copenhagen into still greater dependence upon St. Petersburg. The greatest danger was indeed that the Russians might succeed in taking Finland, finally removing their main source of contention with Sweden and hence their basic motive for an alliance with Denmark.

Involvement in the war threatened moreover to play havoc with internal reform. Available funds would have to be diverted to military needs, which meanwhile would make impossible the economies necessary for Ernst Schimmelmann's reform of the currency and state finances. In Norway the internal situation was still disquieting.

All these factors affected the nature and extent of Danish support for Russia. The crown prince, then visiting Norway, was all for throwing the monarchy's full military strength—40,000 men and forty-six warships—into the fray and seeking from Russia both subsidies and the guarantee of any conquests from Sweden. Bernstorff was determined to restrict participation to the bare minimum required under the Russian alliance: 12,000 men and fifteen warships. Since these were stipulated as an auxiliary force, Denmark need not formally declare war on Sweden. He justified this approach on the grounds that both Britain and Prussia seemed likely to intervene if the odds against Sweden should become too great.

It was Bernstorff's sober view that prevailed, in accord with the mood of the country. At a time when public opinion was coming to play a growing role in public affairs, there was practically no reflection of anti-Swedish sentiment in Denmark or Norway. *Minerva* could well write, "Every honest man in all of Scandinavia wishes for peace between Denmark and Sweden." The Danish government did its best to assure the Swedes that it acted out of necessity and hoped for the speedy return of good relations.[50]

Given its limited scale, the Danish diversionary action would have to be mounted from Norway, making use of the Norwegian part of the army, which in recent years had been badly neglected. Arriving to take command in early September 1788, Prince Carl of Hesse found "everything in complete chaos." The year before, during the peasant uprising, the government had hesitated to strengthen the Norwegian army out of concern over its dependability and had sent Prince Carl on only a short visit, lest as a prince of the blood he be welcomed as a rival focus of loyalty.[51] Nonetheless, by 24 September, after hectic preparations, Prince Carl crossed the Swedish border at the head of 10,000 Norwegian troops and advanced cautiously on Gothenburg. The Swedes were even less prepared, with only some 4,000 poorly equipped troops in that sector. On 29 September, the Norwegians encircled and took prisoner a force of 806 Swedes and ten cannon at Kvistrum.

The Danish-Norwegian intervention had scarcely gotten underway when it was brought to an abrupt halt. Following his return from Finland, Gustav III whipped up Swedish resentment against Danish perfidy and mobilized fresh forces, with which he hastened to the relief of Gothenburg. More important, Denmark's action produced the very reaction that both Bernstorff and Gustav III had anticipated: the intervention of Britain and Prussia. Thus Gustav's optimistic calculations proved largely justified. The initiative came from the British minister in Copenhagen, Hugh Elliott. Acting without the prior knowledge of his government and backed by his Prussian colleague, he demanded that Denmark cease hostilities or face British and Prussian military intervention. Already by 8 October the two ministers mediated an armistice and the withdrawal of the Norwegian force from Swedish territory. The Russians were understandably indignant but impressed with the threat from London and Berlin. By April 1789 Catherine II notified Copenhagen that she would not demand further military support, and in July Denmark declared its neutrality for the rest of the war.[52]

From the strategic viewpoint, Denmark-Norway's brief participation was only a minor episode in the war. Indeed, its greatest effect was to arouse a warlike spirit in Sweden that had heretofore been lacking. Its consequences for the Danish monarchy were meanwhile far from negligible. Although it helped revive Norwegian loyalty following the recent troubles, Gustav III and the Swedes became more hostile to Denmark than ever before and more convinced of the ultimate necessity of seizing Norway, where Gustav continued to seek every opportunity to fish in troubled waters. Worst of all, despite a Russian subsidy of a half-million *rigsdaler*, the financial burden of the war wrecked Schimmelmann's carefully constructed program of financial reform. The opportunity was lost which would thereafter never be regained before Denmark's state finances finally collapsed in 1813. The consequences would be far-reaching. In the short run the financial strain set back the impetus of social and economic reform. Faced with an extraordinary war levy, the *Ritterschaft* in Schleswig-Holstein again demanded recognition of its special corporate status within the state.[53]

Far more than the Danish-Norwegian attack, however, the behavior of the officers in Finland aroused a storm of indignation among the broader masses of Gustav III's realm. On 29 August Colonel Curt von Stedingk wrote to the king that "the old project of M. de Sprengtporten, to make Finland a republic," was gaining ground among his Finnish colleagues. "I see only one way, Sire, to stop the progress of this evil," he urged, "that is to place yourself at the head of the Finnish people. . . . Your Majesty will have all of the people for you. The gentry will have to give in."[54]

The idea can hardly have been a novel one to Gustav III; since the war had failed to unify the nation, he would have to revert to his strategy following the *Riksdag* of 1786, of playing the lower orders off against the aristocracy. Even before he left Finland there was ample evidence that the officers' mutiny had brought to the surface old class antagonisms. Gustav wrote from Åbo on 27 August, "I found, all along my way, clergy and burghers who made the greatest protestations of their inviolable attachment to me and to Sweden, and their horror over what is taking place." By early October Stedingk reported that the insurgents' efforts to gain popular support in Finland were getting nowhere; the common people accused them of cowardice and treason, and emissaries from villages came to Stedingk to assure him of their determination to defend their king.[55]

The Finnish peasantry were particularly outspoken in their loyalty, and numerous parish meetings were held to condemn the treachery of the officers. Behind their reaction there lay not only traditional antipathies toward Russians and aristocrats but also the fear that the Finnish nobility would gladly accept Russian overlordship to gain the same power over the peasantry as the nobles of the Baltic provinces, to whom many were closely related. Thus the village elders of Hollola parish stated:

> We, as simple peasants, cannot comprehend, nor do we wish to speak of that noble-minded attitude, which is alleged to have been behind this otherwise unheard-of action, but consider it the most infamous step, for it was taken, so we have heard, for the purpose of forging chains for us and our children, that under the pretext of calling ourselves independent we thereby become eternal slaves.[56]

The antiaristocratic reaction in Finland was well summarized by Professor Porthan of Åbo University by the end of 1788:

> But if there has been any suspicion that the Finns have felt the least inclination for such a stupid and criminal project, my countrymen have suffered great injustice. Perhaps four to six noble crackpots, who hoped thereby to oppress their countrymen and reduce them to serfdom on the Livonian model, were actually attracted to such an idea, which certain emissaries have dared to present to their confidants; but so crude a trap has been regarded by all thinking persons with as much horror as contempt, and the common people never heard it discussed. Our common people hate the Russians and their protection. . . . Their confidence in the king and mistrust of the gentry is also so great that only the greatest force could create the least inclination for such an insane idea.[57]

In Stockholm there was rioting against resigned officers who had returned from Finland already on 1 August, before the beginning of the Anjala mutiny; it was rumored that Police Master Henrik Liljensparre himself was its secret instigator. Anonymous pamphlets appeared, accusing the officers—and by implication the nobility as a whole—of cowardice and treason, which its victims were likewise convinced were inspired from on high. News of the Anjala Confederation raised emotions to a fever pitch.[58] In October Duchess Charlotta wrote apprehensively in her diary: "The king's action in allowing the people openly to express their views may unfortunately become fatal to him, for it is always dangerous when the mass of the people is permitted to mix in the affairs of state. . . . The masses are much too fickle and can as easily be persuaded to oppose the king as to back him."[59]

Gustav III arrived in Stockholm from Finland on 1 September. He transferred the city's regular garrison to Skåne and confided its defense to its burgher militia, which, the diarist Hochschild sniffed, "went to all the extremes to which military enthusiasm can give rise when combined with the burgher spirit."[60]

The king thereupon departed for Dalarna, where with his sure sense of historical drama he appealed to the local peasantry for their support on 14 September at the same place in Mora where his ancestor, Gustav Vasa, had called upon their ancestors to rise up against the hated Danes in 1520. The response was overwhelming. The Dalecarlians raised a volunteer corps. Their example was quickly followed in neighboring Hälsingland and Värmland, as well as in Gothenburg and Västerbotten.[61]

Alarm and consternation seized the nobility, among whom wild rumors circulated. It was widely feared that Gustav intended to place himself at the head of a peasant host, which would hail him as an absolute monarch, and march on Stockholm. Many nobles hid their valuables and discretely left the capital. Duchess Charlotta believed "the least shift in the wind" might set off an uprising of the Stockholm populace and "horrible atrocities." Nils Rosén von Rosenstein feared all the excesses of the Gordon Riot of 1780 in London. There was talk of bringing over insurgent units of the army from Finland to defend the capital. Throughout the provinces the cry was raised to "break the gentry."[62] From Värmland, Baron Armfelt, in charge of peasant levies, wrote to the king at the end of October, "The time has come when we are more embarrassed by the zeal of your subjects than by the treason of the factious." To his wife, Armfelt confided: "The bitterness among the lower orders against the nobility is so great that one hardly dares to admit to being a baron or a count. They are talking of nothing less than killing and uprooting the whole pack of them. God help us out of this confusion!"[63] Civil war seemed imminent.

In view of Gustav III's recent apprehensions about fomenting peasant uprisings in Norway and the Baltic provinces, he clearly recognized his own appeal to the broader masses in the fall of 1788 as a desperate and risky step. The night before leaving Stockholm for Dalarna in September, he confided to Duchess Charlotta that he had never felt so undecided about what he was going to do.[64] Certainly he had no wish for bloodshed among his own subjects, for the ruin of the nobility, or even for its further alienation from the crown. The peasant and municipal levies unleashed even more frightening class antagonisms than Gustav and his confidants might well have been prepared for. After receiving a heartening demonstration of patriotism and loyalty from them, Gustav made as little use of the volunteer corps as possible. Most never left their home parishes. The aristocracy, meanwhile, could not but be impressed with its isolated and precarious position.

At the same time the king's situation in Finland improved. Even before returning to Sweden, Gustav III had recognized that the Anjala Confederation imposed a de facto armistice on the Finnish front, since St. Petersburg, hard-pressed by the Turkish war, would naturally seek to maintain the goodwill and cooperation of the insurgents.[65] He could thus leave the command in Finland to his brother, Duke Carl, who concluded a formal armistice. When the campaigning season was over by October, he sent most of his units home on winter leave, thereby dispersing them.

Through the late summer and into the fall of 1788, the Anjala confederates vigorously propagated their views within the Finnish and Swedish officer corps and the nobility at large. Their handwritten pamphlets strongly stress concepts of natural law and the social contract. "One must distinguish between legal and natural rights," reasoned "a Patriot." A "Finnish Officer" stated that since the Estates could only meet at the king's pleasure, the army

considered the rights of humanity and regarded with contempt those prejudices which deify the persons of kings and thus revere their whims, even their vices, and weigh them against the nation's will, rights, and consideration for the well-being of posterity. It found the king to be the first servant of the nation, and that his interest may thus never be other than society's, still less in conflict with it. . . . When the foundations of government are shaken, he does best who takes the strongest action to restore them. To condemn such action as illegal is to condemn the law itself, which has not provided any means to uphold the nation's rights.[66]

Numerous constitutional projects were discussed, aimed at limiting arbitrary power, securing the position of the bureaucracy and of regular procedures, largely inspired by the old constitution of 1720.[67]

By September the Anjala insurrection was at its height and probably had the support of most of the army and naval officers in Finland.[68] The duke himself was persuaded to back the demand for a *riksdag*. Yet at that very time, the confederation began to break down under its own internal contradictions. The majority of its adherents sought only what the Liikala note called for: peace, a *riksdag*, and the strengthening of the constitution; at most they also desired some kind of special status for Finland under the existing monarchy. Catherine II's reply to the Liikala note and the intrigues of Sprengtporten and his confidants which followed, however, revealed that they had been manipulated into working toward Finland's complete separation from Sweden. For most, including old General Armfelt, this realization was both disillusioning and humiliating, and they sought individually to make their peace with the king. The Sprengtportians and the Russians had overplayed their hand, and they now turned to rash expedients. In December a few local gentry held a "diet" at Paaso manor on the border, at which they declared Finland's independence, elected Sprengtporten their leader, and appealed to Catherine II for armed support.[69]

The same month, Gustav III issued a proclamation to the Finns, pointing to the sad fates of Poland, Courland, and the Crimea, "which the promise of an illusory independence have misled into helplessness, deprivation, and misery."[70] One may indeed wonder what might have become of Finland had it fallen under Catherine II's suzerainty in 1788, rather than under Alexander I's twenty years later.

By the turn of the year, Gustav III was able to arrest most of the Anjala confederates. Only a few dedicated Sprengtportians, including Jägerhorn, made good their escape to Russia, thereby branding their movement all the more clearly as a foreign intrigue.[71] After two years of hearings, the supreme military tribunal sentenced to death eighty-seven officers, who appealed to the king's mercy. All were pardoned but one, who was to serve as an example. But the execution of Colonel J. H. Hästesko in 1790 left a continuing legacy of bitterness.

On 8 December 1788 Gustav III at last announced the convening of the Estates at the end of January. To fight the Russian war he had incurred large debts, and a new campaigning season was approaching. There was no way out of a *riksdag* to obtain the necessary funds. But circumstances had radically changed since the previous summer. The enemy was in winter quarters; the Finnish insurgents were disconcerted and their leaders arrested; the aristocratic opposition was in ill repute. Rather than forcing a humiliating peace and constitutional restraints, a *riksdag* could now strengthen the nation's defenses and the king himself. If need be, it could provide the opportunity to crush the opposition.

The announcement, according to Duchess Charlotta, came like a "bolt out of the blue." It was feared in aristocratic circles that Gustav intended to seize absolute power, backed by the lower classes.[72] The rumor circulated that he had deliberately provoked the Anjala conspiracy to flush his opponents into the open and brand them with treason. In January 1789 R. F. Hochschild recognized once again the social tensions of the *Riksdag* of 1771–72:

> In connection with the approaching *Riksdag* there arose those questions of the rights of the other estates in relation to those of the nobility, which have ever been so unfortunate for Sweden. They are talking about the right of commoners to hold all official positions, the leveling of those advantages which manors and noble properties enjoy as opposed to other types of land, and similar matters, based upon and sanctioned by the privileges that have always existed, and this can only serve to sow the seeds of discord, with consequences ever perilous for this country.

When a high official sought to remonstrate over the favor he showed toward the other orders, Gustav replied, "What should I do when the nobility want to drive me out of the kingdom?"[73]

The elections, held as quickly as possible, produced the anticipated results: large royalist majorities in three of the Estates. Many of the local electoral assemblies petitioned for the punishment of traitors to the realm; Helsingfors (Helsinki) further instructed its representative to the Burgher Estate to demand an end to all remaining distinctions of birth in civil and military appointments.[74] The nobility, meanwhile, showed that its spirit was by no means broken. Around 900 of its members attended the *Riksdag*, the overwhelming majority belonging to the opposition. They were determined to defend the nation's constitutional liberties and thereby revindicate themselves in the eyes of their countrymen.

Gustav III opened the *Riksdag* in Stockholm on 2 February 1789 with a masterful speech stressing the perils that faced the realm. He pointedly praised the loyalty of his Finnish subjects, "except for a small number of flagrant traitors and criminals," and of the peasantry, who had been the first to rally to their king, as in Gustav Vasa's day. Pursuing this historical analogy, he invoked the memory of

> that frightful century of the Kalmar Union, when we were oppressed by foreign tutelage under the pretext of the defense of our rights, but which had no real effect other than to increase the power of the high and mighty, to serve the ambition of certain individuals, all at the expense of the public good. Remember how much blood these false friends cost you, how much discord and desolation they caused among you; recognize their language and their misleading promises. Compare them with the proposals that the enemy is making to you today.[75]

Gustav's appeal failed to produce the unity of purpose he strove for. His actions showed that he was determined to solve the financial problem as expeditiously as possible by circumventing the noble opposition. Already the following day, the king called for a secret committee to decide with him all matters affecting the independence and security of the realm. Its broadly formulated charge would allow the king to remove from the purview of the *Riksdag* as a whole virtually any question that might be politically explosive, to be dealt with in privileged secrecy by a select group presided over by himself. The Secret Committee, moreover, was now for the first time to include six representatives from the Peasant Estate; thus even if the Nobility elected members of the opposition to its twelve seats on it—as it did—they would still be outnumbered by the eighteen committeemen elected by the other three Estates, since voting on the committee was by head. The noble opposition fought to limit the powers of the Secret Committee. They meanwhile pressed for their vindication by the other Estates against all the unjust accusations against them.

Valuable time was lost, confirming Gustav's belief that the aristocratic opposition must be broken by forceful means. An alleged insult to his handpicked *lantmarskalk*, or speaker of the House of the Nobility, allowed him to bring matters to a head. At a plenary session of the Estates on 17 February, he roundly castigated the nobility for their lack of cooperation, in contrast to the loyalty of the rest of the nation. Their behavior, he warned, showed the "old anarchical spirit, which has long been nurtured in darkness," and which threatened to "revive that aristocratic power which I believed I had crushed already at the beginning of my reign." "Who cannot still recognize here," he continued, "those who, so long as they held power, governed the state with an iron sceptor?" In response to those who accused him of being "Europe's most absolute sovereign . . . I declare to you for the second time . . . that I renounce sovereignty for all time, and that even if disorders should cause it to fall into my power, I will never retain it; I regard it my glory to be the true defender of liberty."[76] His words still have the ring of 1772.

The king commanded the Noble Estate to leave the hall to prepare a formal apology to its *lantmarskalk*, and preemptorily rejected its leaders' requests to speak in its defense. When they had withdrawn, Gustav called upon the other Estates to designate delegates to consult with him concerning the privileges of the nonnoble orders and to enter into a "union, which will guarantee our own and the kingdom's common weal."[77] This formula was the king's answer—on his own terms—to the Anjala "Confederation" of the previous August. The burgher militia, some 3,000 strong, commanded the streets of Stockholm, and 1,200 Dalarna peasants, remobilized by G. M. Armfelt, bivouacked at nearby Drottningholm. Everything now pointed to that royal coup which the opposition had feared for the past year.

Meeting with representatives of the three nonnoble Estates, beginning the same evening, Gustav presented them with the draft of an "Act of Union and Security," which provided for a leveling of corporate privileges in return for greater power to the crown. On 20 February, after the Clerical, Burgher, and Peasant Estates called upon the king to guide the *Riksdag*'s continued proceedings, Gustav arrested and placed in detention nineteen leaders of the noble opposition, including old Count Fersen, to cow his adversaries into submission. This scarcely produced the desired effect; new leaders came to the fore, and many who had formerly sympathized with the king were sorely disillusioned by the *coup de main*, even within the royal family itself.[78]

The day after the arrests, on 21 February, Gustav read to a plenary session of the Estates his Act of Union and Security, and called for its immediate acceptance. This was answered by a great shout, affirmative among the three Estates, overwhelmingly negative among the Nobility. The king declared the Act of Union passed by the votes of three Estates, to which the Nobility could later accede.

The Act of Union amended the constitution of 1772, which otherwise remained in effect. It gave the king "full power to govern and defend the realm," including specifically the right to declare war, conclude treaties and alliances, grant pardons, "dispose of all royal employments," which must, however, be held by Swedish subjects, as well as to "administer justice and provide for the execution of the laws." Other affairs of state were to be "conducted in the manner he judges most useful." "The Swedish people" retained "the incontestable right to discuss and reach agreements with the king on all things concerning subsidies to the state"; the Estates might, however consider only proposals presented by the king.[79]

Important implications emerge from these broad formulations. The king's full disposition of official appointments swept away any constitutional guarantees for the preservation of administrative institutions or security of tenure for individual officials. To a largely office-holding nobility, this meant a deathblow to traditional Swedish liberties. The old royal council (råd), the bastion of aristocratic influence in government, now ceased to exist after five hundred years. A new standing government commission, the Rikets ärenders allmänna beredning, henceforth prepared routine administrative matters for decision by the king, who was free to seek advice when and where he might choose. A separate Ecclesiastical Commission handled church affairs of the same type. The judicial functions of the old council were assumed by a new supreme court (Högsta domstol), half of whose members were commoners.

As for the king's relations with the Estates, he was henceforth free to embark upon an offensive war without the restraint that had embarrassed him a year earlier. He now had the full power of legislative initiative. His unrestricted control over the bureaucracy, moreover, would give him the means to bring greater pressures to bear upon the Estates, particularly the Nobility, whose ranks were largely filled with officials. Yet the Estates were by no means reduced to insignificance. They retained the power of approving taxation, an effective guarantee that they would have to be called on critical occasions, and they could still present to the king petitions which he might find himself well advised to heed.[80]

Of greatest consequence in the long run were the social provisions of the Act of Union. It proclaimed that "all subjects enjoy the same rights, under protection of the laws." All had the right "to possess and acquire land," although the nobility was confirmed in its exclusive possession of immediate manorial demesne (ypperligt frälse). Further, all offices of state were henceforth to be accessible to "all subjects, of whatever birth or condition," excepting only certain "high dignities and principal offices of the kingdom" and court appointments, which were still reserved for noblemen.

The import of these clauses was amplified by specific royal ordinances. On 3 April Gustav issued the "Charter of the Rights of the Swedish and Finnish Peasantry," which granted them the same full disposition over their freehold property as noble proprietors exercised over their manorial tenancies. They were thus finally freed from surviving restrictions affecting their forest, hunting, and fishing rights, the free sale of their property, and their employment of farm laborers. The Act of Union opened up for purchase by commoners most noble land, in the form of outlying manorial tenancies (*frälse strögods*). In a separate ordinance on 21 February, the king confirmed hereditary tenure for peasant tenants of the crown and restored to them the right and first option of acquiring their tenancies through freehold purchase, first granted in 1723, which he himself had suspended in 1773. These provisions would lead to an impressive rise in peasant freeholding and hence in the status and prosperity of the peasantry in Sweden and Finland by the early years of the nineteenth century.[81]

The deceptively moderate language of the Act of Union, its qualifying clauses regarding both land and office, as well as the confirmation of all privileges not affected therein, reflect Gustav's persistent hope that while stripping them of their remaining power, he might still in time reconcile the nobles. The act nonetheless satisfied long-standing demands of the Clerical and Burgher Estates for a career open to talents in the service of the state. The remaining restrictions concerning the highest offices in effect meant little, for the king could—and subsequently did—ennoble bureaucrats of common birth to qualify them for such positions.

Additional concessions to the Clerical and Burgher Estates further rewarded them for their support, even at the cost of compromising to a degree the king's administrative freedom under the Act of Union itself and his earlier economic liberalism. Gustav made assurances of the security of tenure for clergymen and lower functionaries, and permitted the reestablishment of certain town and guild monopolies in trade and manufacture; nevertheless the government thereafter did little to fulfill these promises.[82]

The House of the Nobility stood firm in its rejection of the Act of Union, on valid legal grounds. Its passage had flagrantly violated the constitution of 1772 in three ways: it had not been submitted to the council in advance; it had been passed in plenary session immediately following its proposal; and it affected the privileges of one Estate without its own concurrence.[83] In the end the king's handpicked *lantmarskalk* was induced to sign the act on behalf of the Nobility, which did not, however, accept it formally until the *Riksdag* of 1800.

Gustav III now turned to the financial problem. He revealed to the Secret Committee that by the end of 1788 the national debt had risen to some 10,300,000 *riksdaler*, over four-fifths of which in foreign loans. The expenses of the campaign of 1789 in Finland moreover threatened to double the debt. The Secret Committee prepared a proposal which it submitted to the entire *Riksdag*. Both the old and the anticipated debt, up to the amount of 21,000,000 *riksdaler*, were to be guaranteed by the Estates and administered by a new National Debt Office (*Riksgäldskontor*), controlled by deputies of their own choosing. The

National Debt Office was empowered to raise foreign loans and issue bills of credit (*kreditsedlar*) in the form of interest-bearing bonds, limited "to begin with" to 5–600,000 *riksdaler* and to be redeemed within one or two years. The king bound himself to incur no further debts without the consent of the Estates.

Following hard upon the triumph of the Act of Union, this finance plan required substantial concessions from Gustav III. The precedent was set that budgetary matters could no longer be dealt with in privileged secrecy but were the legitimate concern of the entire *Riksdag*, hence of the nation as a whole. The Estates emerged with greater financial power than ever before.

Only with great difficulty could the Noble Estate be persuaded to join the others in accepting the finance plan. It now prepared to fight a last-ditch battle over the duration of the annual subsidy to the crown. The Nobles demanded that this be granted for two years only, to compel the king to hold a *riksdag* upon its expiration, and on this matter it began to gain some hearing in the other Estates. Gustav countered by invoking his constitutional right to convene the Estates at his own pleasure and insisted that the success of the finance plan required a grant of unrestricted duration. The Clergy and Burghers accepted, after some debate, a subsidy to continue "until the next *riksdag*." When the Peasants hesitated over the size of their share of the proposed taxation, the king summoned them to the royal palace and harangued them into acceptance.

On 27 April Gustav appeared at the House of the Nobility and claimed his seat under the shield of the Vasa family. He appealed for passage of the grant for an unlimited period as essential to the nation's security. On the square outside a large crowd gathered in an ugly mood, once again inspired, it was averred, by Police Master Liljensparre. Hochschild, and surely others as well, feared a "massacre" if the Noble Estate defied the king's demand—although he scoffed afterward, "that miserable rabble could easily have been dispersed by a few courageous souls."[84] In this ominous atmosphere Gustav called for an immediate vote by acclaim, which was answered by mingled "yeas" and "nays," upon which the king declared the motion passed. When he departed, the crowd outside cheered and broke up.

The day after, on 28 April, the *Riksdag* of 1789 was formally dissolved and the last of the detained noblemen were released, only a week before the French Estates-General were to convene at Versailles. Gustav III had gained an impressive victory over his adversaries. "Without money, without support, with an inactive fleet and a half mutinous army," Count Adolf Ludvig Hamilton, one of his bitterest opponents, later wrote, "he had the whole North against him— Russia, Denmark, and Sweden. In a few months the Danish attack was frustrated, Russia still on the defensive, and Sweden . . . in chains at Gustav's feet."[85]

Despite the claims of his enemies, however, the Act of Union and Security of 1789 did not make Gustav a complete autocrat. Nor was it to remain in force for more than a generation in Sweden. Yet for the sake of this incomplete and ultimately transitory concentration of power, Gustav had resorted to drastic and unlawful means when—in contrast to Louis XVI in the months that followed—he deliberately leveled those corporate privileges that underlay the whole aristocratic way of life he himself loved so dearly, to win the support of his common subjects. In the end it was this expedient, rather than the end he sought to gain by it, that proved his most enduring accomplishment in the broader perspectives of Swedish and Finnish history. Gustav III had gone full circle: by his coup in 1772, he had prevented the Younger Caps from leveling privileges; by his coup in 1789, he in effect finally fulfilled their program.[86]

In the process he deepened the chasm that now separated him from those formerly closest to him. ''The true situation can no longer be concealed,'' his own sister-in-law, Duchess Charlotta, wrote in her diary in February 1789, with a sense of historical drama worthy of Gustav himself:

We live in a time of general dissolution and lawlessness. Force and injustice possess the power while innocence vainly cries out for vengeance, a revenge which unfortunately will probably come too late, when the kingdom has been brought to ruin and thousands are reduced to misery. . . . The history of no time can show the counterpart to the horrors I shall now reveal. Ye kings and princes, who shall one day read this, tremble and refuse to take as your example him, who for all time must remain an object of dread and abomination, not only for his own land but for the whole world.[87]

Although the duchess would soon be deploring even greater ''horrors'' in France, the struggle between the king and the aristocracy in Sweden was by no means over.

The years 1786–89 were a climactic period in the Nordic lands, marked by reform, revolt, and war. Between them, obvious similarities and contrasts suggest themselves. There were insurrections in both Norway and Finland, subsidiary domains with particular grievances. Yet in Norway there took place a peasant uprising deriving from an appeal to the autocrat himself, against local conditions and servants of the crown, with social—although not political—implications that pointed toward the future. In Finland it was aristocratic holders of the king's own commission who rebelled in the name of constitutional rights against the attempted autocracy of their monarch, in a way that in essence looked backward socially—but forward politically. Yet this outward contrast can be misleading, for the officers' mutiny in Finland was significant in the context of its time not only in itself, but because of the much greater popular reaction that it aroused. It is this staunchly royalist and socially egalitarian movement in Sweden and Finland, firmly rooted in the radical traditions of the later 1760s and early 1770s, that bears analogy with the peasant insurrection in Norway.

The Northern war that broke out in 1788 has rightly been regarded as a crucial event in the history of the Swedish-Finnish monarchy. Aside from its international consequences, it led, through noble revolt and popular reaction, to the Act of Union and Security in February 1789. In Sweden-Finland war thus opened the way to epoch-making reforms. In Denmark-Norway, it had the contrary effect of slowing the impetus of a vigorous reform movement already underway and weakening its economic foundations for the future.

Events in Scandinavia during these years reflect developments elsewhere in the Western world. The Lofthuus movement in Norway recalls various other peasant uprisings in Europe at that time. Yet, occurring in one of the few societies in Europe that was no longer aristocratic in the traditional sense, it was directed not against noble landowners but against middle-class merchants and public officials. Halvdan Koht has compared it with Shay's Rebellion, which at that very time was taking place in rural Massachusetts.[88] In some ways, too, it would seem to anticipate the antiurban and antibureaucratic rebellion in the Vendée in republican France a few years later.

The Anjala Confederation meanwhile provides a classic example of the later eighteenth-century *révolte nobiliaire*, recalling reactions in defense of traditional liberties in, among other places, the Habsburg lands and in France during the last years of the Old Regime, especially after the convening of the Assembly of Notables in February 1787. The Anjala Confederation calls to mind the "confederations" of the contemporary Polish Republic, with their appeals to Russia to uphold Poland's ancient constitutional rights, such as the Confederation of Bar of 1768 and the later Confederation of Targowica of 1792.[89]

By the time the revolution—properly speaking—began in France during the late spring of 1789, Scandinavia had in effect already undergone its revolution. Here a number of later developments in France were already anticipated: royal reform in the name of efficiency, aristocratic reaction in the name of liberty, popular counterreaction in the name of equality. There was foreign war, the appeal by the defenders of the old order for help from abroad and by their adversaries to "*la patrie en danger*," a kind of "national guard," even the beginnings of a "*levée en masse*," the issuance of "*assignats*" of a type, the radicalization of expectancies, the clamor for the punishment of "aristocrats" and "traitors," and—as suggested—something like a "Vendéean" uprising.

Not all of these developments occurred throughout Scandinavia; they are most notable in Sweden-Finland. Nor did they even there follow what would later come to be regarded as the classic pattern and sequence of the French Revolution. Above all, the epochal reforms of 1786–89 in the Nordic lands were the work of the monarchs themselves. Denmark-Norway was an autocracy in theory, although it had long lacked a vigorous and reform-minded autocrat. Crown Prince Frederik, assisted by exceptionally able advisers and an effective bureaucracy, was thus in a position to undertake the reshaping of society within the kingdom by royal decree. Gustav III was—and even after February 1789 remained—in principle a constitutional monarch. Yet the war and the aristocratic revolt in 1788 allowed him in the spring of 1789 to exercise a Caesarian democracy by imposing reform from above. Under Scandinavian conditions at that time, so basic a restructuring of society could scarcely have proceeded either as far or as rapidly as it did had it not been mandated by an enlightened despotism.[90]

For all the alarms and excursions of these years, the forces were so unevenly balanced that this revolution could be carried out virtually without bloodshed. Its principal victims at the time were the Norwegian peasant Lofthuus, chained to his rock in Akershus fortress in Christiania, and the Finnish nobleman Hästesko, beheaded in Stockholm in 1790, who in themselves represent the antitheses in the great social conflict.

Georges Lefebvre has argued—building upon Alexis de Tocqueville—that the ideals of "liberty" and "equality" belonged before 1789 to different and largely antithetical political traditions, and that these only became linked in the French Revolution because Louis XVI elected to back the aristocracy in the defense of corporate privilege. The Third Estate thus had to win freedom from royal despotism to gain its basic goal of social equality.[91] In Scandinavia the crown placed itself at the head of the nonnoble orders and carried out social reforms that satisfied—in the main—their long-standing aspirations. The Nordic lands thus underwent a "revolution of equality," but not yet of political "liberty," whose aristocratic defenders were struck down by the alliance of crown and commonality.

Even so, the great reforms of 1786–89 did not yet abolish privilege as such. For this, the old traditions of the corporate society remained too deeply rooted, as they had been in 1770–72. What they allowed was the leveling upward of the privileges of the nonnoble orders. Eino Jutikkala has pointed to the paradox that the Swedish and Finnish peasantry emerged in 1789 as a "fully formed Estate," socially as well as politically, at the very time the old Estates system was breaking down at its upper levels, even though the privileges thus gained would ultimately clear the way for the peasant's full integration into national life. The Swedish Act of Union and declaration of peasant rights, like the abolition of the Danish *stavnsbånd*, in this respect differed fundamentally from the French Declaration of the Rights of Man and the Citizen, proclaimed a half a year later, with which it has naturally been compared.[92]

Still, nowhere in the Western world was the Old Regime as radically transformed, before the coming of the French Revolution, as in the Nordic lands. In Denmark-Norway, the strong hand of government created conditions necessary for the social and economic advancement of the mass of the people, particularly through the emancipation and regulation of tenant rights of the Danish peasantry. In Sweden-Finland the social reforms of 1789 formally sanctioned and henceforth encouraged a rise in the status and prosperity of the nonnoble orders which had long been proceeding and which is particularly notable from around 1780 on, following the socially conservative early years of the reign. Gustav III "restored the harmony between fact and law" in 1789, as George Lefebvre wrote of the Revolution in France which broke out later the same year. It was the Act of Union, rather than the coup d'état seventeen years earlier, that constituted Gustav's real "revolution."[93]

Above all, the status of the peasantry, comprising everywhere the overwhelming mass of the population, was improved. Even in Norway, where the Lofthuus movement was followed by a progressive liberalization in the economic sphere, the great reforms of these years represent the great divide in their social, economic, political, and cultural evolution.[94]

Finally, although neither the Lofthuus movement in Norway nor the royalist reaction to the aristocratic revolt in Finland can be regarded as nationalistic, both produced a heightened sense of identity among the peasantries of these lands, within the framework of traditional loyalty to the crown. Lofthuus gave the Norwegian peasants an awareness of their strength and common interests. And just as Gustav III had responded to the Anjala "Confederation" with an Act of "Union" of his own, a petition of thanks presented to Gustav in March 1789 by the Finnish representatives in the Peasant Estate, on behalf of their order throughout the "Grand Duchy of Finland," demonstrated that they too had an emerging sense of their own separate destiny.[95]

# CHAPTER 8

# A New Dawn for Humanity
# 1789–92

The problems confronting the Nordic lands in mid-1789 were their own, arising out of the momentous developments of the years immediately preceding. Yet henceforth they took on new meaning against the background of a vaster conflict of ideals and principles with the outbreak of the revolution in France.

Given France's preeminence in the Western world, no part of it could remain unaffected by the dramatic events taking place there. Yet reactions varied widely, according to place, social milieu, and local circumstance. From what has gone before, it should be evident that Scandinavia, and most particularly Sweden-Finland, should be highly susceptible to the new impulses from France.

The French Revolution was from the beginning a multiple revolution, involving the clash of various largely contradictory forces, and both in France and abroad it could appear in many guises, especially during its first years. In Sweden-Finland it was taken, in the light of its own bitter constitutional struggle, to represent above all the overthrow of royal absolutism, the crushing of "tyranny." It was thus welcomed enthusiastically by aristocratic supporters of the Anjala revolt and of the "Patriot" party in the House of the Nobility during the recent *Riksdag* of 1789.

In Stockholm G. G. Adlerbeth sternly lectured the king on the social contract and the obligations and limits it imposed on royal authority. Malla Montgomery-Silfverstolpe, who as a young girl had come to regard Gustav III as "a tyrant like Tiberius and Christian II" when her father was arrested for his part in the Anjala mutiny, thrilled to "republican principles" from France, while she "dreamed of Sparta and Athens." By the summer of 1791, Duchess Charlotta found "our *enragés*" among the court nobility furious with the younger Count

Fersen for attempting to rescue the French royal family from Paris and jubilant over their capture at Varennes, all the while "making insinuations aimed at our king." A few noble enthusiasts did indeed recognize the social dimension of the revolution but were prepared to accept it; for example, the diplomat Pehr Olof von Asp, an admirer of England, welcomed the voluntary renunciation of its corporate privileges by the French *noblesse* as the necessary price of political freedom.[1] The following chapters will have more to say about the impact of the French Revolution upon its devotees among the Swedish-Finnish nobility.

Less numerous but considerably more articulate was a small group of Stockholm *literati* of generally middle-class origins, dedicated with romantic ardor to the libertarian ideals of the later Enlightenment. Although several had enjoyed favor and patronage from the court, they had become disillusioned in varying degree with Gustav III's autocracy, particularly with his high-handedness at the *Riksdag* of 1789. Their leading figure was Johan Fredrik Kellgren, a stalwart defender of the Enlightenment and former collaborator with Gustav III in his dramatic authorship, whose letters largely summarize the first wave of enthusiasm for the French Revolution in Sweden-Finland.

Few Frenchmen could rejoice more than he, Kellgren wrote to Nils Rosén von Rosenstein, Crown Prince Gustav's preceptor, on 7 August 1789, over the triumph of "the good cause" and the breaking of "long-lived and consecrated oppression" in France. If this demanded the sacrifice of "a few hundred lives," so be it, in contrast to Sweden, which had just drawn "its last breath of freedom" without the courage or will to resist. He feared only that the uprising in France might result only in "needless bloodshed and even greater oppression," in which case "who could then dare to mention the word Enlightenment in connection with a monarchical regime? And would not philosophers, arsonists, and geniuses henceforward be considered as synonymous?" "Now heavens be praised," he wrote more confidently a week later,

> There is still a people on earth who feel themselves to be human beings!
> What matters it to us if they be hundreds of miles away? What lies farther
> than the sun, yet is it not the sun for us all? And for the friend of truth,
> is not the world his fatherland? And have I not wept like a child—like a
> man—at the recounting of this great triumph? Tell me, brother, you who
> are a historian, do Rome or Greece have anything so glorious to reveal?
> . . . This is not the uprising of a mob, which only rages and destroys;
> it is the rising of a people, which overthrows in order to build.[2]

"Who does not recognize the dawning of a philosophic light," proclaimed Carl Fredrik Nordenskiöld in his short-lived journal *Medborgaren* (The Citizen) in January 1790, "spreading its joyous rays to all thinking beings? Ignorance flees like the shades of night. . . . Providence has for all eternity manifestly ordained that Freedom closely follows Enlightenment." An even more exalted visionary was Thomas Thorild. After denouncing the ills of court and society in the tones of a Roman tribune of the people in his soon-suppressed *Den nye granskaren* in the mid-1780s and thereby gaining a following among the king's aristocratic opponents, Thorild had left in disillusionment for England, seeking "to explain all Nature and reform the whole world." In 1790 he returned to Stockholm filled with projects for transforming society, which he was convinced Gustav III, faced with the implied menace of the revolution in France, could not fail to implement through a "Tribunal for Reform and Enlightenment," presided over by Thorild himself as "court philosopher."[3]

Despite bitterness against Gustav III, other politically conscious Swedes took a more sober view of the tumult in France, which placed them in a painful dilemma. In her diary for January 1790, the king's sister-in-law, Duchess Charlotta, expressed a growing alarm over the rising tide of revolution in the Austrian and Dutch Netherlands, Geneva, Bern, Hungary, and elsewhere in Europe. As for France:

> To be sure, the despotism which existed there cried out for reforms, but in its place there has now arisen a crowd of petty tyrants and complete anarchy seems to reign. . . . While the people is thus the absolute master in France, holding its king in what amounts to imprisonment in his own capital, we have a king who under the mask of freedom is the most complete despot. . . . To allow one man alone to determine the destinies of a people cannot be right; there must be a law which imposes a limit to his ambition and injustice. Yet I can no more favor a republican form of government under which despotism can appear in an even cruder form. The best thing is undeniably a well-balanced division of powers, such as we had under the constitution of 1772.[4]

In his memoirs, the historian Erik Gustaf Geijer later wrote of the impressions created in his home in rural Ransäter parish in Värmland:

> War and revolution at a suitable distance may be enjoyed like dessert after a meal. It is remarkable what one can then endure. The most horrible events evoke only a breath of heroism. Frightened we were not. The fair speeches in the French National Assembly—as much of them as echoed far off in the forest—were a source of endless joy to us. We gave little credence to accounts of bloody scenes, since they did not accord with these words.[5]

Geijer was the son of a nonnoble ironmaster and thus belonged to the category of *ofrälse ståndspersoner*, persons of wealth and quality who did not fit into any of the four traditional Estates and thus lacked any political voice—a group in Sweden-Finland particularly susceptible to new ideas. Meanwhile among the broader strata of the burghers, clergy, and peasantry, the French Revolution at first created relatively little stir. Their social and economic grievances had been on the whole satisfied by Gustav III at the *Riksdag* of 1789. They could remain fiercely royalist while observing with benign approval how the French National Assembly sought to realize an apparently similar program of reform.

Among the aristocracy of the Danish monarchy, it was the high German nobility of the capital and the duchies, with their past traditions of imperial liberties, who reacted most enthusiastically to the news from France. "The kingdom of the Lord is at hand!" exulted Countess Luise Stolberg in July 1789, and a few days later:

> The respective ministers of Europe will surely say that the king of France has gotten what he deserved for having helped the rebels in America. . . . In a "well-Bastilled" monarchy the word Freedom must never be uttered under any circumstances: it is a kind of bell-weather which lures slaves to desertion.

Her brother-in-law, the poet Friedrich Leopold Stolberg, declared himself prepared, in this "dawn of a new era," to "sacrifice the ancient arms of the imperial counts of Stolberg to the cause of freedom." Adam Moltke, inspired by the speeches of Mirabeau, eliminated the "von" from his name and accepted disinheritance as a result. Friedrich Christian of Augustenburg, heir to the only ducal title in the realm, "wept like a child" over the fall of the Bastille. To Bernstorff he wrote how events in Versailles and Paris filled him with "horror, agitation, and joy," while to Schimmelmann he expressed his satisfaction that "the mightiest and most arrogant court upon which Despotism has raised its throne is the first of all to bend its neck." When the French complete their great task, wrote Countess Sybille Reventlow to Luise Stolberg in January 1790,

> they will find imitators. That is as it should be. It is in the nature of things. Europe will then come to consist entirely of republics, having gained in wisdom from the experience of so many centuries, through culture and Christianity. We shall perhaps surpass the Greeks, whom we so admire.

Steadfast in her idealism, Countess Charlotte Schimmelmann was heartened in July 1791 that "the Revolution in France shakes the base of the aristocratic hierarchy and its influence spreads throughout the entire region where blindness and the debasement of man prevail."[6]

Others were less sanguine. Count Bernstorff had not been uncritical of the old regime in France, but he had no use for popular movements. Already in 1774 he had perceived a tendency, under the influence of "an unhealthy philosophy which ruins the spirit and corrupts the heart," to "crush civil while appearing to defend personal liberty." The breakdown of respect for the law, the "shield" of the weak and "legitimate restraint" on the strong, would eventually compel all governments to become "military" as the only means to maintain order and public tranquillity. In July 1789 he foresaw dissolution and civil war in France, in July 1791 "a frightful despotism, the antithesis of the liberty to which they aspire." "It is besides," he added, "contrary to human nature to pretend that the people will obey when it believes itself to be the source of the law." Yet he showed at first little concern over the contagion of French ideas, secure in the belief that they could threaten only regimes that oppressed their subjects. Less jubilant than his wife, Charlotte, Ernst Schimmelmann wondered if the French would come to deserve what they sought, although in 1791 he still could not resist privately composing a statement of principles for an improved constitution for France in what a confidant acclaimed as "the true spirit of Rousseau, Mirabeau, and Kant." Ludvig Reventlow contrasted the "glorious" actions of the French with the ignominy of the Swedes, but unlike his intrepid Sybille was disturbed by the excesses of the crowd that stormed the Bastille.[7]

Among the Danish nobles within the kingdom proper, enthusiasm for the French Revolution seems to have been notably absent. Their political power as an estate had been broken in the 1660s, and their interests had by now become essentially those of manorial proprietors, which they shared with a growing number of nonnoble landlords. For this proprietorial class of mixed social origins, the French Revolution represented above all the dissolution of the legal and traditional bonds of discipline and respect in the countryside—bonds which, in their view, had already been dangerously undermined in Denmark by the agrarian reforms of recent years.

Evidence is scanty on their views, but again Ove Høegh-Guldberg, himself a recent *annobli*, would seem representative. Everywhere, he wrote on 6 August 1789, might now seemed to make right.

> In Sweden a king can without fear trample the rights of his people, and do so at a meeting of the Estates through the basest expedients and the manifest use of force. In France, where a king is good enough to revive from the dead the French Estates-General, this first diet is bold enough to strike down the royal authority itself.

After noting fearfully the simultaneous ferment in the Austrian and Dutch Netherlands and in Poland, Guldberg continued:

> A certain spirit of freedom has entirely won the upper hand in Europe and is protected, indeed encouraged, by the princes themselves. . . . It has captivated all, from the heads of states to their lowest and remotest members.[8]

The events in France, Guldberg wrote on 1 September 1789, were "altogether worthy of the 18th century, the philosophic age and its *Aufklärung*"— pointedly using the German word to describe the Enlightenment: despised root of the ills of his time. The lessons of past ages proved that "no constitution but the monarchical is suited to European states, and none can stand without it." Surely he touched upon the heart of the matter in his own mind when he added:

> The common people are little concerned with what form of constitution they live under. Rather, what they crave is to be free from taxes, from requisitions, from the maintenance of troops, from burdens. That is what they call freedom and that is what the French peasantry has now seized for itself. What it will now be interesting to see will be how well the demagogues will succeed in depriving the peasantry of these marvelous gains and in subjecting them once again to law, order, and taxes.[9]

If the Danish proprietors showed little enthusiasm for the French Revolution, the Danish urban middle classes, especially in the intellectual and reform-minded circles of the capital, were all the more likely to welcome the tidings from France. Henrik Steffens later recalled how his father, upon learning of the fall of the Bastille, solemnly gathered his sons around him and proclaimed:

> My children, you are to be envied. What a glorious, happy time lies before you! If you do not succeed in acquiring for yourselves a free and independent position, the fault will be your own. All estates, all the constraining bonds of poverty will disappear, the lowest will enter into equal battle with him who heretofore has been mightiest, a battle with equal weapons, on equal ground.[10]

The same news reached the poet Jens Baggesen in Germany, where he foresaw the leveling of "all Bastilles"; soon in Paris he danced on the ruins of that temple of despotism. Societies like Drejer's Club and newspapers like *Minerva* or *Kjøbenhavns Lærde Efterretninger*, which had already been much concerned with questions of agrarian reform, civic freedom and equality, and attacks on aristocracy, were alive with excitement. Already by the end of 1789, the gregarious Knud Rahbek, co-editor of *Minerva* and very much at the center of Copenhagen's club life, complained wearily:

> In Brabant there rages civil war,
> In France a war of words;
> That seems, I think, so near at hand
> When we are gathered here.

> But let the struggle never reach
> To Médoc, Pontac, and Bordeaux,
> To Épernay, Châlons, and the Rhine
> From whence there comes our wine![11]

Outside Copenhagen, bourgeois enthusiasm for the French Revolution was most manifest in the duchies, particularly in the old Holstein-Gottorp capital and university town of Kiel, and in Norway. From Christiania, *Stiftamtmand* Frederik Moltke wrote in the spring of 1790:

> The only question is how close we are to a revolution. That Norway's bold sons are aware of the progress of freedom in Europe and watch for the moment when they can obtain new advantages, and that they are more drawn to them than ever, seems to me evident.[12]

In Norway the Swedish threat continued to lurk in the background, and a small circle of merchants and entrepreneurs in Østlandet indeed intrigued with Gustav III's agents.[13] Otherwise, however, the middle classes of the Danish monarchy tended to look benignly upon the revolutionary transformation of France in the light of peaceful reforms already well underway under the aegis of a benevolent royal absolutism at home. The journalist Rahbek liked half-jokingly to call himself "a Jacobin in France but a royalist in Denmark"—a description which in general would aptly have fit his peers. Their exultation over the revolution in France thus fortified the popularity and stability of the Danish monarchy, as Bernstorff recognized. The press throughout the realm was filled with fervent protestations of loyalty to the royal house, especially to the crown prince.[14] Yet these very protestations were based upon certain fundamental premises.

Christian Pram, then editor of *Minerva*, wrote in September 1789 that the French people, "weary of the most unbearable oppression, casts off all bonds, that it may in full freedom choose the form of government that best suits the real purpose of all government, the true felicity of the people." The implication behind this and similar statements is clearly that the Danish monarchy, in contrast to the French, was justified because—and as long as—it fulfilled this goal. The idea had indeed been stated clearly by the Norwegian Edvard Storm in a speech celebrating the king's birthday at Drejer's Club in January 1788, printed in *Minerva*. Man, he held, was by nature free; the state was based upon a voluntary contract, "implicit if not explicit"; any act by which the state might limit individual freedom more than the general good required was "tyranny," against which the surest bulwark was "the Patriot's" right to "speak out against manifest abuses, even when these involve the high and mighty."[15] Newspapers and pamphlets, especially in Copenhagen, fill in the essential contours of what the friends of reform expected of the crown. It must be endowed with absolute power to override vested interests for the common weal, yet be ever responsive to the views of an enlightened public as expressed through a free press—what Jens Arup Seip has described as the ideal of "opinion-guided absolutism." These views were, moreover, distinctly antiaristocratic. "While one considered a republic the ideal form of government in principle," the jurist A. S. Ørsted later recalled, "absolute monarchy was considered the next best, for the autocrat could use his power to establish freedom and equality." "True monarchy,"

*Minerva* proclaimed, "is democratic." Increasingly the crown prince was referred to as the "first citizen of the realm."[16]

The underlying premises of this popular royalism nonetheless held implications which could not but eventually appear threatening to the existing state and society. P. A. Heiberg, who in 1787 had fiercely satirized aristocratic pretentions and ignorance in his *Rigsdalerens Hændelser* (The Tale of a *Rigsdaler*), returned to the same theme in a song (*Selskabssang*) for a private gathering in September 1790, which inadvertently came out in print:

> Orders and decorations are hung on idiots,
> Stars and ribbons go to noblemen alone.
>
> . . . . . . . . . . . . . . . . . . . .
>
> We teach no despotic principles,
> It is for equality among men that we strive;
> Nor do we, like the Jutland proprietors
> Wish for slaves and peasants for us to flay.

The same year Heiberg hailed Crown Prince Frederik's marriage with a "Processional Song" (*Indtogsvise*), which in effect publicly lectured the young regent on the views of the more advanced Copenhagen radicals:

> We seek not to censure princes' actions,
> But to warn them against dangerous intrigues.
> Alas! Kings are not gods!—Seldom do they see more
> Than other mortals; indeed, oft times, far less.[17]

Heiberg's reference to Jutland proprietors alluded to the attempt in 1790 of a group of them to remonstrate against the recent agrarian reforms, of which more below. This played directly into the hands of the antiaristocratic camp. Perhaps the most widely noted polemic pamphlet during 1790 was Niels Ditlev Riegels's anonymous *Jule-Mærker fra Land og By* (Christmas Omens from Country and Town), which satirized the Jutland proprietors' desire to reduce the common people to "beasts of burden and slaves." It also went so far as to call for the convening of the defunct Estates of the realm to review the state finances.[18]

Here Riegels tread on dangerous ground, for the very suggestion of a diet called into question royal absolutism under the *Lex Regia* and could be regarded as *lèse-majesté*. His pamphlet caused a sensation, not least in aristocratic circles. Even Countess Charlotte Schimmelmann, considered by her friends "*une furieuse démocrate*," was indignant over the wretched scribblers of the capital.[19] From Aarhus, Guldberg wrote to Bülow in October 1790 that the diet Riegels demanded would unfailingly follow the course of the French Estates-General, stripping the monarch of his power and establishing "French democracy."

My friend will see [he continued] that I have carefully read through this latest piece and have found that the spirit which manifestly prevails in it is the same as that which is now ruining lovely France. And it is just that spirit which reigns . . . in most of the writings in our time from Copenhagen. . . . One shudders to see, in almost every piece, freedom—lawless freedom—praised; all royal revenue called the people's money, which the king has no right to dispose of—a truth which the ruler himself may say to us, but which the people certainly may not say to him; the nobility—our innocent nobility—thoroughly abused; the rights of the peasantry asserted to the extreme, to the point of usurping all other legal rights, so that the great majority in our land . . . may be prepared to break forth, once the battery is prepared, and thus sink Denmark, which hardly possesses a twentieth of France's resources, into an abyss of misery and make us an easy prey for our ever unscrupulous neighbor [Sweden]. At the slightest outbreak Norway will be lost, and will surely become a republic of its own in accordance with the Norwegian-English spirit.

Guldberg's letters thereafter repeatedly dwell upon his alarm and indignation over the clubs and periodicals in Copenhagen—and to a degree in Christiania— as the source of the "light troops" of revolution.[20]

Concern in official quarters over the growing audacity of the press was reinforced by widespread peasant reluctance in Denmark to fulfill manorial labor obligations in anticipation of further, rumored government reforms and by the outbreak of popular disturbances in north Schleswig during 1790. Although these were quite evidently caused by food shortages following poor harvests the year before, the authorities feared wider implications. "Such was then the popular spirit spread by the French Revolution," the *amtmand* in Åbenrå wrote in his report.[21]

The government was vexed by the anonymity behind which the radical pamphleteers took cover. When the printer of Riegels's pamphlet refused to disclose its author's identity, he was fined under the press ordinance of 1773. A new ordinance was at length decreed on 3 December 1790. While it removed the arbitrary powers of Copenhagen's chief of police in press matters and placed them under the law courts, it also warned against the abuse of the press "in violation of the civil laws." The new ordinance was generally welcomed by informed opinion for providing a stable legal foundation for freedom of expression and for rejecting the clamor among conservatives for a return to censorship. Yet it also showed the government's concern about dangerous ideas and outside influences.[22]

The course of internal reform meanwhile continued in the Danish monarchy. State finances and currency naturally received a high priority. The unwelcome expenditures connected with the Swedish-Russian war were at least partially met by a special levy in 1789 upon all classes except the peasantry. The much-heralded finance plan of 1785 had to be abandoned, however, and was replaced in 1791 by a new one, which included the establishment that year of a central bank of issue for the kingdom, corresponding to the recently founded Altona bank in the duchies. While the government strove to economize, it concentrated primarily upon stimulating the national economy.[23]

In Denmark this meant above all continued reforms in the agrarian sector. After a recess of nearly two years, the Great Agrarian Commission reconvened in February 1790 to consider a range of problems connected with the abolition of the *stavnsbånd*. The most basic question was the future relationship between the manorial proprietor and his now emancipated peasant tenant. If the tenant farmer was no longer legally bound to the manor, should the landlord henceforth be bound by any obligations toward the tenant?

In the past the responsibilities of local administration had necessarily devolved largely upon the proprietor, who was compensated by the tax exemption of his demesne (*hovedgård*)—if of requisite size—so long as he maintained the existing number of taxable tenant farms on his manor. His property rights were thus restricted. Moreover, as he was ultimately responsible for the payment of the land tax for his tenant farms, numerous customary arrangements had evolved through which proprietors assisted their tenants in time of need, to keep their tenancies occupied and productive.

Since mid-century at least, an increasing number of landowners had come to recognize that the legal and customary burdens of manorial proprietorship could outweigh the advantages of an assured labor supply under the *stavnsbånd*. Free wage labor, hired as needed, could prove more profitable than the cumbersome and inflexible system of tenant labor obligations. Such landlords looked to England for their inspiration; there the landowner enjoyed the free disposition of his property and could contract freely with tenants and laborers, in accordance with the laws of supply and demand. Freedom, in their view, should work both ways. Such ideas were espoused by champions of peasant emancipation like Tyge Rothe—who somewhat paradoxically defended the restrictive *odelret* in Norway—Ludvig Reventlow, and certain members of the Great Agrarian Commission itself.

Opposed to this viewpoint was the ideal of peasant protection, tracing back to the beginnings of Danish absolutism, inspired first by fiscal and later fortified by humanitarian considerations. It had been exemplified by Henrik Stampe's modest reforms in 1769, which had aimed not only at creating a landowning peasantry but also at protecting it against the rich and powerful. Its leading theorist was the Kiel professor Johann Christian Fabricius, who in his *Von der Volks-Vermehrung insbesonderheit in Dänemark* (1791) attacked the existing manorial system throughout the realm but nonetheless compared Denmark, where the legal protection of tenant farms maintained a sizable rural population, with the duchies, where the absence of such protection resulted in an alarming depopulation of the countryside. Fabricius, too, looked to the English example—which impressed him with the pauperism created by the landlord's unlimited freedom of contract.[24]

On the Great Agrarian Commission, the most outspoken proponent of peasant protection was Christian Colbjørnsen, who since August 1788 was also *general-prokurør*, or juridical counselor to the Danish Chancellery. His basic attitude was summarized already in 1783:

> The rights of the tenant should be specified in law, and this law should, if it is to protect a weaker class against a more powerful one, be given such strength and consistency that the latter shall not be able, through its strength and the other's weakness, to disturb or hinder its effective enforcement.[25]

With the backing of C. D. Reventlow, this viewpoint won the support of the majority on the commission and led to important reforms. On 19 March 1790, a royal ordinance required that all tenancies be granted for the lifetimes of the tenant farmer and his wife. To Ludvig Reventlow, the commission "is too despotic in its attitude, seeks to prescribe everything in hair-splitting, fussy detail, so that everything must depend upon petty functionaries . . . and there is too much animosity and grudge against proprietors in all your undertakings," as he wrote indignantly to his brother, who replied that it was his "confession of faith" that short-term leases would be "the country's ruin."[26]

A year later, on 25 March 1791, Danish landowners were given some compensation when they were permitted, if they could not find a tenant for a farm in good condition, to reallocate its land to other farms, to existing crofts (*huse*) for agricultural laborers with less than three *tønder hartkorn* of land, or to set up two new crofts with six *tønder hartkorn* each. This allowed the proprietor somewhat greater flexibility in the exercise of his property rights, while also providing for the subsistence of the cotter (*husmand*) class, from which it was envisioned that seasonal agricultural labor for both peasant farm and manorial demesne would increasingly be drawn.[27]

With this solution to the problem of rural labor in view, another ordinance of the same date called upon proprietors to negotiate agreements with their tenants fixing the amount and nature of their labor obligations (*hoveri*) on each manor and providing for government mediation if agreement could not be reached. During the years that followed, numerous settlements were concluded. Many tenants commuted labor obligations into money payments, while a growing number purchased their leaseholds and were thereby released from *hoveri* altogether. The same ordinance forbade physical chastisement of the tenant farmer or his wife, as "offensive against the respect due them as themselves the masters and mistresses of households," although not of the tenant's hired help, who in fact performed most of his labor for the manor.[28]

"Except for the agrarian question, there is no topic which has set more hands, pens, and printing presses to work than the improvement of the schools," wrote *Kjøbenhavns Lærde Efterretninger* in 1790.[29] Education was, of course, a central preoccupation of the European Enlightenment. In the minds of the Danish agrarian reformers the cultivator must be literate and informed to profit from emancipation.

As seen, the school ordinance of 1739 had produced only limited results, but various enlightened landlords had interested themselves in the education of their peasants, inspired in part by such continental reformers as Basedow and Pestalozzi. Count Ludvig Reventlow played an innovative role in this respect, establishing model elementary schools on his lands, experimenting with an adult evening school and with teacher training. In his school regulation of 1788 for Brahe-Trolleborg manor, he stated:

> To become a tenant farmer it will henceforth be required, beginning in 1788, that one not only be able to read whatever is set before one, both in print and in script, but that one also be able to write in a good, legible hand and to reckon by the four basic arithmetical modes and [to practice] simple bookkeeping, as well as to understand all that is necessary for rational farming.[30]

His brother, C. D. Reventlow, sought to educate the children on Christianssæde manor "to become good human beings." On 15 August 1788, when he presented the first hereditary leases to crown tenants in north Sjælland, he stressed the importance of education to the success of the other reforms, while holding forth the humanistic ideal that "in all schools the cultivation of the mind and heart is more important than rote learning."[31]

In 1789 the crown appointed a seven-member School Commission, headed by Ernst Schimmelmann, who had likewise established schools on his estates, and including C. D. Reventlow; Ludvig Reventlow—who may at first have seemed too visionary—was added in 1791. In March 1791 the commission established a teachers' training seminary at Blågård, near Copenhagen, following the lead of J. A. Cramer, who had founded such a school in Kiel already in 1781. Admission to Blågård was limited to men of peasant origin, who were trained to teach reading, writing, arithmetic, and singing. The school opened with fourteen students.

From the start, the commission became the battleground of profoundly differing philosophies with far-reaching social implications, which largely deadlocked its deliberations for years at a time. The new *Kulturhumanismus* of the Revent-lows and Schimmelmann clashed with the orthodox traditionalism of Nicolaj Balle, bishop of Sjælland, with its emphasis upon the catechism, and the cautious utilitarianism of Prince Friedrich Christian of Augustenburg, which sought to limit the education of the broader masses to the minimum suitable to their menial vocations. As will be seen, it was not until 1814 that a comprehensive new school ordinance was finally adopted.

The education of the middle classes likewise attracted attention. Because the traditional "learned schools" and the University of Copenhagen remained pri-marily oriented to the training of clergymen and the wealthy employed tutors and sent their sons abroad, there was a growing demand for schools suited to the practical needs of middling men in commerce and the professions. Here again, private initiative took the lead, notably through the establishment in 1786 of the *Efterslægtsselskabets Skole* in Copenhagen, a *Realschule* on the new Ger-man model, by the Society for Civic Virtue (*Selskabet for Borgerdyd*). Govern-ment commissions were established in 1785 and again in 1790 to study secondary and higher education. The second commission was dominated by the bookish prince of Augustenburg, who took a real interest in this sphere of learning. Although little would be accomplished in these areas for some years to come, it was symptomatic of a new spirit that the Sorø *Rytterakademi*, which in 1782 had been opened to commoners, was closed in 1796.[32]

Since 1784, numerous periodicals and pamphlets in the capital hailed the reforms of Crown Prince Frederik and his advisers with the latters' blessings, whereas complaints against them were limited almost entirely to private conver-sation and correspondence. Yet in manor houses throughout Denmark there was clearly much bitterness. Many of the smaller landowners in particular had been economically hard-pressed in recent years. While the abolition of the *stavnsbånd* aroused their consternation, regulation of tenancy contracts caused outright alarm. The peasants seemed increasingly surly and insubordinate, the old rural society on the verge of dissolution. Yet few dared to complain publicly. When some Fyn proprietors held that the ordinances of 8 June 1787 on the rights of manorial tenants threatened to ruin the landowners, the government brought legal action against them, compelling them to beg for pardon.[33]

Proprietorial opposition came to a head in the summer of 1790, at the time of Crown Prince Frederik's marriage to Princess Marie Sophie Frederikke, the daughter of Prince Carl of Hesse. Aroused by the activity of the reconvened Great Agrarian Commission since February of that year, a large gathering of Jutland proprietors in Viborg prepared a message of congratulation to the crown prince; at the same time, *Kammerherre* F. L. K. Beenfelt drafted an accompany-ing statement of grievances signed by 103 proprietors. This document, with a similar message to Prince Carl, who was known for his conservative views, was presented by Beenfelt and *Kammerherre* Tønne Lüttichau on 18 August. It read in part:

> We indeed have cause to fear the general violation of our property, attacks upon our rights, which are sanctioned in law, and the suppression of our liberties, which will in time leave us without bread, lead to general dissolution, bring about the ruin of the land, and wreak misfortune upon posterity. . . . We experience one deprivation of our legal liberties after the other, through which our property rights are violated in what for us is the most humiliating manner.

The proprietors invoked the frightening picture of anarchy in France. They attacked the authors of the reforms, Cølbjørnsen in particular, for not acting as "honest Danish men," and enumerated the harmful effects from which they claimed they already suffered.[34]

The government was prepared to brook no opposition. Crown Prince Frederik promptly stated, "What has been proclaimed by royal decree cannot be changed." He forwarded the letter to the Great Agrarian Commission. Colbjørnsen published it, together with a sharp critique intended for "the tribunal of all just and thoughtful men," branding the proprietors with disloyalty for suggesting that the crown had acted tyrannically. Moreover, he accused the Jutland proprietors of having falsified signatures on their letter to the crown prince. The latter appointed a commission of inquiry, which called Beenfelt and Lüttichau to account and verified the allegation.

Colbjørnsen's attack was a bitter and not altogether scrupulous one, backed by royal approval and well calculated to stir up middle-class support. Indeed, as noted, it stimulated a wave of antiaristocratic pamphleteering, in which Heiberg and Riegels in particular made their mark. The doughty Lüttichau, however, who in 1784 had dared to accuse the government of growing despotism, was not so easily put down. He entered into a heated exchange of pamphlets with Colbjørnsen, who sued him for libel. His defense lawyer complained that society was breaking down into two camps: "He who shows any doubt concerning the rightness of Colbjørnsen's views is given the name of Aristocrat, while he who is of another opinion . . . is called a Democrat."

In the end Lüttichau was heavily fined, and the crown prince deprived him of his title of *kammerherre* for disrespect toward the inquest commission. He left Denmark in disillusionment, with the widespread sympathy of the opponents of reform, including Schack-Rathlou and Guldberg. In Germany he was received as a martyr to the cause of historic rights, was made an imperial count by Emperor Francis II and a privy councillor by the duke of Brunswick. But with his departure, overt opposition to reform among the Danish proprietorial class was effectively broken.[35]

In Sweden, as seen, the French Revolution added to the tensions created by the *Riksdag* of 1789 and the Act of Union and Security. Gustav III found himself largely ostracized by the nobility, many of whom resigned their court positions, and even by members of his own family. To G. G. Adlerbeth, he said in December 1789:

> I know what you think of my behavior at the last *Riksdag*, but I can assure you that I have saved rather than harmed the nobility, for had I not placed myself at the head of the faction which the nobility had then raised against itself, the other Estates would have gone much further. The nobility has meanwhile lost nothing essential.

Turning to events in France, he added: "It was fortunate for the Swedish nobility that those scenes had not yet taken place before the last *Riksdag*. Your fate, gentlemen, would have been worse, and the public's passions toward you harder to manage."[36]

Gustav III's repeated expressions of concern for his nobility in this period reveal his still unshaken conviction that despite its recent behavior it had its vital role—once it could be brought to recognize it. To the French *émigré* Marquis de Bouillé, he wrote in February 1792:

> We are trying to make them understand that in the eighteenth century it is necessary that this first order of the state be sustained by the stability of the throne and by its protection, and not in seeking to fight against it.[37]

Gustav evidently considered the Act of Union of March 1789 as at best a temporary expedient. He told P. O. von Asp the same month that Sweden's present situation allowed no solution other than "full power to the king"; yet he admitted that if the country should not have a "king"—one equal to his task—he could conceive of its eventually becoming a "republic." He was already thinking of reorganizing the Noble Estate or even the entire *Riksdag*, and during the next three years he continued to speculate about constitutional changes. By the end of 1791 he had immersed himself in the study of British institutions, particularly through Jean Louis De Lolme's *Constitution de l'Angleterre* in the Geneva edition of 1790.

By the time he convened his next *Riksdag*, in January 1792, Gustav was considering another coup to establish a new constitution, based on the English. This, it appears, would have created a bicameral legislature, with an upper house of twenty-four "jarls," elected by the nobility, and a lower house of 240, elected by the "people," with substantial property qualifications for both. The king would "communicate" with this legislature through ministers heading specialized government departments. The plan was farsighted and ambitious, anticipating the basic administrative and representational reforms of the nineteenth century in Sweden.

Gustav had early been drawn to the physiocrat Le Mercier de la Rivière's "legal despotism" and derived from him his lasting formula for the "true interests" of peoples—"liberty, security, property." This formula was repeated in Gustav's edict on freedom of the press in 1774 and expressed as "the true freedom of peoples, which is security of persons and property," in his letter to his ambassador, Eric Magnus Staël von Holstein, in Paris in December 1791. He had, however, also been attracted to Montesquieu's concept of an ordered hierarchical monarchy, which likewise underlay De Lolme's idealized description of the British constitution. By 1791 Gustav saw this as a surer means to effective royal authority than theoretical absolutism. "The nobility do not understand me nor do they understand their own interest," he stated early in 1792. "I am the nobles' friend and I cannot be king without a nobility. The king of England has more power than I do under the Act of Security."[38]

Meanwhile there was the continued war with Russia, which still threatened to destroy all he had thus far accomplished. The best he could hope for was to end the war without loss, but Prussian attempts at mediation during the winter of 1789 were contemptuously rejected by Catherine II. Fortunately, the Russians still had to deploy the bulk of their forces against the Turks. But the Swedes, too, were seriously handicapped. Their economic resources were badly strained. A devastating typhoid epidemic killed 10–12,000 people, most of them naval personnel, during 1789–90. An embittered and insubordinate spirit pervaded much of the officer corps, on occasion evidently hampering operations in the field.

In June 1789 Gustav III returned to Finland to take command of his forces. The following campaign was carried on in desultory fashion on land and sea by both sides, without decisive results. At the end of the year, Catherine II declared her conditions for peace to be confirmation of the Treaties of Nystad (1721) and Åbo (1743), amnesty for the Anjala conspirators, and reinstatement of the constitutional prohibition against offensive war without the consent of the Estates. Gustav III published these humiliating demands to steel his subjects for yet another campaign.

In 1790 the Swedes concentrated upon the war at sea to gain control over the Finnish Gulf, the seaward flank of all land operations in southern Finland. Impressive efforts through the winter produced the largest naval force in Sweden's history.

The campaign opened in April with Swedish attacks on Baltischport, Reval, Fredrikshamn, and Kronstadt. The combined Swedish high seas and galley fleets under Gustav III himself next entered Viborg Bay to destroy the Russian galley squadron stationed there, but were trapped there by contrary winds while the scattered detachments of the Russian fleet assembled outside. Virtually the entire Swedish navy, with the king himself and 30,000 men embarked, was cornered. On 3 July, however, the wind changed and the Swedes ran the "Viborg Gauntlet,'' losing nearly a third of their high seas fleet and a score of galleys. They withdrew westward to Svensksund, pursued by the combined Russian fleet. Morale was at a low ebb. J. A. Ehrenström, who himself had been associated with the Finnish independence movement in the mid-1780s, wrote how many officers hoped for a Swedish defeat at Svensksund:

> They imagined that day could not pass without the king's being killed or taken prisoner, that this would lead to peace and that however harmful this might be for the kingdom, they would thereby win their desired goal of vindicating the Anjala Confederation, destroying the royal authority in accordance with the principles of the constitution of 1720, and wreaking vengeance upon the non-noble orders for the devotion they had shown the king.[39]

Such hopes were crushed in the ensuing battle on 9 July. The Swedes under Gustav III trapped and largely destroyed the Russian galley fleet, which lost fifty-three vessels and at last 9,000 men, while Swedish losses were negligible. Svensksund was the Swedish navy's greatest victory, the last, belated triumph of what had long been one of Europe's proud military nations.

In the immediate perspective, Svensksund restored the naval balance lost in 1788 and destroyed Catherine's hopes for a quick and decisive end to the Swedish war. Meanwhile Great Britain, Prussia, and Poland were threatening to join Sweden and Turkey in a grand coalition against Russian expansion. The empress therefore offered Sweden a separate peace on the basis of the *status quo ante bellum*, which Gustav III was glad to accept.

On 14 August 1790 the peace was concluded at Värälä in Finland. Ostensibly it restored the prewar situation, but its deeper significance was not spelled out in its text. By excluding any confirmation of the peace treaties of Nystad and Åbo, it deprived Russia of any legalistic excuse for intervening in Swedish-Finnish internal affairs. The link between the Swedish noble opposition and St. Petersburg was broken. The Danish-Russian alliance had failed the crucial test, and Great Britain and Prussia had shown their determination to maintain the balance of power in the Baltic. But since Finland still remained part of the Swedish realm, the ancient conflict between Sweden and Russia remained unresolved.[40]

Throughout the Russian war Gustav had been, as always, much preoccupied with the situation in France. The convening of the Assembly of Notables in 1787 disturbed him; he knew from experience the ways of "such assemblies," where "they use big words but generally are moved only by personal feelings."[41] He had reacted strongly and promptly to rebellion in America; he now seems to have been the first European monarch to become seriously concerned over the prospect of rebelliousness in France.

One of the king's confidants, Elis Schröderheim, later recalled:

The ceaseless inquietude and remarkable zeal with which King Gustav III followed the disturbances in France could not but amaze and almost irritate. At table almost nothing else was ever discussed. All other reading gave way to the *Moniteur*, the *Journal de Paris*, and the newspapers. The womenfolk tried to reason with him over this and in the council this subject interrupted the deliberations.[42]

Like his own aristocratic opponents, Gustav III saw the revolution in France as above all a struggle over royal authority, with ramifications throughout the European world. Behind the unrest of the time this former enthusiast for the French Enlightenment now perceived the "system of innovation our modern philosophers have introduced," as he wrote to Mme. de Boufflers already in August 1787.

It would be most strange [he continued] if their speculations, which they consider intended for mankind's greatest good, should simply lead to the opposite result and end, in the last analysis, by turning sovereigns—into tyrants, and peoples—into rebels.[43]

"The end of this century is the time of revolutions," Gustav observed in December 1789; an "epidemic," he wrote two years later, which had "spread from the soil of America to France" and which threatened all thrones. In particular he saw the French Revolution in the light of his own recent crisis. Repeatedly he compared his own determined action against the Anjala mutineers and their aristocratic sympathizers with Louis XVI's inept and spineless handling of the contemporary French *révolte nobiliaire*. "See," he wrote to Stedingk in August 1789, "what they are doing to *la délicieuse France*; there is the result of weakness and indecision."[44]

Following the end of the Russian war in August 1790, Gustav III's hostility to the French Revolution became increasingly manifest. Suspecting the revolutionary sympathies of his ambassador to France, Baron de Staël—and especially of his ambitious wife, Jacques Necker's daughter—Gustav made the younger Axel Fersen his secret agent in Paris already in January 1790, opening a direct channel to the French royal family and a steady flow of secret reports bitterly hostile to the revolution. In 1790 and again the following year, Gustav further limited freedom of the press by prohibiting authors or newspapers from referring to the unrest in France or the proceedings of the National Assembly.

Ambitious plans were meanwhile forming in Gustav's mind. To speed the peace negotiations at Värälä in the summer of 1790, the Russians had hinted at an alliance, while in Paris Fersen hoped that peace in the North might help bring "some change" in France. Fersen's reports, Gustav wrote in September to their mutual confidant, Baron Evert Taube, seemed to show the chaos in France at its peak and that a league "like that of the Greeks against Troy" should be formed "to restore order and avenge the honor of crowned heads." "I should like," he added, "to be the Agamemnon of that host."[45]

Throughout late 1790 and early 1791, Gustav III sought to interest Catherine II in a joint action against revolutionary France. Still at war with the Turks, she showed only vague signs of approval until Great Britain and Prussia once again threatened to intervene and angled for Swedish support. This evoked from Catherine a livelier interest in Gustav's speculations. Thus encouraged, on 17 May 1791 he confidently offered to Louis XVI's secret diplomatic agent, the émigré Baron de Breteuil, a Swedish-Russian force to support the king of France, in return for suitable compensation. Breteuil declined for the present because of the danger this might pose for the French royal family in Paris.

By now Gustav knew of the secret preparations by Breteuil, the Baron de Bouillé in Metz, and Fersen in Paris for the escape of the French royal family to France's eastern frontier, where they would appeal both to their own loyal subjects and to the European powers for support. Confident of Russian backing, Gustav departed for Aachen on 24 May to take personal control of his enterprise and to keep Louis XVI and his family, following their escape, from falling under the influence of other monarchs less implacable toward the revolution.

Gustav III's high hopes were foiled by the capture of the French royal family at Varennes on 20 June 1791, after Axel Fersen had successfully spirited them out of Paris.[46] Catherine II's apparent zeal for Russian participation in an intervention in France meanwhile cooled with the passing of the immediate crisis in the East.

Gustav now turned to the idea of a great monarchical crusade, under his own leadership, to attack France before the end of the summer. He sent emissaries to Russia, Britain, Spain, several German principalities, and the French émigrés in Coblenz. Essential to his plan was meanwhile the support of the new emperor, Leopold II, in Vienna, not least to forestall similar initiatives of his own which Gustav feared would acknowledge much of the work of the National Assembly.

The Swedish king sent Axel Fersen, recently escaped from France, to Vienna, thereby introducing a new complication. While officially representing the king of Sweden, Fersen felt personally committed to the interests of the French royal family. Like Marie Antoinette, with whom he remained in secret correspondence, he was convinced that these would best be served by convening a congress of powers, backed by military force, to cow the French into freeing their king and thereafter allowing him to determine the future of the new constitution, rather than by the direct armed intervention that Gustav III strove to organize. The Austrian government inclined toward the idea of such a congress, whereas neither the émigré French princes nor the other European monarchs showed any enthusiasm for accepting the leadership of the quixotic king of Sweden.

By the later summer of 1791, Gustav III was back in Stockholm and soon occupied with fresh plans, first for a Swedish-Russian landing in Normandy, then for a Swedish-Russian-Spanish coalition against France. Preoccupied with the Turkish war and the threat of a revivified Poland, Catherine II vaguely encouraged Gustav's concern with France to distract him from the Baltic. On 19 October 1791, after protracted negotiations, Russia concluded a definitive peace and a defensive alliance with Sweden at Drottningholm. While only vaguely referring to France, it provided for an annual subsidy of 300,000 rubles. The threads of Gustav III's complex counterrevolutionary diplomacy continued to pass largely through the hands of Axel Fersen, now in Brussels, who stubbornly sought to win his king over to the idea of an armed congress. This is where matters stood by the time of Gustav III's death in March 1792.[47]

What lay behind his plans against revolutionary France? Certainly the idea of leading a great monarchical crusade against the revolutionary Hydra appealed strongly to Gustav's romantic sensibilities. He had hoped his Russian war would rekindle the loyal enthusiasm of his nobility, which had cooled in the years preceding; instead it had widened the rift between them. Their alienation deeply grieved him. Yet earlier than most of the Swedish-Finnish nobility, Gustav recognized the social side of the revolution in France, reconfirming his conviction that monarch and nobility must stand or fall together. To Armfelt he wrote of his hope that by participating in a campaign in France, the Swedish nobles would be cured of their opposition by the sufferings and loyalty of the French *noblesse*.[48]

At the same time, Gustav III regarded the revolution as a malady threatening to other lands, not least his own, the latest outbreak of an endemic evil afflicting the European world since even before his own ascent to the throne, which must be cured by drastic means. The king of France must reestablish "royalty in its full powers" and accept no "mixed government." While he took a personal interest in the royal family, he wrote to Stedingk, now ambassador in St. Petersburg, in the summer of 1791,

> that which I take in the public cause, in the private interest of Sweden, and in the cause of all kings is greater yet . . . it may be all the same whether it be Louis XVI or Charles X who occupies the throne, as long as . . . the principles destructive to all authority are uprooted. . . . The only remedy for all this is steel and cannon. It may be that at this moment the [French] king and queen are in danger, but this danger is not as great as that to all the crowned heads that are menaced by the Revolution.[49]

George Washington had observed already in 1784 that since Gustav III had himself so recently changed Sweden's constitution, he was naturally sensitive toward "anything that might have the semblance of republicanism." In April 1788, "one of his less enthusiastic admirers" reportedly said that "the king is

himself nothing more than a revolutionary, although he was favored by success.'' Gustav himself admitted as much to Bouillé in February 1792: "I have
been in the position too often of conducting revolutions or of combating them
not to know that this [enterprise against France] cannot succeed unless led by
a single person.''[50]

Others were less impressed by the revolutionary menace. Duchess Charlotta,
for instance, wrote in September 1791:

> The justification the king gives for his activity, namely the fear that the
> principles of the National Assembly might spread to other lands and even
> to us, seems groundless to me, for a king who lets himself be guided by
> love of justice and freedom should have nothing to fear from anarchy; but
> the despotism for which the king strives is meanwhile fully as great an evil
> as this anarchy, which is indeed the antithesis of freedom and the same as
> the despotism of the many.[51]

Various hardheaded, practical motives may likewise be discerned behind
Gustav's counterrevolutionary plans. Sweden was left diplomatically isolated
and close to bankruptcy following the Peace of Värälä in 1790. Its traditional
ally and source of subsidies, France, was crippled by internal disorder—in
Gustav's mind much as France's ally, Sweden, had been under the constitution
of 1720. If successful, a Swedish-led intervention could ultimately restore
France as the bulwark of Sweden's security.

Such a project meanwhile provided a basis for other possible alliances, particularly with the old enemy, Russia. The Treaty of Drottningholm was the beginning of what might become a real diplomatic revolution in the North. Copenhagen was duly concerned, especially since Bernstorff rejected a Russian feeler
in September 1791 concerning possible Danish participation in a common action
against France, on the grounds that "each nation may give itself its own constitution and govern itself without other powers having the right to intervene"; this
was a principle, he added, which none had more stoutly defended than the king
of Sweden. Gustav did not fail to raise with the Russians the possibility of Sweden's acquiring Norway in return for compensation to Denmark in Oldenburg
and Delmenhorst—at Russia's expense.[52]

By early 1792, Gustav III appeared to some initiates to have lost part of his
zeal for French affairs. Certainly his efforts had met with repeated disappoint-
ment. But there is another explanation. In his memoirs, G. G. Adlerbeth wrote:

> In Sweden several of the king's confidants held that His Majesty was not
> really serious about his armament against France. Some maintained that
> Denmark was the real enemy against which it was intended; that France
> served only as a cover, and that a campaign would be mounted against
> Norway as soon as the season permitted.

Throughout 1790 and 1791 Gustav's agents remained active in Norway, sending the king detailed reports and seeking contact with malcontents. But Adlerbeth's suggestion remains questionable.[53]

Gustav was meanwhile involved in far-reaching speculations about Poland. By the summer of 1790, the Polish Diet, then in the midst of drafting a new constitution, considered an eventual successor to King Stanislaus Poniatowski. In October, following the peace of Värälä, Gustav made known his own candidature. Rumors in Poland that he enjoyed Russian backing, however, put the kiss of death on any Swedish-Polish dynastic union, and in May 1791 the Poles offered the succession to the elector of Saxony. Gustav confided to his minister in Warsaw, Lars von Engeström, that he only contemplated this "sacrifice" for the sake of the strategic and especially the financial benefits it might bring Sweden. The whole scheme may moreover have been only a ploy to allow Sweden to claim compensation in a future partition of Poland; in such an event, he wrote to Stedingk in March 1792, Sweden must be prepared to seize such advantages as the situation might allow. Armfelt later noted that these would have been in "the only area for expansion that would be suitable for him." Again, Norway comes to mind.[54]

Gustav III's motives regarding both France and Poland during 1790-92 were as complex as the man himself. No episodes better illustrate his characteristic mixture of romantic idealism and flexible opportunism.

His foreign policy following the end of the Russian war had been spurred largely by the ruinous condition of Sweden's state finances since the *Riksdag* of 1789. The Estates had then only guaranteed the estimated costs of the campaign for that year. To fill the inevitable deficit and to pay for the war in 1790, the government had resorted to the unrestrained issue of bills of credit, debt notes, and other paper. By the end of the war no one knew the full extent of the national debt. In 1791 redemption of the credit notes, set in 1789 for one to two years, was postponed indefinitely and interest payments on them were suspended.[55] Johan Liljencrantz's great monetary reform of 1776 was drowned in a flood of paper.

Anxious to avoid another *Riksdag*, Gustav III sought for alliances that could provide foreign subsidies. But by the end of 1791 a diet could no longer be postponed. Many dreaded its consequences. Duchess Charlotta feared in December 1791 that "the desperate state of our finances could here, as in France, easily lead to a revolution."[56]

The Estates were summoned to convene on 23 January 1792 in Gävle, to avoid possible disturbances in the capital. In his opening address Gustav III pointed out that, confident of his subjects' loyalty, he had not hesitated to call a *Riksdag* at a time of "fanatical confusion . . . when other kings would have hesitated to expose themselves to the ferment aroused by great assemblies."[57]

He had nonetheless mobilized Gävle's burgher militia and quartered military detachments in the neighborhood.

The king could count on sure majorities in three of the Estates but only upon a small minority of the Nobility. According to the diarist Hochschild, who always had his ear to the ground:

> As many of the Nobility as could turned out for the *Riksdag*, even those who in 1789 had been imprisoned at Fredrikshof, partly to show the nation that they were not causing difficulties, partly at least to be present in case their rights should be called into question and taken from them. The rumor was widely spread that an end to the exclusive right to manorial demesne land might be proposed, together with the equal taxation of land.[58]

As will be seen, the questions of manorial demesne and a uniform land tax would arise seventeen years later, to bedevil the *Riksdag* of 1809-10.

The Gävle *Riksdag* of 1792 went surprisingly smoothly. As in 1789, most of the work was done by the Secret Committee, with a nonnoble majority including Peasant representatives. It estimated the war debts as low as possible at 8.5 million *riksdaler* and the total national debt at 29.5 million—three times as large as at the beginning of the reign—which the Estates were to guarantee and place under the management of the National Debt Office established in 1789. The taxation granted in 1789 was to continue "until the next *Riksdag*." This plan was accepted with little debate outside the Noble Estate. The *Riksdag* could be dissolved already on 24 February 1792.

The king's aristocratic opponents had prudently avoided a confrontation. Anxious to reconcile them, Gustav III had brought up neither his plan for a new constitution nor the question of the Act of Union and Security of 1789, which the Noble Estate had still not accepted. While the noble opposition continued to ostracize him, the other Estates addressed to him a joint petition of thanks, supplemented by an additional one from the Finnish peasant *riksdagsmän*. Altogether Gustav could feel well pleased. Time seemed to be on his side. But this was only the calm before the storm.[59]

In surveying the three years between the spring of 1789 and the spring of 1792, one cannot but be struck by a greater divergence in the focus of national energies within the Nordic world than at any time since the Seven Years' War. Sweden-Finland under Gustav III was above all concerned with war and diplomacy; Denmark-Norway with peaceful internal reform.

As ruling sovereigns, neither Crown Prince Frederik nor Gustav III welcomed the Revolution in France, not least because both had established their positions of power through coups d'etat, or what were often referred to before 1789 as "revolutions." For the time being, Frederik had little to say on the subject. Gustav was older and more experienced in such matters—as well as considerably more articulate. Both the American revolt and the Anjala revolt had well prepared him for his immediate and implacable opposition to the French Revolution.

Although there were some signs of discontent with the recent agrarian reforms in Denmark, the petition of the Jutland proprietors in 1790 and Tønne Lüttichau's feud with Colbjørnsen can hardly compare with the determined— even though seemingly restrained—opposition to Gustav III among a proud nobility with strong constitutional traditions in Sweden and Finland. The relative intensity of reactions to the French Revolution in the two kingdoms must be seen in this light. Largely for internal political reasons Gustav III spun ambitious schemes for intervention against the revolutionary menace; in Denmark Bernstorff saw little to be gained and much to be lost by intervening.

Against the background of its political struggle against Gustav III, the Swedish-Finnish nobility and its intellectual allies welcomed the revolution in France, often with passionate enthusiasm. The Danish proprietorial class seems generally to have reacted negatively to it, from the viewpoint of already beleaguered manorial lords. The German nobles in the Danish kingdom and the duchies, however, reveal a notable similarity to their Swedish and Finnish counterparts, based on their own constitutional traditions. In both monarchies, members of the high court aristocracy, closest to the intellectual currents of the time, were most articulate in their enthusiasm over developments in France. Many of these highborn "*enragés*" were women. "The fair sex," wrote Baron A. L. Hamilton, "which does not love despotism in others  .  .  .  exercised a vast influence upon the attitudes of the younger men, inspiring in them a firmness one would never have expected of folk whose fortunes depended partly on court favor." Perhaps one may here perceive the greater influence of Rousseauian romanticism upon the novel-reading female members of the great families. "Bernstorff said yesterday at court that Rousseau was a scoundrel," wrote Charlotte Schimmelmann to Luise Stolberg in September 1789; "that scoundrel is almost my saint."[60]

The paradoxical aspects of these reactions to the French Revolution in palace and manor house would become evident enough with time. Both Crown Prince Frederik by choice and Gustav III by circumstance were radical social reformers—if not indeed "crowned revolutionaries"—by the later 1780s. By the eve of the French Revolution they had largely accomplished by peaceful means what in France would only be gained by turmoil and bloodshed. Yet neither regarded the French Revolution from this perspective, seeing it instead as a challenge to royal sovereignty. Their opponents among both the Swedish-Finnish and the German aristocracies saw the revolution from the same viewpoint, largely failing at first to recognize that it threatened the very survival of hereditary corporate status. Only the Danish landlord class, represented by Lüttichau and the Jut land proprietors, and Gustav III, who believed he had chastened his nobility only to save it, were evidently fully impressed with this aspect from the beginning. Similarities elsewhere in Europe suggest themselves.[61]

Among the middle classes in both Nordic kingdoms, general enthusiasm for the French Revolution was characteristically combined with strong loyalty to the ruling monarch. This synthesis rested upon an implied social contract, justified by democratic, or at least antiaristocratic, social reforms broadly approved by middle-class opinion. For the present, this dynamic balance provided welcome backing for the crown and a mandate for further reform. But it could in time break down, giving cause for alarm among kings and their ministers.

# CHAPTER 9

# Reform and Radicalism 1792–97

The year 1792 was a turning point for Scandinavia and Europe. In March Gustav III was struck down by an assassin, bringing to an abrupt end one of the most dramatic reigns in the history of the North. Less than a fortnight after his death, France went to war with monarchical Europe, initiating a quarter-century of armed conflict in which the Scandinavian lands would ultimately become involved. War precipitated the fall of the monarchy and the establishment of the republic in France in August and the bloody September massacres which foreshadowed the Reign of Terror of the next two years. In September, too, the French turned back their enemies' advance at Valmy, first revealing to the world the might of the Revolution armed.

In Scandinavia these events showed the French Revolution in a new—and to many, an increasingly ominous—light. As political enthusiasm gave way in aristocratic circles to growing disillusionment and alarm, there was a rising tide of social radicalism among the middle classes. The preromantic temper manifested itself both in the continued glorification of the Enlightenment among the French Revolution's devotees and in a mounting antirationalistic reaction, often with pietistic religious or secular mystical overtones, among its enemies.

The European war once again brought to Scandinavia welcome opportunities for trade, but likewise threats to neutrality and maritime rights. As during the Seven Years' War and the American war, common problems led to cooperation, following a long period of rivalry, which this time inspired a new sense of a shared Nordic identity.

Gustav III died in a manner worthy of the theatrical quality of his life. While attending a masquerade ball at the Stockholm opera on 16 March 1792, he was surrounded by a group of masked figures, one of whom discharged a pistol into his back. Although the assassins escaped, they were soon apprehended. All were noblemen. The aristocratic opposition, which the king and commonality had driven underground in 1788–89, had taken its revenge.

Gustav had been warned of a plot against his life that very day, but disregarded it since the past three years had been rife with such rumors. Already in 1790, there had been talk in Finland of a coup to change the constitution in the event the king were killed or taken prisoner in the Russian war, or even to eliminate him by force. By the time of the Gävle *Riksdag* and thereafter, stories of similar conspiracies were widespread even abroad.[1]

Following the Peace of Värälä, Gustav III's opponents were deeply concerned about the state of Sweden's finances and signs of the king's adventurous speculations in European *grande politique*. Virtually no one in Sweden favored an armed intervention against France. While many feared financial chaos or dangerous dependence upon Russia, the prospect of taking up arms against the very temple of liberty outraged the more idealistic opponents of the king, who saw him as a Swedish "Nero" or "Caligula," at once treacherous, cruel, and decadent. They hoped, J. A. Ehrenström recalled,

> by revealing his warlike intentions toward France to increase their following, not only among friends of the fatherland but among that daily increasing party which, delighted by the eloquent phrases in the speeches from the tribune of the French National Assembly, were filled with enthusiasm for a revolution, of which they expected the rebirth of the world and the golden age of freedom. . . . [They] indeed succeeded in arousing deep fears . . . and in spreading disaffection toward a king who was depicted as a despot, prepared to suppress abroad the regained rights of an oppressed nation, so as to be all the more able to suppress them in his own.[2]

In Stockholm malcontents congregated around General Carl Fredrik Pechlin, a steadfast opponent of strong monarchy during the later Era of Freedom and a master of intrigue. Associated with this circle was Jacob von Engeström, who drafted the outlines of a constitution featuring a strong council, dependent upon the Estates, and securely tenured bureaucracy. Such stipulations recall the old constitution of 1720. Yet Engeström appears also to have envisioned a unicameral legislature, elected by classes based upon property ownership, and the opening of all state employments and categories of land to all citizens. These points call to mind both the Legislative Assembly under the new French constitution of 1791 and Gustav III's own physiocratic emphasis upon property as the basis of representation in his last constitutional plans. Principles aside, the aristocratic conspirators realized they must win over the other Estates from the king. Since the nobility had already lost most of its substantive privileges, Engeström and his friends were evidently prepared to contemplate further sacrifices to restore constitutional freedom.[3]

Separately, another conspiracy formed among men prepared to take the final, desperate step. Gustav's actual assassin, Jacob Johan Anckarström, a former captain of the Guards, was the king's bitter enemy both in principle and over personal grievances. By the winter of 1792, he had confided his views to the young counts Claës Horn and Adolf Ludvig Ribbing; according to the latter, society by then "swarmed with men who wished to play the role of Brutus."[4] At the Gävle *Riksdag* in January 1792, Anckarström and his friends vainly sought an opportunity to strike. Meanwhile, through Ribbing they came into contact with the wider circle of conspirators around General Pechlin, who by March had evidently gathered the various threads of conspiracy into his hands.

It appears that the conspirators planned, after assassinating Gustav III, to seize power with the support of trustworthy military units, to set up a regency for the thirteen-year-old Crown Prince Gustav Adolf, nominally under his mother, to eliminate Gustav's hated henchmen from government and court, and to establish a new constitution. Their plans were, however, frustrated by their failure to kill the king immediately on 16 March and their own rapid arrest. Gustav lingered on until 29 March.[5]

Most of the Swedish and Finnish nobility were aghast at the assassination, and many hastened to make their peace with the dying king. His bitterest enemies were meanwhile jubilant over the fall of what one of them called a despot "surely unrivaled in either ancient or modern history." Naturally French Jacobins were suspected of complicity, a suspicion Gustav himself shared in his final days, doubtful as it now appears.[6]

During the weeks following, the police inquest made alarming progress, implicating an ever-widening circle among the aristocracy. According to a well-informed source, had it continued, every other prominent family would have had cause to "wear mourning."[7] By August the new regent, Gustav's brother, Duke Carl of Södermanland, closed the investigation, claiming that the king had on his deathbed urged leniency toward his assassins. Thus the full scope of the conspiracy remains shrouded in mystery.

Of some forty persons arrested, fourteen were brought to trial. Here Anckarström defended his act as tyrannicide under the social contract:

A king is, in himself, only a sinful mortal like any other, but he has received the nation's mandate to maintain law, peace, and security, and thus to see that all goes well when the nation itself is not convened. . . . Can he be king of the realm who is capable of breaking the oath he has made to the people, to uphold, respect, and govern according to the constitution of 1772, which the king himself had prepared and which was accepted without change by the nation, [he] who can deprive the people of all security? . . . When the king has violated his oath, . . . that of his people is likewise voided. . . . It says in a clause of the constitution . . . that whosoever seeks to change or overthrow that fundamental law shall be considered an enemy of the realm. In consequence thereof, the king has declared himself an enemy of the realm and the people . . . and as a society must defend itself against him who would injure his neighbor's person or property . . . one is justified in opposing force with force.[8]

The court condemned five of those indicted to death, but in August the duke-regent changed four of these sentences to exile. Five others received lesser penalties. Ultimately only Anckarström suffered the supreme penalty. After being publicly whipped on the pillory for three consecutive days, his right hand was struck off and he was beheaded, drawn, and quartered, on 27 April 1792. Sweden's last political execution recalls Struensee's cruel fate in Copenhagen just two decades earlier.

Abroad, news of the assassination caused a sensation. The court of Copenhagen had reason to feel relieved, although in Aarhus Guldberg feared the resulting outcry ''against aristocrats.'' Indeed, signs were not lacking in Sweden that the assassination had again stirred up the class antagonism of recent years. In France there was jubilation among the Jacobins, among whom something of an Anckarström cult flourished.[9]

"If heaven had vouchsafed Gustav III a few more years' peace," Armfelt later wrote, "we would have seen at Haga the philosopher of Sans Souci."[10] In many ways Gustav indeed recalls his uncle, Frederick the Great. As it was, his life was cut short at the age of forty-six. Yet his reign was of great and lasting significance for his nation's future evolution. The Gustavian era remains a golden age of Swedish culture, thanks not least to the king's own passionate interest in literature and the arts. Gustav restored Sweden's strength and self-esteem, and maintained its full, effective independence from the Russian colossus. In the longer perspective, Gustav III, the nobles' friend, left his lasting mark by leveling in drastic fashion the corporate privileges of his subjects. The would-be leader of a monarchical crusade to crush the Hydra of Revolution, Gustav was not altogether blind to this paradox. Once, in 1790, he said—with a prescience he could hardly have appreciated—"I am myself a democrat."[11]

He remains a strange and enigmatic figure, who in adversity showed himself as strong as he had been weak and frivolous in more fortunate times, as J. A. Ehrenström later wrote. He could be hardheaded and opportunistic in politics and diplomacy, and he was among the last European monarchs to command his forces in the field. He was at the same time a man of romantic imagination and grandiose dreams. Historians have never ceased to debate his motives and significance. Yet surely he revealed much of himself when he wrote to his envoy in Warsaw in November 1790: ''We are created to work, to strain our powers, suffer, fight against success, which spoils us, and against adversity, which oppresses us: that is man's lot, as long as he lives, and that is the duty of kings.''[12]

In a codicil to his will, prepared on the day of his death, Gustav III appointed a regency council of five, including Barons Armfelt and Taube, to share authority with the regent, Duke Carl, until Crown Prince Gustav Adolf should come of age four and a half years hence. This arrangement expressed Gustav's misgivings about his brother, who, resentful over the limited role he had heretofore been allowed, had become a natural focal point for the aristocratic opposition. No sooner was Gustav dead than Duke Carl declared the codicil null and void on technical grounds.

While the duke at first retained the appointed council, he summoned to its meetings prominent "Patriots" opposed to Gustavian autocracy. Clearly he had no intention of being guided by his late brother's confidants. In discouragement, Armfelt departed by summer for the Continent. Taube withdrew to private life. Other leading "Gustavians" were sent to minor posts in the provinces.

Although Duke Carl exulted in his newly gained authority, he lacked his brother's qualities of leadership. He was indecisive, indolent, and easily swayed. He tended to be secretive and suspicious. From the start he relied strongly upon unofficial advisers and agents outside the regular structure of government.[13]

In July 1792, Gustaf Adolf Reuterholm, scion of a Finnish noble family of strongly Cap traditions and prominent "Patriot" at the *Riksdagar* of 1786 and 1789, returned to Sweden from semi-exile on the Continent. Like the duke and others in his entourage, he was a passionate devotee of Freemasonry and the occult arts. Inspired by a mystical belief in his own genius and mission, he possessed an energy and strength of will which the duke lacked. Although he accepted only a minor position in the financial administration, Reuterholm soon emerged as the duke-regent's "grand vizier."[14] His position recalls that of Guldberg in Denmark twenty years earlier. The francophile Baron de Staël, recalled from Paris by Gustav III in late 1791, replaced Taube as principal adviser for foreign affairs, without assuming the position of *rikskansler*.

The regency was not a period of constructive government action. For all his ambition, Reuterholm lacked any real program other than to maintain himself in power against his Gustavian rivals. The regime reacted fitfully to alleged Gustavian conspiracies and popular disturbances, as well as to the shifting fortunes of the European war. Thus the really significant developments in Sweden-Finland during these years were the results of private activities, especially in the agrarian sphere.

Gustav III's reforms of 1789 were bearing fruit. There was a steady rise in peasant freeholding through purchase of both crown and manorial tenancies. Peasant holdings likewise increased through internal colonization, particularly in Finland, and the division of existing farms. Freedom, after 1789, from old restrictions on peasant property rights and on the employment of labor promoted increased productivity and land reclamation.[15]

The *Storskifte*, or partial land reallocation, commenced in 1757 and advanced by Gustav III, had resulted by the 1790s in some reduction in the numbers of scattered holdings in about half of Sweden's village lands, although with great regional variations. Nowhere, however, had any village been completely re-structured. Land consolidation had proceeded much further in Denmark and the duchies, whose early agrarian reformers had been in part inspired by the Swedish *Storskifte*.

Not surprisingly, a new movement for consolidation now arose in Sweden's southernmost province of Skåne, an old Danish territory acquired in 1658, where terrain and agrarian conditions closely resembled those across the Sound. The initiative came from Baron Rutger Maclean, a liberal-minded opponent of Gustav III who had welcomed the revolution in France largely for its abolition of old restrictions on property rights. Beginning in 1785, Maclean, inspired by Danish and English examples, had by 1793 reorganized the tenancies on his Svaneholm manor into seventy-five single, compact holdings, in the process breaking up four old villages. These farms were leased out on strict renewable contracts, requiring improved methods of cultivation and commuting all dues and labor obligations to a money rent. Maclean divided his demesne into six farms, worked by hired labor under his own supervision, to provide models for effective agriculture. Eager to raise the cultural level of his tenantry, he estab-lished schools for their chilren, and even sent a young scholar to study the new pedagogy with Heinrich Pestalozzi in Switzerland.

At first the baron had a hard time finding tenants for his farms. Peasants ac-customed to traditional village life were hesitant about moving out to isolated farmsteads or trying new, unfamiliar farming practices. But by the mid-1790s the benefits of the new system were amply demonstrated, not only to the local peasantry but to other landlords in the area. It aroused widespread interest, as evidenced by numerous writings on the subject, and inspired the similar reor-ganization—or *enskifte*—of a number of other manors in the Skåne.[16]

Compact farms and money rents increased the profitability of peasant tenan-cies to both occupant and landlord, while wage labor permitted better cultivation of demesne lands. Dividing the lands of entire villages into compact holdings moreover brought under the plow former common lands that had been too re-mote to cultivate. Land consolidation proved, however, more problematical elsewhere in Sweden and in Finland, where manorial tenancies were widely scattered and their tenants well protected in their traditional rights.

In Sweden—as in Denmark—increased agricultural productivity provided the basis for a growing population, while demanding a large pool of wage labor for peasant farms as well as manorial demesnes. While the number of freehold farmers increased, that of the rural population as a whole increased more rapidly still. A growing proportion were now cotters or *torpare*, who, like Norwegian and many Danish *husmænd*, cultivated parts of farms or manors on revocable leases, in return for labor. There were also increasing numbers of *bakstugusit-tare*, essentially squatters on others' land, without contractual rights and dependent upon casual labor, and of rootless rural paupers. The division of family farms likewise reduced many smallholders to at least part-time wage earners.[17]

In Denmark, the mid-1790s remained a time of vigorous reform under government leadership. While the main emphasis remained the improvement of agrarian conditions, a wide range of problems received attention.

Although there had been a promising beginning in the 1760s, few peasant freehold purchases occurred between 1770 and 1790. Thereafter they increased rapidly and would continue at a high level until Denmark was drawn into the Napoleonic wars in 1807. Following recent reforms, many landlords were now anxious to be rid of their tenant farms, which remained a fiscal liability. By selling them off, they could raise capital to rationalize cultivation of their demesnes, which they were often prepared to reduce to more manageable size. The government encouraged them to do so by granting dispensations allowing them to retain their tax exemptions.

The Credit Bank (*Kreditkasse*), founded in 1786, made credit available to peasant purchasers. An even more important source was the *Almindelige Enke-kasse*, a subscription fund for widows' pensions, after C. D. Reventlow became one of its directors in 1797. Most of the necessary credit was, however, extended by private persons, in particular by the landlords themselves. Mortgages were almost uniformly set at the 4 percent maximum interest permitted by law. Such residual manorial rights as had earlier encumbered freeholds as well as hereditary leaseholds now virtually disappeared in contracts of sale. Within twenty years over half of Denmark's peasant farms passed into freehold ownership.

Peasant tenants were at first often less anxious to buy their farms than their landlords were to sell them. In places the government had reneged on freehold purchases in the 1760s. Many peasants were fearful of payments, interest, and taxes frequently amounting to more than they were accustomed to pay for their leaseholds, or were reluctant to cut themselves off from the landlord's support in time of need. Sale of tenancies might be combined with land reallocation, adding both further expense and the emotional strains of moving away from the old village. Landlords thus often brought pressure to bear through the threat of exact enforcement of tenant obligations, denial of assistance, or prompt collection of outstanding debts. An ordinance in June 1792 permitted proprietors to increase rents for new leases. The main incentive to purchase nevertheless proved to be the obvious success of growing numbers of freeholders.[18]

During the same years land reallocation proceeded rapidly, by now frequently welcomed by the peasantry. An ordinance in June 1792 permitted landlords to charge tenants 4 percent interest on the capital they invested in the process, giving the latter added incentive to purchase. Despite an initial lack of enthusiasm, about half of Denmark's peasant farmholders would relocate outside the old villages by 1807; fortunately, the framework of the old half-timbered buildings could fairly easily be disassembled and moved. This movement brought much former common land within reach for cultivation.[19]

Despite the apprehensions of many proprietors, there proved to be no lack of tenants following the abolition of the *stavnsbånd* in 1788. While that dispensation, reflecting the fears of the 1730s of a paucity of manpower, had bound male peasants to the manors by law, the steady growth of population together with a scarcity of alternative employments made young peasants eager enough to bind themselves to lifetime leases by the 1790s. For the great majority economic security was surely more important than freedom of movement.[20]

The central problem was now the *hoveri*, or manorial labor, required of most tenants, and here the government tread warily. Although it had firmly rebuked the Jutland proprietors who had sought to remonstrate against agrarian reforms in 1790, it was impressed with the widespread discontent among the landlord class this episode revealed and was tacitly prepared to compromise. The situation recalls its combination of public repression and quiet concession in responding to the Lofthuus rebellion in Norway. Its ordinance of June 1791 encouraged landlords and tenants to conclude private settlements based on the existing *hoveri* on each manor—provided only that this did not impede the adequate cultivation of the tenant farms—while strongly stressing the tenant's duty and obedience to the landlord. Proprietors, particularly of smaller manors, hesitated to freeze *hoveri*, even at relatively high levels, so long as it remained in effect the only real source of profit from their tenancies which could be adjusted to keep pace with rising prices and an expanding market. The ordinance of 15 June 1792, permitting freely negotiable rents for consolidated tenant farms, however, not only gave a strong impetus to further land reallocation but provided a welcome, alternative form of profitability to landlords. From their side the deadlock was now broken. An instruction in June 1795 urged the commutation of labor obligations to payments, preferably in money, a solution already then increasingly common. Hoping for a general reduction of *hoveri*, many peasants procrastinated until the government made it known it would mediate, where voluntary settlements were not reached, on the basis of the manor's *hoveri* in 1790. Thus by mid-1795, agreements had been concluded for some 600 of the 759 manors on which tenant labor was performed; in only thirty-seven cases did government mediators thereafter intervene.

Thanks to the expansive agricultural market of recent decades, the government's cautious solution provided substantial benefits to proprietors, for by the early 1790s tenant labor in much of Denmark had reached the highest levels ever. These were now generally frozen by agreement, while the costs to the peasant of either freehold purchase or commutation were correspondingly high.

Still, through these alternatives *hoveri* was removed altogether from about two-thirds of Denmark's peasant farms by the time an ordinance in December 1799 finally made the fixing of tenant labor an absolute requirement, confirming what was then a virtual *fait accompli*. Where still subject to *hoveri*, the tenant could now at least make permanent arrangements to cover it.[21]

The tithe remained a burden to peasant cultivators. Levied for the support of the church, its papal share had been divided at the time of the Reformation between the crown and the local landlord. In part a tax, in part a manorial due, it involved various vested interests. As it was payable in kind—normally in grain—it denied the cultivator profit in time of scarcity. Tithed grain was collected from the field, "in the sheaf," before the rest of the crop could be taken in, causing inconvenient delays and spoilage in wet weather. An ordinance of March 1796 urged titheholders to conclude private agreements with tithable peasants, but such piecemeal, voluntary reforms proceeded slowly.[22]

Except for its relaxation of old restrictions against peasant enterprises outside the towns, following the Lofthuus uprising of 1787, and periodic relief during poor crop years, the government felt little need at this time to concern itself with the Norwegian peasantry. The emancipation of the Danish peasants meanwhile brought to the fore the question of *Leibeigenschaft*, or serfdom, in the duchies.

In Denmark the *stavnsbånd* had been a recent innovation, decreed in 1733 by an absolute monarch free to terminate it at will. In the duchies the king—or rather duke—did not possess unlimited power, and the manorial right of serf-holding was included among ancient privileges repeatedly guaranteed, most recently when ducal Holstein was acquired in 1773. Holstein's ambiguous status as a fief of the Holy Roman Empire and the Schleswig-Holstein *Ritterschaft's* jealous vigilance over local rights further restricted Copenhagen's effective freedom of action.

In this matter—as in others—the government proceeded cautiously, seeking voluntary reform rather than direct confrontation. Since 1765 the crown had sold off much of its domain in the duchies as hereditary leaseholds, whose peasant purchasers were released from serfdom. In 1787 it urged private proprietors to follow suit. Some did so, especially in Schleswig, and many others were attracted to the idea.

The duchies were among the more progressive areas of the German cultural world, a crossroads for cosmopolitan influences. Both Danish and foreign visitors were struck during the 1790s by the prosperity and industriousness they encountered there, in contrast to Denmark itself.[23] The humanitarianism of the French Enlightenment and the new Lutheran pietism, as well as the practical examples of German cameralism and English agronomy all favored the emancipation of the remaining serfs. Early experiments in the duchies had stimulated agrarian reforms in Denmark. Now the Danish program provided a model for the duchies.

Further stimulus came from alarming incidents of social unrest in the duchies. The disturbances in 1790 around Tønder and Åbenrå have already been noted. There were outbreaks in several places in 1794, especially among the cotters near Kaltenkirchen, and the following year a tumult in Flensburg, which had to be put down by the military. Although precipitated mainly by rising prices, this ferment—and the utterances of some of the participants—seemed particularly ominous against the background of the French Revolution. Similar fears were rife in neighboring Mecklenburg and in Swedish Pomerania.[24]

In January 1795, the *non recepti* landowners of the duchies called upon the *Ritterschaft* for common deliberations concerning the abolition of serfdom on all manors within a set period. There ensued a wide-ranging discussion, in which A. P. Bernstorff and Ernst Schimmelmann, who belonged to the *Ritterschaft*, expressed the government's viewpoint, and the brothers Cai and Fritz Reventlow—of the Holstein branch of that widespread family—championed conservative interests. Although there was substantial agreement over the desirability of ending serfdom, the deliberations bogged down over the role to be played by the *Ritterschaft*, in view of its old rivalries with both the *non recepti* and the government in Copenhagen.

At the end of the year, Bernstorff's close collaborator, Professor C. U. D. Eggers of Kiel, came out with his anonymous *Schreiben eines Holsteinischen Edelmanns an seinen Bruder über die Aufhebung der Leibeigenschaft in Holstein*, inferring that if the proprietors did not solve the problem, the ruler (*Landsherr*) could do it for them, and stressing the overhanging threat of social upheaval. Like Bernstorff, Eggers proposed that the *Ritterschaft* elect a deputation to prepare for reform.

When the *Ritterschaft* convened in January 1796, it was acquainted with Eggers's admonition and well understood the official inspiration behind it. It established a commission, including representatives of the *non recepti*, to consider emancipation. Its investigations showed that by early 1797 serfdom no longer existed on many manors, although it still remained on at least thirty-eight in Schleswig and eighty-four in Holstein. In October of that year, after much controversy, the commission submitted its petition to the crown, stating that the proprietors of the duchies, with only one exception, were resolved that serfdom be abolished by a set date, which most agreed should be eight years hence, in 1805. No one had striven with greater tact and determination for this result than A. P. Bernstorff. When he died in June 1797, he had the satisfaction of knowing the commission's decision.[25]

Throughout the monarchy the government's reforms had concentrated upon bettering the conditions—and hence the productivity—of a particular class of peasants: the *gårdmænd*, or farmholders, whether freeholders or leaseholders. The reverse side of the coin was the rapid increase in the lower strata of peasant society.

In Norway the number of crofters grew rapidly, already amounting to some 40,000 by 1792, in which year the government required farmers to conclude written contracts with them. A large class of landless laborers remained subject to the ordinance of 1754, requiring them to accept any available work within their parishes, which they could not leave without permission from the royal bailiff. If complaints were not heard from Norway against such "local slavery"—as the Danish radical Riegels called it—this only shows how well it suited the needs of the farmers. Only by 1799 would this requirement be relaxed by a new militia ordinance. Some relief from population growth was meanwhile provided by internal colonization, particularly in northern Norway.[26]

In Denmark there had been a limited need for wage laborers or cotters while the *stavnsbånd* was in force. But with its abolition, the rise in freeholding, and regulation and commutation of tenant labor, a new source of agricultural labor was essential. The government thus encouraged the formation of a sizable *husmand* class, to be provided ideally with small plots of land—too small to be self-sufficient—in return for labor. In 1791, as noted, it had permitted proprietors under certain conditions to divide up tenant farms into crofts; a further instruction in May 1796 allowed them to create crofts up to the number of their tenant farms. Through these provisions and special dispensations, numerous farms were broken up into new crofts—on Sjælland alone some 30,000 crofts before 1800. Although in principle intended partly to compensate *husmænd* for the loss of customary village rights, land attached to crofts was not usually protected against reallocation by the landlord for other use; nor was it required that most cotters be granted any security of tenure. In time an increasing number of crofts came to have no land at all, or had no more than small garden plots. In this indirect way, much former peasant land was eventually added to manorial demesnes, despite the general prohibition against such engrossments. The cotters meanwhile became increasingly more dependent upon manorial and peasant landowners. In 1791 unmarried laborers were required to seek local employment.[27]

The significant dividing line within Danish rural society moved downward to split the peasantry itself into haves and a growing number of have-nots. In the duchies a similar situation was evolving. A new servitude was emerging to replace the old.

Abolition of the *stavnsbånd* and an increasingly dispersed settlement pattern in the countryside left an administrative vacuum, which was filled partly by the parish pastor, partly by new local officials, most notably the parish bailiff (*sognefoged*) established in 1791, appointed from among the more substantial farmers. Over the years they were charged with a growing number of tasks involving conscription, schools, and relief to the poor, thereby acquiring practical experience in public affairs of increasing significance for following decades.[28]

As agrarian reforms transformed the condition of the majority of the monarchy's inhabitants, the government turned to the problems of other, smaller disadvantaged groups. It relaxed old restrictions against non-Lutheran Christians. A dispute in the 1780s between orthodox and reforming members of the Copenhagen synagogue led to a government commission, which in 1796 recommended that the Jews—heretofore a miniature state within the state—be made entirely subject to the civil laws, except in questions pertaining to the Christian faith. The matter dragged, largely because of disagreements among the Jews themselves, until March 1814, by which time barriers against them had already fallen: they could acquire landed property and were admitted to schools, professions, civil posts, trade guilds, and clubs. Copenhagen's Jews, most of those within the monarchy, estimated in 1800 at about 2,000, by then included many prosperous merchants. "More than anywhere else," Pram made bold to state in *Minerva* in 1797, "we have treated these, our brothers, with a humanity denied them by Europe's other Christians."[29]

The problem of poverty likewise attracted attention. Already in 1787 the government appointed a commission to consider relief to the poor in Copenhagen. An ordinance in March 1792, while leaving a number of details to be resolved, stated the principle that public relief should be available to all in real need.[30]

With the establishment of a new police court (*Politiret*) in Copenhagen in 1793, the policemaster lost his authority to inflict arbitrary punishment, without appeal, for a wide range of offenses, thereby bringing the poorer classes of the capital under the full protection of the law. Numerous reforms in the 1790s meanwhile simplified and speeded legal procedure, prescribed more humane punishments, and improved conditions in the prisons, whose inmates were likewise put to useful work. The establishment of arbitration boards in 1795 greatly reduced the number of civil law suits. A more tolerant attitude allowed an increasing number of divorces after 1790. The appearance of a Society for Saving Lost Citizens on Fyn in 1797 shows a growing public interest in rehabilitating public offenders.[31]

The most wretched inhabitants of the state were the black slaves in the Danish West Indian islands, whose plight aroused a growing sympathy. Debate on the slave trade in the British Parliament stimulated the appointment of a Danish commission, headed by Ernst Schimmelmann, in the fall of 1791. Although the Danes prided themselves on treating their slaves more decently than other nations, the Danish Baltic and Guinea Company had lost some 15 percent of its blacks and a third of its seamen on the Middle Passage, showing little, if any, profit up to its liquidation in 1787. Schimmelmann, who himself had been a director of the company, was conscience-stricken over the trade and sought, on his inherited sugar plantation on St. Croix, to ensure humane treatment of his slaves and their replacement through natural increase alone. The commission concluded that while slavery could not yet be abolished, the condition of the slaves should be improved toward that eventual end through voluntary cooperation of the plantation owners. On 16 March 1792, Denmark was the first Western nation to prohibit the import of slaves into its colonies, as of the beginning of 1803. Through the determined efforts of the planters, implementation was nonetheless delayed until 1807, after Britain had banned the trade. Slavery itself would not be abolished in the Danish colonies until 1848.[32]

Throughout the 1790s, the government sought to stir the old municipal governments to greater activity in Denmark and Norway; in the duchies they had long played a more independent role. In August 1795 it issued new instructions to the Copenhagen magistrature, setting forth its responsibilities in economic matters, welfare, and schools. Whereas in most Danish and Norwegian towns the trend in the later eighteenth century had been from collegial magistrature to mayor (*byfoged*), the councils of "elected men" (*eligerede mænd*) were now given increased powers of surveillance and control.

The government meanwhile strove to make the councils more representative. Beginning in Viborg in 1793, the common pattern came to be the election of councilmen by majority vote of the citizenry (*borgerskab*). In 1797 this became mandatory for all Danish provincial towns and in 1799 for Norwegian towns. In 1800, members of the artisan class were made eligible for Copenhagen's city council, the "Thirty-Two Men."

At the same time, the government encouraged open citizens' meetings to advise and watch over the "elected men." In 1791 provincial town councils were required to consult with the entire citizenry before preparing proposals. An instruction of 1798 mandated open meetings to consider "everything having to do with economic life and governance."

The government meanwhile kept a close watch over municipal affairs, particularly in the capital. Town ordinances required the approval of the local *amtmand* or *stiftamtmand*, and the authorities constantly intervened directly in town affairs. The quickening pace of citizen participation during the 1790s may reflect a public spirit stimulated by the French Revolution, as has been suggested. But it was still far from democratic, and the government was generally more progressive than the burghers themselves. There was, for instance, much opposition among the old oligarchies to broadening representation on the councils in Christiania, Bergen, and Trondheim, which the civic leaders of the last-named town feared would produce "tumultuous scenes and Polish diets," in accordance with the "spirit of the times."[33]

In June 1795 much of central Copenhagen was destroyed by a disastrous fire. The city made extensive arrangements for temporary relief and housing, aided by donations from throughout the monarchy. The well-planned rebuilding of the devastated areas was soon begun, producing some of the city's most characteristic quarters.

In commerce and manufacturing, the government continued its trend toward greater economic freedom, stimulated by opportunities for neutral trade created by the European war. In May 1793 Copenhagen lost its exclusive bonding privileges in the transit trade, which were now extended to virtually all ports in Denmark and Norway. The Finnmark and Iceland, as well as much of the West Indian trade, was opened to all merchants.

The government continued to aid selected manufacturers, but in February 1797 it issued a new tariff ordinance—the most liberal of its time—eliminating most import restrictions and drastically lowering import duties on a wide assortment of foreign wares, thus largely liquidating the old protectionist system and greatly stimulating foreign trade.

A commission to investigate a carpenters' strike in Copenhagen in 1794 took up the whole question of the craft guilds—of which there were then forty-one in the capital—leading ultimately to curtailment of their monopolies in March 1800. Norwegian forest owners were granted full freedom to cut timber in 1795, and in 1799 all types of trade in Christiania were opened to all with burgher rights.[34]

On 21 June 1797, Count Andreas Peter Bernstorff died in Copenhagen at the age of sixty-two. Combining in his hands the direction of foreign policy, the German and—in 1788–89—the Danish Chancelleries, he was the dominant figure on the royal council and had long been recognized, both at home and abroad, as the real head of government in the Danish monarchy, occupying a position of authority and prestige unmatched in its modern history. No less significant were his unwavering dedication to his adopted fatherland, his involvement to some degree in virtually all aspects of its national life, his patient diplomacy and tact. Not only did Bernstorff manage to preserve the monarchy's neutrality and promote its prosperity in a Europe racked by revolution and war; he also conciliated and turned to constructive ends the centrifugal forces of a diverse and fragile dynastic state. He was sincerely mourned in Denmark, Norway, and the duchies alike. His passing marked the end of the era, since 1784, rightly associated with his name, the most creative and dynamic phase of the Danish era of reform.

While various tasks remained to be completed in 1797, few new reforms would thereafter be initiated. How then is the historic significance of the era to be evaluated? The literature on the subject is immense and constantly growing, not least in recent years, but it varies greatly in quality and depth, leaving room for much controversy over basic questions. How bad were the "bad old days" before 1784? How great a role did legislation play in the amelioration of conditions? To what extent did conditions actually improve, and for whom? What were the guiding motives of the reformers and their adversaries? As such questions are by their very nature largely unanswerable, the interpretations offered largely reflect the changing concerns and ideologies of later times, as well as shifting concepts of the potentialities and proper tasks of historical research.

Older accounts, dating back to the period itself, tended to dramatize the reforms of 1784–97 as a unique, sudden, and essentially complete transformation of society. More recent scholarship has made clear that they were in fact none of these things. There had been much speculation about and numerous practical experiments in reform long before A. P. Bernstorff—or indeed Struensee—came to power. More significant, the conditions of the Danish peasantry had steadily improved in important respects since the beginning of the long peace in 1720, particularly in matters of tenure, as Fridlev Skrubbeltrang has shown.[35]

According to Hans Jensen, the reforms demonstrated that by 1784 an increasingly effective bureaucracy had essentially freed the crown from its earlier administrative dependency upon the landlord class. Ole Feldbæk, however, rightly reminds us that as the administrative machine became more complex, Danish society as a whole did likewise. Bernstorff and his associates thus strove pragmatically to balance the competing demands of social justice, the rights of property, and the needs of the state, while seeking to avoid confrontations damaging to the prestige and popularity of the regime. Important reforms could therefore be delayed and compromised in their implementation. If peasant farmholders benefited greatly, the manorial proprietors ultimately benefited as much or more. That improving conditions in the monarchy by the later eighteenth century were due at least as much to rising prices and favorable markets as to government edicts has frequently been observed. The reformers' solutions to old problems meanwhile gave rise to new ones, notably a growing rural proletariat exposed to new forms of exploitation.[36]

The earlier literature presented the reforms of the Bernstorff era in a heroic light, as the work of great men with lofty ideals. Edvard Holm in the 1880s stressed the influence of the European Enlightenment, while V. A. Falbe-Hansen in the same decade saw in them the liberal ideal of personal freedom. Hans Jensen, writing in the troubled 1930s, recognized in the reforms the triumph of a benevolent welfare state over private interests, whereas Albert Olsen, followed by Jens Holmgaard in the 1950s, considered paramount the needs of the national economy and treasury. In the early 1970s, an American, Carol Gold, described the reforms in her doctoral dissertation as "adjustive and diversionary mechanisms," through which a dominant landlord class defused potential social disorder while retaining control of the means of production and the state.[37]

The great reforms represent a classic case of mixed motives. Even the most reactionary could not altogether escape the spirit of the times, as Johan Hvidtfeldt has emphasized, while the men who guided the destinies of the monarchy after 1784 strove with high hopes and enthusiasm to create a more uniform, efficient, and humane society. They naturally gave highest priority to the agrarian problem and were convinced that personal freedom would make the peasant farmer an enterprising, productive, and patriotic citizen. It was likewise evident to them that the reform of peasant agriculture was essential, as Jens Holmgaard has made clear, if the badly depleted treasury were to profit from the later eighteenth-century economic upswing. To have allowed landowners unrestricted disposition of their property at the very time the government was largely dismantling the old protectionist system in manufactures and commerce would have created unemployment and poverty on an unmanageable scale in both town and countryside, Albert Olsen has observed.[38] The reduction of tariffs meanwhile permitted the national economy to benefit fully from the opportunities offered by the European war, while the government sought to relieve such local distress as this readjustment created.

No conspiracy theory is necessary to understand that enlightened and public-spirited men deriving from the old elite should consider themselves the natural leaders of a society whose great majority were only beginning to acquire some rudiments of prosperity, literacy, and awareness of a wider world. They meanwhile strove, as circumstances allowed, to improve the lot of the least favored inhabitants of the state—the Jew, the farm laborer, the pauper, the convict, eventually the West Indian slave—as well as of the peasant cultivator. In sum, ideal motives combined with practical needs to lay the bases of a new way of life.

Internal developments in the North took place against the background of the ongoing revolution in France. The assassination of Gustav III in March 1792 was a profound shock to his Swedish and Finnish subjects, including most of his erstwhile opponents, while the growing violence and radicalism of the French Revolution disillusioned by stages most who had initially welcomed it. As late as January 1793, Gustav III's bitter critic Baron Adolf Ludvig Hamilton could send to the Convention a "Project for the Legislation of the French Republic."[39] But then came the crucial year of the Terror.

Of those still able to keep the faith, many lost it when the revolution thereafter seemed to compromise its earlier ideals. In 1796 the young poet Frans Michael Franzén from Finland arrived in Paris, exhilarated to find himself in "the arena of so many great events and deeds, the mere echo of which in our distant hills was enough to enrapture us," but soon "fell, as if from the heavens, when I did not once encounter in Paris the *republican*, the *public spirit* I had expected," which apparently had expired with Robespierre. Departing from Le Havre, he threw his tricolor cocarde into the sea, with a "certain ceremony and with solemn, rather melancholy feelings." "I am sure," he added wistfully, "the best republicans both within and outside of France would as easily discard their convictions, if circumstances required."[40]

The young regicides involved in Gustav III's assassination had been romantic enthusiasts for both freedom and equality as they saw these ideals embodied in the French Revolution. Around 1794, Count Adolf Ludvig Ribbing would write:

Hasten, Swedish noblemen, to sacrifice freely all that can be called privilege, keep pace with your century, throw to the ground those titles, patents of ennoblement, decorations, that place in society which are demanded as hereditary rights. Blush to have anyone but yourself to thank for any right, any social advantage whatsoever.

Nonetheless, from 1792 there was a growing rift between aristocratic libertarianism and antiaristocratic social radicalism.[41]

Those, meanwhile, who turned against the French Revolution and all its works tended in like measure to repudiate the rationalism of the *philosophes* in favor of religious pietism or secular mysticisms. Among the intellectuals, only a few stout souls, like Nils Rosén von Rosenstein in 1793, still dared uphold the ideals of the Enlightenment by seeking to disassociate them from the excesses of the revolution. By the turn of the century the poet Franzén would elegiacally express their deepening discouragement:

> In vain ye burned the midnight oil, ye wise ones,
> *Locke, Rousseau, Voltaire,* and *Montesquieu,*
> Your efforts are now scattered by the winds.
> While yet the sound of your names we praise,
> In sorrow to your graves takes flight
> The friend of light, who sees the failure of all his hopes
> When *Marat* shares adoration in this world
> With *Cagliostro* and with *Swedenborg.*[42]

G. A. Reuterholm had been among the Swedish "Patriots" of the 1780s inspired by the revolution and had visited Paris in 1789–90. Upon becoming Duke Carl's "vizier" in July 1792, he prepared a grandiloquent edict restoring freedom of the press, which Gustav III had progressively curtailed since 1774.[43] The result was a plethora of new journals and pamphlets glorifying the French Revolution and the rights of man, and in particular attacking the institution of hereditary aristocracy. Most prominent among the radical journalists of 1792 was Lorenz Munter Philipson, who in December declared in his newly founded *Patrioten*:

> No one should hold, much less be born to, any honor but that which he earns through his native and acquired abilities; should own anything but what he himself needs and is not denied to others; permit himself any idleness but that which his nature requires to restore his strength.

While some nobles took up the pen in defense of their order, there were still some who took the popular side. Admiral F. W. Leijonancker even accused the French Revolution of being too moderate and called for a liberty based on economic equality.[44]

Reuterholm, proud aristocrat that he was, had indeed been attracted to the libertarian aspect of the revolution, but by no means to its egalitarian side. The behavior of the unbridled press made him and his friends increasingly uncomfortable. Late in 1792 Thomas Thorild provided an excuse to reimpose controls on the press.

Thorild thirsted, as seen, for the role of court philosopher and prepared ambitious plans for the regeneration of society which he pressed upon Reuterholm, who considered Thorild his protégé. In December 1792, however, Thorild published a pamphlet that appealed for an end to all remaining limitations to freedom of expression, "before it is seized through violence and bloodshed," and offended the dignity of the four Estates by calling them the "kingdom's four states of confusion." "Vanquish," he urged, "these four barbaric nations! Make of us *one* people!" The pamphlet was confiscated and Thorild was arrested, tried, and exiled for four years, amid much public outcry and some rioting in his support—actions which aroused no little attention abroad.[45]

The severity of Thorild's final sentence meanwhile reflected the government's indignation over the execution of Louis XVI in France and its exaggerated fear of "Jacobinism" behind a relatively minor tumult in Stockholm—the so-called Ebel Riot—precipitated by a scuffle between an officer and two local citizens, both of which occurred in January 1793.[46] Already the previous month, the press restrictions of 1774 were restored, and both author and printer were made responsible for violations.

Thus ended, within a scant half-year, Reuterholm's experiment in freedom of expression. Power agreed with him, and he abandoned his old libertarian ideas. Increasingly he was himself regarded as a despot. In 1795, suspicious of "Jacobin" influences, he closed the Swedish Academy, which was only reopened after the end of the regency.

By early 1793, Uppsala University emerged as the new center of Swedish radicalism, with some reverberations at the universities in Lund and Åbo. On New Year's Eve 1792, the Uppsala students held a mock funeral for press freedom. Out of this there developed the so-called Convention—a concept with obvious French republican connotations—which convened frequently at local taverns over the next few months and evidently involved a sizable proportion of the university's roughly 550 students, to the alarm and indignation of conservative circles. Ringing orations were held, republican cocardes worn, and trees of liberty planted. One of the Convention's few preserved speeches asked rhetorically,

. . . is it first in our time that we may courageously declare that those fields of knowledge which are concerned with mankind's, or a people's, true rights and happiness, and with the means to attain them, are the foremost, the most useful and necessary of all? Is it reserved for our time alone

to ask: What is most useful, most necessary? What is true in our understanding? What is noble and touches our hearts? What are the rights of
mankind? What are the laws of God and Nature?[47]

By the end of April 1793, Duke Carl, the university's chancellor, ordered the
Convention dissolved. It offered no resistance, but radical political and social
ideals—characteristically combined with the new Kantian concept of an individual "categorical imperative"—continued to be cultivated the rest of the decade
by a small group of Uppsala intellectuals which came to be called the "Junta."
Many of its members were of noble origin, and several would play important
cultural and political roles in the future. While they tended to be regarded as
flaming "Jacobins," their political liberalism and federalist sympathies were
indeed rather more "Girondin."[48]

Radicalism among middle-class circles, especially in the capital, was by all
evidence distinctly more social in orientation. "The former royalists," R. F.
Hochschild complained in May 1793, "miss the king [Gustav III] and are becoming attached to Jacobinism, going from one extreme to another." The Austrian chargé d'affaires may have been closer to the mark when he reported in
1797 that "French" principles had made great headway among the Swedish
"Third Estate" in connection with "that sort of Jacobinism already fomented
by the late king against the nobility." Leniency toward the regicides in 1792 had
increased resentments against both the aristocracy and the regency itself, while
the fears of the latter were greatly aroused by the Ebel Riot in Stockholm in early
1793.[49]

Fears and accusations of "Jacobinism" likewise loomed large in the bitter
rivalry between the Reuterholm faction and the ousted Gustavians. During 1792
the latter were deeply offended by the new regime's lenient treatment of the regicides, its efforts at rapprochement with France, and the rumor that summer that
a *riksdag* would be called which, like the French Estates-General, they feared
might precipitate revolution. In J. A. Ehrenström's words:

> The ground is already prepared, in my view, for so-called Jacobinism, in
> our land as elsewhere. Inflated ideas of freedom, equality, and the rights
> of the people, which indeed form the Jacobin articles of faith and which
> in practice are so ruinous to all civic order, seem to be carried by the winds
> like a contagion throughout Europe. We have seen a clear enough begin-
> ning of Jacobinism in the writings which came out as soon as freedom of
> the press was allowed.[50]

To the Gustavians, Reuterholm, Staël, even the duke-regent himself were
"Jacobins" in sheep's clothing.

Reuterholm was ever fearful of Gustavian plots. While Baron Taube did indeed quietly cultivate the confidence of the young king, Gustav IV Adolf,
Reuterholm's suspicions focused above all on Baron Armfelt, now minister to

the Italian courts, whose correspondence with Sweden he secretly intercepted. This correspondence contained remarks offensive to himself and the regime. In December 1793 Reuterholm had—or was confident he could find—sufficient evidence to prosecute Armfelt and his closest associates. The latter, including Ehrenström and Armfelt's mistress, Magdalena Rudenschöld, were arrested and brought to trial, although they were first able to burn some of their papers. A warship was dispatched to Naples to arrest Armfelt, who escaped to Russia.

The trial proved an embarrassment to the government for lack of evidence until in April 1794 Reuterholm's agent, the engraver Francesco Piranesi, purloined Armfelt's papers from the safekeeping of the British minister to Florence. These contained a sketchy "plan of revolution," prepared for the eventuality of a *riksdag* in the summer of 1792, whereby the "royalists" (Gustavians), should pretend to come to terms with the "Feuillants" or "Monarchicals" (the old "Patriot" party of 1789), to destroy the "Jacobins" (Reuterholm, Staël, and their friends). At this point, the Russian empress should issue a manifesto guaranteeing Gustav III's political testament and the original regency council. The "royalists" would then break with the "Feuillants" and establish themselves in power.

The anticipated *riksdag* was never held and Armfelt and his confidants apparently did nothing to implement their "revolution," but its discovery gave Reuterholm his revenge. After a parody of a trial, the conspirators were given death sentences, commuted by Duke Carl to imprisonment. The unfortunate Magdalena Rudenschöld was pilloried and committed to a workhouse, arousing much sympathy.[51]

To supporters of the regime, this so-called Armfelt Conspiracy was an odious "Jacobin" attempt to overthrow the legitimate government.[52] Ironies abound. Gustaf Mauritz Armfelt, the "Alcibiades of the North," who had stood by Gustav III in the dark days of the Anjala revolt, looked to the Russian empress for deliverance, while in seeking to crush "Jacobinism" in Sweden, he and his friends were tarred with the same brush.

In the Danish monarchy, an idealistic admiration for the French Revolution long survived among the higher German aristocracy. In the fall of 1792, "all" Copenhagen, which was "very democratic," rejoiced at the French victory at Valmy, according to Jens Baggesen, protégé of the Augustenburgs and Schimmelmanns, who hoped this would strengthen the liberal forces in the Danish government. Countess Sophie, the wife of Christian Ditlev Reventlow, sang "Ça ira" in jubilation and noted the satisfaction of all her friends. Countess Luise Stolberg saw in Valmy the "hand of God," through which the "benign influence" of France would spread to all lands.

"May the French defeat their anarchy within as well as their enemies without, then the last days of crowns and coronets and patents of nobility should be closer at hand than ever," wrote Prince Friedrich Christian of Augustenburg—soon to become a state councillor and the monarchy's only duke—who after suffering much disillusionment with the Revolution in 1791, felt his hopes revived by the "wise and bold" actions of the new French Convention. By December 1792 he could contemplate with philosophic "equanimity" the prospect of losing rank, title, and wealth. Although by the end of 1793 he came to fear "the heaven would be too dearly bought that could immediately arise out of the present Hell" in France, and soon contemplated emigrating to America, his wife, Princess Luise Augusta—sister of the crown prince—stood fast in the faith a year later, when in August 1794 she rejoiced at the triumph of French arms and longed for the day when she might sacrifice her title to the "public good" and "be admitted to the class of Danish citizens, possessing no advantages other than those I am able to acquire myself."[53]

In Holstein, *Amtmann* August Hennings at Plön published in 1792 his polemical *Ueber Adelsgeist und Aristokratismus*, for which he was attacked as a "Jacobin" or "Sansculotte," although he protested that he was rather a "Girondin" in sympathy. Count W. F. von Schmettau, a retired Danish general, attacked the militarism of the monarchy in his *Patriotischen Gedanken eines Dänen* in 1792, setting off a public controversy intensely irritating to Crown Prince Frederik, who for his own part followed the operations of the French armies with keen interest. Nikolaus von Luckner at Blumendorff, son of a general in French service guillotined in 1794, remained an enthusiastic defender of the revolution, although it was noted that his servants still addressed him as "His Grace."[54]

In May 1793 the Prince of Augustenburg wrote to Baggesen that he believed he could get along well with the "Kiel democrats," provided they espoused a "democracy of true cosmopolitans"; he was indeed too much of a *Kulturhumanist* to feel much affinity for the unwashed masses. He was by then in contact with Adam Weishaupt, former leader of the suppressed Order of Illuminati in Bavaria, whom he had long hoped to bring to Denmark to head a secret organization for the spread of true enlightenment.[55] Yet even those among the aristocracy of the duchies who felt little enthusiasm for the revolution as such did not remain unaffected. In 1788 the *Ritterschaft* had declared itself prepared to pay a special levy for the Swedish campaign but had seized the opportunity to reassert its corporate status (*ius subcollectandi*). When in 1792 the government imposed a tax upon the inheritance of estates by collateral heirs, the *Ritterschaft* held this to be a violation of established rights and called for the convening of the long-defunct Schleswig-Holstein *Landtag*, in a manner recalling the French nobility's demand for the Estates-General in 1787–88. As in 1774, however, Bernstorff's determination and tact smoothed the troubled waters.[56] Many landlords were meanwhile impressed by peasant unrest in the duchies with the need for some measure of reform.

Most of the nobility in the duchies, as elsewhere in Europe, regarded the French Revolution with growing repugnance, particularly after 1792. Emkendorf manor in Holstein emerged as the center of a romantic conservatism rooted in an idealization of both Greek antiquity and the High Middle Ages, in classical stoicism and a revived Lutheran piety, implacably opposed to the godless Revolution and the atheistical Enlightenment, with far-reaching influence in the Germanic world. Count Fritz Reventlow of Emkendorf had left the Danish diplomatic service already in 1786 and with his brother, Count Cai Reventlow, assumed leadership of the conservative phalanx of the *Ritterschaft* against the menace of leveling by either Danish absolutism from above or French *Sansculottisme* from below. He was married to Ernst Schimmelmann's sister, Julia, *"die schöne Seele"* of the Emkendorf cult, whose *Weltanschauung* was expressed in a letter to her brother in November 1793:

> The word *Aufklärung* has gradually become quite hateful to me. Never has it been spoken as often as during this shallow century in which no greatness thrives. Every youth, it seems, has it ever on his tongue, while despising the old, true wisdom of life. Oh, that man might once again learn to reform himself and not seek to light the way for others before he has endured this struggle! Oh, that he might once again learn to gather within his soul the blessed inspiration from above and to recognize his own powerlessness when he relies upon himself alone! Then would Peace and Joy embrace once more. One is almost ashamed in our time to be a human being. For in the jungles of Africa there flourish, among lions and tigers, more or less the same kinds of laws, the same liberty and equality![57]

Although Charlotte Schimmelmann had been much disillusioned by the execution of Louis XVI, she was still amused to describe in May 1794 how Guldberg "jeremiadized" against France "like a good Jutlander." His letters are indeed filled with outbursts against France's "metaphysical constitution" and "metaphysical *politici*," as well as dire warnings that Copenhagen was a nest of "Jacobins." His views, it would appear, were characteristic enough, not only of a "good Jutlander," but generally of the Danish proprietorial class. In Denmark, Jakob Baden, a professor of philology at the University of Copenhagen and stout defender of absolutism, and in Norway, Johan Nordal Brun, composer in 1771 of "Norway, Land of Heroes" and now bishop of Bergen, were determined antirevolutionary polemicists.[58]

In the kingdom, as in the duchies, opposition to the revolution was closely linked to antirationalist religious revivalism, not least in response to criticism of orthodox Christian dogma by certain of the Copenhagen radicals. In the capital Bishop Balle began conducting well-attended biweekly Bible reading sessions in 1793 and brought out a devotional journal with some 30,000 subscribers. A visit to Copenhagen in 1793 by the Swiss evangelist and mystic Johann Casper

Lavater, at A. P. Bernstorff's invitation, created a sensation in high aristocratic circles.[59]

Among Copenhagen's substantial bourgeoisie, there remained widespread, if somewhat diffuse, sympathy for the French Revolution, as became evident in 1793, when the French Convention sent the regicide Philippe Grouvelle to Denmark, ostensibly to buy grain. He was lionized by members of the Copenhagen Wholesale Merchants' Society (*Grosserer-Societetet*). They—and particularly their women—were thoroughly charmed by Grouvelle and his companions, whom they affected to see in the guise of heroes of republican Rome. French cocardes were sported and the "Marseillaise" enthusiastically sung.[60]

Thereafter, during the Terror, *Minerva*, which generally mirrored enlightened middle-class opinion, turned sharply critical of the revolution, although it again adopted a more favorable tone following the Thermidorian reaction of mid-1794. Britain's oppressive maritime policies after joining the European war in the spring of 1793 meanwhile stirred old resentments, thereby strengthening sympathy for France, together with the triumphs of French arms against heavy odds. Throughout this period, there are nonetheless signs of a gradual slackening of political engagement among the Danish middle classes as a whole, as reflected, for example, in the waning of club activity in Copenhagen. Already in the winter of 1792, the young historian Frederik Sneedorff, upon visiting France, was disillusioned since the revolution had "made an idol of the rabble, whose altars disgrace and offend the Majesty of the People."[61]

French sympathies meanwhile remained very much the fashion among university students. Henrik Steffens recalled a group popularly known as the "Copenhagen Jacobin Club," to which he belonged and in which hair-raising harangues were heard calling for revolution and the blood of tyrants. Of his student days at the University of Kiel, the Holstein schoolmaster Georg Friedrich Schumacher reminisced:

> War on the palaces, peace to the cottages! This motto we inscribed in our albums, thus we shouted on our nightly excursions through the quiet, deserted alleys. Long live Freedom! Down with Tyrants! So we often bellowed through the night. But when we had properly cursed the palaces, we let them stand in peace. . . . When we had consigned the tyrants to the underworld, we left it to them to find their own way there, having done our part. We sang the *Marseillaise* in exalted voices, *Allons enfants de la patrie*, but went no further than to bed.[62]

Outside Copenhagen, the burghers of the larger towns in the duchies and Norway showed the greatest interest in French developments. By the mid-1790s, growing censorship elsewhere left Schleswig-Holstein with the freest press in the German-speaking world. Certain journals, such as the *Niedersächsischer Merkur* from Hamburg, sought asylum there, while Georg Conrad Meyer's *Der neue Mensch* in Flensburg was particularly outspoken in its republicanism. In Altona and Kiel there were thriving "Jacobin" societies. In 1795 Mary Wollstonecraft found the citizens of Moss in Norway "so determined . . . to excuse every thing, disgracing the struggle for freedom, by admitting the tyrant's plea necessity, that I could hardly persuade them that Robespierre was a monster." A Norwegian study has meanwhile shown how deeply the basic ideals of the revolution had penetrated by the middle of the decade, even into areas of thought where they might hardly be expected; printed sermons and pastoral letters, for instance, show that some of the most articulate spokesmen for egalitarian principles were rationalist clergymen—all, of course, graduates of the University of Copenhagen—even when they condemned revolution as such.[63]

Enthusiasm for the French Revolution remained linked to demonstrative loyalty to the Danish monarchy. "Most of the merchants," Thomas Malthus observed in Fredrikshald (Halden), Norway, in 1799, "seem to be a little inclined to republicanism," but added: "They extoll much the liberty they enjoy under their own government; & say that in England we are comparative slaves." To August Hennings, the absolute monarchy was democracy enthroned. Christian Colbjørnsen best expressed this ideal in a speech to the Agricultural Society (*Landhusholdningsselskab*) in February 1794:

> They are not rulers who through misdeeds have assumed that lofty title.
> . . . No! Ye fathers of your country! It is that power entrusted to you by
> the people that we hail, it is that which we call government, . . . it is
> your glorious deeds that we acclaim when we see you, armed with the
> clear light of Reason, exorcise the specter of Prejudice and, with a mighty
> hand, break the hateful chains of Feudal Tyranny. . . . The rights of the
> throne are inseparable from those of the people. . . . Government is the
> gathering point for the General Will.

"If our famous Colbjørnsen were not deeply involved in public affairs here," Charlotte Schimmelmann wrote to Luise Stolberg, "he would be a dangerous democrat or demagogue; here he is all zeal for the monarchy, while speaking freely of France."[64]

While in Sweden the press was unbridled for only half a year, in 1792, it remained remarkably free in the Danish monarchy throughout the decade, providing a far fuller picture of the evolution of opinion in informed, essentially middle-class circles. Voices praising the revolution in France while condemning "aristocracy" and "tyranny" were well represented. This was no less true of, for instance, *Den snaksomme Bergenser* or *Bergenseren* in Bergen, *Trondhjemske Tidender* or, later, *Quarterbladet* in Trondheim, *Hermoder* in Christiania, or *Schleswigsche Journal* in Altona (later Flensburg), than of *Minerva* or *Kjøbenhavns Lærde Efterretninger* in the capital.[65]

Most of the press accepted the premise implied in Colbjørnsen's speech in 1794: that Danish absolutism accomplished by peaceful means what the revolution in France could only achieve by force, in accordance with the popular will. Such a concept could, however, be a double-edged sword, for it raised critical questions. What was the will of the people and how could it be adequately communicated to the ruler? And was the ruler indeed fulfilling its rightful demands?

Faced with such questions, a small avant-garde of journalists and publicists went over to a republican viewpoint by the mid-1790s and attacked royal absolutism not only in its abuses but in principle. "What is the history of all monarchical governments but a frightful depiction of human misery?" wrote *Politisk og Physisk Magazin* in Copenhagen, following the Terror which it had never ceased to justify, "All hereditary regimes are by their very nature tyrannical." In the same journal, "A Danish Man" stated in 1797 that as an unlimited monarchy, Denmark suffered from all the faults inherent in such a form of government.[66]

Whereas the supporters of enlightened absolutism considered it the sword of democracy, these republican critics condemned it as the shield of privilege. N. D. Riegels complained that in a monarchy, "the monarch's lap dog, or his hairdresser and flunkies, are more important than the nation." This sentiment was widely disseminated by the youthful Malte Conrad Bruun—son of one of the aristocratic Jutland proprietors of 1790—in the first "hymn" of his popular satire *Aristocraternes Catechismus* (The Aristocrats' Catechism) in 1795:

> Oh, Monarchy, our praise to thee!
> Thou shelterst all our guile and treachery.
> What indeed is Aristocracy,
> If *thou*
> doest not uphold it?

In his *Jerusalems Skomagers Rejse til Maanen* (The Jerusalem Shoemaker's Journey to the Moon) the same year, as well as in his newspaper, *Vækkeren*, Bruun held forth the ideal of a republic as the only regime under which morality and virtue could blossom, a vision held by such other radical writers as P. A. Heiberg, N. D. Riegels, M. G. Birkner in Korsør, and G. C. Meyer in Flensburg.[67]

Abroad, liberal opinion hailed Denmark's press freedom as unsurpassed in Europe, while the counterrevolutionary camp saw the Danish monarchy as a dangerous center of Jacobinism. In Denmark conservatives like Guldberg and Schack-Rathlou considered the free press a dire threat to the existing order. Crown Prince Frederik, otherwise no reader, took to avidly following the newspapers, to his mounting indignation. They raised demands, such as for a separate Norwegian university and bank, beginning again in 1793, and criticized sacred cows, as did Count Schmettau in his criticism of the military establishment in the same year. Bruun and Riegels in particular aroused resentment through their attacks on Christian dogma and the religious establishment. In March 1797, 300 burghers of Copenhagen petitioned the crown to protect religion against abuse.[68]

To many, the situation appeared increasingly serious in the light of social disturbances in various parts of the monarchy. Troubles in the duchies in 1794–95 have already been noted. In Norway, there were outbreaks of urban unrest, especially among the miners in Kongsberg in 1794, and conflicts in Østlandet between timber merchants and teamsters. More frightening yet was the so-called Post Office Riot of February 1793 in Copenhagen, set off by an altercation between a student and a Guards' officer. In April 1794 some 2,000 journeyman carpenters in the capital went on strike, encouraged by the radical press, most notably Bruun's *Vækkeren*. Of the strikers, 122—many of them Germans—were exiled for life.[69]

In individual cases the government took action for abuse of press freedom. In 1794 Professor C. F. Cramer was dismissed from the University of Kiel for statements unbefitting a subject of Holstein, which as part of the Holy Roman Empire was technically at war with France. The same year, Heiberg was fined for a satirical song, *"Klubvise,"* insulting to the king of England, and a journeyman printer was prosecuted for a pamphlet ridiculing the doctrines of the state church. Bruun was fined for implying in *Vækkeren*, in connection with the carpenters' strike, that an individual was not bound in obedience to a law or authority he considered unjust. In 1795 he was indicted for attacking the government in his *Aristocraternes Catechismus* and fled temporarily to Sweden.[70]

In the face of a mounting reaction against freedom of expression, its supporters rallied in its defense. The Danish monarch's power, M. G. Birkner argued in a widely disseminated pamphlet in 1797, was in principle as great as the Turkish sultan's or Tipoo Sahib's; without liberty to write about government or administration, there could be no "free citizens," at best only "children under guardianship or leniently, mildly, and humanely treated slaves." While A. P. Bernstorff lived, freedom of expression survived, despite his own antipathy to many of the ideas expressed. But with his passing in the summer of 1797, its days were numbered.[71]

The Danish ultraradicals of the 1790s have naturally received no little attention from the historians. Yet how little impact they had upon the mass of the monarchy's subjects was illuminated, literally and figuratively, by a fire that accidentally broke out in February 1794, destroying Christiansborg palace in Copenhagen. The result was a great wave of public sympathy for the crown prince and his family, as evidenced by private donations, large and small, from throughout the monarchy. The royal family's move to the simpler Moltke and Schack palaces, connected by C. F. Harsdorff's neoclassical colonade, on

Amalienborg Square—where it still resides today—was symbolic of the changed nature of Danish absolutism since Christian VI had built the massive, baroque Christiansborg in the 1730s.[72]

Scarcely a fortnight after Gustav III died, the war he had so avidly sought broke out when France declared war on Austria and Prussia in April 1792. As principalities of the Holy Roman Empire, both Holstein and Swedish Pomerania were nominally involved until 1795, to the extent of modest financial contributions, but this in no way determined policy in Copenhagen or Stockholm. Relieved of the Swedish menace, Denmark held firmly to its neutrality. Gustav III's passing meanwhile led to a diplomatic reversal in Sweden. Duke Carl and his entourage felt a certain sympathy for the French constitutional monarchy. Already in May 1792, France sent a diplomatic agent to Stockholm and secret discussions were begun concerning a possible Franco-Swedish alliance.

Sweden's foreign policy dilemma at this juncture was perceptively described by Duchess Charlotta:

> If the duke-regent should now enter into an alliance with France to seek to obtain a counterweight against Russian power, perhaps the mania for freedom which reigns there might also gain the upper hand in our land, which would indeed be a greater misfortune than any other. If, on the other hand, the duke continues to show himself as submissive to Russia as the late king, one might well fear that Sweden might become a new Poland.[73]

Negotiations with France continued fitfully for over three years, at last resulting in a defensive alliance in September 1795, providing a French subsidy for Sweden to defend its neutral maritime rights.[74]

As always, the outbreak of a major European war created welcome prospects for neutral trade and shipping. Both opportunities and risks increased greatly when Great Britain, the United Netherlands, and Spain entered the conflict in the spring of 1793. France now became heavily dependent upon neutral carriers for provisionment and supply, while British privateers preyed upon Scandinavian ships en route to France. By mid-August the British had seized 189 Danish and Norwegian vessels alone. In so doing, they arbitrarily renounced their treaty of July 1780 conceding Denmark's right to export foodstuffs to Britain's enemies, claiming that the French had now placed themselves outside the bounds of all international law.

In July 1793 Britain offered to buy Danish grain shipments bound for France, but together with Russia demanded an end to all trade with France. Bernstorff stood fast, declaring, "International law is unalterable; its principles do not depend upon circumstances." As expected, Russia was too involved in Poland to back up its demand.[75]

Despite old resentments—especially in Sweden—common commercial interests drew the two Scandinavian kingdoms together. Negotiations commenced in the summer of 1793, leading to the Armed Neutrality Convention signed in Copenhagen on 27 March 1794.[76]

In June 1794 a Swedish squadron of eight ships of the line joined a Danish squadron of the same size to cruise in the North Sea. British visitations in Scandinavian waters ceased, seized vessels were released, and the Danish grain trade with France resumed. Until 1797, combined Scandinavian naval operations continued to produce good effects. Efforts were likewise made in 1794–95 to involve other neutrals, especially the United States, but without result. In 1797 Danish operations against the dey of Tripoli protected a burgeoning commerce in the Mediterranean.[77]

Scandinavian trade flourished. But cooperation in the North did not proceed without friction. As during the American war, Denmark tended to incline toward Britain and Russia, Sweden toward France, largely on the basis of their trade commodities. Sweden's defensive alliance with France in September 1795 moreover called into question its neutral status and led by the spring of 1796 to the threat of war with Russia. France, by now successful on all fronts, showed little concern. Reuterholm, fearful for his native Finland, sought a reconciliation with St. Petersburg. His efforts had met with only limited success when Gustav IV Adolf came of age and assumed personal control in November 1796. The same month, Catherine II died, to the relief of her Nordic neighbors.[78]

The Armed Neutrality of 1780 had revealed the old mistrust between the hereditary enemies of the North, reflected in Johannes Ewald's patriotic anthem, written the year before:

> King Christian stood by the lofty mast,
>     'mid swirling smoke.
> His sword it struck with mighty blows,
>     cleaving Gothic helm and skull.

In contrast, the Armed Neutrality of 1794 showed the growing Nordic sentiment of the later eighteenth century, evident in literature, especially in Denmark, where it was part of the reaction against still powerful German cultural influences. The expressions *Skandinavien* and *Norden* (in an exclusively Scandinavian sense) became increasingly current. In the spring of 1792, the young Danish historian Frederik Sneedorff spoke to a group in London calling itself the Scandinavian Society on ''The Importance of the Union of the Three Nordic Kingdoms''; in this speech he appealed that ''we united Swedes, Norwegians, and Danes consider ourselves as belonging to only one fatherland—Scandinavia.''

While interest was weaker in Sweden, progressive opinion there tended to admire Danish enlightened absolutism. The Scandinavianism of the 1790s was characterized by its affinity for radical social and political ideals and its cosmopolitan view of membership in a larger Nordic community as a step toward the higher goal of world citizenship. It culminated with the establishment in Copenhagen of *Det Skandinaviske Litteraturselskab* (The Scandinavian Literary Society) in 1796.

> Like dew before the sun, all imagined hate
> now disappears;
> See Cimbrian joyfully embracing Goth,
> like a cherished friend.

Thus wrote the Norwegian Jens Zeitlitz in 1794. The contrast to Ewald's warlike anthem of 1779 is striking.[79]

For the later 1780s a notable similarity was observed in the internal development of the two Nordic kingdoms: in both, vigorous and fundamental reforms were then carried out by the crown itself. By the turn of the decade, however, Sweden-Finland, under Gustav III, was occupied primarily by war and diplomacy, whereas Denmark-Norway, under Crown Prince Frederik, continued on the path of reform.

During the years 1792 to 1797, from the death of Gustav III to that of A. P. Bernstorff, there was a further parting of the ways. The reform program of the Danish monarchy was sustained and advanced, while the regency in Sweden was marked by reaction and paranoiac fears. The situation of the two monarchies was now reversed: Gustav III's early reign, after 1772, had been a time of numerous useful reforms in Sweden-Finland, while Denmark-Norway had been governed by the reactionary de facto regency of Juliane Marie.

It was frequently maintained by the thinkers of the Enlightenment that a government should be judged by results rather than form. Scandinavia during these years is a case in point. Subjects of the absolutistic Danish monarchy enjoyed far greater civic liberty—above all, freedom of expression—than those of the Swedish constitutional monarchy, which had evolved into a kind of ad hoc dictatorship. In 1795 Mary Wollstonecraft believed "the inhabitants of Denmark and Norway are the least oppressed people of Europe." The same year, the Swedish regicide Count Ribbing, in exile near Copenhagen, rejoiced to find himself at last in a land where he could "in all justice praise the government," which had "crushed the aristocratic Hydra." Well might Swedish radicals look with envy across the Sound.[80] Meanwhile, as Swedish radicalism took an increasingly social direction, the avant-garde of Danish radicalism now for the first time turned to basic political questions, looking beyond popular autocracy to popular sovereignty.

Despite contrasts between the two regimes, basic similarities can be seen in the economic, social, and cultural evolution of the Nordic lands, especially with regard to the peasant masses. Everywhere freehold ownership was on the rise among a free peasantry, while in the richer agricultural regions land reallocations and the relocation of farmsteads were breaking up the familiar patterns of village and manorial life. Just as the land reforms originating in the duchies and Denmark began to spread to southern Sweden, peasant emancipation inspired by the Swedish-Finnish, as well as the Norwegian and now the Danish model, was gradually extended to the remaining serfs of Schleswig and Holstein. Throughout the Nordic world the rise in numbers and well-being of peasant farmers was meanwhile paralleled by the rapid growth of a rural proletariat of cotters and landless laborers.

The Danish reforms of 1784-97 were neither the first nor even in principle the most radical of their kind in Europe. Extensive and ambitious efforts were made in the preceding decades in Prussia, Austria, and various smaller German and Italian principalities, while enclosures were proceeding in Britain. The Danish reform program, however, continued for a good decade after the outbreak of the French Revolution. Whereas earlier Continental reforms were stopped in midstream or turned back by the rising tide of reaction, the Danish monarchy underwent a greater transformation of existing society than anywhere outside of revolutionary France or French-occupied Europe. Although Crown Prince Frederik was no friend of the French Revolution, it seems not inappropriate that on a visit to Frankfurt-am-Main in 1796 General Jourdan's French troops hailed him as *"Citoyen Altesse."*[81]

Responses to the French Revolution entered into a new phase by 1792. Early "Whiggish" enthusiasm in high aristocratic circles, originally inspired by the French *révolte nobiliaire*, was by now largely disillusioned, especially in Sweden-Finland. Increasingly, Scandinavian "Jacobinism" assumed a bourgeois, socially radical character, directed against all forms of "aristocracy."

To assume thereby that the Scandinavian radicals of the 1790s were "democratic" according to later criteria would naturally be anachronistic. Although they attacked distinctions and privileges based on inheritance, they accepted as a matter of course a "natural" hierarchy of virtue and of accomplishment outside the traditional noble profession of arms. "No one denies the difference between a great merchant and a peddler," declared Berndt Børretzen in 1795, in *Den snaksomme Bergenser*:

> Both, be it understood, may be excellent men and good citizens; both are human beings, conceived in iniquity and born in sin. They should, from that standpoint, be regarded as brothers. But there is still a difference, and we hope it may continue to exist among us to the end of time, for it is ordained by Nature herself and unhappy the land where it disappears! Thus reasonable policy demands that each be treated in daily intercourse accord-

ing to his proper worth, for it is stupid pride, indeed a dangerous, harmful blow to the welfare of the state, when all believe themselves equally distinguished, all demand equal respect.[82]

Børretzen was writing—be it noted—in Norway, where hereditary nobility had long since virtually disappeared. In Sweden, it is related that the merchant Niclas Ebel, arrested in connection with the Stockholm riot that acquired his name in 1793, protested, when taken to jail in the same cart as a shoemaker, that he "did not wish to be equal to any but those above him."[83]

The European war beginning in 1792 brought increasing wealth to the Scandinavian lands, in particular to that urban middle class to which such a natural hierarchy of talent appealed most strongly. It was likewise among the middle class of wealth and intellect that a new sense of common Scandinavian identity emerged in the 1790s, in reaction to the foreign cultural values of the old elite.

CHAPTER 10

# Commerce and Counterrevolution
# 1797–1802

Within a little more than half a year, Gustav IV Adolf's coming of age in November 1796 and A. P. Bernstorff's death in June 1797 brought about effective changes of regime within both Scandinavian monarchies. By this time the European reaction against the French Revolution made itself increasingly felt, leading to repressive measures against native "Jacobins" by the turn of the century. Yet in the two kingdoms, especially the Danish-Norwegian, the course of practical reform continued. Both conservatism and reform meanwhile created reactions of varying types: aristocratic in Schleswig-Holstein, radical in certain Danish and Swedish intellectual circles, evangelistic among a large part of the Norwegian peasantry. Such signs of strain were nevertheless largely dampened for the time being by widespread prosperity created by neutral trade in wartime Europe and beyond. But such a windfall opportunity was precariously dependent upon a disoriented, wider European economy, which could lead to sudden crises, as in 1799, and brought the threat of foreign entanglements, culminating in April 1801 in the first bitter foretaste of seven lean years of war.

Upon assuming personal power at the end of 1796, Gustav IV Adolf dismissed G. A. Reuterholm, who returned to self-imposed exile on the Continent. Duke Carl withdrew into private life. The young king was proud, taciturn, and rather stiffly rectitudinous. He had about him, a British diplomat observed, "more of the Castillian than the Swede."[1] He shunned the ostentatious court life and intellectual brilliance that had so captivated his father, Gustav III, and conscientiously sought to avoid a "reign of favorites."

Gustav IV Adolf inherited a position of power which Gustav III had only managed to win at the cost of internal strife, his own popularity in influential circles, and ultimately his life. The new king was determined to exercise to the fullest the extensive powers afforded him by the constitution of 1772 as amended by the Act of Union and Security of 1789, backed by the growing public reaction against the French Revolution. Yet, although he was no political theorist, he on one occasion around 1799 expressed a rationale for his rule not out of keeping with his times, "having been born free in a kingdom where the king governs according to the laws and where each individual enjoys his rights but knows how to obey," thereby avoiding "licentious liberty," which ultimately makes men "slaves under several or under a single despot."[2] Among his faithful servants, especially among old Gustavians like J. C. Toll and Axel von Fersen, there were meanwhile those who more frankly espoused royal absolutism.[3]

The young king abhorred the French Revolution—convinced as he was that French Jacobins had been behind his father's assassination in 1792—as well as the rationalist philosophy of the Enlightenment, which he considered the root of the present disorders. In religion he held to a strict Lutheran orthodoxy with pietist overtones. Press censorship remained firm.

The markedly conservative features of the reign from its beginning can, however, all too easily obscure the fact that useful and practical reforms were resumed in Sweden-Finland following the end of the regency. Until the final disasters of his reign a decade later, Gustav IV Adolf was able to work far more harmoniously with his bureaucrats than had Gustav III. Despite his fear of "Jacobinism," the king revealed no romantic attachment to the nobility as such, and his top appointments went by preference to men of recent ennoblement and to commoners. Gustav Adolf's interest in aspects of his officials' work could be considerable, if sporadic; ultimately it was he who gave their projects the force of law.

Through various administrative reorganizations, culminating with the restructuring of the old *Kanslikollegium* and the emergence of a separate foreign ministry in 1801, the business of government was steered back into established and now largely rationalized channels. Already in 1796 a new finance committee (*statsberedning*) was set up to regularize the annual budget and adjust expenditures to standing revenues. Gustav III's inflated court establishment and pension list were drastically cut back, while provisions for widows and orphans of public servants were improved. During the first few years careful financial administration combined with favorable economic conditions to return a healthy surplus to the treasury. The restrictive trade policies of the regency were relaxed. A committee, the *Kanslersgille*, was appointed in 1801 to propose reforms for the secondary schools, while private initiative continued to increase the numbers of local parish schools. By 1800 the government was prepared to face the formidable task of monetary reform. The new regime meanwhile showed a strong interest in agriculture, which by 1803 would give rise to important initiatives.

Impressive as A. P. Bernstorff's position had been in the Danish-Norwegian monarchy, his death in June 1797 did not bring any striking and immediate transformation of the regime. Bernstorff himself designated his successors: his son, Count Christian Günther Bernstorff, as foreign minister, and son-in-law, Count Cai Reventlow, as president of the German Chancellery. The latter, who belonged to the Holstein branch, together with Christian Ditlev Reventlow of the Danish branch of that widespread family, was now also appointed to the state council. The Bernstorff-Reventlow-Schimmelmann circle was more firmly ensconced in the seats of power than ever after the passing of its dominant personality.

There were nonetheless portents of change. The new men represented a narrower and more conservative viewpoint, which soon led to friction with the "Men of 1784": C. D. Reventlow, Ernst Schimmelmann, and their friends. Meanwhile, Crown Prince Frederik now felt at the age of twenty-nine that the time had come to take the lead himself. Increasingly, he dealt directly with the government departments and individual state councillors. Although lacking the intellectual brilliance of his leading ministers, the crown prince possessed both willpower and an unflagging sense of duty. By the turn of the century it was clearly he who ruled—and to an almost excessive degree administered—the monarchy.

Much remained to be done if the great task of reform, so well begun during the preceding thirteen years, were to be consolidated and advanced in a time of hardening reaction throughout Europe. While the broader outlines had been established in A. P. Bernstorff's time, difficult questions of implementation remained.

The administrative structure was simplified for the kingdom in 1799 when the Danish Chancellery was divided into four sections—for church and education, justice, social matters, and public institutions—while officials at lower levels were permitted to deal with a wider variety of matters without referring to higher authority.

Administrative rationalization meanwhile largely obliterated the last remaining symbols of Iceland's national past. The *Althing*, which in 1777 had been converted into an eight-member district court for Iceland, met for the last time at Thingvallír in 1798. It was thereafter transferred to Reykjavík and in 1800 dissolved, thereby ending, at least temporarily, its 870-year existence. The ancient Hólar bishopric was discontinued, and the Hólar and Skálholt Latin schools were combined into a single school in Reykjavík, which now emerged as the island's administrative, commercial, and cultural center.

The establishment in 1799 of a special section of the Danish Chancellery for social matters is indicative of the government's growing concern with problems of poverty. Building upon a largely ineffectual ordinance of 1708 for the suppression of beggary and care for the deserving poor, piecemeal reforms in this area had been projected since 1787, as noted in the preceding chapter. Although paupers were officially reckoned at only 3.1 percent of the population of Denmark proper in the census of 1801 (the first since 1787)—as compared with 13 percent in Great Britain in the same year—poverty aroused not only humanitarian concerns but social fears.[4] Late in 1798 *Minerva* wrote:

> The laboring class, which alternately is utilized both by . . . [princes and by other classes], informed by one or the other's faults, has at last learned to know, hence to mistrust, fear, and hate them all. Awaiting only a favorable chance to avenge itself for real and imagined injustices, it stands ready, with the sword of destruction in one hand and the torch of enlightenment in the other.[5]

In 1798 relief to the poor in Copenhagen was transferred from the magistrature to a special commission. A comprehensive ordinance for poor relief in the capital was decreed in 1799, implementing the policy stated already in 1792 that public support be available to all in real need. Work was to be provided, in workhouses if need be, for those capable of performing it, as was modest support for the old and helpless, medical attention for the sick, and elementary schooling, to teach the young useful skills, industry, and good morals. The dependent poor could establish eligibility for direct help after three years' residence, while begging was strictly forbidden. A new emphasis was meanwhile placed upon rehabilitation, in addition to relief, through giving such aid to victims of temporary misfortune as might enable them once again to become useful and productive members of society. Specific revenues, including one-quarter of Copenhagen's port dues, were designated to support the system, which proved adequate at least until the war years after 1807. Similar provisions were extended to the entire kingdom by 1803. During the same years, the training of parish midwives was improved and smallpox vaccination was put to widespread use, as was also the case in the Swedish monarchy. A Board of Health (*Sundhedskollegium*) was established in Copenhagen in 1803, charged with overseeing public hygiene and sanitation, and recalling Struensee's earlier efforts in that direction. An ordinance in 1806 called for the establishment of a modest infirmary in each district (*amt*). In 1799 the School Commission, appointed in 1792, presented an ambitious project for a complete system of rural schools, the universal implementation of which in more modest form was nonetheless delayed by circumstances until 1814.[6]

In 1799 the government opened up all types of trade in Christiania to every person possessing citizen rights in the town. An ordinance in March 1800 curtailed the power of the craft guilds by abolishing their exclusive monopolies and permitting any artisan to qualify as journeyman, and any journeyman to become a "free master" and receive citizen rights in his town after four years. Although the old guilds would remain strong, especially in Copenhagen, for some decades to come, a breach had been made in their privileged position.

By 1797, labor obligations were fixed by contract on all but a very few of the manors in Denmark where they were required of tenants. In December 1799 this was made an absolute requirement by royal ordinance. The economic crisis of 1799—of which more below—meanwhile compelled many proprietors to sell off tenancies to raise ready cash.[7]

The problem of serfdom in the duchies remained complex and difficult. A commission of the *Ritterschaft* had resolved in October 1797 that serfdom should be entirely abolished by around 1805. A number of proprietors in the duchies voluntarily freed their serfs, but otherwise matters languished, while the stoutly conservative Cai Reventlow headed the German Chancellery until 1802—to the mounting impatience of Crown Prince Frederik. After the commission failed to reach any agreement at its last meeting in 1798, the government regulated the military aspects of the problem by unilateral decree in 1800, making little concession to the landowners. It was only a matter of time before it would impose its own solution to the question of serfdom in 1804.

In one respect, however, the Danish reform program was notably unsuccessful. Its early efforts after 1784 to stabilize state finances, as well as the monetary system within the kingdom, had been upset by the brief hostilities with Sweden in 1788. Thereafter, despite the general prosperity of the following years, it failed to balance the state budget or to accumulate any surplus against more difficult times. The government sought above all to increase the nation's wealth and productive capacity to the utmost and therefore declined to tax too heavily. Although revenues increased, expenditures rose more rapidly. For the time being, the financial and monetary situation in the duchies remained more stable than in the kingdom.

Following the unpopular regency, the beginning of Gustav IV Adolf's personal reign aroused high hopes in Sweden-Finland, even among the Uppsala radicals. The latter were soon disillusioned, however, by the young king's patent anti-intellectualism and continued censorship. It soon became evident, too, that he had no immediate intention of convening a *riksdag*.

Despite his wish to avoid favoritism, Gustav Adolf soon came to rely strongly upon the advice of his father's former confidants. Indeed, throughout the regency, Baron Evert Taube, who remained at court, had exercised an occult influence upon him on behalf of the basic tenets of Gustav III's last years: standfast opposition to revolutionary France, close relations with Russia, and hostility toward Denmark, with the ultimate objective of acquiring Norway. In this, he was strongly seconded by Count Fersen, who via Taube sent Gustav Adolf fearsome reports of the spread of the Jacobin menace on the Continent.

Following the end of the regency, Taube was soon recognized as the king's most influential adviser, particularly on foreign policy, while J. C. Toll, an old Gustavian stalwart who proudly called himself "despotism's first-born son," had much to say on internal matters. From 1799 the Russian ambassador, Baron Andrei Budberg, added another strongly reactionary influence, while in Tsar Paul I, whom Gustav Adolf visited in St. Petersburg in late 1800, the Swedish king found in many respects a kindred soul.[8]

The new Swedish regime was soon faced with a serious economic crisis, with alarming social and political repercussions. Harvests were poor in 1798 and 1799, and in the latter year commerce throughout northern Europe was largely paralyzed by the collapse of the Hamburg market owing to an overimportation of British products. During late 1799 and early 1800, there was a wave of rioting in Stockholm, Gothenburg, Norrköping, Linköping, Malmö, and other Swedish towns, although no similar disturbances seem to have occurred in Finland. While observers both then and since tended to consider these outbreaks the result of grain shortages, influential conservatives perceived in them the dark forces of revolution.[9]

During the fall of 1799, General Bonaparte's return to Paris from Egypt was warmly welcomed in many circles. A mixed company of Frenchmen and Swedish "Jacobins" celebrated the event in Stockholm with noisy abandon and "republican cheers," to the mortification of the Swedish government and not least of the Russian ambassador in his reports to St. Petersburg. Gustav Adolf was secretly warned of widespread "Jacobin" sympathies throughout the country, especially in middle-class, commercial circles and at Uppsala University, and that revolution seemed imminent. Disturbing rumors circulated.

Gustav IV Adolf was not one to disregard such alarms, nor was Tsar Paul prepared to let him do so. The military received strict orders to suppress any unrest. For some time, the king had meanwhile been concerned about radicalism at the university in Uppsala. In the face of hardening reaction, persons associated with the so-called Junta, in particular Hans Hierta and Georg Adlersparre, strove between 1798 and 1800 to defend their "zeal for enlightenment in the study of society" against hostile allegations of "Jacobinism."[10] In 1799, just when Count Fersen, returning from the Continent, sought to persuade Gustav IV Adolf to place himself at the head of a secret, international anti-Jacobin league, Hierta wrote a bitter satire on the obscurantism of the new Swedish regime, arousing great indignation in both Stockholm and St. Petersburg.[11]

When students at Uppsala openly celebrated French victories and Bonaparte's return from Egypt in December 1799, Gustav Adolf installed Count Fersen as chancellor. The symbolism implicit in this choice was unmistakable; in G. G. Adlerbeth's words, "a declared *French royalist*" was made "the Swedish Jacobins' schoolmaster."[12]

Fersen strove with a strong hand to stamp out any manifestations of radicalism among faculty and students. The gifted young Kantian philosopher Benjamin

Höijer, considered the radicals' standard-bearer, was denied a permanent chair and departed for the Continent in the spring of 1800 following an obstreperous celebration in his honor. In April an attempt to trick the academic orchestra into performing a composition containing an excerpt from the *Marseillaise* led to the trial and punishment of four known radicals on the faculty, one of whom was dismissed. This rather ludicrous "Music Trial" proved the deathblow to what remained of the lively Uppsala radicalism of the preceding decade. The university, which since Gustav III's death had evolved into the real center of Swedish literary life, now entered what has been called its "Iron Age." The same sobriquet would in retrospect be widely applied to Swedish culture as a whole to the end of Gustav IV Adolf's reign.[13]

Hard times by the turn of the century brought to a head perplexing currency problems. Although the monetary system had been stabilized in 1777, the mass issue of unbacked government credit notes (*riksgäldssedlar*) from 1789, to pay for the Russian war, had undone this much-needed reform. Thereafter, credit transactions, foreign trade, and government finance were severely handicapped, and regular bank notes and metallic coin were driven out of circulation. Gustav IV Adolf sought to contend with the problems of the treasury through strict economies, but poor harvests and declining trade undermined his efforts. It became evident that the currency must be reformed at whatever sacrifice if the state were to be saved from bankruptcy.

Constitutionally, such a measure required the assent of the Estates, which Gustav Adolf had thus far avoided convening. He profoundly mistrusted elected assemblies, at home or abroad, and he lacked both parliamentary experience and his father's striking qualities of leadership. Already in March 1799, R. F. Hochschild wrote in his diary that both "the old Gustavian league and the old, so-called Patriot [party] call for a *riksdag*, each believing that they can lead the Estates." In November he recounted how Baron Fabian Wrede, a conspicuous aristocratic "Jacobin" in the early 1790s, urged the king to convene the Estates, "lest one run the risk that the people, unbidden, assemble."[14] "Who, given the spirit that now prevails, can guarantee that there will not be a general upheaval," wrote Axel von Fersen, for whom the analogy with France on the eve of the Estates-General in 1789 seemed painfully evident.[15]

The king's advisers saw no other way out, and in January 1800 a *riksdag* was announced. As at other critical junctures, it was to be held in a provincial town, Norrköping, to avoid possible turbulence in the capital as well as pressures from foreign diplomats, who were pointedly not invited to attend. Tsar Paul, who pictured Scandinavia as a hotbed of Jacobinism, offered to occupy Finland in case of need. Gustav Adolf, who would have preferred financial aid, tactfully declined but clearly hoped that his close relationship with the tsar might help to overawe any opposition at the forthcoming *riksdag*.

Elections returned solidly royalist majorities for the Clergy and Peasantry, as expected. Although the royalists also dominated the Burgher Estate, its election, especially in the capital, revealed some antigovernment sentiment, even social radicalism. Fersen noted a Stockholm tailor who campaigned for the limitation of all unearned incomes to 1,000 *riksdaler* and the distribution of surpluses to the people.[16]

The Nobility did not attend in force, with less than half the usual number of families represented. Many old "Patriots" were demoralized by Gustav III's later autocracy and the spread of revolution in Europe, and thus left the field to a majority of committed royalists and a minority of enthusiastic but inexperienced young radicals. The former, according to Count Adolf Ludvig Hamilton, "no longer consisted only of courtiers and adventurers," but included many former "Patriots," now convinced that "Jacobinism could not be prevented except by means of the most extensive despotism."[17] The radicals, soon nicknamed the "Mountain," were led by former members of the Uppsala "Junta." While they did not succinctly set forth their ideals, these included, broadly speaking, a balance of power between the crown and an active, regularly convened diet, greater local freedom from bureaucratic constraints, a wider liberty of expression, and some loosening of the traditional corporate structure of society.

The *Riksdag* was officially opened on 15 March 1800 in a generally hopeful spirit. A fortnight later Gustav IV Adolf and Queen Fredrika were at last crowned in Norrköping cathedral, the frugal ceremony reflecting the depleted treasury. The Nobility showed up for the event in fair numbers and now made no difficulties about swearing allegiance to the crown and to the Act of Union and Security of 1789, which as an Estate of the realm they had still not officially accepted.

A secret committee of the Estates, under the chairmanship of the king himself, undertook to prepare a plan for currency reform. Developments at the *Riksdag* meanwhile soon revealed a degree of political radicalism and social ferment that strict press censorship, lifted only briefly in 1792, had largely concealed. In the Noble Estate, the opposition demanded without success that the deliberations of the Secret and Bank Committees be made public. It likewise proposed improvements in the conditions of employment of agricultural laborers, giving rise to heated controversy. Count Hamilton was indignant that "principles of equality, already outmoded at their place of birth and which only served to seduce the worst classes of society" should here be presented with such "zeal and eloquence."[18] The young radicals, according to Count Fersen, sought to outdo each other in outrageous schemes, and " . . . to spew out and spread Jacobin ideas and attitudes among the public. . . . These attitudes, which are destructive of all authority and which have plunged France into ruin, will in the same way lead all other kingdoms to their destruction."[19] Petitions were likewise presented within the Noble Estate for its voluntary renunciation of its exclusive right to own immediate manorial demesne lands; one such petition was endorsed by 332 of its members.[20]

There were signs of unrest outside the noble order, notably within the Peasant Estate. Fersen noted that here there were many who wished to abolish both the Clerical Estate and the remaining privileges of the nobility. The radicals in the Noble Estate made, according to Hamilton, "insinuations to the Estate of the Peasantry that religion, priests, kings were unnecessary, of the sweetness of the words equality and liberty." The diarist Hochschild feared that "lust for revenge" for the assassination of Gustav III would break forth and that "if the nobles commit the least indiscretion, that will do it!"[21]

In May the Secret Committee presented to the Estates its project for monetary reform. Of an estimated 15 million *riksdaler* in national debt notes then in circulation, two-thirds were to be redeemed in bank currency at a discount of one-sixth of face value, by means of a special levy amounting to 2 percent of the total national wealth; the remaining third would be replaced by a new type of credit notes, *courantsedlar*, to be redeemed over fifteen years through regular taxation.

The Clerical, Burgher, and Peasant Estates had no difficulties with the proposal. Among the Nobility, it was also generally accepted. The radical opposition, however, saw its chance to gain political leverage by separating the question of the monetary conversion from that of the regular grant of taxation, upon which it was dependent: by limiting the duration of the grant, it sought to compel the king to convene the Estates at regular intervals.

On 29 May this matter gave rise to such an uproar in the Noble Estate that five of the leading radicals, among them Hans Hierta, dramatically renounced their noble status and left the hall, followed by seven others, including Georg Adlersparre, who refused to participate any longer in the current *Riksdag*. Their gesture created a sensation, as intended, but the "Mountain" thereby virtually abdicated the field to the royalists, who, with the other Estates, accepted both the conversion and a grant of unrestricted duration.

Conservatives were shocked by such goings-on. In Duchess Charlotta's view, the nobility behaved like a "rabble" at Norrköping, and "one must have really low-minded Jacobinical views to wish to renounce one's nobility and change one's name."[22] Following the *Riksdag*, the king ordered the trial of six of the more prominent radicals for offending against the dignity of the *lantmarskalk*, or speaker of the Noble Estate. Several of them thereupon published statements, presenting themselves as martyrs of liberty. Hierta—who now respelled his name Järta—in particular turned the trial into a farce, and in 1802 one defendant was acquitted while four received no more than token sentences. The following year renunciation of noble status was officially prohibited.

The remainder of the *Riksdag* passed relatively smoothly, and much useful business was completed before it was dissolved on 15 June. The king, Duchess Charlotta wrote, had every reason to be satisfied and had "won even greater power than his father had had."[23] Yet the *Riksdag* of 1800 served merely to confirm Gustav IV Adolf in his aversion to elected assemblies. His only *Riksdag*, in 1800, was thus a landmark in the growth of late Gustavian autocracy in Sweden—but also in that of the new liberalism that was to triumph in 1809. It remains of particular interest, too, as a rare example of parliamentary activity in Europe outside of Great Britain, France, and France's satellite republics, around the turn of the century, revealing both indigenous issues and traditions, and powerful influences from a wider world locked in ideological and military conflict.

The conversion plan ultimately failed to solve the monetary problem. Collection of the special levy, which had to be increased by 20 percent, dragged on until 1802, when the government changed the plan without conferring with the Estates, mainly by mortgaging the Swedish enclave of Wismar to the Duke of Mecklenburg-Schwerin—in effect selling it for 1.25 million *riksdaler*—in 1803. In the end, the national bank did redeem the designated amount in national debt notes, before Sweden's war in 1808 once again undermined the currency.

In retrospect, one cannot but wonder at the apparently rapid decline of the flourishing Swedish radicalism of the 1790s. To be sure, an increasingly strict censorship after 1800 would conceal much that would emerge from the shadows nine years later. Yet beneath the surface, other forces were at work by the turn of the century. As seen, early enthusiasm for French liberty among much of the nobility had been chilled by revolutionary "excesses." Even the regicide of 1792, C. F. Ehrensvärd, in exile in Copenhagen, was by now an outspoken proponent of enlightened Danish absolutism, in preference to the French republic.[24] Gustav IV Adolf's strongly bureaucratic regime also helped assuage discontents among the nobility.

The French Revolution was moreover opposed throughout Europe by a growing body of conservative social and political thought; while Edmund Burke was its leading luminary, men iike Mallet du Pan, Sénac de Meilhan, and Abbé Maury held to moderate, constitutional views particularly congenial to former "Patriots" of Gustav III's day. The Uppsala "Junta" itself seems less influenced by outright French revolutionary propaganda than by foreign sympathizers of the revolution, such as Arthur Young or Thomas Paine, and by certain German publications like the *Göttinger Gelehrte Anzeigen*, more "Girondin"—that is, libertarian, antibureaucratic, anticentralist—than "Jacobin" in sympathies.[25]

Even this tempered radicalism in Uppsala was scarcely reflected at the universities of Lund, Åbo, and Greifswald. The Oxford don E. D. Clarke, who at this time considered the Uppsala students debauched by "licentiousness and

Jacobinism,'' was especially impressed by the sound attitudes he encountered in Åbo.[26]

The Consulate in France was, after 1799, unquestionably disillusioning to Swedish, as to other foreign, friends of liberty, while to many conservatives it seemed to presage a restoration of order. "All our Jacobins, who cheered so wildly for Bonaparte, have become very long in the face," Count Fersen noted with satisfaction in January 1800.[27] The first years of the new century were a bleak time for the old radicals of the 1790s, and sensitive souls of a younger generation increasingly took flight into the world of romantic fantasy. Returning to Uppsala from the Continent in 1802, the dismissed philosopher Benjamin Höijer complained that he could no longer find any "tolerable company"–and had "to starve besides"![28]

In Denmark enmity hardened between the government and the small group of radical intellectuals and publicists who with growing audacity attacked the very principle of royal absolutism. A. P. Bernstorff's death in mid-1797 removed the most influential supporter of press freedom, while Crown Prince Frederik's patience with public criticism was rapidly running out.

As in Sweden, tensions were increased by poor crop years in the late 1790s and by the economic crisis of 1799, which caused some thirty commercial bankruptcies in Copenhagen alone and ruined the efforts of the Specie Bank, established in 1791, to maintain order in the monetary system. In 1800 there was another flare-up of peasant unrest near Tønder in Schleswig.[29] Meanwhile, Danish—like Swedish—radicalism seemed to threaten all of northern Europe in the eyes of Tsar Paul, who in 1799 sent Baron B. A. C. von Krüdener to Copenhagen to urge in the strongest terms the curtailment of press freedom. From there, Krüdener sent home alarmist reports on the dangers of Danish and Scandinavian "Jacobinism," including an alleged secret society, *De forenede Skandinaver* (The United Scandinavians), said to be headed by Conrad Malte Bruun and to aspire to a federative Scandinavian republic.[30] Such reports, reinforced by the French émigré General Dumouriez's *Tableau spéculatif de l'Europe*, published in 1798, which depicted Denmark and the duchies as a seedbed of revolution, brought increasing pressures from St. Petersburg.

Beginning already in 1794, the government had, as noted, taken action in individual cases for violation of the press ordinance of 1790. In September 1797 a judicial official, Peter Collet, was dismissed for maintaining in print that a public servant had the same right as any other citizen to express his views on public affairs, even to urge resistance to authority, short of revolt. It is revealing that Collet was dismissed through administrative rather than judicial action, pressed by none other than Christian Colbjørnsen, who was increasingly outraged by attacks upon the reforming monarchy and determined to teach the bureaucracy a lesson in discipline. The following month, a government commission was appointed to consider new press regulations. Although this caused consternation among the radicals, the commission's recommendations, submitted in January 1798, were modest enough and rejected actual censorship.[31]

Most of the radicals—including doubtless the most original thinkers among them, M. G. Birkner and N. D. Riegels—henceforth tread warily. After 1797, the limelight fell above all on the two most conspicuous radical publicists, P. A. Heiberg and M. C. Bruun. Heiberg, whose bitterness against the regime became irreconcilable after it blocked his appointment to a municipal post in Copenhagen in 1798, belabored it with massive scorn and irony, whereas the younger Bruun attacked it with boyish impudence and lighthearted satire. During 1798 Heiberg criticized the government's finances and the un-Danish nature of the administration. Shortly after the establishment of the commission on the press, he counterattacked with *En Draabe i det store Hav af Skrifter om Skrivefriheden* (A Drop in the Great Sea of Writings on Press Freedom), intimating the legitimacy of revolt and maintaining that revolutions were precipitated not by peoples but by their rulers.

In February 1799 the government brought Heiberg to trial, demanding that his earlier writings also be examined for subversive ideas. Heiberg struck back in the journal *Læsning for Publikum* with thinly veiled attacks on Colbjørnsen, whom he now despised as a renegade.

By 17 August 1799, Crown Prince Frederik had had enough.

It is offensive to me [he stated] that the [Danish] Chancellery should have so much to do with the scribblers. . . . These people have to be cowed. Why should such nonsense have to appear in a state where everyone may receive justice and where the way to the throne is open to all? I demand that the Chancellery take these gentlemen in hand. Show no leniency and the matter will be taken care of.[32]

The result was the press ordinance of 27 September 1799. While this stated that free discussion should continue to spread enlightenment and useful knowledge, and to suggest practical improvements in state and society, anonymity was prohibited, all publications of fewer than twenty-four pages were to be approved by Copenhagen's policemaster or, in cases of doubt, by the Danish Chancellery, and those condemned in press cases were to be placed under permanent censorship.[33] A similar ordinance in November extended the same restrictions to the duchies.

These provisions were not altogether illiberal for Europe at that time. Certainly the press remained freer in principle in the Danish than in the Swedish monarchy. The government nonetheless added point to its new policy by increasing the charges against Heiberg and by bringing Bruun to trial. Applying the new ordinance retroactively, the court sentenced Heiberg to permanent exile in December 1799. Bruun received the same sentence a year later, in December 1800. Both thereafter made their way to Paris. After 1799 criticism of established authority virtually vanished in the Danish press.

Ove Høegh-Guldberg, never a friend of the unbridled press, claimed that the Russian tsar had been midwife to the ordinance of September 1799. Russian pressures over the past year had indeed been considerable. Yet in the Danish monarchy, as in the Swedish, opinion had been changing, and signs were not lacking that much of the reading public itself was ready to welcome restraints on the radical press. The Terror, the decline of political liberty in France, French privateering—all contributed to disenchantment with republican France. Even the impetuous Jens Baggesen, who in 1792 had ecstatically hailed the establishment of the French Republic as Humanity's greatest triumph, after visiting Paris in May 1795—in time to experience the uprising of 1 Prairial—wearily admitted the following year that he now regretted the effort he had expended in seeking to comprehend and explain the "chaos" in France.[34] The ongoing reform program at home meanwhile continued to enjoy general support. Among the Copenhagen intelligentsia itself, more moderate men like Rahbek, Pram, Baggesen, Rasmus Nyerup, and Jens Kragh Høst were warily disassociating themselves from the hotheads.

The notable decline of club life in Copenhagen by the later 1790s reveals a growing apathy toward political questions among a bourgeoisie now occupied above all by the pursuit of profit on the wartime European market. It is likewise indicative of changing social mores. Women, who had taken no part in the clubs, were assuming an ever more active role in both social and cultural life, reinforced by the idealization of womanhood and domesticity in literature and art.[35] By the turn of the century, the homes of prominent burghers, like Constantin Brun's Sophienholm, where his wife Friederike presided over a circle of refined souls, and of *literati* like Knud Rahbek, at whose Bakkehuset the charming Kamma held sway after 1798, were becoming the centers of literary and artistic coteries. Heiberg's former wife, Thomasine, remarried in 1802 to the Finnish regicide, C. F. Ehrensvärd, had her devoted following. One thinks, too, of such muses as Constantine de Steensen-Leth, mistress of Egelykke manor on Langeland, for whom the young N. F. S. Grundtvig pined in secret love, of Countess Julie Reventlow at Emkendorf, who inspired her circle of German poets with the dream of an idealized medieval age of faith and hierarchical social harmony, and of the French émigrée Marquise de Tessé at Wittmoldt in Holstein, whose coterie included her nephew, General de Lafayette.

In Sweden, Anna Maria Lenngren, a frequent contributor to *Stockholms Posten* who ridiculed the pretentions of the aristocracy, decried prevailing prejudices against her sex, and warmly praised the newer Danish literature, enjoyed growing respect, and Malla Montgomery-Silfverstolpe's celebrated salon was soon to become the temple of Uppsala romanticism. To be sure, Thomas Malthus was struck in 1799 by a lack of "literary female characters" in Norway, while Mary Wollstonecraft, who was much interested, four years earlier found Danish women—as well as their Scandinavian sisters in general—to be "simply notable housewives; without accomplishments, or any of the charms that adorn more advanced social life."[36] Yet from an internal perspective, the change is unmistakable, as is its growing influence upon the cultural life of the North.

The return of Henrik Steffens from Jena to Copenhagen in 1802, filled with the romantic theories of Fichte and Schelling, and his encounter with the young Adam Oehlenschläger, which left the latter a wholehearted convert to the new *Weltanschauung*, were milestones in the blossoming of full-blown romanticism in Denmark, with Oehlenschläger as its standard-bearer. The civic-minded ethos of past decades was here, as elsewhere, dissolving before shining visions of a distant past.

Responsibility for suppression of the press cannot, meanwhile, be attributed solely to conservative currents at home and abroad. The struggle over the press was waged above all, as Edvard Holm has pointed out, within the progressive camp itself.[37] All its adherents desired a regime of justice and material well-being, and all had been comrades-in-arms in the heady, early years of reform. By the turn of the century they had divided irreconcilably into those who like Crown Prince Frederik, C. D. Reventlow, and Christian Colbjørnsen occupied the citadel of power and held fast to the ideal of enlightened absolutism, and those like P. A. Heiberg and C. M. Bruun who ultimately could be satisfied only with a government by—as well as for—the people.

If the friends of reform within the Danish monarchy idealized Crown Prince Frederik as democracy enthroned, the *Ritterschaft* in the duchies feared him for that very reason. Frederik could speak, as he did in a letter to Schimmelmann in 1803, of the power he "received from the nation," but he mistrusted and disliked the aristocratic defenders of local, corporate privileges in Schleswig-Holstein for essentially the same reason as he did the ultraradicals in Copenhagen, for both contested the ideal of rationalist, reforming absolutism.[38] While considering themselves implacable foes of the French Revolution, both the crown prince and the *Ritterschaft* represented forces inherent in the revolution itself, and for that very reason mistrusted and feared each other.

A. P. Bernstorff, the great conciliator, had managed to tread a narrow path between Danish centralism and Schleswig-Holstein particularism, and had enjoyed the confidence of the *Ritterschaft*. While he was succeeded at the German Chancellery by the strongly conservative Holsteiner Count Cai Reventlow, Bernstorff's death also cleared the way for Crown Prince Frederik's increasingly direct rule over the entire monarchy. Conflict between two opposed concepts of state and society could not long be postponed.

Under such circumstances, the question of serfdom in the duchies proved an increasingly difficult bone of contention. Many noble proprietors in the duchies, including both Cai and his brother Fritz Reventlow, were genuinely concerned with the welfare of their peasants and by no means opposed to serf emancipation as such, but they stoutly denied the right of the central government in Copenhagen to impose a solution in violation of their immemorial privileges. Cai Reventlow regarded the relationship between lord and peasant as a "purely domestic matter which ought not, so to speak, cross the threshold of my house," as he had written to Schimmelmann in 1795. "Just because the dukes of Holstein have become kings of Denmark," his brother Fritz, the master of Emkendorf, wrote to Cai in 1798, "this gives them no right to tear the province away from the Germanic empire and govern it according to Danish laws, customs, and ideas."[39] As noted, the eight years set in 1797 for the completion of emancipation passed amid a growing deadlock.

Emkendorf manor became ever more the capital of an aristocratic state within the state, in rivalry with Copenhagen, bitterly opposed to democracy in either its French republican or its Danish autocratic guise, a citadel of German romanticism in both literature and politics. It led opposition in the duchies to religious rationalism and despite its Lutheran orthodoxy opened its doors to sincere Roman Catholics, including various French émigré nobles, as allies against indifferentism and unbelief. In 1799 Count Friedrich Leopold Stolberg embraced the Roman faith, bringing accusations of crypto-Catholicism against Emkendorf from the opposing camp. Cai Reventlow counterattacked by arranging for Fritz's appointment in 1800 as curator of the University of Kiel, where like Count Fersen at Uppsala he waged a determined battle against the new ideas.

In Norway the ironmaster and merchant Jacob Aall would later look back with nostalgia to the years around 1800:

> Nowhere were the effects of the French Revolution felt less than in Norway, and nowhere did ideas of liberty cause less ferment. . . . There was no wish for any change and . . . the great mass of the inhabitants had long enjoyed in effect that freedom and equality in the conditions of civil life which other nations waged a bloody struggle to win. No nation in the North was less concerned over that revolution in the form of government than Norway, which just at the beginning of this [the nineteenth] century was in the midst of the most advantageous period of activity its history can reveal. It felt the spur of no oppression; its taxation was light and by no means in proportion to what the nation was able to bear, and any sort of change in its official or political status seemed to forbode a loss rather than a gain.[40]

These were indeed prosperous times for Norwegian merchants and mariners. The small radical journals in Christiania, Bergen, and Trondheim—loyal as they had always remained to the monarchy—were gone by 1800. Yet Aall's bright description had little to say about the Norwegian peasantry, whose old conflicts with merchants and officials, doubtless exacerbated in places by poor harvests between 1800 and 1804, found during these very years a new outlet in a great pietistic revival movement led by a man from its own ranks, Hans Nielsen Hauge.

By the middle 1790s signs were not lacking of a religious awakening in various parts of the monarchy, although this was at first generally limited to the upper levels of society: the aristocracy, the urban middle classes, some of the clergy. By the end of the decade, however, attempts by the Lutheran state church to introduce a more rationalistic liturgy and devotional books began to encounter peasant resistance, in Jutland as well as in the duchies, where it was encouraged by the aristocratic Emkendorf circle, and even in Iceland. For social as well as religious reasons, however, the strongest reaction took place in Norway.

Rationalism had been gaining ground in the theological faculty of the University of Copenhagen, and in consequence throughout the Danish and Norwegian clergy, since mid-century. By the 1790s it had reached its apogee. Its proponents, in parsonages throughout the far-flung kingdom, included many admirable men distinguished as much—if not more—through zeal for peasant literacy or improved farming methods as for the cure of souls. In most rural parishes the pastor was the most conspicuous and active bearer of enlightenment, culture, and practical reform. But he was, by the same token, the foremost representative of outside officialdom, hence of the power of the state and of the upper classes. In Norway this circumstance alone was enough to cause frequent difficulties between pastors and their flocks. Many peasants resented the constant, nagging efforts of the clergy to change their accustomed ways, which threatened to involve risks and expense. At the same time, the dry rationalism of the later eighteenth century failed to satisfy yearnings for a richer, more emotional religious experience.[41]

At this point Hans Nielsen Hauge emerged from the obscurity of rural Østlandet. In 1796 he experienced a religious awakening and took to the road to preach his message of personal conversion, simple piety, and strict Christian morality far and wide throughout Norway. Already in 1799 he was arrested for the first time, for violating the ordinance of 1754 requiring farm laborers to take local service. By then Hauge had already won over several thousand "Friends," as they called themselves, many of whom became missionaries for the new awakening.

Hauge's writings show their author's lack of book learning and systematic theology. They are poorly written, often obscure, sometimes inconsistent. He made no attempt to found a new and separate sect, in violation of the Conventicle Law of 1741, seeking rather to establish a company of the righteous within the state church—ever an uncomfortable situation both for the few and for the many.

The writings were meanwhile relatively insignificant compared with the man

himself, for Hauge combined in remarkable fashion the qualities of the charis-
matic visionary and of the practical man of affairs. He recognized the need for
a strong economic base for his evangelistic movement. ''The worldly wise, false
and evil,'' he wrote in 1804, had possessed themselves of the goods of this
world; the godly should therefore ''put a stop to the prideful luxury of the
rich.''[42] Worldly success among the faithful he considered a sign of God's
grace. For a time in 1800–1801 he considered the idea of a community of property among the ''Friends''; although he soon gave it up, they frequently pooled
their resources with telling effect in common business ventures. In 1801 Hauge
was able to establish himself as a merchant and citizen of Bergen through funds
raised by his followers. The ''Friends'' acquired or founded a number of enterprises, including Christiansand's only newspaper and two paper mills—important for the printing of Hauge's writings.

The Establishment became increasingly concerned as Hauge and his peasant
following seemed to threaten both clerical and secular authority and the economic privileges of the urban merchant oligarchy.[43]

The later 1790s were a particularly prosperous period for Scandinavian—
especially Danish-Norwegian—maritime commerce. After Austria made peace
with France at Campo Formio in October 1797, the European war turned into
a bitter and closely matched maritime struggle between Great Britain on the one
side and France, Spain, and the Batavian Republic on the other. According to
a Danish government report in 1798:

France's commerce has come to a complete halt, Britain's trade in the
Mediterranean has stopped, the formerly so extensive Dutch carrying
trade has been ruined, Venice's political existence has been destroyed, and
the other Italian states are concerned above all with their self-defense.[44]

The Scandinavian kingdoms—with the United States—remained the principal
neutral carriers and profited accordingly. The Danish monarchy maintained
close to 3,000 seagoing vessels, of which more than half were Norwegian,
around the turn of the century, whereas Sweden-Finland had somewhat less than
half that number.[45] In addition to carrying their own products and those of the
Baltic region, they assumed much of the carrying trade both in Europe and beyond. Most of the Mediterranean trade now fell into Scandinavian hands, as did
a growing volume of business with North America.

A lively commerce passed through Denmark's colonies in the West Indies
and in India—and on a more modest scale through Swedish St. Barthélemy—
consisting largely of goods belonging to citizens of the belligerent powers seeking the protection of neutral flags. The Danish Asiatic Company entered into its
era of greatest prosperity. Danish ships called frequently at isolated French Île
de France. In February 1797 the Dutch-born Copenhagen merchant Frédéric de

Coninck negotiated the so-called Batavian Contract with the Dutch East India Committee to buy up the latter's accumulated wares in the East Indies for 19 million *gulden*—secretly provided by the Dutch themselves—and ship them, under the Danish flag, to Copenhagen, from whence they could be profitably sold on the Continent. Foreign merchants invested heavily in Danish commercial ventures, and despite the efforts of the Danish government, an undeterminable number of foreign ships were registered as Danish, or at least flew the Danish flag, which Thomas Malthus considered "much prostituted during the war." French, Dutch, and Spanish privateers put into Norwegian ports, where local middlemen carried on a thriving business selling captured ships and their cargoes back to their owners.[46]

Statistics on Scandinavian trade during these years are incomplete, especially for Denmark-Norway after 1794. But the prosperity it brought was unmistakable. Copenhagen emerged by the turn of the century as the great emporium of neutral commerce in Europe, even though in total value this evidently did not quite reach the level of 1782–83, during the American war. Other seaports, like Altona, Flensburg, Bergen, Arendal, Christiansand, Christiania, Stockholm, and Gothenburg, also thrived.

Such commerce was, however, necessarily risky. Reinforced by Dutch and Spanish naval power, France sought to press its advantage through the edict of 29 Nivôse, Year VI (18 January 1798), according to which neutral vessels together with their cargoes would be forfeit if they carried any British goods whatsoever. Because British shipping was largely convoyed by the Royal Navy, French and allied privateers preyed mainly upon the neutrals trading with Britain.

Privateering caused a growing demand among Scandinavian merchants for regular convoying of their shipping. By the early summer of 1798 Sweden commenced convoy operations, followed soon after by Denmark. Dismissing Foreign Minister Christian Bernstorff's apprehensions, Crown Prince Frederik and his admiralty instructed escort commanders to resist seizure of ships under their protection after guaranteeing that they did not carry contraband. Cooperation under the armed neutrality agreement of 1794 revived, and ships of the two Scandinavian powers sailed in each others' convoys.

Having responded to French privateering, the Scandinavians quickly ran afoul of the British navy, not least of all as the Swedes refused to regard naval stores as contraband. In June 1798 the first of the Swedish convoys, consisting of eighteen merchant vessels, was seized by the British, followed in August by another Swedish convoy of thirty-eight ships. Forty-three vessels and their cargoes were declared forfeit by a British admiralty court, after long delays, in June 1799. Since Sweden was then facing mounting economic difficulties, the loss was heavy. Despite his natural gallophobia, Gustav IV Adolf was aroused to profound indignation.

Following General Bonaparte's coup d'etat of 18 Brumaire in November 1799, France, now facing the combined might of the Second Coalition, adopted a more conciliatory stance toward the maritime neutrals, while Britain held to its hard line and was increasingly aroused over enemy overseas trade under neutral flags. In March 1799 the British admiralty required strict enforcement of boarding and inspection of neutral merchant ships. Already by July this resulted in an encounter in the Channel between four British frigates and the Danish escort vessel *Freja*, whose commander, Captain Peder Greis Krabbe, became the hero of the hour throughout the Danish monarchy. In December 1799 the Danish *Havfruen* sought to defend its convoy off Gibraltar.

While Denmark concentrated upon safeguarding neutrality and commercial interests, Sweden's foreign policy during the first years of Gustav IV Adolf's personal reign followed an erratic course determined by both principle and opportunism, as well as by the vagaries of European great-power politics.

The conclusion of peace between France and Austria in 1797 provided for a congress at which France and the Germanic states were to work out a territorial settlement for the Holy Roman Empire. As both ruler of Swedish Pomerania and as co-guarantor (with France) of the Peace of Westphalia of 1648, Gustav Adolf, encouraged by Austria, saw an opportunity for Sweden to defend the integrity of the empire and thus oppose the further spread of revolution, and appointed Axel von Fersen his ambassador to the congress, which convened at Rastadt in December 1797. When Vienna quickly abandoned its opposition to a French annexation of the Rhineland, Fersen found himself in an untenable position and was browbeaten in humiliating fashion by the ranking French envoy, General Bonaparte himself.

The same month, in December 1797, Gustav IV Adolf appointed as his acting foreign minister Fredrik Wilhelm von Ehrenheim, who favored accepting the apparently inevitable territorial reshuffle in Germany and turning it to Sweden's advantage. He now held out to the young king the beguiling prospect of acquiring Norway in return for compensation to Denmark in Germany. While he surely realized how totally unacceptable such a scheme would be to Copenhagen, it enticed Gustav Adolf out of an impossible, if not dangerous, position at Rastadt, and Count Fersen was quietly removed from the congress.

Already by the spring of 1798 it was evident even to Gustav Adolf that there was no immediate prospect of obtaining Norway as part of a wider territorial settlement on the Continent. Austria again shifted ground, the Congress of Rastadt became deadlocked, and Europe drifted toward a new war. Alarmed by reports from Count Fersen of the continued spread of French influence and ideas on the Continent, the king reverted to his natural anti-French stance, encouraged by Tsar Paul, who by the end of the year brought Russia into the Second Coalition and thus for the first time into the struggle against revolutionary France.

By April 1799 Gustav Adolf was negotiating secretly with the tsar concerning Sweden's entry into the new coalition. The same month his envoy to the Germanic diet at Regensburg made a ringing appeal for resistance against French encroachments. The allied campaign was strikingly successful during the summer of 1799, and conservatives everywhere exulted at the prospect of the imminent collapse of the revolution.

On 29 October 1799 Sweden concluded the Gatchina Treaty with Russia. Ostensibly a defensive alliance like Gustav III's Drottningholm Treaty of 1791, it contained secret clauses committing Sweden to put at the tsar's disposal a Swedish auxiliary corps of 8,000 men for the war against France, in return for "suitable compensation," by which Norway was doubtless intended. Gustav IV Adolf now stood prepared to take up his father's crusade and, if possible, to unite the Scandinavian peninsula in the process.[47]

In the summer of 1799 Tsar Paul, aroused by the specter of Danish "Jacobinism," pressured Copenhagen not only to muzzle its press but also to join the Second Coalition against France, even without direct participation in the war, adding emphasis through a temporary embargo on Danish vessels in Russian ports. Given this threatening situation, the Danish government reluctantly acceded in principle, in a memorandum to St. Petersburg dated 27 September.[48]

The picture was soon radically transformed when the Russian tsar fell out with his Austrian and British allies and withdrew from the Second Coalition by the beginning of 1800. Both Sweden and Denmark were thus fortuitously released from any obligation to join the struggle as the advantage now passed to the French. While at home official repression of native "Jacobinism" reached its climax by 1800, the main concern of the Northern monarchies in the international arena became once again Britain's tyranny on the seas.

Aroused in particular over the two convoys seized by the British in 1798, the Swedish government proposed to St. Petersburg a commercial treaty in June 1800 including the revival of the program of the League of Armed Neutrality of 1780. In August, after the *Freja's* engagement with the British in the Channel, Copenhagen sent a similar suggestion to the Russian government, followed by a second feeler from Stockholm. Tsar Paul responded enthusiastically with a proposal to the Scandinavian kingdoms and Prussia for resurrecting the League of Armed Neutrality, behind which lay even more ambitious plans for an alliance system—the "Northern League"—hostile to Great Britain. In November he seized all British ships in Russian ports. Gustav IV Adolf visited him in St. Petersburg in December, and by the end of the month Sweden, Denmark, and Prussia joined Russia in a new league based on the principles of 1780 and specifically stipulating armed resistance to the visitation of convoyed merchant vessels, following assurance that they did not carry contraband. The participating powers sought to broaden the league and negotiated to that end with Portugal and especially the United States. In 1801 Denmark accredited its first minister to Washington.[49]

As in the American war twenty years before, the new armed neutrality posed a grave threat to Great Britain. Austria could not alone keep up the struggle by land against France and concluded peace at Lunéville in February 1801. At sea Britain's naval resources were strained to the limit by the combined fleets of France, Spain, and the Batavian Republic. The armed neutrality now threatened not only to break the blockade of France and throttle Britain's vital trade with the Baltic, but—given Tsar Paul's emotional anglophobia—to destroy Europe's precarious balance of naval power altogether, bringing into existence a vast Continental fleet capable of covering the invasion of the home islands themselves.

The British responded with alacrity. On 14 January 1801 they seized all vessels belonging to the armed neutrals in British ports; those from Denmark-Norway alone amounted to 149 ships. As rapidly as communications would permit, they occupied the Danish Virgin Islands and Swedish St. Barthélemy, followed by Danish Tranquebar and Frederiksnagore in India. On 12 March a British naval force of 53 sail, including twenty ships of the line, put to sea under Sir Hyde Parker to break up the League of Armed Neutrality by intimidation or force.

The Scandinavians found themselves dangerously exposed. France had given them no assurance of support. Although the Russian fleet appeared formidable on paper, it was of poor quality and still frozen into its ports. Both Nordic states made hectic efforts to fortify their far-flung coastlines, but owing to financial weakness their navies, upon which their defenses above all depended, were not up to strength. Denmark hastily organized a *landeværn*, or militia. Meanwhile many warships lay decommissioned and unrigged in Copenhagen's naval dockyard while their crews were furloughed and away serving on merchant vessels.

To protect their capital by sea, the Danes deployed a line of nineteen unrigged warships, anchored bow and stern, to serve as floating gun platforms, supported by smaller craft and covered in part by land fortifications, especially on Tre Kroner Island in the roadstead, the key point of the defense. With trained naval personnel in short supply, the blockships were largely manned by commandeered land troops, reinforced by city militia and an enthusiastic crowd of volunteers, including students from the university.

There was meanwhile little collaboration between the two Scandinavian kingdoms. As the British fleet passed the Sound on 30 March, it kept out of cannon range of Kronborg Castle at Helsingør on the Danish side by hugging the Swedish shore. The Swedes did not fire on it since Crown Prince Frederik deliberately declined to request such support, fearing it might later encourage the Swedes to demand exemption from the Danish Sound dues in return. The Swedish fleet remained weatherbound at Karlskrona, occupied with its own feverish preparations, while the Russians were immobilized in Reval and Kronstadt.

Britain now presented its ultimatum demanding that Denmark withdraw from the armed neutrality. When this was refused, Admiral Parker detached the greater part of his force, some thirty vessels including twelve ships of the line, under his second-in-command, Sir Horatio Nelson, the recent hero of Aboukir Bay, to smash Denmark's naval capacity. Negotiating the tricky eastern approach to Copenhagen Roads, Nelson was able to attack the line of Danish blockships at its weakest point on the morning of 2 April, but the ensuing battle proved far harder than the attackers had anticipated. Although both unmaneuverable and outgunned, the Danish blockships resisted valiantly, their guns manned by successive relays of fresh volunteers from the shore who replaced the fallen. The British were forced to operate in hazardously close quarters, some of their ships grounded in shoal waters, and they were dangerously exposed when they came within range of the Danish shore batteries, covering their line of retreat to leeward. Prevented by wind and tide from joining in, the anxious Parker signaled vainly for Nelson to break off the engagement.

By mid-afternoon, impressed by the growing seriousness of his situation, Nelson sent word to Crown Prince Frederik that in the event of further resistance he would be compelled to set fire to the ships now in British hands, "without having the power of saving the brave Danes who have defended them."[50] The threat produced the desired effect. Denmark had done more than honor required in defending the armed neutrality against superior force. A number of the Danish ships had not yet come under attack and could be saved. Without consulting his military commander, who favored further resistance, the crown prince accepted a truce. No sooner was it signed than four of Nelson's ships ran aground within easy range of Tre Kroner's batteries.

"I have been in a hundred and five engagements," Nelson wrote, "but that of to-day is the most terrible of them all."[51] Casualties had been heavy on both sides: the Danes lost 375 dead, 670 wounded, and 1,984 prisoners and missing; the British, 350 dead and 850 wounded. Much of the Danish fleet was destroyed or damaged, and the League of Armed Neutrality collapsed, as it turned out, almost immediately thereafter. Yet the bloody Second of April, 1800, aroused throughout the Danish monarchy a wave of patriotic fervor unparalleled since the heroic defense of Copenhagen against the Swedes in 1658–60. Adam Oehlenschläger and his literary friends, who had served as volunteers, glorified in verse and prose the martial valor of a nation that had enjoyed virtually unbroken peace for over eight decades. Countess Sophie Reventlow saw in the battle a new "Thermopylae." And in Holstein, the Kiel medical professor Georg Heinrich Weber could write—in German—"Our national honor stands in all its glory. This every good Dane feels with noble pride . . . for we too are good Danes![52]

The sequel to the Battle of Copenhagen Roads is quickly told. While the truce with Denmark was extended from day to day, Parker's force proceeded to Karls-krona to deal with the Swedes. As both sides girded for battle, the news arrived that Tsar Paul had been assassinated in St. Petersburg. His successor, Alexander I, was disposed to negotiate with Great Britain, and since the Scandinavian powers could only follow suit, Parker's naval force left the Baltic. A British-Russian convention in June 1801 recognized Britain's right to visit and search neutral vessels, even if convoyed, and tacitly surrendered the principle that free ships made free goods. In separate conventions Sweden and Denmark thereafter acknowledged the same conditions, and the occupied Scandinavian overseas colonies were returned. By the summer of 1801 Scandinavian maritime trade was once again thriving. Gustav IV Adolf returned to speculating over ways to acquire Norway, even sounding out Paris on this matter. In March 1802 the Treaty of Amiens between Britain and France at last restored peace throughout Europe after a decade of war.

The years from 1797 to 1802 reveal once again a close parallelism of de-velopments within the two Nordic states for both internal and external reasons, following the divergences noted in the preceding decade. There are striking similarities between both the ruling princes and their regimes after 1796–97. In his retiring nature, distaste for courtly pomp and state extravagance, impatience with high aristocratic pretentions, pedantic concern for detail, above all military, and rather dogmatic self-righteousness, Gustav IV Adolf closely resembled his cousin, Crown Prince Frederik. Both stood at the head of dedicated and hard-working bureaucracies, to which they entrusted the administration of their realms and which soberly and unostentatiously carried on the work of practical reform initiated earlier by more brilliant and imaginative leaders. Both mean-while determinedly silenced any voices that presumed to question the authority or legitimacy of their regimes.

The Danish press ordinance of 1799 and the exile of Heiberg and Bruun had their counterpart in Gustav IV Adolf's suppression of the Uppsala "Junta," while his confrontation with the aristocratic liberals of the "Mountain" at the Norrköping *Riksdag* in 1800 recalls the mounting conflict between Crown Prince Frederik and the Schleswig-Holstein *Ritterschaft* which would culminate in 1802. In both monarchies the rapid subsidence of native "Jacobinism" after 1799–1800 shows how far the avant-garde had by then gone beyond educated opinion as a whole. Religious unrest among the Norwegian peasantry and polit-ical discontent among the Schleswig-Holstein nobility meanwhile sprang from deeper roots.

Scandinavian internal developments in these years reflect those occurring elsewhere in the Western world. Everywhere a conservative reaction against revolutionary radicalism was evident. One recalls the suspension of the Habeas Corpus in 1794 and the Seditious Meetings and Treasonable Practices Acts of

1796 in Britain, the so-called Jacobin Trials of 1795 in Vienna, the Alien and Sedition Acts of 1798 in the United States. Count Fersen became convinced by 1798 that the French Directory, no less than other European regimes, was itself threatened by the destructive force of Jacobinism, and the coup d'etat of 18 Brumaire, which brought General Bonaparte to power in November 1799, was indeed intended to forestall a resurgent neo-Jacobinism.[53] The banishment of Heiberg and Bruun from Denmark recalls not only that of Thorild from Sweden in 1793, but also such contemporary political refugees as Joseph Priestley, Wolfe Tone, Vittorio Alfieri, Tadeusz Kosciuszko. The Haugian revival in Norway, like English Wesleyanism and a variety of German pietisms, reflected in part the growing self-awareness of simple people whose traditional patterns of life and belief were under the pressures of change. Among the educated classes, the conservative trend of backward-yearning romanticism calls to mind such European figures as Goethe, Tieck, Novalis, Wordsworth, Coleridge, Chateaubriand.

In international affairs there were greater contrasts between the Nordic kingdoms, with precedents extending back to the early seventeenth century: Sweden under Gustav IV Adolf followed an adventurous and at times opportunistic course, in which the hope of acquiring Norway and thereby creating a strong and secure Scandinavian power provided the leitmotif, whereas Denmark held to its traditional policy of preserving its existing territory and exploiting the blessings of neutral trade in wartime. The economic crisis of the later 1790s was international in scope, and the Swedish monetary conversion of 1800 recalls that of the French Directory in 1798. Scandinavian maritime trade faced the same problems as that of the greatest of the maritime neutrals, the United States, during the years of its "quasi-war" with France and of growing friction with Britain.

Buffeted by the epic struggle of the great powers, the Scandinavian kingdoms were narrowly spared from involvement in the war against France by 1800, but were in turn precipitated into a conflict with Britain which led to the baptism of fire at Copenhagen Roads by the spring of 1801. A precarious peace was reestablished in Europe a year later, but it was not destined to last long. In the next round of hostilities the Scandinavian lands would be drawn into the maelstrom itself.

# CHAPTER 11

# At the Crossroads
# 1802–7

Following the often dramatic clash of principles and personalities up to the turn of the century, an unnatural stillness rests over the next few years in the Nordic lands. In both kingdoms the heavy hand of censorship silenced political and social debate after 1800. Only among the proud German aristocrats of the duchies and Swedish Pomerania, and the Norwegian peasant followers of the evangelist Hans Nielsen Hauge was opposition to a growing political and cultural autocracy still evident. Yet this was also a time of ongoing structural changes in both monarchies, especially in the economic and social spheres, and events occurring only a few years later would reveal that the radical heritage of recent decades still glowed beneath the ashes.

After a brief respite, the European conflict resumed again in the spring of 1803. Two years later, Sweden joined in the attack upon revolutionary France. Denmark remained neutral, profiting as before from wartime commerce, while attempting against mounting odds to avoid its pitfalls. By 1807 both Scandinavian states were faced with international forces that threatened to overwhelm them.

During these years Gustav IV Adolf ruled Sweden with a strong hand, loyally supported by his capable bureaucracy. The work of useful improvement in state administration and finance, in the monetary system, and in education, discussed in the preceding chapter, was continued with good results. The most basic reforms in this period meanwhile affected agrarian life.

Minor improvements limited the distances within which manorial tenants had to deliver their dues *in natura* and allowed for free wage agreements between master and man by eliminating fixed maximum wages. Most significant, however, was a new movement to consolidate landholdings.

The problems connected with scattered and intermixed holdings had long been evident. The Swedish government had attempted through the *Storskifte* ordinances of 1757 and 1762 to reduce somewhat the fragmentation of village lands. These measures had provided some inspiration for the more thoroughgoing Danish land consolidations, especially from 1781 on, which in turn had set an example for Baron Rutger Maclean and his friends on their estates in Sweden's southernmost province of Skåne across the Sound, beginning in 1785.

While Baron Maclean was *persona non grata* with Gustav IV Adolf for his supposedly "Jacobin" political views, his rational reorganization of Svaneholm manor into consolidated tenancies of practicable size, as well as the Danish land reforms, greatly impressed influential members of the government in Stockholm, leading by March 1803 to the *Enskifte* ordinance for Skåne.

This provided for the creation of farms consolidated into single blocs of land. Any landowner could upon demand withdraw from his village community (*byalag*) and have his holdings thus concentrated. While other village landholders were not obliged to follow suit, the surveyors and outside referees called in to effect the necessary land exchanges would prepare a plan for the reorganization of all the village lands and encourage its adoption. In practice, despite apprehensions, pressures from social superiors and officials induced numerous villages to undergo complete reorganization; by 1807, 194 villages in Skåne had at least commenced the process. A second ordinance in 1804 extended *enskifte* to Västergötland. A third in 1807 applied to the rest of the kingdom, except for Dalarna, the northernmost provinces (Norrland), and Finland. A new forest ordinance in 1805 provided for the division of village woodlands upon the demand of any village landowner. In 1827 a new *Laga Skifte* ordinance would provide somewhat greater flexibility by allowing consolidation of farms into more than one bloc to accommodate the rugged topography of much of Sweden.

As in Denmark—and Great Britain—the process of land consolidation and enclosure would continue long into the nineteenth century, gaining momentum with the development of commercial agriculture and in the process transforming both rural life and the very appearance of the countryside. For many it brought material and psychological hardship, reducing as it did many marginal members of the old village communities, who had previously benefited from common lands and common rights, to the meaner status of landless wage laborers, and largely breaking up the old close-knit rural society. For holders of both freehold and leasehold farms, the agrarian reorganization brought possibilities for new wealth, comfort, and social standing. Much new land was now cleared and cultivated, while the fallow was gradually reduced with the spread of more intensive systems of crop rotation. The enlargement of landholdings with portions of former common lands encouraged their division into smaller, more easily workable units or the sale of part of the land to pay the costs of surveying and enclosing, thereby increasing the total numbers of farms and crofts. All of this resulted in a great increase in food production, which by the 1820s would allow Sweden to export surplus grain for the first time since the 1680s. The rural population grew rapidly, but the increase was greatest among the poorer, landless strata of the peasantry. Parallels with both Denmark and Great Britain are evident.[1]

Crown Prince Frederik's increasingly personal autocracy is no less apparent than Gustav IV Adolf's. His growing impatience with contrary opinions and inclination to deal directly with individual subordinates raised apprehensions in various quarters. This is most evident among the German nobility in the duchies, and indeed during these very years issues arose that sorely tried their attachment to the crown. Yet on the Danish council itself frictions are apparent. C. D. Reventlow came to regard himself as the principal defender of its traditional, quasi-constitutional power and dignity, while he became increasingly solicitous of individual rights, leading to admonitions that the crown prince found tiresome.[2]

Increasingly, Frederik filled the higher administrative posts with professional bureaucrats, such as Frederik Moltke, president of the Danish Chancellery, 1799-1804, Frederik Julius Kaas, his successor, and Johan Sigismund von Møsting, president of the German Chancellery after 1802. Characteristically these men were Danes, commoners, or both, rather than independently wealthy and prominent noble German landowners like those of the Bernstorff-Reventlow-Schimmelmann circle, which had dominated after 1784. They had made their way in royal service, often as provincial governors (*amtmænd*), and were dependable instruments of the regent's will.

After the resumption of the Anglo-French conflict led to a French occupation of neighboring Hanover in 1803, Crown Prince Frederik mobilized an army of observation in Holstein, with which he spent much of his time during the following years, while the council in Copenhagen faded into the background. It was widely believed, at the time and since, that Frederik fell at this time under the influence of a camarilla of military adjutants at his headquarters in Kiel, popularly known as "The Red Feathers" for their plumed headgear, but later historical opinion has tended to discount their probable significance.[3]

What occurred was the reemergence of cabinet, as opposed to conciliar, government, such as had evolved during the Struensee and Guldberg eras in the 1770s and 1780s, with the important difference that power was exercised directly by the rightful heir to the throne.

For the time being, however, Frederik's personal autocracy proved an asset in carrying on the program of reform. In accordance with the decree of 1792, the slave trade was ended in the Danish colonies in 1807. Commerce was consistently encouraged and the tariff systems of the kingdom and the duchies were largely equalized in 1803. A forest ordinance in 1805, prepared by C. D. Reventlow, allowed the government extensive control over private woodlands to ensure their rational management. The higher schools were placed under a new Directorate for the University and Learned Schools in 1805, freeing them from the control of the state church. An important landmark was reached in the evolution of the national army when it was decreed in 1804 that henceforth all recruitment would consist of the enlistment or conscription of subjects of the crown. Most important of all was the emancipation of the serfs in the duchies by 1805, of which more below.

There has been a tendency in the older historiography to contrast an earlier, creative period of reform led by A. P. Bernstorff up to his death in 1797 with an arid period that followed under the crown prince's personal autocracy. The studies of Axel Linvald in particular have meanwhile shown that such a contrast is in the main untenable. Although Frederik lacked the brilliance and imagination of an A. P. Bernstorff or a C. D. Reventlow, he was firmly committed to the ideals they represented and indeed would seem even to have surpassed them in the warmth of his sympathy for his humbler subjects. "Every citizen without exception stands under the protection of the laws," he declared. And on another occasion:

> Were it not so much against the prevailing spirit, I would never exempt either the nobility or those of equivalent privileges from conscription, for when these sons of the people are destined neither for naval nor military careers nor for studies, I consider them, when they do not learn even the simplest handicrafts, useless members of the state.[4]

After 1797 it was above all the crown prince himself who provided the impetus not only to new reforms but to the consistent implementation of those already undertaken, and who broke the deadlocks impeding their progress, overriding the protests of vested interests and the cautious apprehensions of his advisers. The burden of responsibility his self-willed autocracy imposed upon him was, however, at times more than Frederik could manage—not least in view of his personal limitations, his long absences from Copenhagen, and sometimes the indifference or tacit opposition of his officials. This could on occasion thwart his good intentions, as in the case of his attempt to forbid the physical chastisement of crofters in 1807.[5]

Christian Colbjørnsen might still inveigh, as he did in 1803, against "that proud nobility of birth which from the days of the Waldemars has oppressed the nation by weakening the royal authority" and warn that the "spirit of aristocracy . . . lurks within the ruins of the fearsome temple of wicked feudalism." His polemics echo the storms of the previous decade, which his own support for the press ordinance of 1799 had helped to still. But by now the aristocratic bogey no longer excited much concern within the kingdom.[6]

Aristocracy as such remained far more vigorous in the duchies, in the face of mounting frictions with the crown during these very years. Following the British naval attack on Copenhagen Roads in 1801, the government in its pressing need for new revenues decreed in 1802 a new supplementary tax (*kontribution*) levied upon real property throughout the monarchy, except Finnmark and the Atlantic Islands. In the duchies this increased the taxation set "once and for all" as long ago as 1652, and was extended to both persons and forms of property, urban and manorial, that had previously been exempt. To the *Ritterschaft*, the new surtax represented a flagrant violation of its historic rights and a perilous precedent. Cai Reventlow resigned in December 1802 as president of the German Chancellery in ill-concealed protest.

Unity within the *Ritterschaft* over the taxation issue, however, began to break down when it was unable to agree on an appeal to the crown prince in January 1803. Most of its Schleswig members, with some Holsteiners—as well as the majority of the *non recepti* in both duchies—feared a direct confrontation and backed down. Most of the Holstein *Ritterschaft* at first favored a direct appeal to the *Reichskammergericht* or Imperial Cameral Tribunal, but confidence in the institutions of the Holy Roman Empire waned following the Peace of Lunéville in February 1801 and in the end nothing came of it.

Count Fritz Reventlow, the lord of Emkendorf and leader of the intransigents in the taxation controversy, was meanwhile chancellor of Kiel University since 1800, providing another source of contention with Copenhagen, especially when he appointed the ultrareactionary Prussian H. D. Hermes to head the Kiel Teachers' Seminary in 1804. This caused such a furor in the rationalist camp that the government intervened and dismissed Hermes after a year. The Emkendorf circle had suffered yet another defeat in a matter of principle and prestige. By 1808 Fritz Reventlow resigned his chancellorship.

Since the issue of emancipation of the serfs in Holstein and Schleswig had first been raised in 1795, many manorial lords had voluntarily freed their serfs. In Schleswig serfdom had virtually disappeared. Yet the *Ritterschaft*, jealous of its ancient rights, remained apprehensive of any solution imposed from above.

After lengthy delays, the matter was revived within the German Chancellery by C. D. Reventlow in May 1803, leading to protracted negotiations with the superior courts of Glückstadt and Gottorp and with the *Ritterschaft*, which now focused primarily upon the question of the manorial proprietor's free disposition of his property following emancipation. Like many Danish landowners in the later 1780s, the manorial lords in the duchies sought to gain unrestricted property rights, whereas the government favored some degree of protection for the peasantry, as in Denmark.

Crown Prince Frederik at length determined in November 1804 that the number of peasant holdings on each manor not be reduced and that all future manorial labor obligations (*Frondienst*) be fixed in amount. At Møsting's urging, this formula was modified somewhat to allow proprietors to attach parts of their tenancies to their demesne, provided this were controlled and the number of tenant farms were not thereby reduced. The final emancipation ordinance was endorsed by the council and signed on 19 December 1804; it abolished all remaining *Leibeigenschaft* in the duchies as of 1 January 1805.

The ordinance had been somewhat hastily put together at the last moment and it contained certain ambiguities, not least because of the government's desire not to offend needlessly the nobility in the duchies. On the whole it provided the peasantry with somewhat less protection than in the kingdom. C. D. Reventlow in particular was dissatisfied with it. Yet the government by no means let matters go at that. If any former serf were deprived of his farm or croft as a result of emancipation, it required that the proprietor provide him and his widow with an income for life equal to that produced by the tenancy. Manorial labor requirements were regulated by an ordinance in July 1805, based on the Danish ordinance of 1791 and largely prepared by C. D. Reventlow, which calmed a certain ferment among the disoriented former serfs following emancipation.

Whatever its shortcomings, the emancipation must be considered one of the monarchy's greatest agrarian reforms. Some 100,000 serfs—about one sixth of the population of the duchies—at last gained their personal freedom under protection against both outright expropriation of their tenancies and arbitrary labor obligations.[7] While term leases, rather than hereditary leaseholds (as in Denmark), remained the norm in the duchies, in practice the same families generally continued to occupy the same holdings. And while proprietors could somewhat enlarge their demesne, peasant land henceforth remained on the whole in peasant hands. One need only compare the flourishing class of large and middling peasant farmers of the following decades in the duchies—where many, be it recalled, had long been freeholders—with the desolation in the same period of the old peasant society in much of northern Germany and the Baltic region, where proprietors were left free to incorporate tenant farms into the demesne, thereby reducing the peasantry to an impoverished rural proletariat. A notorious example of this process of *Bauernlegen* is provided by neighboring Mecklenburg, from which many peasants came to seek a better life in Holstein and Schleswig.[8]

The government's proceedings regarding emancipation and peasant protection could not but rankle the more intransigent elements of the *Ritterschaft*, for which they represented the inexorable advance of Danish absolutism. But worse was yet to come. On 6 August 1806, following the Peace of Pressburg, Emperor Francis II laid down the imperial crown, thus dissolving the ancient Holy Roman Empire, under which Denmark held Holstein in fief. Prussia, now anticipating war with France, sought to organize a north German league including Holstein. The French foreign minister, Talleyrand, countered by assuring the Danish minister in Paris that France would favor direct Danish sovereignty over Holstein.

This situation suddenly offered Crown Prince Frederik the chance to realize his dearest wish: the final, complete consolidation of the monarchy. Time was of the essence. From Kiel, he wrote on 29 August to Duke Friedrich Christian of Augustenburg as the senior state councillor, directing the council to prepare a proclamation by which "Holstein is incorporated and integrated entirely and without any reservation whatsoever into Denmark."[9]

These instructions set off a complex conflict of wills, matching principles against expediency. The crown prince stood for a well-established objective of Danish statecraft, and he was staunchly backed by the presidents of the Danish and German Chancelleries, Kaas and Møsting, as well as by much Danish-national sentiment within the kingdom. Unfortunately, however, Frederik had only two living children, both daughters, and he was not expected to produce further heirs. The duke of Augustenburg consequently had the dynastic interests of his own, younger branch of the Oldenburg house to uphold, since the old Salic law had heretofore prohibited succession through the female line in Holstein. He was particularly affronted that Frederik should pass on through him the order that the council prepare an ordinance barring him and his heirs from their rightful claims.

After presenting the directive, the duke withdrew from the council's deliberations and sent a memorandum to the crown prince, bluntly expressing incredulity that the "reputation of a government renowned for its wisdom and integrity" could be called into question through the "theft" of the rightful succession in Holstein. Instead, he proposed that Holstein be declared a sovereign duchy, closely federated with Denmark, but preserving the existing order of succession and the traditional rights and privileges guaranteed by the exchange treaties with Russia of 1767 and 1773. This was of course the last thing Crown Prince Frederik wanted. To his sister he declared himself to be the "sworn enemy of the Germanic constitution" and to feel "great satisfaction" over the demise of the empire. He was incensed by the duke's memorandum, complaining that while every "patriot, cosmopolitan, and true subject" recognized the need for the incorporation, "my brother-in-law has secretly set aside his patriotic pose and his old Holstein hatred of the Danish royal house, imbibed with his mother's milk, reveals itself all too clearly."[10]

In this, the crown prince judged too harshly, for the duke was caught in a painful dilemma. But others on the council, in particular Christian Bernstorff and Ernst Schimmelmann, also had reservations. The treaties with Russia in 1767 and 1773 had stipulated the reversion of ducal Holstein to the Russian imperial house if the male line of the older, royal branch of the Oldenburg dynasty should fail, and Sweden, too, claimed reversionary rights for its Holstein-Gottorp kings. The outright annexation of the duchy was bound to alienate even further the aroused *Ritterschaft*. Christian Bernstorff and Schimmelmann had, moreover, a certain sentimental fondness for Holstein's old Germanic liberties.

The royal declaration of 9 September 1806 somewhat softened Crown Prince Frederik's hard line with studied ambiguity. It acknowledged the existence of a "duchy of Holstein," which comprised "in every respect a fully unseparated [*ungetrennter*] part" of the Danish state, which in consequence was "hencefor-ward subject only to Our own unlimited authority."[11]

Reactions were accordingly mixed. Russia and Sweden evoked their rever-sionary rights, but only *pro forma*. Joachim Bernstorff wrote dejectedly to his brother, Christian, on 2 September that the idea "that the Holsteiners should re-joice over this reunion, based upon the destruction of their German fatherland by lawless outside force, I consider an unheard-of expectation." Christian replied a few days later that the declaration "in no way united Holstein with the Danish kingdom as such through a complete incorporation," but this could only be wishful thinking. Crown Prince Frederik had precisely the opposite view, and in directing the German Chancellery—henceforward called the Schleswig-Hol-stein Chancellery—to prepare a new law code for Holstein, he spoke of the duchy's "inseparable [ *unzertrennliche*] union with Denmark."[12] He was warmly sympathetic to the urgings of various of his confidants that Holstein be completely Danicized, in language as well as law. The Copenhagen journal *Nyeste Skilderie af Kjøbenhavn*, wrote enthusiastically on 13 September:

> Our fellow citizens in Holstein will become accustomed through the new ordinance to consider themselves not simply the *subjects* of one king, but also as one *people* under the king, who should forget their German origin and their former relationship to Germany. They will learn to see that they never honor themselves more than when they honor the Danish people, its language, and customs. May Denmark, Norway, and Holstein ever remain a single state, unified by the closest bonds of blood, brotherhood, and just laws! May this be the warmest wish of every friend of the Fatherland.[13]

In Holstein itself, while it aroused no great manifestations of enthusiasm, the incorporation was apparently accepted easily enough in bourgeois circles of rationalist bent, to which it seemed a logical solution and a welcome deliverance from Prussian designs. But more evident are the fears it aroused in more roman-tically minded, aristocratic society, above all at Emkendorf. Denmark's involve-ment in the European conflict after 1807 would for the time being hold its griev-ances in abeyance; yet it would also prevent the peaceful structural reforms which alone might have consolidated Holstein's new status. Otto Brandt's thesis that the origins of the nineteenth-century Schleswig-Holstein separatist move-ment must be sought in this period thus seem amply borne out.[14]

The incorporation issue of 1806 largely alienated Crown Prince Frederik from the aristocratic German members of his council, thus in effect from the council as a whole, an important step toward its eventual suspension in 1808.

The crisis also opened a fateful breach between the crown prince and the duke of Augustenburg.

In Norway the government continued to face the perplexing religious awakening among the peasantry led by the evangelist Hans Nielsen Hauge, which expressed other discontents with the existing authoritarianism. The Norwegian "Brethren" were increasing in numbers and, especially after their leader established himself as a merchant in Bergen in 1801, were rapidly building up a coordinated and mutually supportive network of economic enterprises in town and countryside.

Since the Haugians did not secede from the state church, it is impossible to judge their numbers with anything approaching accuracy. At the height of the movement, Hauge's writings were, however, being printed in editions of 50,000 to 60,000 copies.[15] No doubt there were considerable numbers of passive sympathizers.

The movement gave rise to mounting consternation and alarm in the upper levels of Norwegian society, for in various ways it appeared to threaten the vested interests of the entire Establishment. Hauge's strong emphasis upon, in effect, Luther's doctrine of the priesthood of all true believers—upon individual repentance and conversion, lay preaching, private devotions, and the ministry of useful work in this world—called into question the authority of the ordained and appointed parish pastor, the hierarchy, the entire institutional church. The weakening of ecclesiastical discipline, a pillar of the absolutist state, in turn undermined the authority of the civil bureaucracy as well as respect toward persons of quality and their established prerogatives. Insolence, it seemed, was fortified by blind and willful fanaticism, even though Hauge himself dismissed the fears of those who believed "all will go here as in France if we are successful."[16] The burgher class felt threatened by a movement that strove to break down traditional barriers between privileged towns and their rural hinterlands, between commerce and agriculture, between individual enterprise and an organized, collective competition.

Complaints accumulated. Hauge and various of his followers were repeatedly arrested on diverse charges. In 1804 Bishop Peder Hansen of Christiansand, an enlightened rationalist who had done much to improve popular education in his diocese, sent an alarming report on Hauge's religious fanaticism to the Danish Chancellery in Copenhagen. This was supplemented by the testimony of twenty-four leading citizens of Christiansand that the "Friends" threatened to disrupt economic life and even to precipitate civil or religious war. The Chancellery solicited reports from other officials, clerical and secular, in Norway.

In October 1804 Hauge was arrested and his property was confiscated upon government orders. While he was held in confinement, a commission of inquiry was appointed and heard some three hundred witnesses over the next three years before preparing charges that Hauge had violated the Conventicle Ordinance of 1741, had sought to found a sect with its own separate social order while seeking his own private gain, had spoken and written in a manner offensive to both civil and ecclesiastical authority, and had presented doctrines "which mislead the less enlightened masses into unsuitable brooding over the truth of the Christian religion."[17]

The government took its time, hoping that deprived of its leader the movement would fade away. The trial did not begin until 1809, a year after the commission's report, and it took another three years. Hauge was treated leniently in prison and was even released for a time in 1809 to help organize wartime saltpeter production. At last the court passed judgment in December 1813: nine years after his arrest in 1804, Hauge was sentenced to two years in a workhouse and to pay the costs of his trial. An appeal to the Superior Criminal Court (*Overkriminalret*) in Christiania, by that time Norway's highest tribunal, in December 1814 reduced the sentence to a fine of 1,000 *rigsdaler* plus court costs. Looking ahead, the Norwegian *Storting* or parliament would grant Hauge a small compensation of 2,600 *rigsdaler* in 1820, four years before his death. By the end of his life he showed little of his old fire.

The object of these proceedings against Hauge had been, as Frederik VI wrote in 1808, "to prevent the further spread of this fanaticism."[18] Yet persecution only strengthened the religious movement by making a martyr of its leader. Haugianism would remain a strong spiritual tradition among much of the Norwegian peasantry throughout the nineteenth century, and its influence lives on today. It meanwhile gave a higher moral sanction to a mounting social reaction against bureaucratic controls and urban monopolies, such as had underlain the Lofthuus rebellion in 1786. It represents a vital stage in the evolution of a self-conscious peasant movement that would find political expression already in the Norwegian constitutional convention of 1814. Unlike earlier manifestations of peasant unrest, which had always been more or less local in character, Haugianism quickly spread throughout Norway. In proclaiming the Word and in managing a variety of worldly enterprises, the "Friends" acquired a new self-confidence and a new mobility, established widespread contacts, and gained considerable practical organizational experience. Their puritan work ethic surely underlay, in no small measure, the economic advancement of numerous peasant families from this time forward.[19]

In its social and economic aspects, the Haugian movement seems more clearly progressive than had the Lofthuus uprising more than a decade before, which had shown a certain ambivalence toward transforming the old peasant society. The Haugians strove not only to break down occupational barriers but also, in their pietistic zeal, to eradicate much in the ancient folk culture that they dismissed as worldly or sinful: fiddle playing and the singing of old ballads, dances and games, ornate festive dress, ostentation in food and drink, old stories and legends. "From a purely religious-historical point of view," Halvdan Koht has written, "it may be said that the Haugian movement carried through what rationalism had undertaken: to put an end to all old superstition. . . . many shadows fell over the earthy vitality and aesthetic creativity that until recently had distinguished peasant culture."[20] The price could not but be high for liberation from old, previously accepted restraints and, in consequence, from the traditions of a largely self-contained society.

The brief respite in the European wars ushered in by the Peace of Amiens in March 1802 proved a somewhat mixed blessing for the Scandinavian lands. While the perils of neutrality now ceased, so too did the advantages that wartime commerce offered to neutral carriers.

Sweden remained on bad terms with Great Britain. The Anglo-Russian convention of June 1801, to which the Nordic states were invited to adhere, had accepted the neutrals' demand that a blockade, to be honored, must be effective rather than simply proclaimed, but rejected the principle that free ships made free goods while accepting Britain's right to visit and search neutral merchantmen. Gustav IV Adolf refused to accept the terms of the convention, even after the British returned St. Barthélemy in May 1802, hoping to gain compensation for the two convoys and numerous other vessels seized by the British since 1798, as well as a more favorable definition of contraband.

The danger of Sweden's diplomatic isolation meanwhile became painfully apparent in April 1803, when a petty border dispute at Abborfors in Finland promptly led to a Russian ultimatum. After bidding proud defiance, Gustav IV Adolf accepted a face-saving solution, after which the whole affair soon blew over. Russian motives remain unclear, but they seem to be connected with the possibility that a resumption of Anglo-French hostilities would soon involve Russia as an ally of Britain, again exposing St. Petersburg to attack from a potentially hostile Sweden, as in 1788. Perhaps the Abborfors crisis was only intended as a precautionary warning to Stockholm. It was nonetheless a reminder that the Russian government still by no means considered the problem of Finland resolved.

Gustav IV Adolf meanwhile revealed an increasingly paranoiac fear of the Jacobin peril, perceiving it even in most unlikely places. In September 1802 Alexander I carried out far-reaching administrative reforms in Russia, increasing the powers of the Senate and allowing both it and the provincial nobility certain rights of remonstrance. According to G. G. Adlerbeth, Gustav IV Adolf, who had the "most exalted concept of the royal prerogative," perceived therein "Jacobinical principles and a threat to all governments." It was a curious reversal of roles since Tsar Paul's day, only a few years previously. In 1803 Gustav Adolf was alarmed to discover in the royal palace itself a small circle of occultist adepts around Duke Carl, which he imagined to be dangerous "Illuminati."[21]

The British declaration of war against France on 16 May 1803 eased Sweden's situation to some degree. It evidently helped smooth over the recent Swedish-Russian crisis. Stockholm gained a stronger bargaining position vis-à-vis London, leading at last to a commercial convention in July 1803, exempting both metals and timber (except oak) from contraband and granting Sweden generous compensation for the convoys of 1798. For the next two years, Sweden did a good business with both sides, especially with Britain, producing a favorable balance of trade up to 1807, despite growing competition to its principal export industry from Britain's increasing production of coke-smelted iron.[22]

In July 1803 Gustav IV Adolf and Queen Fredrika departed for a visit to Germany. The queen had long desired to revisit her childhood home at the court of Karlsruhe in Baden, but the king had his political interests as well, which would cause mounting anxiety at home during the eighteen long months before he returned. Already in October 1803 Duchess Charlotta noted rumors in Stockholm that Gustav Adolf sought in Germany to "form a league against France and that the allies would choose him their leader."[23] The situation was, however, at first more complex. While he associated with French émigrés and counterrevolutionaries who eagerly sought his support, Gustav Adolf also carried on secret negotiations with French agents in Germany concerning a possible alliance with a view to obtaining Norway, at least through the end of 1803.

This interval of watchful opportunism ended abruptly when French troops violated the territory of neutral Baden to abduct the duc d'Enghien, a close relative of the French royal family, who was summarily tried and executed in Paris in March 1804. The incident caused an uproar throughout monarchical Europe. To the distress of his advisers in Stockholm, Gustav Adolf in Karlsruhe recalled his minister from Paris. Tsar Alexander did the same. By the end of March both Sweden and Russia sounded each other out regarding an anti-French alliance, and in April both refused to recognize Napoleon Bonaparte's self-proclaimed imperial title. Their recent mutual suspicions were quickly forgotten.

In August 1804 the *Moniteur* in Paris ridiculed Gustav IV Adolf as a vain and childish fool, the misfortune of the "brave and loyal" Swedish nation.[24] This article circulated in translation in Sweden, together with other, surreptitious attacks on the king. Already in February Gustav Adolf had forbidden the import of Danish newspapers into Sweden. In August new French books and journals were banned, as was any mention in the Swedish press of events in France. Diplomatic relations with Paris were now broken off altogether.

Gustav Adolf had meanwhile entered into negotiations with the British, even before finally returning to Stockholm in February 1805. Britain and Russia concluded an alliance against France in April, soon to be joined by Austria, thus forming the Third Coalition. A new continental war was bound to break out shortly. Yet Sweden's negotiations with Russia and Britain proceeded slowly, for Gustav IV Adolf proved an astute bargainer. Although Sweden could contribute only limited military resources, its strategic position on the Sound and the Baltic offered the allies an important asset. In particular, Swedish Pomerania, with the fortified port of Stralsund, could provide the necessary bridgehead for operations against the French in northern Germany. Gustav Adolf could hold out for high subsidies, thus avoiding a *riksdag*. He also long insisted that the allies commit themselves to restoring the Bourbons in France, producing further delays which made the allies ever more disposed to make concessions regarding the respective sizes of the Swedish military contingent and the British subsidy.

At length, through a series of agreements culminating with the Treaty of Bäckaskog on 3 October 1805, Sweden undertook to augment its garrison at Stralsund to 8,000 men, half of them to be subsidized by Britain at nearly twice the standard rate per man to be paid to Russia and Austria, and to provide a field army of 10,000 (formally 12,000) troops at the standard subsidy. Counting additional sums for armaments and transport, Sweden was to receive a monthly subsidy from Britain of some 20,000 pounds. The allies gained access to Swedish Pomerania, while the Swedish king was to command the combined allied forces in northern Germany. Peace was to be concluded only by common agreement. There was no mention of the Bourbons.[25]

On 31 October Sweden declared war on France. A decade and a half after Gustav III had sought to organize a great monarchical crusade, his son at last brought Sweden into the great struggle against France. His purpose, Gustav Adolf wrote on 7 October, was to "resist and obstruct the brutal system of encroachment and oppression of French despotism."[26] The die was cast. The neutrality of the Scandinavian world, so long preserved, was breached.

In view of the ignominious outcome of Sweden's role in the War of the Third Coalition and of its aftermath, Gustav IV Adolf's entry into the European conflict has traditionally been condemned as folly, if not outright madness. The decision was his own and was favored by none of his principal advisers. Yet in the fall of 1805 both ideal and practical arguments could be made in its favor. Napoleonic France did indeed threaten all of Europe. As Duchess Charlotta—who was by no means uncritical of her nephew—saw it in December, Sweden had only three options: to side with France, to remain neutral, or to join Britain and Russia. The first alternative was impossible, for experience showed that the combined enmity of the British on the seas and the Russians on the Finnish border would be ruinous, while with their backing, Sweden was shielded from direct attack. Neutrality would naturally be preferable, but could it ultimately be maintained? To be sure, both Prussia and Denmark still remained neutral, but, the duchess added prophetically, "we have not yet seen the end of this war." Sweden was meanwhile compensated by considerable foreign subsidies and was able to fight on its own terms on foreign ground.[27] When the allies won the victory they had every reason to expect, Sweden could demand its just rewards.

Early in the present century, some efforts were made to revindicate Gustav IV Adolf's war policy in 1805 by seeking to show that it was motivated by a practical concern for Sweden's commercial interests, but this view is now generally discounted. "It is impossible to speak with the king about commercial interests," Gustaf af Wetterstedt would complain in 1807, "he can never believe they are of any benefit to the state."[28]

Gustav IV Adolf arrived in Pomerania at the beginning of November 1805 to assume overall command of the allied forces there, including some 12,000 Swedes and 17,000 Russians. The latter advanced into Hanover, and a small British force landed at the mouth of the Elbe. Gustav Adolf was meanwhile held back by his mistrust of still-neutral Prussia, which mobilized a 30,000-man army of observation on the Pomeranian border and also sent troops into Hanover as the French withdrew.

Ill will between Sweden and Prussia was of long standing, tracing back to the seventeenth century and exacerbated in the Seven Years' War. Berlin was ever watchful for its chance to acquire Swedish Pomerania. Since the accessions of Gustav IV Adolf and Frederick William III, friction had increased over questions of neutral trade and German affairs.

Fearful for its growing domination in neutral northern Germany, Berlin had sought to sabotage the recent Swedish-Russian rapprochement. Gustav Adolf was offended by Prussia's recognition of Napoleon's imperial title, leading to the breaking of diplomatic relations between Berlin and Stockholm at the very time the Third Coalition was forming.

Upon arrival in Pomerania, Gustav Adolf demanded a clarification of his intentions from the Prussian king. His personal envoy arrived in Berlin just as Tsar Alexander was negotiating a provisional alliance with Prussia, signed on 3 November; in the excitement the Swedish note remained unanswered. Gustav Adolf was outraged by this new sign of Prussian duplicity, as well as by his allies' apparently greater solicitude toward Frederick William than toward himself.

Under these circumstances, the Swedish army did not receive orders to march into Hanover until 3 December. Already the day before, the main Austrian and Russian armies were crushed by Napoleon at Austerlitz in Bohemia. There ensued a kind of *drôle de guerre*, as the allies in the north awaited the outcome of confused developments in the south. Prussia made a sudden about-face: on 15 December, the very day it had undertaken to join the coalition, it concluded an agreement with France allowing for a Prussian occupation of Hanover.

The British and Russians withdrew from northern Germany, but Gustav Adolf continued to occupy the small Hanoverian territory of Lauenburg, on the right bank of the Elbe. The Swedish presence there provided him with a legalistic justification to seek British and Russian backing in his defiance of Prussia, as well as to extort from Britain some still unpaid subsidies. London and St. Petersburg urged him to abandon an untenable situation. When Prussia announced its formal annexation of Hanover in March 1806, Gustav Adolf warned that an attack on Lauenburg would be tantamount to an attack on Sweden itself, although he prudently reduced his force there to a token 300 men.

The line was drawn. Under growing pressure from France, the Prussians could hardly fail to cross it. In April they marched into Lauenburg, from which the small Swedish force retreated after offering a symbolic resistance. Gustav Adolf responded by clamping a naval blockade on Prussia's Baltic ports.

The escalating Swedish-Prussian dispute was a constant irritant to the British and Russians. Gustav Adolf had riled the Prussians at the very time their active participation in the coalition hung in the balance. His blockade of the Prussian ports in the spring and summer of 1806 seriously disrupted British and Russian commerce in the Baltic. Repeated British and Russian efforts at mediation, in hopes that Prussia might yet be won back into the allied camp, stranded mainly on Gustav Adolf's intransigence.

During the summer of 1806, however, friction between France and Prussia reached its breaking point. A Prussian-Russian alliance was concluded in August, and Frederick William withdrew his troops from Lauenburg, which Gustav Adolf promptly reoccupied, permitting him to celebrate what G. M. Armfelt wryly called the "triumph of obstinacy."[29] The whole dispute with Prussia vanished almost miraculously in the face of the far greater menace from the west.

While Gustav IV Adolf was engaged in his quasi-war with Prussia, a crisis arose in his own German dependency of Pomerania when he undertook to augment his forces by creating a Pomeranian *Landwehr* through conscription on the French model in the early summer of 1806.[30] The Pomerania Estates (*Landstände*) protested that this violated the established privileges of the duchy and—more audacious than the Schleswig-Holstein *Ritterschaft* in 1802—they appealed to the imperial *Reichskammergericht* in Wetzlar. The king thereupon declared Pomerania's ancient constitution and privileges null and void on 26 June 1806. Following the formal dissolution of the Holy Roman Empire a few weeks later, in August, he proceeded to reorganize and reform the province to his own taste. The old Germanic institutions were replaced by the Swedish constitution and laws. These did not allow for the existence of personal servitude, and Gustav Adolf abolished serfdom (*Leibeigenschaft*) in the province. Swedish ecclesiastical and educational institutions were introduced.

In August the king convened a special Pomeranian *Landtag* in Greifswald, organized on the Swedish four-Estates model, which accepted the new dispensation and guaranteed the debts of the Pomeranian treasury. Ambitious plans were meanwhile being considered for creating new farms on the royal domain and for land reallocation and consolidation such as was then being carried out in Sweden. The king's aim in Pomerania in 1806, Sten Carlsson has written, was "clearly a free and independent peasantry on the Swedish model."[31]

Gustav IV Adolf's actions in Swedish Pomerania in 1806, as well as the aristocratic opposition they aroused, bear obvious similarities with the Danish government's reforms in the duchies during the same period. Yet while Swedish Pomerania was considerably smaller in area, population, and relative importance to the state as a whole, its defense of its corporate privileges was more determined and the program of reforms that destroyed them was at once more sudden and more radical than in Schleswig and Holstein. Lars Dalgren, the leading authority on the subject, did not hesitate to call it the "coup d'etat of 1806," thereby bringing to mind Gustav III's coup at the *Riksdag* of 1789 which produced the Act of Union and Security.[32] Like his father in Sweden, Gustav IV Adolf in Pomerania combined social with constitutional objectives, although in the latter's case a more clearly antiaristocratic stance is apparent. Similarly, Gustav Adolf's high-handed proceedings did not fail to create much bitterness among the Pomeranian *Junkers*.

In September 1806 Gustav IV Adolf returned to Stockholm, well pleased with his recent triumphs over Frederick William III and the Pomeranian *Landstände*. Soon thereafter, Prussia declared war on France on 9 October. Five days later, its main armies were smashed by the French at Jena and Auerstädt. Frederick William retreated with the remnants of his forces to East Prussia and the protection of his Russian ally. The small Swedish detachment in Lauenburg was trapped and capitulated.

Swedish Pomerania now lay isolated far behind the front. Napoleon sent peace feelers to Gustav Adolf, who peremptorily rejected them. The king made strenuous efforts to assemble 30,000 men, frustrated by constitutional limits to his authority to raise revenues without convening a *riksdag*. Early in 1807 he confiscated 375,000 pounds in British subsidies then crossing Sweden on the way to Russia, claiming that the Russians owed him that amount. It has been suggested that Alexander I foreclosed on this debt in Finland the following year.[33]

In January 1807 the French attacked Swedish Pomerania in force, but encountering stout resistance, they were prepared to conclude an armistice in April when all their available forces were needed in the east.

During the respite, Gustav Adolf managed to arrange for increased British subsidies and for the reinforcement of Swedish Pomerania with British and Prussian troops. He likewise intrigued with a variety of French counterrevolutionaries urging daring projects and sought to recruit French émigrés under his banner.

The Swedish king was in an exalted frame of mind by the summer of 1807. Always seriously religious with strong pietistic and mystical leanings, he began by now, if not before, to recognize in Napoleon the biblical Beast of the Apocalypse as interpreted by the German mystic Johann Heinrich Jung-Stilling; he feared that by negotiating with Napoleon he would condemn himself to both temporal and eternal woe.[34] There was now speculation, both at home and abroad, about his sanity, a question which has since perplexed historians.

Counting British and Prussian reinforcements and Pomeranian *Landwehr*, Gustav Adolf had hopes of fielding 36,000 men, and on 3 July 1807 he announced that he would terminate the armistice after the stipulated two weeks. Unfortunately the situation was already then beginning to change radically. The Russians were defeated by the French at Friedland on 14 June. By 7–9 July, Alexander I concluded both peace and an alliance with Napoleon at Tilsit. Prussia made peace and recalled its troops from Swedish Pomerania, and the British detachment also withdrew. The French attacked in overwhelming force on 13 July. Stralsund quickly capitulated. The last Swedish troops evacuated the island of Rügen in late September. In all, some 10,000 returned, leaving behind at least 6,000 dead or prisoners of war.[35]

Thus ended Sweden's ill-starred campaign in Germany. Despite it all, it had not been insignificant. Without Sweden's participation, Alexander I hesitated to commit Russia to the struggle and Napoleon later admitted that the Pomeranian redoubt on his flank had tied down sizable French forces.

The Swedish king had nonetheless been plagued by misfortune: Austerlitz ended his first attempt to go on the offensive, Friedland his second. More alarmingly, he manifestly lacked those qualities his difficult situation demanded, while possessing others that under the circumstances were dangerous. His dogmatic intransigence prevented compromise with either the Prussians or the French, to the detriment of both Swedish and allied interests. The price Sweden itself paid for its failure and that of its allies by the end of 1807 was not excessive in material terms; even Swedish Pomerania was eventually recovered through the fortunes of war. Sweden's greatest sacrifice was the loss of confidence in the sovereign by both his allies and his own subjects. And in the months ahead he would be overwhelmed by far greater problems.

Denmark, in the meantime, maintained its neutrality as the tides of war once again engulfed Europe. When the French, following the outbreak of hostilities, occupied Hanover, Denmark mobilized an army of observation of 16,000 men in Holstein. Like Sweden, it had cause to watch Prussia closely, for should they be drawn into the war on opposite sides, Prussia would surely seize the duchies—as it was to do some sixty years later. Despite much sympathy in the Danish government for the Third Coalition, mistrust of Prussia played perhaps a decisive role in keeping Denmark on the sideline, Edvard Holm has suggested.[36] As during the Seven Years' War, the price of military preparedness on the southern border meanwhile came high.

There was once again the matter of neutral commerce. Denmark had adhered to the Anglo-Russian convention of June 1801 in October of that year. When the Anglo-French war resumed in the spring of 1803, the Danish government issued strict regulations to prevent misuse of the Danish flag and ships' papers by foreigners.

Danish commerce was at first little disturbed. During the first two years of hostilities, Napoleon, concentrating on his intended cross-Channel invasion of England, was little concerned with commercial warfare, while the British, initially assured of their command of the seas, showed greater leniency toward neutral shipping. At first the British blockaded only France itself, then Spain from 1804.

Danish commerce once again flourished, reaching a peak by 1806. Visitors to Copenhagen were struck by the prosperity of the city arising in more imposing grandeur than ever following the great fire of 1795. The old dream of earlier decades was revived of making Copenhagen the great entrepôt of trade between northern and southern Europe.

Following the British naval victory at Trafalgar and the French triumphs by land at Austerlitz and Jena-Auerstädt in 1805-6, however, both sides turned to economic warfare to force a decision. In November 1806, after bringing most of the European coastline from the Adriatic to the Baltic under French dominance, Napoleon issued his Berlin Decree, establishing his Continental System: Great Britain was declared to be under blockade, and all ports under his control were closed to vessels proceeding from Britain or its colonies. The British naval blockade had meanwhile been progressively extended along the coastlines of French-controlled Europe, and in January 1807 a British Order in Council prohibited neutral trade between enemy ports or with ports from which the British were denied entry. During the following year both sides tightened their restrictions to the point where any neutral vessel trading with one belligerent was liable to seizure and confiscation by the other.

A swarm of British privateers took to the seas to enforce Britain's effective blockade of the enemy to their own profit, while French privateering had by now become relatively ineffectual. Danes and Norwegians continued to carry on a sizable trade with Britain, which above all needed imports of grain and timber. But the British blockade of the Continent hurt other Danish interests, particularly in the Mediterranean, where the thriving neutral carrying trade was largely ruined. In negotiations with Britain—such as those concerning the closing of the Elbe, which cut off the trade of Altona and Glückstadt in Holstein—Crown Prince Frederik and Christian Bernstorff held to a rigidly legalistic interpretation of Denmark's neutral rights, rather than seeking to accommodate to the practical realities of Britain's strategic situation and command of the seas. In dealing with France, they tended to be more pragmatic, in view of the immediate proximity of Napoleon's Grand Army in Germany. All of this could not but cause mounting exasperation in London. Upon becoming Britain's foreign minister in March 1807, George Canning ominously decided that Denmark was not to be relied upon.

Throughout the years from 1802 to 1807, the internal development of the two Scandinavian monarchies continued along remarkably similar lines. Both saw the progressive emergence of an autocracy at once personal and bureaucratic, despite formal constitutional differences. The lines of authority tended increasingly to run from the crown to the individual officials and government bureaus, whose established procedures it generally respected, in the process bypassing such intermediate bodies as formally continued to exist. The Swedish council had been suspended by Gustav III in 1789, and Gustav IV Adolf avoided calling another *riksdag* after 1800. Following A. P. Bernstorff's death in 1797, Crown Prince Frederik relied less and less upon the Danish state council until it too was suspended in 1808. Both Holstein and Swedish Pomerania were at last deprived of their special status and integrated into their respective kingdoms. The suppression of the Haugian movement in Norway meanwhile upheld the sanctity of both clerical and bureaucratic authority. In both states the voice of dissent was stifled by tight press controls. The lengthy absences of both rulers from their capitals further reinforced the trend toward a personal and bureaucratic autocracy.

Yet this autocracy remained a benevolent one, for all its cultural obscurantism, and it carried out important internal improvements. In both Sweden and Denmark the tendency has long been to emphasize earlier reforms under the aegis of Gustav III and A. P. Bernstorff, at the expense of those later carried out by the less glamorous Gustav IV Adolf and Crown Prince Frederik, both of whom were moreover later burdened with the stigma of their unfortunate foreign policies. Yet the liberation of the serfs in Holstein and Swedish Pomerania and the program of land consolidation in Sweden easily bear comparison with earlier accomplishments. Both Crown Prince Frederik and Gustav IV Adolf revealed a strong dislike for aristocratic privilege and a warm sympathy for the common man.[37] It is worth noting that peasant emancipation and agrarian reforms in Denmark's and Sweden's German provinces provided useful precedents for Prussia in the era of Stein and Hardenberg following the defeat at Jena and Auerstädt in 1806.

In foreign policy, however, the two Nordic states continued to follow separate paths. Gustav IV Adolf, unreconciled to Sweden's role as a minor power, followed an adventurous course which by 1805 involved his reluctant nation in the European war. Denmark remained neutral and sought to profit from wartime commerce. Both the Swedish king and the Danish crown prince-regent took an uncompromising stance in seeking to uphold what they considered their just rights. Still, to both Scandinavian governments it was becoming painfully evident by the fall of 1807 that their destinies lay increasingly outside their own control.

# CHAPTER 12

# Into the Maelstrom
# 1807–10

Following the resolution of the Franco-Russian conflict in July 1807, both Scandinavian monarchies found themselves faced with dire threats to their security and integrity. Within a month Denmark was drawn into the European war as an ally of France and Russia. The conflict changed character for Sweden, which remained Britain's only ally, besides Portugal, resulting in a disastrous defeat, the loss of Finland, and a change of regime. Under the strains and shifting circumstances of a war dividing Scandinavia against itself, Finland gained for the first time an autonomous existence, while in Norway, Iceland, and the German provinces old ties to the central regimes were weakened in varying degree, with important implications for the future.

The Copenhagen journal *Nyeste Skilderie af Kjøbenhavn* might still proclaim in January 1807 that future generations would admire how Denmark, a land unthreatened by its neighbors' ambitions, "like a frail vessel amidst the storm was kept from foundering by the hand of a wise helmsman, while the proudest monarchs of the waves were crushed on the rocks and swallowed up by an all destructive Maelstrom."[1] But it was soon evident that this was not to be, for the Tilsit alliance of 9 July between France and Russia posed the gravest threat to Denmark's neutrality. The new allies were determined to close the continent to British commerce, and Denmark-Norway, extending from the Elbe to the Barents Sea, commanded close to half of Europe's western coastline. If Denmark refused to join the Continental System, the duchies, Jutland, and even Fyn lay exposed to invasion and occupation by overwhelming French land forces, even if the other Danish islands, Norway, and the Atlantic dependencies might be protected by a strong fleet, presumably reinforced by the British. If Denmark

275

joined the Continental System, the maritime trade upon which Denmark—and particularly Norway—depended so heavily would be swept from the seas, Norway would be cut off from Denmark by the British navy and a hostile Sweden, the Atlantic islands and overseas colonies would be isolated and defenseless, while even communications in Danish home waters would be precarious. In the balance, Crown Prince Frederik and his advisers inclined toward the British Scylla rather than the French Charybdis, as they clearly signaled to London already by the beginning of 1807.[2]

The outcome was decided otherwise thanks to George Canning, the new British foreign minister since March 1807. Danish protests over neutral rights had quickly convinced him that Denmark was not to be relied on, and the Tilsit alliance immediately aroused his apprehensions over the Danish fleet, which had proved its mettle at Copenhagen Roads six years before. If joined with other continental naval forces, it might threaten the decisive but now ever more thinly spread British command of the seas following Trafalgar.

Already around 10 July 1807, just as the first rumors reached London that a Franco-Russian rapprochement was impending, Canning received a report from a traveling British diplomat that the Danish fleet was being mobilized, while the British resident in Altona feared the Danes might close the Holstein ports and that the duchy might be occupied by the French. Both reports were mistaken, but Canning decided that Britain must strike hard and fast.[3] On 18 July he secured orders for a large naval expedition against Denmark. Sir Francis Jackson was appointed special envoy to deal with the Danes. When the main British force sailed from Yarmouth on 26 July, no one embarked knew its destination except Jackson and its commander, Admiral James Gambier. But to many it appeared to be the greatest expedition to set forth from Britain's shores in the struggle against Napoleon. The fleet, which entered the Sound during the first days of August, included twenty-four ships of the line, twenty-two smaller naval vessels, and a host of troop transports.

What followed was a tragic comedy of errors. Only after the expedition had sailed did Canning receive reports from the British minister in Copenhagen strongly denying the veracity of the reports he had received. Jackson was under strict instructions to demand that the Danish fleet be placed at Britain's disposal until the end of the war, possibly through an Anglo-Danish alliance. He presented his proposals to Christian Bernstorff and to Crown Prince Frederik on 7–8 August in Kiel. Outraged, the crown prince departed for Copenhagen to see to its defenses. Jackson followed after, arriving in the capital after Frederik had returned to Kiel, and thus vainly negotiated with Joachim Bernstorff, who had no authority to grant the assurances he demanded. In exasperation, Jackson broke off negotiations on 13 August and rejoined the British fleet in the Sound.

The British now landed 30,000 troops on Sjælland—including the force just withdrawn from Swedish Pomerania—beginning on 16 August. In command was General William Cathcart, and among his subordinates was Arthur Wellesley, the future duke of Wellington. Opposing them were only some 5,500 Danish regulars—since the Danish main force was in Holstein—backed by peasant and burgher militias, a total of some 13,000 men. Copenhagen's land defenses had been neglected for the past century. Morale in the city nevertheless remained remarkably high at first, not least among the high-spirited corps of student volunteers, some 800 strong.

After encircling the city on its landward side, the British demanded its surrender upon pain of bombardment on 20 August. A pitiful force of Sjælland militia was handily routed near Køge on 29 August. Jackson pressed for bombardment of Copenhagen. Reluctantly Cathcart agreed.

The ordeal began on 2 September, causing great destruction. The new Congreve incendiary rockets proved particularly effective, and large areas of the city were devastated by fire. Under growing pressure from the magistrature, the wounded commandant agreed to an armistice on 5 September, and a council of war in the capital undertook to negotiate the surrender of the fleet to the British. Crown Prince Frederik, who on 16 August had declared war on Britain, was outraged by Copenhagen's early capitulation.

The armistice was concluded on 7 September, to last until 19 October. The British sought to be tactful in their occupation, and Copenhageners were bemused at the sight of kilted Highlanders encamped in their city's parks. British naval personnel meanwhile worked furiously to rig the Danish fleet before the armistice expired. On 20 October the entire British force on Sjælland embarked and departed. Their armada now included eighty warships and 243 transport vessels, several of which were lost on the stormy return voyage. It included virtually the entire Danish fleet: seventeen ships of the line, seventeen frigates, eight brigs, eight smaller vessels, and twenty-six cannon boats. Before departing, the British destroyed a ship of the line and three other vessels in dry dock.[4]

Behind them they left a city badly devastated. Recovery during the hard times after 1807 would be slow, and empty lots could still be seen twenty or thirty years later. The British attack upon a major European capital meanwhile caused a furor throughout the Continent and aroused no little indignation in Britain itself. Canning was accused of having acted irresponsibly, and Jackson was ostracized by George III and polite society.

For the Danish monarchy, the British attack meant more than humiliation and the loss of the fleet. It was thereby precipitated into the European conflict on the side of Britain's enemies, with fateful consequences for its future existence. At this critical juncture, the course of events might have been very different. On 2 August Napoleon had written to Marshal Jean-Baptiste Bernadotte, his commander in Hamburg, that if Denmark would not go to war with Britain, he would declare war on Denmark.[5] On 31 October Denmark concluded a formal alliance with France, which Crown Prince Frederik was thereafter determined to uphold at any cost.

Gustav IV Adolf meanwhile held staunchly to his British alliance, which following Tilsit and Denmark's entry into the war on the other side placed Sweden and Finland in a particularly hazardous position, once again encircled by a reconstituted, hostile Russian-Danish entente. Alexander I made what seemed simply *pro forma* soundings to urge his brother-in-law, Gustav IV Adolf, to abandon Britain and join the Continental System. Only by late January was Stockholm apprised of alarming Russian military preparations. On 21 February the Swedish ambassador in St. Petersburg was handed an ultimatum demanding that Sweden make common cause with Russia and Denmark. On the same day Russian troops crossed the Finnish border. Three weeks later, on 14 March, Stockholm received Denmark's declaration of war.

By attacking during the winter the Russians enjoyed the advantage that Finland could not be reinforced from Sweden until after the spring thaw. However, owing to problems of provisioning and communications in Finland's rugged and thinly settled terrain, they at first committed only 24,000 troops to the campaign under General F. W. von Buxhövden, a veteran of the Russo-Swedish war of 1788–90; the aging G. M. Sprengtporten, leader of the Finnish autonomist movement of the 1780s, accompanied him as his adviser. The Finnish army was not much smaller, amounting to some 22,000 men. The Russian troops were, however, seasoned veterans, capably commanded, and backed by large reserves, whereas few of the Finns had yet seen combat and their officers were all too often inexperienced, superannuated, and defeatist in attitude. A third of the Finnish army was immobilized in Sveaborg fortress in the Helsingfors archipelago.

For centuries Sweden's defense of its trans-Baltic possessions had been based on the concept of a strategic retreat to coastal redoubts, from which counterattacks could be mounted after reinforcement by sea. The construction of Sveaborg in the mid-eighteenth century had been based on this strategy, which was reiterated in instructions to the Finnish command at the beginning of 1808.

In issuing these instructions, Gustav IV Adolf stressed the importance of a fighting retreat. Following the Russian attack, however, the Finnish field army of some 12,000 men, under the elderly General W. M. Klingspor, withdrew rapidly to northern Österbotten on the Bothnian coast, offering practically no resistance. The main Russian force advanced along the south coast. By 2 March it entered Helsingfors, thereby isolating Sveaborg. By 22 March the Russians had taken Åbo. On 12 April they landed on the Åland Islands.

As long as Sveaborg, the "Gibraltar of the North," held out, the Russian hold on southern Finland remained precarious. Considered one of Europe's most impregnable fortresses, it protected a sizable galley fleet and was garrisoned by some 7,000 men. The Russians began serious siege operations in mid-March with a force roughly equal to that of the defenders. Their first summons to surrender were rejected, and their bombardment from nearby islands caused little damage. But morale among the higher officers of the garrison soon eroded. Unaccustomed to land operations of this type, Sveaborg's commander, Vice-Admiral C. O. Cronstedt, relied upon the advice of subordinates who considered resistance futile. On 6 April he was persuaded to conclude an armistice with the Russians, according to which he would capitulate on 3 May if the fortress were not relieved before that date.

The agreement entailed serious risks owing to the unpredictability of the spring thaw, which indeed came late that year. No relief expedition was yet being prepared in Sweden. Cronstedt was allowed to send couriers to Stockholm, but the Russians found ways to delay them. News of the armistice first reached the Swedish capital the very day Sveaborg surrendered.

Word of the impending capitulation aroused great indignation among the garrison, and some of the junior officers vainly sought to organize a mutiny. With the fortress the Russians took 110 vessels and over 2,000 cannon. The garrison was released on parole, although many of the men later rejoined the Finnish field army. Cronstedt remains in historical memory a Finnish Benedict Arnold.[6]

The war, however, was not yet over, especially since Russia's concerns in Central Europe and on the Black Sea immobilized the greater part of its military might. Klingspor's army commenced its two-pronged counteroffensive from Ösberbotten by July, advancing down the west coast and inland toward the Russian supply lines in Karelia. Until mid-September it penetrated far to the south, supported by peasant partisans behind the enemy's lines.

Finland could not, however, be regained unless the Finnish counteroffensive from the north were supported by an even larger-scale attack from Sweden in the south. Following the surrender of Sveaborg, this necessarily involved difficult and risky landing operations, although prospects improved when a local uprising drove the Russians out of the Åland Islands in May and the combined British and Swedish fleets took control of the Baltic.

Gustav IV Adolf meanwhile made great efforts to raise troops. To supplement an existing military establishment of 66,000 (including 20,000 Finns), he created a new militia, the *Lantvärn*, based on conscription of unmarried men between the ages of nineteen and twenty-five. This levy, which recalls Gustav IV Adolf's Pomeranian *Landwehr* in 1806, provided an additional 30,000 men. Sweden-Finland thus fielded a total force of close to 100,000, although its training, armament, and supply presented serious problems.

Swedish attempts at landing operations in southwestern Finland were delayed until August and September, when they were disrupted by stormy weather on the Baltic. By then the Russians had already turned back Klingspor's counteroffensive. No lasting bridgehead could be established in the south. In his rage Gustav Adolf stripped the three elite guards' regiments of their special status and distinctions.

Had the Swedes shown greater skill and determination, the Finnish peasantry might have risen up against the occupier, as was taking place in Spain at that very time. But by the late fall of 1808 the chance was lost. The British navy withdrew from the Baltic for the winter. The Russian army, increased to some 55,000 men, pressed steadily northward against the dispirited and dwindling Finnish force. On 19 November its command concluded a convention for the evacuation of northern Finland, and on 13 December the last of some 10,000 Finnish troops crossed the Kemi River into Sweden proper.

Sweden meanwhile faced its enemy to the west, and it was here that Gustav IV Adolf at first concentrated his attention. Denmark was the weaker foe, and the old Gustavian dream of acquiring Norway was never far beneath the surface. In the fall of 1807, Canning had raised the idea of a Swedish occupation of Sjælland until the end of the war. Although nothing came of this somewhat nebulous scheme, London thereafter held out to Gustav IV Adolf the prospect of British support against Denmark to help Sweden acquire Norway. In view of this enticement, Sven G. Trulsson has recently argued that Gustav Adolf, aware that a continued British alliance must surely bring war with Russia and Denmark, was prepared to "maximize risks" to "maximize his gains," with Finland as his "stake" in the gamble. Alarmed by Sweden's manifest designs against Norway, Crown Prince Frederik, following the outbreak of the war, in turn aspired to regain the old "East Denmark": the Scanian provinces lost to Sweden in the seventeenth century.[7]

Denmark was under strong French pressure to attack Sweden. Napoleon made Marshal Bernadotte's army corps available for an offensive across the Sound, provided Bernadotte be placed in command. In early March the marshal entered Denmark with a force including several Spanish regiments, hostages for the good behavior of an uncertain ally. His troops took up quarters in the duchies, Jutland, and Fyn, where they could be provisioned at Denmark's expense. The appearance of Spanish troops in Rendsburg literally frightened Christian VII to death on 13 March, and the crown prince at last became King Frederik VI.

The projected invasion came to naught. Only two Spanish regiments crossed the Great Belt to Sjælland, from whence the attack on Sweden was to proceed, before the spring thaw allowed the British fleet to return to Danish waters. Soon thereafter, the British got word of the national uprising in Spain, beginning in May, to most of the Spanish units in Denmark before the French could secure their oath of allegiance to Joseph Bonaparte. In early August the Spaniards mutinied. The British fleet succeeded in evacuating most of them, some 9,000 men, and took them home to Spain to fight against their erstwhile allies. In the meantime, they had been surprisingly popular with the local population.

The mutiny, as well as problems of coordination, supply, and naval support, ended for the time being any prospect for an attack across the Sound. Already concerned mainly with the Iberian peninsula, it seems most probable that Napoleon—unlike Bernadotte—intended the troop movements in Denmark simply to encourage the Danes and Russians while distracting the British and Swedes, without really intending to follow through.[8] Bernadotte's corps returned to Germany, to the relief of the Danes, who were surely mindful of what Spain's French allies had undertaken there while en route to Portugal. Denmark's war against Sweden could now be carried on only from Norway, which, isolated by the British fleet, involved serious difficulties and risks.

To cover its western front, Sweden at first assembled 7,000 men in Skåne to oppose a landing from Denmark, and some over 15,000 men on the Norwegian frontier, of which 13,400 in the southernmost sector, the traditional invasion route. The Norwegian army amounted to 35,800 men, but since much of it was dispersed along the long coastline or in fixed fortifications, Prince Christian August of Augustenburg, the commander in southern Norway, had a field army of only 9-10,000 men.

Both Swedes and Norwegians were plagued by logistical problems. Moreover, following generations of peace—broken only by the brief conflict in 1788—neither army showed much enthusiasm for what now seemed a fratricidal war. A cautious Swedish advance into southern Norway was repelled by a limited Norwegian counterattack in the spring, after which operations virtually ceased.

Gustav IV Adolf had far more ambitious plans. Convinced that the Finnish army would offer stouter initial resistance to the Russians and that Sveaborg would stand fast, he favored from the start a holding action in the east while he directed his main effort to a rapid conquest of Norway. Developments in Finland undermined this strategy, yet the king persevered. On 17 May a convoy carrying 11,000 British troops under Lieutenant-General Sir John Moore arrived in Gothenburg. It was intended primarily to protect that essential seaport and the Swedish west coast against invasion from Denmark or Norway, but Moore's rather vague instructions permitted him to consider other objectives. The opportunity thus provided was lost, however, when the king refused to allow the British troops to debark until Moore recognized him as their commander-in-chief and agreed to his own proposals for an Anglo-Swedish landing on Sjælland or in Norway. Negotiations broke down amid mutual recriminations, and after six weeks Moore's troops departed Gothenburg en route to Spain on 3 July. As in the case of the Spanish units in Denmark, the Iberian Peninsula again played its part in the war in the North. There could now be no immediate hope of winning

Norway, while the chance was lost for an effective seaborne counterattack in Finland.

As 1808 drew to a close, Sweden's enemies laid plans for their knockout blow. While a small Russian force advanced around the Gulf of Bothnia to the north, larger units would land in the Umeå area and just north of Stockholm. The Danes would land in Skåne while a new attack would be mounted from Norway. In actuality, the coordination of so vast a strategy proved impossible. In late January and briefly in March the Sound froze over, offering the Danes their chance, but since their preparations were not complete they lost it. Lack of supplies hindered any attack from Norway. The Russians were unable to begin their offensive before the middle of March.

Gustav IV Adolf remained as determined as ever to carry on the fight. Troops were not lacking, but without adequate supplies, especially following poor harvests in 1808, the newly raised *Lantvärn* and the remnants of the Finnish army in the north in particular suffered serious deprivation and were decimated by disease. Existing tax revenues and an annual British subsidy of 300,000 pounds left a rapidly mounting deficit. On 7 January 1809, the king on his own authority decreed a new wartime levy, amounting to five times the existing taxation granted by the *Riksdag* in 1800. This was done over the unanimous opposition of his advisers, arousing widespread consternation, especially among the propertied classes. While Sweden—now minus Finland and Pomerania—was doubtless capable of greater sacrifices, the scale of the increase was alarming. Moreover, under the constitution the Estates were empowered to levy taxes or grant credit. By adamantly refusing to call a *riksdag* in the nation's hour of peril, Gustav Adolf revealed the depth of his mistrust of his own subjects.

The king's pressing demands for increased British subsidies brought no satisfaction, and in February 1809 London tactfully suggested that it would not object to Sweden's making a separate peace. Clearly Britain no longer considered Sweden's services worth the price. Gustav Adolf became so incensed that his advisers could barely restrain him from breaking immediately with his only ally and offering peace and an alliance to Denmark to bar the British from the Baltic.

A curious and revealing episode seems to have played its part in dissuading Gustav Adolf from so desperate a course. Word reached him of a printed proclamation being scattered in Skåne by means of Danish hot air balloons. This so-called Balloon Proclamation had been composed by the exiled Finnish regicide of 1792, C. F. Ehrensvärd, long resident in Copenhagen and an enthusiastic Pan-Scandinavianist. After painting a dark picture of Sweden's perilous situation, it urged that it reject its present "foreign" dynasty and accept "Frederik of the North" as its king. The proclamation gave assurances that under such a Scandinavian union Swedish law, or at least the "good part" of it, as well as a *riksdag* controlling taxation, would be combined with the enlightened features of the Danish regime. King Frederik, it added, "recognized the true principle that all citizens of the state should on the same basis bear the burdens of the state and enjoy rights in relation to their usefulness to the common good." Such a union would ensure the future peace and prosperity of the North.[9]

Few copies of the "Balloon Proclamation" seem to have reached Skåne, and it apparently had no effect on public opinion in Sweden.[10] It is meanwhile difficult to judge the extent to which Frederik VI and his advisers considered it something more than opportunistic wartime propaganda. To be sure, as long ago as 1790 Frederik had played with the idea of a unifed "Kingdom of Scandinavia" under himself, at a time when Gustav III had already engaged in somewhat similar speculations from a Swedish perspective.[11] Thereafter, he seems to have given little thought to such ideas, despite the lively Scandinavianism in Copenhagen literary circles. Certain of his advisers were, however, apparently interested in the prospect of a Nordic dynastic union.[12]

By the beginning of 1809, Gustav IV Adolf, at best never a popular monarch, faced a rising tide of disaffection among influential classes of his subjects. His foreign policy had drawn Sweden into a ruinous war, pitting him against Napoleon—the apparent arbiter of the new Europe—and had largely disenchanted his only ally, Great Britain. His military command had resulted in repeated fiascoes. Pomerania and Finland were lost. What remained of the Finnish army and the new *Lantvärn* were decimated by deprivation and disease.

The ordeal of the war years had aliented the upper bureaucrats, who sought to curb him in the fall of 1808 by urging a *riksdag* and a settlement with Sweden's enemies. A committee to investigate war finances purposefully overestimated the costs of the following year's campaign to make him see reason; instead he imposed what seemed a crushing special war levy and demanded increased subsidies from Britain. In desperation, leading officials considered a kind of bureaucratic general strike, such as those that had compelled the convening of a *riksdag* in 1769 and the French Estates-General in 1789.

The possibility of a coup d'etat had been bruited about in military circles since the inglorious siege of Stralsund in the summer of 1807. Concern over Gustav Adolf's military ineptitude had greatly increased during 1808, and his arbitrary degradation of the 120 officers of the elite guards regiments in September had spread resentment throughout widespread aristocratic circles.

As it was, Gustav Adolf inspired little love among the nobility. According to Count H. G. Trolle-Wachtmeister, one of his bitterest critics, Gustav Adolf spoke in November 1808 of consulting directly with "the Swedish people," thereby bypassing the Estates, over means to continue the war. The king, he claimed, hoped for an outbreak among the "higher classes" to provide "an opportunity to appeal to the people against their *masters*, throw all the blame on them, and seal his power in blood." Opposition to the special war levy could be represented to the "rabble" as collusion between the "distinguished" classes and the Russians, "under whose dominion the lord is *powerful*, but the *peasant a slave*."[13]

Early in 1809 a group of subordinate officers and bureaucrats conspired to seize Gustav Adolf in Stockholm. The attempt was called off by Hans Järta, a former leader of the radical opposition at the Norrköping *Riksdag* of 1800 with close connections in the upper bureaucracy, who saw that it was too poorly planned to succeed.

The initiates in this plot meanwhile included Lieutenant-Colonel Georg Adlersparre in Värmland, recently relieved of a command on the Norwegian front. Upon learning that the coup in Stockholm had fallen through, he determined to act himself, with the support of like-minded fellow officers. After claiming he had arranged a tacit armistice with the Norwegians, he issued a manifesto in Karlstad dated 7 March, calling in high-flown rhetoric for peace, a *riksdag*, the rescinding of the special war levy, and a "change of system," in a manner consciously recalling William III's proclamation to the English in 1688.[14] He thereupon marched on Stockholm at the head of an insurgent force of 3,000 men.

In the capital Gustav Adolf at first dismissed rumors of Adlersparre's revolt. Not until 12 March did he realize the seriousness of the situation. After midnight, he determined to confiscate the remaining reserves of the national bank and withdraw with his family, court, and the Stockholm garrison to join up with the army commanded by the staunch old royalist J. C. Toll in Skåne.

To a number of higher army officers in Stockholm who had thus far remained uncommitted, it became clear that the moment had come for quick and decisive action if civil war, in the midst of foreign war, were to be averted. Urgency was heightened by renewed Russian attacks on Sweden. These men likewise mistrusted Adlersparre, who at the turn of the century had edited the "Jacobin" journal *Läsning i blandade ämnen*, had been a conspicuous member of the "Mountain" at the *Riksdag* of 1800, and was feared to hold dangerous democratic ideas.

At the head of six other high officers, General Carl Johan Adlercreutz, a hero of the Finnish campaign, demanded an audience with Gustav IV Adolf at the palace early on the morning of 13 March. After the king angrily refused their demand for a *riksdag*, the officers placed him under arrest. The same day, his uncle, Duke Carl of Södermanland, assumed the regency, as he had in 1792. Gustav Adolf and his family were confined in Gripsholm Castle.[15]

A provisional government was formed, including most of the king's former advisers, together with Generals Adlercreutz and Klingspor, and Count Axel von Fersen. This miscellaneous group, popularly called "Noah's Ark," was clearly constituted largely for its symbolic value, to reassure all classes that what had occurred was a coup necessitated by special circumstances, rather than a revolution. Censorship was lifted, resulting during the following months in a rapid revival of political journalism.

On 22 March Adlersparre made a rather anticlimactic entry into the capital at the head of his private army. Here he established his headquarters, from which he exercised for some weeks a kind of quasi-independent authority, arousing the hopes of the increasingly vocal radical wing of the opposition to the late regime.

On one point virtually all shades of opinion were agreed: a *riksdag* must be convened. Already on 14 March the provisional government issued its summons for 1 May. The problems the Estates would have to face were many and serious. Above all they included the succession to the throne, the constitution, and peace.

These questions were closely interwoven. Adlercreutz, Klingspor, and their friends had intended only to take power from a monarch they felt could no longer manage it, naturally assuming that he would be succeeded by his son, the nine-year-old Crown Prince Gustav. Recent Danish and British experience offered precedents for such a situation. Duke Carl wished at first only to serve as regent for his grandnephew, who was favored by most of the provisional government, as well as by broad strata of public opinion. Gustav Adolf showed a surprising readiness to cooperate, having indeed considered abdication. On 27 March he offered to vacate the throne for his son.

By this time, however, Georg Adlersparre, with two strong supporters, had been added to the provisional government, where they gained a growing influence. Although a man of considerable talents, both idolized and feared as a radical standard-bearer, Adlersparre was fearful and suspicious, obsessed with protecting himself against future retribution by excluding from the throne both Gustav IV Adolf and all his heirs. By arranging a mission to Napoleon to seek mediation with Russia as well as to determine his views on the Swedish succession, the Adlersparre faction gained precious time. Upon the return of the Swedish envoys in early May, Adlersparre's supporters were able to construe Napoleon's noncommittal remarks as disapproval of Prince Gustav. They meanwhile stressed the perils of a long and uncertain regency for the young prince. Duke Carl was at length persuaded to accept the throne as King Karl XIII, but since he was by then sixty years old and childless, the ultimate solution to the succession problem would only thereby be postponed.

The *Riksdag* convened on 1 May. Ten days later, the Estates, meeting in plenary session, resolved by acclaim to exclude Gustav IV Adolf and his heirs permanently from the Swedish throne. No voice was raised in defense of the crown prince. The Gustavian legitimists feared both for themselves and for the royal family. But they would not forget that passage of a resolution by acclaim was not legally valid in *riksdag* proceedings.

A committee appointed by the provisional government had prepared a draft constitution for Duke Carl to promulgate as legitimate heir to the throne, thereby stressing the legal continuity of the regime and forestalling more radical initiatives. Led by the Nobility, the Estates rejected this draft and elected its own committee—six Nobles and three from each of the other Estates—which notably did not include Adlersparre, to prepare another.

The new committee presented its draft to the Estates on 1 June, a little over a fortnight after it convened. Although it did not keep minutes, it is evident that its proposals were to a considerable degree the work of its secretary, Hans Järta, who likewise presented a memorandum explaining and justifying the committee's draft.

The new constitution was clearly intended to prevent abuses of monarchical power such as had occurred under Gustav III's constitution of 1772 and Act of Union and Security of 1789. Yet the lessons of the preceding Era of Freedom, during which the authority of the crown had been fatally weakened, were not forgotten. "Warned by a double experience," in Järta's words, the committee sought "to protect the nation against oppression from either of the two powers within society which during a single lifetime have prevailed, each in its own direction and each to hateful extremes, equally unrestrained and equally devastating."[16]

Like Gustav III in 1772, the constitution-makers assumed the previous existence of a just polity, which from the later seventeenth century had repeatedly been upset by cycles of royal despotism and licentious liberty, and thus sought to emphasize the native Swedish background to their proposals. Yet in 1809—as in 1772—the propaganda value of such a nationalist stance must be taken into account. Foreign ideas and examples could not but play an important role. In particular the British constitution, as interpreted by Locke, Montesquieu, J.-L. De Lolme, Blackstone, and J. J. Mounier, evidently provided much inspiration. Similarly the American federal and state constitutions afforded positive examples, and various of the French revolutionary constitutions negative ones.[17]

The resulting constitutional proposal was thus cautious and moderate in its approach, which Hans Järta explained in classic fashion in his accompanying memorandum:

> The committee does not propose great and brilliant changes to the ancient foundations of our constitution. It has felt that such principles should not be lightly transformed, least of all during the first days of a regained freedom, when opinion must unavoidably be divided. It has believed what the example of Europe's freest state likewise demonstrates, that there is no surer protection for the general rights of the nation and for the citizen's personal liberty than these foundations, surrounded by the sanctity of centuries and fortified by a common national force, which works through them.[18]

In its actual stipulations this draft constitution did not differ greatly from that previously prepared by the provisional government's committee, which the Estates had rejected. Their own constitutional initiative was thus based upon the principle that the new constitution must emanate from the elected representatives of the nation and that Duke Carl must accept it as the condition of his accession. "By such a loosening of all constitutional bonds," Baron Lars Mannerheim wrote the duke, "the nation, through its representatives, has regained its original right alone to give itself a king and another constitution." This position was soon summarized by the slogan "Constitution first, then king."[19] It was a stand reminiscent of past accession charters, not least between 1719 and 1772, as well as of England's Glorious Revolution of 1688, as its proponents were quick to point out. "The revolution whereby James II was expelled from the English throne," exulted Count Trolle-Wachtmeister in May, "shall now no longer be admired as the only one of its kind."[20] They were rather less eager to recall Louis XVI's forced acceptance of the French constitution of 1791.

The constitution-makers strove for a balance between the traditional elements of Swedish state power: Crown, Council, and Estates. Hans Järta explained his colleagues' intentions:

> The committee has sought to establish an executive power, acting within set forms, united in its decisions and with full means to carry them out; a legislative power, acting with all due deliberation but firm and steadfast in resistance; a judicial power, independent under the law, but without arbitrary authority over it. It has moreover sought to organize these powers in such fashion that they maintain a surveillance over each other, that they hold each other in check, without mixing them together, without allowing the restraining power any of the authority appertaining to the power it restrains.[21]

Under this formulation, the crown was to remain strong, with "undivided authority to administer" the realm. In some respects, its power became even greater than under the constitution of 1772. Because of the difficulty of distinguishing between defense and offense, the assent of the Estates was no longer required to declare war. Most earlier restrictions concerning the bureaucracy were removed, and new categories of higher officials were made freely removable at royal pleasure. The tenure of judges was meanwhile strengthened by making them replaceable only through specified judicial action.

The crown was, however, counterbalanced by reestablishing the *statsråd*, or state council, discontinued by Gustav III after 1789, and requiring that all state business be submitted to its consideration. The nine councillors were to be freely appointed by the monarch but accountable to the Estates, either for the advice they gave or for remaining silent when they should give warning. This was intended to forestall the biased information and unofficial advisers so evident under the Gustavian regime. State secretaries, in charge of government departments, as well as the generals-adjutant for the army and navy, sat with the council in matters affecting their fields of competency, but without vote. However, except on questions of war and peace, all the councillors were not required to meet as a body, and in the interests of secrecy, the monarch could consult with only the secretary for foreign affairs or the generals-adjutant on diplomatic or military matters.

The monarch was to relinquish governing authority to the council when outside the country. If he remained abroad for more than a year, the Estates were empowered to decide on the nation's future government.

The Estates were to meet regularly every five years and remain in session for at least four months after the government presented its proposals; the monarch might also summon extraordinary meetings. The Estates and most of their committees were forbidden to deliberate or vote in the monarch's presence, to forestall royal pressure of the type exercised by both Gustav III and Gustav IV Adolf. Both crown and Estates were empowered to initiate and veto legislation.

Control over all taxation, loans, the state bank, and national debt office was vested in the Estates, while various tolls and excises which formerly provided a standing revenue to the crown now became part of the regular taxation. The Estates furthermore obtained widespread controls over the specific expenditures of the government.

They reviewed not only the government's accounts but also the minutes of the state council. If they judged a councillor to have been derelict in his duties, they could petition the monarch for his removal or impeach him before a special tribunal, the *riksrätt*, composed of certain high officials, sitting *ex officio*. The constitution could be amended by two successive *riksdagar*, upon the initiative of either the crown or the constitutional committee of the Estates. To insure the individual citizen against bureaucratic or judicial abuse, the constitution provided for an independent official, the judicial *ombudsman*, with direct access to all levels of government. The citizen's right to express himself freely on all matters of public concern was specifically guaranteed.

The new constitution was not without its flaws. In particular, the revived state council was placed in an ambiguous position. Because its members were to be appointed by the monarch but answerable to the Estates, they were neither *riksdagsmän* nor the responsible heads of administrative departments, and they were only exceptionally required to function as a group. Rolf Karlbom has indeed described 1809 as the great break in Sweden's constitutional development, through which the ancient tripartite balance between Crown, Council, and Estates finally and definitively gave way to that dualism between monarch and legislature which would thereafter prevail into the twentieth century.[22] Their respective powers were moreover so evenly opposed to each other as to impede cooperation, and thus prompt and decisive action. Since the Estates remained much divided between and within themselves, effective national leadership would still necessarily depend in high degree upon the personal qualities of the monarch.

Important questions remained unanswered, which threatened the establishment of a stable regime, as quickly became apparent with the relaxation of censorship. Anxious above all to provide a rudderless Sweden with a new, workable constitution as quickly as possible in a perilous situation, the *Riksdag* committee understandably steered clear of controversies that could hazard that objective. It proposed, and the *Riksdag* concurred, that special committees of the Estates be elected to prepare separate statutes on freedom of the press, representation in the *Riksdag*, and the succession to the throne during the current session, following acceptance of the constitution; these statutes were to have the force of constitutional law.

Behind these divisive issues loomed greater and more fateful questions of the survival of those corporate privileges that still remained even after Gustav III's parliamentary coup of 1789: above all the reservation of certain high dignities and of immediate manorial domain (*yppersta frälse*) lands to the nobility. Already in June the Noble Estate voluntarily relinquished these rights, thus at last giving full access to all public employments and categories of land to all citizens. The Nobles held adamantly, however, to the special tax exemptions attached to manorial lands no matter in whose possession, on the grounds that they constituted a legitimate form of property.

Whereas the other three Estates accepted the new constitution early in June, the Peasantry held out for a revision requiring the equal taxation of all landed property, led by prosperous members of the Estate particularly resentful of surviving distinctions. According to Count Trolle-Wachtmeister, passions reached the point where the more radical peasant leaders spoke of ''turning us into a republic under a president, like in North America,'' since without the desired taxation reform Sweden could not afford the monarchy. This agitation, he added ironically, ''has brought some measure of moderation to the more stormy members of the nobility, who want no one but themselves to act as revolutionaries and are more devoted to their manors than to democracy.'' Many of the latter were now prepared to accept ''any constitution whatsoever'' to put an end to the wrangling in the *Riksdag*.[23]

Only after much pressure and bribery from the other Estates and a royal dressing down by Duke Carl on 27 June did the Peasants give way and accept the constitution in return for minor concessions on the tax obligations of manorial lands and on the promise that taxation would continue to be discussed in the future. The old system of taxation would survive until 1891.

The new constitution was at last accepted by all four Estates. Despite its weaknesses, but perhaps largely thanks to its studied ambiguities and possibilities for amendment, it would endure for more than a century and a half, until 1975.

The way was now cleared for crowning the new king, Karl XIII, on 29 June, and for the selection of his successor. Adlersparre and his friends were quick to propose a candidate from an unlikely quarter: Prince Christian August of Augustenburg, the Danish commander in southern Norway. Adlersparre had secretly negotiated with the prince concerning an armistice before his march on Stockholm, at which time the possibility had been raised of Christian August's candidature for the Swedish succession. The Adlersparre circle knew him to be a capable and inspiring leader of men—in striking contrast to the deposed Gustav IV Adolf.

Yet considerably more was involved than Christian August's personal qualities. Nothing might better establish a new dynasty in Sweden than the acquisition of Norway, following the loss of Finland. Christian August was immensely popular in Norway, where wartime hardships had revived old grievances against Copenhagen. The Adlersparre faction thus had high hopes that if Christian August accepted the Swedish succession, he might bring Norway with him.

The prince, however, had an even more grandiose vision, unbeknown to his Swedish backers. Already on 10 March—three days after Adlersparre had raised the standard of revolt in Karlstad—Christian August wrote to his brother, Duke Friedrich Christian in Copenhagen, that he hoped to "perform a brilliant service for our king and fatherland," the details of which he wrote on 6 April. The "close union of the three Nordic realms under one scepter" would be the only means to save the Danish-Norwegian monarchy from "dissolution." Its basis should be a common, moderate constitution, drafted by delegates from all three kingdoms in consultation with the king. "This revolution" would have to come about "from above," through the sacrifice of unlimited sovereignty by the monarch, who should nonetheless remain powerful enough to ensure "the felicity and security of the land."[24]

On 11 March, Christian August reported to Frederik VI on his indirect negotiations with Adlersparre's envoy, predicting a "civil war, which will bring a completely devastated Sweden to Your Majesty's feet."[25] He thereafter continued to urge upon Frederik a Scandinavian union under his rule.

Despite the recent balloon proclamation calling for union under "Frederik of the North," the latter seems to have been taken by surprise by the Swedish revolution of 13 March and to have found it not altogether to his liking. He was reluctant to abandon the projected joint Danish-Russian offensive. When a Swedish delegation arrived to inform him of Duke Carl's regency and evidently to sound him out concerning a union as well, Frederik expressed his repugnance at dealing with "insurgents."[26]

During the ensuing weeks Frederik, influenced both by Christian August and advisers in Copenhagen enthusiastic for a Nordic union, began to warm to the idea, even though the constitutional problem bothered him. His inclination in recent years had been toward the restoration of personal absolutism in his own domains. He would be prepared, he wrote Christian August on 18 April, to allow the Swedes no more than "the appearance of freedom," while maintaining absolute sovereignty in Denmark and Norway. On 24 May, Christian August, in a last-minute effort to sway the Swedish *Riksdag*, urged a "modified and uniform constitution for the whole of Scandinavia."[27] This was more than Frederik could contemplate.

The *Riksdag's* election of Karl XIII came as a shock. Frederik VI was outraged, believing the Swedes had intentionally duped both Christian August and himself. He had ever regarded them as an unruly and unreliable people. No friend of aristocracy at home, he felt a particular antipathy toward the Swedish nobility, for whose proud constitutional traditions he had neither sympathy nor understanding. Behind the overthrow of the autocratic Gustav IV Adolf he discerned the specter of aristocratic resurgence, the reimposition of a "system of oppression" upon the common people. With Karl XIII as king he saw "aristocracy at its height," a view generally shared by his ministers and Danish liberal opinion. Christian August too put his confidence in "the lower classes, that is, the greater part of the nation," expected little enthusiasm for union among the "privileged," and had repeatedly urged upon Frederik a constitution for Sweden conferring "equal rights without regard to estate."[28]

The Danish king now returned determinedly to the idea of the outright conquest of as much Swedish territory as possible with Russian support. He now envisioned not only the recovery of the lost Scanian provinces but a new frontier along the Klara River. "It is deplorable," he wrote to Christian August on 28 June, "that what the Swedes could have done voluntarily to their own advantage, circumstances will compel them to do; and when Finland goes to Russia and part of southern Sweden falls to Denmark, Karl XIII's kingdom will become very small and scarcely possible for him to sustain in the long run."[29] He thereafter sent repeated orders to Christian August to attack.

The latter found himself in a difficult quandary. He was already deeply involved in secret negotiations with the Swedes, and although disappointed by their election of Karl XIII, he still hoped to work for Frederik VI's eventual succession in Sweden. He was moreover hesitant to support a Russian offensive, which might bring all of Scandinavia under "that barbaric yoke." Its only salvation, he remained convinced, lay in a strong Nordic union, "which can, in its time, shake the throne of Russia."[30]

On 18 July, The Swedish *Riksdag*, under the vigorous prodding of the Adlersparre faction and lacking any other viable candidate, elected Christian August as Swedish crown prince. The latter agreed provisionally to come to Sweden once peace was concluded, if Frederik VI would permit this. To the dismay of Adlersparre and his friends, however, he refused to hear of any insurrectionary schemes concerning Norway.

The Swedish-Russian war meanwhile dragged on in desultory fashion. Early in March 1809 the Russians mounted a two-pronged attack over the ice of the frozen Gulf of Bothnia. The Swedes were dislodged from the Åland Islands, and a small Russian detachment seized Grisslehamn in the northern Stockholm Archipelago. A larger Russian force crossed over to Umeå. The decimated and demoralized Swedish-Finnish force at the head of the Gulf was thereby isolated, and in late March its commander capitulated under terms paroling his Swedish troops while permitting their Finnish comrades to return to their homeland. Although the Russians withdrew from Grisslehamn, a long stretch of Sweden's northern Bothnian coastline was now in enemy hands.

There followed something of a lull in the hostilities as all parties sought to interpret the significance and potentialities of the Swedish revolution of 13 March. The provisional government in Stockholm appealed, as seen, to Napoleon for mediation, but the emperor simply referred it to Tsar Alexander's noble generosity. Operations languished until August, when 7,500 Swedes landed to the north of Russian-occupied Umeå, but within a few days they were outmaneuvered and forced to debark.

Stockholm could now only seek peace on the best terms it could get. Informal feelers since March gave way to hard negotiating at Fredrikshamn (Hamina) in Finland. The Russians were by now eager to end the northern war, which proved a heavy burden and a strategic liability since their relations with Napoleon were badly deteriorating. Had the Swedes been more fully aware of this, they might have held out for better terms.

On 17 September 1809 Sweden concluded peace with Russia. It ceded to the tsar all of Finland plus part of the province of Västerbotten lying east of the Torne and Muonio Rivers; although the Swedish negotiators strove to save the Åland Islands, considered essential for the defense of Stockholm, the Russians refused to take the "trunk" without the "keys." Sweden thus relinquished roughly a third of its territory and a quarter of its population. The consequences for both Finland and Sweden would be profound, for unlike many of the other great *renversements* of the Napoleonic era the Peace of Fredrikshamn would not thereafter be undone. An immediate result was that Sweden now pledged itself to join the Continental System.

As long as Russia had remained in the field, Frederik VI had wanted to continue the war against Sweden. By late summer, however, the Russians made it clear that they would support Denmark's claim only to such Swedish territory as it succeeded in occupying itself. Norway was now Frederik's only feasible base of operations against Sweden, but Prince Christian August was reluctant to attack the land that chose him as its crown prince. Frederik's repeated orders to Norway show his rising exasperation. Still, political considerations aside, the Norwegian army, cut off by sea from Denmark, was so poorly equipped and provisioned that any effective offensive was out of the question. Following the Swedish-Russian peace in September, Copenhagen could only follow suit. On 10 December 1809 Denmark and Sweden made peace at Jönköping on the basis of the status quo antebellum. Soon thereafter Sweden concluded the Peace of Paris with France on 6 January 1810, by which Sweden formally entered the Continental System and regained Swedish Pomerania.

Denmark meanwhile remained at war with Britain, although this now involved few actual hostilities. The British took the island of Heligoland in the North Sea in September 1807, and on Christmas Day of that year occupied the Danish West Indies, whose largely English-speaking planter class thereafter profited from the high price of sugar on the London market. In March 1808 Denmark's last ship of the line, the *Prins Christian Frederik*, which had been in Norway, was trapped by a British squadron off Sjælland and forced to strike its flag after a stiff fight. More than a year later, in May 1809, the British seized the island of Anholt in the Kattegat to control its vital lighthouse.

Denmark made great efforts to rebuild its fleet, supported by generous private donations, although by the end of the war in 1814 only four frigates had been completed. More important at the time was the construction of nearly two hundred oared cannon boats. Manned by twenty or more men and mounting one or two relatively large-bore guns, such craft could wreak considerable destruction upon becalmed enemy merchantmen and on occasion fought pitched battles with convoying British warships or their longboats. In Norway five brigs managed in June 1810 to seize a British convoy of forty-seven ships. During the course of the war, the Danes and Norwegians captured or sank several smaller British naval vessels. From 1808 Denmark also provided crews for two French warships in the Scheldt estuary.

The government meanwhile issued letters of mark and reprisal to enterprising shipowners, and close to 600 privateers were fitted out during the war years. Many were provided by joint stock companies, whose shares sold at inflated prices, although the great mercantile houses, anxious to preserve international goodwill for the future, remained aloof. Enormous gains were to be made through privateering against British (and Swedish) commerce, and with the wartime slump in foreign trade it bid fair by around 1810 to become the monarchy's most profitable activity.

Copenhagen would long remember the colorful ostentation of newly rich privateers of humble origins, although few of their quickly won fortunes would survive the war. Privateering would prove a mixed blessing at best. While it inflicted damage upon enemy commerce and tied down enemy naval forces, the men, weapons, and money expended upon it might well have been more effectively utilized by the meagerly supported Danish-Norwegian military forces. In seizing British merchantmen flying the neutral American flag, Danish privateers also captured some American ships, resulting in a controversy only finally resolved in 1830 when Denmark paid an indemnity to the United States.[31]

The war ruined the flourishing overseas trade the monarchy had enjoyed during the long years of neutrality. Its merchant marine was swept from the seas, much of it confiscated in British ports or permanently blockaded in Continental ones, while thousands of Danish and Norwegian seamen were interned on British prison hulks. During the course of the war the British seized some 1,400 Danish-Norwegian vessels on the high seas. The shock to the great mercantile houses in Copenhagen was buffered somewhat by the large supplies of Far Eastern goods on hand in 1807, which could be disposed of through Baltic ports over the next few years. British colonial wares were meanwhile smuggled into the duchies via Heligoland, from whence they found their way into Germany.[32]

Although harvests remained generally good, there were heavy demands for grain, in Norway and, for a time, to provision Marshal Bernadotte's French and Spanish troops. Coastal and inter-island transportation was meanwhile badly disrupted, stimulating the development of internal waterways, especially on Sjælland to provide Copenhagen with food, fodder, and fuel. Under the strains of war the government was compelled to abandon its recent economic liberalism and impose extensive controls.

The war encouraged Frederik VI to complete his concentration of personal power. On 19 March 1808, immediately following his succession, he informed the departments of the central administration that they were henceforth to receive their instructions directly from him. The state council was effectively suspended.

Yet the wartime disruption of seaborne communications with outlying parts of the monarchy, such as Bornholm, the Færøes, and Iceland, had by then already compelled the government to grant extensive powers to local authorities and to relax its efforts, begun in 1806, to integrate the duchies into the kingdom. The greatest administrative problems were meanwhile posed by Norway, across the Skagerrak, where an interim Government Commission (*Regjeringskommisjon*) of four, presided over by Prince Christian August, was established already on 24 August 1807, followed by a provisional superior civil court, admiralty court, and exchequer for Norway. The necessities of war forced the government to break, in effect, with its traditional policy of centralization.[33]

The new Government Commission in Christiania faced grievous problems, for the greatest burden of Denmark's alliance with France necessarily fell upon Norway. Norwegian trade, far more than Danish, dealt in local products and depended primarily upon the British market, while a disproportionately large part of the monarchy's merchant marine was Norwegian.

More serious still was the problem of provisioning a land never at best self-sufficient in grain. Denmark, especially Jutland, was Norway's natural bread-basket, but shipment across the enemy-controlled Skagerrak was hazardous. Few skippers were prepared to chance it, and of the grain sent from Denmark to Norway at least a quarter ended up in British or Swedish ports.[34] Internal communications via Norway's long coastline were badly disrupted, and the Far North was virtually isolated.

Most ruinously affected were the South and Southeast, Christiansand and Akershus *Stifter*, which together accounted for over half of Norway's population, 84 percent of its merchant shipping, 92 percent of its timber exports, and all of its iron and glass production.[35] Not only were their trade, manufacture, and shipping devastated, they also suffered the greatest grain shortages. Harvests in the north and west were generally good and were supplemented by Russian grain from Arkhangelsk, even as far south as Bergen. In Akershus *Stift*, where there were widespread crop failures, the supply of grain declined to only one-sixth of the normal level during 1808, accompanied by an alarming rise in local mortality rates.[36] Privateering provided some profits in Christiansand *Stift*. The situation was grimmest in Akershus *Stift*, which moreover bore the brunt of the war with neighboring Sweden.

The repulse of the brief Swedish offensive in the spring of 1808 created an initial wave of patriotic fervor but also strengthened an impression among the Norwegians that they stood virtually alone against the British and Swedish foes. Faced with the imminent economic ruin of the classes and starvation of the masses, influential members of the patriciate in Østlandet began to reflect seriously on Norway's position within the dual monarchy.

In December 1808 the youthful Count Herman Wedel Jarlsberg was appointed to the Government Commission. One of the few Norwegians to bear a noble title, Wedel Jarlsberg had spent much of his youth in England and combined a warm love for his native Norway, to which he had returned two years before, with a deep admiration for British parliamentary liberty. Since the outbreak of the war he had distinguished himself through several hazardous trips to Denmark to organize relief shipments of grain. By the time he first appeared in the Government Commission in January 1809, he had concluded that only a change in the monarchy's foreign policy with regard to Norway, exempting it from the Continental System and restoring peace with Sweden, could save the country from total disaster. The following month, on 17 February, the Government Commission, evidently under Count Wedel's strong influence, appealed to Frederik VI to delegate to it the authority to conclude a separate armistice with Britain and Sweden.

The king remained determined to hold strictly to the Continental System and was by no means prepared to permit the provisional Government Commission in Christiania to make policy on its own. His rejection of its proposal arrived in early March, at the very time Christian August was first approached by Adlersparre's emissaries about his possible candidature to the Swedish throne and right before the coup d'etat in Stockholm.[37]

For Wedel and certain influential members of the patriciate in Østlandet with whom he enjoyed close relations, these developments—in close apposition—proved decisive. Wedel was now persuaded that Norway's immediate and future salvation lay in its own self-government under a liberal constitution. The Swedish coup in March at first encouraged him to hope for a union of the three Scandinavian kingdoms, each under its own constitution, and he strongly urged Prince Christian August in this direction. Already by late April, however, Wedel recognized that Frederik VI could not be counted upon to realize such an ideal. In consultation with Swedish envoys of the Adlersparre faction, he now put his hopes in a voluntary Norwegian-Swedish dynastic union, to be brought about through Christian August's election as Swedish crown prince and a Norwegian insurrection to make him king of Norway. Central to Wedel's plan was a separate constitution for Norway, to be framed prior to union with Sweden and to be its essential precondition.[38]

Although Christian August accepted election as successor to the Swedish crown in July, he refused to place himself at the head of a Norwegian uprising against Denmark, as seen. Wedel did not lose hope, and an undated letter to a Swedish correspondent reveals much about his thinking by the late summer of 1809. It would be well, he wrote, if Denmark might now "make common cause with us in establishing the internal and external freedom and independence of the North under Prince Christian's leadership, which little by little forms closer bonds between the nations."

> Otherwise, Norway will in a few weeks be obliged to speak forcefully. This seems the most likely. . . . Once the Norwegian nation has clearly expressed its will, I am convinced Prince C. can make no more difficulties over assuming the rule over both nations. This must, however, come about in such fashion that Norway has its own representation on the basis of equality, its own laws, finances, etc. We have almost no nobles, and those we have must either content themselves with becoming like their fellow citizens or move to other places better suited to their exalted nature. Your constitution may be very good under present circumstances for Sweden, but it does not suit Norway, which will create entirely new institutions for itself.

If Frederik VI's "stupidity and conceit" should lead shortly to a Norwegian insurrection, Wedel nonetheless warned against any overt Swedish intervention, particularly through armed force, which could be ruinous to the great goal. Wedel here set forth the essential principles he would uphold through the fateful years to follow. During the summer and fall of 1809, he and his friends strove to foment a Norwegian uprising. A letter to Georg Adlersparre from one of his agents on the border meanwhile summarized in late September the hopes of their faction in Sweden

> that a speedy peace with Denmark [will have] the double good effect that our crown prince will leave Norway, which is now threatened by famine after a total crop failure, [and that this,] together with the war with England which still continues for them and in consequence the strictest blockade of their coasts will cause the Norwegians to cast themselves into the arms of their friends the Swedes.

But despite a well-advertised surplus of grain in Sweden, it was all ultimately to no avail.[39]

By this time, informed opinion in Norway was in considerable ferment. Christian August held to the ideal of a constitutional Scandinavian state, whereas Wedel and his friends on both sides of the Keel aspired to the more limited goal of a Norwegian-Swedish federation. Others still hoped for greater autonomy and separate institutions under the Danish crown. Common to them all, however, was the growing conviction that what they increasingly referred to as their "fatherland" was, in fact and by right, a separate national entity with its own legitimate interests.

By August, Frederik VI came to realize he would have to make concessions to save Norway. It was apparent that further military action against Sweden could be expected neither from the Russians nor from the Norwegians. He at last permitted licensed trade with Great Britian in Norway, although not in Denmark and the duchies. He temporarily forbade further privateering and entered into negotiations with Sweden leading to peace in December. In return, the British relaxed their blockade, allowing foreign trade and grain shipments from Denmark. In effect, Frederik VI adopted the separate policy for Norway proposed by the Government Commission in February.

Norway's economic situation improved almost miraculously during the fall of 1809. Within months sizable fortunes were accumulated through trade under British and French licenses—many skippers carried both—in disregard of the Continental System. Much clandestine trade with the British was now also carried on through Gothenburg in Sweden, which during the war years became a thriving entrepôt. Recent political discontents were generally soon forgotten—at least for the time being.

It is easy in retrospect to overestimate political disaffection in Norway during the crisis of 1809, especially in view of developments there five years later. It was essentially limited to a small elite of merchants and officials, mainly in the southeast. Above all, there was little the patriciate could do without the support of the peasant masses. Between them lay a social cleavage which recent decades had only deepened, and despite their own tribulations the Norwegian peasantry remained steadfastly loyal to the crown. To reinforce its position, the government in Copenhagen declined to raise the Norwegian peasants' tax burden—while increasing that of the Danish peasantry. The raising of revenue through tolls, loans, and inflation meanwhile affected the peasants but little. As for union with Sweden, the Norwegian peasants were soon made aware that their Swedish brethren were more heavily taxed than themselves.

The immediate crisis had passed. Yet neither patrician nor peasant could thereafter conceive of their homeland in quite the same terms as before. "What has Norway been; what is it; what can it become?" wrote Jacob Aall in a pamphlet entitled *Fædrelandske Ideer* (Ideas on the Fatherland) in December 1809, echoing the Abbé Sieyès's famous appeal to the French Third Estate in 1789.[40]

There were intimations of an answer when Wedel and his friends capitalized on the wave of patriotic fervor surrounding Christian August's departure for Sweden to establish, without royal permission, a Society for Norway's Welfare (*Selskabet for Norges Vel*) on 29 December 1809. Its manifesto made no mention of Denmark or the monarchy as a whole, only of Norway, "our proud and ancient mountain home, [which] once again shall arise in renewed glory" as its "honor and well-being shall be the first thought and highest goal of Norway's sons." On its first day it had 200 members, a year later nearly 1,500, in a network of local committees throughout the land. Ostensibly it was devoted to economic and cultural advancement, but Frederik VI was under no illusions as to the threat it posed to the centralized monarchy, even though he sought to preserve appearances by adding "Royal" to the Society's name.[41]

The Atlantic islands, cut adrift by the war, evolved their own *modus vivendi* with the enemy. They suffered serious shortages and were defenseless against landing parties from British vessels. The British made no attempt to occupy them but felt under no compulsion to respect established Danish trade monopolies. In Iceland British merchants and skippers soon gained control of overseas trade, despite the efforts of local officials.

Early in 1809 Captain George Jackson of the *Clarence*, a ship belonging to the London merchant Samuel Phelps, obtained an agreement permitting British merchants to establish themselves in Reykjavík, upon pain of bombardment of the town. Jackson's interpreter was the renegade Danish adventurer Jürgen Jürgensen, who in June 1809 returned to Iceland, together with Phelps. With a band of armed men they seized the Danish *stiftamtmand* in Reykjavík. On 26 June Jürgensen issued a proclamation that all Danish authority in Iceland had ceased, that a national government would be established under British protection, with Icelandic laws such as they had been at the time of the union with Norway—in 1262!—and that all further contacts with Denmark were forbidden.

On 12 July Jürgensen declared himself "protector" and commander of the armed forces by land and sea. All officials were required to swear allegiance, and British subjects were granted the right to trade and reside in Iceland. Jürgensen promised to relinquish authority before 1 July 1810, after a constituent assembly established a new government. He thereupon set off at the head of his armed retinue to confiscate the property of Danish merchants.

The British government was not prepared to countenance a filibustering expedition which could complicate an eventual peace settlement with Denmark. On 14 August the British man-of-war *Talbot* arrived in Reykjavík. Its captain negotiated an agreement with Phelps and the brothers Stephan and Magnus Stephensen by 22 August, declaring Jürgensen's actions null and void. The regular administration and officials were reinstated, and Danish property was restored, although British subjects retained the right to trade and settle in Iceland. On 4 September the *Talbot* departed for Britain carrying Phelps and Jürgensen, leaving the Stephensen brothers in temporary charge of affairs.

Thus ended Iceland's brief revolution in 1809. Upon his return to England, Jürgensen was imprisoned. He later became a gambler in the more conventional sense and was deported to Tasmania, where he ended his days.[42]

By the Peace of Fredrikshamn Sweden ceded Finland to the Russian tsar in September 1809. Yet the original intentions of the secretive and often vacillating Alexander I remain a matter of some controversy.[43] Ostensibly the Russian attack in February 1808 was intended to force Sweden into the Continental System, and initially the Russians declared that Finland would be occupied only temporarily. The extension of Russia's frontier to the Gulf of Bothnia had nonetheless had its proponents in St. Petersburg since Peter I had opened his "window to the West." At the end of 1807, G. M. Sprengtporten prepared a memorandum for the Russian government urging the conquest of Finland and its establishment as an autonomous buffer state under a member of the Russian imperial house.[44]

Already on 1 April 1808 Tsar Alexander declared Finland a part of the Russian empire. On 17 June he proclaimed that its religion, laws, and corporate privileges would be respected. At the same time, the Russians demanded that the Finns swear fealty to the emperor, as they had during the Russian occupation in 1741–43.

Whatever Alexander's original intentions, it became clear during 1808 that once having taken Finland he did not intend to relinquish it. At his Erfurt meeting with Napoleon that fall—if not before—he had learned that Russia's enforcement of the Continental System in the North would bring no concessions from France in the Balkans, but that Russia had a free hand in Finland.

The behavior of the upper classes in occupied Finland could not but encourage Russian aspirations. Defeatism was rife within the Finnish officer corps. The civil administration continued to function without interruption, and the church admonished cooperation with the occupiers, who in turn maintained discipline and good order. Few members of the elite hesitated to swear the required oath during the summer of 1808, at the very time the Finnish army was counterattacking from the north. Few attempted to flee to Sweden.

Behind this tame acquiescence lay generations of growing fatalism vis-à-vis the Russian threat. Combined with this were old traditions of political opportunism inherited from the Era of Freedom, and the pragmatic utilitarianism of the later Enlightenment, with its conviction that government must be judged by the human needs it fulfilled rather than on the basis of history and tradition. There was moreover a growing confidence during the cosmopolitan eighteenth century that a civil population would remain undisturbed if it did not offer resistance, even under a sovereign of a different religious faith. Acceptance was eased—at the time and since—by emotional resentment against Sweden, and especially Gustav IV Adolf, for its meager support during the war. "We were separated from Sweden," wrote Carl Johan Walleen of the Åbo Court of Appeals, "because that land in the most craven fashion abandoned us to our fate," although he admitted that the Finns, "guided by that worldly wisdom which distinguishes our age," had done little enough to ward off the flood that had overwhelmed them.[45]

The war of 1808-9, however, again revealed the same social cleavages as had Gustav III's war of 1788-90: whereas the Swedish-speaking elite showed a widespread willingness to cooperate with the Russians, the peasantry, both Finnish- and Swedish-speaking, displayed a firm determination to defend its native soil against the hereditary foe, spurred by fears that they would fall under the same oppression as their brethren in Old Finland, or worse yet, the Baltic provinces. The men in the ranks fought stubbornly despite often poor and dispirited leadership, while peasant partisans caused both the Russians and upper-class Finns who had sworn allegiance to them serious concern in several areas. A young student wrote how "there was a general fear of the common people, when the Russian army under Prince Bagration finally entered Åbo and freed its inhabitants from this justifiable fear." To Finland's elite, Russia offered the inducements of both future peace and social stability. Its defenders justified acquiescence as true devotion to the fatherland, the highest patriotism.[46]

On 1 December 1808 Alexander I announced that he would govern Finland directly as an autonomous principality under its existing constitution. In so doing, he opted essentially for the proposal made the preceding winter by G. M. Sprengtporten, whom he now appointed as his governor-general in Finland. He thereby rejected the view of many of his principal advisers, and even of certain Finns, that Finland should be annexed outright to the empire, even if allowed certain privileges, as in Old Finland and the Baltic provinces.[47]

Both ideal and practical motives were surely involved in this solution. Alexander was at the height of his youthful "liberalism," and under the influence of Mikhail Speransky and Prince Adam Czartoryski was prepared to consider moderate constitutional regimes in peripheral territories under Russian overlordship, as experiments for an eventual federative reorganization of the empire. In Finland the Pole Czartoryski could hope for useful precedents for his own unfortunate homeland.

The tsar was apparently also impressed by the spirited resistance of the Finnish army during the summer of 1808 and the hazards of inciting a "Spanish" peasant insurrection. Moderation toward the Finns in their hour of defeat could win their future loyalty while enhancing Russia's credit in enlightened European opinion—not least in Poland. As an autocrat at home, it would have been difficult for Alexander to decree constitutional laws and civil rights for a conquered people. Gustav III's constitution of 1772, as amended in 1789, however, already provided ample authority in Finland.

In January 1809, Alexander called for a meeting of the Finnish Estates, which convened in Borgå (Porvoo) on 22 March. Three days later Alexander appeared before them and proclaimed:

> We, Alexander I, . . . have desired, by the present act, to confirm and ratify the religion and fundamental laws of the land, as well as the privileges and rights which each Estate in the said Grand Duchy in particular, and all the inhabitants in general, be their position high or low, have hitherto enjoyed according to the constitution. We promise to maintain all these benefits and laws firm, unchanged, and in full force.[48]

On 29 March the Finnish Estates swore their fealty to their new grand duke. It would be a salve to their consciences that the Swedish revolution earlier the same month had absolved them of their allegiance to Gustav IV Adolf, and indeed developments in Sweden would thereafter tend to solidify the new regime in Finland by appearing dangerously "Jacobin."

The Borgå diet adopted a plan for Finland's higher administration prepared by Matthias Calonius. The tsar was represented by a governor-general, who presided over a council (renamed the Senate in 1816). A state secretary for Finland stationed in St. Petersburg presented matters requiring his decision to the tsar-grand duke. Beneath this new superstructure, the existing bureaucratic, judicial, and ecclesiastical organs continued to function as before. Because convening the Estates was the prerogative of the sovereign under the constitution of 1772, no diet would thereafter be called until 1863, under Alexander II. Thus Finland was in effect governed by its bureaucracy, which continued to use Swedish as the official language.

At the conclusion of the Borgå diet in June, Alexander predicted that his Finnish subjects would be grateful to Providence for having placed Finland "in the rank of nations, governed by its own laws."[49] Finnish nationalist historians, in their struggle to assert their national identity, would later make much of the diet of 1809, seeing in it the actual beginning of their country's separate existence. It cannot, however, be regarded as an initiative by the Finns themselves. Tsar Alexander had declared the main outlines of Finland's autonomous status in December—if not already in June—1809. It was he who called together the Estates and determined what matters they might consider. The Peace of Fredrikshamn, moreover, made no mention of Finland's position under the tsar, which thus remained an essentially domestic matter. Yet the Borgå diet had great symbolic value, both internally and externally: it proclaimed to Sweden and the world Finland's acceptance of its new situation while fostering a sense of direct participation among Finland's politically influential classes.[50]

Faced with deteriorating relations with France, Alexander showed a particular solicitude for the Finns in the period that followed. It was his intent, he wrote to his governor-general in 1810, "to give this people a political existence in such a way that it does not regard itself as conquered by Russia but on the contrary as attached to it by the bonds of its evident interests." Finland's internal organization should therefore offer "incomparably greater advantages than they would have had under Swedish domination."[51]

The creation of a new central administration brought new opportunities. Although the Finnish government played no part in the affairs of the empire as a whole, Finns were welcomed into the imperial service and before long would join it in considerable numbers. Meanwhile, except for the governor-general, no Russian might hold office in Finland.

Salaries for bureaucrats in Åbo were raised to almost double those of their Swedish and far above those of their Russian colleagues. In 1809 a provincial governor had urged the importance of assuring "the future destiny of our unfortunate but above all honorable military establishment, perhaps I sould say the future survival of our class." In March 1810 Alexander guaranteed former officers and noncommissioned officers of the disbanded Finnish army retention of their previous incomes and assigned farms. Already in the summer of 1808 the University of Åbo was instructed to plan for a sizable expansion, implemented by early 1811. Numerous titles and dignities were distributed. Between 1808 and 1816, twenty families were raised to noble status. In 1809 the retired major Berndt Aminoff had confided to his diary, "There now remains for me only the painful memory that I once was a happy Swede." Soon after, he considered Finland "the most fortunate land in Europe."[52]

While Alexander's policy of pacification concentrated primarily upon the small elite, he sought to reassure the broader masses by changing existing conditions as little as possible. After the reestablishment of normal relations with Sweden in the fall of 1809, St. Petersburg meanwhile sought to make clear that the cause of future discord was now eliminated and it refrained from any attempts to fish in the troubled waters of Swedish internal politics.

In Sweden, economically crippled, defeated in war, mutilated through the loss of Finland, and deadlocked in political and social strife, the ship of state drifted without strong leadership or a clear sense of national priorities.

The provisional government had immediately rescinded Gustav IV Adolf's special war levy of January 1809. But war deficits, combined with the loss of British subsidies after March 1809 and of tax revenues from Finland, compelled the *Riksdag* to increase regular taxation to more than twice what it had been at the beginning of 1808. Foreign trade meanwhile languished. Continental markets were cut off, while iron exports faced British domestic competition. The export of Swedish bar iron declined by 1809 to about half of its 1800 level.[53] Sweden was flooded with more British imports than it could dispose of owing to the Continental System, despite much clandestine trade. Merchant shipping was harried by Danish and French privateers. The currency, laboriously stabilized in 1800–1803, again fell into disarray. Economic hardship gave a keener edge to social and political antagonisms.

The surrender of Finland meant more than the loss of manpower, resources, and revenues. For over six hundred years it had been an integral part of the realm. Innumerable bonds of blood and sentiment spanned the Bothnian Gulf. The Russian colossus was moreover now within immediate striking distance of the Swedish heartland, giving rise to much the same fears as the territorial losses of 1721 and 1743 had earlier created in Finland, that the land now lay exposed and essentially undefendable. Following ratification of the new constitution in June 1809, the Estates turned to questions of immediate concern. Not only was taxation increased, but a uniform, graduated income tax was enacted, ranging from .25 to 10 percent of income, without reference to social status.[54] The establishment of a permanent standing debt on the British model was approved. Restrictions of 1800 on household distillation were removed. The Estates endorsed the construction of the Göta Canal, which via Lakes Vättern and Vänern would bypass the strategically exposed Sound and long provide a major artery of transport. A system of national conscription, establishing a reserve of 50,000 men, was passed by three Estates against the opposition of the Peasantry. A statute on freedom of the press, based on the law of 1766, was enacted in March 1810.

The Estates had convened amid high hopes in May 1809, and much more might surely have been accomplished during the following year had the *Riksdag* not soon broken down into increasingly hostile factions over issues that were as much social as political.

The revolution of 1809 had been first and foremost the work of members of the nobility, as members of that Estate pointedly reminded the others at the beginning of the *Riksdag*, and until its dissolution in May 1810 its leadership in all camps—conservative, liberal, radical—was provided almost entirely by noblemen.[55] The nobility thus maintained, under new and trying conditions, its traditional role as the political class above all others.

The "Men of 1809," including such divergent personalities as Georg Adler-sparre and Hans Järta, were essentially liberals in the classic sense: upholders of personal rights and of constitutional government regulated by checks and balances. Since these moderate and, in the Swedish context, largely traditional objects were quickly attained following the revolution, the liberal bloc soon became anxious to prevent any further transformation of state or society. Its leaders, the old "Jacobins" of the 1790s, reveal clearly enough the overall trend since that time of Swedish—and Scandinavian—radicalism, away from social toward purely political objectives. Looking back on the student radicalism of his youth, Count Trolle-Wachtmeister would write in the 1840s that he and his friends would now be ridiculed as "doctrinaires" and "adherents of the *juste-milieu,*" revealing "our present-day reformers' contempt for the constitution of 1809, which is the realization of Swedish Jacobinism."[56]

"One has a fatherland under a good regent, but not under a bad one," one of their leading ideologues, Axel Gabriel Silfverstolpe, had written in Adler-sparre's journal, *Läsning i blandade ämnen* already in 1800, echoing the British Lockean tradition and foreshadowing the rationalizations of his Finnish peers in 1808-9. No one, he continued, could love a land that it was not in one's interest to love; hence there was no basis for the state but a contract freely accepted by its inhabitants, which they might freely renounce. The fatherland was therefore not necessarily the land where one was born, but that in which the individual might expect that felicity to which all were entitled.[57]

Flanking this liberal bloc in the *Riksdag* was a varied and growing opposition. Following their initial confusion and discouragement, the Gustavian legitimists began to take heart during the summer of 1809. Led by Counts Jacob De La Gardie and Eric Ruuth, they sought to disconcert the "Men of 1809" at every turn, often joining forces with those who believed the revolution had not gone far enough, making it at times difficult to distinguish "right" from "left" in the opposition.

What the Gustavian faction had in common was above all its continuing support for Prince Gustav of Vasa's hereditary right to the throne and, generally, for a strengthened royal power, rather than for a specific social orientation. Its leading figures were titled and economically independent landed magnates, largely from Skåne, in contrast to the lower service nobility who predominated among the "Men of 1809." While some, such as Count Hans Axel von Fersen and Baron G. M. Armfelt, were social conservatives, Counts De La Gardie and Ruuth, Baron Rutger Maclean, and others showed an apparently greater receptivity to social change than the leading revolutionaries of 1809.

During the fall of 1809 a group of Gustavians, including De La Gardie, Ruuth, Adlercreutz, and Klingspor, planned secretly with Karl XIII for a coup d'etat to change the constitution and increase royal authority, in the process restoring the legitimate succession. Significantly, they were able to gain support among some of the more radical members of the Peasant Estate, who had suffered defeat over the land taxation issue in June 1809. For the "Men of 1809," alarmed by vague reports from informers, this revived the old specter of a union between the crown and the populace, still vivid in memory from 1788–89 and with antecedents stretching far back into Sweden's past.

There were meanwhile intimations of what such a coup could mean in sociopolitical terms. Already in June 1809 Baron Maclean had proposed the abolition of the clause in the new constitution requiring the assent of all four Estates to changes affecting corporate privileges. It was largely through De La Gardie's initiative that the uniform progressive income tax was established.

On 13 January 1810 De La Gardie hurled a bombshell at his rivals by proposing in the Noble Estate that his peers renounce all their remaining privileges providing the other Estates did likewise, that all land be reassessed and taxed on an equal basis, and that a more modern and equitable system of representation be adopted in the *Riksdag*. The "Men of 1809" counterattacked bitterly, both in the *Riksdag* and through personal slander. De La Gardie was denounced for his "aristocratic-demagogic" spirit and compared with the "deserter" Count Mathieu de Montmorency, who in 1789 had so lightheartedly renounced for his Estate the privileges of the French *noblesse*.[58] The constitutional committee refused to consider the proposal after A. G. Silfverstolpe demonstrated to its satisfaction that virtually all surviving privileges were now property rights, accessible to all citizens. The Clerical and Burgher Estates revealed a marked reluctance to surrender their established privileges and the Peasant Estate was fearful that a new assessment might increase its tax burden.

The intended Gustavian-royalist coup d'etat was planned for 13 March 1809, the anniversary of the revolution of the preceding year. But at the last moment the sickly and indecisive Karl XIII lost his nerve.

Representational reform had been under consideration since the spring of 1809 by the Constitutional Committee, which received numerous proposals: for enlarging the existing Estates, for adding a fifth Estate, for devising an entirely new system. The matter seemed pressing. Petitions to the committee pointed out that in 1809 some 70,000 "nonnoble persons of quality" (*ofrälse ståndspersoner*) lived in Sweden proper; although more numerous than any of the three higher Estates and accounting for a sixth of the regular taxation, this group was debarred from membership in any of the Estates. In addition, a half million others, including soldiers, miners, and nonagricultural laborers, lay outside the existing Estates system.[59] Individual Estates undertook some reforms on their own initiative. The Nobility abolished the three-class voting procedure established by Gustav III in 1778, restoring the "noble democracy" of the Era of Freedom. The Peasantry now admitted certain categories of "gentlemen farmers'' previously excluded. In general, the Nobility showed the greatest concern for the representation of essentially middle-class nonnoble persons of quality.

In April 1810 the constitutional committee at last presented its proposal: for the replacement of the four Estates by a bicameral legislature, including an upper house, elected on the basis of taxable property, and a lower house, based on population, although elected by voters qualified by property ownership. While a notable departure from Swedish political tradition, the proposal was scarcely democratic in spirit, for it would reinforce the political power of the wealthiest magnates. What it envisioned was well expressed by A. G. Silfverstolpe in February 1810, in language that revealed the hardening social conservatism of the revolutionaries of 1809 and which could have been taken almost verbatim from Montesquieu:

> The monarch has a natural interest in being as powerful as he possibly can; his inclination should be recognized as despotism. . . . The representatives of the people (Commune, lower house, or whatever one may call them) have a natural interest in limiting the monarch's power. . . . Both of these forces tend toward the dissolution of the state. Something is needed to hold them together. That is the intermediate power, which may here be called the aristocratic [upper house].[60]

The proposal was passed by the *Riksdag*, but as an amendment to the constitution it required the endorsement of the following diet. Subsequently, it was ignored by the *Riksdagar* of the summer of 1810, 1812, and early 1815, and was quietly shelved in an atmosphere of growing conservatism.

On 2 May 1810 the long *Riksdag* at last dissolved. Amid mounting disillusionment and political conflict, all parties had meanwhile come increasingly to place their hopes in the new crown prince. Christian August made his sentimental departure from Norway in January 1810. Arriving in Sweden, he adopted the more Swedish name Karl August and quickly became as popular as he had been across the Keel. Thanks to his simple habits and unaffected manner, it was soon widely believed among a populace again aroused by old social antagonisms that he was the enemy of the old aristocracy. He showed, however, political acumen in winning over various influential elements in the Swedish political establishment. He quickly gained the affection of Karl XIII and Queen Charlotta. He was naturally on good terms with the Adlersparre faction, which had secured his election, but he avoided its more obvious attempts to dominate him. Before long he also managed to gain the respect of leading Gustavians.

At first the new crown prince continued to hope for a constitutional Scandinavian union. Since he was still a bachelor, he envisioned his possible future abdication of the Swedish crown in favor of the king of Denmark, in return for a liberal constitution or constitutions for all of Scandinavia. Frederik VI meanwhile came to accept Karl August's new position as a guarantee of improved Swedish-Danish relations.

Only gradually did Karl August come to realize the depth of anti-Danish sentiment in Sweden, revived by the recent war, and turn to other thoughts. He hinted to the Gustavian leaders that he considered eventually abdicating in favor of Prince Gustav. Only after his last-minute discovery of their plan for a coup d'etat in March 1810 did he begin to resign himself to the idea of marrying and establishing his own dynasty.

On 28 May 1810, only four months after his arrival in Sweden, Crown Prince Karl August fell from his saddle while attending army maneuvers in Skåne and expired within half an hour. Although an autopsy revealed that he had died of a stroke, word quickly circulated that he had been poisoned. Since January it had been rumored in Stockholm that the Gustavians conspired to do away with the crown prince, evidently spread by Carl August Grevesmöhlen, a journalist and political jobber of shady background, to discredit the opponents of the dominant party. As news of Karl August's death reached the capital, suspicion focused on Count Axel von Fersen and his sister, largely through an anonymous satirical poem, "*Räfvarne*" ("The Foxes"), in the radical journal *Nya Posten*.

There followed three weeks of feverish agitation, and on June 20 Karl August's body reached Stockholm. As it was escorted to the royal palace by an impressive cortège, an aroused crowd set upon Count Fersen, who took part as grand marshal, hauled him from his coach, and trampled him to death, despite the presence of military units. Rioting continued late into the night, by now largely directed toward the homes of wealthy and powerful persons, until the troops fired into the crowd, causing an unknown number of casualties.

A prolonged inquiry into the events of 20 June ultimately revealed little about its causes and probable instigators, which ever since have remained the objects of much speculation. Karl XIII, various of his councillors, as well as the Adlersparre faction generally, were convinced—or found it politically expedient to suspect—that the Fersen family was implicated in Karl August's untimely death, which would account for the curious passivity of the troops until after the rioting had gotten out of hand, as well as for the apparent efforts of the "highest authority" to suppress certain evidence in the inquest.

Antipathy was meanwhile widespread among the middle classes toward the nobility as a whole, including the oligarchs of 1809, heightened by economic dislocations, disillusionment with the results of the recent *Riksdag*, and crushed hopes in the new crown prince. Obviously middle-class persons were much in evidence in the violence against Fersen. Their involvement was apparently coordinated in advance by a small circle of radicals around C. A. Grevesmöhlen. An anonymous report to St. Petersburg perceived behind the tumult a "revolutionary party," led by "certain bourgeois," which sought to "overthrow entirely the whole order that had recently been reestablished in the country." The

Danish minister reported that ambitious burghers aspired to "introduce a complete equality within society."[61]

Behind them stood the poorer classes of the capital, who gave weight and impact to the rioting but whose resentments, under mounting economic hardship, were directed more toward all who possessed wealth and authority than toward the nobility as such. Among the broader masses of both town and countryside, the revolution of 1809 had aroused little enthusiasm, and the deposed Gustav IV Adolf—who like Karl August had been widely regarded as the people's friend—met with many signs of popular sympathy as he and his family were escorted through Sweden and Swedish Pomerania into exile in December 1809. Among those who murdered Count Fersen, J. A. Ehrenström wrote in August 1810,

> were surely many who with sheep-like stupidity imagined that in him they avenged, besides the poisoning of the crown prince, Gustav III's assassination, the deposition of his son, the exclusion of the latter's family from his hereditary rights, and even the abandonment of Sveaborg and the loss of Finland. It was necessary to put such ideas into circulation to set the masses in motion.[62]

The Fersen murder was one of the great political assassinations of the revolutionary and Napoleonic era, and the rioting that attended it was the largest and bloodiest popular uprising in Scandinavia during the entire period. It seemed to symbolize the nadir of Sweden's degradation, following over a year of revolution, social and political conflict, military defeat, and inept leadership. Rumors were rife of future dissentions. To many, both at home and abroad, the nation's future seemed dark. In neighboring Denmark, C. D. Reventlow saw in the "fearsome" events across the Sound "a late imitation of the French Revolution." Napoleon lectured the Swedish minister to Paris on the dangers of the "Jacobin" avalanche. "He must indeed be sanguine," wrote the English traveler E. D. Clark, "who can hope to see *Sweden* regenerated and her glory restored."[63]

By the fall of 1807, all of Scandinavia was involved in the European conflict, and although the Swedish and Danish monarchies took different sides, the immediate consequences were largely similar for both. Throughout the North, the pressures of war moreover precipitated basic changes that had long been preparing.

The economic impact of war was devastating. Up to 1807 the Scandinavians had prospered in international trade. In the fall of that year, however, Hans Järta observed:

> Surely a worse and more worrisome situation for commerce than at present has never existed. If peace does not intervene, by spring either our

own ports will be blockaded or all other ports will be closed to us, depending upon the political course we take.[64]

In the event, Sweden suffered from the latter consequences, Denmark from the former. Faced with similar dilemmas, the remaining neutrals, Portugal and the United States, would likewise soon be drawn into the fray.

The war led to a de facto decentralization of power in both Nordic kingdoms, following periods in which personal autocracy had reached its height. In Sweden military defeat resulted in the loss of the eastern third of the realm, which now for the first time became self-governing, as well as in a new constitution for Sweden proper which imposed a system of checks and balances. The attempt to incorporate Swedish Pomerania directly into the kingdom was frustrated by its occupation by the French in 1807–10. In the Danish monarchy, Frederik VI at last dispensed with his state council, but he was forced to grant a wide measure of local initiative to officials in his outlying domains, particularly Norway, and largely to suspend his efforts to integrate the duchies. In Finland, Norway, and even Iceland, under the strains of war members of the local elites now found themselves prepared to think the unthinkable: of a national destiny separate from the old metropolises.

Gustav IV Adolf and Frederik VI were enemies by 1808, each bent on the conquest of territory from the other. Yet in personality and attitudes Gustav IV Adolf surely resembled his older Danish cousin, Frederik VI, more than he did his father, Gustav III. He was hardly the "charmer king" Gustav III had been, and he did nothing to gain for posterity the gratitude and praise of courtiers, artists, and literati. After the revolution of 1809 his reputation was systematically blackened by Sweden's new masters.[65]

Still, there is more to a reign than the personality of the monarch, and there remains a basic unity to the Gustavian period, particularly with respect to Sweden's social and economic development from 1789 on. Gustav IV Adolf was in effect the executor of Gustav III's Act of Union and Security and Charter of the Rights and Liberties of the Swedish and Finnish Peasantry of 1789. Through his practical, pragmatic internal reforms, his reign went in significant respects beyond his father's.[66]

Gustav IV Adolf's sobriety, thrift, personal piety, sense of justice, mistrust for the old aristocracy, and concern for his humbler subjects were surely more to the taste of the broader masses than Gustav III's often exotic ways, and indeed their affection for him largely survived the essentially oligarchic revolution of 1809. Again, these are qualities that recall Frederik VI.

If Gustav IV Adolf's mismanagement of the war led to his deposition in March 1809, in the long run Frederik VI's wartime leadership in Denmark would result in even greater national calamities. But in Denmark the absolute monarchy was far more solidly entrenched than Gustav IV Adolf's makeshift autocracy in Sweden, the aristocracy had long since ceased to be a political force, and the long series of reforms had firmly established Frederik in the affections of his nation. Frederik would thus weather the storm and be remembered for firmness, attachment to principle, steadfastness in the face of national misfortune, whereas Gustav Adolf has been branded with inflexibility, dogmatism, quixotic refusal to face reality. The first remains associated with a "golden age," the latter with an "iron age" in the cultural life of their respective lands.

In Sweden, following the adoption of the new constitution in 1809, there was much speculation about abolishing all surviving corporate rights and establishing a system of parliamentary representation without regard to social status. In Norway new liberal constitutions were likewise envisioned within broader Scandinavian frameworks. Although they remained unrealized at the time, all these projects looked essentially toward a social and political order based on class rather than estate. In all, moreover, the innovative role played by great noblemen—Prince Christian August of Augustenburg, Count Wedel Jarlsberg, Count De La Gardie, Baron Maclean—is unmistakable; by contrast, there is a notable lack of initiative among other classes—with the partial exception of the Swedish Peasant Estate—to dismantle what remained of the corporate structure of society. One is reminded of the role of the great reforming magnates of the Bernstorff-Reventlow-Schimmelmann circle in Denmark a generation earlier. In Finland, meanwhile, all the Estates clung firmly to the existing order at the Borgå diet, to forestall any restructuring under Russian auspices.

It is ironic yet revealing that the pressures precipitating these developments resulted largely from a war between the two Nordic monarchies which by that time was considered so unnatural that a Danish-Schleswig noble could be elected crown prince of Sweden and ambitious projects for a union of the Scandinavian crowns could be considered while it was still going on. That such ideas were more than a passing dream the future would show.

CHAPTER 13

# The Resolution
# 1810–15

The sudden death of Crown Prince Karl August of Sweden in May 1810 once again threw all of Scandinavia into uncertainty. A new crisis over the Swedish succession led to revived hopes in Sweden for the recovery of Finland and in Denmark for a greater Scandinavia. But the triumph of a dark horse candidate dashed all such speculations and determined the course of the North's political evolution.

The crisis immediately stirred up the bitter rivalry between the Gustavians, now presented with the opportunity to revive the claims of Prince Gustav, and the Men of 1809, determined to prevent a restoration of the old dynasty. The agitation against the Gustavians that culminated in the Fersen Riot on 20 June was widely understood to have been inspired by leading Men of 1809, and indeed no serious attempt was thereafter made to support Prince Gustav. Georg Adlersparre meanwhile lost no time in advancing the candidacy of the late crown prince's elder brother, Duke Friedrich Christian of Augustenburg.

Other possibilities meanwhile suggested themselves. The Danish envoys to Stockholm and Paris, Counts Magnus Dernath and Niels Rosenkrantz, immediately saw a renewed opportunity to obtain the Swedish succession for Frederik VI, thereby creating the Scandinavian union envisioned the year before. The views of Napoleon again seemed paramount, and the Swedish and Danish governments sounded out the emperor regarding Duke Friedrich Christian and King Frederik, respectively. Preoccupied with the Continental Blockade and improving his strategic position for an eventual showdown with Russia while not provoking the Russians prematurely, Napoleon seemed to indicate a vague but noncommittal approval of either solution, arousing hopes on both sides. Meanwhile,

311

one of his own marshals, Jean-Baptiste Bernadotte, Prince of Ponte Corvo, revealed surprisingly that he had been urged to stand as a candidate for the Swedish succession.

The election of a new crown prince called for a special *riksdag*, convened in July in Örebro. Frederik VI at first hesitated to advance his candidacy in Sweden. Thus no official Danish measures were taken in that regard before the beginning of July, when Count Rosenkrantz returned from Paris to replace Christian Bernstorff as foreign minister. Believing Napoleon's goodwill to be assured, Rosenkrantz initiated a vigorous campaign to secure his king's election as Swedish crown prince. Ernst Schimmelmann and Frederik Moltke, with a number of pro-Scandinavianist literati in Denmark, wrote pamphlets—generally under pseudonyms—to persuade their Swedish brethren that a Scandinavian union was essential to their future security, prosperity, and happiness, using arguments recalling the "Balloon Proclamation" of 1809 and anticipating almost all the traditional Scandinavianist ideas of the nineteenth century.[1] At last on 18 July Frederik VI wrote to Karl XIII, formally proposing his candidacy. Count Dernath sought support on the Swedish state council, making it known that his monarch was prepared to accept the Swedish constitution of 1809 for Sweden, although not for Denmark or Norway. Prominent Danish aristocrats and men of letters toured Sweden to arouse enthusiasm among their respective peers.

Reactions in Sweden were, however, mainly negative or indifferent. The Swedes retained bitter memories of the medieval Kalmar Union, mistrusted Danish absolutism, feared economic and cultural domination and the eclipse of Stockholm by Copenhagen. The recent war had revived old prejudices against the perfidious "Jute." Danish and Norwegian privateers continued to prey on Swedish vessels trying to run the Continental Blockade. While union with Norway would clearly strengthen Sweden, there were fears that Denmark, especially Jutland and the duchies, would prove a strategic liability. Since the preceding year, the person of Frederik VI had become distasteful to most politically conscious Swedes; to many he seemed, in Lolo Krusius-Ahrenberg's words, "a Gustav IV Adolf in Danish guise."[2] A way out of this dilemma appeared to some to be the election of Frederik's cousin and heir presumptive, the young Prince Christian Frederik, but Frederik VI's own announced candidacy stood in the way.

On 10 August the Secret Committee of the Estates, charged with nominating a successor, endorsed the Duke of Augustenburg, who despite strained relations with Frederik VI had himself shown interest in a greater Scandinavia and made references to a union along the lines conceived by his brother, Karl August, that is, one endowed with a common, liberal constitution. He pointedly told Frederik VI that he saw little chance of his election and that he himself would not refuse the Swedish crown from a "higher hand."[3] Frederik became increasingly exasperated, seeing in the duke the main obstacle to his own election, and in August sent a military detachment to Als to "protect" the duke from being "abducted" to Sweden by the Adlersparre faction. Relations between the Danish royal house and the Augustenburg family, already embittered by Holstein's incorporation into the realm in 1806, henceforth became irreconcilable, with fateful consequences for the Schleswig-Holstein dispute of the mid-nineteenth century.

This strife between the royal brothers-in-law largely canceled out whatever support either might have hoped for in Sweden, thereby clearing the way for the improbable candidacy of the French Marshal Bernadotte. On 10 August—the same day the Secret Committee endorsed the duke of Augustenburg—the marshal's personal emissary, J. A. Fournier, arrived in Örebro. Although he carried no written message from Bernadotte, he gained credence by showing miniature portraits of the latter's wife Desirée and son Oscar. Assurances of the marshal's interest had meanwhile reached Sweden from Paris. Fournier strongly hinted that his master enjoyed official French support; the effect was reinforced by dispatches in the same vein from the Swedish minister in Paris, Baron Gustaf Lagerbjelke. Fournier moreover gave assurances that Bernadotte was prepared to offer Sweden substantial economic benefits, including a loan of eight million francs.

The government was thus persuaded to refer the matter back to the Secret Committee, which already on 14 August shifted its support to Bernadotte. A week later he was unanimously elected crown prince by the Estates. "All the Scandinavian voices did not prevail against a single Gallic one," wrote the Swedish unionist C. V. Broocman to his Danish colleague Rasmus Nyerup. "We are now considered quite fortunate. God grant that this be so!"[4]

"No one has fulfilled a destiny like mine," said Bernadotte at the end of his long life in 1844.[5] He was born in Pau in Béarn, the son of a petty lawyer (*procureur*), in 1763 and began his military career as a private soldier in 1780. He was commissioned a lieutenant in 1791 and rose to major-general already by 1794. After serving as French ambassador to Austria and as war minister, as well as in the field, Bonaparte appointed him to his *Conseil d'État* in 1800, made him a marshal in 1804, and Prince of Ponte Corvo in 1806. His first contact with the Nordic world came in November 1806 when he took Lübeck by storm; among the enemy units there taken prisoner was a small Swedish force, whose officers the marshal treated with a courtesy that would not be forgotten in Swedish higher society. As French administrator over the Hanseatic Cities—Hamburg, Bremen, and Lübeck—Bernadotte revealed both administrative skill and consideration for their inhabitants. As noted, he commanded the French and Spanish force that moved into Denmark in 1808 in anticipation of a Danish-French attack on Sweden.

The death of Crown Prince Karl August quickly aroused interest in certain

Swedish circles in a Napoleonic marshal as the new successor. In particular, some of the younger military officers of progressive views sought for a military leader of proven capabilities and on close terms with Napoleon to avenge the recent defeat by Russia and recapture Finland. Certain academics and radicals in Uppsala and Stockholm hoped that a crowned Jacobin would level the last vestiges of aristocratic privilege. Although much of the background to the Fersen Riot of June 1810 remains obscure, it is apparent that C. A. Grevesmöhlen and his friends hoped through it to clear the way for the election of a French marshal. An article in *Nya Posten*, probably by Grevesmöhlen, in October acclaimed Bernadotte's election as "in actuality a greater revolution than that which took place on 13 March 1809," which would end "*aristocratic* oppression, which of all forms is that which the Swedish people can least endure."[6] Of the French marshals, none was better known than Bernadotte, whose martial skills and qualities of leadership stood in striking contrast to both the pedantic Frederik VI and the schoolmasterish Duke Friedrich Christian.

Once Bernadotte's candidacy became known at the Örebro *Riksdag*, he appeared to many in a new light as the strong-willed man of order who alone could restore discipline to a society badly shaken by the recent Fersen Riot. A few days after that event, Count Dernath wrote to Copenhagen:

> The crime committed has opened the eyes of those thoughtless men who give encouragement to a dangerous delusion but who are far from wishing the overthrow of the social order. They have drawn closer than ever to the government.

Gustav Lagerbjelke wrote to Karl XIII from Paris in July that Providence itself seemed to have permitted this "deplorable event," to provide "a government, as firm as it is enlightened, the *opportunity* and *justification* for developing that power, authority, and indeed that salutory severity the general good unfailingly demands." Count Trolle-Wachtmeister, who himself had been something of a "Jacobin" in his day, later recalled how the tumult had given a horrifying glimpse into the abyss of social dissolution:

> The weak government could not possibly have held in check the parties already then emerging, which, through their dissension opened the way for a democratic or anarchical league, to which a Gustavian faction had attached itself, which would have stirred up popular uprisings, after which we would perhaps in the end have seen the Russians come to put an end to anarchy and civil war. . . . All, despite their differing views, came [to Örebro in 1810] determined, in electing a successor, to unite around a person who could protect them against popular revolution and who was strong enough to prevent anarchy. All party interests made way for the personal concern not to be killed in the open street.[7]

The Fersen Riot in Stockholm marked the beginning of a long era of political reaction in early nineteenth-century Sweden, as would become evident soon enough. On a smaller scale, it recalls the pivotal impact of the Gordon Riots in London, twenty years earlier, upon British political opinion.

The invitation to seek the Swedish succession reached Bernadotte in most irregular fashion. A young officer, Lieutenant Count Carl Otto Mörner, sent to Paris with the message that his government intended to back Duke Friedrich Christian, obtained a private meeting with Bernadotte on 25 June and proposed that he should be Sweden's next crown prince. Ostensibly Mörner was acting on his own, yet he had influential connections at home. He was promptly joined in his representations to the French marshal by General Fabian Wrede, also in Paris at that juncture.

The offer was clearly made in the firm belief that Bernadotte enjoyed the full confidence of the emperor Napoleon, his brother-in-law. In actuality, relations between them were never cordial and frequently strained. A vehement dispute between them during the Austrian campaign in July 1809 had led to Bernadotte's return to Paris in disgrace. Still, the day after Lieutenant Mörner's visit, Bernadotte informed Napoleon of the offer made him and asked permission to accept it. The emperor did not refuse, but he made no direct effort to support Bernadotte's candidacy.

There has been much speculation about Napoleon's actual views on the Swedish succession in 1810.[8] It seems, however, reasonable to accept Baron Lagerbjelke's opinion that Napoleon could not openly back Bernadotte lest he prematurely alarm the Russians.[9] While a more or less unified Scandinavia under Frederik VI or Duke Friedrich Christian might prove an asset if allied with France, neither was an effective military leader. A divided North might more easily be dominated. Napoleon may have been under no illusions regarding Bernadotte's loyalty to his person, but he surely counted on his patriotism toward France and on Sweden's natural *revanchisme* toward Russia. To the Austrian ambassador, Prince Metternich, he said, "If the Swedes take a [French] marshal as their king, it will be to reconquer Finland; if they choose the Prince [*sic*] of Augustenburg, they will devote themselves to peace." To which he added, soon after, that Bernadotte was a "good soldier," but lacked "any talent for ruling."[10] He thus seems to have been confident that the ex-marshal would be a tractable satrap and Sweden a dependable adjunct to the Grand Empire, even though he considered extracting a promise from Bernadotte that he would never bear arms against France, when the latter departed for Stockholm at the end of September.[11]

Arriving in Helsingør, Bernadotte was received into the Lutheran faith on 19 October 1810, before setting foot for the first time on the soil of his new patrimony the following day. He entered Stockholm on 2 November and three days later was proclaimed Karl XIII's adopted son under the name Karl Johan.

Upon first meeting the new crown prince, Gustav III's dowager queen, Sophia Magdalena, is said to have exclaimed, "He is marvelously like the late king."[12] Indeed, Karl Johan's similarity to Gustav III is in many ways as striking as it was unexpected. He had, to be sure, been an enthusiastic enough supporter of the revolution that had opened his way to advancement: in 1798 Axel von Fersen had called him "one of the raging Jacobins," and to his dying day he reputedly bore on his chest the tattoo, *"Mort a roi [sic]."*[13] Yet before his arrival in Sweden he had evolved into a firm upholder of the existing social order. Four days before his election in Örebro, Hans Järta wrote, with clear allusion to young Carl Otto Mörner, "What most appeals to me is the conviction that under him, more than any other, lieutenants will remain lieutenants."[14] Grevesmöhlen and his fellow radicals who had labored covertly for his election received scant reward. Nor did Karl Johan seek or find support primarily among the Men of 1809. Instead he relied from the start upon tried and true officials from the Gustavian era to implement what would in time prove to be essentially Gustavian policies.

Like Gustav III, he was a consummate political opportunist who whenever possible kept several irons in the fire. Though voluble, often in the extreme, his utterances could on occasion be both misleading and bewilderingly inconsistent. His innermost thoughts he kept to himself, and unlike Gustav III he was not given to putting on paper general statements of political philosophy. His temper was mercurial, although behind his celebrated *"gasconnades"* one could frequently perceive well-timed, calculated dramatic effects. He had a sure sense for the telling gesture and the uses of propaganda, produced for him by hired pens — including Grevesmöhlen. For these reasons, interpretation of Karl Johan's motives and intentions must be based largely upon conjecture — essentially upon deeds more than words — leaving ample room for controversy on almost every significant point.

What is indisputable is that Karl Johan assumed a commanding position almost from the moment he arrived in Stockholm. With tact and deference, he quickly overcame the misgivings of King Karl and Queen Charlotta over his common origins and checkered past, while his forceful personality overshadowed both the aging monarch and his ministers. When Karl XIII was incapacitated by a stroke less than four months later, in March 1811, Karl Johan declared himself regent, disregarding the constitution of 1809 which conferred such powers on the council. This action would be symptomatic of his tendency in following years to adjust the constitution to his own needs—again recalling Gustav III. Although the regency ended officially in January 1812, Karl Johan remained Sweden's real ruler; in this respect his accession to the throne as Karl XIV Johan in 1818 simply confirmed the position he had long held.

In no respect has there been greater controversy than over Karl Johan's foreign policy. His election had been fervently supported and enthusiastically welcomed by those in Sweden who saw in him Finland's redeemer. It was increasingly evident that the Tilsit alliance would sooner or later break down, offering Sweden its chance to recover its ancient eastern domain.

This prospect aroused considerable concern, not only in Russia but among those in Finland who found it beneficial to come to terms with the new order in their land and who had compromised themselves by doing so. Their alarm was increased by the knowledge that many Finns still regarded Sweden as the true fatherland. Throughout 1810–11 there were rumors of pro-Swedish conspiracies.

Bernadotte's election, however, presented another possibility. "If ever our greatest political concern, Norway's union with Sweden, can be realized," wrote Gustaf Lagerbjelke to Karl XIII already on 17 August, "it will be through a French prince."[15] The Danish minister to St. Petersburg quickly sensed this danger and warned his government of it. Prince Christian Frederik, the Danish successor, saw his country faced with a "great fight for life or death" and proposed grandiose plans for invading Sweden to create a Nordic union by force.[16] Frederik VI and his foreign minister, Rosenkrantz, were at first not much impressed. Frederik assumed Bernadotte to be, like himself, firmly in Napoleon's camp and received the marshal cordially in Copenhagen on his way to Sweden.

During the two years following Bernadotte's election there would emerge the outlines of a new foreign policy for Sweden. What came to be called the "Policy of 1812" meant accepting the loss of Finland with Norway as compensation, to be obtained in alliance with Russia and Great Britain against France and Denmark. The acquisition of Norway—although not the ultimate relinquishment of Finland—was of course a long-standing Swedish aspiration, cherished by both Gustav III and Gustav IV Adolf, and most recently championed by Georg Adlersparre and his friends in 1809. At Fredrikshamn, the Russian peace negotiators had moreover hinted in September 1809 that Sweden might find compensation for Finland in Norway.

As a foreigner, Bernadotte had no sentimental attachment to Finland, while as a hardheaded soldier-statesman of the French revolutionary school he could not but be impressed by the plain facts of geography: Finland would be hard to reconquer and harder to retain, whereas Norway, easier to acquire, would ensure Sweden's security within natural frontiers. Knowing Napoleon's Grand Empire from within, he was surely less certain than most Swedes or Danes of its ultimate survival. To tie himself to France to reconquer Finland would keep him Napoleon's vassal; an alliance with Russia and Britain, and the acquisition of Norway, would give both Sweden and himself greater strength and independence in the European arena.

Significant questions nonetheless remain. At what point did Bernadotte first conceive the "Policy of 1812"? When did he, at least in his own mind, commit himself to it? How firm was this commitment at any given point? How consistently did he hold to it? Clear answers can hardly be expected. Torvald Höjer and Sten Carlsson, for instance, tend to stress his opportunistic turns and shifts in response to changing circumstances, whereas Sam Clason, Jörgen Weibull, and Päiviö Tommila emphasize the early beginnings and underlying consistency of Karl Johan's foreign policy.[17]

Much can be said for both views. As early as November 1806, Bernadotte allegedly told a Swedish officer taken prisoner at Lübeck that it was unnatural for Norway to belong to Denmark and that it ought rightfully to be annexed to the Swedish king's domains. Lagerbjelke reported from Paris in August 1810 that he was aware the marshal had spoken to Napoleon about Norway.[18] Bernadotte was at that very time passing on to Alexander I assurances of his goodwill and apparent disinclination to regain Finland, through Colonel I. A. Chernychev in Paris, and indeed the tsar, unlike many of his advisers, showed remarkable equanimity over Bernadotte's election. Considering, however, the strength of *revanchiste* sentiment in Sweden and its importance in his election, the new crown prince could scarcely reveal prematurely the idea of so startling a reversal of policy. As long as France and Russia remained at peace, there was moreover always the chance they might reconcile their differences, leaving Sweden exposed, and until they actually came to blows it would be impossible to judge the relative likelihood of victory for either side. To be sure, the advantages of gaining Norway were manifest. But for a self-made prince there were even greater concerns at stake. A striking triumph would consolidate his position in his adopted land. More essential still, however the great power contest should end, was that he should be on the winning side. His political survival and that of his dynasty depended upon biding the right moment for action and keeping his options open.

Bernadotte had scarcely arrived in Stockholm before he was faced with a serious challenge from his former master. Sweden had undertaken in the peace treaties of Fredrikshamn and Paris, in September 1809 and January 1810, to adhere to the Continental System, but this commitment had been honored mainly in the breach. Despite initial fears, Britain had not retaliated. Admiral Sir James Saumarez, dispatched to Northern waters in March 1810 with instructions to act according to circumstances, avoided provocation and helped the Swedes to carry on business as usual. Although officially blockading Sweden, he established covert relations with local officials, of which Stockholm remained officially ignorant, and his ships quietly provisioned along the Swedish coast, to the profit of its inhabitants. As long as Swedish ships flew a neutral flag—usually the American—their origins were not questioned and licenses were required only if they were trading with the Continent. Swedish vessels from the Baltic even sailed in British convoys, while British exporters often transported goods for Baltic destinations overland across Sweden to avoid Danish privateers. Swedish imports from Britain thus amounted in 1810 to nearly 7,000,000 *riksdaler* in value, to which may be added around 2,000,000 *riksdaler* in imports from the United States, mostly destined for reexport to the Continent. The same year Sweden sent some 3,750,000 *riksdaler* in exports to Pomerania and other German destinations alone.[19]

Napoleon was determined to apply the Continental Blockade with maximum effect and thus to prevent violations in northern Europe. During the summer of 1810 he annexed directly to France both Holland and the north German coast as far as Lübeck. This established a land frontier with Denmark, largely ending the profitable smuggling trade from Holstein. On 13 November a French ultimatum reached Stockholm, demanding that Sweden declare war on Britain, together with notification of Karl Johan's forfeiture of his continental appanages as Prince of Ponte Corvo. Napoleon clearly sought to force his brother-in-law's hand and commit him publicly to the French camp before he had any chance to strike out on any independent line of his own. Under the circumstances, Sweden could only accede. The new crown prince, however, declined to play any part in the decision, while protesting to the French minister and assuring the council that although born French, he was now "Swedish in heart and soul."[20]

London was naturally apprehensive at the election of a French marshal to the Swedish succession, which in turn aroused fears in Sweden. Yet nothing was to be gained on either side by active hostilities. By treating the state of war as a mere formality, it still proved possible to carry on no small amount of contraband trade in quiet agreement with Admiral Saumarez.[21]

Already in February 1811—even before becoming regent—Karl Johan entered into secret negotiations with Napoleon for an alliance in return for subsidies and increased territory, above all in Norway. The emperor categorically opposed such an arrangement. The Swedes, he took for granted, must naturally desire revenge against Russia, the Finns to rejoin Sweden, and the Russians to prevent a Norwegian-Swedish union. Once the crisis in Franco-Russian relations of the spring of 1811 had passed, he let the matter drop.

The reasons for these negotiations remain obscure.[22] Yet from Karl Johan's standpoint they could for the time being reassure *revanchiste* sentiment in Sweden, while giving Napoleon notice of his primary objective—the acquisition of Norway—and of his determination to pursue an independent policy. He probably neither expected nor perhaps even hoped the emperor would accept his proposal; it could later be evoked as evidence of his desire for good relations, and its rejection could subsequently be blamed on France. Not least, Karl Johan gained valuable time to follow developments on the European scene and quietly prepare opinion for a change of course.

He meanwhile kept his line open to St. Petersburg. By the fall of 1810 the Russian government began seriously to consider the Norwegian question, seeing a real need to compensate Sweden for Finland. Already in December Colonel Chernychev turned up in Stockholm, where he apparently encouraged Karl

Johan in this hope. The lead thus provided was not immediately followed up while the crown prince pursued his negotiation with France, but thereafter relations became increasingly cordial beween Russia and Sweden in the fall of 1811. By the turn of the year the Russian chargé d'affaires in Stockholm was instructed to explore the possibility of a Russo-Swedish alliance.

At this point Napoleon played into Karl Johan's hands. In January 1812, incensed over continued Swedish evasions of the Continental System, he occupied Swedish Pomerania and sent its captured garrison as prisoners of war to France. This aroused a wave of indignation throughout Sweden, clearing the way for a reversal of policy. Karl Johan lost no time in negotiating with Russia and declaring Sweden's neutrality in the Anglo-French conflict. His position was further strengthened when Denmark concluded a new alliance treaty with France on 3 March 1812, placing at Napoleon's disposal a force of 10,000 men for use in Northern Germany.

On 5 April a secret Swedish-Russian treaty was signed in St. Petersburg, by which Alexander I undertook to obtain Norway for Sweden through negotiation or force, providing in the latter case 15-20,000 men and naval forces for the purpose, *after which* Karl Johan, at the head of this force augmented by 25-30,000 Swedes, would undertake a diversion against the French in northern Germany. The treaty likewise contained a mutual guarantee of both powers' existing territories. For Sweden this meant nothing less than a formal renunciation of Finland. Napoleon sought in March to offer Karl Johan the return of Finland if Sweden joined him against Russia, which simply strengthened the crown prince's hand vis-à-vis St. Petersburg and London. In June 1812 Britain concluded peace with both Sweden and Russia in Örebro. But Karl Johan prudently did not sever connections with Paris until the Grand Army invaded Russia the same month.

Sweden and Russia prepared to attack Sjælland in the spring of 1812, causing alarm in Denmark and relief in upper-class circles in Finland. A sizable Russian army was assembled in Finland by the time the French crossed the Niemen, but the Swedes were still not ready to act. Yet more than practical logistical problems would seem to have delayed the project. For the Russians, a Scandinavian diversion could be hazardous in the face of imminent French attack. Karl Johan was surely not anxious to break with France before Alexander did and must have wished to assure himself of the probable outcome of the Franco-Russian contest before irrevocably committing himself. In the meantime he reactivated Adlersparre's propaganda and intelligence network in Norway.

As the Grand Army plunged deep into Russia, Sweden's goodwill became increasingly vital to Alexander I, who in August arranged a personal meeting with Karl Johan in Finland. Their conversations, held in Åbo, were mainly tête-à-tête and unrecorded, but significant details emerge. Alexander offered Karl Johan command of a Russian field army. The latter countered by proposing immediate Swedish military aid to Russia in return for a temporary Swedish occupation of Finland, as a gage for Sweden's future acquisition of Norway, and perhaps the cession of the Åland Islands. Alexander rejected this proposal, as Karl Johan surely expected. They meanwhile discussed an idea urged upon the tsar by the ubiquitous Mme. de Staël, which the crown prince must already have contemplated: that Karl Johan might become France's new ruler following Napoleon's defeat.[23]

The secret Swedish-Russian agreement signed in Åbo on 30 August 1812 amplified the St. Petersburg treaty of five months earlier, calling for a joint expedition against Sjælland, now to include 35,000 Russians, to obtain for Sweden not only Norway but Sjælland and Bornholm, the keys to the Baltic, for which Denmark was to receive compensation in northern Germany; thereafter, Sweden would join the war against France. It also included a family pact, requiring both parties to oppose any attempt by a third power to disturb the security or tranquillity of each others' domains.

The Åbo meeting failed, not surprisingly, to bring about a speedy attack on Denmark. Russia was naturally unprepared to spare troops for such a venture while fighting for survival, as Alexander officially informed Karl Johan after the French occupied Moscow a fortnight later. Karl Johan's gains at Åbo were less direct. He was able to maintain and through personal contact to strengthen his alliance with Alexander I, while postponing direct Swedish involvement before the outcome of the war in Russia became clear. A new factor involved was a desire to delay or minimize open war with France to protect his popularity there against the day when he might conceivably be called to its throne. Meanwhile, the family pact at Åbo gave Karl Johan's succession in Sweden the indispensable backing of a great European power. It would be upon this rock that the survival of his dynasty and forty years of Swedish-Russian amity would be based. Russia also remained committed in principle to Sweden's acquisition of Norway.

For his part, Alexander was reassured of Finland's security, permitting him to send the Russian forces assembled there to the relief of Riga, while simply by meeting with him at this juncture Karl Johan sufficiently compromised himself to bar any future return to the Napoleonic camp.

During the fall of 1812 Sweden made military preparations, arousing fears in Denmark and some dissatisfaction at home, since they were costly but led nowhere. Very likely they were intended largely to demonstrate to St. Petersburg Sweden's seriousness about the Norwegian project and to London its need for subsidies.

It may be asked whether Karl Johan did not lose his most favorable opportunity to seize Norway on his own terms that fall, even without Russian support, for with the French retreat from Moscow and the Russian advance into northern Germany by early 1813, Sweden quickly lost much of its strategic value to both

Russia and Britain, depriving Karl Johan of much of the leverage upon which his "Policy of 1812" was predicated. His position was moreover morally equivocal, for while other powers fought to regain what they had lost, he was prepared only to fight to gain a land Sweden had never possessed. He now faced a hard dilemma: to join the allies in the war would brand him as a traitor to his native land, diminishing his chances for the French throne; to fail to do so would cost him the support of the allies, the chance to gain Norway, and probably the insecure Swedish crown itself. By the winter of 1813 a Swedish army of 30,000 men began to assemble in Swedish Pomerania, evacuated by the retreating French.

Karl Johan's anxieties greatly increased when the allies around the turn of the year began making discreet overtures to Denmark, whose strategic importance waxed as Sweden's waned. Opinion in Denmark had become increasingly skeptical of the French alliance during 1812 as the Swedish threat to Norway became apparent. On 19 September 1812 the Norwegian-born foreign minister, Niels Rosenkrantz, alarmed by armaments across the Sound, had urged that only by breaking with Napoleon and joining the allies might Denmark be saved from being "stricken from the number of independent states, for nothing less is at stake." Frederik VI had then remained firm. The French, he replied, would in such a case surely occupy the duchies and Jutland, and Norway would be lost should it become dependent upon other sources of provisionment outside the monarchy. "Sjælland would, perhaps, be all I would have left." Moreover, honor demanded that he stand by his ally.[24] Napoleon's crushing defeat in Russia by the end of the year nonetheless caused him to waver, and he did not reject the allies' approaches in early 1813.

The success of Karl Johan's grand design depended above all upon keeping Denmark in the enemy camp. On 3 March 1813 he scored a crucial success with the conclusion in London of an Anglo-Swedish alliance treaty. In return for Sweden's participation in the war against "common enemies" with at least 30,000 men, Britain would provide diplomatic and naval support for the acquisition of Norway, a subsidy of 1,000,000 pounds, and the French West Indian island of Guadeloupe. At this point the allies crossed their signals, for on 22 March Prince Sergei Dolgoruki, a confidant of the tsar, arrived in Copenhagen, where he intimated that Russia would not press for Sweden's accession of Norway if Denmark joined the coalition. Frederik VI was persuaded to send envoys to London and St. Petersburg. As he got wind of these developments, Karl Johan protested furiously and broke diplomatic relations with Denmark on 21 April. Tsar Alexander recalled Dolgoruki and disavowed his actions. St. Petersburg and London would now only offer Frederik VI compensation for Norway in Germany or Holland. This, the Danish envoy explained to the tsar, would make the Danish king "a Dutch or German prince. . . . The victors would be lost among the vanquished," whereas "Danes and Norwegians comprised a single nation."[25] Negotiations broke down.

A curious incident suddenly threatened to upset the calculations of all parties. In May the French counterattacked toward Hamburg, which was then occupied by a Danish force whose commander, uncertain of his government's position, prepared to defend the city and appealed to the Swedish commander in Pomerania for support. A small Swedish force set forth before being furiously recalled by Karl Johan, who arrived in Pomerania on 17 May to take personal command. On 10 June 1813 Denmark concluded a new alliance treaty with France, providing an auxiliary corps of 12,500 men in northern Germany.

Although the immediate threat to Karl Johan's policy had passed, he found himself compelled to give ground on important points. Transferring the main Swedish army to northern Germany meant abandoning a landing on Sjælland and hence the possibility of acquiring that island and Bornholm, along with Norway, as envisioned at the Åbo meeting. Denmark would have to be attacked through the duchies and Jutland. Soon after his arrival in Germany, however, the British and Russians made it clear the Karl Johan would have to join the campaign against the French without further delay, postponing the solution of the Norwegian question.

On 4 June Russia and Prussia without warning concluded an armistice with France, followed by negotiations for a compromise peace. At last fully committed to enter the fray and thus compromised on all sides, Karl Johan found himself dangerously exposed. He was now prepared to limit his demands to Trondheim *Stift*, together with gages in northern Germany which he contemplated retaining if he could not later acquire the rest of Norway.[26] Frederik VI naturally stood fast. Austria sought to mediate between France and the allies, and Austria was known to be pro-Danish. After a year, Karl Johan's "Policy of 1812" lay in apparent ruin and was subject to growing criticism in Sweden. Worse still, he was haunted by the recurrent specter of a new "Tilsit" at Sweden's expense. His very political existence seemed to hang in the balance.

Karl Johan nevertheless still had his battlefield experience and inside knowledge of Napoleonic strategy. When the peace negotiations led nowhere and Britain pushed for resumption of the war, the Russian and Prussian monarchs invited him to Trachenburg in Silesia on 9–12 July to consider strategy. The plan adopted was mainly Karl Johan's and placed him at the head of the allied Northern Army, consisting of 158,000 Russians, Prussians, and Swedes. The armistice ended on 10 August, and Austria joined the coalition two days later.

The Northern Army played a decisive role in the ensuing campaign, leading up to the defeat of the French at Leipzig on 16–19 October. Karl Johan's sparing use of his own Swedish troops meanwhile caused much bitterness among his allied subordinates. During the entire German campaign of 1813, Sweden lost only some 1,200 men.[27] He sought to preserve his force for the sake of his popularity both in Sweden and in France, and for the long-awaited blow against Denmark. Sweden declared war on Denmark on 3 September, and the Battle of the Nations at Leipzig in October crushed the Danes' last slender hopes.

During these years the Swedish crown prince was mainly occupied with questions of diplomacy and war. Yet he by no means neglected internal affairs. Indeed, Sweden's effectiveness in the international arena was largely dependent upon its internal strength, tranquillity, and resources. Serious problems confronted the government: the disruption of trade, inflation of the currency, falling prices for agricultural produce and raw materials, declining state revenues and mounting expenditures, continued unrest and internal opposition due to both foreign and domestic policies.

Since 1807, Sweden's overseas commerce had suffered badly. Trade with Great Britain had, as seen, continued at a high level through 1810, despite Sweden's formal commitments to the Continental System. The enforced Swedish declaration of war on Britain at the end of the year by no means eliminated this trade, but it declined in 1811 to about half of what it had been the year before, while reexports from Sweden fell by more than four-fifths. During 1812 trade began to recover, although imports by now greatly exceeded exports.[28]

The issue of unbacked paper money during the war years had long since devastated the monetary reform of 1800, creating a mounting inflation. From 1809 to 1812, the exchange rate for the Swedish *riksdaler* rose from 55 to 90 per Hamburg *Thaler banco*, the usual standard of comparison; by late 1814 it had reached 100. Rising prices encouraged wild speculation, which collapsed with crop failures in 1811 and 1812. Thereafter, between 1812 and 1815 grain prices fell by nearly one-third, creating a serious crisis in agriculture. Economic stagnation and inflation, with the loss of accustomed net surpluses from Finland, caused the government's revenues to decline while its expenditures increased by a third from 1810 to 1812.[29]

Karl Johan's ambitions for an active foreign policy called for adequate military forces. A proposal for a French-style national conscription had been defeated in the *Riksdag* in 1809, mainly through the opposition of the Peasant Estate. In the spring of 1810 the *Riksdag* approved a more conservative measure, allowing the crown to raise a reserve of up to 50,000 men between the ages of twenty and forty-five, excluding officials, students, and burghers, as well as the cultivators of farms. The burden was to be borne by manorial and nonmanorial land alike.

In the spring of 1811 the government attempted to raise 15,000 men under these provisions. Its decree, insufficiently explained, aroused immediate unrest among the peasantry. The necessary redistricting was not yet completed, giving rise to suspicions that the upper classes would evade their share of the cost.

Since recruitment by lot was left to parish councils composed of exempted farmers, ferment was greatest among the landless laborers, who had bitter memories of the unfortunate *lantvärn* of 1809. Unrest was most widespread where social cleavages in the countryside were widest. Queen Charlotte feared an outbreak of smoldering "Jacobinism."[30] In Skåne a military force attacked a crowd of some 800 peasants at Klagerup, near Lund, in July. Thereafter hundreds of persons were brought to trial and two farm laborers were executed. This brutal overreaction reflects the new crown prince's sense of insecurity and his suspicion—often revealed in later years—of Gustavian or foreign conspiracies behind popular unrest.

In January 1812 the need for increased revenues and for strengthening the military caused the government to call an extraordinary *riksdag*, again in Örebro, which opened on 13 April. With much effort, a considerably augmented budget was hammered out. Appropriations were increased, as were sea tolls; the old land tolls had been abolished in 1810, and the graduated income tax of that year, which had proved fairly ineffective, was now repealed, evidently as a concession to an increasingly conservative mood. Following the example of France, which in the Peace of Paris in January 1810 had renounced 3,500,000 *francs* in government debts to Swedish subjects, the *Riksdag* repudiated some 7,500,000 *riksdaler* owed by the Swedish government to citizens of France and French vassal states. The savings of nearly a half-million *riksdaler* in interest payments allowed the National Debt Office to make further advances to the crown.

The *Riksdag* meanwhile vested the financial administration of St. Barthélemy—and all other possible overseas acquisitions—directly in the crown. Because St. Barthélemy had by 1811 begun to operate at a profit, this concession provided welcome resources for secret diplomatic and propagandistic purposes.

A new conscription law was passed in May, authorizing the crown to call up, as needed, men between the ages of twenty and twenty-five, by "class" according to year of birth, for military training. All in fit condition were liable for service, although those called could provide voluntary substitutes to serve in their place. Eventually purged of this loophole, the conscription law of 1812 remains the basis of Sweden's present-day universal military service. The *Riksdag* likewise approved the construction of permanent barracks in several towns and appropriations for new equipment.

Karl Johan, at that very time negotiating a rapprochement with Russia based on the renunciation of Finland, was anxious to shield himself from the criticism of a press virtually uncontrolled under the constitutional law of March 1810. By reviving and amending a tabled resolution on the press of quite a different nature from the Örebro *Riksdag* of 1810, the government circumvented the constitutional requirement that an amendment to fundamental law be passed by two successive *riksdagar*, to put through a new, restrictive press ordinance in July.

This permitted the government to close down any periodical considered "harmful to public security or offensive to personal rights without reason or proof, or of a consistently abusive nature."[31]

As the weeks dragged by, the crown prince, his attention keenly engaged by developments on the Continent, felt growing frustration with the restrictions on royal power and the cumbrous workings of the *Riksdag* under the constitution of 1809. He found, Queen Charlotta noted, that while "the Swedes are good-natured as individuals," when convened in a *riksdag* they were "certainly neither humble nor amiable." With certain higher officials of Gustavian background he speculated over a new constitution to strengthen the crown.[32]

In the end, Karl Johan let the project drop. He hardly needed to risk his popularity in such fashion, given his striking success at the *Riksdag* that ended in August 1812. It had revealed that he now enjoyed the solid backing of the old Gustavians, who saw in him the redeeming man of order, whereas the Men of 1809, owing to growing public disillusionment with their earlier failings, played only a modest role. They dared not even openly oppose the repressive press ordinance.

Karl Johan was much interested in economic affairs, particularly agriculture, which he tended to regard in the physiocratic tradition as the true basis of national wealth. In 1811 he founded the Royal Agricultural Academy (*Kungliga Landtbruksakademien*) as a semi-official department of government and in 1813 economic societies (*hushållningssällskap*) in each of Sweden's twenty-four counties (*län*). Political calculations were, as usual, not absent, for the economic societies, chaired and partly appointed by the county governors, allowed the central government greater control over county affairs through the unpaid efforts of local notables.[33] The crown prince meanwhile actively encouraged sheep raising, flax cultivation, herring fishing, and saltpeter production, as well as the construction of roads, barracks, and the Göta Canal. Thus, before the great European conflict ended in 1815, important steps had been taken toward Sweden's economic recovery.

Through the Peace of Paris in January 1810, Sweden regained its Pomeranian dependency. The new regime in Stockholm did not attempt to carry through Gustav IV Adolf's interrupted revolution from above. Instead of a four-Estate *Landtag* on the Swedish model, the province was now granted a single-chamber diet, elected by class, giving wider preponderance to the wealthier elements, especially the landed proprietors, and allowing greater local autonomy. Since there was no protection for peasant tenancies on private manors, landlords freely compensated themselves for the loss of serf labor by absorbing them into the demesne, reducing tenants to landless laborers, whose obligations to take regular service were set forth in new ordinances in 1810 and 1811.[34]

Despite Karl Johan's assurances of goodwill and the St. Petersburg alliance in March 1812, Alexander I continued to court the loyalty of his new Finnish subjects. In the winter of 1812, the *guberniya* of Viborg—consisting of those parts of southeastern Finland ceded to Russia by the Peace Treaties of Nystad and Åbo in 1721 and 1743—was reunited with the new grand duchy. The peasants of the region were thereby guaranteed their former liberties, to the ill-concealed chagrin of Russian landowners there and elsewhere in the empire.

To reorient Finland's new administration toward the east, Alexander transferred its capital from Åbo to Helsingfors in April 1812. Following his meeting with Karl Johan in Åbo in August, the tsar-grand duke authorized the reestablishment of a small Finnish army, initially three regiments, which replaced Russian forces withdrawn from Finland and St. Petersburg to fight the French, and which demonstrated, both at home and abroad, his confidence in Finland's loyalty. The new Finnish regiments were equipped largely through voluntary contributions in the grand duchy itself.

These developments in 1812 were largely due to the efforts of Baron Gustaf Mauritz Armfelt—Gustav III's former favorite—who like other highly placed Finns in Swedish service had faced the difficult choice of retaining his position in Sweden or his properties in Finland. A visit to Finland in the spring of 1810 had dispelled his former anti-Russian prejudices while news of the Fersen Riot in the Swedish capital in June had shocked and revolted him, evoking in his mind the horrors of revolutionary Paris. He was disgusted by Sweden's declaration of war against Britain in December of that year, and after urging an anti-French stance upon Karl Johan, he departed Sweden in March 1811 for St. Petersburg and swore fealty to the tsar. An implacable foe of Napoleonic France, Armfelt found a sympathetic hearing in the Russian capital and quickly gained the confidence of Tsar Alexander, with important consequences for both Finnish and foreign policy. For Armfelt, the two were closely connected: satisfying the Finns by generous concessions would encourage Sweden to turn to Norway for compensation, thus paving the way for Russian-Swedish cooperation in the war against Napoleon. Already in June 1811 he presented to Alexander a lengthy memorandum urging peace with Turkey and alliance with Britain and Sweden against France, the policy in fact followed in 1812.

Meanwhile, Armfelt became the tsar-grand duke's indispensable adviser on Finnish affairs. From late August 1812 until April 1813, he served as Finland's acting governor-general. Thereafter, he managed Finnish affairs from St. Petersburg, virtually independently of the Russian imperial administration, during Tsar Alexander's long absence in Germany and France, until his own death at Tsarskoe Selo in August 1814.[35]

Among numerous others of Finnish origin who left Swedish service to return to their homeland was the old Gustavian Johan Albrekt Ehrenström, an erstwhile participant in the "Armfelt Conspiracy" of 1793–94, under whose supervision Finland's new capital, Helsingfors, would be rebuilt by the 1820s in the neo-classical style as a miniature St. Petersburg.

Finland was finding its place in the new order of things. "Many still believe they should be Swedes and not Finns, which they confuse with Russians, which we ought not be except in wishing them all success for our own sake," commented Colonel A. F. Palmfelt in 1811. "The emperor wants to make good Finns of us," wrote Armfelt that summer, "and in God's name let us fulfill our destiny." To the Swedish chargé d'affaires in St. Petersburg in November, the "dominant spirit" in Finland appeared so "Russian" that it would now be beyond reason to shed a drop of Swedish blood to recover it. The social realities of the situation are meanwhile glimpsed in a letter from the old Gustavian J. F. Aminoff to Armfelt in July 1812:

> On all the better people I think we can surely count, [although] never in any land on the common people or mob, especially here, where the weight of centuries has attached them to the former overlordship. They are best kept in hand with sternness and justice. The Greencoats [Russians] hold them best to order and obedience.[36]

Denmark's war with Great Britain dragged on, essentially as a *guerre de course* against British merchantmen and Swedish blockade-runners. Privateering was temporarily suspended in the summer of 1809, to permit the the provisioning of Norway, but resumed the following spring. In March 1811 the Danes vainly attempted to recover the island of Anholt in the Kattegat, which the British had occupied in 1809, in the last real encounter between Danish and British forces.

Although uneventful, the war was ruinous for Denmark. Its fleet was gone, much of its merchant marine confiscated in enemy ports, its colonies occupied, its foreign trade cut off, its sea lanes to Norway and the Atlantic islands largely severed, its inter-island communications in constant jeopardy. By the spring of 1811 the smuggling trade through Holstein was largely suppressed, and privateering became increasingly hazardous and unprofitable. While Norway could not obtain enough grain, Jutland and the duchies could not dispose of their surpluses.

State revenues fell as expenditures increased, and the government—to an even greater degree than in Sweden—sought to fill the gap by printing unbacked paper money. Silver and copper currency disappeared from circulation. Already by 1807 the paper *rigsdaler* had sunk to a third of its silver value, by 1812 to a fourteenth.[37] That summer a commission was appointed to consider the problem. It soon convinced itself that only the most draconian measures would suffice.

On 5 January 1813 the inhabitants of the realm were stunned by a government ordinance reorganizing the entire monetary system. A new state bank (*Rigsbank*) was established, superseding all existing credit institutions. All types of paper currency then in circulation were to be replaced by a new *rigsbankdaler*, without a metallic base but on the security of all real property at the rate of six old *rigsdaler* to one *rigsbankdaler*. Payable *daler* for *daler* in the new currency, existing taxes were increased six times over in real value, while converted to the new exchange rate the national debt was reduced to one-sixth of its former real value. Complicated provisions were made for the settlement of personal debts, depending on monetary values on the dates incurred. The silver value of the old *rigsdaler* soon declined further to about one-tenth of the new *rigsbankdaler*.[38]

To the effects of devaluation and enormously increased tax rates there was now added a special levy of 6 percent on all real property in the realm, assessed at its silver value and with 6 1/2 percent interest on deferred payment, to provide backing for the new banknotes. Large numbers of investors, creditors, and savers were ruined, producing bankruptcies and much personal distress. Not until 1838 would Denmark's currency finally be stabilized at its silver value, at the cost of a deflationary policy that kept the economy depressed for a generation.

Although the war had hurt the economy of the duchies, the well-managed *Giro- und Leihbank* in Altona, established in 1776, had kept their own separate currency remarkably stable, while that of the Kingdom went to ruin. Increasingly the Copenhagen government intervened in the operations of the Altona bank, violating its guarantee of 1788. The ordinance of January 1813 finally abolished the duchies' separate monetary status and confiscated the holdings of the Altona bank, thus confronting their inhabitants for the first time with the full economic brunt of the war.

Although Ernst Schimmelmann was convinced as finance minister that this measure was unavoidable, it went against the grain of his own warm concern for the duchies and numerous personal ties there. In Kiel, Countess Luise Stolberg was mortified that he should have signed "so ignominious a decree," and in February she wrote to A. P. Bernstorff's widow, "I do not think Denmark will have any joy of this in the long run, rather I see more and more clearly that that country and ours cannot have the same interests. They are too different in all respects." To Schimmelmann, his brother-in-law Fritz Reventlow wrote in righteous indignation from Emkendorf on 29 January:

Have we not simply been sacrificed to the envy of the Danes, as hateful as it is misinformed? . . . One asks oneself whether the Terrays, the Maupeous, the Calonnes, those precursors of the French Revolution, ever made greater encroachments upon the rights of property, imposed heavier and more oppressive taxes, brought more confusion and ruin to the fortunes of the individual, offended more openly against the most sacred obligations of the state toward those who give it their trust and the guaranteed rights and fundamental laws of the provinces!

"Our land, I speak here only of the duchies," Count Christian Stolberg warned in June, would be "irretrievably lost" unless the ordinance were repealed; otherwise nothing could secure the "Fatherland" against an uprising in the near vicinity of 20,000 Swedish troops commanded by a true son of the revolution.[39] Another grievous blow had widened the chasm between Copenhagen and the proud Holstein nobility, which Schimmelmann's dismissal for the sake of public opinion in December 1813 did nothing to bridge.

While war and economic breakdown brought widespread distress in Denmark, one important element of society fared remarkably well: the peasant farmers. The rapidly inflating currency after 1807 progressively lightened the burden of taxation and of mortgage payments for those purchasing freeholds, while as creditors, many of their former landlords suffered accordingly. Neither the monetary crash of 1813 nor the loss of the Norwegian market had a very great impact upon farmers still largely geared to self-sufficiency. They were thus strengthened for times to come. The lot of cotters and landless laborers on both manors and peasant farms was less enviable, particularly where they were dependent upon occasional work at money wages, which rose more slowly than prices for produce.

Neither war nor economic crisis ended the work of internal reform in Denmark before the last of its long-considered projects were completed. Among these was the matter of the tithe, which had long remained unresolved. It has been seen that the government sought, in characteristic fashion, to encourage private agreements between titheholders and farmers, beginning in 1796. At last on 8 January 1810 a new ordinance established a uniform annual tithe in grain, which the farmer could commute to a money payment based on a sliding scale according to current grain prices. In 1853 all remaining tithes in kind would be commuted to money payments, the last of which were made as late as the 1970s.

The School Commission, established in 1789, finally completed its labors in 1814, after long delays due mainly to philosophical differences between the cultural idealism of Ludvig and Christian Ditlev Reventlow, the clerical traditionalism of Bishop Nicolaj Balle, and the socially conservative utilitarianism of Duke Friedrich Christian of Augustenburg. The commission's initial proposal, submitted in 1799, contained an ambitious curriculum for elementary instruction, inspired by the Reventlows, including natural history, civics, music, and gymnastics in addition to reading, writing, reckoning, and religion. This formed the basis for the program of the Copenhagen schools established under the ordinance of July 1799 on poor relief in the capital, which proved largely unpracticable, and it came under such strong criticism, not least from official quarters, that the commission lapsed into inactivity. It was thereafter revived mainly by Bishop Balle, whose influence, with that of Duke Friedrich Christian, now gained ground.

The duke expressed his views clearly in a memorandum of April 1802:

The instruction of the youth in the village schools must aim at developing basic human understanding. Everything must be excluded that does not contribute to making them upright, sensible country folk, suited for and active in their occupations. Any education going beyond the sphere of their future activity would be harmful, for it implants the seeds of dissatisfaction with one's station in life, encourages a restless striving to raise one's lot, creates distaste for physical labor, and becomes the source of foolish desires and decisions.[40]

C. D. Reventlow protested angrily that the duke sought to divide the population into the "civilized" and the "uncivilized."[41] Yet the latter's viewpoint reflected widely held, traditional social apprehensions both at home and abroad. The educational system adopted provisionally in the islands in 1806 and throughout the kingdom in 1814 was thus a compromise: in its simplified curriculum it leaned toward the conservative values of the bishop and the duke, while adapting to economic austerity; yet in mandating a comprehensive system of compulsory schooling it realized one of the cornerstones of the whole program of reforms conceived by the Reventlows and their friends in the 1780s.

The ordinances issued on 29 July 1814 stated that it was the purpose of popular education to make children "good, law-abiding people, in accordance with the teachings of the evangelical Christian religion, as well as to bring them the skills and proficiencies which are necessary for them to be useful citizens of the state."[42] They required the establishment of a fixed school in each parish, rural and urban, and the erection of suitable buildings, although ambulatory teachers could also be employed in large parishes. Costs were to be met through parish taxation and a modest tuition, from which poor families were exempted. Children were required to attend from the age of six or seven until they received confirmation at thirteen. Instruction was to include religion, reading, writing, reckoning, singing, and where possible some Danish history and geography, and gymnastics. In towns boys were to be taught wood and metal crafts, and girls needlework; an optional additional class, intended primarily for middle-class pupils, taught basic commercial subjects to boys and domestic skills to girls. Teachers were to be trained in teachers' seminaries or to take examinations in basic subjects, although decades would pass before these stipulations could be fully met; in the meantime the English "Lancaster" system, using older pupils to help instruct younger ones, was widely employed, involving much rote drilling and marching about in groups. A separate ordinance of the same date set essentially similar requirements for elementary schools in the capital. Parents who could afford it were permitted to educate their children at home through private tutors or in private schools, subject to suitable controls.

In sum, the ordinances of 1814 were the decisive step toward the progressive enlightenment of the broader masses. They established the first comprehensive system of public education in Scandinavia—Sweden would follow suit in 1842, Norway in 1860, and Finland in 1865—and one of the earliest in the Western world. The higher, or Latin, schools and the universities in Copenhagen and Kiel meanwhile remained unconnected with the new system, and from the mid-eighteenth until well into the nineteenth century the number of university students of peasant or artisan background declined in Denmark and Norway, in contrast to Sweden, where their proportion rose from the 1780s on.[43]

It has been seen that Denmark's small Jewish community had, since the 1790s, gradually been freed from numerous old restrictions, both legal and customary. A government commission had recommended in 1796 that the Jews, who hitherto had largely managed their own affairs, be made fully subject to Danish law, except where it pertained to the Christian religion.

Owing largely to divisions within the Jewish community itself, the government put off taking action. The legal emancipation of the Jews in France in 1791 and in French-dominated Holland, Italy, and western Germany in 1796 meanwhile encouraged a formal resolution of the matter. Napoleon's efforts in 1806-7 to work out a "Jewish Concordat" for the Grand Empire aroused fears in Denmark, as elsewhere, that he sought the allegiance of Jews everywhere. The Danish government was also apprehensive lest the French initiatives revive the authority of the rabbis and of Mosaic law.

Following the so-called Jewish Feud in 1813, when the rising prominence of Jews in Copenhagen's economic life led to overt manifestations of anti-Semitism under the impact of widespread distress, the government at last took action. In its ordinance of 29 March 1814 it proclaimed the Jews in the kingdom—although not yet in the duchies—to possess equal rights with all other subjects, under the civil law of the land, against which no appeal could be made to Mosaic law; it also gave the state certain controls over the practice of Judaism, similar to those it held over both the state church and other Christian religious bodies.[44] The ordinance of 1814 granted in effect official sanction to what was already a virtual fait accompli, and following generations would witness a steady integration of Jews into Danish national life. Their full civic equality would be confirmed by the Danish constitution of 1849. In Norway they would attain comparable status by 1851 (at which time they were also first permitted to settle in the country), in Sweden by 1860, and in Finland following independence from tsarist Russia in 1918.

Upon acceding to the throne in March 1808, Frederik VI had announced he would deal directly with the various government departments, thereby effectively suspending the state council, which ceased to meet. During the next five years the king exercised a *Kabinettsregiment* reminiscent of the Struensee and Guldberg eras. In the crisis caused by the Swedish attack and demand for the cession of Norway in December 1813, however, Frederik called together a "council of good men" ("*de Gode mænds råd*"), presaging the end of the long trend toward personal autocracy. From April 1814, the state council again met regularly and the king abandoned direct intervention in government affairs through cabinet orders. Counts C. D. Reventlow and Ernst Schimmelmann remained on from the old council; the former no longer participated much, but Schimmelmann remained active until his death in 1831. Its dominating members were meanwhile the new men of recent years, stout Danes, competent and obedient bureaucrats, men not unlike the former Gustavian functionaries surrounding Karl Johan in Sweden. The day of the reforming cosmopolitan *grands seigneurs* was now past.

The Peace of Jönköping with Sweden and the permitting of Norwegian licensed trading with Britain in the fall of 1809 had for the time being reestablished more or less normal communications across the Skagerrak and ended, almost miraculously, Norway's threatening crisis of that year. Through Prince Christian August's successor in Christiania, Prince Frederik of Hesse, the Copenhagen government lost no time in dissolving the emergency Government Commission set up in 1808, and in reasserting its traditional policy of centralization. "Everything," the king instructed him, "that does not contribute to the closest relationship and union of the entire monarchy must go."[45]

That such a situation could no longer satisfy Norway's upper classes was soon demonstrated by a revival of the old demand for a separate Norwegian university, which quickly turned into a demonstration of popular sentiment. The matter had been raised by Count Wedel and his friends in connection with the organization of the Society for Norway's Welfare in December 1809. One of its first acts was to sponsor an essay contest on the university question, won by Nicolai Wergeland, who spoke of Denmark as though it were a foreign land. In April 1810 Frederik VI announced that an academic institution would be established at the existing school of mines in Kongsberg, allowing students to complete their arts (*artium*) degree in Norway. This was both too little and too late, particularly since Wedel and others who still aspired to a constitution and union with Sweden were deliberately exploiting the issue to mobilize opinion in Norway. In June 1810 supporters of a true university began collecting voluntary contributions toward its establishment; within two years this campaign brought in some 781,000 *rigsdaler*, plus quantities of grain.[46]

Early in 1811 Frederik VI commanded Wedel to appear before him in Copenhagen, evidently hoping to regain his support. What was said at their meeting on 1 March is not known, but doubtless dealt largely with the university question, by now a highly emotional issue in Norway. The king directed Wedel to consult with the consistory of the University of Copenhagen, which recommended that Norway be given its own university.

Frederik feared, as he wrote to Frederik of Hesse the same month, that a Norwegian university would encourage "that harmful tendency toward separation of the two kingdoms, which is so prevalent."[47] The ongoing collection campaign in Norway, attended by much publicity, nonetheless forced his hand. On 2 September 1811 he at last signed a decree authorizing the establishment of a complete university in Christiania. The event was celebrated throughout Norway with exuberant manifestations of both national pride and gratitude toward the monarch. "It has been reserved for our generation," wrote a pastor in Stavanger, "to see our fatherland raised to equal rank in culture and learning with the other enlightend nations of the world."[48] When the new institution at last opened its doors in 1813, it was called the Royal Frederik University.

By early 1812 Norway's brief revival of prosperity was beginning to flag. Fishing was poor, the market for timber falling off, British licenses harder to obtain. The renewed Franco-Danish alliance pact of 3 March led to stricter prohibitions against British imports, hurting timber exports from Østlandet, since the British demanded that Norway import British wares in return. Increasingly Canadian timber was replacing Norwegian in the British market. The licensed trade collapsed as the British renewed their blockade. By summer it was apparent that Norway faced the worst crop failure in living memory, at a time when grain imports were again cut off. The winter of 1812–13 brought growing misery throughout the land. On top of everything came the state bankruptcy and monetary conversion in January 1813, bringing commercial confusion and greatly increased taxation, which were especially burdensome to Norway with its lack of credit facilities.

Georg Adlersparre's agents in Norway reported by the spring of 1813 that resentments were rapidly mounting against Denmark.[49] Such discontent was expressed most vocally by the merchant class, but it was geographically more widespread than in 1809. Again misgivings were expressed over Norway's future fate in union with Denmark. Wedel and his friends continued to look to a connection with Sweden. There was some speculation in mercantile circles about establishing an independent Norway under British protection.

Hunger stirred up endemic social tensions. During the spring and summer of 1813, there were outbreaks of peasant unrest in a number of towns, directed against merchants and officials suspected of hoarding grain. In Toten, Arendal, and Trondheim, troops were used to restore order. During these disturbances, the peasants expressed no real discontent with the existing regime, and the outbreaks petered out after a good harvest in 1813. Yet they added to the disaffection of the upper classes toward Copenhagen and its ruinous foreign policy.

On 5 April 1813 Prince Frederik of Hesse wrote from Christiania that

Norway had never been "in such an unfortunate situation as at this moment and help must come immediately if it is still to be saved from ruin."[50] The following month Frederik VI, after long hesitation, replaced him with his cousin and heir presumptive, the twenty-four-year-old Prince Christian Frederik, as *statholder* in Norway.

Christian Frederik, who three years earlier had aroused some hopes during the Swedish succession crisis of 1810, had long shown a strong interest in Norway, largely inspired by his close friend Carsten Anker, the great Christiania merchant, who had lived periodically in both Copenhagen and London. At his enthusiastic reception in Christiania on 22 May 1813, the prince announced that the "[king's] command shall be my law, to win your confidence my endeavor."[51] Given existing circumstances, such a program could not but imply certain contradictions, of which Christian Frederik was already well aware. In an undated memorandum to Frederik VI, evidently from the winter of 1813, he had envisioned the situation that might arise if Sweden, backed by the coalition powers, demanded the secession of Norway:

I will not here consider philosophically a monarch's right to cede a kingdom to another state. When he renounces his right to the throne, when his dynasty does likewise for all time, the right to choose its king must revert to the nation, and surely the Norwegians would not elect a French soldier, even if he wears a Swedish coat and bears a Swedish sword; this land may be conquered for a time, but the nation will never submit. Unless it starves and as long as it has anything to live on, the war against its oppressors will be like the Spanish. Such a nation, true to its king and royal house, will not abandon Your Majesty.

On 30 April 1813, Carsten Anker wrote to the prince in the same vein:

No devil is going to persuade me to be untrue to my king. . . . [But] if he loses Norway, that is, if he is compelled elsewhere by force of arms to cede it, then for God's sake hurry up here and save us from Sweden, come up with your [claim to] your fathers' patrimony, so that Norway may become independent until the storm has passed and Norway can again be united with Denmark.[52]

By the end of 1813 it would be apparent that a number of prominent Norwegians were thinking of making the prince-*statholder* their king.

Frederik VI was surely aware of the chance he took in making Prince Christian Frederik in effect his viceroy in Christiania. He had long hesitated, despite constant urging, to replace his vice-*statholder*, Frederik of Hesse, with someone capable of inspiring the same kind of personal following as the popular Prince Christian (Karl) August in 1808–9. In 1811 and 1812, Christian Frederik had begged to be sent to Norway. By the spring of 1813, faced with alarming discontent in Norway and the growing threat of a showdown with Sweden, Frederik VI overcame his apprehensions and sent the prince to Christiania, armed with wide discretionary powers. In so doing, it seems not inconceivable that he was now prepared tacitly to envision as an extreme solution what he had until then most feared: Norway's separation from Denmark, perhaps for the rest of his own lifetime, until Prince Christian Frederik ascended the Danish throne by hereditary right.[53]

To deal with the new wartime crisis, Christian Frederik set up several central judicial and fiscal institutions in Christiania and planned to revive the Government Commission of 1808-9. A particular problem was an acute shortage of currency and credit, which again raised the old question of a separate Norwegian bank. The prince considered establishing a new loan and discount office (*Lån- og diskontokasse*) and in mid-December 1813 convened a meeting in Christiania of seventy-two of Norway's leading merchants to prepare its statutes. At length, Copenhagen was prepared to go even further and authorize an essentially complete and separate bank for Norway, which might issue its own banknotes. Following shortly the opening of the new university in Christiania, this concession to a century-old Norwegian demand marked another important step toward what might have become a new federative structure for the Danish monarchy, a turning point which outside events soon prevented from turning.

The bank meeting was a crucial move in Christian Frederik's astute campaign to gain the goodwill of Norway's merchant patriciate, that key element which in recent years had been most disgruntled over the effects of Danish foreign policy, in contrast to Frederik of Hesse, who had favored the bureaucrats and peasants. Not least, he attempted to win over Count Wedel and his following among the greater merchants. By the time the bank meeting ended on 5 January 1814, not only had the participants enthusiastically pledged their guarantee of the new bank's initial capitalization, but many had privately discussed acclaiming Christian Frederik as Norway's king, thereby cutting adrift from the sinking Danish ship of state. The meeting in Christiania was thus of more than merely financial significance: it was a portent of the restoration of representative institutions in a land ruled by royal absolutism for the past century and a half.

Following their victory at Leipzig in mid-October 1813, the allies began to show differences in war aims. The Austrian chancellor, Prince Metternich, fearful of strengthening Russia and Prussia, again sought a negotiated peace, whereas Russia, Prussia, and Britain were for pursuing the retreating French across the Rhine. The resulting hiatus presented Karl Johan with his long-awaited opportunity. While he sent Prussian and Russian units into Holland, he marched north with his main Swedish and Russian force. Driving a wedge between Marshal Davout's French corps, which fell back on Hamburg, and Frederik of Hesse's Danish force, he invaded Holstein on 5 December.

The Danish troops fought stoutly but were poorly led and no match for the Swedish and Russian veterans. After a lifetime of organizing and exercising his beloved army, Frederik VI hesitated to throw it into an all-out trial of arms. The Swedes and Russians advanced into Schleswig. Already on 15 December, Frederik VI obtained an armistice.

Upon the advice of the "council of good men" assembled to consider the crisis, the Danish king accepted mediation from Austria, which proposed that Denmark surrender Trondheim *Stift* to Sweden and join the anti-French coalition. Frederik VI bridled at such terms, and Karl Johan threatened to renew the war unless he received all of Norway. Denmark's strategic situation meanwhile deteriorated, and Austria abandoned mediation. Frederik VI saw no alternative but direct negotiations with Sweden.

On the night of 14–15 January 1814, Denmark concluded the Peace of Kiel with Sweden, surrendering all of Norway in full sovereignty to the king of Sweden, in return for Swedish Pomerania and Rügen. Denmark undertook to join the coalition with a corps of 10,000 men, for which Sweden would provide a subsidy of one million *riksdaler*; Sweden also pledged itself to seek additional territorial compensation for Denmark in northern Germany at the final European peace settlement.

Certain features of the peace treaty are worthy of special note. While the first Swedish proposal for Article IV called for Norway's direct incorporation into the Swedish state, this was revised on Karl Johan's own initiative to specify that Norway was ceded to the king of Sweden, to comprise a separate realm in union with Sweden (*"un Royaume, et reuni à celle de la Suède"*).[54]

The earlier and final versions of Article IV reflect long-standing differences of view within the Swedish government. Gustav III had quite evidently aspired to the direct incorporation of Norway into the Swedish state by right of conquest, like the provinces taken from Denmark and Norway in 1645 and 1658, and various of Karl Johan's advisers continued to uphold this concept. Already in 1800, meanwhile, an unidentified expert had counseled Gustav IV Adolf in a long memorandum that Norway could only be won with the support of its inhabitants, to be gained by promising autonomy in their internal affairs. Count Wedel had made it clear in 1809 that a separate constitution would be the indispensable condition for a union with Sweden, and this position was firmly backed by the Adlersparre faction across the Keel. Already in December 1810, only a few weeks after arriving in Stockholm, Karl Johan secretly intimated his support for such a program to sympathetic Norwegians. From that time forward, he sent repeated assurances to his contacts there that Norway would have its own constitution and institutions in a federative union with Sweden, especially through Georg Adlersparre's revived intelligence and propaganda network from the spring of 1813.[55]

Knowing the strength of Swedish chauvinism, Karl Johan evidently did not divulge his views on this matter indiscriminately at home. Still, by January 1814, he was morally committed to Sweden's friends in Norway. Through generous terms, he might hope to reconcile the Norwegians to a change of dynasty, as Tsar Alexander had so successfully done in Finland. Critical opinion in Britain might be assuaged. Such an approach might also favorably impress liberals in France, opposed to both Napoleon and the Bourbons, thereby improving his chances for the French throne. Finally, considering the evident insecurity of his position in the face of growing conservative legitimism in Europe, a separate Norwegian kingdom might conceivably offer him and his heirs a retreat in the case of an eventual Vasa restoration in Sweden. In any event, a federative union would suffice to ensure the strategic unity of the Scandinavian peninsula, ending the old threat of Sweden's encirclement.

It may have been largely due to the historical ignorance of the Swedish negotiators that Denmark retained Norway's ancient dependencies—Iceland, the Færøes, and Greenland. In any case, time was of the essence. The allies, who in December had resumed their offensive against France, needed Karl Johan's forces and brought diplomatic pressure to bear on both sides to end the northern stalemate. On 14 January there arrived in Kiel a British note threatening to cut off subsidies if the Swedes did not immediately rejoin the allies. Six hours after the peace was signed, Karl Johan broke camp and began to evacuate his forces from the duchies. A more determined Danish resistance could have caused him incalculable difficulties.

Like the Treaty of Fredrikshamn five years earlier, that concluded in Kiel in January 1814 would prove one of the most drastic, as well as one of the most permanent, of the peace settlements of the Napoleonic era, depriving the Danish state of the greater part of its European territory and more than one-third of its population. In Denmark, now reduced to a small remnant of the former kingdom, it left deep bitterness and despair. Word reached Christian Frederik in Norway that "a frightful spirit prevails in Copenhagen. . . . The state seems to have broken down; it is like an interregnum."[56] The popularity of the regime had reached its lowest ebb.

In the duchies reactions were more mixed, particularly among a higher nobility long at odds with Copenhagen. Not long before, Princess Luise Augusta of Augustenburg had written:

> In this war I feel like the famous donkey between two haystacks. I do not know whom I should wish to win. In my German heart, and indeed as a cosmopolite, I tremble lest Napoleon should bring about his universal monarchy, and my Danish heart trembles for our fatherland lest he should be defeated.[57]

By 1813 some of the Holstein nobility no longer had any doubt that their sympathies lay with the coalition and separation from Denmark. "How can our hearts not beat faster at [the thought of] breaking such bands?'' wrote Luise Stolberg in April:

> To be sure, the duchies would gladly belong to Denmark if they were not so basely treated. To see our rights and privileges denied—our contributions multiplied—a conscription more vicious than the Evil One—all decency offended—even our language threatened—how can all this affect [our] dependency?[58]

Amid the German War of Liberation in 1813, the publicist August Wilhelm Schlegel, now serving as Karl Johan's private secretary, called upon the Holsteiners to rise in rebellion and join forces with Karl Johan, the new Gustav Adolf the Great, to throw off Danish despotism and reclaim their old rights. The Emkendorf circle welcomed the Swedish-Russian occupation of Holstein. On 30 December 1813 a delegation of the *Ritterschaft*, including Cai Reventlow and Christian Stolberg, called on the Swedish crown prince to seek through him to obtain a reduction in taxation for the duchies. If they had further, ulterior motives, Karl Johan was evidently not prepared to listen. The day had not yet come to realize the dream of Emkendorf.

After departing Kiel on 15 January 1814, Karl Johan moved with all due deliberation across Germany into Belgium, where he established his headquarters in Liège at the end of February. Here he played for more time as he was visited by various Frenchmen connected with the group around Mme. de Staël and Benjamin Constant interested in his candidacy for the French throne. He held back from a direct attack on French soil and vocally opposed depriving France of its natural frontiers. His resentful allies withdrew Prussian and Russian units from his command and relegated Sweden to the coalition's minor powers.

News from Norway was meanwhile disquieting by early March, giving Karl Johan all the more reason to husband his Swedish forces. The Norwegians refused to accept the transfer of their allegiance. Again, Karl Johan faced a hard dilemma: to take immediate action in Norway would forfeit any chance for the French crown and the necessary support of his allies, whereas further delay would give the Norwegians the chance to establish a regime of their own and prepare to defend it. Under such circumstances Karl Johan made his belated entry into Paris on 12 April, in the wake of his victorious allies. Already on 3 April the French senate had declared Napoleon deposed and the Bourbon pretender King Louis XVIII. Karl Johan and his Swedish army were already on their way home to face the situation across the Keel by the time the coalition concluded the first Peace of Paris on 30 May.

Although Norway had been alive with rumors for the past month, news of the Peace of Kiel struck like a thunderbolt, creating both confusion and indignation.[59] On 24 January 1814 a courier arrived in Christiania bearing the Danish king's written instructions to Prince Christian Frederik to turn over the border fortresses to the Swedes and return to Denmark, to which was added an oral admonition not to place himself at the head of a Norwegian national uprising. The prince reacted indignantly. "The king has sacrificed Norway for all time," he wrote the same evening in his diary, "and it will most certainly be lost to our family if I do not hold on to it."[60]

The question is what Frederik VI himself really intended at this point. Already on 2 November 1813, immediately upon receiving rumors of Napoleon's defeat at Leipzig, Christian Frederik had proposed that Norway negotiate its own peace with Britain. To separate Norway from Denmark would be too dangerous, Frederik replied on 30 November. Yet this was a stratagem that could not be put out of mind. It had been in the air since the previous spring at least. General A. W. C. Kardorff urged it upon the king on 30 November, and a few days later the Austrian envoy, seeking to mediate with Sweden on the basis of Denmark's cession of Trondheim *Stift*, pointed out how Austria had relinquished the Tyrol in 1809 to preserve the state, but had since regained it. On 7 December Frederik wrote to Christian Frederik that even if Trondheim *Stift* were formally ceded, its loss could be prevented "if the Trondheimers said, 'We will stand by our king!' " This, he hoped, might win the goodwill and support of the coalition powers, as they now knew Karl Johan to be "a braggart and most contemptible man."[61]

Christian Frederik had thereupon seized the opportunity to write the king on 25 December:

> If Denmark's salvation now unavoidably requires separation from a part of the realm, and if that part of the realm does not wish for such a separation, I ask, and await Your Majesty's reply: should I act independently of the connection with Denmark, or should I condemn Your Majesty's most faithful subjects for disobedience and abandon a kingdom I could no longer govern in your name? . . . It would in any case be better that I retained authority, rather than anyone else. When the storm had passed and Norway saved, or another ruler were on Sweden's throne, then Frederik VI would again be hailed [as king].[62]

The courier who had borne this message at length returned and caught up with Christian Frederik in Trondheim on 7 February with the full text of the Treaty of Kiel and an oral reply from Frederik VI. "The king accepted all the proposals I had made to him," the prince noted in his diary; "in the worst case I should place myself at the head of the Norwegian nation as its chief or its king." It was evident, too, that Frederik would give what covert support he could.[63] An uprising in Norway at this juncture might by no means be a hopeless cause. It could at least buy valuable time, during which much could happen. Napoleon might yet turn the tables upon his enemies. The allies might fall out among themselves. They might abandon the former French marshal Bernadotte. Karl Johan might leave Sweden to become king of France. If the Swedish succession should again fall vacant, might not Prince Christian Frederik yet gain his chance to unite the three Nordic kingdoms? To succeed, Christian Frederik and the Norwegians would have to take full responsibility, while Frederik VI maintained the appearance of scrupulously upholding the Treaty of Kiel. It was a gamble, but the stakes were too high not to take it.

Frederik VI's initial instructions to Christian Frederik may well have reflected the strain and exhaustion of the moment. More likely they were intended as apparent evidence, promptly communicated to Stockholm, of Denmark's good faith toward the peace settlement. There are, however, aspects of the Treaty of Kiel that may best be understood as part of a last, desperate gamble. Denmark did not hold out for the immediate cession of Trondheim *Stift* alone, which thus allowed an intact Norway to form a common front against the Swedes, while obtaining Karl Johan's immediate withdrawal from the duchies, lest they be held as a gage for Norway. The raising of the British blockade meanwhile permitted large shipments of Danish grain across the Skagerrak, thus forestalling any immediate possibility that Norway could be starved into submission. This, above all, proved Denmark's greatest contribution to Norway in 1814: without such provisionment, Knut Mykland has said, there could have been "no national assembly, no elected king, no 17th of May."[64]

Sweden, with its crown prince and main army in Belgium, was for the time being powerless to take effective action. A governor-general was appointed for Norway, but he could only bide his time across the border. Karl XIII, in a somewhat vague declaration dated 19 February, promised the Norwegians their own constitution.[65] Karl Johan made repeated diplomatic representations to Copenhagen, seeking to curb Christian Frederik in Christiania.

Encouraged by some of his leading bureaucrats, Prince Christian Frederik considered proclaiming himself king of Norway by right of succession and with absolute sovereignty under the *Lex Regia* of 1665, pending the grant of a constitution. The legitimate succession was indeed crucial to his ultimate aim of reuniting the Danish and Norwegian crowns. A tour through Østlandet to Trondheim, however, revealed strong sentiment for a constitution.

In mid-February Christian Frederik held a meeting of twenty-one prominent Norwegians at Carsten Anker's country house at Eidsvoll to sound their opinion. At this "assembly of notables," Professor Georg Sverdrup of the new university argued effectively that the *Lex Regia* lost its force in Norway when Frederik VI renounced his sovereignty, returning to the Norwegian people their right to choose their own government. If they freely exercised this right, however, they would surely elect Christian Frederik as their king.[66] This implied "state of nature" recalls the Swedish *Riksdag's* demand in 1809 for "constitution first, then king."

The result was a compromise: the prince would serve as regent while convening a constitutional convention empowered to elect the monarch. His proclamation of 22 February—three days after Karl XIII's—was used as a kind of basic referendum to strengthen his position. It was promulgated on or around 25 February in all parishes, at which time their members were invited immediately to swear to uphold and defend Norway's independence, and thereafter to elect delegates to the constitutional assembly.

There followed a widespread mood of euphoria, after weeks of uncertainty. In his diary Pastor Claus Pavels, the prince's chaplain, in Christiania, caught the mood of those February days:

> What I dreamed of as a youth at the time of the French Revolution, that I might one day come to attend and speak in a national assembly, it seems will soon be fulfilled. . . . It is a wonderful age we live in. There are surely many lands whose climates I wished to exchange for our cold and discomfort, but I know no realm in Europe or the world where I would rather be a citizen than Norway.[67]

This wave of nationalistic fervor nevertheless concealed some sober apprehensions. On his tour Christian Frederik saw much misery in the timber-cutting regions of Østlandet. There a group of peasants asked him if Norway were now at peace with Britain, which would be their "greatest good fortune."[68] In so doing, they put their finger on the Achilles's heel of his policy, for what Norwegian did not know from bitter experience the meaning of a British naval blockade?

What meanwhile of those who favored union with Sweden? It was surely fortunate for Christian Frederik that Count Wedel was in Denmark in January 1814, leaving his following leaderless at this critical juncture. A recently discovered draft from early February, in *Kammerherre* Severin Løvenskiold's hand and addressed to the king of Sweden, nonetheless shows the direction of their thinking. It states in the name of the "Norwegian government" that through Frederik VI's renunciation of sovereignty, Norway was now in the "original state" of a nation free to form its own government. It would be prepared to accept union with Sweden on the basis of complete equality, with adequate guarantees for its separate national existence. But if Sweden refused such conditions, the Norwegians would resist by every means, leaving only a "devastated and depopulated land."[69] This program is reminiscent of both Professor Sverdrup's argument to Prince Christian Frederik and—more remotely—the Liikala Note in 1788 from the Finnish Anjala conspirators to Empress Catherine II.

The breakup of the ice on the Skagerrak finally permitted Count Wedel to return by late February to Christiania, where he inveighed against the stupidities of his moonstruck compatriots. He vainly urged Christian Frederik to keep open the channels of negotiation with Stockholm. He and his supporters meanwhile prepared for the approaching constitutional convention. The day was not yet lost, for although they now swam against the emotional tide, Norway might yet be compelled to give way to *force majeure* and accept a union with its more powerful neighbor to the east, as any thoughtful citizen could not but realize.

While there was little advance notice and preparation, elections for the constituent assembly generally proceeded smoothly. Christian Frederik now found it prudent to seek new sources of support. In 1813 he had concentrated on the merchant patriciate, but here, too, Count Wedel had the base of his support and as the weeks passed the prince saw himself abandoned by a number of influential merchants. He now set his main hopes on the public officials and peasants—as Frederik of Hesse had done before him—and used his control of the mainly indirect and on some points rather vague electoral procedures in their favor.

The delegates who assembled at Eidsvoll on 8–9 April 1814 totaled 112, of whom none came from remote Nordland or Finnmark. The rural districts were represented by fifty-four delegates, the towns by twenty-five, the army and navy by thirty-three. More than half—fifty-seven of them—were public officials (including military officers and clergymen), thirty-seven were peasant landholders, thirteen were merchants.[70] Two factions quickly emerged: the "Independence" and "Union" parties. These names are misleading, for many of the Independence men aspired to eventual reunion with Denmark, whereas the Unionists, considering complete independence unattainable, sought a separate existence for Norway as the sine qua non of a union with Sweden. As Yngvar Nielsen put it, "What Count Wedel had sowed in 1809 was for the time being harvested by Christian Frederik." Since the prince, after opening the assembly on 10 April, absented himself from its sessions, Christian Magnus Falsen emerged as the tactical leader of the Independence party, which could generally muster up to eighty votes. Wedel naturally led the Unionists, who could command some thirty votes. Both vied for support among the undecided.[71]

The basic task at hand was to draft a constitution with the least delay. To this end, a committee of fifteen was appointed, including Falsen, Sverdrup, Wedel, Jacob Aall, and Nicolai Wergeland; fourteen were public officials; four were Unionists, the rest, Independence men. By 15 April the constitutional committee was able to present its preliminary proposals. These were then debated in the assembly while the committee received and considered numerous constitutional drafts. The most significant of these, containing 250 paragraphs, was submitted by Falsen and Johan G. Adler. On 2 May the committee presented its own final draft in 112 paragraphs, which as modified in ensuing debate was adopted by the assembly.

As a compromise document, Norway's new constitution contained a minimum of political philosophizing, although it rested firmly upon the principle of popular sovereignty, over which both the Independence and Union parties were in full agreement. It is thus an unadorned statement of fundamental law, reminiscent, in Sverre Steen's view, of the old Norse law codes in its straightforward simplicity.[72] Yet its structure reveals the underlying model of the French constitution of 1791, while details show influences from the Batavian and American constitutions—both federal and state—and the Swedish constitution of 1809, as well as the old *Lex Regia*. It would prove amenable to adaptation to changing circumstances. Since Sweden adopted a new constitution in 1975, Norway's remains the oldest in the world, after the American.

Like both the American and Swedish constitutions, the Norwegian sought a separation between the executive, legislative, and judicial functions. The crown was granted extensive powers, particularly regarding the appointment of officials, the military forces, foreign relations, war and peace. A state council (*statsråd*) of five, appointed by and responsible to the crown, was to advise or to fulfill such assignments as the crown might delegate.

In comparison, the legislature, named the *Storting*, was endowed with relatively limited powers. It was to meet every three years, unless specially convened by the crown, without whose permission its sessions could not exceed three months. While the *Storting* possessed legislative power, the crown held a suspensive veto and was authorized to issue decrees concerning internal order, commerce, customs duties, and economic matters in general. The *Storting* had the power of taxation, whereas the crown had virtually free disposition over revenues, subject to the *Storting*'s review of its accounts. A special state tribunal (*riksrett*) might remove state officials for cause. Judges were assured of the security of tenure essential to an independent judiciary.

The *Storting* was organized on the basis of a modified unicameralism. While all its members were to be elected on the same basis, it thereafter itself elected one-quarter of its membership to a *Lagting* to review and confirm legislation passed by the remaining three-quarters of the *Storting*, which comprised the *Odelting*. If the *Lagting* twice rejected a proposal, it was then voted on in a plenary session of the entire *Storting*, at which a two-thirds majority was required to pass the measure.

The right to vote was conferred upon all males over the age of twenty-five who had resided in the country at least five years; who had served as public officials, owned or for more than five years leased taxable rural land, or held burgher rights in a town in which they owned property worth at least 300 *riksbankdaler* in silver; and who swore to uphold the constitution. Although this franchise was limited, it was substantially wider than in any other European country at that time. Stein Kuhnle has recently calculated that 45.5 percent of all Norwegian men over the age of twenty five, or 10.3 percent of the total population, received the vote in 1814. In contrast, Louis XVIII's Charter, promulgated at the same time, enfranchised only 0.3 percent of France's population; the First British Reform Bill, 10 percent in 1832; the Belgian constitution of 1840, 1.15 percent; and the Swedish electoral reform of 1866, 5 percent.[73] Candidates for the *Storting* were to be residents of their districts, of which two-thirds were to be rural and one-third urban.

In no area was there greater unanimity than regarding basic civil rights and obligations. The constitution guaranteed freedom of expression and from arbitrary arrest, as well as the sanctity of personal property, including the venerable *odel* and *åsete* rights protecting family farms. No new restrictions might be imposed upon economic activity. Freedom of worship was permitted to all Christians, although after some debate Jews and Jesuits were forbidden to enter the kingdom and public officials were required to belong to the Lutheran state church. No new nobles might be created or manorial rights granted. The principle of universal conscription was established, although as in Sweden two years earlier certain exemptions were allowed in practice.[74]

The debates over the constitution, which at times waxed hot, illuminate the conflict between the two factions at Eidsvoll. The Unionists fought stoutly to exclude hindrances to a dynastic union with another state; in this they had some success, for the Independence party did not want to close the door to a possible future reunion with Denmark. But the rivalry concerned not only home rule, but who should rule at home. The Unionists strove vainly for a strong state council and a bicameral legislature with greater powers to counterbalance royal authority. They likewise favored restrictive property qualifications for the vote, which did not exclude a patriarchal concern for the welfare of the common people. They meanwhile succeeded in putting off consideration of existing noble and economic privileges, as well as special exemptions from conscription, until the new *Storting* should meet. Some of these ideas found support within the Independence party as well: the Falsen-Adler draft constitution included a bicameral legislature and would have excluded about half the peasant farmholders from the vote, while Christian Frederik considered a nobility essential to a monarchy. In the main, however, the Independence men were for a strong royal authority and dependent state council, together with a basically unicameral legislature elected by a wide popular franchise.[75]

In this rivalry one may discern differing political temperaments, opposing hardheaded "realists" to warmhearted "romantics." "Should a good cause count for nothing if one cannot calculate with pen and paper the outcome of the struggle?" Claus Pavels mused in April. "If enthusiasm be called day-dreaming and a religious-poetic viewpoint arouse derisive laughter, then farewell human dignity and human felicity."[76] Sectional cleavages are also apparent, with the greatest support for the Union party in Østlandet, the region most dependent upon foreign trade and most affected by war with Britain and Sweden.

But more than that, the Unionists strove to preserve a more "aristocratic" social order—the Norwegian context—whereas the Independence party sought to create a more "democratic" dispensation. In this regard, the social composition of the two factions seems revealing. The leading Unionists were wealthy men of private means: great merchants, ironmasters, landowners. The core of the Independence party consisted of public officials, and although it too included some merchants and even some titular nobles like Falsen, none were as rich as the most prominent Unionists. Knut Mykland thus speaks of what may be called the "patrician" and "bureaucratic" parties. From this perspective their respective orientations toward Sweden and Denmark become more comprehensible. While both parties aspired to constitutional self-government, Sweden had proud traditions of aristocratic parliamentarianism, Denmark of strong kingship and bureaucratic rule. The constitution adopted in May 1814 inclined largely in the latter direction, establishing a powerful royal prerogative and a securely tenured officialdom. In his diary the Unionist G. P. Blom wrote bitterly that the "royalists" had now built "a veritable temple to a new sovereignty upon the burial mound of that which apparently had expired."[77]

The constitution raises a fundamental question. How, Halvdan Koht has asked from his Marxian perspective,

> could the upper classes holding power in Norway in 1814—the bureaucratic and burgher classes—bring themselves to establish a democracy which would *necessarily*—sooner or later—deprive them of their own power? Or more succinctly put: Why did they grant so wide a franchise to the peasant class?[78]

For this there would seem to be various explanations. There was a pressing need for national solidarity in a time of emergency; hence winning the backing of the peasant masses was indispensable. But one may also perceive, as Koht did not, the effects of a long-term tendency—since the administrative reforms following the Lofthuus revolt in 1787—toward a pragmatic alliance between the bureaucracy and the peasantry versus the merchant oligarchy, strengthened by economic conflicts during the years of neutral trade and especially by the recent wartime crises of provisionment in 1808–9 and 1812–13. The so-called Peasant Paragraph of the constitution, allotting two-thirds of the *Storting* seats to the rural districts, was astutely predicated upon the assumption that enfranchised peasant farmers would tend to elect local officials, which indeed was the case for some decades to come.

As in Denmark, the representative of the crown had come to be perceived by the peasant farmer as his advocate against selfish interests, rather than as their defender. The new Norwegian regime was thus in essence the realization of that democratic royalism implicit in the ideal of an "opinion-guided absolutism" as described by Jens Arup Seip, which, he argues, must largely explain how in

1814 Norway could so rapidly metamorphose from part of Europe's theoretically most absolutistic state into its most democratic.[79]

The peasant delegates at Eidsvoll were among the most prosperous and best informed of their class. Among them were parish functionaries, schoolteachers, and noncommissioned officers. Several had been active Haugians. In general, they played little part in the factional rivalry. Most, it would appear, had little interest in constitutional government as such and held instinctively to their traditional belief in a strong and benevolent king. Few, however, voted with the Union party, since the Independence leaders played skillfully upon their prejudices against the hereditary foe, impressing upon them that the Swedish peasant was burdened with far heavier taxes, oppressed by an arrogant nobility, and subject to military service in foreign lands.[80]

Peasant mistrust toward the burghers meanwhile came to the fore. Although the "Peasant Paragraph" of the constitution assured rural voters control of a two-thirds majority of the *Storting* seats, the one-third of the seats to be filled by the far less numerous urban voters gave the latter five times as much representation in proportion to the total population. It was therefore vigorously opposed by the peasant delegates, and indeed only passed by one vote.

The peasant representatives meanwhile had more concrete concerns. A local officer of the peace (*lensmann*), Anders Lysgaard, proposed a whole program of reforms, including the abolition of all hereditary privileges; reduction of the bureaucracy; prohibition of the possession of more farm land than the owner was capable of working with his own hired folk and cotters; restoration of the *odel* right in its older, more restricted form; and an end to controls on sawing timber and distilling alcohol. Demands were thereafter raised among the peasant delegates that only peasants should be entitled to possess and cultivate farmland; that agriculture and the cutting and sawing of timber be reserved for them; that nonpeasants be prohibited from acquiring farms as absentee owners, as well as forest lands or sawmills; and that all remaining church benefices be sold to raise bank capital. None of these proposals passed, nor was the question of exemptions from conscription, which the peasants and military officers strongly opposed, fully settled at Eidsvoll. In effect, the peasant representatives revealed a greater concern with economic and social than with political questions, and while they sought to level the privileges of those above them, they attempted to fortify their own position through new privileges of their own. But as yet they were too few and too inexperienced. Their day would come in the 1830s.

On 17 May 1814 the new constitution was signed and the assembly unanimously elected Christian Frederik to the throne, after a last-minute attempt by the Unionists to defer the election until after the peace. He swore to uphold the constitution and dissolved the Eidsvoll assembly on 19 May. Pastor J. H. Darre of the Independence party privately noted that the assembly, "on the nation's behalf, elected a king—if perhaps only an interim king!"[81]

Indeed, amid the joyous celebration of the Seventeenth of May—which has remained Norway's national holiday—there was much cause for apprehension. Napoleon had abdicated the day after the Eidsvoll assembly had convened. In Paris Karl Johan was able, despite recent frictions, to gain the assurances of his allies, now including Austria, to honor their commitments to help him acquire Norway, thanks largely to Tsar Alexander's support. A Russian corps, encamped outside Hamburg, was placed at his disposal to bring pressure to bear against Denmark. Britain again blockaded Norway by late April and continued its subsidy to Sweden. Karl Johan contemplated a Swedish-Russian attack through Jutland and thence against Norway, after which Denmark might be completely partitioned, leaving Sweden with Sjælland, Fyn, and Bornholm. But the British were opposed to allowing any one power to control both shores of the Sound. On 28 May the crown prince arrived back in Sweden, followed by the main Swedish army.

Both sides sought to promote their goals through negotiation. Already in March Christian Frederik, convinced that Britain's position was critical, had sent Carsten Anker to London. Lord Liverpool's cabinet found it convenient to regard the Norwegian revolt as a Danish conspiracy to obstruct fulfillment of the Peace of Kiel and declined to receive him. Unofficially, Anker was advised that Britain would seek favorable conditions from Sweden, provided the Norwegians repudiated Christian Frederik. Meanwhile, he aroused much sympathy for Norway both inside and outside Parliament.[82] Christian Frederik's soundings elsewhere fared no better. It was apparent that no European government was prepared to recognize Norway's complete independence.

In Copenhagen the Swedish minister made repeated demands that the Treaty of Kiel be fulfilled. On 14 March Frederik Moltke of the revived council strongly urged upon Frederik VI a national *levée en masse*, to bid defiance and defend Denmark's independence and honor. But the latter had by now lost heart and a week later wrote to Christian Frederik, counseling him to transfer Norway to Swedish control as part of a "federative state," to forestall his being deprived by the great powers of the Danish succession.[83] In May commissioners from the great coalition powers arrived in Copenhagen to obtain compliance with the Treaty of Kiel. Alarmed by their representations and by the Russian army corps near Hamburg, Frederik VI forbade all further communication between Denmark and Norway. The great gamble of January had turned into a nightmare.

Christian Frederik meanwhile kept his options open. He was concerned about the allied threat to Denmark, he wrote to Frederik VI on 2 April, but could not deny Norway's right to devise its own government. Honor required that he accept its crown if offered him—if only to establish his son's dynastic claim. Yet if "all Europe" united against Norway, "only this or another assembly could decide whether the nation should by necessity enter into a union with Sweden, . . . and if I could no longer accomplish anything here, I would return to my beloved Denmark."[84]

In the summer of 1813, shortly after Christian Frederik's arrival in Norway as Frederik VI's *statholder*, Count Wedel reputedly told him that if he did not place himself at the head of an independent Norway, expel Karl Johan from Sweden, and unite the Peninsula, the reverse would take place. By the spring of 1814 the prince was increasingly preoccupied with the hope that neither the coalition powers nor the Swedish people could long abide Bernadotte, and that once he fell with the other "Napoleonides," the way would be cleared for his own election as successor in Sweden and thus for a federative Scandinavian union. In June C. M. Falsen published an impassioned appeal for resistance to union with Sweden under a "true French military despotism," while holding out the prospect of a free and honorable union under the "Nordic" Prince Christian Frederik. Pastor Pavels, stirred by reports from Copenhagen, meanwhile envisioned a possible popular uprising in Denmark, leading to a constitution and reunion with Norway.[85] But ultimately the decision remained with the great powers.

On 31 May a special envoy reached Christiania from London, bringing assurance of Britain's support for Norway's autonomy under its own constitution in a union with Sweden. At a meeting of the state council a week later, the decision was made to convene the *Storting* to consider the British proposal. To give a show of determination, however, the government mobilized the army to confront the Swedish forces now assembling across the border.

The allied commission arrived from Copenhagen on 30 June, and Christian Frederik appealed to principles their own governments had recently proclaimed:

> I must avow that I have put my confidence in the great powers, that the same principles that have guided them in their efforts to liberate other peoples should likewise determine their conduct toward the Norwegian people, that they should not, at the very moment they are restoring freedom to the peoples of Germany and Spain, put the Norwegians in chains.

It was to no avail. The coalition powers, faced with the reconstruction of Europe following the Napoleonic maelstrom, were not to be impressed with such rhetoric. "Public opinion and the rights of peoples," Christian Frederik noted dejectedly, "seem to mean nothing to these gentlemen. Several times I heard Steigentisch [the Austrian commissioner] say scornfully: 'The people, bah! The people have nothing to say in the sovereigns' councils; that would turn the world upside down.' "[86] And he himself had abandoned the high ground of legitimism in February for the revolutionary principle of popular sovereignty.

Sympathetic as some of its members were toward Norway—or unsympathetic toward Bernadotte—the commission could only offer to seek favorable terms from Sweden. Christian Frederik could not refuse their mediation. It was no longer a question of whether he should abdicate, but when and under what conditions.

Through the allied commission Christian Frederik offered his terms. He was prepared to relinquish the crown to Karl XIII if the *Storting* convened and demanded his abdication, provided Norway remained a separate realm under its new constitution. He declined to turn over the border fortresses to the Swedes in the interim and demanded an immediate end to the blockade.

Karl Johan broke off negotiations and on 26 July launched an attack on Norway. The Norwegian army fought bravely, but its adversary was superior in numbers—some 45,000 versus 25,000 men—as well as in matériel, experience, and leadership. Secretly informed of the Norwegians' defensive plans, the Swedes handily outmaneuvered them.

Already a few days after the hostilities began, Karl Johan secretly initiated negotiations for an armistice on the basis that Christian Frederik immediately abdicate executive power to the state council and leave Norway. The latter, although no general, was an astute negotiator. Karl Johan offered a highly significant concession: Norway might retain the Eidsvoll constitution, subject only to revisions permitting a union with Sweden, the latter to be worked out between the king of Sweden and the *Storting*.[87] While he had repeatedly promised Norway its own constitution, he had not previously recognized that prepared by what he considered an insurgent assembly. On these terms an armistice was concluded in the Convention of Moss on 14 August, less than three weeks after the outbreak of hostilities. Christian Frederik had rendered his last service to Norway, the news of which was received with mingled incredulity, outrage, and relief. In the event, the armistice ended Sweden's last war in modern times, and Norway's, until the German invasion of 1940.

One cannot but wonder why Karl Johan broke off negotiations so abruptly and resorted to war, then on his own initiative so promptly offered the Norwegians peace on essentially the same basis as previously, indeed on terms similar to what Christian Frederik himself had finally been prepared to concede, when he could have pressed his military advantage and imposed harsher conditions. Again, sources are lacking for any direct answer, but several important considerations suggest themselves.

Christian Frederik could surely have been compelled to offer further concessions, but negotiations would have dragged out in time, and time was crucial. If military action were to cut the Gordian knot, it would have to be taken promptly, before the end of the brief Nordic summer. Not only was Karl Johan's sensitive personal prestige at stake—within chauvinistic circles in Sweden as well as abroad—but mediation by the coalition powers might lead to binding restrictions upon a Norwegian-Swedish union. Moreover, as Karl Johan had stated repeatedly, it was Frederik VI's obligation under the Treaty of Kiel to deliver Norway to Karl XIII; thus Sweden would not be bound to fulfill its commitments to Denmark under the treaty if it had to use force to acquire Norway. By resorting to war, Sweden could quickly consummate the union without foreign intervention and it could avoid relinquishing its Pomeranian territory and paying a subsidy to Denmark of one million *riksdaler*. In Norway, despite widespread defeatism, national pride meanwhile required that honor be upheld, however briefly.

The basic purposes of the war for both sides were thus accomplished virtually with the first shot. Karl Johan still hoped to win over the Norwegians through liberal concessions. He thus refrained from inflicting a humiliating defeat upon them and offered union under face-saving conditions preserving the appearance of popular consent. While the Swedes had quickly demonstrated their military superiority, they had no assurance of a prompt or easy victory should the Norwegians continue the fight from the mountainous interior, especially with the approach of winter. The behavior of the coalition powers was unpredictable in the event of a prolonged crisis in the North, while the widespread popularity of the Norwegian cause in Britain was particularly disquieting. The powers were furthermore due to meet shortly in Vienna to work out a general European peace settlement, and Karl Johan could count on scant sympathy at what promised to be a strongly legitimist conclave. Finally, too, he was informed by Mme. de Staël and others in France that the restored Bourbon monarchy was by no means secure. Liberal behavior in Norway might yet prove a strong recommendation in France if its throne should again fall vacant.

The Norwegian state council called for elections to a *storting*, which convened in Christiania on 7 October. Of its seventy-nine members, no fewer than fifty were public officials, whereas eighteen were peasants, nine merchants, and three mariners; again time was too short to obtain representatives from the two northern *stifter*. Only eighteen of its members had been at Eidsvoll. Of the leading Unionists who had been there, only Wedel was reelected, although he was naturally destined to play a leading role.[88] The large majority, composed of former supporters of the Independence party, found a new leader in Wilhelm Christie from Bergen. Wedel, disillusioned by what he considered his countrymen's quixotic irresponsibility and the personal abuse he had received from his opponents, had come to favor a close union with Sweden through the revision of both countries' constitutions to make them essentially similar, a demand which now held little appeal for either side.[89] Christie and his followers—like their Finnish colleagues at the Borgå diet in 1809—strove to protect and strengthen the existing constitution as the bulwark of autonomy within a union with a stronger power.

Already on 10 October the *Storting* received Christian Frederik's abdication and the latter departed for Copenhagen. After a lively debate, distinguished by ringing declarations of Norway's rightful freedom, the *Storting* on 20 October voted, by a majority of seventy-two to five, to accept union with Sweden. Significantly, however, it deferred consideration of any constitutional changes and of the formal election of the king—in that order. It was apparent that, like the Eidsvoll assembly, it would follow that good Swedish maxim from 1809: "constitution first, then king."

Karl Johan, in nearby Frederikshald, communicated with the *Storting* through a Swedish commission in Christiania. To prepare the way for a closer union in the future, he sought in particular to obtain the right of the crown to create new nobles in Norway, to grant or deny naturalization as Norwegian citizens, to appoint subjects of one kingdom to positions in the other, to name the speaker of the *Storting*, and to dispose freely over the military forces of both kingdoms. He nonetheless hesitated to push the *Storting* too hard, lest this produce further delay. As long as it accepted Karl XIII as king, he did not care whether this were through "recognition" or "election." Provided the vital interests of Sweden and the union were protected, Karl Johan left it to the discretion of his commissioners "to agree to anything which, by contributing to mutual confidence between the nations, may further convince the Norwegian people that it is not its oppression but rather the mutual advantages of both kingdoms that is the object of the desired union."[90] For the present he was satisfied that the Eidsvoll constitution allotted extensive powers to the crown, especially in foreign policy and military matters. The experience of the past quarter-century meanwhile convinced the former Napoleonic marshal that there was no constitution that could not eventually be modified.

Christie and the majority in the *Storting* skillfully exploited Karl Johan's anxiety to avoid delay and on one point after the other exacted concessions. The Swedish commissioners backed down regarding new ennoblements, naturalization, mutual eligibility for official appointments, and the speaker of the *Storting*, while only after hard bargaining and Karl Johan's threat to end the armistice did it agree to allow small detachments of the Swedish and Norwegian armies to exercise together at stated intervals and the use of Norwegian troops in an offensive war outside Norway with the consent of the *Storting*. The Swedish commissioners also accepted the stipulation that the crown consult with the Norwegian, as well as the Swedish, state council before declaring war or concluding peace. Thus both the council and the *Storting* gained a stronger and more independent position than originally envisioned at Eidsvoll. It would indeed appear that the Swedish commission, which included members of the Swedish state council, did not vigorously oppose—or that it even quietly encouraged—these checks and balances, owing to apprehensions over the crown prince's autocratic propensities in Sweden.[91]

Karl Johan's patience grew thin with the approach of winter and of the Congress of Vienna. At last, on 4 November, the *Storting* "elected and recognized"

Karl XIII as Norway's king.[92] Five days later, Karl Johan made his long-awaited entry into Christiania.

Thus the Norwegian-Swedish union was finally realized, although under singularly ambivalent circumstances. Karl Johan himself had guaranteed Norway a separate constitution in the Treaty of Kiel but seven months later had concluded the Convention of Moss with a de facto Norwegian government and recognized its constitution without reference to the Kiel treaty. The juridical status of the union thus remained open to future controversy, with the Swedes claiming that the *Storting* had "recognized" their rightful king under the Treaty of Kiel and the Norwegians maintaining that it had freely "elected" him under the existing Eidsvoll constitution.

For both sides, the union was both a victory and a defeat. Although Norway had been unable to maintain complete national sovereignty, its inhabitants could find much consolation. The diarist Pavels, who in June had feared "heavier chains than we have ever borne before," could ask himself in August why Norway should continue to fight:

To be called Norwegian rather than Swede? We retain that name as long as the constitution is honored with as much right as when we were under Denmark's sovereign king, and when personal respect no longer binds us to an individual, it is quite incidental where the constitutional king lives or what his name is. . . . It might happen that he later tries to slip the fetters of slavery onto us, but where the nation, under the constitution, has so much to say, it would immediately notice and condemn any attempt upon our rights—and if they are not then respected, then let it rise up en masse![93]

In February 1814 Baron Armfelt in St. Petersburg had foreseen that "Norway will be more of an encumbrance than a gain to Sweden." Karl XIII, who according to his queen had hoped at first "to rule over the Norwegians on the same basis as the king of Denmark," and much chauvinist opinion in Sweden were greatly upset by the lenient Convention of Moss and final form of the union. In late September Hans Järta asked prophetically, if "Sweden's and Norway's constitutional, moral, and economic conditions are not woven together early, what can, after a century or perhaps before, keep the Norwegian people from resuming the fight for independence it has now attempted?"[94]

For the present, however, the union was the great personal triumph Karl Johan considered essential to consolidate his position in Sweden and Europe, and it at last secured lasting peace and security to the Scandinavian peninsula after centuries of conflict.

An epilogue to the Norwegian *Storting*, which Karl Johan dissolved in person on 26 February 1815, was the special Swedish *Riksdag* convened in the same month to confirm the union. The constitutional relationship between the two kingdoms was set forth in an Act of Union, which following review by the *Storting* was promulgated on 6 August 1815.

The *Riksdag* of 1815 was otherwise necessarily concerned mainly with financial matters, in the lively discussion of which a new parliamentary leader, Count Fredrik Boguslaus von Schwerin, emerged in the Noble Estate. He had opposed press controls at the *Riksdag* of 1812 and now undertook to form a "loyal opposition" on the British model, evoking Karl Johan's memorable outburst: "*Opposition, c'est conspiration!*"[95] The small opposition in 1815 made no appreciable difference, but it was the harbinger of a revival of Swedish party politics within the following decade.

Both Sweden and Denmark were reckoned among the smaller powers at the Congress of Vienna, held between September 1814 and June 1815, but both had vital interests to protect. Karl Johan in Stockholm was anxious that neither Norway's new status nor Sweden's refusal to compensate Denmark according to the Treaty of Kiel after the Norwegian campaign be called into question. He was meanwhile apprehensive of reported legitimist cabals against him in Vienna.

In the end, he need not have worried. For Tsar Alexander, the union of Norway with Sweden and the stability of the Bernadotte succession were his firmest guarantees for the union of the Grand Duchy of Finland with the Russian Empire, hence of the future stability of the North. As he explained to Lord Castlereagh:

> My capital had become impregnable, while Sweden, better concentrated, no longer had anything to fear. In this way both sides gained in security and all cause for dissention and alarm had been eliminated. If the laws of balance are not to be found herein, I know not where to look for them.[96]

Although Finland's new situation, like Norway's, was kept off the agenda in Vienna, it played its indirect role by demonstrating the type of regime Alexander I envisioned for the new Congress Poland.

Denmark seemed to be faced with even greater perils by the early fall of 1814. It had been grievously mutilated by the loss of Norway. Not only did Sweden now refuse to give the compensation promised in the Treaty of Kiel, but it proclaimed the treaty itself invalidated, thus technically renewing a state of war. Russia had still not ratified a peace treaty with Denmark, and a Russian corps of some 45,000 men, encamped on Holstein soil following the French capitulation of Hamburg, stood at Karl Johan's disposal, which might overrun the duchies and Jutland. Denmark's military situation was hopeless; its finances in ruins. It was meanwhile feared that the Congress of Vienna would construct a new Germany including Holstein. Rumors were rife. The monarchy's very existence seemed in jeopardy.

Actually, the danger was by this time more apparent than real. The allied commission that visited Copenhagen in May and June 1814 had reported Denmark to be innocent of violating the Treaty of Kiel, while Britain had vetoed Karl Johan's flight of fancy concerning an invasion and partition of the Danish monarchy—thus to some imponderable degree making late amends for the attack on Copenhagen in 1807 and the disasters that had followed.

Frederik VI was still sufficiently alarmed to depart—secretly and uninvited—for Vienna in early September 1814. There was little he could do but wander the corridors of power, a forlorn but not unsympathetic figure, seeking to buttonhole any available listener. At last he returned to Copenhagen the following spring, leaving Denmark's interests in Vienna to Christian Bernstorff.

The congress was interrupted by Napoleon's return from Elba in March 1815 and the ensuing "Hundred Days." The allies quickly renewed their coalition, this time including Denmark but not Sweden. Faced with its staggering treasury deficits, Denmark was reduced to begging the allies to let its troops participate so that they might be supported by a British subsidy. Although they arrived too late for Waterloo, a small Danish contingent took part in the allied occupation of northern France in 1815–18. Karl Johan again entertained some hope that the call might come from France, but Louis XVIII was restored to his unstable throne.

Through bilateral agreements the final settlement in the North was reached in June 1815. Sweden sold Swedish Pomerania and Rügen to Prussia for 3,500,000 Prussian *Reichstaler* (4,800,000 *riksdaler*), from which were debited 430,000 *Reichstaler* toward Prussia's compensation to Denmark for failing to acquire those lands. Prussia also secretly undertook to pay 1,550,000 *Reichstaler* (2,125,714 *riksdaler*) to Karl Johan personally, while Russia canceled Sweden's debt of 1,500,000 rubels (700,000 *riksdaler*) for loans under the Åbo agreement, in favor of the Swedish king and crown prince. Because Britain, contrary to the Anglo-Swedish alliance pact of March 1813, had returned Guadeloupe to France, it paid 4,000,000 *riksdaler* in compensation directly to Karl Johan, to whom the *Riksdag* of 1812 had allotted all income from overseas possessions. These personal payments provided de facto compensation to Karl Johan for the sacrifice of his imperial appanages in 1810. Since the "Guadeloupe Fund" was promptly used to liquidate Sweden's foreign debt, the *Riksdag* of 1815 undertook to pay the sum of 200,000 *riksdaler* annually to the royal family in perpetuity. It continues to be paid today.

Denmark received from Prussia the small duchy of Lauenburg, bordering on Holstein, and some 3,000,000 *rigsdaler*, including the amount debited against Prussia's payment to Sweden. Britain retained Heligoland, while returning Denmark's East and West Indian possessions. Although the king of Denmark remained duke of Holstein, that duchy and Lauenburg, which had previously both belonged to the Holy Roman Empire, were included in the new Germanic

Confederation, which involved an obligation to establish representative assemblies there, a commitment long unheeded in Copenhagen.[97]

Throughout the period from 1760 to 1815, no half-decade was more momentous than that which brought the era to its close. During these years the great transformation of the political geography of the North which had begun with Finland's separation from Sweden and attachment to the Russian Empire was completed by Norway's separation from Denmark and attachment to Sweden. As had long been foreseen, both were inextricably bound together, parts of a single process of territorial and strategic realignment.

In the process, internal changes took place throughout the North. The loss of Finland had precipitated a libertarian revolution in Sweden, but while the new Swedish constitution of 1809 was retained, it came by 1815 to be applied in a far more conservative spirit than its framers had intended.

Although the Norwegians—like the Finns before them—had not themselves sought to break their ancient political ties, Norway, like Finland, obtained its own constitution, and indeed one more liberal than any in the Europe of that time. It was, moreover, drafted with remarkably little friction. Historians have often attributed much of the tumult of revolutionary France to a lack of political experience under the old regime. From this perspective, the political maturity and realism shown by Norway's leaders in 1814 is impressive. Yet for all their factional disputes, they belonged to a small elite—the "Generation of 1814"—largely homogeneous socially and culturally, indeed often interrelated, within an administratively unified land.

The remainder of the Danish monarchy was likewise transformed to a high degree. Already in the spring of 1813, Fritz Reventlow of Emkendorf wrote to his brother Cai that "next to separation from Denmark," the Duchies could wish for nothing better than for Denmark to lose Norway in return for compensation in Germany, so that the resulting combination "could not be separated from the Germanic body." The balance between Danes and Germans would thereby be redressed in favor of *Deutschtum*.[98] His hopes—and Frederik VI's apprehensions—would be largely fulfilled. The inclusion of Holstein in the Germanic Confederation of 1815 thereafter prevented any direct incorporation of both Holstein and Schleswig into the kingdom. Frederik VI's policy of 1806 was thus decisively defeated, despite later nineteenth-century attempts to promote a *helstat*, or integral state. The duchies, including Lauenburg, now comprised close to half the monarchy's European territory and more than 40 percent of its reduced population of about one and a half million. This would set the stage for an increasingly intransigent confrontation between Dane and German within what had become an essentially federative union, not unlike the others that had just come into existence in the North.

In pondering the events of the Scandinavian world in these years, one cannot but again reflect upon the role of the individual in history. Without discounting long-term geopolitical trends, it is virtually impossible to envision the actual course of events apart from the actions in particular of Napoleon and Alexander I without, and of Karl Johan, Christian Frederik, and Frederik VI within.

Of Karl Johan, it has been said that in electing him their crown prince, the Swedes guessed wrong but chose right.[99] Surely nothing would have seemed more obvious in 1810, when Napoleon was at the zenith of his power, than that his former marshal should join in the assault on Russia and restore Finland to Sweden. That he should instead defy both his own and his adopted country's traditional loyalties was one of the most dramatic *renversements* of the Napoleonic era and surely something no one else could have accomplished. In retrospect it is tempting to see in it an essential turning point in Napoleon's fortunes, as both contemporaries and later historians in Sweden have often tended to do. "Those familiar with events, and especially circumstances in 1812 and 1813," wrote Count Trolle-Wachtmeister in his memoirs, ". . . know that Napoleon would not have fallen if the crown prince had not cooperated." On St. Helena in 1816, Napoleon himself called Bernadotte "the snake we sheltered in our bosom" and "one of the chief active causes of our ruin," who had given his enemies "the key to our policies and to the tactics of our armies" and "showed them the roads across the sacred soil."[100] While the importance of his role remains imponderable in this respect, he would prove to be the only "Napoleonide" to retain a European crown and found a lasting dynasty. Meanwhile, by combining constancy of purpose with flexibility of means, Karl Johan succeeded, against heavy odds, in unifying the Scandinavian peninsula. That the old Jacobin should furthermore prove a stern authoritarian conservative was also something various of his backers in 1810 had hardly reckoned on.

Christian Frederik has received his share of criticism, at the time and since, for shortcomings of both character and policy.[101] Yet the twenty-four-year-old prince, who previously had been excluded from any real responsibility, emerged in 1813–14 as a political leader of impressive ability. Although his efforts did not succeed in preserving Norway's dynastic tie with Denmark, they did permit the Norwegians to create their own state and thereafter to negotiate for an acceptable union with Sweden.

In contrast to these two practitioners of politics as the art of the possible, Frederik VI is significant during these years mainly for his failings as a statesman and general. Stubbornly attached to absolutism, centralization, and the integrity of the existing monarchy, he consistently gave way too late and only half-heartedly to the imperative pressure of events. He failed to act promptly and imaginatively in the Swedish succession crises of 1809 and 1810; to undercut Sweden by joining its allies in early 1813; or later the same year to permit Norway to do so separately. One wonders, for instance, what might have happened if he had encouraged Christian Frederik to proclaim a separate kingdom in Norway—to be reunited with Denmark upon his succession there—*before*, rather than after, the Peace of Kiel. But such a bold move was quite beyond him. There was little he could do to support his cousin in 1814, and in Vienna he cut a pitiful figure. Yet upon his return to Denmark in the spring of 1815, he was enthusiastically welcomed by his people, for whom he had ever remained a symbol of pride and rectitude in the face of overwhelming odds. His limitations and misjudgments in the international arena did not dim the accomplishments of the enlightened autocrat, who even in 1814—amid military defeat and financial ruin—could still complete the great edifice of internal reform he had begun as a young prince in happier times.

CHAPTER 14

# Conclusions
# Scandinavia by 1815

In July 1815, the month after Napoleon's final defeat at Waterloo and the conclusion of the Congress of Vienna, Frederik VI held his belated coronation in
Roskilde cathedral, surrounded by medieval pageantry and the tombs of his
ancestors since the days of the Valdemars. This costly ritual—against the background of Denmark's postwar exhaustion and impoverishment—may stand as a
milepost, not only in Denmark but throughout the North. It would be followed,
three years later, by the crowning of King Karl XIV Johan in the medieval cathe-
drals of Stockholm and Trondheim. The revolutionary era had run its course.
"At times my diary arouses sensations like those I imagine must be felt upon
treading Classic ground," Claus Pavels reflected in March 1815, "and if one
compares its present low, prosaic tone with the great events it once displayed
. . . generations seem to lie between these two periods—and yet it is only a few
months!"[1] As elsewhere in Europe, the decade and a half beginning in 1815
would be a time of cautious political and social conservatism, of economic stagnation and slow recovery, following the Napoleonic upheaval. Not until the
1830s would the pulse of economic and political life again begin to quicken.

Thus 1815 clearly marks the end of an era. Because the Nordic lands lay on
the periphery of the European continent, outside the well-beaten thoroughfares
of diplomacy and war, because they were too sparsely populated and poor in
resources to weigh heavily in the balance of power, because their voluminous
historical literatures remain largely locked away in languages known to few
foreign scholars, this epoch—like most others in their history—remains generally *terra incognita* to the outside world. Little has been said about the North
in the general histories, and what has been said has all too often been erroneous.

Jacques Godechot largely summarized the view of international scholarship when he stated in 1956 that Scandinavia during this era "remained calm."[2]

The present study should surely have disabused the reader of any such conception. The period is, however, of great significance, for although the Nordic lands were never invaded, occupied, or reorganized by revolutionary or Napoleonic France, they underwent by 1815 as fundamental a transformation—territorially, dynastically, constitutionally, economically, socially, and culturally—as any part of the Western world.

In the first volume of his *Age of the Democratic Revolution*, R. R. Palmer argued in 1959 that the whole of Western civilization was swept during the last four decades of the eighteenth century by

> a single revolutionary movement, which manifested itself in different ways and with varying success in different countries, yet in all of them showed similar objectives and principles. . . . Revolutionary aims and sympathies existed throughout Europe and America. They arose everywhere out of local, genuine, and specific causes; or, otherwise, they reflected conditions that were universal throughout the Western World.[3]

By the same token, the forces of conservatism and counterrevolution rallied around the same standards throughout the West. Palmer's thesis has not lacked its critics.[4] Yet the example of the Nordic lands—particularly when the period is extended to 1815—substantiates Palmer's basic view to a considerably greater degree than he himself realized when he formulated it. Not least, his concept of a three-cornered struggle between autocracy, aristocracy, and democracy (in the eighteenth-century sense) is repeatedly illustrated in both Scandinavian monarchies.[5]

The essential problems confronting the North were recognized already by 1760: in Denmark and the duchies the peasant problem called for reform, on both practical and ideal grounds; in Sweden parliamentary liberty was degenerating into party strife, cut across by social conflict, hazardous to both public order and national security; Norway, Finland, and the duchies were restive within their traditional subordinate status; the independence and integrity of both Scandinavian monarchies were increasingly precarious within the European arena, due in large part to persistent rivalry and suspicion between them. The basic solutions to these problems were likewise envisioned during the crucial decade of the 1760s, even if their realization was sometimes long delayed.

Scandinavia, in common with the rest of the Western world, was subjected to the effects of war, at home and abroad, in 1757–63, 1775–83, 1788–90, 1792–1815, including erratic swings between prosperity and impoverishment, and effective pressures for internal reforms to provide for military needs. At the same time, the North was open and receptive to the intellectual crosscurrents of the secular Enlightenment, religious pietisms, and romantic sensibility. Political and social crises abroad—especially in Britain, America, France, and French-dominated Europe—intensified and dramatized its own domestic conflicts and rivalries.

The economic transformation then gaining momentum, most notably in Great Britain, made deep inroads into an ancient and traditional way of life in Scandinavia. Although its industrial side would hardly affect the Nordic lands before the mid-nineteenth century, in its agrarian aspect it strikingly illustrates E. J. Hobsbawn's view of the sociopolitical and the economic revolutions of the period, centered on opposite sides of the Channel, as the "twin crater" of a single "larger regional volcano," whose eruption basically transformed life in the Western world.[6]

Certainly the most visible changes of the period were territorial. In no other part of Europe was the map redrawn in more drastic or lasting fashion. Both Sweden and Denmark lost vast domains, ancient and integral parts of their respective realms. Yet while Sweden ceded Finland to the Russian tsar and Denmark relinquished Norway to the Swedish king, both these lands gained self-rule under their own constitutions. Norway thus recovered an autonomy lost in 1536, whereas Finland became a separate political entity for the first time in its history. In effect, the two Scandinavian monarchies of 1760 had become by 1815 four Nordic nations under three monarchs.

By the 1790s a new idea gained currency, that of uniting the existing kingdoms to form a greater Scandinavian state. While this appealed on cultural grounds to many intellectuals, especially in Copenhagen, it also offered the obvious practical solution to the perennial weakness of the North in the face of the greater European powers. Unsuccessful attempts were made to bring such a Scandinavian union into being in connection with the Swedish succession crises of 1809 and 1810. Their failure was nonetheless no foregone conclusion under the unsettled conditions of those years, and a united Scandinavia might well have proved more durable in the long run than the Finnish-Russian, Norwegian-Swedish, or indeed the Irish-British or Belgian-Dutch unions established in that period.[7]

From the geopolitical standpoint, however, the territorial reorganization of 1809–15 realized the essential objectives of political Scandinavianism, since it established natural frontiers between formerly rival powers and removed the underlying bases of their enmity in Finland and Norway. Strategically, the Scandinavian peninsula became an "island," surrounded on three sides by water and on the fourth by a sub-Arctic wilderness. Sweden's cession of Ducal Pomerania in 1815 eliminated its last foothold on the far side of the Baltic and a potential source of conflict with Prussia.

By 1815, Sam Clason wrote, "Sweden, the Baltic state, was dead, the peninsular state had been born." Indeed, the territorial settlement transformed both

Denmark and Sweden from extended maritime to concentrated continental states.[8]

Geopolitical reorganization led to ethnic consolidation. While neither of the older monarchies were seriously disturbed by separatist discontents, awareness of cultural and historical distinctiveness had been growing in both Finland and Norway throughout the period and would, sooner or later, have led to mounting friction with Sweden and Denmark respectively. What this might eventually have involved is suggested by the subsequent history of the Norwegian-Swedish union until its dissolution in 1905 and of the Finnish-Russian union until it ended in 1917, as well as by Iceland's relations with Denmark until it achieved full independence in 1944.

In the event, the emergence of five fully sovereign Nordic states by the present century has provided a firm foundation for what presently amounts to a kind of super-state in the North, through voluntary cooperation on a basis of national equality.

Meanwhile, the most pronounced ethnic schism of the period 1760–1815, between Danes and Germans, did not result in separation by 1815. The Danish monarchy, with the duchies, remained the exception in the North, being in effect less ethnically consolidated than before during the next half-century, until the loss of the duchies to Prussia in 1864. Denmark's southern frontier would not be redrawn along ethnic lines until 1920, finally completing the process begun in the North in 1809–15.

The overall results of territorial and ethnic concentration would be the long peace in the North and the possibilities for internal development it allowed. Sweden has not fought a war since 1814; Norway and Finland were spared until World War II. Denmark, owing to the problem of the duchies, would be less fortunate, having to fight rear-guard actions in 1848–49 and in 1864, before it too was drawn into World War II. Not disregarding these exceptions, the long Pax Nordica has been of inestimable importance for the evolution of a distinctive way of life and values in the North.

No less significant were the political and administrative developments of the period. The Napoleonic wars brought about changes of dynasty in Sweden, Finland, and Norway, replacing Vasas and Oldenburgs with Bernadottes and Romanovs. Only Denmark remained under its old royal house.

The years between 1760 and 1815 bear witness to profound changes of attitude toward the state. No longer could it be regarded as no more than the sum total of the ruling prince's domains and as such the extension of the sovereign and his dynastic interests. Increasingly the state emerged in informed public opinion as a whole greater than its parts, distinct from the monarch and his particular regime, a means to the public weal rather than an end in itself. "Must one serve the king? Must one serve the state?"[9] Thus the younger Count Fersen expressed the dilemma confronting himself and his peers in 1789. It was a central question many others—in the North and beyond—would find themselves asking in the troubled years up to 1815.

Such a shift from traditional to conditional loyalties has been seen in different contexts and judged accordingly. Finnish historians of the older school stressed the weakening of the moral fiber of the Swedish-Finnish state through the individualistic and utilitarian values of the Enlightenment, leading to the ignominy of 1808-9.[10] Conversely, the Danes have taken pride in steadfast loyalty to their king in the face of adversity. Historians in Sweden, Norway, Schleswig-Holstein, and even Iceland—like their English, American, and French counterparts—have tended to vindicate the concept of a revocable social contract based on the natural rights of the individual and the common good.

Among contemporary European monarchs, none identified himself with the ideal of the "first servant of the state" more conscientiously than Frederik VI. He himself recognized, at least obliquely, what others in his lands on occasion expressed more directly: that his regime legitimized itself only so long as it provided for the welfare of the nation and its citizens. In Denmark there were few murmurs of discontent, even amid the tribulations of war and economic collapse. In the duchies, however, there were those who denied that the government served their best interests and who were prepared to conclude that they would be morally justified in seceding from the Danish state.

Having been seized from Sweden by military force, Finland in 1809 was permitted by its new sovereign, the autocrat of all the Russias, to retain Gustav III's constitution of 1772, as amended in 1789, the first of the Nordic constitutions of the period. Under the impact of military defeat, the Swedes in 1809 renounced the same constitution in favor of a new one restoring a balance between the crown and the nation's representatives. The Norwegians went farthest in 1814, repudiating Europe's theoretically most complete absolutism for the last constitution of this era and the most liberal in Europe in its time.

Norway established a semi-unicameral legislature elected on a broad liberal franchise. Sweden would not abandon representation through its four Estates until they were replaced by a bicameral legislature in 1866, whereas Finland—the last European country to retain the medieval Estates system—would make the full jump to a unicameral legislature elected through the universal suffrage of both sexes in 1906, a leap comparable to Norway's nearly a century earlier.

Throughout the period there are striking parallels between Finland and Norway. A question that has much concerned historians has been the degree to which the Finns and the Norwegians during the eighteenth century—in particular after 1760—evolved into self-conscious and self-sufficient national entities, capable of managing their own affairs and both preserving and developing separate cultures by 1809-14. It has been seen how the populations and economic importance of both lands increased greatly during the period. In many respects they became more closely integrated than ever before, administratively, eco-nomically, and culturally, with Sweden and Denmark, as Lars G. von Bonsdorff in particular has argued for Finland and Hans Jensen for Norway.[11]

Yet at the same time, growing population, wealth, and relative importance within their respective realms also brought increased awareness in both Finland and Norway of particular regional interests, thus grievances against the central-izing policies of Stockholm and Copenhagen, especially in times of economic or military crisis. The pre-romantic mood, from the 1760s on, fostered a height-ened pride in the unique cultural values preserved in rich folk traditions, and in Norway's case in a proud medieval past before the union with Denmark. In both Finland and Norway, small coteries among the elite classes—nobility and patri-ciate, respectively—felt moved, already in the 1770s and 1780s, to speculate about breaking old political bonds to form new unions with Russia and Sweden, anticipating the final settlement of 1809–14. Yet surely more significant was a growing and assertive self-awareness among the broader strata of society, mani-fested by the Lofthuus and Haugean movements in Norway and, as Pentti Ren-vall has argued, by an increasingly self-conscious solidarity among the Finnish representatives in the Swedish *riksdagar* between 1762 and 1800, particularly within the Peasant Estate.[12] No less important were the high and constantly ris-ing proportions of native-born civil, ecclesiastical, and military officials at all levels in both Finland and Norway during the period, as well as their evidently growing preference to serve at home, rather than in Sweden or Denmark.[13]

There can be little doubt that had the Russians retained all of Finland in 1721 or 1743, the country would scarcely have been prepared to undertake the man-agement of its own affairs; Swedish Finland would surely have been reduced by necessity to the same status as Russian "Old" Finland or the Baltic Provinces. According to Einar Juva, Finland was no better prepared in 1788.[14] Similarly, had Karl XII seized Norway in 1718 or Gustav III done so in 1772, its incorpora-tion in a manner similar to the Danish and Norwegian provinces annexed by Sweden in the seventeenth century might not have been out of the question.

With few exceptions, neither Finns nor Norwegians had desired to break their existing ties in 1809–14. But when compelled by circumstance to assume re-sponsibility for their separate political existence, they proved admirably pre-pared by the experience of recent decades. Until the end of the eighteenth cen-tury, political tutelage under Stockholm and Copenhagen had served them well in fostering their internal growth and development. But by then they were reach-ing the point of diminishing returns, after which their subordinate status within larger, centralized states would have impeded progress. For the immediate future internal autonomy within federative unions would provide scope for their ongoing development.

By 1815 there were constitutional regimes in three of the Nordic lands: most conservative in Finland, most liberal in Norway, with Sweden in between. Denmark remained the exception: just as it retained its old dynasty, it would continue to be ruled under the royal absolutism established in 1660 for the next thirty-four years. Yet underlying similarities with the other Nordic countries were greater than they might seem. In 1813–14 Frederik VI abandoned his attempts at personal autocracy and restored the Danish state council; in 1815 he was compelled to accept practical limitations to his powers in the duchies. Thereafter, it was above all the bureaucracy that governed the Danish state—as it had, less effectively, in 1760. The same was no less true in Finland, where the tsar-grand dukes did not see fit to convene the Estates from 1809 until 1863. Sweden, after 1809–14, was essentially more administered than ruled until the *Riksdag* gradually assumed a more active and independent role by the 1830s, while the commanding position of the bureaucracy in Norway, both in drafting the constitution of 1814 and in the *Storting* for at least the next decade and a half is unmistakable. In both kingdoms the strong hand of Karl Johan would be everywhere apparent to the end of his reign in 1844.

It seems paradoxical that the period associated with the birth—or rebirth—of constitutional liberty likewise witnessed the culmination of the bureaucratic state (the *embedsstat* or *ämbetsstat*) throughout the North. This latter development was, of course, part of an overall growth of administrative power and efficiency throughout the Western world between the Seven Years' War and the end of the Napoleonic conflict, arising both from military demands upon the state and from the appeal of the Enlightenment for strong government as the necessary instrument of humanitarian reform. While the Swedish and Danish monarchies engaged in protracted hostilities only during the last years of the period, impending threats to Finland and Norway, Schleswig-Holstein and Swedish Pomerania, as well as to neutral commerce, placed a premium upon effective government. The implementation of the great reforms of the period, ameliorating the social, material, and cultural conditions of the Nordic peoples as a whole, in turn depended upon the power of the crown and the competence, dedication, and honesty of its servants.

Royal autocracy and centralization reached their height in the North in 1806, when both Gustav IV Adolf and Crown Prince Frederik resolutely governed without benefit of councils or estates and incorporated Swedish Pomerania and Schleswig-Holstein directly into their domains. By 1815 a retreat from this advanced position was already well under way. The bureaucratic state, as experience in Sweden, Finland, and Norway—to say nothing of elsewhere in Europe—had shown, was capable of functioning, if need be, independently of the crown. The apparent paradox, suggested above, was ultimately resolved by the monarchs and their functionaries themselves, who through their effective reforms and firm political tutelage cleared the way, whether intentionally or not, for the exercise of popular sovereignty.

Sweden, after veering between the extremes of an exuberant but ineffectual

rule by the Estates before 1772 and the severe limitation of their powers thereafter, established in 1809 a viable balance of political forces as the basis for a
stable and effective parliamentary life from at least the 1830s on. By the same
decade, parliamentary activity was on the increase in Norway. The Swedish and
Norwegian constitutions of 1809 and 1814 would thereafter prove adaptable to
a broadening democratization down to the present.

In 1831, under pressure to establish the *Landtag* required by the Germanic
Confederation for Holstein, Frederik VI established four local consultative
assemblies (*stænderforsamlinger*): for Holstein and Lauenburg, Schleswig, Jutland, and the islands (including Iceland and the Færøes). By the end of his life
in 1848, Christian VIII—who had been Norway's elected king in 1814—considered a constitution for Denmark. This was granted by his successor, Frederik
VII, in June 1849, at a time of renewed revolution throughout much of Europe,
finally ending 189 years of royal absolutism. It was the measure of its success
that it had itself created the conditions which rendered it obsolete, thereby laying
the foundations for what would in time become—together with the other Nordic
nations—a showcase of working democracy. In 1863 Alexander II at last revived
the Finnish diet. By 1874 Iceland, too, would be granted its own separate constitution and legislative assembly with the ancient name of the *Althing*.

Throughout the North old "Jacobins" of the 1790s and their political heirs
remained standard-bearers of the liberal cause in the early nineteenth century.
Well could Count Trolle-Wachtmeister describe the Swedish liberalism of the
1840s as the "realization" of the "Swedish Jacobinism" of his youth.[15] Count
Adolf Ludvig Ribbing, the Swedish regicide of 1792, then editor of the journal
*Le vrai liberal* in Brussels, could still proudly describe himself in 1817 as a
"sworn enemy of oppression and despotism of any hue, be it the imperial green,
the monarchial blue, or Robespierre's tricolor," and at the end of his life in 1838
he called himself the last of "those frightful men of 1792, whom some regarded
as arch-aristocrats and others as Jacobins."[16]

The quickening of parliamentary life in the North from the 1830s on coincided with the emergence of the peasantry as a major political force, reflecting
its steady advancement in prosperity, enlightenment, social standing, experience
in public affairs, and self-awareness. The Swedish Peasant Estate at last gained
full parity within the *Riksdag* in 1809. The Norwegian and Danish constitutions
of 1814 and 1849 provided for broad, liberal franchises without reference to
Estate, which gave land-holding farmers a predominance they soon learned to
exploit. The political role of agrarian parties would loom large in the North
through much of the nineteenth century and beyond.

Throughout the period, not only wider European but specifically Nordic
interactions are manifest. The example of the freeholding Norwegian *odelbonde*
provided a model for peasant reforms in Denmark, which in turn spurred emancipation in the duchies. This step toward a basic social leveling called forth re-

actions in German aristocratic circles on the social, political, and cultural levels. German cultural predominance in the mid-eighteenth century precipitated a Danish national reaction, while German resistance to Danish absolutism in the duchies, together with Swedish and particularly Norwegian examples, would inspire Danish liberalism by the 1830s. Liberals and nationalists in Finland and Iceland could draw similar sustenance from the other Scandinavian lands.

In the period 1760–1815 there was a dynamic growth in economic activity and productivity in the North, together with a considerable reorientation from predominantly subsistence toward largely market economies. Behind these developments lay a rapid increase in population. We have estimated a total population for the region of something under 4,000,000 around the middle of the eighteenth century. By the beginning of the nineteenth century, this had increased to around 5,875,000: by then the Danish monarchy had a population of circa 2,410,000, of which 925,680 in Denmark (1801), 883,353 in Norway (1801), and 604,085 in the duchies (1803); the approximately 3,465,000 inhabitants of the Swedish kingdom in 1805 included 2,425,000 in Sweden, 895,000 in Finland, and 45,000 in Pomerania.[17] Thus in a half-century roughly corresponding with that considered here, the Nordic population had grown by at least a third. The rate of increase was greatest in Finland and Norway, smallest in Iceland; overall, it accelerated during the later decades, toward the peak years of the mid-nineteenth century.

Population growth most strongly affected agriculture and its traditional subsidiary occupations, including forestry and fishing, which throughout the period continued to employ the overwhelming majority. This marked predominance of agriculture has tended to obscure the overall scope of economic growth in Scandinavia at this time, thanks to the present-minded tendency of historians to evaluate economic development since the mid-eighteenth century in primarily *industrial* terms, with the British Industrial Revolution as their model. Manufacturing generally declined in the Scandinavian kingdoms by the end of the period, with the abandonment of mercantilistic policies. Yet as in Britain and elsewhere, a transformation to a more productive, more market-oriented agriculture would be the indispensable precondition for industrial development, occurring in the Nordic lands from the mid-nineteenth century on.

Agriculture underwent important structural changes. In no part of Europe outside of Great Britain were enclosure and land consolidation more widely carried out before 1815 than in the Scandinavian lands, despite wide local variations. The practice was at first most widespread in the duchies—as Thomas Malthus observed in 1799—but by 1807 some two-thirds of the land on the Danish islands and about one-half on Jutland was reallocated. By 1837 only an estimated 1 percent of Denmark's land remained unaffected. In Sweden the practice was well advanced under the enclosure (*Enskifte*) ordinance of 1803 in the southernmost province of Skåne, where a good two-thirds of all agricultural land in Malmöhus County (*län*) would be consolidated by 1822, although in those areas of the country covered by the ordinances of 1804 and 1807 the process was still only beginning.[18] Norrland, the northern two-thirds of the land, was still exempted, as was the province of Dalarna, where in places fragmented and scattered holdings still exist. In Finland land consolidations continued to be governed by the older *Storskifte* ordinances until well into the nineteenth century. Similarly, Norway was not subject to the Danish enclosure ordinances, with the result that land consolidations scarcely began before the 1820s. The Atlantic islands, with their particular forms of sub-Arctic livestock raising, were never really touched by these developments, and in the Færøes an ancient system of communal agriculture with widespread common lands is still practiced.

Enclosures in the more fertile areas resulted in both more extensive and more intensive types of arable farming, through a more widely dispersed settlement pattern on individual farmsteads which brought new land under the plow and by the more constant utilization of the soil made possible by new techniques of crop rotation. Yet even outside the areas of large-scale land consolidations, farming was becoming more extensive and more intensive in varying degree. Widespread internal colonization proceeded apace in northern Norway, Sweden, and especially Finland, creating from the beginning farms of the newer type. Population pressures in old areas of settlement with limited arable land meanwhile led to divisions of family farms into smaller and smaller holdings, requiring more labor-intensive forms of cultivation.[19] In parts of western Norway, for instance, the plow was abandoned in favor of the spade on the steeper hillside fields. Throughout the North the potato gained ground, thanks to the plentiful nourishment it could provide from small patches of poor soil.

Farming was becoming increasingly commercial in the richer and more accessible areas, producing not only for urban markets but for sizable segments of the rural population unable to provide fully for their own basic needs. The dependence of much of the Norwegian peasantry upon supplies of Danish grain, even after the end of the Danish grain monopoly in 1788, is the classic case in point. Meanwhile, Denmark and the duchies were able to export produce abroad. Large estates, now purchasable by any enterprising citizen, consolidated and enclosed, and employing wage labor and rational methods, continued to play a leading role in production for the market and in local encouragement of improved peasant farming. The trend toward commercial cultivation led in some areas to the abandonment of old subsidiary occupations associated with subsistence farming.

Agricultural yields were greatly increased. By around 1800, Sweden was importing no more than 2–3 percent of its grain consumption, of which much was used for distillation. The ratio of seed planted to grain harvested in Denmark is estimated to have increased on the average to around 5:1, or by some 25 percent in the twenty years after 1788, during which both yields and exports of grain approximately doubled. Thanks largely to the cultivation of clovers and grasses through crop rotation, the number of cattle in Denmark rose by a third between 1770 and 1800. In Norway grain production by 1814 was double that estimated for 1723 and would by 1835 be calculated at two and a half times as large.[20]

While there were good crop years and bad, there were much more erratic swings in other areas of the economy, resulting above all from the vagaries of war and peace in Europe. The war years 1757–63, 1775–83, and 1792–1807 brought great prosperity to neutral Scandinavian merchants and shippers. The involvement of the region itself in hostilities by 1807 proved devastating. After 1815 the fabled days of commercial prosperity remained no more than a memory. The great merchant houses were bankrupted or reduced to a modest trade in indigenous products, impeded after 1814 by new tariff barriers dividing the formerly interdependent Danish and Norwegian markets.

Decline in trade after 1815 meanwhile reflected contracting markets abroad for Nordic goods and services. Great Britain, the major customer, was by now mining and smelting its own iron and importing Canadian timber, as well as shipping in its own bottoms. Swedish ironmasters and Norwegian sawmill operators, shipowners, and fishermen suffered accordingly. A generation would pass before new technologies would enable them to recover lost ground.

The war years between 1807 and 1814 ruined painstaking efforts to stabilize state finances and monetary systems. Thereafter the destruction of neutral commerce and the loss of foreign markets made financial recovery especially arduous before the general European upswing by mid-century.

The real and solid gains of the period thus remain in agriculture, and these not even the long post-1815 recession would obliterate. It would be upon this firm foundation that the future economic development and prosperity of the North would build.

Surely the most far-reaching transformations of the period were those affecting social structure. Count Anders Fredrik Skjöldebrand recalled in later life a time, in the 1750s and 1760s, when Sweden still had "magnates" who "enjoyed the consideration due to princes." In 1803 Christian Colbjørnsen still perceived a "spirit of aristocracy" lurking within the "ruins of the fearsome temple of wicked feudalism."[21] Both commentaries would apply on both sides of the Sound. Although the aristocratic spirit was not dead, "feudalism"—to the extent that flexible concept applied to Nordic society—lay in "ruins" by 1815.

Nobility as such did not disappear. The old titles remained—and remain today—in Denmark, Sweden, Finland, and the former German provinces. Noblemen would long preserve the greater part of the old manorial lands, often protected by entail. As proprietors they had by no means suffered in the long run from agrarian reform. Speaking of the abolition of the *stavnsbånd* in Denmark, the poet Jens Christian Hostrup held that "those who lost the battle only gained thereby."[22] Release from public responsibilities and liabilities, land consolidation, the largely unregulated use of wage labor, the formation of new cotters' holdings from peasant tenancies and frequently their eventual absorption into the demesne—all proved more than adequate compensation for lost prerogatives in Denmark, Sweden, and the German lands, allowing for profitable large-scale commercial agriculture, in many cases down to the present day. Noblemen likewise continue to play a prominent role in politics, government service (especially the officer and diplomatic corps), social and cultural life. They would be represented by their own Estate in the Swedish *Riksdag* until 1866 and in the Finnish diet until 1906.

Yet by 1815, no form of manorial property or public appointment remained their exclusive privilege in either Denmark or Sweden. In Finland, Schleswig-Holstein, and the former Swedish Pomerania, such vestigial privileges as still existed in 1809 and 1815 would be more gradually eliminated. In Norway, where nobility scarcely existed, further ennoblements were prohibited by the constitution in 1814, and noble status would be abolished entirely in 1821, over Karl XIV Johan's indignant veto. In the Atlantic islands, a native nobility was never established.

The decline of the nobility reflects the transformation of the Scandinavian kingdoms from expansive powers in the seventeenth century, requiring the services of a numerous administrative and military class and with ample means to reward it, to minor and contracting powers in the eighteenth. For Denmark, the Peace of Lübeck in 1629 marked the crucial turning point, for Sweden, the Peace of Nystad in 1721. The preconditions for a golden age of aristocracy, such as still existed in much of eastern Europe and to a degree in Great Britain, no longer prevailed in Scandinavia by the 1760s.[23]

There seems a notable disparity between the relatively modest differences in privilege separating nobility from the upper levels of the commonality by the 1760s and the intensity of antiaristocratic passions in the North. One is reminded of Alexis de Tocqueville's view that the essential similarity of the upper classes in all but legal status was itself a powerful stimulus to class antagonism in pre-revolutionary France.[24]

In the event, the Scandinavian nobility lost almost entirely such special status as it possessed between 1760 and 1815, not through the abolition of its existing privileges but through the granting of similar privileges to the other social orders. Opportunities for advancement and social standing were opened up to burghers, clergy, lower officials, and in Sweden and Finland, to those numerous "nonnoble persons of quality" (*ofrälse ståndspersoner*) who did not fit into any of the old Estates but who constituted an increasing proportion of the emerging, amalgamated middle classes. The most momentous changes nonetheless affected the peasantries. The differences in their conditions in the various Nordic lands had never been greater than they had become by the mid-eighteenth century. By 1815, their legal status had become essentially similar throughout the North, while their economic and cultural differences were rapidly disappearing.[25]

In Denmark a virtual serfdom under the *stavnsbånd* of 1733 was declared abolished by degrees in 1788 and ceased to exist altogether in 1800. The remaining serfs (*Leibeigne*) in the duchies were liberated in 1805. Approximately 60 percent of Denmark's peasant farms had become freeholds already by 1807, compared with around 3 percent in the mid-eighteenth century, while the very concept of freehold property had been progressively freed from vestiges of manorial control.[26] Freehold purchases eliminated manorial labor obligations for most peasant farmers; where such obligations still survived, they were regulated, as was the tithe.

In Sweden and Finland the last restrictions on peasant freehold rights were removed in 1789. At the same time, the sale of crown land to peasant tenants, periodically suspended in the past, was resumed on a large scale, and general and immediate manorial lands (*allmänt* and *ypperligt frälse*) were made freely purchasable by all citizens in 1789 and 1809, respectively. In Sweden proper the number of peasant farms increased between 1751 and 1810 from around 190,000 to 220,000; in Finland, where population grew even more rapidly, from roughly 31,000 to 52,000, including some 6,000 newly cleared holdings in the forests, from 1750 to 1805. By 1809 some 30 percent of the manorial lands in Sweden proper had passed into the hands of commoners, of which at least a third went to peasant landowners. By 1815, Eli F. Heckscher estimated, 52.6 percent of the matriculated land in Sweden consisted of peasant freeholds, whereas another 14.5 percent comprised crown tenancies. Although in Finland retention of the Gustavian constitution in 1809 formally preserved, for the time being, the noble monopoly on immediate manorial demesne, this meant less than it would have in Sweden, owing to the far smaller amount of manorial land and the generally smaller size of individual manors. In Norway, where the only manors were those of Jarlsberg—belonging by 1815 to Count Wedel—Larvik, and Rosendal, peasant purchases of former leaseholds continued throughout the period, especially in Østlandet, where this brought control of profitable forest lands. Between 1723 and 1802 the number of farms increased from circa 65,000 to around 79,000.[27]

The basic similarity of the Nordic peasantries by 1815 was secured not only through emancipation from old restrictions, but in the Danish monarchy by protection of the peasant from the free play of economic forces. Whereas most peasant farmers in Norway, Sweden, Finland, and the Atlantic Islands were freeholders or crown tenants at the beginning of the period, the overwhelming majority in Denmark and the duchies were manorial tenants. The emancipation of the peasantry there, as in much of Europe, was attended by strong pressures to compensate manorial proprietors by permitting them the unrestricted disposition of their property. Had this come about, the results in Denmark and the duchies would doubtless have been similar to those in much of northern Germany. There, manorial lords, to expedite large-scale commercial demesne farming, carried out mass evictions of their peasant tenants, as in neighboring Mecklenburg, or compensated themselves for the loss of tenant labor with a sizable part of each former tenancy, as in Prussia, including the former Swedish Pomerania.[28] In Denmark, and to only a slightly lesser degree in the Duchies, peasant lands remained in peasant hands, either as freeholds or as regulated tenancies.

Eli F. Heckscher has meanwhile compared the social results of enclosure in Great Britain and Sweden. Whereas in Britain most of the agricultural land already belonged to a handful of large landlords, who could consolidate their lands following enclosure into a limited number of fairly large and economically profitable tenant farms, in Sweden over half the land was held by peasant freeholders before the Enskifte ordinances of 1803–7, which therefore increased peasant landholding through the division of common lands and of existing properties.[29] The North, like France and adjoining areas reorganized by revolutionary and Napoleonic France – but unlike Britain and most of eastern Europe – would thus remain a stronghold of independent smallholders.

In Denmark, the duchies, and Sweden, enclosure and land consolidation broke up old, tight-knit village communities and the social solidarity and interdependency they had preserved. The appearance of entire regions was changed as settlement dispersed from compact villages and hamlets to individual farmsteads. By 1807 three-quarters of the peasant farms on the Danish islands and half of them on Jutland had been consolidated, and about half of the peasant farmers had relocated on their new holdings.[30] At the same time, the dividing-up of former common lands deprived numerous poor peasants without land of their own of such rights of usage as they had customarily enjoyed in the past.

The Nordic peasantries were thus becoming increasingly stratified between haves and have-nots. The former, be it noted, included leaseholders, who if they farmed substantial, indivisible tenancies, could often be more prosperous and respected than the owners of small, frequently divided freeholds. The have-nots included cotters or crofters—husmænd in Denmark or Norway, Häusler or Kossäten in the German provinces, torpare in Sweden, torparit in Finland—who occupied cottages on farms and manors, with perhaps a small plot of land attached, in return for stipulated labor obligations. In addition there was a variety of hired hands, day laborers, and paupers.

Enclosure and land consolidation, together with more intensive cultivation through crop rotation and the attendant increase in livestock, created a growing need for farm labor, especially in Denmark. The Danish census of 1801 showed that along with their families, there were 261,307 persons in the farmer class, as against 322,587 in the cotter and 123,147 in the servant class of live-in hired help. Whereas the first and third of these groups had remained fairly constant, the cotter class had increased by nearly a quarter since 1787. On Sjælland cotters outnumbered farmers by two to one. Nor did native farm labor fill the need, at least in good times, for there was a certain immigration of Holsteiners, Norwegians, and Swedes; in 1802 some 6,000 Swedish farm laborers were estimated to be employed on Sjælland alone. Because the total number of farms could increase only slowly at best, the rapid population growth of the period accrued almost entirely to the landless classes of the countryside. By 1801 about one-third of the cottages had no land attached.[31]

As manorial proprietors lost the compulsory labor services of farmers by selling off tenancies or entering into binding *hoveri* settlements with their remaining leaseholders, they became increasingly dependent upon the labor obligations of their cotters. Peasant farmers set up cotters of their own on similar terms. The burden of compulsory labor did not disappear; it shifted primarily from the farmer to the cotter.

Although softened by more available land for clearance and new settlement, as well as by the freer division of existing farms, a similar agrarian restructuring was taking place elsewhere in the North. In Norway there were 11,814 crofts with land attached, mainly in Østlandet, in 1723; the census of 1825 showed some 48,700 *husmenn* with some land to cultivate, in addition to 42,500 male persons classified as landless *husmenn*, day laborers, and the like. The ordinance of 1754, requiring landless rural inhabitants to accept available employment from farmers in their district, would remain unchanged until 1818. In Sweden the number of crofts increased from just under 28,000 in 1751 to over 64,500 by 1800, in Finland from around 3,000 to nearly 25,000 between 1750 and 1805. The number of cotters and landless laborers practically doubled in Sweden between 1760 and 1810, while the total rural population grew by about two-fifths.[32] Here, as in Finland, new crofts were established in large numbers on outlying, frequently undeveloped parts of existing farms, often for younger family members.

In sum, the agrarian reforms of 1760–1815 raised the legal, economic, and social status of a large part of the peasantry of the Nordic lands, creating a kind of "rural bourgeoisie," to use a concept Georges Lefebvre applied to France in that period, or what Kåre D. Tønnesson has called a "kulak" class, using a more recent analogy. Scandinavian historiography has traditionally tended to emphasize this positive side of the picture. Yet the same reforms largely created a new problem in the form of a rapidly growing rural proletariat, which by the end of the period outnumbered, or in places would soon outnumber, the farming class. "The relations between the peasant farmers and their cotters reflect the seigneurial regime on a lower level," Tønnesson has commented. In the mid-nineteenth century the Norwegian scholar Ivar Aasen called the larger peasant farmers "petty barons and lords." For Ole Feldbæk it was the cotter class that "paid the price" for Danish absolutism's compromise with the manorial proprietors and the establishment of the new farmholding class.[33] The greatest problems facing Nordic society after 1815 would thus come to be rural overpopulation and poverty, to be only gradually ameliorated by emigration, industrialization, and social reform.

The reforms of 1760–1815 did not create equality of condition, nor were they so intended, but they did provide an essential equality of opportunity, removing social and religious barriers to talent and ambition, and to the free circulation of wealth and property. The result was a society already by 1815 based primarily upon functional status and personal attainment and wealth, rather than upon birth and breeding: on "class" in the modern sense, rather than "estate" in the earlier tradition.

To be sure, the tendency was generally for the middle classes of town and countryside to seek to level upward, rather than downward: the Stockholm patrician Niclas Ebel in 1793 was not alone in not wishing "to be equal to any but those above him," as Baron Lars von Engeström alleged. In Scandinavia, as elsewhere in Europe, middle-class foes of aristocracy were often enough "inattentive to the sense of the common people," as the American John Adams, himself no social leveler, claimed in the case of the Dutch "Patriots" in 1787.[34]

History is, moreover, seldom a matter of straight-line progressions. Some ground was unquestionably lost during the lean years of the early nineteenth century, as is most evident in Denmark. There, freehold purchases virtually stopped for three decades or more after 1807: of some 66,500 farmers in 1835, over a third, or around 24,800, were still tenants, including some unsuccessful former freeholders. The number of cotters grew as the proportion with some land to till declined, and until 1848 they had little protection against arbitrary treatment. In 1838 the government permitted landlords to appropriate to the demesne limited parts of their tenant farms if they released the occupants from labor obligations. Schools and relief to the poor suffered from insufficient means. Press controls were again tightened in May 1814.[35]

Yet in Denmark—as elsewhere in the North—the ideals and patterns of social reform were set by 1815, the essential groundwork for the progressive democratization of society, to be taken up again by the 1830s. In 1800 the Swede Axel Gabriel Silfverstolpe hailed Andreas Peter Bernstorff, "Denmark's glory," for having "striven, in the right order, to make his nation one day worthy to receive freedom and capable of maintaining it."[36] His words would apply to the reformers of the period throughout the North.

The ordinance of 1799 on relief to the poor in Copenhagen meanwhile embodied a principle likewise foreshadowing the Scandinavia of today: the state's commitment to provide either employment or material support for its needy citizens—a concept recalling the abortive French constitution of 1793. "If expressed in the language of our day," Kjeld Philip wrote in 1947, the ordinance "could have been written today and could in general serve to characterize the social policy of our time."[37]

Developments in the political, economic, and social spheres both reflected and affected those occurring in cultural life between 1760 and 1815, including the spread of literacy among the population at large and the conflict of ideas and values among the educated and influential.

Throughout the period, much thought was given to education, especially of the broader masses. Opinion on its proper scope and content varied greatly, emphasizing state or social utility, religious doctrine, or individual self-realization. The overall result was nevertheless a steady increase in the number of primary schools, both rural and urban, throughout the North. In principle this fulfilled long-standing requirements set forth in the Swedish and Danish ordinances of 1723 and 1739, which called for some modicum of local instruction but provided neither means nor sanctions. New schools came about through the local initiatives of dedicated pastors, landowners, and private societies.

Progress was greatest in Denmark, where not only some very advanced schools by the standards of the time but also teachers' training seminaries were established, culminating with the ordinance of July 1814, mandating the first comprehensive system of primary education in the North and recalling recent parallels in, for example, Prussia and France. In offering evening classes for both young and old on their manors, Ludvig and Christian Ditlev Reventlow meanwhile anticipated the characteristic Nordic folk high schools of a later day.[38] In Sweden, even without a corresponding school law before 1842, progress had also been considerable. It has been estimated that while in 1768 only some 10 percent of the rural parishes had either "fixed" or "ambulatory" schools—the latter an itinerant schoolmaster—by 1802 the proportion had increased to at least 15–20 percent, and by 1814 to a good 45 percent. Parish schools remained, however, unevenly distributed according to population density and local wealth, from Visby diocese on the island of Gotland, where all parishes maintained schools, to the northern diocese of Härnösand, with only one fixed and fourteen ambulatory schools in 1814.[39]

Nonetheless, in 1768, when the bishop of Härnösand could report no parish schools at all in his diocese, many of the peasants there could read and write.[40] In Iceland literacy was understood to be practically universal, without benefit of any parish schools. Literacy in the North, thanks mainly to family instruction, was thus much greater than the number and distribution of primary schools would suggest. Carlo M. Cipolla has estimated that by 1850—less than a decade after the school law of 1842—adult literacy in Sweden was as high as 90 percent.[41]

Although the content of popular instruction remained rudimentary at best, it opened broader horizons to the common man. It was, moreover, conceived as an essential part of the agrarian reforms aimed at creating independent, enterprising, and productive peasant farmers, above all in Denmark and the duchies. The Danish School Ordinance of 1814 was thus the capstone of an integrated program of social amelioration. Through broadening literacy, the guiding ideas of the age filtered down from the classes to the masses. Slogans of the French Revolution echoed in the streets of Åbenrå and Tønder during the disturbances of the early 1790s and in Stockholm during the fearsome Fersen Riot in 1810. More significant in the long run, the vision of secular progress was beginning to counteract traditional acceptance of this world as a "vale of tears," as would soon be demonstrated by the mass emigration of Scandinavian peasants across the ocean to the New World in search of a new and better life, from the later 1830s on.

At the secondary level of urban *borgerskoler* and *gymnasier*, there were modest efforts from the 1790s to introduce curricula better suited to careers in commerce and public service. Characteristically for that age, it was the universities that remained most firmly wedded to past traditions of learning. In Sweden, meanwhile, a growing number of aspirants to the secondary schools and universities came from peasant backgrounds.

No less influential than the spread of literacy—and closely related to it—were popular movements of religious pietism. Of these, the greatest in this period was Haugianism in Norway, beginning in 1796, but it was by no means an isolated phenomenon. Moravian pietism was already well established by the 1760s, mainly in urban centers, throughout the North. Already in the 1750s there had been a wave of emotional evangelism among the Finnish peasantry. The 1780s witnessed the rise and fall of Åke Svensson's small peasant perfectionist sect in southern Sweden, and the following decade an upsurge of peasant pietism in Fyn, Jutland, and the duchies, as well as Bishop Balle's revival movement in Copenhagen. With local Moravians, the Scottish Congregationalist John Patterson in 1808–9 founded Stockholm's Evangelical Society, which by 1814 counted some 400 members. Throughout the nineteenth century the Nordic lands would be swept by powerful waves of evangelical revivalism, on occasion assuming the form of separatist cults.[42]

These movements, among both the urban middle classes and the rural peasantries, at once stimulated a sense of group solidarity, a concern with public questions beyond the bounds of the local parish, organizational initiative and experience, and a tendency toward private judgment and the rejection of traditional authority in secular as well as spiritual matters. They were the first of the great folk movements which over the following century would play so conspicuous a part in the democratization of state and society in the North. Characteristically, the new pietism welcomed the temporal success of the godly in this world.

Whereas pietism frequently condemned old practices, the growing prosperity of the farmholding peasants would for some time to come generally serve to reinforce the traditional folk cultures and provide the means for their final flowering. The mid-nineteenth century would thus be the golden age of Nordic peasant culture in all its characteristic manifestations. But by that time it was sustained by the agricultural profits of a market economy, which within a few generations would largely destroy it through industrialization and emigration.

For the educated classes, the decades between 1760 and 1815 were a time of complex intellectual and cultural crosscurrents. The European Enlightenment reached its zenith in outreach and influence at the very time its "disaggregation"—as Paul Hazard has called it—began.[43]

In Scandinavia the work of such eminently rationalist bodies as the Swedish *Riksdag* of 1809–10, the Borgå diet in Finland in 1809, and the Eidsvoll assembly in Norway in 1814 should serve to recall that the party of Enlightenment by no means lost its vitality by the early nineteenth century. Nonetheless, the complex of forces that would come to comprise an "Anti-Enlightenment"—Pre-Romantic sensibility, religious pietism, and a variety of secular mysticisms—were already well developed in the North by the 1760s, as Martin Lamm has shown in fascinating detail in the case of Sweden in particular. As the preromantic synthesis of emotional enthusiasm for the light of Reason and a new dawn for Humanity broke down amid the grim realities of the French Revolution and the European war, an increasingly bitter battle was joined between what now emerged as antithetical *Weltanschauungen*. In 1798 the poet Frans Michael Franzén, recently returned to Åbo from the Continent, eulogized:

> In awesome beauty, like a ship aflame,
> E'en now this century passes by,
> Spreading glare and horror along its course,
> Upon the night-enshrouded shore.[44]

By the end of the period, the new romanticism was in full flood. While those still holding to the Enlightenment credo represented a chastened optimism in future progress through human reason—and generally classical canons of taste as well—the romantics in their flight from the present turned from the future to the past. Yet within the romantic camp in the North there came to be a significant cleavage, again perhaps best illustrated in Sweden. In Uppsala a coterie around Per Daniel Amadeus Atterbom violently attacked both the Enlightenment and classicism in his journal, *Phosphorus*, between 1810 and 1814, creating a furor in established literary circles. Looking to Germany for inspiration, the young "Phosphorists" extolled the Christian Middle Ages and contemptuously rejected the new materialism and liberalism. In their escapism they recall such European contemporaries as Chateaubriand, Tieck, Wackenroder, and Wordsworth in his later years.

Simultaneously there emerged in Uppsala another circle of young romantics, whose influence upon national cultural life was more profound and long-lasting, who looked even further back for their heroic age. Founding the "Gothic Society" (*Götiska förbundet*) in 1810, they idealized the pre-Christian North, finding there an antithesis virtually unique in the European world to its common background in Greco-Roman antiquity and the inspiration to moral regeneration in the future. Through their journal, *Iduna*, founded in 1811, the "Gothicists," above all Erik Gustaf Geijer and Esaias Tegnér, the leading Swedish poets of their day, painted a glowing picture of a hardy Nordic race tilling the ancestral soil in health and contentment, uncorrupted by the civilization of more southerly climes. The implication was that by returning to the simple tastes and rude virtues of their forefathers, the Swedes might rise again from defeat and moral decay to build a better and more firmly grounded future. It was a message old even in Rousseau's day, but it now provided the central core, in Sweden and elsewhere, for the vital and creative national romanticism of the following century. By hard work and sacrifice, Tegnér admonished his countrymen in 1811 to "reconquer Finland within Sweden's boundaries" in his epic poem "Svea."

When arms speak the Muses fall silent, according to an old Latin dictum. Yet this was scarcely the case in Denmark, any more than in Sweden: in both countries the years of national tribulation witnessed the beginning of a great age in literature and the arts. Nor, surely, was this fortuitous, for in Denmark, too, the challenge of adversity evoked an appeal to moral renewal and national solidarity. Serving with the student corps during the British naval attack on Copenhagen in 1801, young Adam Oehlenschläger, Denmark's foremost poetic talent of the time, was moved to write:

> A divinity sweeps over Copenhagen
> all pettiness, all grudges die today
>
> . . . . . . . . . . . . . . . .
>
> the spirit of yore has awakened from its slumber.[45]

Returning to Denmark after four years abroad in 1809, Oehlenschläger turned, like the Swedish Gothicists, to Nordic antiquity as a source of strength and inspiration for the future. Similarly, Nicolai Frederik Severin Grundtvig, beginning his long career as a pivotal figure in Denmark's nineteenth-century cultural life, looked upon Napoleon as God's chosen instrument for the regeneration of nations.

It was in this vein that Frederik Stoud, a Danish government official writing under the pseudonym "Frederik Cortsen," in April 1815 published his *Tabet af Norge til Medborgernes Eftertanke* (Norway's Loss for the Reflection of Citizens), urging that the Danes make up for Norway by reclaiming their own undeveloped wastelands. Abandoning past dreams of easy commercial and colonial wealth, "we must conquer our own country." His words recall both his contemporary Tegnér's in Sweden and his later compatriot H. P. Holst's celebrated admonition in 1864, following Denmark's loss of Schleswig-Holstein, that "what has been lost without must be won within."[46]

It was thus on a note of quiet but determined optimism that the Nordic peoples prepared to face an uncertain future by 1815. The same impression is thereafter reinforced by the visual arts, then best represented in the serene and sunny domesticity portrayed by the painters of the Danish "Golden Age," such as C. V. Eckersberg, Christen Købke, and Constantin Hansen, in contrast to the medieval otherworldliness or exotic and violent theatricality of such Continental contemporaries as Caspar David Friedrich (a native of Swedish Pomerania) in Germany, and Théodore Géricault and Eugène Delacroix in France.[47]

Given the prevailingly positive response of Scandinavian romanticism to the challenge of the future, it seems not unnatural that Erik Gustaf Geijer, the acknowledged high priest of Uppsala Gothicism, should make his celebrated apostasy to political liberalism in 1838, recalling the conversion of such leading European conservative romantics as Victor Hugo by or during the 1830s.

Neither Finland nor Norway were quick to embrace the romantic mood. By 1815 facing new challenges and the search for new identities, they held firmly to the Enlightenment faith in reasoned progress. For generations their educated classes would continue to look to Stockholm and Copenhagen respectively for cultural inspiration, thereby reinforcing their distinctiveness within new political unions.[48] But by the mid-nineteenth century, both would be caught up in the creative surge of national romanticism, to the incalculable enrichment of their emerging national cultures.

Thus in all areas of life the Nordic lands were profoundly affected by the developments of the revolutionary era, each in ways reflecting its own conditions and traditions. It may, in conclusion, be asked to what extent Scandinavia itself underwent a "revolution" in these years.

The answer is, of course, largely a matter of definitions. The term "revolution" in present usage is generally taken to mean the violent overthrow of an existing social and political order, involving the active participation of large masses of people, as in the classic case of the French Revolution. It may, however, also describe a transformation, not necessarily violent, in some area or related areas of life so profound as to affect significantly society as a whole, like the Industrial Revolution occurring in the same period. Despite palace revolutions and parliamentary coups, the assassination of one monarch, the deposition of another, the popular election and abdication of a third, the abrogation of old constitutions and the drafting of new, aristocratic conspiracies, popular rioting, war and deprivation, Scandinavia cannot be said to have experienced revolution in the first and more specific sense of the term. Yet in the second sense, which stresses results as opposed to process, it may well be argued that Scandinavia was "revolutionized" during this period.

The eminent American historian of the period, Leo Gershoy, has summarized the "epochal social consequences" of the impact of the French Revolution upon Europe in 1789–99 as "the overthrow of feudalism, the vast transfer of real property, the winning of civil rights and liberties, and the opening of careers to talents, at least the talents of the propertied classes."[49] These criteria apply no less to the Nordic lands than to any other part of Europe, except France itself, and without the intervention of the French.

Scandinavian historians have not hesitated to employ the term or concept of revolution in discussing events and developments in their countries during this period. Swedes speak traditionally of the revolutions of 1772 and 1809. Sverre Steen has called Norway's Eidsvoll constitution of 1814 the "last offshoot of the great French Revolution."[50] In this period, Hans Jensen has written of Denmark, there took place

the overthrow of the previous framework of society. Something new and significant was established in almost every area, and the total result was a strongly renewed, far more rationally ordered society. This was in truth the Danish revolution, which was accomplished under peaceful, bloodless forms; it produced consequences for the people corresponding to these obtained by the French people through contemporary developments during the great Revolution and the Napoleonic period, developments which demanded colossal sacrifices in blood.[51]

If "revolution" this be, it was for the most part a "silent revolution." Considering in particular the final denouement in Sweden, Finland, and Norway between 1809 and 1814—at the very end of the period—one is reminded of John Adams's observation that the real American revolution was "effected" before the war for independence ever began.[52]

At the same time, it was in large measure "revolution from above." The role played by strong royal authority has been emphasized more than once in this study. French historians, notably Alexis de Tocqueville in the nineteenth century and Georges Lefebvre in the twentieth, have stressed that in France a revolution of liberty preceded a revolution of equality.[53] In Scandinavia the process was the reverse: it was the monarchs themselves who leveled most of the old corporate privileges, before political insurrections in 1809, 1814, and 1849 would found liberal constitutions.

In all of this one cannot but reflect again upon the relative importance of revolution "from above" versus revolution "from below" in the shaping of the modern Western world. One must again ponder Martin Göhring's thesis that reform by royal authority strong enough to override vested interests represents the mainstream of progressive change in eighteenth-century Europe as a whole and that the French Revolution was in this sense the great aberration.[54] Axel Linvald called the Danish agrarian reforms

> the manifestation of the freeing of state power from the landowning class as necessary intermediaries between the government and the peasantry and the building of a bureaucracy and administration sufficiently independent of class interests as to be capable of completing the break with the feudal order begun in 1660, which has been the greatest internal accomplishment of Danish absolutism.[55]

The Scandinavian experience is thus of considerable though generally neglected relevance to the ongoing debate among historians over the concept of "enlightened despotism." This has tended to concentrate upon the practice of royal autocracy in the larger, primarily eastern European monarchies. Because these were also great military powers, it has been easy enough for critics of the concept—chiefly of the Anglo-Saxon and French libertarian schools—to claim that concrete military needs, rather than enlightened humanitarian considerations, were the "real" levers of reform in the period, on the basis of a kind of unstated moral Gresham's Law whereby more mundane motives ipso facto invalidate more ideal ones. The examples of the Scandinavian monarchies, even though *quantitatively* affecting only a small part of Europe's population, add to a more finely shaded *qualitative* understanding of both the ethos and the practice of enlightened government in the eighteenth century.[56]

Since the Nordic lands were not great military powers, the demands of war, while not absent, were not their constant and predominating concern. The close examination of their programs of reform reveals what common sense suggests: that mixed motives were ever present, then as now. It is meanwhile naturally assumed that the ideals of enlightened absolutism derived from the secular rationalism of the Enlightenment. This seems evident enough in the brief, feverish career of Johann Friedrich Struensee in Denmark and in the longer and more variable career of Gustav III in Sweden.[57] Yet the Danish monarchy in particular offers some rather different perspectives of interest and surely wider relevance.

The great trio of dedicated reformers, Counts A. P. Bernstorff, C. D. Reventlow, and Ernst Schimmelmann, seem, as high aristocrats and deeply religious men, curiously inappropriate to their roles as the instigators of far-reaching social change—according, that is, to the conventional preconceptions about enlightened absolutism. Although familiar with the secular values of Enlightenment thought, their guiding inspiration came quite evidently from other sources, in part a revivified aristocratic ideal of *noblesse oblige*—fortified by Montesquieu's concept of a vigorous, serving nobility as the mainstay of monarchy—in part a warm religious piety combining orthodox Lutheranism with the new pietist activism, with its stress upon walking humbly with thy God and loving thy neighbor as thyself. The role of "enlightened aristocracy" and of the new pietism as driving forces for humane reform in later eighteenth-century Europe are facets of the debate on "enlightened despotism" thus far scarcely conceived, let alone examined.

The actual accomplishments of reforming government in Scandinavia were notable in Europe by any standard, in part because the way had been prepared by earlier monarchs and their ministers. Again Denmark since 1660 offers the best, though not the only, example. According to Axel Linvald:

> Many different conditions gave the Danish Age of Enlightenment its particular distinctiveness. One factor is, however, decisive. Round about in Europe's various countries the task at hand was to assure the ultimate victory of state power over the survivals of the old medieval social order. In Denmark, absolutism had long since overcome these forces. In most countries under enlightened despotism the work of practical reform had to take second place; in Denmark it gave the period its character.[58]

Scandinavian examples likewise illustrate how the transformations finally effected bore the imprint of opposing forces and ideals. In Sweden Gustav III and Gustav IV Adolf leveled social barriers while despising the revolution in France. Their aristocratic opponents meanwhile hailed the French Revolution in the name of a political liberty at last secured for the future in 1809, while generally seeking to defend established privileges. Similarly, in the duchies liberty and reform were the rallying cries of opposing camps. While liberal reformers finally gained the emancipation of the peasantry from the *stavnsbånd* in Denmark and from *Leibeigenschaft* in Schleswig-Holstein, the Danish government characteristically adjusted the pace and scope of agrarian reform to allow the accommodation of existing property owners while itself largely assuming the protective role of the ideal manorial lord toward his tenantry espoused by thoughtful conservatives.

Consideration of reforms "from on high" must raise fundamental questions concerning their ultimate effectiveness in bringing about the changes that manifestly took place, perhaps most notably in Denmark. Earlier historians, such as Hans Jensen and Axel Linvald, quoted above, have traditionally attributed the leading role to government and its farsighted leadership. Sir James Mackintosh's description in 1791 of the French Revolution as a "grand experiment to ascertain the portion of freedom and happiness that can be created by political institutions" may well be applied to the Danish reforms of the period. A recent tendency is to stress long-term economic trends affecting population growth, expanding markets, and rising prices. Already in 1891 Christen Christensen (Hørsholm) emphasized the Danish peasants' own efforts to improve their lot from the 1760s. In his great survey of Danish agrarian society from 1500 to 1800, published in 1978, Fridlev Skrubbeltrang was concerned primarily with "normal developments," rather than "acute situations." Birgit Løgstrup and Thorkild Kjærgaard have stressed the proprietors' own growing inclination to divest themselves of increasingly complex and burdensome public functions and to face a conversion from tenant to wage labor. In 1982 Ole Feldbæk stated that "so central — and vastly oversimplified — a question as whether it was legislation that brought about social and economic changes, or vice versa, can still only be answered by suppositions"; he sees in the period 1730–1814, "an interplay between the general economic and social development and Danish absolutism's attempts to guide society."[59] For Scandinavia, as elsewhere, the question must largely remain open, shading as it does into the imponderable enigma of free will versus determinism in history.

Scandinavian historians have long been much concerned with the question of indigenous impulses versus foreign influences behind the reforms and conflicts of the era.[60] It should be clear at this point that both were involved. Yet it is striking that virtually all of the most advanced ideas emerged in the North already by the 1760s and early 1770s, and that in retrospect these ideas were distinctly radical, not only for Scandinavia but for the wider Western world of that time.[61] In Scandinavia they would provide the blueprint for the controversies and projects of the next half-century.[62] Moreover, most of the basic social and economic reforms of the period were initiated in the North before the French Estates-General convened at Versailles in May 1789. The Younger Caps, according to P. E. Brolin, already in the 1760s "represented the men of the American and French Revolutions on Swedish soil."[63] Across the Sound, the "party of Saint-Germain" and Dr. Struensee were no less radical.

The American and French Revolutions thus encouraged but did not greatly change the basic goals and ideals of Scandinavian reformers and radicals. There are indeed suggestions that the most active phase of popular radicalism had already passed by the end of the 1780s in both the Swedish and Danish monarchies.[64] Yet the great reforms of that crucial decade, while satisfying to most Scandinavians, left enough undone to fuel discontents among radical minorities inspired by the French Revolution up to the years of resolution between 1809 and 1815, and to some degree beyond.[65]

How much of a watershed do the decades between 1760 and 1815 form in the broader perspective of the evolution of modern Scandinavia? Certainly to single out any limited span of years as the crucial divide must be to some degree arbitrary, cutting out both earlier and later developments. "To think," Ortega y Gasset once wrote, "whether you want to or no, is to exaggerate."[66] Yet bearing this qualification in mind, it is hard to discern a more momentous half-century in the entire history of the North. In all areas of Scandinavian life during the past two centuries essential lines of development can be traced to ideals formulated and in large part realized in government and society between the Seven Years' War and the end of the Napoleonic conflict.

# Notes

# ABBREVIATIONS

DHG  Aksel E. Christensen, et al., eds., *Danmarks historie*, 4 ( + ) vols. Copenhagen: Gylendals Forlag, 1977– . Vol. IV: Ole Feldbæk, *Tiden 1730-1814* (1982).

DHP  J. Danstrup and H. Koch, eds., *Danmarks historie*, 14 vols. Copenhagen: Politikens Forlag, 1963–66. Vol. IX: Svend Cedergreen Bech, *Oplysning og tolerance 1721-1784* (1965); Vol. X: Jens Vibæk, *Reform og fallit 1784-1830* (1964).

DNH  Edvard Holm, *Danmark-Norges Historie fra den Store nordiske Krigs Slutning til Rigernes Adskillelse 1720-1814*, 7 vols. Copenhagen, 1891–1912.

GSH  Volquart Pauls, et al., *Geschichte Schleswig-Holsteins*. Neumünster, 1957– . Vol. VI: Olaf Klose and Christian Degn, *Die Herzogtümer im Gesamtstaat 1720-1830* (1960).

HTD  *Historisk tidsskrift* (Danish).

HTF  *Historisk tidskrift för Finland*.

HTN  *Historisk tidsskrift* (Norwegian).

HTS  *Historisk tidskrift* (Swedish).

NFLH  E. Bull, et al., *Det norske folks liv og historie gjennem tidene*, 11 vols. Oslo, 1930–38. Vol. VI: Sverre Steen, *Tidsrummet 1720 til omkring 1770* (1932); Vol. VII: Sverre Steen, *Tidsrummet 1770 til omkring 1814* (1933).

NH  Knut Mykland, ed., *Norges historie*, 13 vols. Oslo, 1976–79. Vol. VIII: Ståle Dyrvik, *Den lange fredstiden 1720-1784* (1978); Vol. IX: Knut Mykland, *Kampen om Norge 1784-1814* (1978).

SDH  A. Friis, et al., *Schultz Danmarkshistorie*, rev. ed., 6 vols. Copenhagen, 1941–43. Vol. III, part 4: Hans Jensen, "Christian VI's og Frederik V's Tid"; Vol. IV, part 1: Axel Linvald, "Oplysningens Tidsalder"; Vol. IV, part 2: T. A. Müller, "Oplysningstidens Aandsliv."

SEH  Eli F. Heckscher, *Sveriges ekonomiska historia från Gustav Vasa*, 2 vols. in 4. Stockholm, 1935–49.

SEHR  *Scandinavian Economic History Review.*

SHVD  Emil Hildebrand, ed., *Sveriges historia till våra dagar*, 14 vols. Stockholm, 1919–26. Vol. IX: Ludvig Stavenow, *Frihetstiden* (1922); Vol. X; Ludvig Stavenow, *Den gustavianska tiden 1772-1809* (1925); Vol. XI: Sam Clason, *Karl XIII och Karl XIV Johan 1809-1844* (1923)

SUPH  Nils Ahnlund, ed., *Den svenska utrikespolitikens historia*, 5 vols. Stockholm, 1951–61. Vol. II, part 2: Olof Jägerskiöld, *1721-1792* (1957); Vol. III, part 1: Sten Carlsson, *1792-1810* (1954); Vol. III, part 2: Torvald Höjer, *1810-1844* (1954).

VFH  T. Dahl, et al., eds., *Vårt folks historie*, 9 vols. Oslo, 1961–64. Vol. V: Axel Coldevin, *Enevoldstiden* (1963).

# Notes

## CHAPTER 1. THE SETTING: SCANDINAVIA AROUND 1760

1. On the colonies, see esp. Johannes Brøndsted, ed., *Vore gamle tropekolonier*, 2 vols. (Copenhagen, 1952-53; 2d ed., 1966-68, in 10 vols.); Finn Gad, *Grønlands histore* (Copenhagen, 1946).

2. W. R. Mead, *An Economic Geography of Scandinavia and Finland* (London, 1958), 19-20.

3. *Ibid.*, 13.

4. *Ibid.*, 45—47; Hans Chr. Johansen, *En samfundsorganisation i opbrud 1700-1870*, Dansk socialhistorie, 4 (Copenhagen, 1979), 15-23.

5. Feldbæk, *DHG*, 122; Karen Larsen, *A History of Norway* (New York, 1948), 327; Kurt Samuelsson, *From Great Power to Welfare State* (London, 1968), 72; Sten Carlsson, *Svensk historia*, II (Stockholm, 1961), 33.

6. Knut Gjerset, *History of Iceland* (London, 1922), 322.

7. Einar W. Juva, *Finlands väg från Nystad till Fredrikshamn 1721-1809* (Stockholm, 1947), 36-37; Gustaf Utterström, "Two Essays on Population in Eighteenth-Century Scandinavia," in D. V. Glass and D. E. C. Eversley, eds., *Population in History* (Chicago, 1965), 523-48; Eino Jutikkala, "Finlands Population Movement in the Eighteenth Century," in *ibid.*, 549-69; Johansen, *En samfundsorganisation i opbrud*, 39-104; Michael Drake, *Population and Society in Norway, 1735-1865* (Cambridge, 1969); Magnus Stephensen, *Island i det 18. Aarhundrede, historisk-politisk skildret* (Copenhagen, 1808), 16. See also Hans Finsen, *Om Folkemængdens Formindelse ved Uaar i Island* (Copenhagen, 1831).

8. Ragnhild Hatton, *Europe in the Age of Louis XIV* (New York, 1969), 10; Gjerset, *History of Iceland*, 321-22; Bech, *DHP*, IX, 276-79.

9. Juva, *Finlands väg*, 13.

10. Claude Nordmann, *Grandeur et Liberté de la Suède (1660-1792)* (Paris and Louvain, 1971), 251, 291; Linvald, *SDH*, IV:1, 191; Larsen, *History of Norway*, 304, 327.

11. Axel Linvald, "Hvem ejede Danmarks Jord omkring Midten af det 18. Aarhundrede?" in *Til Edvard Holm paa hans 80-aarige Fødelsedag den 26. Januar 1913*, supplement to *HTD*, 8:4 (1913), 148; Gunnar Olsen, *Hovedgård og bondegård* (Copenhagen, 1957), 69-71; Heckscher, *SEH*, II:1, 270-71; Samuelsson, *From Great Power to Welfare State*, 74; Larsen, *History of Norway*, 310-11.

12. V. Falbe-Hansen, *Stavnsbaands-Løsningen og Landboreformerne set fra Nationaløkonomiens Standpunkt*, 2 vols. (Copenhagen, 1888-89), I, 39-44; Hans Jensen, "Godsejerklassen og

Herregaardene i historisk Belysning," in Therkel Mathiasen, ed., *Herregaardene og Samfundet* (Copenhagen, 1943), 13–92; Birger Planting, *Baroner och patroner* (Stockholm, 1944).

13. Falbe-Hansen, *Stavnsbaands-Løsningen*, I, 2. See also E. Ingers and Sten Carlsson, *Bonden i svensk historia*, 3 vols. (Stockholm, 1943–56), II (Ingers), 113. On yield ratios, cf. Ditlev Skrubbeltrang, *Det danske landbosamfundet 1500–1800* (Copenhagen, 1978), 243–44.

14. On the *Storskifte*, see Heckscher, *SEH*, II:1, 241–56; Eirik Hornborg, *Finlands hävder*, 4 vols. (Helsingfors, 1929–33), III, 304–5.

15. Heckscher, *SEH*, II:1, 172.

16. Samuelsson, *From Great Power to Welfare State*, 87–93. Cf. H. S. F. Kent, *War and Trade in Northern Seas: Anglo-Scandinavian Economic Relations in the Mid-Eighteenth Century* (Cambridge, 1973).

17. Heckscher, *SEH*, II:2, chap. 9, esp. 600–601, 604, 640–42; Per Nyström, *Stadsindustriens arbetare före 1800-talet* (Stockholm, 1955), esp. 138–43, 151–56, 162, 187, 391–92n. Bech, *DHP*, IX, 355–59; Klose [ Degn, *GSH*, VI, 108–9.

18. Jon J. Aðils, *Den danske Monopolhandel paa Island 1602–1787* (Copenhagen, 1926).

19. Coldevin, *VFH*, V, 410.

20. See *ibid.*, 36–39; Klose & Degn, *GSH*, VI, 5; Jensen, "Godsejerklassen og Herregaardene," 26–30. Also Nils G. Bartholdy, "Adelsbegrebet under den ældre enevælde," *HTD*, 12:5 (1971), 577–650.

21. Hugo Valentin, *Frihetstidens riddarhus* (Stockholm, 1915), esp. 1, 81, 88–89. See also Sten Carlsson, *Ståndssamhälle och ståndspersoner* (Lund, 1949); Michael Roberts, "The Swedish Aristocracy in the Eighteenth Century," in his *Essays in Swedish History* (Minneapolis, 1967), 269–85.

22. Linvald, "Hvem ejede Danmarks Jord?"; Carlsson, *Ståndssamhälle och ståndspersoner*, chap. 6. Cf. Skrubbeltrang, *Det danske landbosamfund*, 237–39.

23. Carlsson, *Ståndssamhälle och ståndspersoner* (rev. ed., 1973), 250–51; Svend Cedergreen Bech, ed., *Breve fra Dorothea. Af Charlotta Dorothea Biehls historiske breve* (Copenhagen, 1975), 128–29.

24. See Tom Söderberg, *Den namnlösa medelklassen* (Stockholm, 1956), 173, 186.

25. See *ibid.*, chap. 7; Sten Carlsson, *Byråkrati och borgarstånd under frihetstiden* (Uppsala, 1963).

26. See Carlsson, *Ståndssamhälle och ståndspersoner*.

27. *Ibid.*; Söderberg, *Den namnlösa medelklassen*, chap. 7; Steen, *NFLH*, VII, 12–13; Linvald, *SDH*, IV:1, 223: Albert Olsen, *Bybefolkningen i Danmark paa Merkantilismens Tid* (Aarhus, 1932).

28. Linvald, *SDH*, IV:1, 192; Olsen, *Bybefolkningen*; Samuelsson, *From Great Power to Welfare State*, 73; Gjerset, *History of Iceland*, 344.

29. Sten Carlsson, "Bondeståndet i Norden under senare delen av 1700-talet," *Scandia*, 19 (1948–49), 196–213.

30. Christen Christensen (Hørsholm), *Agrarhistoriske Studier*, 2 vols. (Copenhagen, 1886–1891), II, 1–26; Olsen, *Hovedgård och bondegård*, 13–27.

31. Falbe-Hansen, *Stavnsbaands-Løsningen*, I, 16.

32. Much has been written about the *stavnsbånd*. In addition to Falbe-Hansen, *Stavnsbaands-Løsningen*, see esp. J. A. Fridericia, ed., *Aktstykker til Oplysning om Stavnsbaandets Historie* (Copenhagen, 1888); Johan Hvidtfeldt, "Stavnsbaandet, dets Forudsætninger og Virkninger," *Vejle Amts Aarbog 1938* (Vejle, 1938), 4–49, and "Kvindestavnsbånd i 1750erne og 1760erne," in *Festskrift til Erik Arup* (Copenhagen, 1946), 250–65; Gunnar Olsen, "Stavnsbåndet og tjenestekarlene," *Jydske samlinger* (1950), 197–218.

33. Falbe-Hansen, *Stavnsbaands-Løsningen*, I, 11–16; Hans Jensen, *Chr. D. Reventlows Liv og Gerning* (Copenhagen, 1938), 34; Vibæk, *DHP*, X, 68–69.

34. See Hans Jensen, *Dansk Jordpolitik 1757–1919*, 2 vols. (Copenhagen, 1936, 1945), I, 13–17, 240; Sigurd Jensen in Sigurd Jensen et al., *Ståndssamhällets upplösning i Norden* (Åbo, 1954), 8; Christensen, *Agrarhistoriske Studier*, II, 249–54. Cf. Birgit Løgstrup, *Jorddrot og offentlig administrator* (Copenhagen, 1983). A *tønde hartkorn* was a fiscal assessment unit consisting of enough land to produce a standard barrel of rye, oats, or barley, thus varying in size in different parts of the country.

35. Skrubbeltrang, *Det danske landbosamfund*, part IV, esp. 214, 236. The best treatment of

*hoveri* is Thorkild Kjærgaard, *Konjunkturer og afgifter. C. D. Reventlows betænkning af 11. februar 1788 om hoveriet* (Copenhagen, 1980). Regarding manorial discipline and punishments, cf. Gunnar Olsen, *Træhesten, hundehullet og den spanske kappe* (Copenhagen, 1960).

36. Paul Jørgensen, *Danmarks Retshistorie* (Copenhagen, 1947), 554–55; Linvald, "Hvem ejede Danmarks Jord?" 148. On contemporary concepts of peasant freeholding, see Sigurd Jensen, *Fra patriarkalisme til pengeøkonomi* (Copenhagen, 1950), 15–33. See also J. A. Jørgensen, *Bornholms Historie*, 2 vols. (Rønne, 1901), II, 98–101, 126–27, 134–41, 155–59.

37. See esp. Fridlev Skrubbeltrang, *Husmand og Inderste* (Copenhagen, 1940); Kjeld Philip, *Staten og Fattigdommen* (Copenhagen, 1947).

38. Klose & Degn, *GSH*, VI, 94–96; Olsen, *Hovedgård og bondegård*, 18–19; Johan Hvidtfeldt, *Kampen om ophævelsen af livegenskabet i Slesvig og Holsten 1795–1805* (Aarhus, 1963), 5–22.

39. Coldevin, *VFH*, V, 118–22, 200–202, 208; Larsen, *History of Norway*, 310–11. See also Halvdan Koht, *Norsk bondereising* (Oslo, 1926), 198–99; O. A. Johnsen, *Norges bønder* (2d ed., Oslo, 1936), 300–301; Hans Jensen, *Dansk-norsk Vekselvirkning i det 18. Aarhundrede* (Copenhagen, 1936), 23; Andreas Holmsen, "The Transition from Tenantry to Freehold Peasant Ownership in Norway," *SEHR*, 9 (1961), 152–64.

40. Kåre D. Tønnesson, "Problèmes de la féodalité dans les pays scandinaves," *Annales historiques de la Révolution française* (1969), 339–42; Sølvi Sogner, "Freeholder and Cottar," *Scandinavian Journal of History*, I (1977), 184; Holmsen, "Transition."

41. See Sogner, "Freeholder and Cottar."

42. Steen, *NFLH*, VII, 190; Johnsen, *Norges bønder*, 304; Jensen, *Dansk-norsk Vekselvirkning*, 119–22.

43. Johnsen, *Norges bønder*, 335. See also Steen, *NFLH*, VII, 200, 355–56; Halvdan Koht, "Verknaden av unionen med Danmark på det norske bondestande," *Scandia*, 8 (1935), 197–209.

44. Gjerset, *History of Iceland*; Jón Jónsson, "Fæstebondens Kaar paa Island i det 18. Aarhundrede," *HTD*, 6:4 (1892–94), 563–645; John F. West, *Faroe: The Emergence of a Nation* (London, 1972).

45. Ingers, *Bonden i svensk historia*, II, 200–206. This work is basic for the Swedish peasantry. On the manorial peasants in the former Danish provinces, see also Staffan Smedberg, *Frälsebonderörelser i Halland och Skåne 1772–76* (Uppsala, 1972), chaps. 4–5. Specifically on the Finnish peasantry, see Eino Jutikkala, *Bonden i Finland genom tiderna* (Stockholm, 1963).

46. Tønnesson, "Problèmes de la féodalité," 336–39; Ingers, *Bonden i svensk historia*, II, 212–17; Eino Jutikkala, "Finnish Agricultural Laborers in the Eighteenth and Nineteenth Centuries," *SEHR*, 10 (1962), 203–19.

47. Ingers, *Bonden i svensk historia*, II, 212–17; Alfred Kämpe, *Svenska allmogens frihetsstrider* (Stockholm, 1974), 55–95; Arthur Montgomery, "Tjänstehjonsstadgan och äldre svensk arbetarpolitik," *HTS*, 53 (1933), 245–76. Cf. Gustaf Utterström's magisterial study of the Swedish rural proletariat in the eighteenth and nineteenth centuries, *Jordbrukets abetare*, 2 vols. (Stockholm, 1957).

48. Olsen, *Hovedgård og bondegård*, 19; Lars Dalgren, *Sverige och Pommern 1792–1806* (Uppsala, 1914), 15–18; Carl Johannes Fuchs, *Der Untergang des Bauernstandes und das Aufkommen der Gutsherrschaften. Nach archivalischen Quellen aus Neu-Vorpommern und Rügen* (Strassburg, 1888).

49. See West, *Faroe*, 16; Jørgensen, *Bornholms Historie*, II, 59–60.

50. Johannes Steenstrup, *Den danske Bonde og Friheden* (3d. ed., Copenhagen, 1912), 168–73; Klose & Degn, *GSH*, VI, 96; Jerome Blum, *The End of the Old Order in Rural Europe* (Princeton, 1978), 54; Skrubbeltrang, *Det danske landbosamfund*, 250; Heckscher, *SEH*, II:1, 201.

51. See Ernst Ekman, "The Danish Royal Law of 1665," *Journal of Modern History*, 29 (1957), 102–7.

52. Bech, *DHP*, IX, 104–18; Linvald, *SDH*, IV:1, 225.

53. See R. R. Palmer, *The Age of the Democratic Revolution*, 2 vols. (Princeton, 1959–64), I, chap. 2.

54. T. K. Derry, *A Short History of Norway* (London, 1957), 87–89.

55. Jensen, *Dansk-norsk Vekselvirkning*, 32–41, 48, 112–13.

56. Steen, *NFLH*, VI, 306.

390    NOTES TO PP. 31–42

57. See esp. Klose & Degn, *GSH,* VI, 11–37, 46–60, 90–94; Otto Brandt, *Geistesleben und Politik in Schleswig-Holstein um die Wende des 18. Jahrhunderts* (Kiel, 1927), 5–11. On the relationship of the duchies to the *Lex Regia,* see H. V. Gregersen, *Slesvig og Holsten før 1830* (Copenhagen, 1981), 375–78, 423–24.

58. See Steen, *NFLH,* VI, 379–90; Falbe-Hansen, *Stavnsbaands-Løsningen,* I, 16–19; Jensen, *SDH,* III:4, 567–70.

59. See Michael Roberts, "Charles XI," in his *Essays in Swedish History,* 226–68.

60. Fredrik Lagerroth, *Frihetstidens författning* (Stockholm, 1915), *passim;* Ludvig Stavenow, "Det 18:de århundradets parlamentarism i Sverige," *Uppsala universitets årsskrift 1923,* Program I, 32 pp.; Eino Jutikkala, *A History of Finland* (London, 1962), 144–45, 157–58. Michael Roberts, *Swedish and English Parliamentarianism in the Eighteenth Century* (James Ford Special Lecture at Oxford University, 1973) (Belfast: The Queen's University, 1973).

61. Michael Roberts, "On Aristocratic Constitutionalism in Swedish History, 1520–1720," and "The Swedish Aristocracy in the Eighteenth Century," in his *Essays on Swedish History,* 14–55, 269–85.

62. Valentin, *Frihetstidens riddarhus,* 1, 81, 88–95.

63. For the political order during the "Era of Freedom," see esp. Carlsson, *Svensk historia,* II, 96–106; Roberts, *Swedish and English Parliamentarianism.*

64. See Carlsson, *Byråkrati och borgarstånd.* Cf. Roberts, *Swedish and English Parliamentarianism,* 14–16; Söderberg, *Den namnlösa medelklassen,* 201–9. On the historiography of the period, see Hugo Valentin, *Frihetstiden inför eftervärlden* (2d ed., Stockholm, 1964).

65. On Finland's position, see Jutikkala, *History of Finland,* 142–44, 153; Juva, *Finlands väg,* 165–73; Sten Carlsson, "Finlands ämbetsmän och Sveriges rike under 1700-talet," in his *Grupper och gestalter* (Stockholm, 1964), 60–74. On Finnish participation in the *Riksdag,* see Pentti Renvall, *Finsk representation i Sveriges riksdag* (Stockholm, 1967); and Toivo J. Paloposki, *Suomen talonpoikaissäädyn valtiopäiväedustus vapaudenajalla* (Helsinki, 1961), the latter on Finns in the Peasant Estate. Paloposki estimates (p. 462) that about 2/5 of the Finnish population, of which 91.5% were peasants, enjoyed political representation.

66. Dalgren, *Sverige och Pommern,* 1–14.

67. See my "Russia and the Problem of Sweden-Finland, 1721–1809," *East European Quarterly,* 5 (1972), 431–55.

68. Juva, *Finlands väg,* 47, 55–66, 182–83; Hornborg, *Finlands hävder,* III, 521–25.

69. The ethnic-linguistic boundaries between Dane and German in Schleswig are the subject of a voluminous and largely polemic literature. See, however, Linvald, *SDH,* IV:1, 234–36; Klose & Degn, *GSH,* VI, 114–24.

70. From his *Regni Suecie geographica et politica descriptio,* quoted in Carlo Cipolla, *Literacy and Development in the West* (Harmondsworth,1966), 54n. Steen, *NFLH,* VI, 345; G. S. Mackenzie, *Travels in the Island of Iceland during the Summer of the Year 1810* (2d ed., Edinburgh, 1812), 310.

71. See Wilhelm Sjöstrand, *Pedagogikens historia,* 3 vols. (Lund, 1945–65), III:1; Mauno Jokipii and Ilka Nummela, eds., *Ur nordisk kulturhistoria. Läskunnighet och folkbildning före folkskoleväsendet* (Jyväskylä, 1981); my "Popular Education in Eighteenth-Century Sweden: Theory and Practice," in James A. Leith, ed., *Aspects of Education in the Eighteenth Century,* Studies in Voltaire and the Eighteenth Century, 167 (Oxford, 1977), 523–41; Steen, *NFLH,* VI, 338–50.

72. Mackenzie, *Travels,* 310–11; Juva, *Finlands väg,* 179–82.

73. Stephensen, *Island i det 18. Aarhundrede,* 154–65.

74. Torben Holck Colding, et al., *Akademiet og Guldalderen 1750–1850* (Copenhagen, 1972); Andreas Lindblom, *Sveriges konsthistoria* (Stockholm, 1947); Carl Laurin, et al., *Scandinavian Art* (New York, 1922).

75. Francis Bull, *Fra Holberg til Nordal Brun* (Christiania, 1916), 163–65.

76. See J. W. Eaton, *The German Influence in Danish Literature in the Eighteenth Century* (Cambridge, Mass., 1929); cf. Bull, *Fra Holberg til Nordal Brun,* 36–38, 223–24.

77. Heinrich Steffens, *Was ich erlebte,* 10 vols. (Breslau, 1840–44), II, 135.

78. See Bull, *Fra Holberg til Nordal Brun,* 28–29.

79. Ingemar Carlsson, *Olof Dalin och den politiska propagandan inför "lilla ofreden"* (Lund,

1966), chaps. 2–3, and *Frihetstidens handskrivna politiska litteratur. En bibliografi* (Göteborg, 1967).

80. See Per-Erik Brolin, *Hattar och mössor i borgarståndet 1760–1766* (Uppsala, 1953), 314–15; Edvard Holm, *Om det Syn paa Kongemagt, Folk og Borgerlig Frihed der udviklede sig i den dansk-norske Stat i Midten af 18de Aarhundrede* (Copenhagen, 1883).

81. Steffens, *Was ich erlebte*, II, 57. On rationalism in the Danish church, cf. T. A. Müller, *SDH*, IV:2, 304–9.

82. Cf. Ludwig Selmer, *Oplysningsmenn i den norske kirke* (Bergen, 1923).

83. On eighteenth-century Scandinavian topographical literature, see Mead, *Economic Geography*, 86–89.

84. See A. Pontoppidan Thyssen, et al., "De religiosa folkrörelserna och samhället ca. 1750–1850," *Historiallinen arkisto*, 62 (1967), 7–112. On reactions against the Enlightenment in general, see Martin Lamm, *Upplysningstidens romantik*, 2 vols. (Stockholm, 1918–20).

85. Brolin, *Hattar och mössor i borgarståndet*, 391; Lagerroth, *Frihetstidens författning*, 570–71, 575; Steffens, *Was ich erlebte*, II, 135.

86. Rutger Fredrik Hochschild, *Memoarer*, ed. H. Schück, 3 vols. (Stockholm, 1908–9), I, 51. Cf. my "Gustav III of Sweden and the Enlightenment," *Eighteenth-Century Studies*, 6 (1972), 24–25.

87. Brandt, *Geistesleben und Politik*, 54–55.

88. On eighteenth-century nationalism in Scandinavia, see *ibid.*; Paul Koopmann, *Deutsch und Dänisch um die Wende des 18. Jahrhunderts* (Neumünster, 1939); Andreas Elviken, *Die Entwicklung des norwegischen Nationalismus* (Berlin, 1939), condensed in the same author's "The Genesis of Norwegian Nationalism," *Journal of Modern History*, 3 (1931), 365–91; John H. Wuorinen, *Nationalism in Modern Finland* (New York, 1931), 12–28; Pentti Renvall, "Ueber die Wurzeln der finnischen Autonomie im 18. Jahrhundert," *Sitzungsberichte der finnischen Akademie der Wissenschaften 1960* (Helsinki, 1960).

89. Montesquieu, *L'Esprit des lois* (1748), Bk. XVII, chaps. 2, 5.

90. See esp. Anton Blanck, *Den nordiska renässansen i sjuttonhundratalets litteratur* (Stockholm, 1911). Cf. Pierre van Tieghem, *Le Préromanticisme*, 3 vols. (Paris, 1929–48), I.

91. Bull, *Fra Holberg til Nordal Brun*, 24–42, 233–38; Albert Olsen, *Danmark-Norge i det 18. Aarhundrede* (Copenhagen, 1936), 91–93; Gösta Lext, *Bok och samhälle i Göteborg 1720–1809* (Göteborg, 1950); Brolin, *Hattar och mössor i borgarståndet*, 309–19, 398, 408; Söderberg, *Den namnlösa medelklassen*, 245–57.

92. Carl Michael Bellman's ever-popular ballads affectionately satirize the social pretentions of Stockholm's lower classes in the later eighteenth century. See Paul Britten Austin, *Carl Michael Bellman* (New York, 1967).

93. Juva, *Finlands väg*, 170–71.

94. On Fougner, see Bull, *Fra Holberg til Nordal Brun*, 60–71.

## CHAPTER 2. THE WINDS OF CHANGE, 1760–70

1. See my "Russia and the Problem of Sweden-Finland," 444; R. Nisbet Bain, *Peter III, Emperor of Russia* (London, 1902), 112–22; Erik Amburger, *Russland und Schweden 1762–1772. Katharine II., die schwedische Verfassung und die Ruhe des Nordens* (Berlin, 1934), 47–60.

2. Klose & Degn, *GSH*, VI, 41–45.

3. Jørgensen, *Bornholms Historie*, II, 155–59.

4. See [J. Chr. Berg, ed.,] "Efterretninger om Opløbet i Bergen 1766 i Anledning af Extra-skatten," *Saga*, 3 (Christiania, 1820), 307–526; Georg Sverdrup, "Strilekrigen. Bondeopløbet i Bergen 1765," *Skrifter utgivne av Bergens historiske forening*, 25–26 (Bergen, 1921), 9–107.

5. Koht, *Norsk bondereising*, 303–4. Cf. Steen, *NFLH*, VI, 401–2, 404–5, 408–9; Bull, *Fra Holberg til Nordal Brun*, 10, 17–18.

6. See esp. K. C. Rockstroh, *Udviklingen af den nationale Hær i Danmark i det 17. og 18. Aarhundrede*, 3 vols. (Copenhagen, 1909–16), III, 196–261, *passim*; Jens Johansen, *Frederik VI.s Hær 1784–1814* (Copenhagen, 1948), 7–14.

7. See Holm, *DNH*, IV:1,12–13, 74–75, 221–23, 229, 232–34; Bech, *DHP*, IX, 306–9, 401–3, 437; Knud J. V. Jespersen, "Claude Louis, Comte de Saint-Germain: Professionel soldat, dansk

militærreformator og fransk krigsminister," *Scandia*, 48 (1983), 87-102. Much of the correspondence of the Saint-Germain circle is printed in Holger Hansen, ed., *Inkvisitions-Kommissionen af 20. Januar 1772*, 5 vols. (Copenhagen, 1927-41), vols. 2-5.

8. E. S. F. Reverdil, *Struensee og det danske Hof*, trans. and ed. P. L. Müller, ed. Louis Bobé (Copenhagen, 1916), 58-59.

9. Carl Gustaf Malmström, *Sveriges politiska historia från konung Karl XII:s död til statshvälfningen 1772*, 6 vols. (2d ed., Stockholm, 1893-1901), V, 259.

10. Brolin, *Hattar och mössor i borgarståndet*, 355. See also Roberts, *Swedish and English Parliamentarianism*, 10-12.

11. Carlsson, *Svensk historia*, II, 165.

12. Carlsson, *Ståndssamhälle och ståndspersoner* (2d ed., 1973), 249-51; Sten Carlsson, "Sweden in the 1760s," in Steven Koblik, ed., *Sweden's Development from Poverty to Affluence, 1750-1970* (Minneapolis, 1975), 21-22; Lagerroth, *Frihetstidens författning*, 636; Valentin, *Frihetstidens riddarhus*, 88, 229, 234-35, 279, 285, 289-92.

13. Brolin, *Hattar och mössor i borgarståndet*; Carlsson, "Sweden in the 1760s." Cf. Lamm, *Upplysningstidens romantik*, I, chap. 4.

14. See Arndt Öberg, *De yngre mössorna och deras utländska bundsförvanter 1765-1769* (Stockholm, 1970), 62-69. Also Daniel Mornet, *Les origines intellectuelles de la Révolution française, 1715-1787* (Paris, 1933), 20-25, 105-19, 125-27; Lamm, *Upplysningstidens romantik*, I, 244, 248. Cf. Brolin, *Hattar och mössor i borgarståndet*, 410-13.

15. Cf. Brolin, *Hattar och mössor i borgarståndet*, 410-13.

16. On Nordencrantz, see Lagerroth, *Frihetstidens författning*, 508-42; Brolin, *Hattar och mössor i borgarståndet*, 261-74, 386-88; Öberg, *De yngre mössorna*, 62-79; P. J. Edler, *Om börd och befordran under frihetstiden* (Stockholm, 1915), 137n. Carlsson, "Sweden in the 1760s," 24-25; Michael F. Metcalf, "Challenges to Economic Orthodoxy and Parliamentary Sovereignty in 18th Century Sweden," *Legislative Studies Quarterly*, 7 (1982), 252-54.

17. Brolin, *Hattar och mössor i borgarståndet*, 376-80; Edler, *Om börd och befordran*, 136-37.

18. See esp. Michael Roberts, *British Diplomacy and Swedish Politics, 1758-1773* (Minneapolis, 1980); Michael F. Metcalf, *Russia, England and Swedish Party Politics, 1762-1766* (Stockholm, 1977).

19. Brolin, *Hattar och mössor i borgarståndet*, 25-26, 97-102, 140-41, 288-93; Söderberg, *Den namnlösa medelklassen*, 168-69, 225-26, 232, 236-37; Carlsson, "Sweden in the 1760s," 26, 28-30.

20. Anders Chydenius, *Politiska skrifter*, ed. E. G. Palmén (Helsingfors, 1880), 117.

21. On Chydenius, see Eli F. Heckscher, "Anders Chydenius," in *Svenskt biografiskt lexikon*, 8 (Stockholm, 1929), 516-32; Carl Uhr, "Anders Chydenius, 1729-1803," *Western Economic Journal*, 2 (1964), 85-116; Brolin, *Hattar och mössor i borgarståndet*, 389-90; Lagerroth, *Frihetstidens författning*, 577; Carlsson, "Sweden in the 1760s," 27; Metcalf, "Challenges," 254-55.

22. Gustaf Fredrik Gyllenborg, *Mitt lefverne 1731-1775*, ed. Gudmund Frunck, (Stockholm, 1885), 59-60. Cf. Metcalf, *Russia, England and Swedish Party Politics*, 155-69.

23. Holm, *DNH*, IV:1, 234.

24. Bech, *DHP*, IX, 424.

25. Holm, *DNH*, IV:1, 17.

26. On Christian VII's early peculiarities, see esp. Reverdil, *Struensee og det danske Hof*, 1-16 passim. His condition has been retrospectively diagnosed as *dementia præcox*. See V. Christiansen, *Christian 7.s Sindssygdom* (Copenhagen, 1906).

27. Tønnesson, "Problèmes de la féodalité," 333.

28. See Wolfgang Prange, *Die Anfänge der grossen Agrarreformen in Schleswig-Holstein bis um 1771* (Neumünster, 1971); Blum, *End of the Old Order*, 324-25.

29. Aage Friis, "Andreas Peter Bernstorff og 'den nye Indretning i Landbruget' paa Bernstorff," in *Til Edvard Holm paa hans 80-aarige Fødelsedag den 26. Januar 1913*, supplement to *HTD*, 8:4 (1913), 98-114; Aage Friis, *Bernstorfferne og Danmark*, 2 vols. (Copenhagen, 1902-19), II, 361-86; L. Gotfredsen, *Bernstorffs bønder* (Hellerup, 1965).

30. Holm, *DNH*, IV:1, 309-12; Christensen, *Agrarhistoriske Studier*, II, 10-11; Hvidtfeldt, *Kampen om ophævelsen*, 48-49.

31. The relative importance of German, as opposed to English and French ideas, in Denmark, is maintained by Johan Hvidtfeldt in *Kampen om ophævelsen*, esp. 23–31; this is contested by C. O. Bøggild-Andersen in his review of Hvidtfeldt's study, in *HTD*, 12:1 (1964), 354–56.

32. The classic work on the debate over agrarian reform in Denmark remains Edvard Holm's *Kampen om Landboreformerne i Danmark i Slutningen af 18. Aarhundrede (1773–1791)* (Copenhagen, 1888), upon which the relevant sections of his *DNH* are based. See also Jensen, *Dansk Jordpolitik*, I, esp. 88–94, 242–43; Albert Olsen, "Samtidens Syn paa den danske stavns-bundne Bonde," *Scandia*, 12 (1939), 99–139. Skrubbeltrang estimates that two-thirds of the approximately 5,000 works on agriculture printed in Denmark, 1750–1815, are on practical matters. (*Det danske landbosamfund*, 267.) For Lehn's comments, Bech, *DHP*, IX, 453; cf. Jensen, *Reventlow*, 68–69.

33. Reverdil, *Struensee og det danske Hof*, 4–5, 48–49, 53–54, 57–58. On Reverdil's and Saint-Germain's positions, see also Jensen, *Dansk Jordpolitik*, I, 48–52, 57–58, 64; Jensen, et al., *Stånd-samhällets upplösing i Norden*, 12.

34. Reverdil, *Struensee og det danske Hof*, 60–61; Fridericia, ed., *Aktstykker*, 196, 198, 199, 201, 202–6, 207, 219, 226.

35. Fridericia, ed., *Aktstykker*, 183–92; Reverdil, *Struensee og det danske Hof*, 53, 58, 78–80.

36. See Jensen, *Dansk Jordpolitik*, I, 52–56, 75–86, 241–42.

37. My "Gustav III and the Enlightenment," 2–4.

38. Roberts, *British Diplomacy and Swedish Politics*, 227, 314–15.

39. Malmström, *Sveriges politiska historia 1718–1772*, VI, 83–84.

40. *Borgmästarens och Riksdags-Fullmäktigens ifrån Lovisa Stad, Herr And. Keppleri Memorial rörande Privilegier för Borgare och Bonde-Stånden* (Stockholm, 1770). See Göran von Bonsdorff, "En finländsk insats i frihetstidens statsrättsliga diskussion. Kring Alexander Kepplerus' memorial angående privilegier för de ofrälse stånden." *Skrifter utgivna av Svenska litteratursällskapet i Finland*, 335 (Helsingfors, 1952), 315–58; Gunnar Kjellin, "Kring Alexander Kepplerus' memorial," *HTS*, 75 (1955), 276–91; Lagerroth, *Frihetstidens författning, 637–40;* Edler, *Om börd och befordran*, 161–65; Renvall, *Finsk representation*, 330; Metcalf, "Challenges," 257.

41. Malmström, *Sveriges politiska historia 1718–1772*, VI, 192–93; Adolf Ludvig Hamilton, *Anekdoter till svenska historien under Gustaf III:s regering*, ed. O. Levertin (Stockholm, 1901), 52. See also Carlsson, *Ståndssamhälle och ståndspersoner* (1973 ed.), 249–50; Ingvar Elmroth, *Nyrekryteringen till de högre ämbetene 1720–1809* (Lund, 1962), esp. 263–65.

42. My "Russia and the Problem of Sweden-Finland," 445–46.

## CHAPTER 3. THE FIRST ASSAULT ON PRIVILEGE, 1770–72

1. On Struensee generally, see Reverdil, *Struensee og det danske Hof*; Jens Kragh Høst, *Geheime Kabinettsminister Grev Johann Friedrich Struensee og hans Ministerium*, 3 vols. (Copenhagen, 1824); Karl Wittich, *Struensee* (Leipzig, 1879); Henry Steele Commager, "Struensee and the Reform Movement in Denmark" (unpublished Ph.D. dissertation, University of Chicago, 1928); Svend Cedergreen Bech, *Struensee og hans tid* (Copenhagen, 1972); Ludvig Koch, "Struensees Parti," *HTD*, 6:5 (1894–95), 63–120.

2. Much has naturally been written about this relationship, including popularizations and historical novels. See esp. Christian Blangstrup, *Christian VII og Caroline Mathilde* (3d ed., Copenhagen, 1894) and W. H. Wilkins, *A Queen of Tears*, 2 vols. (London, 1904).

3. Bech, *DHP*, IX, 435–36.

4. *Ibid.*, 436. See also W. F. Reddaway, "Struensee and the Fall of Bernstorff," *English Historical Review*, 27 (1912), 274–86.

5. Bech, *DHP*, IX, 449.

6. The cabinet orders are contained in Holger Hansen, ed., *Kabinetsstyrelsen i Danmark 1768–1782. Aktstykker og Oplysninger*, 3 vols. (Copenhagen, 1916–23). On the possible extent of the king's personal role during Struensee's first months in power, see W. F. Reddaway, "King Christian VII," *English Historical Review*, 31 (1916), 59–84.

7. On the influence of Saint-Germain, see L. Koch, ed., "Breve fra Slutningen af det 18. Aarhundrede," *Dansk Magazin*, 5:3 (1893–97), 38–40; Commager, "Struensee," 21–22; Bech, *Struensee*, 215.

394 NOTES TO PP. 71–80

8. Fridericia, ed., *Aktstykker*, 252–56. Cf. *ibid.*, 246–50, 256–58; Skrubbeltrang, *Det danske landbosamfund*, 364–67; Feldbæk, *DHG*, 151; Olsen, "Samtidens Syn," 115–16.

9. Cf. Eigill Snorrason, *Johann Friedrich Struensee, læge og geheimestatsminister* (Copenhagen, 1968), on medicine and public hygiene.

10. Reverdil, *Struensee og det danske Hof*, 161–64. See also Reddaway, "King Christian VII."

11. On these writings, see Edvard Holm, *Nogle Hovedtræk af Trykkefrihedens Historie 1770–1773* (Copenhagen, 1885), upon which the more abridged treatment in his *DNH*, IV:2, is based.

12. Gerhard Schøning, *Norges Riiges Historie*, 3 vols. (Sorø, 1771–81).

13. See Holm, *Nogle Hovedtræk*, 66–86.

14. Holm, *DNH*, IV:2, 294.

15. Cf. [S. O. Falckenskiold], *Mémoires de M. de Falckenskiold* (Paris, 1826), 150.

16. On Guldberg's role, see Bech, *Struensee*, 316–17, 322, 324, 409, 412.

17. Bech, ed., *Breve fra Dorothea*, 294.

18. The documents of the inquest and trial of Struensee and Brandt are given in Hansen, ed., *Inkvisitions-Kommissionen*. A selection is also given in Victor Lange, *Fra Struenseetiden* (Copenhagen, 1926).

19. Cf. Reverdil, *Struensee og det danske Hof*, 131–32, 254–56, 263–64; Holm, *DNH*, IV:2, 402–17; Linvald, *SDH*, IV:1, 66–67; Bech, *Struensee*, 394, 403.

20. See Henry Steel Commager, "Struensee and the Enlightenment," in his *The Search for a Usable Past and Other Essays in Historiography* (New York, 1967), 350–51.

21. *Ibid.*, 353.

22. Reverdil, *Struensee og det danske Hof*, 102.

23. My "Gustav III and the Enlightenment," esp. 7; Henrik Schück, ed., *Gustaf III:s och Lovisa Ulrikas brevväxling*, 2 vols. (Stockholm, 1919), I, 261–62.

24. Edler, *Om börd och befordran*, 171.

25. J.-B. Dechaux, ed., *Collection des écrits politiques, littéraires et dramatiques de Gustave III, roi de Suède, suivie de sa correspondance*, 5 vols. (Stockholm, 1803–5), I, 87.

26. My "Gustav III and the Enlightenment," 9–10. See also Beth Hennings, "Gustav III och författningen," in her *Fyra gustavianska studier* (Stockholm, 1967), 7–94; Birger Sallnäs, "England i den svenska författningsdiskussionen 1771–72," *Vetenskapssocieteten i Lunds årsbok 1958–59* (Lund, 1959), 19–31; Gunnar Kjellin, "Gustaf III, den patriotiske konungen," in *Gottfrid Carlsson 18.12.1952* (Lund, 1952), 323–38.

27. My "Gustav III and the Enlightenment," esp. 10, 12–13, 33.

28. Lagerroth, *Frihetstidens författning*, 637–41, 671–73; Edler, *Om börd och befordran*, 161–67, 183–94. On the peasants' demands specifically, see Ingers, *Bonden i svensk historia*, II, 84–85; Erland Alexandersson, *Bondeståndet i riksdagen 1760–1772* (Lund, 1975).

29. L. Bonneville de Marsagny, *Le comte de Vergennes: son ambasade en Suède, 1771–1774* (Paris, 1898), 140.

30. Edler, *Om börd och befordran*, 136–37, 152, 243–44; Lagerroth, *Frihetstidens författning*, 644–45.

31. Dechaux, *Écrits de Gustave III*, I, 89–92; Alexandersson, *Bondeståndet i riksdagen*, 209.

32. Lagerroth, *Frihetstidens författning*, 665.

33. Schück, *Brevväxling*, II, 135.

34. Malmström, *Sveriges politiska historia*, VI, 242–44, 276.

35. Edler, *Om börd och befordran*, 158–59, 168–69, 200–201.

36. Lagerroth, *Frihetstidens författning*, 702–3, 709.

37. Jacob Wallenberg, *Min son på galejan* (Stockholm: Prisma ed., 1960), 10; translation by Michael Roberts in his *Swedish and English Parliamentarism*, 26. On reactions against partisan politics, cf. Roberts, *ibid.*, esp. 40; Michael F. Metcalf, "Freedom of the Press and Attitudes toward Party in Sweden, 1766–72," in Warren F. Spencer, ed., *Proceedings of the Twelfth Consortium on Revolutionary Europe, 1750–1850* (Athens, Ga., 1983), 180–204.

38. Malmström, *Sveriges politiska historia*, VI, 343.

39. See Crown Prince Gustav's justification of dissimulation under certain circumstances to his

governor, C. F. Scheffer, in 1759, in Dechaux, *Écrits de Gustave III*, IV, 3. On French pressure for a coup, see Roberts, *British Diplomacy and Swedish Politics*, 370–73, 390–92.
40. Schück, *Brevväxling*, II, 135–36.
41. Aurélien Vivie, ed., *Lettres de Gustave III à la comtesse de Boufflers et de la comtesse au roi* (Paris, 1898), 51.
42. R. M. Klinckowström, ed., *Riksrådet och fält-marskalken m. m. Fredrik Axel von Fersens historiska skrifter*, 8 vols. (Stockholm, 1867–72), III, 84; Metcalf, *Russia, England and Swedish Party Politics*, 168.
43. See Roberts, *British Diplomacy and Swedish Politics*, 373; Gabriel Nikander, "Filosofi och politik i Gustav III:s Finland," in his *Gustaviansk politik i Finland. Essäer* (Åbo, 1958), 15. Cf. Gunnar Suolahti, *Sprengtportens statskupp och andra essayer* (Helsingfors, 1919).
44. Vivie, *Lettres*, 51. For a comparison of Sweden's and Poland's situations, see Ladislaus Konopczyński, "Polen och Sverige i det adertonde århundradet. En historisk parallel," *HTS*, 45 (1925), 101–31; the same author's "Svensk-polska analogier," *Svio-Polonica*, 8–9 (1946–47), 5–17; Amburger, *Russland und Schweden 1762–72*, 267–68.
45. On the historiography of the Swedish revolution of 1772, see Herman Schück, *Gustaf III:s statsvälvning 1772 i berättande källor och äldre litteratur*, Historiskt arkiv, 4 (Stockholm, 1955).
46. Dechaux, *Écrits de Gustave III*, I, 102–5.
47. Klinckowström, ed., *F. A. von Fersens historiska skrifter*, III, 115.
48. See Birger Sallnäs, "Det offrälse inslaget i 1772 års revolution," *HTS*, 74 (1954), 139–40; Roberts, *Swedish and English Parliamentarianism*, 40–41.
49. Dechaux, *Ecrits de Gustave III*, I, 107.
50. On the background to the constitution, see C. T. Odhner, *Sveriges politiska historia under konung Gustaf III:s regering*, 3 vols. (Stockholm, 1885–1905), I, 112–13; Folke Almén, *Gustav III och hans rådgivare 1772–1789* (Uppsala, 1940), 9–51; Hennings, "Gustav III och författningen," 24–31. On the foreign powers, see Amburger, *Russland und Schweden*, 208–13, 219–20; Michael Roberts, "Great Britain, Denmark and Russia, 1763–1770" in Ragnhild Hatton and M. S. Anderson, eds., *Studies in Diplomatic History: Essays in Memory of David Bayne Horn* (London, 1970), 236–67.
51. The official English translation of the constitution of 1772 is given in full in William Coxe, *Travels into Poland, Russia, Sweden and Denmark*, 4 vols. (London, 1787), IV, 429–47; quotation from *ibid.*, 433–34.
52. Schück, *Brevväxling*, II, 255.
53. E. G. Geijer, ed., *Konung Gustaf III:s efterlemnade och femtio år efter hans död öppnade papper* (2d. ed., Stockholm, 1876), 59; Almén, *Gustav III och hans rådgivare*, 43, 45–46, 51 (quotation).
54. Almén, *Gustav III och hans rådgivare*, 52.
55. My "Gustav III and the Enlightenment," 14–15; Amburger, *Russland und Schweden*, 266; Klinckowström, ed., *F. A. von Fersens historiska skrifter*, III, 131; [John Louis Delolme], *A Parallel between the English Constitution and the Former Government of Sweden* (London, 1772), esp. 34, 49.
56. See, for instance, Odhner, *Gustaf III:s regering*, I, 241; Ludvig Stavenow, *Den gustavianska tiden 1772–1809* (Stockholm, 1925), 11–13; Almén, *Gustav III och hans rådgivare*, 40–41, 51, 53; Hennings, "Gustav III och författningen," 30, 36–37. For the historiography on Gustav III, see Georg Landberg, *Gustaf III inför eftervärlden* (Stockholm, 1968).
57. See Valentin, *Frihetstiden inför eftervarlden*; Roberts, *Swedish and English Parliamentarism*; Roberts, *British Diplomacy and Swedish Politics*, esp. 227, 381; Lagerroth, *Frihetstidens författning*, esp. 709, 712, 733–35; Michael F. Metcalf, "The First 'Modern' Party System? Political Parties, Sweden's Age of Liberty and the Historians," *Scandinavian Journal of History*, 2 (1977), 265–87; and "Structuring Parliamentary Politics: Party Organization in Eighteenth-Century Sweden," *Parliaments, Estates & Representation*, 1 (1981), 35–49; Carlsson, "Sweden in the 1760s," 20.
58. Amburger, *Russland und Schweden*, 266; Elof Tegnér, "Bidrag till kännedom om Sveriges yttre politik närmast efter statshvälfningen 1772," in his *Valda skrifter*, V (Stockholm, 1906),

97-192; Michael Roberts, "Great Britain and the Swedish Revolution, 1772-73," in his *Essays in Swedish History*, 286-347; Holm, *DNH*, V, 43-50.

59. See Holm, *DNH*, IV:2, 147-48; Linvald, *SDH*, IV:1, 11-12; Bech, *DHP*, IX, 437; Lagerroth, *Frihetstidens författning*, 712, 718-19, 733-35; Edler, *Om börd och befordran*, 171, 255; Brolin, *Hattar och mössor i borgarståndet*, 376, 396-97, 417; Carlsson, "Sweden in the 1760s," 17-18, 32-33, 35; Öberg, *De yngre mössorna*, 83-84. Cf. Commager, "Struensee and the Enlightenment," 352-53, 358.

## CHAPTER 4. THE RALLYING OF THE OLD ORDER, 1772-76

1. Aage Friis, *Andreas Peter Bernstorff og Ove Høegh Guldberg. Bidrag til den guldbergske tids historie* (Copenhagen, 1899), 3-5, 54-58; Holm, *DNH*, V, 19-20, 211. For examples of the suspicions against Juliane Marie, see Charlotta Dorothea Biehl's letters in Bech, ed., *Breve fra Dorothea*, esp. 284, 286, 289-94, 296, 300-302.

2. Holm, *DNH*, V, 21-23, 211-12.

3. Friis, *Bernstorff og Guldberg*, 61-62; Holm, *DNH*, V, 105-6, 218, 221.

4. Holm, *DNH*, V, 36.

5. For a summary of what was revoked and what retained from the Struensee regime, see Commager, "Struensee," 279-99.

6. Skrubbeltrang, *Det danske landbosamfund*, 366-70; For Guldberg's views on agriculture, see esp. J. B. Bang, ed., "Breve fra Ove Høegh-Guldberg til Johan v. Bülow," *HTD*, 4:1 (1868-70), 164-70; Jensen, *Dansk Jordpolitik*, I, 103-9.

7. Holm, *Nogle Hovedtræk*, 128.

8. On press opinion, see esp. *ibid.*, 98-119. On the conspiracy around Caroline Mathilde, see Holm, *DNH*, V, 235-45. Cf. Nathanael Wraxall, *Memoirs* (London, 1884).

9. Bech, *DHP*, IX, 492, 500; cf. Bech, ed., *Breve fra Dorothea*, 218, 229, 289-94.

10. Holm, *DNH*, V, 148, 153-54.

11. Holm, *Nogle Hovedtræk*, 99-108.

12. Bang, *"Breve til Bülow,"* 178-79; Bech, *DHP*, IX, 499.

13. See Olsen, *Bybefolkningen*, 84-85; Rockstroh, *Udviklingen af den nationale Hær*, III, 279; Johansen, *Frederik VI.s Hær*, 11-14.

14. Friis, *Bernstorff og Guldberg*, 68; Brandt, *Geistesleben und Politik*, 54-55.

15. Brandt, *Geistesleben und Politik*, 255, 257; Friis, *Bernstorff og Guldberg*, 157.

16. On the duchies in this period, see esp. Brandt, *Geistesleben und Politik*, 18, 26-41, 53; Friis, *Bernstorff og Guldberg*, 118-42; Klose & Degn, *GSH*, VI, 11-12, 41-47, 84-88, 180-81.

17. Mykland, *NH*, IX, 28-36; Steen, *NFLH*, VII, 68.

18. See esp. Holm, *Nogle Hovedtræk*, 131-59.

19. Wallenberg, *Min son på galejan*, 37.

20. Geijer, ed., *Gustaf III:s efterlemnade papper*, 154-57.

21. Holm, *DNH*, V, 47.

22. See Lydia Wahlström, "Gustaf III och norrmännen," *Nordisk tidskrift* (1907), 56-61. For greater detail, cf. Yngvar Nielsen, "Gustav III's norske politik," *HTN*, II:1 (1877), 1-308.

23. Geijer, ed., *Gustaf III:s efterlemnade papper*, 58, 60 (quotation), 61. On the influence of Montesquieu, see my "Gustav III and the Enlightenment," 12-13.

24. Stig Boberg, *Gustaf III och tryckfriheten 1774-1786* (Göteborg, 1951), 139-43; Geijer, ed., *Gustaf III:s efterlemnade papper*, 155-56.

25. Vivie, *Lettres*, 51.

26. Tom Söderberg, *Två sekel svensk medelklass från gustaviansk tid till nutid* (Stockholm, 1972), 9. Cf. Carlsson, *Ståndssamhälle och ståndspersoner*, 250-51. R. R. Palmer, in *The Age of the Democratic Revolution*, I, 99-103, implies that Gustav III's coup of 1772 was actually antiaristocratic in nature. See my "Scandinavia and the Atlantic Revolution," in Warren F. Spencer, ed., *Proceedings of the Twelfth Consortium on Revolutionary Europe, 1750-1850* (Athens, Ga., 1983), esp. 149-50.

27. Valentin, *Frihetstidens riddarhus*, 284-85; Carlsson, *Ståndssamhälle och ståndspersoner*, 251; Söderberg, *Den namnlösa medelklassen*, 32, 178.

28. Carlsson, *Ståndssamhälle och ståndspersoner*, 250-51. On Gustav III's court, see esp. Beth

Hennings, *Gustav III* (Stockholm, 1957). R. Nisbet Bain's now largely obsolete *Gustavus III and His Contemporaries*, 2 vols. (London, 1894), gives many details, based on the memoir literature of the time.

29. Odhner, *Gustaf III:s regering*, I, 302–7, 337–39; Ingers, *Bonden i svensk historia*, II, 316–22; Johan R. Danielson-Kalmari, *Finland under gustavianska tiden*, 2 vols. (Stockholm, 1926), 96–100; Smedberg, *Frälsebonderörelser i Halland och Skåne*. On manifestations of peasant unrest in Denmark in this period, see Holm, *DNH*, V, 387–88.

30. For Gustav III's reforms in general see esp. Odhner, *Gustaf III:s regering*, I. For a good brief survey, see also Nordmann, *Grandeur et Liberté de la Suède*, 338–51.

31. See Erik Anners, *Humanitet och rationalism* (Stockholm, 1965); my "Gustav III and the Enlightenment," 16.

32. My "Gustav III and the Enlightenment," 17.

33. Odhner, *Gustaf III:s regering*, I, 352.

34. See Hornborg, *Finlands hävder*, III, 304–5, 516–17; Sven Ulric Palme, "Gustav III och Finland," *Nordisk tidskrift*, 49 (1973), esp. 147–49; Stewart P. Oakley, "Gustavus III and Finland in 1775," *Scandinavian Studies*, 51 (1979), 1–12; Jutikkala, *Bonden i Finland*, 272–76.

35. Carlsson, *Svensk historia*, II, 209. Cf. Söderberg, *Två sekel*, 16–17.

36. Cf. Palme, "Gustav III och Finland," 149, 151, which stresses the ties between domestic reform and military strength.

37. Odhner, *Gustaf III:s regering*, I, 274–75.

38. Dechaux, *Écrits de Gustave III*, I, 234–40.

39. Odhner, *Gustaf III:s regering*, I, 279–80; Boberg, *Gustav III och tryckfriheten*, 43–55.

40. Nils Staf, *Polisväsendet i Stockholm 1776–1850* (Uppsala, 1950), 47–55.

41. Boberg, *Gustav III och tryckfriheten*, esp. 56–57, 76. Cf. S. U. Palme, "Filosofen på tronen," in his *Vår tids hjältar* (Stockholm, 1953), 86–89; Landberg, *Gustav III i eftervärldens dom*, 121–24.

42. Dechaux, *Écrits de Gustave III*, I, 222.

43. My "Gustav III and the Enlightenment," esp. 17.

44. Birger Sallnäs, "Gustav III som inrikespolitiker—hatt eller mössa?," in *Gottfried Carlsson 18.12.1952* (Lund, 1952), 339–48. Cf. Carlsson, "Sweden in the 1760s," 35.

45. Renvall, *Finsk representation*, 354.

46. Schück, *Brevväxling*, I, 223.

## CHAPTER 5. THE CLASH OF ARMS AND IDEAS, 1776–83

1. *Fredmans testamente*, No. 1, quoted in Amandus Johnson, *Swedish Contributions to American Freedom, 1776–1783*, 2 vols. (Philadelphia, 1953–57), I, 148.

2. Thorkild Kjærgaard, *Denmark Gets the News of '76* (Copenhagen, 1976), esp. 9–19; Vivie, *Lettres*, 101–2.

3. Aage Friis, ed., *Bernstorffske Papirer*, 3 vols. (Copenhagen, 1903–13), III, 498. Regarding Schimmelmann, see Friis, *Bernstorff og Guldberg*, 115.

4. My discussion of Swedish opinion, like much of the material on Sweden-Finland in this chapter, is based on my article, "Sweden and the War of American Independence," *William & Mary Quarterly*, 3d series, 23 (1966), 408–30.

5. G. F. Schumacher, *Genrebilder aus dem Leben eines siebzigjährigen Schulmannes* (Schleswig, 1841), 147.

6. Klose & Degn, *GSH*, VI, 108.

7. *Ibid.*, 189.

8. Friis, *Bernstorff og Guldberg*, 153–55.

9. The whole conflict is best described in Klose & Degn, *GSH*, VI, 185–90.

10. Holm, *DNH*, V, 263.

11. *Ibid.*, 268; Bech, *DHP*, IX, 519.

12. See esp. Friis, *Bernstorff og Guldberg*, 64–71.

13. *Ibid.*, 76–77, 97–117; Holm, *DNH*, V, 88–92, 246–51; Klose & Degn, *GSH*, VI, 165–75. Cf. Fritz Valjavec, *Die Entstehung der politischen Strömungen in Deutschland 1770–1815* (Munich, 1951), 130–31.

14. Bech, *DHP*, IX, 517-19; Friis, *Bernstorff og Guldberg*, 72-77; Holm, *DNH*, V, 263-66, 269; Klose & Degn, *GSH*, VI, 175-78; Gregersen, *Slesvig og Holsten før 1830*, 428.

15. Georg Schauman, "Till religionsfrihetsfrågans historia vid 1778-1779 års riksdag," *HTS*, 18 (1898), 49-59, 328-38.

16. See my "Popular Education in Sweden," esp. 532.

17. Chydenius, *Politiska skrifter*, ed. Palmén, 339-68.

18. Geijer, ed., *Gustaf III:s efterlemnade papper*, 249-50.

19. Schauman, "Till religionsfrihetsfrågans historia," 338; Odhner, *Gustaf III:s regering*, II, 3.

20. See my "Gustav III and the Enlightenment," 18-20.

21. See Jägerskiöld, *SUPH*, II:2, 271-72, 278-80; Ingegerd Hildebrand, *Den svenska kolonin S:t Barthélemy och Västindiska kompaniet fram till 1796* (Lund, 1951), 2-5, 12-13n49; Wahlström, "Gustaf III och norrmännen," 57-59.

22. My "Sweden and the War of American Independence," 412-26; *Danske i Amerika*, 2 vols. (Minneapolis, 1907-16), I, 89-93; Johnson, *Swedish Contributions*, I, 188-89, which gives an admittedly partial listing of Danish and Norwegian officers in French (p. 12) and Dutch (p. 6) service; J. O. Bro-Jørgensen, ed., *Ove Høegh Guldbergs og arveprins Frederiks brevveksling med Peter Christian Schumacher 1778-1807* (Copenhagen, 1972), 60.

23. Bang, ed., "Guldberg til Bülow," 162.

24. Hildebrand, *S:t Barthélemy*, 41-43, 315; Johnson, *Swedish Contributions*, I, 542-52, 564-65; Jägerskiöld, *SUPH*, II:2, 285.

25. My "Sweden and the War of American Independence," 412.

26. Holm, *DNH*, V, 528-29. Cf. Coldevin, *VFH*, V, 350. Julius Schovelin, *Fra den danske Handels Empire*, 2 vols. (Copenhagen, 1899-1900), I, 218-61, gives detailed statistics.

27. Holm, *DNH*, V, 517.

28. Regarding Danish colonial trade during the American war, see esp. Ole Feldbæk, *Dansk neutralitetspolitik under krigen 1778-1783* (Copenhagen, 1971) and *India Trade under the Danish Flag, 1772-1808* (Copenhagen, 1969).

29. Steen, *NFLH*, VII, 80-90.

30. West, *Faroe*, 45-48; Aage Rasch, *Niels Ryberg 1725-1804, Fra bondedreng til handelsfyrste* (Aarhus, 1964), 170-74.

31. Jägerskiöld, *SUPH*, II:2, 280.

32. Johnson, *Swedish Contributions*, I, 538.

33. On the League of Armed Neutrality of 1780, see my "Sweden and the War of American Independence," 423-25. The most important studies are Paul Fauchille, *La diplomatie française et la Ligue des neutres de 1780 (1776-1783)* (Paris, 1893); Samuel Flagg Bemis, *The Diplomacy of the American Revolution* (New York, 1935), chaps. 9-12; Isobel de Madariaga, *Britain, Russia and the Armed Neutrality of 1780* (New Haven, 1962); and Johnson, *Swedish Contributions*, I, chap. 9.

34. Bech, *DHP*, IX, 521-22; Friis, *Bernstorff og Guldberg*, 101, 233-38; Holm, *DNH*, V, 340-42.

35. Friis, *Bernstorff og Guldberg*, 69.

36. For Guldberg's later summation of his economic philosophy, see Bang, ed., "Guldberg til Bülow," 159-62; on the canal, see Klose & Degn, *GSH*, VI, 200-203.

37. Olsen, *Bybefolkningen*, 34-36. Cf. Steen, *NFLH*, VII, 68-69.

38. Johnson, *Swedish Contributions*, I, 144.

39. Friis, ed., *Bernstorffske Papirer*, III, 541-42.

40. Fauchille, *La diplomatie française*, 17.

41. My "Sweden and the War of American Independence," 419-21. Cf. Bernhard von Beskow, *Gustaf III såsom konung och menniska*, 5 vols. (Stockholm, 1860-69), III, 131, 160-61.

42. Beskow, *Gustaf III*, III, 162-63; John C. Fitzpatrick, ed., *Writings of George Washington*, 27 (Washington, D. C., 1937), 458.

43. See esp. Johnson, *Swedish Contributions* and Adolph B. Benson, *Sweden and the American Revolution* (New Haven, 1926).

44. My "Sweden and the War of American Independence," 412-16. Cf. my *Count Hans Axel von Fersen: Aristocrat in an Age of Revolution* (Boston, 1975), 24-25. On Fibiger, see *Danske i Amerika*, I, 91-93.

45. Comte de Biörnstierna, ed., *Mémoires posthumes du feldmaréchal Comte de Stedingk*, 2 vols. (Paris, 1844–47), I, 19, 28; Catherine Prescott Wormely, ed. and trans., *Diary and Correspondence of Count Axel Fersen* (Boston, 1902), 19–20; H. L. von Dardel, *Fältmarskalken von Stedingks tidigare levnadsöden* (Örebro, 1922), 75 (quotation).

46. Dardel, *Stedingks tidigare levnadsöden*; F. U. Wrangel, ed., *Lettres d'Axel de Fersen à son père pendant la Guerre d'Amérique* (Paris, 1929). Cf. my *Fersen*, 31–36.

47. Harald Elovson, *Amerika i svensk litteratur 1750–1820* (Lund, 1930), 87; my "Sweden and the War of American Independence," 413–14, 416.

48. Elovson, *Amerika i svensk litteratur*, 121.

49. *Ibid.*, 93–95, 131–35; my "Sweden and the War of American Independence," 428; *Statsrådet Johan Albert Ehrenströms efterlemnade historiska anteckningar*, ed. S. J. Boëthius, 2 vols. (Stockholm, 1883), I, 29, 31.

50. *Medborgaren* (Stockholm), No. 2, 9 January 1790, p. 6; Auguste Geffroy, *Gustave III et la cour de France*, 2 vols. (Paris, 1867), II, 112.

51. See Elovson, *Amerika i svensk litteratur*, 171–90.

52. Edvard Holm's valuable series of monographs on Danish public opinion in the second half of the eighteenth century, cited in notes to other chapters, unfortunately leaves a gap for the period 1772–84. For some details see, however, Kjærgaard, *Denmark Gets the News of '76*. Johnson, in *Swedish Contributions* (I, 188), wrote that in 1912 he had transcriptions made in Copenhagen of reports and letters from Danish officers in French service during the war, but that these were destroyed by a fire in 1918, before he could prepare an intended study based on them.

53. *Frederik Sneedorffs samlede Skrifter*, 4 vols. (Copenhagen, 1794–98), III:2, 152.

54. *Minerva* (Copenhagen), XIV:2 (Oct. 1798), 17; Schumacher, *Genrebilder*, 146.

55. Steffens, *Was ich erlebte*, I, 30, 77–81, 114, 234–35.

## CHAPTER 6. CHANGING BEARINGS, 1783–86

1. Gjerset, *History of Iceland*, 321–22, 343; Pálmi Einarsson, "Island," in Fridlev Skrubbeltrang, et al., *Jordpolitiken i Norden* (Stockholm, 1955), 87–88; Holm, *DNH*, V, 585–86. Cf. Finsen, *Om Folkemængdens Formindelse ved Uaar i Island*.

2. Holm, *DNH*, V, 468–73, 523–26, 538–45; VI:1, 164–75; Bech, *DHP*, IX, 525; Steen, *NFLH*, VII, 93–95, 139.

3. Holm, *DNH*, V, 427–30, 569; VI:1, 115–17; Steen, *NFLH*, VII, 91–93.

4. Steffens, *Was ich erlebte*, II, 108.

5. Knud Bokkenheuser, *Drejers Klub* (Copenhagen, 1903), 33–34.

6. *Ibid.*, 44–47.

7. " . . . at fremme al mulig Nytte." (Holm, *DNH*, V, 556.)

8. Cf. Christensen, *Agrarhistoriske Studier*, II, 252–53.

9. See esp. Holm, *Kampen om Landboreformerne*; Olsen, "Samtidens Syn paa den danske stavnsbundne Bonde"; cf. Carol Gold, "The Danish Reform Era, 1784–1800" (unpublished Ph.D. dissertation, University of Wisconsin, Madison, 1975), esp. 53–57.

10. Holm, *DNH*, V, 710.

11. Cf. Friis, ed., *Bernstorffske Papirer*, III, 696.

12. Vibæk, *DHP*, X, 27.

13. Holm, *DNH*, V, 218. Cf. Hansen, ed., *Kabinetsstyrelsen i Danmark 1768–1782*.

14. Jensen, *Reventlow*, 80, 83.

15. Friis, ed., *Bernstorffske Papirer*, III, 696. See also Friis, *Bernstorff og Guldberg*, 147–49.

16. See Vibæk, *DHP*, X, 35–48, 104, 110; Linvald, *SDH*, IV:2, 86–87. Also Friis, *Bernstorfferne og Danmark*, II, esp. chap. 10; Jensen, *Reventlow*.

17. L. Bobé, ed., *Efterladte Papirer fra den Reventlowske Familiekreds*, 10 vols. (Copenhagen, 1895–1931), I, 87–89.

18. "Undersøgelse om ikke almindelig Oplysning er en farlig Sag," *Minerva*, I:1 (July 1785), 1–27.

19. Bokkenheuser, *Drejers Klub*, 34–37; Holm, *DNH*, VI:2, 377–87; Klose & Degn, *GSH*, VI, 207.

20. On Maclean's reforms, see chap. 9. On Reichenbach, Fuchs, *Untergang des Bauernstandes*, 194–98.

21. See Stewart Oakley, "Gustavus III's Plans for War with Denmark, 1783–84," in Ragnhild Hatton and M. S. Anderson, eds., *Studies in Diplomatic History* (London, 1970), 168–86.

22. See Henning Stålhane, *Gustaf III:s resa till Italien och Frankrike* (Stockholm, 1953); my "Gustav III and the Enlightenment," 20–24.

23. See Hildebrand, *S:t Barthélemy*.

24. Holm, *DNH*, VI:1, 206–33.

25. Wahlström, "Gustaf III och norrmännen," 63.

26. Odhner, *Gustaf III:s regering*, II, 353–55.

27. See Klinckowström, ed., *F. A. von Fersens historiska skrifter*, IV, 56–58.

28. *Hedvig Elisabeth Charlottas dagbok*, ed. Carl Carlsson Bonde & Cecilia af Klercker, 9 vols. (Stockholm, 1902–42), II, 5, 41.

29. Sten Carlsson, et al., *Den svenska historien*, 10 vols. (Stockholm, 1966–68), VII: *Gustavianska tiden 1772–1809*, 111.

30. See Elmer Nyman, *Indragningsmakt och tryckfrihet 1785–1810* (Stockholm, 1963).

31. Beth Hennings, ed., *Ögonvittnen: om Gustav III* (Stockholm, 1960), 183. On Armfelt, see Elof Tegnér, *Gustaf Mauritz Armfelt*, 3 vols. (Stockholm, 1883–87).

32. Danielson-Kalmari, *Finland under gustavianska tiden*, I, 248–61. J. M. Sprengtporten died in 1786; it is unclear whether the king actually read his critique. On his dissatisfaction, cf. Nikander, "Filosofi och politik," 21.

33. Georg Hindric Jägerhorn, "Lefvernes Beskrifning," *Historiallinen arkisto*, 8 (1884), 129.

34. Ehrenström, *Historiska anteckningar*, I, 30–31.

35. Bruno Lesch, *Jan Anders Jägerhorn* (Helsingfors, 1941), 120.

36. Renvall, *Finsk representation*, 374–76.

37. See my "Russia and the Problem of Sweden-Finland," esp. 439.

38. Danielson-Kalmari, *Finland under gustavianska tiden*, I, 279.

39. Lesch, *Jägerhorn*, chap. 3.

40. Cf. Danielson-Kalmari, *Finland under gustavianska tiden*, esp. 81–82, 290–91; Lesch, *Jägerhorn*, esp. 103–4, 146; Hornborg, *Finlands hävder*, III, 494–98.

41. Klinckowström, ed., *F. A. von Fersens historiska skrifter*, VI, 96.

42. Dechaux, ed., *Écrits de Gustave III*, I, 135–38.

43. *Ibid.*, IV, 190–91.

44. Jutikkala, *History of Finland*, 162. Cf. the physiocratic slogan: "Tout pour le peuple, rien par le peuple."

45. Odhner, *Gustaf III:s regering*, II, 519.

46. Cf. Palmer, *The Age of the Democratic Revolution*, I.

47. On the rise of the middle class, see esp. Carlsson, *Ståndssamhälle och ståndspersoner*; Söderberg, *Två sekel svensk medelklass*; Palme, "Gustav III och Finland," 159–60; Olsen, *Bybefolkningen*. Cf. B. J. Hovde, *The Scandinavian Countries, 1720–1865: The Rise of the Middle Classes*, 2 vols. (Boston, 1943), esp. I.

## CHAPTER 7. ENLIGHTENED DESPOTISM AND REVOLT, 1786–89

1. Holm, *Kampen om Landboreformerne*, 98–99.

2. *Minerva*, IV:2 (Oct. 1788), 1–7. Cf. Gold, "Danish Reform Era," 219–21.

3. Holm, *DNH*, VI:1, 58; Gold, "Danish Reform Era," 76–78; Jens Holmgaard, "De nordsjællandske landboreformer og statsfinanserne," *Erhvervshistorisk årbog*, 4 (1954), 59–78.

4. Vibæk, *DHP*, X, 74; Jensen, *Reventlow*, 103–4. Cf. Olsen, "Samtidens Syn paa den danske stavnsbundne Bonde," 101.

5. Fridericia, ed., *Aktstykker*, 276–77; *Den for Landboevæsenet nedsatte Commissions Forhandlinger*, 2 vols. (Copenhagen, 1788–89), I, 4. Cf. Gold, "Danish Reform Era," 77.

6. Holm, *Kampen om Landboreformerne*, 120–23.

7. Fridericia, ed., *Aktstykker*, 277.

8. Skrubbeltrang, *Det danske landbosamfund*, 320; Fridericia, ed., *Aktstykker*, 295; Bro-Jørgensen, ed., *Brevveksling*, 319–21, 335–36; Bang, "Guldberg til Bülow," 163–70.

9. Holm, *DNH*, VI:1, 36–42, 58–64, 87–96, 375; Bang, "Guldberg til Bülow," *passim*, esp. 156; Bokkenheuser, *Drejers Klub*, 119–20, 134–35.

10. Fridericia, ed., *Aktstykker*, 297–302. On the military implications in the context of the progressive nationalization of the army, see Holm, *DNH*, VI:2, 601–29.

11. See esp. Holm, *Kampen om Landboreformerne*, 127–30; Falbe-Hansen, *Stavnsbaands-Løsningen*; Jensen, *Dansk Jordpolitik*, I, 13–19, 240–41, 245, 247, and *Reventlow*, 54, 137–38. Cf. Skrubbeltrang, *Det danske landbosamfund*, 265.

12. Falbe-Hansen, *Stavnsbaands-Løsningen*, I, 62; Bang, "Guldberg til Bülow," 202–3, 246, 271.

13. Regarding the courts, see Olsen, "Samtidens Syn paa den danske stavnsbundne Bonde," 119.

14. Falbe-Hansen, *Stavnsbaands-Løsningen*, I, 63. Cf. Jensen's criticism of this liberal view in *Dansk Jordpolitik*, I, 1–11, 153, 242, 324.

15. Klose & Degn, *GSH*, VI, 204–6; Bang, "Guldberg til Bülow," 143.

16. Hans Chr. Johansen, *Dansk økonomisk politik i årene efter 1784*, 2 vols. (Aarhus, 1968, 1980), esp. I, 8, 11–14, 211, 216–24, 264, 322; Gjerset, *History of Iceland*, 343–45; Holm, *DNH*, VI:1, 104–9.

17. Holm, *DNH*, VI:1, 110–14; Steen, *NFLH*, VII, 143–47.

18. Holm, *DNH*, VI:1, 134, 139, 178–79.

19. See Steen, *NFLH*, VII, 104–5; Johnsen, *Norges bønder*, 330–33; Coldevin, *VFH*, V, 377–78.

20. Jensen, *Dansk-norsk Vekselvirkning*, 149; Koht, *Norsk bondereising*, 311–12.

21. Georg Sverdrup, *Lofthusbevægelsen* (Oslo, 1917), 104–5.

22. Jensen, *Dansk-norsk Vekselvirkning*, 148.

23. Steen, *NFLH*, VII, 104.

24. Koht, *Norsk bondereising*, 312–14; Steen, *NFLH*, VII, 113–14; Sverdrup, *Lofthusbevægelsen*, 78–79, 86–87.

25. Mykland, *NH*, IX, 48.

26. Coldevin, *VFH*, V, 380.

27. Steen, *NFLH*, VII, 121.

28. See Holm, *DNH*, VI:1, 123–33; Sverdrup, *Lofthusbevægelsen*, 248–49.

29. Ludvig Daae, *Det gamle Christiania* (3d ed., Oslo, 1924), 224.

30. Steen, *NFLH*, VII, 126–27.

31. Wahlström, "Gustaf III och norrmännen," 63. Cf. chap. 6.

32. Ehrenström, *Historiska anteckningar*, I, 127; *Hedvig Elisabeth Charlottas dagbok*, II, 182–83.

33. Holm, *DNH*, VI:1, 240, 242–60.

34. *Minerva*, III:2 (Oct. 1787), 128.

35. See my "Gustav III of Sweden and the East Baltic, 1771–1792," *Journal of Baltic Studies*, 7 (1976), 14–17, 24–25.

36. *Ibid.*, 17–24.

37. E. L. Birck, *General Tolls krigsplan år 1788* (Helsingfors, 1944), 3–89 *passim*; A. Brückner, "Russland und Schweden 1788," *Historische Zeitschrift*, 22 (1869), 312–402; my "Gustav III and the East Baltic," 16, 24–25.

38. My *Fersen*, 42; Elof Tegnér, ed., *Konung Gustaf III:s bref till friherre G. M. Armfelt*, Historiska handlingar, XII:3 (Stockholm, 1883), 11, 14–15.

39. For the Swedish ultimatum, see *Hedvig Elisabeth Charlottas dagbok*, II, 294–97. Cf. my "Gustav III and the East Baltic," 24.

40. Hornborg, *Finlands hävder*, III, 319–20.

41. See Stavenow, *SHVD*, X, for a good brief account of the Swedish-Russian war of 1788–90. Cf. R. C. Anderson, *Naval Wars in the Baltic, 1522–1850* (London, 1910), 241–93; this work covers the entire period, 1760–1815, in considerable detail.

42. Hochschild, *Memoarer*, I, 131; Klinckowström, ed., *F. A. von Fersens historiska skrifter*, VII, 14 (quotation), 23–24, 30–31; *Hedvig Elisabeth Charlottas dagbok*, II, 231, 235–37.

43. Danielson-Kalmari, *Finland under gustavianska tiden*, II, 158–59.

44. See my "Russia and the Problem of Sweden-Finland, 1721-1809," 431-46. On the role of social contract theory, cf. Stig Jägerskiöld, "Tyrannmord och motståndsrätt 1792-1809," *Scandia* (1962), esp. 132, 136-37.

45. Danielson-Kalmari, *Finland under gustavianska tiden*, II, 182-84.

46. There is a large literature on the Anjala Confederation. In addition to *ibid.*, see my "Russia and the Problem of Sweden-Finland, 1721-1809," 448-49; A. Brückner, "Der Anjalabund in Finnland 1788," *Baltische Monatsschrift*, 19 (1870), 309-54. Documents connected with the insurrection are printed in the original Swedish, French, and German in A. R. Cederberg, *Anjalan liiton historialliset lähteet* (Helsinki, 1931), 233-326.

47. Bruno Lesch, in *Jägerhorn*, 214-15, 226, seeks to defend Jägerhorn against the traditional accusation that he intended from the beginning to go beyond the Liikala note by encouraging Finland's separation from Sweden. This view is refuted, convincingly I feel, by Einar Juva in *Finlands väg*, 228-29, 232.

48. Danielson-Kalmari, *Finland under gustavianska tiden*, II, 173-74, 177-79.

49. Gudmund Göran Adlerbeth, *Historiska anteckningar*, ed. Elof Tegnér, 2 vols. (2d ed., Stockholm, 1892), I, 46.

50. Holm, *DNH*, VI:1, 255-69, 290-91; *Minerva*, IV:2 (Dec. 1788), 386.

51. Holm, *DNH*, VI:1, 281 (quotation); Steen, *NFLH*, VII, 127.

52. Holm, *DNH*, VI:1, 293-300.

53. *Ibid.*, 201-4, 320; Klose & Degn, *GSH*, VI, 214.

54. Biörnstierna, ed., *Mémoires posthumes de Stedingk*, I, 123.

55. Klinckowström, ed., *F. A. von Fersens historiska skrifter*, VII, 165; Biörnstierna, ed., *Mémoires posthumes de Stedingk*, I, 132-33. Already at the *Riksdag* of 1778-79, Gustav had revealed a special solicitude for the good opinion of the Finnish peasantry. (Renvall, *Finsk representation*, 355-58).

56. Nikander, "Filosofi och politik," 34.

57. Hornborg, *Finlands hävder*, III, 507-8.

58. Staf, *Polisväsendet*, 133-38. Cf. Hochschild, *Memoarer*, I, 142-43; Klinckowström, ed., *F. A. von Fersens historiska skrifter*, VII, 57-59, 70.

59. *Hedvig Elisabeth Charlottas dagbok*, II, 407.

60. Hochschild, *Memoarer*, I, 153-54.

61. Hennings, ed., *Ögonvittnen om Gustav III*, 279-81. On the peasant volunteer corps, see Elof Tegnér, "Folkväpningen i Sverige 1788," *HTS*, 1 (1881), 213-46.

62. *Hedvig Elisabeth Charlottas dagbok*, II, 339, 350-51, 354-55; Hochschild, *Memoarer*, I, 153-54; Elof Tegnér, ed., *Elis Schröderheims skrifter till konung Gustaf III:s historia jämte urval ur Schröderheims brefväxling* (2d ed., Stockholm, 1892), 265-66, 272; Tegnér, "Folkväpningen," 235; Staf, *Polisväsendet,* 138-43.

63. Tegnér, ed., *Gustaf III:s bref till Armfelt*, 51; Tegnér, "Folkväpningen," 240.

64. *Hedvig Elisabeth Charlottas dagbok*, II, 350. Cf. Tegnér, "Folkväpningen," 215.

65. Tegnér, "Folkväpningen," 214.

66. Fredrik Lagerroth, *Konung och adel* (Stockholm, 1917), 80, 82-83. Cf. Adlerbeth, *Historiska anteckningar*, I, 43-44.

67. See, for example, the draft constitution in Cederberg, *Anjalan liiton historialliset lähteet*, 266-67.

68. Nikander, "Filosofi och politik," 34.

69. C. T. Odhner, "Ett bidrag till Anjalaförbundets historia," *HTS*, 2 (1882), 70-76; Stavenow, *SHVD*, X, 163-66, 170; Hornborg, *Finlands hävder*, III, 334; Jutikkala, *History of Finland*, 170.

70. Juva, *Finlands väg*, 216.

71. The expatriate Jägerhorn was later involved in Wolfe Tone's Irish conspiracy of 1797-98. See Lesch, *Jägerhorn*, ch. 12.

72. *Hedvig Elisabeth Charlottas dagbok*, II, 443.

73. Hochschild, *Memoarer*, I, 169.

74. Lagerroth, *Konung och adel*, 85-86.

75. Dechaux, ed., *Écrits de Gustave III*, I, 139-48.

76. *Ibid.*, 149-62.

77. Stavenow, *SHVD*, X, 177.
78. See my *Fersen*, 79-81.
79. The Act of Union and Security is given in Palmer, *Age of the Democratic Revolution*, I, appendix III, 512-13.
80. See esp. Renvall, *Finsk representation*, 384-85, 416.
81. Ingers, *Bonden i svensk historia*, II, 375-77, 381, 387-92; Heckscher, *SEH*, II:1, 272-73, 280-83; Jutikkala, *Bonden i Finland*, 317-27; Tønnesson, "Problèmes de la féodalité," 338.
82. On commercial and manufacturing policy, see Söderberg, *Två sekel svensk medelklass*, 33.
83. Stavenow, *SHVD*, X, 179; Hornborg, *Finlands hävder*, III, 336-37.
84. Hochschild, *Memoarer*, I, 236. Cf. Staf, *Polisväsendet*, 151-52.
85. Adolf Ludvig Hamilton, *Anekdoter till svenska historien under Gustaf III:s regering*, ed. O. Levertin (Stockholm, 1901), 129. My account of the events of the *Riksdag* of 1789 is based largely upon Stavenow, *SHVD*, X, 172-87.
86. Cf. Sallnäs, "Gustav III som inrikespolitiker—hatt eller mössa?" 346-47; Söderberg, *Två sekel svensk medelklass*, 29-31.
87. *Hedvig Elisabeth Charlottas dagbok*, III, 16.
88. Koht, *Norsk bondereising*, 11-12.
89. Palmer, *Age of the Democratic Revolution*, I, 399, 411-35.
90. Holm, *DNH*, VI:1, 380-81; Ingers, *Bonden i svensk historia*, II, 387-88; Söderberg, *Två sekel svensk medelklass*, 29-31.
91. Georges Lefebvre, "La Révolution française dans l'histoire du monde," in his *Études sur la Révolution française* (Paris, 1954), 315-26. Cf. Alexis de Tocqueville, *L'Ancien Régime et la Révolution française* (Paris, 1856).
92. Jutikkala, *Bonden i Finland*, 317. Cf. Sjöstrand, *Pedagogikens historia*, III:1, 52; Palmer, *Age of the Democratic Revolution*, I, 400.
93. Georges Lefebvre, *The Coming of the French Revolution*, trans. R. R. Palmer (New York, 1957), 4; Carlsson, *Ståndssamhälle och ståndspersoner*, 254-59.
94. Carlsson, "Bondeståndet i Norden under senare delen av 1700-talet"; Tønnesson, "Problèmes de la féodalité."
95. Renvall, *Finsk representation*, 386-87.

## CHAPTER 8. A NEW DAWN FOR HUMANITY, 1789-92

1. Adlerbeth, *Historiska anteckningar*, I, 192; *Malla Montgomery-Silfverstolpes Memoarer*, ed. Malla Grandinson, 4 vols. (Stockholm, 1908-11), I, 46, 49-50; Alma Söderhjelm, *Sverige och den franska revolutionen*, 2 vols. (Stockholm, 1920-24), I, 160, 235-39.
2. Henrik Schück, ed., *Nils von Rosensteins brefsamling* (Stockholm, 1905), 240-45, 248-49. Cf. Otto Sylvan, *Johan Henric Kellgren* (2d ed., Stockholm, 1939), 163-66; Lamm, *Upplysningstidens romantik*, II, 115-16.
3. *Medborgaren* (Stockholm, 9 Jan. 1790), p. 6; Stellan Arvidson, *Thorild och den franska revolutionen* (Stockholm, 1938), 6-30; Lamm, *Upplysningstidens romantik*, II, 115-17, 510-25; Lagerroth, *Konung och adel*, 59-69.
4. *Hedvig Elisabeth Charlottas dagbok*, III, 228-29.
5. Söderhjelm, *Sverige och den franska revolutionen*, I, 157. Cf. Erik Gustaf Geijer, *Samlade skrifter*, I (Stockholm, 1875), 5-6.
6. Bobé, ed., *Efterladte Papirer*, III, 55; IV, 165-66; IX, 65; Hans Schulz, ed., *Aus dem Briefwechsel des Herzogs Friedrich Christian zu Schleswig-Holstein* (Stuttgart, 1913), 74-75. Cf. Klose & Degn, *GSH*, VI, 208-9; Renate Erhardt-Lucht, *Die Ideen der Französischen Revolution in Schleswig-Holstein* (Neumünster, 1969). Cf. Valjavec, *Die Entstehung der politischen Strömungen in Deutschland*, which places the pro- and anti-revolutionary trends in Schleswig-Holstein into a wider German context.
7. Friis, ed., *Bernstorffske Papirer*, III, 316-17; C. U. D. Eggers, *Denkwürdigkeiten aus dem Leben des Grafen von Bernstorff*, 2 vols. (Copenhagen, 1800), I, 232-34; Erhardt-Lucht, *Ideen*, 18-22; Schulz, ed., *Briefwechsel*, 76, 98; Bobé, ed., *Efterladte Papirer*, II, 87-88, 91; VII, 9-10; Hans Schulz, ed., *Timoleon und Immanuel. Dokumente einer Freundschaft. Briefwechsel zwischen Friedrich Christian zu Schleswig-Holstein und Jens Baggesen* (Leipzig, 1910), 23-24.

8. Bang, "Guldberg til Bülow," 263-65.

9. *Ibid.*, 268-69. .

10. Steffens, *Was ich erlebte*, I, 363-64.

11. Edvard Holm, *Den offentlige Mening og Statsmagten i den dansk-norske Stat i Slutningen af det 18de Aarhundrede (1784-1799)* (Copenhagen, 1888), 59-70. The sections in Holm's *DNH*, VI:1-2, dealing with public opinion in this period are based on this monograph. Also Jens Baggesen, *Labyrinten*, ed. L. L. Albertsen (Copenhagen, 1976), 163; *Minerva*, V:1 (Aug.-Sept. 1789), 281-91, 417-24; VI:2 (Dec. 1790), 273-300; VII:3 (Mar. 1792), 305-30; Frederik Bajer, *Nordens politiske Digtning 1789-1804* (Copenhagen, 1878), 23.

12. Klose & Degn, *GSH*, VI, 209-10; Schumacher, *Genrebilder*, 193-98; Ludvig Daae, ed., *Af Geheimraad J. v. Bülows Papirer* (Christiania, 1864), 29.

13. Steen, *NFLH*, VII, 136-37; Mykland, *NH*, IX, 73-78.

14. Holm, *Den offentlige Mening*, 84-94; Hans Kyrre, *Knud Rahbek, Kamma Rahbek og Livet paa Bakkehuset* (Copenhagen, 1914), 129.

15. *Minerva*, III:3 (Jan. 1788), 72-90; V:1 (Sept. 1789), 417.

16. See Jens Arup Seip, "Teorien om det opinionsstyrte enevelde," *HTN*, 38 (1957-58), 397-463. Also Holm, *Den offentlige Mening*, 94; Holm, *DNH*, VI:1, 151-53, 379-87; Klose & Degn, *GSH*, VI, 209; Erik Vea, *Likhetsidéen i Norge i 1790-årene* (Oslo, 1956), 25-27; A. S. Ørsted, *Af mit Livs og min Tids Historie*, 4 vols. (Copenhagen, 1851-57), I, 16.

17. Bajer, *Nordens politiske Digtning*, 28, 30-31.

18. Holm, *DNH*, VI:1, 392-94.

19. *Ibid.*, 395; Bobé, ed., *Efterladte Papirer*, IV, 121, 136-37.

20. Bang, "Guldberg til Bülow," 294-96. Cf. *ibid.*, 330, 333-36, 355.

21. Johan Hvidtfeldt, "Social og politisk uro i Sønderjylland paa revolutionstiden," *Sønderjyske Aarbøger* (1945), 128-69; H. V. Gregersen, "Optøjerne i Åbenrå 1790," *ibid.* (1956), 209-14.

22. Holm, *DNH*, VI:1, 395-98.

23. *Ibid.*, VI:2, 429-31; Steen, *NFLH*, VII, 139-41.

24. Holm, *DNH*, VI:1, 80, 340-41; Hvidtfeldt, *Kampen om Ophævelsen*, 63; Olsen, "Samtidens syn paa den danske stavnsbundne Bonde," 109, 115-17; Jensen, *Dansk Jordpolitik*, I, esp. 1-11, 85-94, 113-15, 161-67, 242-45.

25. Holm, *DNH*, VI:1, 66. Cf. *ibid.*, 70-74, 81; Jensen, *Dansk Jordpolitik*, I, 133, 245; Jensen, *Dansk-norsk Vekselvirkning*, 127-33.

26. Jensen, *Dansk Jordpolitik*, I, 159-60, 168-71; Bobé, ed., *Efterladte Papirer*, II, 157.

27. *Ibid.*, 179-82.

28. *Ibid.*, 185-205; Falbe-Hansen, *Stavnsbaands-Løsningen*, I, 64-66; Christensen, *Agrarhistoriske Studier*, II, 176.

29. Holm, *DNH*, VI:2, 511.

30. *Ibid.*, 522.

31. *Ibid.*, 516; Jensen, *Reventlow*, 189, 199-200.

32. See Sjöstrand, *Pedagogikens historia i Norden*, III:1, 213-15, 251, 253.

33. Holm, *DNH*, VI:1, 86-87.

34. Christian Colbjørnsen, *Betragtninger i Anledning af endeel jydske Jorddrotters Klage* (Copenhagen, 1790), esp. 6, 24, 26, 34, 36, 40, 42, 44. Cf. Holm, *Kampen om Landboreformerne*, 197-225; Jensen, *Dansk Jordpolitik*, I, 172-78.

35. Colbjørnsen, *Betragtninger*, esp. 3, 9, 11, 15, 17, 19, 27, 29; Holm, *DNH*, VI:1, 355-62, 424; Jensen, *Dansk Jordpolitik*, I, 175-78; Vibæk, *DHP*, X, 98.

36. Adlerbeth, *Historiska anteckningar*, I, 191.

37. *Mémoires du marquis de Bouillé*, ed. M. F. Barrière (Paris, 1859), II, 141. Cf. Adlerbeth, *Historiska anteckningar*, I, 228-29.

38. See my "Gustav III and the Enlightenment," esp. 26-27, 33. Also "A. B—z" (Axel Brusewitz), "Till frågan om Gustaf III:s sista författningsplaner," *HTS*, 32 (1912), 210-16.

39. Ehrenström, *Historiska anteckningar*, I, 292-93.

40. On the Swedish-Russian war in 1789-90, see Stavenow, *SHVD*, X, 187-203. Cf. Jutikkala, *History of Finland*, 172-74.

41. Vivie, *Lettres*, 386.

42. Tegnér, ed., *Schröderheims skrifter*, 102.
43. Vivie, *Lettres*, 386.
44. My "Gustav III and the Enlightenment," 27–28; Biörnstierna, *Mémoires posthumes de Stedingk*, I, 206.
45. My *Fersen*, 110.
46. On Fersen and the Flight to Varennes, see *ibid.*, chap. 5.
47. For Gustav III's attempts to organize a counterrevolutionary crusade, see esp. Nils Åkeson, *Gustaf III:s förhållande till den franska revolutionen*, 2 vols. (Lund, 1885–86); Erland Hjärne, "Gustav III och franska revolutionen," *Svensk tidskrift*, 19 (1929), 502–22; Söderhjelm, *Sverige och den franska revolutionen*, I, chap. 5; my *Fersen*, chaps. 5–6.
48. Tegnér, ed., *Gustaf III:s bref till Armfelt*, 193–94.
49. My *Fersen*, 129–30.
50. Fitzpatrick, ed., *Writings of George Washington*, XXVII, 453 (cf. chap. 5.); *Hedvig Elisabeth Charlottas dagbok*, II, 221; Bouillé, *Mémoires*, II, 140.
51. *Hedvig Elisabeth Charlottas dagbok*, III, 376.
52. Bang, "Guldberg til Bülow," 344, 350–51; Signe Carlsson, "Till frågan om Sveriges utrikespolitik efter freden i Värälä 1790," in *Gottfrid Carlsson 18.12.1952* (Lund, 1952), 348–76; Holm, *DNH*, VI:2, 5–10.
53. Adlerbeth, *historiska anteckningar*, I, 265. Åkeson, in *Gustaf III:s förhållande*, II, 220–21, and Söderhjelm, in *Sverige och den franska revolutionen*, I, 301–9, argue that Gustav III never gave up the idea of intervening in France.
54. My "Gustav III and the East Baltic," 22–26. Cf. *Hedvig Elisabeth Charlottas dagbok*, III, 328.
55. See Stavenow, *SHVD*, X, 207–10.
56. Tegnér, ed., *Bref till Armfelt*, 193–96; *Hedvig Elisabeth Charlottas dagbok*, III, 391–92.
57. Dechaux, ed., *Écrits de Gustave III*, I, 173–74.
58. Hochschild, *Memoarer*, II, 210.
59. On the *Riksdag* of 1792, see Stavenow, *SHVD*, X, 214–18.
60. Hamilton, *Anekdoter*, 168; Bobé, ed., *Efterladte Papirer*, IV, 120.
61. See Palmer, *Age of the Democratic Revolution*, I.

## CHAPTER 9. REFORM AND RADICALISM, 1792–97

1. Nikander, "Filosofi och politik," 36; my *Fersen*, 154–55; Ehrenström, *Historiska anteckningar*, I, 379–80; Jägerskiöld, "Tyrannmord och motståndsrätt," 137n.
2. Ehrenström, *Historiska anteckningar*, I, 375–76. On the ideological background to Gustav III's assassination, see esp. Lolo Krusius-Ahrenberg, *Tyrannmördaren C. F. Ehrensvärd* (Helsingfors, 1947), chaps. 1–4; Jägerskiöld, "Tyrannmord och motståndsrätt." Cf. R. Nisbet Bain, "The Assassination of Gustavus III of Sweden," *English Historical Review* (1887), 543–52.
3. Lolo Krusius-Ahrenberg, "Jacob von Engeström," *Svenskt biografiskt lexikon*, XII (1950), 612–26; Krusius-Ahrenberg, *Tyrannmördaren*, 179–82, 189, 193; Ludvig Stavenow, "Till diskussionen om Jacob von Engeströms författningsprogram och dess beroende av franska revolutionsidéer," *Uppsala universitets årsskrift 1923*, Program 4 (17 pp.); Fredrik Lagerroth, "Var det von Engeströmska författningsförslaget reaktionärt?" *Statsvetenskaplig tidskrift* (1936), 304–435.
4. Elof Tegnér, "Ur Adolf Ludvig Ribbings papper," *HTS*, 12 (1892), 58.
5. Krusius-Ahrenberg, *Tyrannmördaren*, 184–98.
6. *Ibid.*, 132–33; my *Fersen*, 154–55; Hamilton, *Anekdoter*, 19–20; Olof Dixelius, *Den unge Järta* (Uppsala, 1953), 65–66.
7. Sten Carlsson, "Hans Gabriel Wachtmeisters dagbok 1807–1809," *Vetenskaps-Societeten i Lund årsbok 1943* (Lund, 1944), 56. Cf. Ehrenström, *Historiska anteckningar*, I, 379.
8. Jägerskiöld, "Tyrannmord och motståndsrätt," 153–54.
9. Holm, *DNH*, VI:2, 12; Bang, "Guldberg til Bülow," 363; Söderhjelm, *Sverige och den franska revolutionen*, II, 14, 25–29.
10. Hennings, ed., *Ögonvittnen om Gustav III*, 317.
11. Hennings, *Gustav III*, 233.
12. Ehrenström, *Historiska anteckningar*, I, 294–95; Landberg, *Gustaf III inför eftervärlden*;

Ladislaus Konopczyński, "Lars von Engeströms mission i Polen 1787-1791," *HTS*, 44 (1924), 46.

13. On Duke Carl, see G. Iverus, *Hertig Carl av Södermanland*, I: *Till ryska kriget* (Uppsala, 1925); Alma Söderhjelm, *Gustav III:s syskon* (Stockholm, 1945).

14. On Reuterholm, see Martin Nylund, G. A. *Reuterholm under förmyndaretiden 1792-96* (Uppsala, 1917).

15. Heckscher, *SEH*, II:1, 270-72; Carlsson, *Ståndssamhälle och ståndspersoner*, 261; Jutikkala, *Bonden i Finland*, 276-83.

16. Heckscher, *SEH*, II:1, 253-58; Ingers, *Bonden i svensk historia*, II, chap. 13, also 462-63; Inge Svensson, "Rutger Maclean som lanthushållare," in *Från Fugger till Kreuger. Studier tillägnade Oscar Bjurling* (Lund, 1957), 15-34; Alf Åberg, *När byarna sprängdes* (new ed., Stockholm, 1979), 65-73.

17. Heckscher, *SEH*, II:1, 273-74, 280-83; Jutikkala, *Bonden i Finland*, 282-83. Cf. G. Utterström, "Population and Agriculture in Sweden circa 1700-1830," *SEHR*, 7 (1961), 167-94.

18. Falbe-Hansen, *Stavsbaands-Løsningen*, I, 79-81, 106-10; Jensen, *Fra patriarkalisme til pengeøkonomi*. Cf. Bro-Jørgensen, ed., *Brevveksling*, 525-26.

19. Falbe-Hansen, *Stavnsbaands-Løsningen*, I, 69-73, 74-78; Vibæk, *DHP*, X, 85-90; Skrubbeltrang, *Det danske landbosamfund*, 293. Cf. Christian B. Reventlow, *En dansk statsmands hjem omkring år 1800*, 2 vol. (Copenhagen, 1902-3), I, 153.

20. Skrubbeltrang, *Det danske landbosamfund*, 391, 431.

21. *Ibid*, 367-91. Cf. Falbe-Hansen, *Stavnsbaands-Løsningen*, I, 64-68; Jensen, *Dansk Jordpolitik*, I, 194-205; Kjærgaard, *Konjunkturer og afgifter*, 40-53, 64-70.

22. Falbe-Hansen, *Stavnsbaands-Løsningen*, II, 12-14; Vibæk, *DHP*, X, 82-83.

23. Cf. Baggesen, *Labyrinten*, esp. 27; Frans Michael Franzén, *Resedagbok 1795-1796*, ed. Anders Hernmarck (Stockholm, 1977), 33-36; Mary Wollstonecraft, *Letters Written during a Short Residence in Sweden, Norway and Denmark* (1796), ed. Carol H. Poston (Lincoln, Nebr., 1976), 177-79, 183; *The Travel Diaries of Thomas Malthus*, (1799), ed. Patricia James (Cambridge, 1966), 45-52.

24. Hvidtfeldt, "Social og politisk uro i Sønderjylland." Cf. Fuchs, *Untergang des Bauernstandes*, 189-90.

25. See esp. Hvidtfeldt, *Ophævelsen*. Also Holm, *DNH*, VI:2, 446-50; Klose & Degn, *GSH*, VI, 243, 251.

26. Coldevin, *VFH*, V, 416-18; Jensen, *Dansk-norsk Vekselvirkning*, 119-22. Cf. Simen Skappel, *Om husmandsvæsenet i Norge. Dets oprindelse og udvikling* (Kristiania, 1922).

27. Falbe-Hansen, *Stavnsbaands-Løsningen*, I, 127-44; Holm, *DNH*, VI:2, 344-45, 416-17; Jensen, *Dansk Jordpolitik*, I, 206-16; Christensen, *Agrarhistoriske Studier*, II, 13-14, 17-19; Skrubbeltrang, *Det danske landbosamfund*, 299, 415. The classic on this subject is Fridlev Skrubbeltrang, *Husmand og Inderste* (Copenhagen, 1940).

28. Johansen, *En samfundsorganisation i opbrud*, 125-27.

29. Holm, *DNH*, VI:2, 600-601; Gold, "The Danish Reform Era," 130-42; Axel Linvald, "Af Jødernes Frigørelseshistorie," *Tidsskrift for jødisk Historie*, 3 (1921-25), 333-424; *Minerva*, XIII:1 (July, 1797), 17.

30. Holm, *DNH*, VI:2, 495-510; Johansen, *En Samfundsorganisation i opbrud*, 289-95.

31. Holm, *DNH*, VI:2, 471-93; Vibæk, *DHP*, X, 111, 114-15.

32. Holm, *DNH*, VI:2, 267-74; Gold, "Danish Reform Era," 121-28. Cf. C. A. Trier, "Det danske vestindiske Negerindførselforbud af 1792," *HTD*, 7:5 (1904-5), 405-508; S. E. Green-Pedersen, "The Scope and Structure of the Danish Negro Slave Trade," *SEHR*, 19 (1971), 149-97. Slavery was abolished on Swedish St. Barthélemy in 1847.

33. Holm, *DNH*, VI:2, 356-60, 406-13; Steen, *NFLH*, VII, 202-8.

34. Holm, *DNH*, VI:2, 276-84, 314-21, 334-38; Steen, *NFLH*, VII, 170-76; Johansen, *Dansk økonomisk politik*, I, 254-64, 327.

35. Skrubbeltrang, *Det danske landbosamfund*, esp. 214, 217, 236, 339, 429. Cf. Fridlev Skrubbeltrang, "Developments in Tenancy in Eighteenth-Century Denmark as a Move towards Peasant Proprietorship," *SEHR*, 9 (1963), 165-75.

36. Jensen, *Dansk Jordpolitik*, I, 13–19, 231–45, and *Reventlow*, 54, 223; Hvidtfeldt, *Ophævelsen*, 94–95; Skrubbeltrang, *Det danske landbosamfund*, 265, 320, 390, 394–95, 435; Kjærgaard, *Konjunkturer og afgifter*, 35–38, 70; Feldbæk, *DHG*, IV, 70, 71, 156, 171, 180, 188, 191, 312.

37. See Holm, *Kampen om Landboreformerne* (1888); Falbe-Hansen, *Stavnsbaands-Løsningen*, I (1888); Jensen, *Dansk Jordpolitik*, I (1936); Olsen, "Samtidens Syn paa den danske stavnsbundne Bonde" (1939); Holmgaard, "De nordsjællandske landboreformer" (1954); Gold, "The Danish Reform Era" (1975). Gold's dissertation uses the model provided by Harry Eckstein's "On the Etiology of Internal Wars," in *Studies in the Philosophy of History*, ed. George H. Nadel (New York, 1965). Cf. Skrubbeltrang, *Det danske landbosamfund*, 262–71, for a brief discussion of the historiography of the reforms, especially agrarian.

38. Hvidtfeldt, *Ophævelsen*, 1; Holmgaard, "De nordsjællandske landboreformer," 59; Olsen, "Samtidens Syn paa den danske stavnsbundne Bonde," 117. Cf. Jens Holmgaard, "Landboreformerne—drivkræfter og motiver," *Fortid og Nutid*, 27 (1977), 37–47.

39. Hamilton, *Anekdoter*, xxx-xxxi.

40. Franzén, *Resedagbok*, 123, 134, 168–69.

41. Tegnér, ed., "Ur Adolf Ludvig Ribbings papper," 55–56. Cf. Krusius-Ahrenberg, *Tyrannmördaren*, 177–78; Rolf Karlbom, *Bakgrunden till 1809 års regeringsform* (Göteborg, 1964); my "Late Gustavian Autocracy in Sweden: Gustav IV Adolf and His Opponents, 1792–1809," *Scandinavian Studies*, 46 (1974), 269–71.

42. Cf. Nils Rosén von Rosenstein, *Försök til en afhandling om upplysningen* (Stockholm, 1793). Cf. Ehrenström, *Historiska anteckningar*, I, 487–94; Lamm, *Upplysningstidens romantik*, II, 117–21.

43. Given in Söderhjelm, *Sverige och den franska revolutionen*, II, 118–19. On the radical journalism which followed during 1792, see esp. *ibid.*, 119–78.

44. *Ibid.*, 152; Arvidson, *Thorild och den franska revolutionen*, 199–200; Nordmann, *Grandeur et Liberté*, 440.

45. Arvidson, *Thorhild och den franska revolutionen*, esp. 233–84; Lamm, *Upplysningstidens romantik*, II, 525–31. Cf. *Samlade skrifter av Thomas Thorild*, ed. Stellan Arvidson, III (Stockholm, 1944), 257–90. In 1795, Reuterholm had Thorild quietly appointed librarian at Greifswald University in Swedish Pomerania; he never returned to Sweden.

46. On the Ebel riot, see Staf, *Polisväsendet*, 215–20.

47. Söderhjelm, *Sverige och den franska revolutionen*, II, 197. On student unrest, see *ibid.*, 178–205; A. Grape, "Tidsrörelser inom studentvärlden i Uppsala 1792–1794," *Samlaren* (1923), 185–234; Nils Afzelius, "Konventvisor och andra politiska dikter från revolutionsåren 1792–1793," *Samlaren* (1923), 235–47; Sven G. Svenson, "Studentens klang- och jubeltid," in *Uppsalastudenten genom tiderna* (Uppsala, 1950), 73–90.

48. Svenson, "Studentens klang- och jubeltid," 90–91; Dixelius, *Den unge Järta*; Gunnar Kjellin, "'Hvem äro de sannskyldige Jacobinerne?'—sengustavianska opinioner och stämningar," *HTS*, 83 (1963), 188–96.

49. Hochschild, *Memoarer*, III, 43; Richard Nordin, "En österrikisk diplomat om Sveriges inre förhållanden år 1797," *HTS*, 31 (1911), 49–50. See also Staf, *Polisväsendet*, 237–43.

50. Ehrenström, *Historiska anteckningar*, II, 145–47.

51. On the Armfelt Conspiracy, see Tegnér, *G. M. Armfelt*, II, chaps. 1–4, esp. 179–84; my *Fersen*, 186–94; Staf, *Polisväsendet*, 243–64.

52. Cf. my *Fersen*, 191.

53. Bobé, ed., *Efterladte Papirer*, IX, 78–79; Hans Schulz, ed., *Aus dem Briefwechsel des Herzogs Friedrich Christian zu Schleswig-Holstein-Sonderburg-Augustenburg mit König Friedrich VI. und dem Thronfolger Prinzen Christian Friedrich* (Leipzig, 1908), 37–38; Schulz, ed., *Timoleon und Immanuel*, 150, 212; Reventlow, *En dansk statsmands hjem*, I, 180; Hans Schulz, *Friedrich Christian, Herzog zu Schleswig-Holstein. Ein Lebenslauf* (Leipzig, 1910), 147; Schulz, ed., *Briefwechsel*, 86, 95–96, 106–7, 137–38.

54. Klose & Degn, *GSH*, VI, 208, 271–73; Hvidtfeldt, *Ophævelsen*, 100–101. Cf. Erhardt-Lucht, *Ideen*.

55. Schulz, ed., *Briefwechsel*, 90–92; Schulz, ed., *Timoleon und Immanuel*, 158, 179, 186, 201.

56. Klose & Degn, *GSH*, VI, 214-15.

57. Bobé, ed., *Efterladte Papirer*, VIII, 344. On the Emkendorf circle, see Brandt, *Geistesleben und Politik*, 169, 261-62, 267; Klose & Degn, *GSH*, VI, 163, 277-83.

58. Bobé, ed., *Efterladte Papirer*, IV, 136-37, 152; Bang, "Guldberg til Bülow," *passim*; Holm, *DNH*, VI:2, 151; Vea, *Likhetsidéen i Norge*, 39-53.

59. Holm, *DNH*, VI:2, 574-94; Steffens, *Was ich erlebte*, II, 177-81. Cf. J. C. Lavater, *Rejse til Danmark i Sommeren 1793*, ed. Louis Bobé (Copenhagen, 1898); Schulz, ed., *Timoleon und Immanuel*, 174-77, 180-81.

60. See J. Clausen & P. F. Rist, eds., *Grandmamas Bekiendelser* (Copenhagen, 1906), 42-51, 74-94.

61. Holm, *DNH*, VI:2, 121-29, 145-46; Bokkenheuser, *Drejers Klub*, 208-9, 218-23, 266; Steffens, *Was ich erlebte*, II, 240-41; *Minerva*, VII:3 (Mar. 1792), 359-60.

62. Steffens, *Was ich erlebte*, II, 247-50, 258-59; Schumacher, *Genrebilder*, 197.

63. Klose & Degn, *GSH*, VI, 208-13; Hvidtfeldt, *Ophævelsen*, 100; Hvidtfeldt, "Social og politisk uro i Sønderjylland," 148-69; Erhardt-Lucht, *Ideen*, esp. chap. 3; Walter Grab, *Norddeutsche Jakobiner* (Frankfurt a/M, 1967); Valjavec, *Die Entstehung der politischen Strömungen in Deutschland*, esp. 187-88, 223-24, 424-26; Wollstonecraft, *Letters*, 116; Steen, *NFLH*, VII, 182-89; Vea, *Likhetsidéen i Norge*, esp. 14-15.

64. Malthus, *Travel Diaries*, 92; Holm, *DNH*, VI:2, 152-53; Bobé, ed., *Efterladte Papirer*, IV, 153. Cf. *Minerva*, VII:3 (March 1792), 305.

65. For the Norwegian radical journals, see Vea, *Likhetsidéen i Norge*.

66. Holm, *DNH*, VI:2, 129-44, 165-66; Vibæk, *DHP*, X, 189.

67. Holm, *DNH*, VI:2, 124-25, 132, 141-42; Vibæk, *DHP*, X, 208; Klose & Degn, *GSH*, VI, 209; Erhardt-Lucht, *Ideen*, 151-58.

68. Holm, *DNH*, VI:2, 166-205, 215-16; Vibæk, *DHP*, X, 194; Steen, *NFLH*, VII, 162-63, 220-23.

69. Mykland, *NH*, IX, 93, 100-101, 124; Steen, *NFLH*, VII, 165-69; Holm, *DNH*, VI:2, 206-10, 331-34; Steffens, *Was ich erlebte*, II, 280-306.

70. Holm, *DNH*, VI:2, 210-15; Klose & Degn, *GSH*, VI, 209-10.

71. Holm, *DNH*, VI:2, 210, 217-19.

72. Holm, *DNH*, VI:2, 155-60; Steffens, *Was ich erlebte*, II, 306-9; Vibæk, *DHP*, X, 141-43.

73. *Hedvig Elisabeth Charlottas dagbok*, IV, 6-7.

74. Carlsson, *SUPH*, III:1, 24-35, 38-40.

75. Holm, *DNH*, VI:2, 20-27.

76. *Ibid.*, 29-39; Carlsson, *SUPH*, III:1, 33-35.

77. Holm, *DNH*, VI:2, 42-50, 54-63, 76. Cf. Samuel Flagg Bemis, "The United States and the Abortive Armed Neutrality of 1794," *American Historical Review*, 24 (1918), 26-47.

78. Holm, *DNH*, VI:2, 40-41, 50-54, 70-73; Carlsson, *SUPH*, III:1, 44-47.

79. See Julius Clausen, *Skandinavism historisk fremstillet* (Copenhagen, 1900), 1-20; Krusius-Ahrenberg, *Tyrannmördaren*, 299-310, 319-30, 395, 400-403. Cf. my article, "The Swedish Succession Crises of 1809 and 1810, and the Question of Scandinavian Union," *Scandinavian Studies*, 42 (1970), 311-13.

80. Holm, *DNH*, VI:2, 77-78, 167; Wollstonecraft, *Letters*, 66; Tegnér, ed., "Ur Adolf Ludvig Ribbings papper," 62.

81. See, for instance, Olsen, "Samtidens Syn paa den danske stavnsbundne Bonde," 107, 114, 135; Hvidtfeldt, *Ophævelsen*, 34-39. Holm, *DNH*, VI:2, 64. For a wider European perspective, including Denmark and the Duchies, cf. Blum, *The End of the Old Order in Rural Europe*.

82. Vea, *Likhetsidéen i Norge*, 37.

83. Lars von Engeström, *Minnen och anteckningar*, ed. Elof Tegnér, 2 vols. (Stockholm, 1876), I, 199. Cf. Söderberg, *Två sekel svensk medelklass*, 22-24, 38-41; Ørsted, *Af mit Livs og min Tids Historie*, I, 12-13.

## CHAPTER 10. COMMERCE AND COUNTERREVOLUTION, 1797-1802

1. Great Britain, Historical Manuscripts Commission, *The Manuscripts of J. B. Fortesque Preserved at Dropmore*, 10 vols. (London, 1892-1927), VI, 65.

2. Sven G. Svenson, *Gattjinatraktaten 1799* (Uppsala, 1952), 95.

3. Fersen is hereafter no longer designated as "the younger," since his father had died in 1794.

4. Johansen, *En samfundsorganisation i opbrud*, 179. Cf. Gold, "The Danish Reform Era," 108.

5. *Minerva*, XIV:2 (Nov. 1798), 163.

6. On social welfare reforms, see esp. Johansen, *Dansk økonomisk politik*, I, 265–75, and *En samfundsorganisation i opbrud*, 289–97; Philip, *Staten og Fattigdommen*.

7. Falbe-Hansen, *Stavnsbaands-Løsningen*, I, 65.

8. Cf. Adlerbeth, *Historiska anteckningar*, II, 394–95.

9. See Erik Elinder, "Adolf Ludvig Hamiltons minnesanteckningar från 1800 års riksdag," *Personhistorisk tidskrift*, 52 (1954), 92–93.

10. Dixelius, *Den unge Järta*, 293.

11. *Några tankar om sättet att åter upprätta och befästa den urgamla franska monarkien* (1799); in Hans Järta, *Valda skrifter*, ed. H. Forssel, 2 vols. (Stockholm, 1882–83), I, 3–39.

12. Adlerbeth, *Historiska anteckningar*, II, 53–54.

13. My *Fersen*, 280. Cf. Lamm, *Upplysningstidens romantik*, II, 599.

14. Hochschild, *Memoarer*, III, 304, 318.

15. Söderhjelm, ed., *Axel von Fersens dagbok*, IV, 58.

16. *Ibid.*, IV, 65.

17. Elinder, "Hamiltons minnesanteckningar," 98.

18. *Ibid.*, 18.

19. Söderhjelm, ed., *Axel von Fersens dagbok*, IV, 107.

20. See Carlsson, *Ståndssamhälle och ståndspersoner*, 327.

21. Söderhjelm, ed., *Axel von Fersens dagbok*, IV, 84, 89–91; Elinder, "Hamiltons minnesanteckningar," 109; Hochschild, *Memoarer*, III, 327.

22. *Hedvig Elisabeth Charlottas dagbok*, VII, 31.

23. *Ibid.*, 39.

24. See Krusius-Ahrenberg, *Tyrannmördaren*, 316–26.

25. See esp. Kjellin, "'Hvem äro de sannskildiga Jacobinerna?'" 192–95. Cf. Palmer, *Age of the Democratic Revolution*, I, II.

26. E. D. Clarke, *Travels in Various Countries of Scandinavia Including Denmark, Sweden, Norway, Lapland and Finland*, 3 vols. (London, 1838), III, 327.

27. Söderhjelm, ed., *Axel von Fersens dagbok*, IV, 55. Cf. *Hedvig Elisabeth Charlottas dagbok*, VII, 297.

28. Svenson, "Studentens klang- och jubeltid," 100.

29. Holm, *DNH*, VI:2, 637–45; Hvidtfeldt, "Social og politisk uro i Sønderjylland," 145–48.

30. Holm, *DNH*, VI:2, 691; Krusius-Ahrenberg, *Tyrannmördaren*, 340.

31. Holm, *DNH*, VI:2, 668–72, 679–80; A. Jantzen, "Collett, Peter," *Dansk biografisk leksikon*, ed. Povl Engelstoft et al., 27 vols. (Copenhagen, 1933–44), V, 385.

32. Holm, *DNH*, VI:2, 697.

33. The press ordinance of 1799 is given in English in Gold, "Danish Reform Era," Appendix G, 232–33.

34. Holm, *DNH*, VI:2, 699; Schulz, *Timoleon und Immanuel*, 149, 352.

35. See esp. Bokkenheuser, *Drejers Klub*, 272–74. Cf. Kyrre, *Knud Lynne Rahbek*.

36. Malthus, *Travel Diaries*, 120*n*, 137; Wollstonecraft, *Letters*, 15, 25, 34–35, 145, 152.

37. Holm, *DNH*, VI:2, 709–10.

38. Axel Linvald, *Kronprins Frederik og hans Regering 1797–1807* (Copenhagen, 1923), 27.

39. Klose & Degn, *GSH*, VI, 253; Hvidtfeldt, *Ophævelsen*, 101.

40. Jacob Aall, *Erindringer som Bidrag til Norges Historie fra 1800 til 1815* (2d ed., Christiania, 1859), 17, 18–19.

41. On the religious awakening throughout the North in this period, see Thyssen, et al., "De religiösa folkrörelserna"; "Nordiska historikermötet, Helsingfors 1967. Plenardebatter," *Historiallinen arkisto*, 63 (1968), 13–23. Cf. Gregersen, *Slesvig og Holsten før 1830*, 137–39; Gjerset, *Iceland*, 349.

42. Coldevin, *VFH*, V, 434.

43. On the Haugian movement, see esp. Andreas Aarflot, *Hans Nielsen Hauge: His Life and Message* (Minneapolis, 1979); Dagfinn Breistein, *Hans Nielsen Hauge, "Kjøbmand i Bergen"* (Bergen, 1955); Johan Schreiner, "Hans Nielsen Hauge og 'samfunnets felleskasse'," *HTN*, 29 (1930), 383–401.

44. Holm, *DNH*, VI:2, 289.

45. Coldevin, *VFH*, V, 407–8; Svenson, *Gattjinatraktaten*, 151.

46. See esp. Feldbæk, *India Trade under the Danish Flag, 1772–1808* and "Dutch Batavia Trade via Copenhagen, 1795–1807," *SEHR*, 21 (1973), 43–75. Cf. Malthus, *Travel Diaries*, 48. On Denmark's wartime trade, Schovelin, *Fra den danske Handels Empire*, II, is still useful. See also Ernst Ekman, "St. Barthélemy and the French Revolution," *Caribbean Studies*, 3 (1964), 17–29.

47. On Gustav IV Adolf's foreign policy in this period, see esp. Svenson, *Gattjinatraktaten*. Cf. my *Fersen*, chaps. 10–11.

48. Holm, *DNH*, VI:2, 693–96.

49. Cf. Alexander De Conde, *The Quasi-War* (New York, 1966), esp. 298–311.

50. Oliver Warner, *A Portrait of Lord Nelson* (Harmondsworth, 1963), 254.

51. Arthur Bryant, *The Years of Endurance, 1793–802* (Glasgow, 1961), 386. For a detailed account of the battle, cf. Anderson, *Naval Wars in the Baltic*, 303–12. (See chap. 7, note 41.)

52. Adam Oehlenschläger, *Meine Lebens-Erinnerungen*, 4 vols. (Leipzig, 1850), I, 172–74; Reventlow, ed., *En dansk statsmands hjem*, II, 15; Brandt, *Geistesleben und Politik*, 325. For other expressions of "Danish" patriotism in Holstein during the 1790s, see Gregersen, *Slesvig og Holsten før 1830*, 436.

53. See my *Fersen*, 258.

## CHAPTER 11. AT THE CROSSROADS, 1802–7

1. On the Swedish *enskifte*, see esp. Heckscher, *SEH*, II:1, 157–83, 172–73; Ingers, *Bonden i svensk historia*, II, 461–502; Åberg, *När byarna sprängdes*.

2. Cf. Linvald, *Kronprins Frederik*, 75–76, 83–84.

3. See esp. *ibid.*, 22–96; Linvald, *SDH*, IV:1, 90–95; Klose & Degn, *GSH*, VI, 297. On the adjutants see Linvald, *Kronprins Frederik*, 63–64.

4. Linvald, *Kronprins Frederik*, 263; Linvald, *SDH*, IV:1, 180–81. On military reforms, see Johansen, *Frederik VI.s Hær*, 62–63, 114–15.

5. See Linvald, *Kronprins Frederik*, esp. vii–ix, 22–24, 227–36, 259–63, 381–82. Cf. Hvidtfeldt, *Ophævelsen*, 432–33; Christensen, *Agrarhistoriske Studier*, II, 176–79; Skrubbeltrang, *Det danske landbosamfund*, 414–15.

6. Linvald, *Kronprins Frederik*, 88–89.

7. Klose & Degn, *GSH*, VI, 262.

8. *Ibid.*, 257–65; Hvidtfeldt, *Ophævelsen*, 423–29. Cf. Blum, *End of the Old Order in Rural Europe*, part III.

9. Aage Friis, "Holstens Indlemmelse i Danmark i Aaret 1806," *HTD*, 7:6 (1905–6), 23.

10. Schulz, ed., *Briefwechsel mit Friedrich VI*, 257–61; Klose & Degn, *GSH*, VI, 300, 301.

11. Schulz, ed., *Briefwechsel mit Friedrich VI*, 267–69.

12. Schulz, *Friedrich Christian*, 296; Friis, "Holstens Indlemmelse," 55, 56.

13. Friis, "Holstens Indlemmelse," 98–99.

14. Brandt, *Geistesleben und Politik*, vii–viii.

15. "Nordiska historikermötet, Helsingfors 1967. Plenardebatter," 18.

16. Mykland, *NH*, IX, 126.

17. Coldevin, *VFH*, V, 436.

18. Koht, *Norsk bondereising*, 349.

19. See Dagfinn Mansaker in A. Thyssen, et al., "De religiösa folkrörelserna," 48–49.

20. Koht, *Norsk bondereising*, 338. Cf. Thyssen, et al., "De religiösa folkrörelserna," 30–33. For general sources on Haugianism, see chap. 10, note 43.

21. Adlerbeth, *Historiska anteckningar*, II, 294–95. On the alleged "Illuminati," cf. my *Fersen*, 311–12.

22. Carlsson, *SUPH*, III:1, 79–82; Clason, *SHVD*, XI, 22–24, 30–34.

23. *Hedvig Elisabeth Charlottas dagbok*, VII, 257.

24. *Ibid.*, 307-11, gives the text of the *Moniteur* article of 14 August 1804.
25. Carlsson, *SUPH*, III:1, 92-99.
26. *Ibid.*, 99.
27. *Hedvig Elisabeth Charlottas dagbok*, VII, 391-94.
28. See esp. Sam Clason, *Gustaf IV Adolf och den europeiska krisen under Napoleon* (Stockholm, 1913); Herbert Lundh, *Gustaf IV Adolf och Sveriges utrikespolitik 1801-1804* (Stockholm, 1926). Cf. Carlsson, *SUPH*, III:1, 106-7.
29. R. Carr, "Gustavus IV and the British Government," *English Historical Review*, 60 (1945), 50.
30. Gustaf Björlin, *Sveriges krig i Tyskland åren 1805-1807* (Stockholm, 1882), 116-18.
31. Sten Carlsson, "Schweden und Pommern in der neueren Geschichte," *Zeitschrift für Ostforschung*, 15 (1966), 274.
32. Lars Dalgren, *Sverige och Pommern 1792-1806. Statskuppen 1806 och dess förhistoria* (Uppsala, 1914), subtitle and *passim*. In addition to this work, see Fuchs, *Untergang des Bauernstandes*, esp. 227-38.
33. Björlin, *Sveriges krig i Tyskland*, 194.
34. See Seved Johnson, "Legend och verklighet kring Gustaf IV Adolfs brytning med Napoleon," *Svensk tidskrift*, 37 (1950), 461; Å. V. Ström, "Gustav IV Adolf och vilddjuret," *Svenska dagbladet* (Stockholm), 31 Jan. 1937.
35. Björlin, *Sveriges krig i Tyskland*, 225. On Sweden in the War of the Third Coalition, see also my *Fersen*, chap. 14.
36. Holm, *DNH*, VII:1, 148-49, 160.
37. On the significance of internal reform under Crown Prince Frederik and Gustav IV Adolf and their solicitude for the common man, see esp. Linvald, *Kronprins Frederik*, vii-ix, 22-23, 381-82; my "Late Gustavian Autocracy in Sweden: Gustav IV Adolf and His Opponents, 1792-1809," *Scandinavian Studies*, 46 (1974), 265, 275-77, 279-80.

## CHAPTER 12. INTO THE MAELSTROM, 1807-10

1. Holm, *DNH*, VII:1, 214-15.
2. *Ibid.*, 2, 7-18, 224-25.
3. On scholarly debate over Canning's actions, see esp. Feldbæk, *DHG*, IV, 308-9; Mykland, *NH*, IX, 152. Cf. A. N. Ryan, "The Causes of the British Attack on Copenhagen in 1807," *English Historical Review*, 68 (1953), 37-55; Sven G. Trulsson, *British and Swedish Policies and Strategies in the Baltic after the Peace of Tilsit in 1807* (Lund, 1976), chap. 2.
4. Vibæk, *DHP*, X, 299-300.
5. Holm, *DNH*, VII:1, 265-66.
6. See Wilhelm Odelberg, *Viceamiral Carl Olof Cronstedt* (Helsingfors, 1954); also Eirik Hornborg, *När riket sprängdes* (Stockholm, 1955), a good account of the Finnish campaign of 1808-9.
7. Holm, *DNH*, VII:1, 377-79, 389-94; R. Carr, "Gustavus IV and the British Government," 45-58; Trulsson, *British and Swedish Policies*, chaps. 3-7, esp. 126-27, 133-35, 142-45, 154, 159-60; Lars Tangeraas, "Canning og Norge," *HTN*, 52 (1973), 293-313.
8. On the failure of the Franco-Danish invasion plan, see esp. Holm, *DNH*, VII:2, chaps. 4, 6; Torvald T:son Höjer, *Carl XIV Johan. Den franska tiden* (Stockholm, 1939), 368-84, esp. 370-84.
9. The "Balloon Proclamation" in P. Wieselgren, ed., *DeLaGardiska arkivet. Handlingar ur grefliga DeLaGardiska biblioteket på Löberöd*, 20 vols. (Stockholm, 1831-44), XX, 242-56 (corrected pagination). Cf. Krusius-Ahrenberg, *Tyrannmördaren*, 397, 404-10.
10. Wieselgren, ed., *DeLaGardiska arkivet*, XX, 410; Krusius-Ahrenberg, *Tyrannmördaren*, 411.
11. Holm, *DNH*, VI:1, 207, 211-14; VI:2, 79-80.
12. Krusius-Ahrenberg, *Tyrannmördaren*, 406, 411.
13. Hans Gabriel Trolle-Wachtmeister, *Anteckningar och minnen*, ed. Elof Tegnér, in Elof Tegnér, *Valda skrifter*, 6 vols. (Stockholm, 1904-6), IV, 67, 100-101, 115, 128-29, 132-33. Cf. my "Late Gustavian Absolutism," 276.

14. C. A. Adlersparre, *1809 och 1810. Tidstaflor*, 3 vols. (Stockholm, 1850), I, 163; Birger Sjövall, *Georg Adlersparre och tronfrågen 1809* (Lund, 1917). On the alleged armistice, see J. S. Worm-Müller, *Norge gennem Nødsaarene 1807–10* (Kristiania, 1917), 256–70.

15. On the coup d'etat of 13 March 1809, see esp. Sten Carlsson, *Gustaf IV Adolfs fall* (Lund, 1944).

16. Järta, *Valda skrifter*, II, 566.

17. Concerning the historiographical debate on the role of foreign ideological influences on the Swedish revolution and constitution of 1809, see Stefan Björklund, ed., *Kring 1809* (Stockholm, 1965), especially the essays by Fredrik Lagerroth, Gunnar Brusewitz, and Gunnar Heckscher. See also Karlbom, *Bakgrunden till 1809 års regeringsform*.

18. Järta, *Valda skrifter*, I, 45–46.

19. Sigfrid Andgren, *Konung och ständer 1809–1812* (Lund, 1933), 16; Clason, *SHVD*, XI, 102.

20. Trolle-Wachtmeister, *Anteckningar och minnen*, 184; my "Late Gustavian Autocracy," 268.

21. Järta, *Valda skrifter*, I, 44.

22. Karlbom, *Bakgrunden till 1809 års regeringsform*, 315, 341.

23. See Ingers, *Bonden i svensk historia*, II, 239–48; Trolle-Wachtmeister, *Anteckningar och minnen*, 190–92.

24. Schulz, ed., *Briefwechsel*, 243–46. Cf. Worm-Müller, *Norge i Nødsaarene*, 271–98; Leland B. Sather, "The Prince of Scandinavia: A Biography of Prince Christian August of Schleswig-Holstein-Sonderburg-Augustenburg, 1768–1810" (unpublished Ph.D. dissertation, University of California, Santa Barbara, 1975); my "Swedish Succession Crises."

25. *Meddelelser fra Krigsarkiverne. Udgivne af Generalstaben*, IV, ed. C. T. Sørensen (Copenhagen, 1890), 211.

26. *Ibid.*, 218.

27. *Ibid.*, 228, 258.

28. *Ibid.*, 221–22, 230, 236, 248, 256, 268.

29. *Ibid.*, 282.

30. *Ibid.*, 252, 263.

31. Arne Hall Jensen, *Den dansk-amerikanske Historie* (Copenhagen, 1937), 40. On Danish-Norwegian commerce raiding and British countermeasures, see A. N. Ryan, "The Defense of British Trade with the Baltic, 1808–1813," *English Historical Review*, 84 (1959), 443–66.

32. Vibæk, *DHP*, X, 302; Feldbæk, *DHG*, IV, 296; Klose & Degn, *GSH*, VI, 320–21. Cf. Roland Ruppenthal, "Denmark and the Continental System," *Journal of Modern History*, 15 (1943), 7–23.

33. Mykland, *NH*, IX, 155. The most detailed study of Norway in this period is still Worm-Müller, *Norge gennem Nødsaarene*.

34. Vibæk, *DHP*, X, 319.

35. Steen, *NFLH*, VII, 284.

36. *Ibid.*, 288.

37. *Meddelelser fra Krigsarkiverne*, IV, 149–54. On Wedel, see Yngvar Nielsen, *Lensgreve Johan Caspar Herman Wedel Jarlsberg*, 3 vols. (Christiania, 1901–2). Cf. Worm-Müller, *Norge i Nødsaarene*, 242–44.

38. Nielsen, *Wedel Jarlsberg*, I, 169–331 passim.

39. *Ibid.*, I, 257–60; cf. Worm-Müller, *Norge i Nødsaarene*, esp. 417–74; Sam Clason and Carl af Petersens, eds., *För hundra år sedan. Skildringar och bref från revolutionsåren 1809–1810*, 2 vols. (Stockholm, 1909–10), II, 37.

40. Mykland, *NH*, IX, 72–73; Worm-Müller, *Norge i Nødsaarene*, 556.

41. Mykland, *NH*, IX, 208–9; Steen, *NFLH*, VII, 325–27; Nielsen, *Wedel Jarlsberg*, I, 344–52.

42. Gjerset, *History of Iceland*, 352–59; Holm, *DNH*, VII:2, 277–84.

43. See, for instance, Hornborg, *Finlands hävder*, III, 402–3; L. G. von Bonsdorff, *Den ryska pacificeringen i Finland 1808–09* (Helsingfors, 1929), 7–9; Päiviö Tommila, *La Finlande dans la politique européene en 1809–15* (Helsinki, 1962), 18–20.

44. Bonsdorff, *Den ryska pacificeringen*, 50–52, 57.

45. See Carl von Bonsdorff, *Opinioner och stämningar i Finland 1808–1814* (Helsingfors, 1918), esp. chaps. 1 and 2; quotations, *ibid.*, 33. Cf. Gabriel Nikander, "Akademisk syn på krigs-året 1808," in his *Gustaviansk politik i Finland*, 40–46.
46. Hornborg, *Finlands hävder*, III, 465. Cf. Bonsdorff, *Opinioner och stämningar*, 49, 54–55, 79–80, 93, 223. On conditions in Russian Old Finland, see the special issue of *HTF*, 67 (1982), esp. Yrjö Kaukiainen, "Bidrag till bondens historia i Gamla Finland," 4–31, and I. M. Bobovič, "Donationsgodsen i Gamla Finland fram till mitten av 1800-talet," 34–47.
47. Cf. Bonsdorff, *Den ryska pacificeringen*, 58–62; Hornborg, *Finlands hävder*, III, 494–98.
48. Wuorinen, *History of Finland*, 114.
49. *Ibid.*, 116.
50. See Tommila, *La Finlande*, 28–39.
51. *Ibid.*, 46.
52. *Ibid.*, 48–99. On Alexander I's policy of conciliation, see esp. L. G. von Bonsdorff, *Den ryska pacificeringen* and C. von Bonsdorff, *Opinioner och stämningar*. Quotations from the latter work, 75, 79, 106.
53. Clason, *SHVD*, XI, 33–34.
54. Cf. Sune Åkerman, *Skattereformen 1810. Ett experiment med progressiv inkomstskatt* (Uppsala, 1967).
55. Jöran Wibling, *Opinioner och stämningar i Sverige 1809–10* (Uppsala, 1954), 87–88. On the factions at the *Riksdag*, cf. Andgren, *Konung och ständer*.
56. Trolle-Wachtmeister, *Anteckningar och minnen*, 6.
57. "Försök om Patriotismen," *Läsning i blandade ämnen*, 42 (1800), 1–55, esp. 6–8. Cf. Clason, *SHVD*, XI, 52–53; Nikander, "Filosofi och politik," 25–26, and "Akademisk syn på krigs-året 1808," 42.
58. Bernhard von Schinkel, *Minnen ur Sveriges nyare historia*, ed. C. W. Bergman, 10 vols. (Stockholm, 1852–68), V, 137; S. J. Boëthius, ed., *Bihang till Minnen ur Sveriges nyare historia*, 2 vols. (Stockholm, 1880–83), II, 157.
59. Clason, *SHVD*, XI, 108.
60. Andgren, *Konung och ständer*, 52–53.
61. My *Fersen*, 384–85.
62. G. Andersson, ed., *Handlingar ur Brinkman'ska arkivet på Trolle-Ljungby*, 2 vols. (Örebro, 1859–65), II, 365.
63. Reventlow, *En dansk Statsmands Hjem*, II, 137; Trolle-Wachtmeister, *Anteckningar och minnen*, I, 253n; Clarke, *Travels*, III, 155. On the Fersen Riot, see my *Fersen*, chaps. 15 and 16.
64. Clason, *SHVD*, XI, 34.
65. For the historiography on Gustav IV Adolf, see Sture Bolin, "Gustaf IV Adolf i svensk historisk opinion," *Svensk tidskrift*, 28 (1941), 323–36; Sten Carlsson, *Gustaf IV Adolf. En biografi* (Stockholm, 1946), 348–55; Svenson, *Gattjinatraktaten*, 9–30.
66. See my "Late Gustavian Autocracy," esp. 277–80.

### CHAPTER 13. THE RESOLUTION, 1810–15

1. See my "Swedish Succession Crises," 325–26.
2. Krusius-Ahrenberg, *Tyrannmördaren*, 423.
3. Schulz, ed., *Briefwechsel mit Friedrich VI*, 372–76, 379–83, 511–29.
4. Karl Warburg, "Rasmus Nyerups svenska brefväxling," *Samlaren*, 15 (1894), 99n.
5. Sven Åstrand, "Karl XIV Johan," in *Svenskt biografiskt lexikon*, 20 (Stockholm, 1975), 697.
6. Wibling, *Opinioner och stämningar*, 303.
7. C. J. Anker, ed., *Utdrag ur danska diplomaters meddelanden från Stockholm 1807–1808, 1810 och 1812–13*, trans. F. U. Wrangel (Stockholm, 1898), 73; Boëthius, ed., *Bihang till Minnen*, II, 223; Trolle-Wachtmeister, *Minnen och anteckningar*, 217–18.
8. See esp. Tommila, *La Finlande*, 76–105.
9. Boëthius, ed., *Bihang till Minnen*, II, 229.
10. Tommila, *La Finlande*, 103–4.
11. Torvald T:son Höjer, *Carl XIV Johan. Kronprinstiden* (Stockholm, 1945), 31–33.

12. Wahlström, "Gustaf III och norrmännen," 76.
13. Söderhjelm, ed., *Axel von Fersens dagbok*, III, 224; *Dagens nyheter* (Stockholm), 25 September 1966, 8.
14. Clason & af Petersens, eds., *För hundra år sen*, II, 124.
15. Boëthius, ed., *Bihang till Minnen*, II, 264.
16. Christian VIII, *Breve 1796-1813*, ed. Axel Linvald, 2 vols. (Copenhagen, 1965), I, 55-63.
17. See, for instance, Höjer, *Carl XIV Johan. Kronprinstiden*; Carlsson, et al., *Den svenska historien*, VIII; Clason, *SHVD*, XI; Jörgen Weibull, *Carl Johan och Norge 1810-1814* (Lund, 1957); Tommila, *La Finlande*.
18. Trulsson, *British and Swedish Policies*, 158; Boëthius, ed., *Bihang till Minnen*, II, 264.
19. Clason, *SHVD*, XI, 193-94. Cf. A. N. Ryan, ed., *The Saumarez Papers: The Baltic, 1808-1812* (London, 1968).
20. *Hedvig Elisabeth Charlottas dagbok*, VIII, 614-15.
21. See Ryan, ed., *The Saumarez Papers*, esp. 161-64, 176-79, 182, 185-86.
22. Regarding controversy on this point, see Tommila, *La Finlande*, 160-61.
23. On Karl Johan's French ambitions, see esp. Franklin D. Scott, "Bernadotte and the Throne of France, 1814," *Journal of Modern History*, 5 (1933), 465-78.
24. *Meddelelser fra Krigsarkiverne*, V, 261-64, 353.
25. C. T. Sørensen, *Kampen om Norge i Aarene 1813 og 1814*, 2 vols. (Copenhagen, 1871), I, 136-38.
26. In 1803, Trondheim's *Stift*, hitherto comprising all of northern Norway, was reduced by the detachment of the northernmost *amter* of Nordland and Finnmark to form the new Tromsø *Stift*.
27. Clason, *SHVD*, XI, 245.
28. *Ibid.*, 193, 203, 277-78. See also diagram maps on British trade with northern and western Europe, 1809-12, in Tommila, *La Finlande*, 197, based on François Crouzet, *L'Economie brittanique et le Blocus continental (1806-1813)*, 2 vols. (Paris, 1958). See also Anne-Marie Fällström, "Kontinentalblockaden och de sociala förhållandena i Göteborg," in Hans Anderson, ed., *Historia kring Göteborg* (Stockholm, 1967), 132-57.
29. Clason, *SHVD*, XI, 211-12, 276-79.
30. *Hedvig Elisabeth Charlottas dagbok*, VIII, 699-701, 708.
31. Clason, *SHVD*, XI, 217.
32. *Hedvig Elisabeth Charlottas dagbok*, IX, 3; Andgren, *Konung och ständer*, chap. 5, appendix I.
33. Cf. Jan Stattin, *Hushållningssällskapen och agrarsamhällets förändring* (Uppsala, 1980).
34. Carlsson, "Schweden und Pommern," 276; Fuchs, *Untergang des Bauernstandes*, 237-55, 268.
35. Cf. Tegnér, *G. M. Armfelt*, III, chaps. 6-9; Tommila, *La Finlande*, 201-37.
36. Bonsdorff, *Opinioner och stämningar*, 45, 154, 224; Tommila, *La Finlande*, 267.
37. Vibæk, *DHP*, X, 378.
38. *Ibid.*, 383-86; Steen, *NFLH*, VII, 341-43. The most detailed study of Denmark's wartime finances is provided by Marcus Rubin, *1807-14. Studier til Københavns og Danmarks Historie* (Copenhagen, 1892).
39. Bobé, ed., *Efterladte Papirer*, VII, 290, 295; VIII, 311, 313; III, 245. On the impact of the state bankruptcy in the duchies, cf. Gregersen, *Slesvig og Holsten før 1830*, 454-55.
40. Schulz, *Friedrich Christian*, 239.
41. Holm, *DNH*, VI:2, 546.
42. Ordinance on rural schools, 29 July 1814, quoted in Gold, "Danish Reform Era," 166-67.
43. Sjöstrand, *Pedagogikens historia*, III:1, 180-81, 289; Carol Gold, "Educational Reform in Denmark, 1784-1814," in James A. Leith, ed., *Facets of Education in the Eighteenth Century*, Studies in Voltaire and the Eighteenth Century, 167 (1977), 49-64; Carlsson, *Ståndssamhälle och ståndspersoner* (1973 ed.), 220-21, 227-28.
44. The ordinance is given in English in Gold, "Danish Reform Era," 223-24. See also Linvald, "Af Jødernes Frigørelseshistorie," esp. 391-415.
45. Mykland, *NH*, IX, 199.
46. Steen, *NFLH*, VII, 333.

47. Coldevin, *VFH*, V, 465.
48. Mykland, *NH*, IX, 214.
49. Weibull, *Carl Johan och Norge*, 101–2. On Swedish activities in Norway in this period, see also Sven Eriksson, *Skandinaver emellan* (Stockholm, 1957).
50. Holm, *DNH*, VII:2, 400.
51. Mykland, *NH*, IX, 269.
52. Christian VIII, *Breve*, I, 70, 237.
53. See esp. Sørensen, *Kampen om Norge*, I, 135, 344–46.
54. Weibull, *Carl Johan och Norge*, 171–72.
55. There is an extensive literature on Karl Johan's and his advisers' views toward union with Norway. See Eriksson, *Skandinaver emellan*, esp. 28–29, 51; Nielsen, *Wedel Jarlsberg*, I, esp. 396–98, 413–22, 446–54; Weibull, *Carl Johan och Norge*, esp. 44–47, 58–59, 67–72, 104–12, 132–42, 163–74, 182–89. Weibull identifies Foreign Minister Lars von Engeström as the leading Swedish "amalgamationist" (see esp. 163–74), which is disputed by Henrik A. Olsson in "Karl Johan, Lars v. Engeström och den norska statusfrågan 1810–1814," *HTS*, 78 (1958), 377–402.
56. [Christian VIII], *Kong Christian VIII.s Dagbøger og Optegnelser*. I. *1799–1814*, ed. Axel Linvald (Copenhagen, 1943), 337.
57. Schulz, *Friedrich Christian*, 319. Cf. Schumacher, *Genrebilder*, 406.
58. Brandt, *Geistesleben und Politik*, 345. Cf. Gregersen, *Slesvig og Holsten før 1830*, 456–58.
59. The literature on 1814 in Norway is immense. For a brief but useful bibliographical orientation, see Knut Mykland, ed., *Omkring 1814* (Oslo, 1967), esp. introduction, 5–10.
60. *Meddelelser fra Krigsarkiverne*, IX, 154–55; Christian VIII, *Dagbøger og Optegnelser*, 323.
61. *Meddelelser fra Krigsarkiverne*, VII, 449–55, 462–63; X, 403–4; Sørensen, *Kampen om Norge*, I, 387, 394–95.
62. *Meddelelser fra Krigsarkiverne*, IX, 141.
63. Christian VIII, *Dagbøger og Optegnelser*, 336. This diary entry would seem to refute Georg Nørregård's contention, in "Den danske regering og den norske selvstændighedsrørelse 1814," *Nordisk tidskrift*, new ser., 40 (1964), 156–74, that Frederik was opposed to the Norwegian independence movement.
64. Mykland, *NH*, IX, 408. For Frederik VI's behavior toward Norway in early 1814, see esp. Knut Mykland, "Medens der endnu er tid," *HTN*, 41 (1962), 1–41. Cf. *Meddelelser fra Krigsarkiverne*, IX, 172, 189.
65. Cf. Aall, *Erindringer*, 749–50.
66. Christian VIII, *Dagbøger og Optegnelser*, 341–43.
67. Claus Pavels, *Biografi og Dagbøger*, ed. Claus Pavels Friis (Bergen, 1864), 144, 150.
68. Christian VIII, *Dagbøger og Optegnelser*, 339–40.
69. Mykland, *NH*, IX, 317–18. Cf. Pavels, *Biografi og Dagbøger*, 139; Nielsen, *Wedel Jarlsberg*, II, 68.
70. Sverre Steen, *1814* (Oslo, 1951), 135.
71. Nielsen, *Wedel Jarlsberg*, II, 105, 150–51. Cf. Knut Mykland, "Grunnlovens far og kongemaktens forsvarer," *Samtiden* (1964), 276–91.
72. Steen, *NFLH*, VII, 386.
73. Stein Kuhnle, "Stemmeretten i 1814," *HTN*, 51 (1972), 373–90.
74. See T. Andenæs, ed., *The Constitution of Norway and Other Documents of National Importance* (2d ed., Oslo, 1960).
75. Cf. Nielsen, *Wedel Jarlsberg*, I, 357, 360; II, 94, 194–96, 200–204, 226–32; Aall, *Erindringer*, 403; Christian VIII, *Dagbøger og Optegnelser*, 388; Halvdan Koht, "Trongen til demokrati i 1814," *HTN*, 34 (1947), 143, 149–51.
76. Pavels, *Biografi og Dagbøger*, 173–74.
77. Mykland, *NH*, IX, 380; Ludvig Daae, ed., "Gustav Peter Bloms Dagbog under Rigsforsamlingen paa Eidsvold," *HTN*, 3:1 (1888), 106.
78. Koht, "Trongen til demokrati," 133.
79. Seip, "Den opinionsstyrte enevelde," esp. 397–98, 443. Cf. also Steenstrup, *Den danske Bonde og Friheden*, 168–71.
80. On anti-Swedish propaganda in 1813–14, see Eriksson, *Skandinaver emellan*, 56–73; Niel-

sen, *Wedel Jarlsberg*, II, 105, 239–40; Christian Magnus Falsen, *Hvad har Norge at haabe* . . . ? (Christiania, 1814, 22 pp.); Steen, *1814*, 113.
  81. Chr. Thaulow, ed., "Sognepræst J. H. Darres Dagbog under Rigsforsamlingen paa Eidsvold," *HTN*, 4 (1877), 411.
  82. Cf. Terje I. Leiren, "1814 and British Opinion," *Scandinavian Studies*, 47 (1975), 364–82; Lars Tangeraas, "Castlereagh, Bernadotte and Norway," *Scandinavian Journal of History*, 8 (1983), 193–223; Eriksson, *Skandinaver emellan*, chap. 5.
  83. *Meddelelser fra Krigsarkiverne*, IX, 174, 177.
  84. *Ibid.*, 208–10. Cf. Christian VIII, *Dagbøger og Optegnelser*, 367, 371.
  85. Nielsen, *Wedel Jarlsberg*, II, 16–17, 168–70, 243, 248–49, 268; Aall, *Erindringer*, 308n.; *Meddelelser fra Krigsarkiverne*, IX, 209–10; Christian VIII, *Dagbøger og Optegnelser*, 280, 285, 371, 406, 411; Falsen, *Hvad har Norge at haabe?*; Pavels, *Biografi og Dagbøger*, 178, 180.
  86. Christian VIII, *Dagbøger og Optegnelser*, 419.
  87. Weibull, *Carl Johan och Norge*, 286–87.
  88. Steen, *1814*, 233.
  89. Nielsen, *Wedel Jarlsberg*, I, 430; II, 203–4, 271–80.
  90. Höjer, *SUPH*, III:2, 215.
  91. Weibull, *Carl Johan och Norge*, 296–301, 309–10, 314, 317–18, 329–30, 335–36, 338–40.
  92. Höjer, *SUPH*, III:2, 215.
  93. Pavels, *Biografi og Dagbøger*, 237.
  94. Bonsdorff, *Opinioner och stämningar*, 171; *Hedvig Elisabeth Charlottas dagbok*, IX, 269, 351n., 353; Weibull, *Carl Johan och Norge*, 290–93.
  95. Clason, *SHVD*, XI, 282.
  96. Tommila, *La Finlande*, 417.
  97. Johan Feuk, *Sverige på kongressen i Wien 1814–1815. Ett bidrag till kännedom om Karl Johans yttre politik* (Lund, 1915); Georg Nørregård, *Danmark og Wienerkongressen 1814–15* (Copenhagen, 1948).
  98. Brandt, *Geistesleben und Politik*, 341–42.
  99. Sir Dunbar Plunket Barton, quoted in Ragnar Svanström and C. F. Palmstierna, *A Short History of Sweden* (Oxford, 1934), 324.
  100. Trolle-Wachtmeister, *Anteckningar och minnen*, 218; Emmanuel, comte de Las Cases, *Le Mémorial de Sainte Hélène*, ed. Jean Prévost, 2 vols. (Paris, 1935), II, 51, cf. 488–89.
  101. See Mykland, *NH*, IX, 261–64.

### CHAPTER 14. CONCLUSIONS: SCANDINAVIA BY 1815

  1. Claus Pavels, *Dagbog-Optegnelser 1815–1816*, ed. C. P. Friis (Christiania, 1867), 43–44.
  2. Jacques Godechot, *La Grande Nation*, 2 vols. (Paris, 1956), I, 200.
  3. Palmer, *Age of the Democratic Revolution*, I, 4, 7.
  4. See, for instance, Peter Amann, ed., *The Eighteenth-Century Revolution* (Boston, 1963).
  5. See my "Scandinavia and the Atlantic Revolution, 1760–1815." Cf. Kåre D. Tønnesson, "Nye arbeider om den franske revolusjon," *HTN*, 45 (1966), 271–72.
  6. E. J. Hobsbawm, *The Age of Revolution, 1789–1848* (London, 1962), 2.
  7. See my "Swedish Succession Crises," esp. 331–33.
  8. Clason, *SHVD*, XI, 265. Cf. my "Russia and the Problem of Sweden-Finland," 431, 455.
  9. My *Fersen*, 81, 399.
  10. See, for instance, Hornborg, *Finlands hävder*, III, 428–30, and *När riket sprängdes*, 263.
  11. Lars G. von Bonsdorff, *Stämningar och förhållanden i Finland före skillsmässan från Sverige* (Stockholm, 1949); H. Jensen, *Dansk-norsk Vekselvirkning*.
  12. See Koht, *Norsk bondereising*, esp. 364–65; Renvall, *Finsk representation*, 416–19, 425–29.
  13. Juva, *Finlands väg*, 72–81; Carlsson, "Finlands ämbetsmän och Sveriges rike"; H. Jensen, *Dansk-norsk Vekselvirkning*, 38–41, 112–13; Steen, *NFLH*, VIII, 350–51. Nielsen, *Wedel Jarlsberg*, I, 62.
  14. Juva, *Finlands väg*, 236–37.
  15. Trolle-Wachtmeister, *Anteckningar och minnen*, 6.
  16. Tegnér, ed., "Ur Adolf Ludvig Ribbings papper," 65, 69.

17. See chap. 1; Linvald, *SDH*, IV:1, 191; Clason, *SHVD*, XI, 9-10.
18. Malthus, *Travel Diaries*, 47-52; Feldbæk, *DHG*, IV, 176; Falbe-Hansen, *Stavnsbaands-Løsningen*, I, 89; Heckscher, *SEH*, II:1, 259.
19. See Heckscher, *SEH*, II:1, 264; Jutikkala, *Bonden i Finland*, 282-83.
20. Clason, *SHVD*, XI, 16-18; Falbe-Hansen, *Stavnsbaands-Løsningen*, I, 105-6; Holm, *DNH*, VI:2, 440; Johnsen, *Norges bønder*, 317-18.
21. *Excellensen A. F. Skjöldebrands memoarer*, ed. H. Schück, 5 vols. (Stockholm, 1903-4), IV, 101-2; Linvald, *Kronprins Frederik*, 89.
22. Skrubbeltrang, *Det danske landbosamfund*, 320; cf. 435. See also Kjærgaard, *Konjunkturer og afgifter*, 69-70; Feldbæk, *DHG*, IV, 174, 188.
23. Carlsson, *Ståndssamhälle och ståndspersoner*, 348-51.
24. Tocqueville, *L'Ancien Régime et la Révolution française*, part II, chaps. 8-9.
25. Carlsson, "Bondeståndet i Norden."
26. Falbe-Hansen, *Stavnsbaands-Løsningen*, I, 80-81; Jensen, *Fra patriarkalisme til penge-økonomi*.
27. Ingers, *Bonden i svensk historia*, II, 221, 257-68; Hornborg, *Finlands hävder*, III, 512-15; Carlsson, *Ståndssamhället och ståndspersoner*, 153-54, 178; Heckscher, *SEH*, II:1, 270-73; Jensen, et al., *Ståndssamhällets upplösning i Norden*, 123; Coldevin *VFH*, V, 428.
28. See Jensen, *Dansk jordpolitik*, I, 1-11, 85, 93-94, 133, 153, 178, 234, 241-42. Cf. Skrubbeltrang, *Det danske landbosamfund*, 394-95. Also Hvidtfeldt, *Kampen om ophævelsen*, 32-34, 416-29; Fuchs, *Untergang des Bauernstandes*, 238-39.
29. Heckscher, *SEH*, II:1, 270. Cf. Jutikkala, *Bonden i Finland*, 273.
30. Vibæk, *DHP*, X, 85-86.
31. Skrubbeltrang, *Husmand og inderste*, 67; Falbe-Hansen, *Stavnsbaands-Løsningen*, I, 125, 133-34; Feldbæk, *DHG*, IV, 178-79.
32. Skappel, *Om husmandsvæsenet i Norge*, 33, 85, 91; Johnsen, *Norges bønder*, 302-4; Heckscher, *SEH*, II:1, 282; Ingers, *Bonden i svensk historia*, II, 268-80; Hornborg, *Finlands hävder*, III, 414-15.
33. R. R. Palmer, "Georges Lefebvre: The Peasants and the French Revolution," *Journal of Modern History*, 31 (1959), 329-42; Tønnesson, "Problèmes de la féodalité," 334, 342; Feldbæk, *DHG*, IV, 188.
34. Engeström, *Minnen och anteckningar*, I, 199; George Rudé, *Revolutionary Europe, 1783-1815* (Cleveland, 1964), 46.
35. See esp. Christensen, *Agrarhistoriske Studier*, II, 12-19, 169; Jensen, *Dansk Jordpolitik*, II, 116, 118; Johansen, *En samfundsorganisation i opbrud*, 296-97.
36. Silfverstolpe, "Försök om patriotismen," 45.
37. Philip, *Staten og Fattigdommen*, 29.
38. Cf. Skrubbeltrang, *Det danske landbosamfund*, 422.
39. My "Popular Education in Sweden," 536.
40. *Ibid.*, 538-39. Cf. Jokipii & Nummela, eds., *Ur nordisk kulturhistoria*.
41. Cipolla, *Literacy and Development in the West*, 115. Cipolla lists Denmark, the Færø Islands, Finland, Iceland, and Norway among countries with less than 30% adult illiteracy around 1850. (*Ibid.*, 113.)
42. See Thyssen, et al., "De religiösa folkrörelserna."
43. Paul Hazard, *European Thought in the Eighteenth Century from Montesquieu to Lessing* (Cleveland & New York, 1963), part III.
44. Lamm, *Upplysningstidens romantik*; Franzén's verse, *ibid.*, II, 503.
45. Vibæk, *DHP*, X (chapter on literature by Mogens Brøndsted), 388, 405.
46. *Ibid.*, 418-20.
47. See, for instance, Laurin, et al., *Scandinavian Art*; Colding, et al., *Akademiet og Guldalderen 1750-1850*.
48. Cf. Nikander, "Akademisk syn på krigsåret 1808"; Knut Nygaard, *Nordmenns syn på Danmark og danskene i 1814 og de første selvstendighetsår* (Oslo, 1960).
49. Leo Gershoy, review of Jacques Godechot, *La Grande nation* (see chap. 14, note 2), in *Journal of Modern History*, 29 (1957), 376.

50. Steen, *NFLH*, VII, 392.

51. H. Jensen, *Reventlow*, 222-23. Cf. Jensen, *Dansk Jordpolitik*, I, 232-33, 238.

52. Clinton Rossiter, *The First American Revolution* (New York, 1956), flyleaf.

53. Tocqueville, *L'Ancien Régime et la Révolution française*; Lefebvre, *The Coming of the French Revolution*.

54. Martin Göhring, *Geschichte der grossen Revolution*, 2 vols. (Tübingen, 1950), I, 380-403.

55. Linvald, *SDH*, IV:1, 150-51. Cf. Jensen, *Dansk Jordpolitik*, I, 231-33, 240-41, 246-47.

56. For this debate, see Roger Wines, ed., *Enlightened Despotism: Reform or Reaction?* (Boston, 1967). Cf. essays on enlightened despotism in the Nordic lands by Axel Linvald, "Comment le despotisme éclairé s'est présenté dans l'histoire du Danemarck," *Bulletin of the International Committee of Historical Sciences*, 5 (1933), 714-26; Ludvig Stavenow, "Der aufgeklärte Absolutismus des 18. Jahrhunderts in Schweden," *ibid.*, 762-72; P. O. von Törne, "Les effets du despotisme éclairé en Finlande," *ibid.*, 49-55; Kåre D. Tønnesson, "L'Absolutisme éclairé: le cas danois," *Annales historiques de la Révolution française*, 238 (1979), 611-26.

57. Cf. my "Gustav III of Sweden and the Enlightenment."

58. Linvald, *SDH*, IV:1, 10. Cf. Jensen, *Dansk Jordpolitik*, I, 18-19.

59. Franklin L. Ford, *Europe, 1780-1830* (London, 1970), 141; Christensen, *Agrarhistoriske Studier*, II, 8-9; Skrubbeltrang, *Det danske landbosamfund*, 419; Løgstrup, *Jorddrot og offentlig administrator*, 298, 359-79; Kjærgaard, *Konjunkturer og afgifter*, 35-38, 69-71; Feldbæk, *DHG*, IV, 191, 311; Claus Bjørn, "The Peasantry and Agrarian Reform in Denmark," *SEHR*, 25 (1977), 117-37. Cf. Tønnesson, "L'Absolutisme éclairé," 622-25.

60. See, for instance, the essays in Björklund, ed., *Kring 1809*, esp. those by Axel Brusewitz, Fredrik Lagerroth, Gunnar Heckscher, and Rolf Karlbom.

61. Cf. esp. Lagerroth, *Frihetstidens författning*, 733-35; Edler, *Om börd och befordran*, 255.

62. See Söderhjelm, *Sverige och den franska revolutionen*, II, 138-40, on the selective response in Sweden to those French revolutionary ideas relating to earlier Swedish internal conflicts.

63. Brolin, *Hattar och mössor i borgarståndet*, 417.

64. See Lagerroth, *Frihetstidens författning*, 735; Bokkenheuser, *Drejers klubb*, 223, 266.

65. Tønnesson, "Problèmes constitutionnels," 225.

66. José Ortega y Gasset, *The Revolt of the Masses* (New York, [1932], 1960), 131-32.

# Selected Bibliography

# Selected Bibliography

Aall, Jacob. *Erindringer som bidrag til Norges historie fra 1800 til 1815.* 2d ed., Christiania, 1859.
[Adlerbeth, G. G.] *Historiska anteckningar af Gudmund Göran Adlerbeth.* Ed. Elof Tegnér. 2d ed., 2 vols. Lund, 1892.
Åkeson, Nils. *Gustaf III:s förhållande till franska revolutionen.* 2 vols. Lund, 1885–86.
Almén, Folke. *Gustav III och hans rådgivare 1772–89.* Uppsala, 1940.
Andgren, Sigfrid. *Konung och ständer 1809–1812. En studie i maktfördelningstillämpning.* Lund, 1933.
Bain, R. Nisbet. *Gustavus III and His Contemporaries.* 2 vols. London, 1894. Still the only English-language biography of Gustav III. Badly outdated.
Bang, J. B., ed. "Breve fra Ove Høegh-Guldberg til Johan v. Bülow." *Historisk Tidsskrift* (Dan.), Række IV, bd. 1 (1869–70), 125–466.
Barton, H. Arnold. *Count Hans Axel von Fersen: Aristocrat in an Age of Revolution.* Boston, 1975.
———. "The Danish Agrarian Reforms, 1784–1814, and the Historians." As yet unpublished.
———. "Gustav III of Sweden and the East Baltic, 1771–1792." *Journal of Baltic Studies*, 7 (1976), 13–30.
———. "Gustav III of Sweden and the Enlightenment." *Eighteenth Century Studies*, 6 (1972), 1–34.
———. "Late Gustavian Autocracy in Sweden: Gustav IV Adolf and His Opponents, 1792–1809." *Scandinavian Studies*, 46 (1974), 265–84.
———. "Popular Education in Eighteenth-Century Sweden." James A. Leith, ed., *Aspects of Education in the Eighteenth Century*, Studies in Voltaire and the Eighteenth Century, 167 (1977), 523–41.
———. "Russia and the Problem of Sweden-Finland, 1721–1809." *East European Quarterly*, 5 (1972), 431–55.
———. "Scandinavia and the Atlantic Revolution, 1760–1815." Warren F. Spencer, ed., *Proceedings of the Twelfth Consortium on Revolutionary Europe, 1750–1850*, (Athens, Ga., 1983), 145–58.
———. "Sweden and the War of American Independence." *William & Mary Quarterly*, 3d. ser., 23 (1966), 408–30.
———. "The Swedish Succession Crises of 1809 and 1810, and the Question of Scandinavian Union." *Scandinavian Studies*, 42 (1970), 309–33.
Bech, Svend Cedergreen. *See* Cedergreen Bech, Svend.
Benson, Adolf B. *Sweden and the American Revolution.* New Haven, 1926.
Blum, Jerome. *The End of the Old Order in Rural Europe.* Princeton, 1978. Includes Denmark, Schleswig-Holstein, and Swedish Pomerania.

Bobé, L., ed. *Efterladte Papirer fra den reventlowske Familiekreds.* 10 vols. Copenhagen, 1895-1931. Important collection of letters, almost exclusively in German and French, between members and friends of the Bernstorff-Reventlow-Schimmelmann-Stolberg circle in Denmark and the duchies.

Bokkenheuser, Knud. *Drejers klub.* Copenhagen, 1903.

Bonsdorff, Carl von. *Opinioner och stämningar i Finland 1804-1814.* Skrifter utgivna av Svenska litteratursällskapet i Finland, 141. Helsingfors, 1918.

Bonsdorff, L. G. von. *Den ryska pacificeringen i Finland 1808-1809.* Lovisa, 1929.

Brandt, O. *Geistesleben und Politik in Schleswig-Holstein um die Wende des 18. Jahrhunderts.* Kiel, 1927.

Breistein, Dagfinn. *Hans Nielsen Hauge, "Kjøbmand i Bergen." Kristen tro og økonomisk aktivitet.* Bergen, 1955.

Brolin, P. E. *Hattar och mössor i borgarståndet 1760-1766.* Uppsala, 1953.

Brøndsted, Johannes, ed. *Vore gamle tropekolonier.* 2 vols. Copenhagen, 1952-53.

Bull, Edvard, et al., eds. *Det norske folks liv og historie.* 10 vols. Oslo, 1929-38. *See* Steen, Sverre.

Bull, Francis. *Fra Holberg til Nordal Brun.* Kristiania, 1916.

Carlsson, Sten. "Bondeståndet i Norden under senare delen av 1700-talet." *Scandia,* 19 (1948-49), 196-213.

———. "The Dissolution of the Swedish Estates." *Journal of European Economic History,* I (1972), 574-624.

———. *Gustav IV Adolf. En biografi.* Stockholm, 1946.

———. *Ståndssamhälle och ståndspersoner 1700-1865.* Lund, 1949; 2d. ed., Lund, 1973. Essential study of the breakdown of the estates in Sweden and rise of social mobility. Summarized in the author's "Dissolution of the Swedish Estates" (q.v.).

———. *Svensk historia. Tiden efter 1718.* Stockholm, 1961. Vol. 2 of Jerker Rosén and Sten Carlsson, *Svensk historia,* 2 vols. Stockholm, 1961. Presently the standard text. Contains useful historiographical discussions following chapters.

———. *Den svenska utrikespolitikens historia,* III:1, *1792-1810.* Stockholm, 1954.

———. "Sweden in the 1760s." In Steven Koblik, ed., *Sweden's Development from Poverty to Affluence* (Minneapolis, 1975), 17-35.

———. et al. *Den svenska historien.* 10 vols. Stockholm, 1966-68. Expanded and lavishly illustrated version of Rosén and Carlsson, *Svensk historia* (q.v.), with additional sections by various authors on special topics, but without the bibliographical surveys contained in the original work.

———, and Ingers, E. *See* Ingers, E.

Cedergreen Bech, Svend. *Oplysning og tolerance 1721-1784.* Danmarks historie, eds. John Danstrup and Hal Koch, 9. Copenhagen, 1965.

———. *Struensee og hans tid.* Copenhagen, 1972.

Christensen, Aksel E., et al., eds. *Danmarks historie,* 4 (+) vols. Copenhagen, 1977- . *See* Feldbæk, Ole.

Christensen (Hørsholm), Christen. *Agrarhistoriske Studier,* 2 vols. Copenhagen, 1886-91. Vol. II: *Danske Landboforhold under Enevælden.*

[Christian VIII, king of Denmark.] *Dagbøger og Optegnelser.* I. *1799-1814.* Ed. Axel Linvald. Copenhagen, 1943.

Clason, Sam. *Karl XIII och Karl XIV Johan.* Sveriges historia till våra dagar, ed. E. Hildebrand and L. Stavenow, 11. Stockholm, 1923.

Clausen, Julius. *Skandinavismen historisk fremstillet.* Copenhagen, 1900.

Coldevin, Axel. *Enevoldstiden.* Vårt folks historie, ed. Thorleif Dahl, et al., 5. Oslo, 1963.

Colding, Torben Holck, et al. *Akademiet og Guldalderen 1750-1850.* Dansk kulturhistorie, ed. Vagn Poulsen et al., 3. Copenhagen, 1972.

Commager, Henry Steele. "Struensee and the Reform Movement in Denmark." Unpublished Ph.D. dissertation, University of Chicago, 1928.

Dahl, Thorleif, et al. *Vårt folks historie.* 9 vols. Oslo, 1961-63. *See* Coldevin, Axel.

Dalgren, Lars. *Sverige och Pommern 1792-1806. Statskuppen 1806 och dess förhistoria.* Uppsala, 1914.

Danielson-Kalmari, Johan R. *Finland under gustavianska tiden.* 2 vols. Helsingfors, 1925-26.

Danstrup, John, and Koch, Hal, eds. *Danmarks historie*. 14 vols. Copenhagen, 1964. *See* Ceder-green Bech, Svend; Vibæk, Jens.
Dyrvik, Ståle. *Den lange fredstiden 1720–1784*. Norges historie, ed. Knut Mykland, 8. Oslo, 1978.
Edler, P. J. *Om börd och befordran under frihetstiden*. Stockholm, 1915.
[Ehrenström, J. A.] *Statsrådet Johan Albert Ehrenströms efterlemnade historiska anteckningar*. Ed. S. J. Boëthius. 2 vols. Stockholm, 1883.
Elovson, Harald. *Amerika i svensk litteratur 1750–1820*. Lund, 1930.
Erhardt-Lucht, Renate. *Die Ideen der Französischen Revolution in Schleswig-Holstein*. Quellen und Forschungen zur Geschichte Schleswig-Holsteins, 56. Neumünster, 1969.
*Excerpta Historica Nordica*. Ed. Povl Bagge et al. Copenhagen, 1955– . Occasional series, provid-ing useful summaries of Scandinavian historical books and articles in English, French, and German.
Falbe-Hansen, V. *Stavnsbaands-Løsningen og Landboreformerne set fra Nationaløkonomiens Stand-punkt*. 2 vols. Copenhagen, 1888–89.
Feldbæk, Ole. *Tiden 1730–1814*. Danmarks historie, eds. Aksel E. Christensen et al., 4. Copen-hagen, 1982.
Fridericia, J. A., ed. *Aktstykker til Oplysning om Stavnsbaandets Historie*. Copenhagen, 1888.
Friis, Aage. *Andreas Peter Bernstorff og Ove Høegh-Guldberg. Bidrag til den Guldbergske Tids Historie (1772–1780)*. Copenhagen, 1899.
———. *Bernstorfferne og Danmark*. 2 vols. Copenhagen, 1903–19. Also in German translation, *Die Bernstorffs* (Leipzig, 1905), vol. I only. Important for background on the Bernstorff family and eighteenth-century Denmark, but completed only up to the end of J. H. E. Bernstorff's political career in 1770.
– – – . *Bernstorffske Papirer. Udvalgte Breve og Optegnelser vedrørende Familien Bernstorff i Tiden fra 1732 til 1835*. 3 vols. Copenhagen, 1904–13. Important collection of sources for Den-mark and the Bernstorffs, in the original French and German, but completed only up to 1783. German edition, *Bernstorffsche Papiere* (3 vols., Copenhagen [ Christiania, 1904–13) gives the author's text in translation; otherwise pagination and the numbering of documents is identical with the original Danish edition.
Friis, Aage, Linvald, Axel, and Mackeprang, M., eds. *Schultz Danmarks historie. Vort Folks His-torie skrevet af danske Historikere*. 6 vols. Copenhagen, 1941-43. *See* Linvald, Axel; Müller, Th. A.
Fuchs, C. J. *Der Untergang des Bauernstandes und das Aufkommen der Gutsherrschaften. Nach archivalischen Quellen aus Neu-Vorpommern und Rügen*. Abhandlungen aus dem Staatswissen-schaftlichen Seminar zu Strassburg, 6. Strassburg, 1888.
Geijer, E. G., ed. *Konung Gustaf III:s efterlemnade och femtio år efter hans död öppnade papper*. 2d. ed., in *Erik Gustaf Geijers samlade skrifter*, supplement 1. Stockholm, 1876.
Gjerset, Knut. *History of Iceland*. London, 1922.
Gold, Carol. "The Danish Reform Era, 1784-1800." Unpublished Ph.D. dissertation, University of Wisconsin, 1975.
Gregersen, H. V. *Slesvig og Holsten før 1830*. Copenhagen, 1981.
Gustafson, Alrik. *A History of Swedish Literature*. Minneapolis, 1961.
[Gustav III, king of Sweden.] *Collection des écrits politiques, littéraires et dramatiques de Gustave III, roi de Suède, suivie de sa correspondance*. Ed. J.-B. Dechaux. 5 vols. Stockholm, 1803-5.
[———.] *Konung Gustaf III:s bref till friherre G. M. Armfelt*. Ed. Elof Tegnér. Historiska hand-lingar, XII:3. Stockholm, 1883. Gustav III's letters to Armfelt, mainly in French.
Hansen, H., ed. *Kabinetsstyrelsen i Danmark 1768-1782. Aktstykker og Oplysninger*. 3 vols. Copenhagen, 1916-23. Cabinet orders from the Struensee and Guldberg periods in Denmark, from the Struensee years mainly in German.
Heckscher, Eli F. *Sveriges ekonomiska historia från Gustav Vasa*. 4 vols. Stockholm, 1935-49. A compendious study of Sweden's economic history since the sixteenth-century, unparalleled in the other Nordic countries.
Hedemann-Heespen, Paul von. *Die Herzogtümer Schleswig-Holstein und die Neuzeit*. Kiel, 1926. A vast but uneven work. Interesting material on the Schleswig-Holstein *Ritterschaft* in the period.

[Hedvig Elisabeth Charlotta, queen of Sweden.] *Hedvig Elisabeth Charlottas dagbok.* Ed. Carl Carlsson Bonde & Cecilia af Klercker. 9 vols. Stockholm, 1902–42. A fascinating, richly detailed, and remarkably well-informed secret chronicle covering the years 1775–1817; published together with valuable documents (in Swedish) in notes and appendixes.

Hennings, Beth. *Gustav III.* Stockholm, 1957.

Hildebrand, E. and Stavenow, L., eds. *Sveriges historia till våra dagar.* 15 vols. Stockholm, 1919–45. *See* Stavenow, Ludvig; Clason, Sam.

Hjärne, Erland. "Gustav III och franska revolutionen." *Svensk tidskrift,* 19 (1929), 502–22.

Hobsbawm, E. J. *The Age of Revolution, 1789–1848.* London, 1962.

Höjer, Torvald T:son. *Carl XIV Johan.* 3 vols. Stockholm, 1939–60. The definitive biography of Bernadotte. In somewhat abridged French translation, *Bernadotte: Maréchal de France, Roi de Suède* (2 vols., Paris, 1971). The crucial years, 1810–15, are covered in vol. 2 of the Swedish edition, *Kronprinstiden* (1945), and divided between the two volumes of the French edition.

———. *Den svenska utrikespolitikens historia,* III:2, *1810–1844.* Stockholm, 1954.

Holm, Edvard. *Danmark-Norges Historie fra den Store nordiske Krigs Slutning til Rigernes Adskillelse 1720–1814.* 7 vols. Copenhagen 1891–1912. The most monumental Scandinavian work for this period, it comprised virtually its author's life work, since almost all his other voluminous writings were essentially preliminary studies for it. Vols. IV–VII (in 7 parts) cover the period 1766–1814, although Vol. VII deals only with foreign affairs, for Holm died before he could write a projected additional volume on internal affairs in the Danish monarchy in 1800–14. Although superseded in matters of detail, Holm's great work remains indispensable and virtually the only source for many developments in the period.

Hornborg, Eirik. *Finlands hävder.* 4 vols. Helsingfors, 1929–33. Vols. III–IV.

Hovde, B. J. *The Scandinavian Countries, 1720–1865: The Rise of the Middle Classes.* 2 vols. Boston, 1943. A meticulous labor of love by an American scholar, topical in approach and covering a broader period than the present study, though concentrating on Denmark, Norway, and Sweden only. A mine of information.

Hvidtfeldt, Johan. *Kampen om ophævelsen af livegenskabet i Slesvig og Holsten 1795–1805.* Aarhus, 1963. A work of wider significance than its title suggests, it deals with the ideological background of agrarian reform in the Danish monarchy in its European context, as well as peasant emancipation in the duchies.

Ingers, E. and Carlsson, Sten. *Bonden i svensk historia.* 3 vols. Stockholm, 1949–56. Vols. I and II by Ingers; Vol. III by Carlsson.

Jägerskiöld, Olof. *Den svenska utrikespolitikens historia,* II:2, *1721–1792.* Stockholm, 1957.

Jägerskiöld, Stig. "Tyrannmord och motståndsrätt 1792–1809." *Scandia,* 25 (1962), 113–66.

Jensen, Hans. *Chr. D. Reventlows Liv og Gerning.* Copenhagen, 1938.

———. *Dansk Jordpolitik 1757–1919.* 2 vols. Copenhagen, 1936. Vol. I. A basic work on the Danish agrarian reforms.

———. *Dansk-norsk Vekselvirkning i det 18. Aarhundrede.* Copenhagen, 1936.

Jensen, Sigurd. *Fra patriarkalisme til pengeøkonomi.* Copenhagen, 1950.

———, et al., *Ståndssamhällets upplösning i Norden.* Åbo, 1954.

Johannesson, Þorkell, *Tímahilið 1770–1830. Upplýsingaröld.* Saga Íslendinga, 7. Reykjavík, 1950. For those who read Icelandic, the standard work on the period in Iceland.

Johansen, Hans Chr. *Dansk økonomisk politik i årene efter 1784.* 2 vols. Aarhus, 1968, 1980. I: *Reformår 1784–88*; II: *Krigsfinansierings problemer 1789–93.*

———. *En samfundsorganisation i opbrud 1700–1870.* Dansk socialhistorie, 4. Copenhagen, 1979.

Johansen, Jens. *Frederik VI's Hær 1784–1814.* Copenhagen, 1948.

Johnsen, Oscar Albert. *Norges bønder. Utsyn over den norske bondestands historie.* 2nd ed. Oslo, 1936.

———. *Norwegische Wirtschaftsgeschichte.* Jena, 1939.

Johnson, Amandus. *Swedish Contributions to American Freedom, 1776–1783.* 2 vols. Philadelphia, 1953–57.

Johnson, Seved. *Sverige och stormakterna 1800–1804.* Lund, 1957.

Jokipii, Mauno, and Nummela, Ilka, eds. *Ur Nordisk kulturhistoria. Läskunnighet och folkbildning före folkskoleväsendet.* Studia Historica Jyväskyläensia, 22:3. Jyväskylä, 1981.

Jónsson, Jón. "Fæstebondens Kaar paa Island i det 18. Aarhundrede." *Historisk Tidsskrift* (Dan.), 6:4 (1892–94), 563–645.

Jutikkala, Eino. *Bonden i Finland genom tiderna*. Stockholm, 1963.

——, with Piranen, Kauko. *A History of Finland*. London, 1962.

Juva, Einar W. *Finlands väg från Nystad till Fredrikshamn 1721–1809*. Stockholm, 1947.

Karlbom, Rolf. *Bakgrunden till 1809 års regeringsform. Studier i svensk konstitutionell opinionsbildning 1790–1809*. Studia historica Gothoburgensia, 3. Göteborg, 1964.

Kjærgaard, Thorkild. *Konjunkturer og afgifter. C. D. Reventlows betænkning af 11. februar 1788 om hoveriet*. Copenhagen, 1980.

Klinckowström, R. M., ed. *Le comte de Fersen et la cour de France*. 2 vols. Paris, 1877–78. Document collection, including much material, in French, on Gustav III's attitudes and policies toward the French Revolution.

——, ed. *Riksrådet och fält-marskalken m. m. Fredrik Axel von Fersens historiska skrifter*. 8 vols. Stockholm, 1867–72. Memoirs of one of the leading Swedish parliamentary leaders; extensive appendixes contain important documents (in Swedish).

Klose, Olaf, and Degn, Christian. *Die Herzogtümer im Gesamtstaat 1720–1830*. Geschichte Schleswig-Holsteins, begründet von Volquart Pauls, 6. Neumünster, 1960.

Koht, Halvdan. *Norsk bondereising. Fyrebuing til bondepolitikken*. Oslo, 1926. An interesting and thought-provoking work on peasant movements in Norwegian history down to 1814. In French translation, *Les luttes des paysans en Norvège du XVI^e au XIX^e siècle* (Paris, 1928).

Krusius-Ahrenberg, Lolo. *Tyrannmördaren C. F. Ehrensvärd*. Helsingfors, 1947.

Lagerroth, Fredrik. *Frihetstidens författning*. Stockholm, 1915. An important study of the Swedish constitution of 1720 and Sweden's political history, 1720–72.

——. *Konung och adel*. Stockholm, 1917.

Lamm, Martin. *Upplysningstidens romantik*. 2 vols. Stockholm, 1918–20.

Lamminen, Paavo. *Suomen historiallinen bibliografia 1951–1960*. Helsinki, 1968.

Landberg, Georg. *Gustav III i eftervärldens dom*. Stockholm, 1945.

Laurin, Carl, Hannover, Emil, and Thiis, Jens. *Scandinavian Art*. New York, 1922.

Lesch, Bruno. *Jan Anders Jägerhorn. Patriot och världsborgare, separatist och emigrant*. Helsingfors, 1941.

Lindblom, Andreas. *Sveriges konsthistoria*. Stockholm, 1947.

Linvald, Axel. *Kronprins Frederik og hans Regering 1797–1807*. Copenhagen, 1923. This important study of Crown Prince Frederik's regime, 1797–1807, fills part of the gap left by Edvard Holm's death before completing his treatment of internal affairs in his *Danmark-Norges Historie* (q.v.).

——. *Oplysningens Tidsalder*. Schultz Danmarkshistorie, eds. Aage Friis et al., IV:1. Copenhagen, 1943.

Løgstrup, Birgit. *Jorddrot og offentlig administrator*. Copenhagen, 1983.

Maliniemi, Aarno, and Kivikoski, Ella. *Suomen historiallinen bibliografia 1901–1925*. 2 vols. Helsinki, 1940.

Malmström, C. G. *Sveriges politiska historia från konung Karl XII:s död till statshvälfningen 1772*. 2d ed., 6 vols. Stockholm, 1893–1901. The classic work on Sweden during the "Era of Freedom," 1720–72.

Mead, W. R. *An Economic Geography of Scandinavia and Finland*. London, 1958.

*Meddelelser fra Krigsarkiverne. Udgivne af Generalstaben*. [Eds. C. T. Sørensen, et al.] 9 vols. Copenhagen, 1880–1902. Important collection from the Danish War Archives of documents, in various languages, for the years 1794–1814.

Müller, Th. A. *Oplysningstidens Aandsliv*. Schultz Danmarkshistorie, IV:2. Copenhagen, 1943.

Mykland, Knut. *Kampen om Norge 1784–1814*. Norges historie, ed. Knut Mykland, 9. Oslo, 1978.

——, ed. *Norges historie*. 13 vols. Oslo, 1976–79. *See* Dyrvik, Ståle; Mykland, Knut.

Nielsen, Axel. *Dänische Wirtschaftsgeschichte*. Jena, 1933.

Nielsen, Yngvar. *Lensgreve Johan Caspar Herman Wedel Jarlsberg*. 3 vols. Christiania, 1901–2.

Nikander, Gabriel. *Gustaviansk politik i Finland. Essäer*. Åbo, 1958.

Nordmann, Claude. *Grandeur et Liberté de la Suède (1660–1792)*. Paris & Louvain, 1971.

Odhner, C. T. *Sveriges politiska historia under konung Gustaf III:s regering*. 3 vols. Stockholm,

1885-1905. A classic on the political history of Gustav III's reign, completed only through the end of 1788.

Olsen, Albert. *Bybefolkningen i Danmark paa Merkantilismens Tid.* Acta Jutlandica, 4:2. Aarhus, 1932.

——. *Danmark-Norge i det 18. Aarhundrede.* Copenhagen, 1935.

——. "Samtidens Syn paa den danske stavnsbundne Bonde." *Scandia,* 12 (1939), 99-139.

Olsen, Gunnar. *Hovedgård og bondegård. Studier over stordriftens udvikling i Danmark i tiden 1525-1774.* Copenhagen, 1957.

Palmer, R. R. *The Age of the Democratic Revolution.* 2 vols. Princeton, 1959-64.

Pavels, Claus. *Biografi og Dagbøger.* Ed. Claus Pavels Friis. Bergen, 1864.

Pederson, Bente, ed. *Dansk historisk årsbibliografi.* Copenhagen, 1972 et seq. For period from 1967.

Peterson, Carl S., and Andersen, Vilhelm, eds. *Illustreret dansk Litteraturhistorie.* 4 vols. Copenhagen, 1929-35. Vol. II (Andersen).

Philip, Kjeld. *Staten og Fattigdommen.* Copenhagen, 1947.

Prange, Wolfgang. *Die Anfänge der grossen Agrarreformen in Schleswig-Holstein bis um 1771.* Quellen und Forschungen zur Geschichte Schleswig-Holsteins, 60. Neumünster, 1971.

Renvall, Pentti. *Finsk representation i Sveriges riksdag.* Stockholm, 1967.

——. "Ueber die Wurzeln der finnischen Autonomie im 18. Jahrhundert." *Sitzungsberichte der finnischen Akademie der Wissenschaften,* 1960 (Helsinki, 1961), 185-204.

[Reverdil, Élie Salomon François.] *Struensee et la cour de Copenhague, 1760-1772. Mémoires de Reverdil.* Ed. A. Roger. Paris, 1858. Highly valuable memoirs for the early reign of Christian VII, including the Struensee era, in Denmark. Annotated Danish translation, *Struensee og det danske Hof,* trans. Paul Læssø Müller, ed. Louis Bobé (Copenhagen, 1916).

Rosén, Jerker, and Carlsson, Sten, et al. *Den svenska historien.* 10 vols. Stockholm, 1966-68. An expanded, illustrated version of Rosén and Carlsson, *Svensk historia,* with supplementary articles by other authors. (*See* under Carlsson, Sten.) Vol. VI, *Frihetstiden;* VII, *Gustavianska tiden;* VIII, *Carl Johanstiden och den borgerliga liberalismen 1809-1865.*

Rubin, Marcus. *1807-14. Studier til Københavns og Danmarks Historie.* Copenhagen, 1892. A compendious work, filling part of the gap in Danish internal history left by Edvard Holm's death before completion of his *Danmark-Norges Historie* (q.v.).

Samuelsson, Kurt. *Från stormakt till välfärdsstat.* Stockholm, 1968. English translation, *From Great Power to Welfare State.* London, 1968.

Schück, Henrik, and Warburg, Karl. *Illustrerad svensk litteraturhistoria.* 3d ed., 8 vols. Stockholm, 1926-49. Vol. III, *Frihetstiden* (1927); IV, *Gustavianska tiden* (1928).

Schulz, Hans. *Friedrich Christian, Herzog zu Schleswig-Holstein. Ein Lebenslauf.* Leipzig, 1910.

Scott, Franklin D. *Bernadotte and the Fall of Napoleon.* Harvard Historical Monographs, 7. Cambridge, Mass., 1935.

Seip, J. A. "Teorien om det opinionsbestemte enevelde." *Historisk tidsskrift* (Nor.), 38 (1958), 397-463.

Sjöstrand, Wilhelm. *Pedagogikens historia.* 3 vols. Lund, 1945-65. Vol. III:1, *Sverige och de nordiska grannländerna under frihetstiden och gustavianska tiden* (1965).

Skappel, S. *Om husmandsvæsenet i Norge. Dets oprindelse og utvikling.* Kristiania, 1922.

Skrubbeltrang, Fridlev. *Det danske landbosamfund 1500-1800.* Copenhagen, 1978. Presently the authoritative survey of Danish agrarian history in the early modern period.

——. *Husmand og Inderste.* Copenhagen, 1940.

Söderberg, Tom. *Den namnlösa medelklassen.* Stockholm, 1956.

——. *Två sekel svensk medelklass från gustaviansk tid till nutid.* Stockholm, 1972.

Söderhjelm, Alma. *Sverige och den franska revolutionen.* 2 vols. Stockholm, 1920-24.

Sørensen, C. T. *Kampen om Norge i Aarene 1813 og 1814.* 2 vols. Copenhagen & Christiania, 1871.

Stavenow, Ludvig. *Frihetstiden.* Sveriges historia till våra dagar, eds. E. Hildebrand & L. Stavenow, 9. Stockholm, 1922.

——. *Gustavianska tiden 1772-1809.* Sveriges historia till våra dagar, eds. E. Hildebrand & L. Stavenow, 10. Stockholm, 1925.

Steen, Sverre. *Det frie Norge.* I: *1814.* Oslo, 1951.
——. *Tidsrummet 1720 til omkring 1770.* Det norske folks liv og historie, eds. Edvard Bull et al., 6. Oslo, 1932.
——. *Tidsrummet 1770 til omkring 1814.* Det norske folks liv og historie, eds. Edvard Bull et al., 7. Oslo, 1933.
Steffens, Heinrich [Henrik]. *Was ich erlebte.* 10 vols. Breslau, 1840–44. Vols. I and II contain fascinating glimpses of radical and romantic circles in Denmark, especially Copenhagen, in the 1780s and 1790s.
Stephensen, Magnus. *Island i det 18. Aarhundrede, historisk-politisk skildret.* Copenhagen, 1808. Uniquely valuable study of Iceland in the eighteenth century by one of the island's most active public and literary figures of the age.
*Svensk historisk bibliografi* [1771 et seq.]. Ed. Kristian Setterwall et al. Stockholm, 1923 et seq.
Svenson, Sven G. *Gattjinatraktaten 1799. Studier i Gustav IV Adolfs utrikespolitik 1796–1800.* Uppsala, 1952.
Sverdrup, Georg. *Lofthusbevægelsen.* Avhandlinger fra universitetets historiske seminar, 3. Oslo, 1917.
——. "Strilekrigen. Bondeopløpet i Bergen 1765." *Skrifter utgivne av Bergens historiske Forening,* 25–26 (1921), 9–107.
Tegnér, Elof. *Gustaf Mauritz Armfelt. Studier ur Armfelts efterlemnade papper samt andra handskrifvna och tryckta källor.* 3 vols. Stockholm, 1883–87.
Thyssen, A. Pontoppidan, et al. "De religiösa folkrörelserna och samhället ca. 1750–1850." *Historiallinen arkisto,* 62 (1967), 7–112.
Tommila, Päiviö. *La Finlande dans la politique européene dans 1809–1815.* Helsinki, 1962.
Tønnesson, Kåre D. "Problèmes de la féodalité dans les pays scandinaves." *Annales historiques de la Révolution française* (1969), 331–42.
——. "Problèmes d'histoire constitutionelle en Scandinavie à l'époque de la Révolution et de l'Empire." *Annales historiques de la Révolution française,* (1967), 221–50.
[Traustedt, P. H., ed.] *Dansk litteraturhistoria.* 4 vols. Copenhagen, 1967. Vols. I, II.
Utterström, Gustaf. *Jordbrukets arbetare.* 2 vols. Stockholm, 1957.
Valentin, Hugo. *Frihetstidens riddarhus. Några bidrag till dess karakteristik.* Stockholm, 1915.
Vallinkoski, J., and Schauman, Henrik. *Suomen historiallinen bibliografia 1926–1950.* 2 vols. Helsinki, 1955–56.
Vea, Erik. *Likhetsidéen i Norge i 1790-årene.* Avhandlinger utgitt av universitetets historiske seminar, 11. Oslo, 1956.
Vibæk, Jens. *Reform og fallit 1784–1830.* Danmarks historie, ed. John Danstrup & Hal Koch, 10. Copenhagen, 1964. Section on literature by Mogens Brøndsted.
Weibull, Jörgen. *Carl Johan och Norge 1810–1814.* Bibliotheca Historica Lundensis, 6. Göteborg, 1957.
West, John F. *Faroe: The Emergence of a Nation.* London, 1972.
Wibling, Jöran. *Opinioner och stämningar i Sverige 1809–10.* Uppsala, 1954.
Wittich, Karl. *Struensee.* Leipzig, 1879.
Worm-Müller, J. S. *Norge gennem Nødsaarene 1807–10.* Kristiania, 1917.

Index

# Index

Aall, Jacob, 245, 298, 343
Assen, Ivar, 373
Abborfors, 265
Åbenrå (Åbenråde), 183, 209, 376
Åbo (Turku), 65, 80, 157, 278, 298, 302,
    320–21, 327, 377; Agreement of *1812*,
    320–21, 323, 355; Peace of, 138, 190,
    191, 327; University of, 39, 40, 43, 137,
    162, 217, 240, 302
Adams, John, 374, 380
Adler, Johan G., 343
Adlerbeth, Gudmund Göran, 175, 189,
    195–96, 265
Adlercreutz, General Carl Johan, 284, 285,
    304
Adlersparre, Georg, 236, 239, 284, 285–86,
    290–91, 295–97, 304, 306, 311, 313,
    317, 320, 334, 337
Adolf Fredrik (king of Sweden), 37, 64, 77
Africa, 4, 27, 47, 119, 149, 221
Åland Islands, 278, 279, 292, 321
Alexander I (emperor of Russia), 165, 253,
    265, 270–71, 278, 299–302, 318, 320–21,
    327, 354, 357
Alexander II (emperor of Russia), 301, 366
Almén, Folke, 83
Altona, 13, 14, 17, 30–31, 67–68, 107, 108,
    115, 116, 124, 148, 184, 223, 248, 272,
    276, 329
*Altonaischer Mercurius*, 107

Amager, 20, 22
Amalienborg Palace, 225–26
America, 85, 107–9, 111, 114–17, 119–25,
    126, 135–36, 141, 172, 192, 198, 220,
    227, 247, 254, 286, 289, 294, 318–19,
    344, 360–61, 363, 383
Amiens, Peace of, 265
Aminoff, Berndt, 302
Aminoff, J. F., 328
*Amt* (Danish administrative unit), 29
Anckarström, Johan Jakob, 202–3
Anholt, 293, 328
Anjala Confederation. *See* Finland
Anker, Bernt, 153
Anker, Carsten, 98, 335, 341, 348
Arendal, 150, 151–52, 248, 334
Armed Neutrality, 47, 117–18, 227, 248,
    250–52
Armfelt, Baron Gustaf Mauritz, 135, 156,
    163, 167, 194, 196, 203, 204, 218–19,
    269, 304, 327–28, 353. *See also* Sweden:
    Armfelt Conspiracy
Armfelt, General Carl Gustaf, 158, 164–65
Asp, Per Olof von, 176, 189
Atterbom, Per Daniel Amadeus, 377
Auerstädt, Battle of, 270, 272
Augustenburg, Prince Christian (Karl) Au-
    gust, 142, 291–98 *passim*, 308, 310, 333;
    candidacy of, for Swedish succession,
    290–91; as Danish commander in southern

431

H. Arnold Barton earned his doctorate in history at Princeton University in 1962 and has taught since 1970 at Southern Illinois University, where he became professor of history in 1975. Barton edited and translated *Letters from the Promised Land: Swedes in America, 1840–1914* (Minnesota, 1975) and is the author of *Count Axel von Fersen: Aristocrat in an Age of Revolution* (1975) and *The Search for Ancestors: A Swedish-American Family Saga* (1979). He has served as editor of the *Swedish-American Historical Quarterly* since 1974.

# SCANDINAVIA, 1760–1815

0    100    200    300
MILES

ICELAND

Reykjavík

NORWEGIA

60

FÆRØ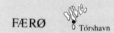

Tórshavn

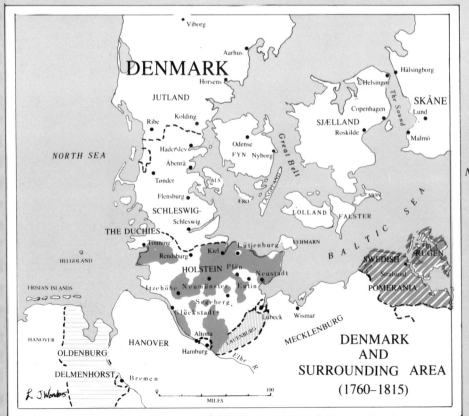

Viborg

Aarhus

DENMARK

Horsens

Hälsingborg

JUTLAND

Helsingør

SKÅNE

Ribe    Kolding

Copenhagen    Lund

SJÆLLAND

Odense    Roskilde

Malmö

Haderslev

FYN    Nyborg

Åbenrå

ALS

Tønder

NORTH SEA

Flensburg

ÆRØ

MØN

NORT

SCHLESWIG-

LOLLAND    FALSTER

SEA

Schleswig

THE DUCHIES

FEHMARN

HELGOLAND

Tønning

Lütjenburg

BALTIC SEA

RÜGEN

Rendsburg    Kiel

SWEDISH

For de

HOLSTEIN    Plön

Stralsund

of this a

Neustadt

see

FRISIAN ISLANDS

Itzehöhe    Neumünster    Eutin

POMERANIA

Segeberg

Glückstadt    Lübeck    Wismar

MECKLENBURG

Altona    LAUENBURG

DENMARK

HANOVER    HANOVER    Hamburg    Elbe R.

AND

OLDENBURG    SURROUNDING    AREA

DELMENHORST    Bremen    (1760–1815)

0    100

MILES

L. J. Wonders